MW00628915

Indigenous Intellectuals

In the United States of America today, debates among, between, and within Indian nations continue to focus on how to determine and define the boundaries of Indian ethnic identity and tribal citizenship. From the 1880s and into the 1930s, many Native people participated in similar debates as they confronted white cultural expectations regarding what it meant to be an Indian in modern American society. Using close readings of texts, images, and public performances, this book examines the literary output of four influential American Indian intellectuals who challenged long-held conceptions of Indian identity at the turn of the twentieth century. Kiara M. Vigil traces how the narrative discourses created by these figures spurred wider discussions about citizenship, race, and modernity in the United States and elsewhere. By setting them in dialogue with white American culture, Vigil demonstrates how these figures deployed aspects of Native American cultural practice to authenticate their status both as indigenous peoples and as citizens of the United States.

Kiara M. Vigil is an assistant professor of American studies at Amherst College and specializes in teaching and research related to Native American studies. She is a past recipient of the Gaius Charles Bolin fellowship from Williams College, as well as fellowships from the Mellon Foundation, the Autry National Center, the Newberry Library, and the Rackham Graduate School at the University of Michigan.

Studies in North American Indian History

Editors

Frederick Hoxie, *University of Illinois, Urbana-Champaign*
Neal Salisbury, *Smith College*
Tiya Miles, *University of Michigan*
Ned Blackhawk, *Yale University*

This series is designed to exemplify new approaches to the Native American past. In recent years scholars have begun to appreciate the extent to which Indians, whose cultural roots extend back for thousands of years, shaped the North American landscape as encountered by successive waves of immigrants. In addition, because Native Americans continually adapted their cultural traditions to the realities of the Euro-American presence, their history adds a thread of non-Western experience to the tapestry of American culture. Cambridge Studies in North American Indian History brings outstanding examples of this new scholarship to a broad audience. Books in the series link Native Americans to broad themes in American history and place the Indian experience in the context of social and economic change over time.

Also in the Series:

Lucy Murphy *Great Lakes Creoles: A French-Indian Community on the Northern Borderlands, Prairie du Chien, 1750–1860*

Richard White *The Middle Ground: Indians, Empires, and Republics in the Great Lakes Region, 1650–1815*, second edition

Gary Warrick *A Population History of the Huron-Petun, A.D. 500–1650*

John Bowes *Exiles and Pioneers: Indians in the Trans-Mississippi West*

David J. Silverman *Faith and Boundaries: Colonists, Christianity, and the Community among the Wampanoag Indians of Martha's Vineyard, 1600–1871*

Jeffrey Ostler *The Plains Sioux and U.S. Colonialism from Lewis and Clark to Wounded Knee*

Claudio Saunt *A New Order of Things: Property, Power, and the Transformation of the Creek Indians, 1733–1816*

Jean M. O'Brien *Dispossession by Degrees: Indian Land and Identity in Natick, Massachusetts, 1650–1790*

Frederick E. Hoxie *Parading through History: The Making of the Crow Nation in America, 1805–1935*

Colin G. Calloway *The American Revolution in Indian Country: Crisis and Diversity in Native American Communities*

Sidney L. Harring *Crow Dog's Case: American Indian Sovereignty, Tribal Law, and United States Law in the Nineteenth Century*

Indigenous Intellectuals

Sovereignty, Citizenship, and the American Imagination, 1880–1930

KIARA M. VIGIL

Amherst College

CAMBRIDGE
UNIVERSITY PRESS

CAMBRIDGE
UNIVERSITY PRESS

University Printing House, Cambridge CB2 8BS, United Kingdom

One Liberty Plaza, 20th Floor, New York, NY 10006, USA

477 Williamstown Road, Port Melbourne, VIC 3207, Australia

4843/24, 2nd Floor, Ansari Road, Daryaganj, Delhi - 110002, India

79 Anson Road, #06-04/06, Singapore 079906

Cambridge University Press is part of the University of Cambridge.

It furthers the University's mission by disseminating knowledge in the pursuit of education, learning and research at the highest international levels of excellence.

www.cambridge.org
Information on this title: www.cambridge.org/9781107656550

© Kiara M. Vigil 2015

This publication is in copyright. Subject to statutory exception and to the provisions of relevant collective licensing agreements, no reproduction of any part may take place without the written permission of Cambridge University Press.

First published 2015
First paperback edition 2017

A catalogue record for this publication is available from the British Library

Library of Congress Cataloging in Publication data
Vigil, Kiara M., 1975–
Indigenous intellectuals : sovereignty, citizenship, and the American
imagination, 1880–1930 / Kiara M. Vigil, Amherst College.
pages   cm. – (Studies in North American Indian history)
Includes bibliographical references and index.
ISBN 978-1-107-07081-3 (hbk.)
1. Indians of North America – Biography.   2. Intellectuals – United States –
Biography.   3. Indians of North America – Intellectual life.   4. Indians of
North America – Politics and government.   I. Title.
E89.V53   2015
970.004′97–dc23   2015002193

ISBN 978-1-107-07081-3 Hardback
ISBN 978-1-107-65655-0 Paperback

Cambridge University Press has no responsibility for the persistence or accuracy of URLs for external or third-party internet websites referred to in this publication, and does not guarantee that any content on such websites is, or will remain, accurate or appropriate.

In loving memory of
R. Max Vigil
Father, artist, and intellectual

Contents

Figures

Acknowledgments

I could never have completed this book without a tremendous amount of scholarly and personal support from other people. In particular, I am grateful to my colleagues at Amherst College, especially those in the American Studies Department. Professors Lisa Brooks and Kevin Sweeney offered me feedback on certain parts of the manuscript in its final stages that I know has made for a better book. I am equally indebted to Karen Sanchez-Eppler and Barry O'Connell for their inspirational work as researchers, teachers, and mentors. My colleagues in American Studies have done well to provide me time and support to finish this book; thank you to: Carol Clark, Frank Couvares, Robert Hayashi, Sujani Reddy, Molly Mead, Solsi Del Moral, Leah Schmalzbauer, and Wendy Bergoffen. Much gratitude goes to our staff members Karen Graves and Lisa Ballou for managing the nitty-gritty of my life at Amherst when it counts. I am also grateful to Ted Melillo for his words of wisdom and kindness, as well as to Eunmi Mun and Sahar Sadjadi for their friendship. In addition to faculty and staff, I am very thankful for the help I received from Amherst College's students, in particular the efforts of my incredibly smart and capable research assistants who helped find images for this book. A very special thanks to: Julian Roberson, Holly Burwick, and Francheska Santos – you are all wonderful scholars in the making and I cannot wait to see what you will do in the future!

I am also indebted to the faculty and staff in the American Culture Department at the University of Michigan, where this project began as a dissertation under the guidance of Philip Deloria, June Howard, Magdalena Zabarowska, and my outside reader, Matthew Briones, now at the University of Chicago. All four of my readers were instrumental in guiding my research, writing, and thinking about this work. Phil in particular has remained steadfast as a mentor and inspiration; words cannot possibly capture what his work and friendship have meant to me and this project. Working in the field of Native American and Indigenous studies (NAIS) has also enabled me to find a wide range of mentors and colleagues whose scholarship, leadership, and guidance have greatly shaped the path taken to complete this book. I will forever be thankful to: Neal Salisbury, Tiya Miles, Ned Blackhawk, Fred Hoxie, Phil Deloria, Jean O'Brien, and Robert Warrior; and to J. Kēhaulani Kauanui, Beth Piatote, Chad Allen, Meg Noodin, Michael Witgen, Vince Diaz, and Kathleen Washburn; as well as to my fellow graduate students from Michigan whose work in NAIS is crucial to our field, John Low, Veronica Hutch, Angela Parker, and Kelly Fayard. Most recently I have had the pleasure of sharing my work with NAIS colleagues from across the Five Colleges in the Connecticut River Valley and I am grateful for their guidance and encouragement, with many thanks to: Neal Salisbury, Kathleen Brown-Perez, Sonya Atalay, Lisa Brooks, Christine DeLucia, Alice Nash, and, of course, Ron Welburn.

The research for this book would not have been possible without help from an array of talented archivists and librarians. All of the librarians working at Dartmouth College's Rauner Library should be given special recognition for their knowledge of the collection and availability to help with just about any item that one might need. I especially want to thank Andi Bartelstein, Sarah Hartwell, Jay Satterfield, and Joshua Shaw. Huge thanks also to Katherine Kominis at the Howard Gotlieb Archival Research Center at Boston University and Amy Hague from the Sophia Smith Collection at Smith College and all of their staff. Thanks so much to John Cahoon at the Los Angeles County Museum of Natural History; Cheryl Gunselman at the Washington State University Library; Kevin Bradley at the National Archives and Records Administration in College Park, Maryland; and Ashley Adair at the Dolph Briscoe Center for American History at the University of Texas at Austin, as well as to Sarah Allison and Gwido Zlatkes at the Rupert Costo Library of the American Indian at the University of California at Riverside. A special thanks also to Brigham Young University's well-organized and highly trained staff who work with BYU's special collections and who helped with Gertrude Bonnin's personal papers; the friendly and helpful staff at the Center for Southwest Studies in Durango, Colorado; and the incredibly capable staff at the Wisconsin Historical Society in Madison, Wisconsin, as well as the librarians of the Newberry Library in Chicago for their assistance with Carlos Montezuma's personal papers. Of course thanks go to the many dedicated and highly trained librarians and archivists who work at the Hatcher Graduate Library of the University of Michigan, the Bentley Historical Library (especially Karen Jania), and the Clements Library. Thank you also to the staff and librarians at the Gene Autry National Center and the Braun Research Library of the Southwest Museum of the American Indian, especially Marva Felchlin and Liza Posas. An important thank you also goes to Kate Boyle and the Jones Library in Amherst, Massachusetts, for helping me with images related to Charles Eastman's family. Finally, a special thank you to the library staff of Amherst College's Archives and

Special Collections, including Mike Kelly and Rebecca Henning, and the important work they have begun by acquiring and building on the new Kim-Wait/Pablo Eisenberg Native American Literature Collection, which arrived at the College shortly after I did and has been invaluable to me in finishing this book.

My many research trips were well funded because of numerous travel grants, beginning with support from the Department of American Culture and the Rackham Graduate School at the University of Michigan. Most recently my final research was supported (in part) by a grant from the Amherst College Faculty Research Award Program, as funded by The H. Axel Schupf '57 Fund for Intellectual Life. In addition, I received funding support from the Westerners' Corral of Los Angeles to enable me to be in residence at the Autry National Center's research libraries, which helped strengthen the fourth chapter. While still writing the dissertation that preceded this monograph, I received funding from the Newberry Library and a Frances C. Allen Fellowship as well as support from Williams College, where I was the Gaius Charles Bolin Fellow in American Studies. At Williams I worked closely with faculty who helped me develop and grow as a scholar and I would like to thank Liza Johnson, Mark Reinhardt, Merida Rua, Cassandra Cleghorn, Dorothy Wang, Ji-Young, Maria-Elena Cepeda, Jackie Hidalgo, Nick Howe, Vince Schleitwiler, and Scott Wong for their guidance and their friendship. In addition to colleagues, student researchers, archivists, and librarians, this project would not have come to fruition without extraordinary editorial support from Deborah Gershenowitz of Cambridge University Press. I am also thankful for the help of Dana Bricken in securing proper permissions for my images and in assisting to ensure the quality of their resolution.

The vast majority of research for this project took place across the United States. I am thankful for the hospitality of Chris and Sarah in Durango and Claire Decoteau and Andy Clarno for hosting me during a short (but productive) stay in Chicago. And, of course, to Paul Farber for a place to stay in DC. Thank you also to my academic friends who read parts of the manuscript at various stages; your keen insights have made all the difference. Thank you, Matt Duques, for still reading so much of my work. Thank you, Jenn Solheim, my dear writing confidante, for our thought-provoking feedback sessions; you are a treasure! A very special thanks too to Heather Houser for helping me refine my thinking in key places and for being an extra mentor at crucial moments throughout this arduous process. Along with these colleagues and friends, I am especially grateful for those who have remained true intimates and whose kindness nourished my soul so I could complete this book. To all those who continue to inspire me every day, thank you so very much: Kathleen Tipler, Denise Bailey, Miriam Stanton, Miki Yagi, Talia Senders (and her family: Josh, Nate, and Jack!), Orlena Yee, Molly Keehn, Julia McQuade, Emily Lordi,

Jennifer Garcia Peacock, and Sarah Jacobson – I am very fortunate to have you all in my life.

A final thank you to my family: my mom, Dr. Terry Anne Vigil; my brother, Dr. Ryan Vigil; and my partner, Blake Johnson. All three of you are smart people who continue to push my intellectual growth. Thank you especially to the Vigils, who are superb editors and who have read or listened to a lot of this work with a generosity of spirit that is unmatched. I am very grateful to them for their insightful feedback, which has deepened my commitment and has encouraged me to write for a wide audience because the stories of these Native peoples' lives are worth hearing and worth repeating. Finally, a depth of gratitude for Blake because without your deep love, support, pet care, and cooking, this book (while keeping me happy and healthy) would never have been realized. Any errors are, of course, my own.

Introduction

A Red Man's Rebuke

The American government is one where the voice of the people is heard. It is therefore not a radical step nor a presumption for the native Red Man today to raise his voice about the welfare of his race. The Red Man has been mute too long. He must speak for himself as no other can, nor should he be afraid to speak the truth and to insist upon a hearing for the utterance of truth can harm no one but must bless all mankind.[1]
– Zitkala-Sa, *American Indian Magazine*, July–September (1918)

On the morning of October 9, 1893, Potawatomi political leader Simon Pokagon rang a facsimile of the Liberty Bell to open Chicago Day at the World's Columbian Exposition.[2] He had been invited by Chicago's mayor, Carter Harrison, who imagined that the ceremony might illustrate an important cultural connection between the rise of the great city of Chicago and the region's Indian people.[3] Yet as Pokagon, dressed in a suit like most white men that day although distinguished by a feathered cap, struck the bell, his appearance at the Fair offered a far more complex range of meanings.[4] Although Chicago Day may have been a high point for the mayor and others, commemorating as it did the anniversary of the Great Chicago Fire of 1871, the moment was a very different one for Pokagon.[5] His appearance at the Fair represented a critical, and urgent, opportunity.[6]

As a public Indian intellectual,[7] Pokagon aimed to engage the Fair's audiences in rethinking the very premise of the Exposition, namely, that America's origins and history could be represented through impressive displays of architecture, celebrations of scientific discovery, the marketing of new food products, and the articulation of white cultural supremacy through the displays along the Midway. This part of the fairgrounds embodied an arrangement of diverse cultures that followed an evolutionary logic for displaying humanity using a scale that measured human beings according to stages from "less" to "more" civilized. Within a mile-long strip of populist display the Midway relied on discrete ethnographic exhibitions of nonwhite people

performing in their "native" costumes to reiterate a social Darwinist understanding of progress. Pokagon saw things differently. He sought to show the
irony of Indians' participation in these celebrations of America when they
had lost both the political rights and the economic resources needed to claim
sovereignty over land and culture.[8]

As Pokagon ascended the stage to begin his opening address, he faced dignitaries who had traveled to Chicago from all over the world. Surveying his
audience, Pokagon began, "Where these great Columbian show-buildings
stretch skyward, and where stands this 'Queen City of the West' once stood
the red man's wigwams;"[9] His address aimed to fix the site of the Fair in
Indian terms. He did not celebrate the Expo, or praise Chicago Day, or
recall the events of the 1871 fire. Instead, he looked to an earlier time and
lamented the unfulfilled principles that lay behind democratic freedom and
the historical legacy of Columbus's journey to the Americas. His speech continued, "here met their old men, young men, and maidens; here blazed their
council fires."[10]

Chicago had once belonged to the Potawatomi. Pokagon's speech
remembered this past, as it baldly criticized American imperialism and the
tide of civilized white settlers that washed over – and displaced – indigenous peoples across the continent. His pointed and public counter-history
ignited controversy: Who invited *him* to the party? And how dare he
take the opportunity to impugn the message of the Exposition, the message – after all – of America itself? Contemporary readers might well
ponder the same question. Why *was* a Native American man chosen to
open Chicago Day in the first place? Pokagon was a trophy, an authentic
connection to the past, a piece of local nostalgia, a gesture toward irony,
a figure associated with a primitive freedom that was understood to be
American – and more.

This book is not about Simon Pokagon at all. But it is about the storm
of meanings, urbanism, industrialism, and imperialism that Indian public
performances elicited at the end of the nineteenth century. Surrounding
Pokagon's performance on that October day was an American cultural repertoire that Indians would have to confront, assimilate, master, defy, and
perform for the next several decades. This moment was strikingly different
from the America that earlier generations of Indian people, living during the
beginning of the nineteenth century, had to navigate. For the group of Indian
intellectuals who followed Pokagon had to face this new storm of meanings,
and their histories demonstrate the limits and opportunities to be found in
doing so. Pokagon was hardly the first Indian to grapple with an American
public, but he may have been the first to do so under the bright lights of
modernity,[11] and among the first to embody the profound question Gerald
Vizenor has posed to scholars of Native American studies: "What did it
mean to be the first generation to hear stories of the past, bear the horrors
of the moment, and write to the future?"[12]

This book aims to provide a collective cultural biography of four Indian intellectuals who followed in Pokagon's footsteps: Charles Eastman, Carlos Montezuma, Gertrude Bonnin (also known as Zitkala-Sa), and Luther Standing Bear. Pokagon's history, like theirs, concerned self-fashioning and the struggle to define oneself for a wide array of audiences. The ambivalence Pokagon's performance produced at the Fair connects him to these other individuals, as a pre-figure, a prototype, a near-ancestral figure.[13] Pokagon offered the opening scene, a moment of self-representation that foreshadowed the how and why of Native public performances, whether written or spoken, that began to flourish during the early decades of the twentieth century, and that helped define public perceptions of *Indianness*.[14]

Throughout the nineteenth and twentieth centuries, dramatic staged performances of Native Americans for non-Native commercial audiences became popular through Wild West shows, circuses, fairs, exhibitions, vaudeville, and burlesque, as well as in museums and tourist venues. In these acts of nostalgia, Native people were honored as romantic, brave, and spiritual, but doomed to extinction because of their inability to adapt to a modern world. During the century following, Native artists and intellectuals have increasingly taken control of Native performances, molding drama, music, dance, performance art, and film to conform to their own needs and values. Pokagon's opening asks us to turn to a much earlier period in the history of Native performance, and to consider if and how Native speakers, writers, actors, and activists were able to strategically harness the expectations of largely non-Native audiences on behalf of themselves and Indian Country. Unlike earlier Native public figures, like William Apess (1798–1839), Pokagon found himself working in a time when dominant expectations of Indians situated him in an already-doomed-to-vanish position that seemed to require a strategic performance of Native culture to assert an indigenous present and future. By the turn of the twentieth century, the stakes for Native public figures had shifted when it came to performance and representation. Despite this shift, Pokagon and the Indian intellectuals after him used the forms of writing introduced by European colonizers, in ways similar to that of their Native predecessors, to record their own histories, write petitions, and compose political tracts and speeches.[15] This latter generation of Native intellectual leaders faced a new challenge: how to claim their rights as modern, American citizens who wanted to use citizenship to intervene in the affairs of a government that had already been intervening in Native peoples' affairs for far too long. At the same time, Native leaders were also navigating the occasions when they were called upon to perform Indianness according to primitivist ideologies that aimed to define Indianness only in terms of the past – and a past as largely imagined by white audiences who romanticized the "noble savage" figure who was now in decline.[16] For Native intellectuals at the turn of the twentieth century, their representational politics revolved around how to retain their own definitions of indigenous sovereignty while fighting for political citizenship that was not about integration but rather a means for tipping the balance of power in their favor.[17]

For many non-Native people in the audience that day in 1893, Pokagon's appearance signified the power of pacification and the closing of the frontier.[18] How better to celebrate American progress and the triumph of modern democracy than by witnessing a Native man strike the Liberty Bell, a visual and aural reminder of the promises of democratic freedom? In addition, Indianness more generally enabled many white viewers, from different backgrounds, to celebrate a particular narrative of American freedom, one that disavowed the violence of colonialism and slavery on which the country's history rested.[19] Pokagon at the Columbian Exhibition tied together: America's founding, the industrial site of Chicago, an ancient Indian past, and a structural and ideological disavowal of the consequences and legacies of the actual Columbian encounter.[20]

Pokagon's rhetoric demonstrated the inextricable relation between the American nation and Indian people, so that white middle-class Americans could reimagine the so-called Indian Problem. With his gaze fixed toward the fairgrounds, Pokagon continued his critique: "The world's people, from what they have so far seen of us on the Midway will regard us as savages; but they shall yet know that we are human as well as they.... The Red Man is your brother, and God is the Father of all."[21] As they were confronted by Pokagon's narrative, many listeners might be moved to see the Fair through his eyes. Speaking on this global stage, he sought empathy, sympathy, and understanding as he gave voice to a lost, or rather neglected, history. For although his audience may have desired a romantic version of colonial grandeur, he remembered things differently. His speech highlighted the construction of this cultural space as a merger of spectacle and anthropological didacticism, in which "Columbian show buildings" erected to celebrate modern American civilization resulted in an erasure of "the red man's wigwam," an overwriting of Potawatomi claims to the land. He may have nodded, in his opening remarks, to Chicago as the "Queen City of the West," but Pokagon's speech also critiqued the hegemonic practices of racialization and cultural hierarchization that were built into Chicago Day's events and the Fair's displays, ready to be consumed by fairgoers.[22]

Pokagon's speech was not the only act of performance as resistance at the Fair. In fact, when the address was over he walked the fairgrounds with other Potawatomi to sell his published treatise, "The Red Man's Rebuke."[23]

For Pokagon, it was not just remembering or living in the moment, but writing for both the present and the future that mattered. Writing, in this sense, is actually a performance, and a central theme of this book. All four main subjects who came after Pokagon were part of a Native intellectual network who utilized different kinds of writing: the memoir, the letter, the tract, the polemic, the children's story, the opera, and so forth. Understanding

FIGURE 1. "The Red Man's Rebuke" pamphlet cover (1893).
Bentley Historical Library, University of Michigan, Ann Arbor, MI.

these writings – and the way they emerged out of intellectual circuits – is key to understanding the cultural politics Pokagon epitomized at the Exposition, and how his rhetoric prefigured that of Eastman, Montezuma, Bonnin, and Standing Bear.

In mass producing his "Rebuke," which was printed on birch bark and sold as a souvenir, Pokagon exemplified the strategies later Indian intellectuals would use to make their voices heard.[24] In effect, he is the first member of the cohort that this book follows. His allusions are not accommodationist as much as aggressive and forward cultural politics. His "Rebuke" makes this point plain: "On behalf of my people, the American Indians, I hereby declare to you, the pale faced race that has usurped our lands and homes, that we have no spirit to celebrate with you the great Columbian Fair now being held in this Chicago city, the wonder of the world."[25] So the real legacy of Pokagon at the Fair might be how he expanded the boundaries of oppositional discourse and did so on a stage and in writing. Despite the use of celebratory rhetoric situating Chicago as "the wonder of the world," the rest of the rebuke lamented the imperial logic of the Fair.[26]

The "Rebuke" also positioned Pokagon as a representative figure for Indian people. Just as Pokagon was tribally transcendent in his writing, so too were the four figures I trace, who often tended to speak not for the

tribe or for a specific Indian nation but for their "race."[27] This was a crucial strategy for individuals interested in acquiring the rights of citizenship
in the United States, not merely to become a part of the nation but rather
to have more tools in their arsenal ready to critique and reshape the nation
that continued to threaten indigenous sovereignty. Nowhere did Pokagon's
"Rebuke" specify his connection to the Pokagon band of Potawatomi, but
instead he used the more general category of "American Indian" to assert
his position and his politics. When he writes, "on behalf of my people," he
means – and was read to mean – Indian people writ large. This type of categorization enabled Pokagon to juxtapose Indianness with American whiteness. For then and now Indianness mattered and so, as Robert Warrior has
argued in *Tribal Secrets*, it was less a matter of emphasizing "Indian" in
essentialist terms and more a matter of disentangling it from questions of
authenticity by looking to different modes of performance; education, writing, lecturing, and performing (acting).[28] Furthermore, when the text references the "pale faced race" Pokagon is hailing a white audience. His rebuke
becomes even more personal and emphatic by using the phrase "declare
to you" in order to appeal to his audience through their shared humanity.
Within this personal hailing, however, is always the voice of collectives, both
Indian and white, where the dispossession of Indian lands is a real problem
given that "we" (Indian people) "have no spirit to celebrate" the Fair or the
city of Chicago as any kind of "wonder of the world." Pokagon's assertions
offered a powerful counter-narrative to the one embodied in the gleaming
neoclassical buildings of the White City that were built in contrast to exhibits of lesser, nonwhite cultures along the Midway. Such distinctions could
not enthrall Pokagon; he performed at the Fair with a keen awareness that
the Exposition's aims were not his own.[29]

The Columbian Exposition had certainly succeeded in including if also
misrepresenting indigenous people in several important ways: first, through
inaccurate ethnological displays that characterized indigeneity as linked to
primitivism; second, through staged reproductions of Indian schoolhouses
on the Midway that argued Indian people must Americanize or disappear;
and third, through the appearance of Simon Pokagon, whose performance,
at least in part, pushed back against these other forms of representation.
The bold claims of "The Red Man's Rebuke," therefore, put forth Pokagon's
argument that European conquest ought not be celebrated but rather seen in
terms of infestation and disease as he described early colonists as pests and
parasites who infected Native people. Pokagon's rebuke ends by referring to
Judgment Day, when God will say to the white man:

I shall forthwith grant these red men of America great power, and delegate them
to cast you out of Paradise, and hurl you headlong through its outer gates into the
endless abyss beneath – far beyond, where darkness meets with light, there to dwell,
and thus shut you out from my presence and the presence of angels and the light of
heaven forever, and ever.[30]

Concluding with a reference to Christian theology, with his Potawatomi spin on it, Pokagon urges white readers to consider revising their views on American history in relation to the usurpation of indigenous lands and culture. For Pokagon's "Rebuke" makes clear that Christianity's God will most certainly recognize the sins of Euro-American colonization to grant Native people the power to punish those who have oppressed them, as the red man casts the white man out of Paradise "forever, and ever." Beyond Pokagon's speech and selling his keepsake, there is yet another moment from the Fair that offers a different, and somewhat contradictory, example of the presence and possible futures for Native people at the turn of the twentieth century. For Pokagon was not alone in using *this* cultural space to perform Indianness and to criticize American culture and society, and to use white and Christian rhetoric to do so.[31]

It was Wednesday, July 12, 1893, around ten o'clock in the morning, when the president of the Minnesota branch of the Chicago Folk-Lore Society gave his address to fairgoers, titled "Sioux Mythology." No doubt attendance was high given the topic and the "Indian craze" to see and hear authentic Indian talks during this period.[32] The speaker listed on the program, for the International Folklore Congress that day, was Dr. Charles A. Eastman. He was the only other Native person invited to present a formal speech at the Fair. Unlike Pokagon, his address was marked neither by pageantry nor by nostalgia but instead framed by the practical eye of scientific discourse.

Eastman's remarks began by invoking the rhetoric of social Darwinism. Although his key terms appeared trapped in a binary structure, civilized in opposition to savage, this familiar, if also problematic, framing would have gotten the attention of his audience. When discussing the American citizen, for example, Eastman employed subtlety to shift between sacred and secular registers. This shifting enabled him to suggest that in fact, the aborigines of the United States, like all human beings, possessed the same mind "equipped with all its faculties" to make them capable "even in ... [an] uncultured state" of the important "process of reasoning." Eastman's speech worked through the language of white civilization and racial uplift to craft a rational argument for why Indian people ought to have the same political rights as any other American citizen.[33]

Like Pokagon's Liberty Bell address, Eastman's participation at the Fair through the Folklore Congress afforded him a space to be strategic in his self-presentation. He was a member of the Sisseton-Wahpeton tribe and he was emerging as a well-known public intellectual, as Dartmouth's Indian no less, so he could draw on all these aspects of his identity to educate his audience about the past and present of Indian people. Considering that Eastman's speech cast Indians in scientific terms it is curious that it also briefly touched on spiritual beliefs. At the end of his talk, after listing the names of Sioux deities in connection to water and land, Eastman abruptly concluded with a subtle reference to a comparison between American society and the Sioux Nation. We might wonder if Pokagon sat among the audience trying to make sense of these closing remarks:

These few hurriedly collected facts concerning the mythology of the Sioux Nation will tend to show that the American Indian, *before the coming of the whites*, had a great faith in his "unknown God," whose colossal power, physical, moral, and mental, was so impressed upon his untutored mind and made him so conscious of his own sinful life, that he felt he was not warranted to approach Him direct, but through some mediator, who will intercede for him with his Great Mystery.[34] [emphasis mine]

Eastman's reference to "facts" seems to situate him and his topic within a social scientific discourse more than the study of folklore. When he suggests that the mythology of the Sioux Nation was quite different "before the coming of the whites," he deftly participates in a cultural logic that similarly underpinned Pokagon's critique of American civilization. Both speeches refer to loss. For Eastman, faith is at stake, and for Pokagon, land. In both instances the "coming of the whites," which we might read as the arrival of Columbus to the Americas and the occasion for the Fair itself, is to blame for cultural and physical dispossession. Eastman's conclusion also implies that Native people were, prior to colonial contact, more humble in their engagements with the Great Mystery. One might then infer that this relationship was changed and corrupted after "the coming of the whites."

Both talks by Eastman and Pokagon operated within an imagined nostalgia promoted by the Fair's organizers, who sought to recall an America long gone, but both men also had an eye to the future. For these Indian intellectuals, the past they mourned was neither that of Frederick Jackson Turner's closed frontier nor a Puritan New England. In addition, their future was concerned neither with the extension of American influence abroad nor a conquest of territories, but rather focused on overcoming and overturning a history of fraught interactions between whites and Indians that had resulted in so many losses, in people, in faith, and in land.

For Eastman, the Fair marked the beginning of a career as a public speaker, a writer, and an educator. In a similar fashion to Carlos Montezuma, Gertrude Bonnin, and Luther Standing Bear, he moved from the specific site of the Folklore Congress to other cultural spaces to push beyond the limits of Indianness defined by types, such as "noble savage," "wild Indian," and "warrior." Instead, Eastman and other Native intellectuals found ways to represent a range of ideas about the roles Indian people could play as political and cultural citizens of the United States, and as members of Native communities. Their intellectual work did not capitulate to the ideology of the Fair, but rather sought to remember and create an American nation that acknowledged the conquest of Native lands *and* the necessary presence of

Indian people in its future. These were the stakes and claims Eastman's generation of Native intellectuals set forth.

Why Collective Cultural Biography?

This history begins with Charles Eastman, the Native physician well known for tending to survivors of the Wounded Knee massacre in 1890, just three years before his presentation at the Chicago Fair, before he became active as a writer of autobiographies, political tracts, and young adult books. The next chapter turns to another member of this cohort, Carlos Montezuma (Yavapai), who, like Eastman, trained as a doctor. Unlike Eastman, however, Montezuma did not move around different reservations in search of work or rely on white progressive allies in the Northeast, but succeeded in his medical career based out of Chicago. Perhaps Montezuma was among the fairgoers in 1893 who witnessed Pokagon's speech or came to hear Eastman talk. Living in Chicago for most of his life, Montezuma was an active member of local professional groups, and able to self-publish a Native newsletter circulated throughout the United States to Indian and non-Indian readers alike. Montezuma no doubt drew on similar sorts of networks that had supported Pokagon's writing and speaking career through the patronage of white men and women among Chicago's Gold Coast "high society" and the Chautauqua literary circuit and "Friends of Indians" groups nationwide.[35] The third chapter of this book moves to a friend of Eastman and the former fiancée of Montezuma, Gertrude Bonnin (Yankton Sioux). Often known as Zitkala-Sa, after she began publishing short stories, Bonnin also became active as a lobbyist in Washington, DC. Bonnin's story also brings us to the West Coast, specifically Utah, where she and her husband, Raymond, lived and worked among the Ute. There she collaborated with William Hanson, a professor of music at Brigham Young University, to produce an opera titled *The Sun Dance* in 1910, before she relocated to Washington, DC, to found and become president of the National Council of American Indians, a position in which she served until her death. The fourth and final chapter of this book is largely centered on activities of performance on the West Coast, in California, and on the acting and activist career of Luther Standing Bear (Oglala Sioux). Beginning with his education at the Carlisle Indian Industrial School (where Bonnin had taught, Eastman had worked as a recruiter, and Montezuma had been the resident physician for the well-known football team), Standing Bear first became acquainted with Carlisle's headmaster, Richard Pratt, who would help shape the young man's future. The fourth chapter continues by examining the ways Standing Bear maneuvered Pine Ridge as a teacher before being hired as a translator and performer by William "Buffalo Bill" Cody, which set the stage for his work in the emergent film industry of Hollywood.[36] Examining all four of these

individuals in detail, while also attending to their points of intersection and
disjuncture, reveals the different strategies Native intellectuals used as public figures during the early twentieth century.

All four of them were active as writers. Therefore, I turn to the work
of American Indian literary critics, such as Robert Warrior, Philip Round,
and Penelope Kelsey, who have focused on the subversive potential of the
writing Native people produced.[37] I focus on these four writers in particular because some of their political works have been understudied and they
have also been criticized for advocating assimilation, despite the fact that
they invariably had tribal-centered agendas, which contradicted arguments
in favor of acculturation. My choice to examine them together contributes
to this scholarship as much as it also reflects the work of historians of the
Progressive Era. This book builds on the work of Frederick Hoxie, who
has highlighted the importance of these individuals, and the recent work of
Cathleen Cahill, whose social history of the Indian Service examines Native
and non-Native employees and broader issues related to governance, colonialism, and gender (*Federal Fathers & Mothers* [2011]). In addition, Jean
O'Brien's *Firsting and Lasting: Writing Indians out of Existence in New
England* (2010), which looks to an earlier time period and focuses on the
ways that local histories written by European Americans operated to assert
their own modernity while simultaneously denying it to Indian people, has
influenced how I analyze these Native intellectuals and their engagement
with modernity. This book, like these other histories, aims to push back
against dominant trends in American historical writing that have suggested
the period between the 1880s and the 1930s be understood as a decline
in Native activities because of either population decreases or the so-called
success of assimilation practices. The collective nature of this history aims
to showcase quite the contrary, that there were a diversity of ways Native
intellectuals participated in American society with regards to politics and
culture during the early twentieth century.[38]

My examination of the cohort of Indian cultural producers in the
pages that follow links their work to political changes, like the Dawes Act
(1887), the Indian Citizenship Act (1924), and the Indian Reorganization
Act (1934) to add to the scholarship of Robert Berkhofer, Brian Dippie,
Philip J. Deloria, and others.[39] These scholars have successfully traced the
origins and movements of white attitudes and representations of concepts
like "vanishing Indian" or "playing Indian" that appeared in science, literature, art, and popular culture, while also influencing federal Indian policy. Inspired by these earlier studies, but with attention more focused on
Native responses to white perceptions and utilizing Deloria's theorization
of dominant American cultural "expectations," I consider the ways that
American cultural ideologies helped shape policy formation to point out
how this intersection contributed to the emergence of pan tribal[40] networks,
which affected changes in federal policy. Indians perceived this early, as Lisa

Brooks' and Matt Cohen's work examining the Northeastern networks of the eighteenth and early nineteenth centuries demonstrates,[41] but this later generation – through writing, lobbying, and performance – saw a real opportunity to shape white culture and federal Indian policy. At the same time, they could not miss the possibility of shaping a broad "race" defined by pan-Indian culture. So their project rapidly became dense and complicated and contradictory. Through pan-tribal alliances, these Indian intellectuals responded to threats posed by a coercive and oppressive federal bureaucracy and educational system, by articulating a common Indian identity that ran counter to dominant narratives regarding Native savagery or disappearance. At the same time, pan-tribal organizations such as the Society of American Indians (SAI) formed when similar sorts of progressive reform groups, created by white social activists, aimed to reshape cultural practices and politics. The strategies used by different pan-tribal groups and the ways these groups accessed Native and non-Native networks fit within a history of political organizing from the early twentieth century, while simultaneously emphasizing the issues and concerns affecting indigenous communities. The choice to focus on Native writers who had political concerns also aligns with Beth Piatote's recent work. In *Domestic Subjects: Gender, Citizenship, and Law in Native American Literature* (2013), Piatote examines both literary texts and legal discourses, in Canada and the United States, which she argues intersected in a struggle between Native and non-Native people. In particular she emphasizes how by the late nineteenth century this struggle had shifted from what she terms the "tribal-national domestic" to the space of the Indian home or "intimate domestic." For the four subjects of this book, the shifting Piatote mentions is most evident in the autobiographical writings of Bonnin.[42]

By taking the form of a collective cultural biography, I redefine how we might think of this group of early twentieth-century intellectuals.[43] One way to consider the work of Indian intellectuals during this period is as a network of nodes and hubs, with a rich texture of multiple connections. Certainly Eastman, Montezuma, Bonnin, and Standing Bear's writings and political ideas circulated in just this way. They can also be viewed as a cohort of people with enough social and cultural commonality that they found themselves acting – not always together – in similar arenas and with similar goals. Put another way, they functioned as a community collective, at times working together with intent and planning, and in other moments as a circuit, a series of stops and positions along which individuals traveled. All of these metaphoric descriptions hold true, and yet none quite captures accurately the dynamics involved in their representational politics. Thus, in turning to the genre of collective cultural biography they can be studied as individuals and also read together to give us a new picture of the history of Indian intellectuals within the United States and the world during the early twentieth century.[44]

One way to examine them together is to focus on the shared circuits they
traveled through; for instance a lecture circuit like those begun by the lyceum
movement and those operated by the Chautauqua assemblies, or a literary
circuit like those established through publishing houses based in Boston
and New York. These public cultural sites were linked by non-Native and
Native peoples' participation in them as contributors (lecturers or writers)
and through booking arrangements and publishing ventures. Apart from
distinctly cultural circuits, there were well-worn, and at times coercive, circuits operated and maintained by the Bureau of Indian Affairs (or as it was
known during this era, the Office of Indian Affairs), such as the educational
circuits built around Indian boarding schools, like Carlisle, and efforts to
recruit and retain Native students. In choosing these four figures, it is important to note that all of them worked for the Indian Service at one time or
another. As Cahill has shown, "Their employment experiences gave them
firsthand knowledge about the Indian Office and reinforced their recognition of the shared concerns of Native people."[45]

In addition to circuits, I trace the networks accessed, created, and maintained by Native intellectuals from this period. Networks have a somewhat
more organic connotation and for the purposes of this book, at times, an
ambivalent function. A network is a structure, with individual centers of
gravity (the BIA, SAI, publishing companies like Little Brown and Company,
museums, Hollywood, etc.). Everyone had a network, but it is the nodes
where they overlap that are interesting. In a network, ideas flow through
both interpersonal and mediated communication. A circuit, then, reflects
the patterns that most often come up in a network: Native people who
meet every year at the SAI, publish in the same magazines, go to Boston to
speak in the same churches or at the same schools, publish books with the
same presses, and correspond with the same people at the BIA. When Indian
people travel the same circuit, we can think of them as a cohort, and thus a
group of people who are not necessarily like-minded but who are nonetheless similar and connected. They don't have to be friends, and they don't
even have to be social, but they are part of the same visible group. Then,
finally, when they become engaged, or break bread together, they can be seen
as a community. The four central figures chosen for this collective biography cover the waterfront. Viewed from Standing Bear's position, they are a
cohort at best. Viewed from Bonnin and Montezuma's, they are more like
a community. Viewed from Eastman's perspective, they are introduced as
people on a network and a circuit who might even be understood as founders of a Native rights movement.

Working within the genre of collective cultural biography enables me to
focus on both categorization and comparison, so that each chapter examines the specificities of an individual's life while remaining attentive to collective and cultural aspects that demonstrate the different relationships that
can be drawn between all four figures. They were performers. They worked

in the Indian Service. They were writers. Both Eastman and Bonnin worked
in a print culture driven by Northeastern publishing companies and the circulation of national periodicals, such as *Harper's* and the *Atlantic Monthly*,
whereas Montezuma created his own newsletter, *Wassaja*, and Standing
Bear mainly found support from white editors and writers based out of the
West Coast.

Certainly there are other Indian intellectuals, Seneca archaeologist Arthur
C. Parker, Ho-Chunk artist Angel de Cora-Dietz, or Wisconsin Oneida
Laura Cornelius – the sole female founder of the SAI – from this period that
could be at the center of this book. In many cases, these other people were
part of the same networks that Eastman, Montezuma, Bonnin, and Standing
Bear helped to establish. In fact, there were a compelling number of Native
anthropologists, like Meskwaki scholar William Jones (1871–1909), an
undergraduate at Harvard before studying with Franz Boas at Columbia
University, and Ella Cara Deloria (1889–1971), another Boas student, who
traveled throughout Indian Country studying Native traditions and languages to become influential in crucial ways. There were also other Native
artists, like Wa-Wa-Chaw, who came in contact with white intellectuals and
leaders of the day like Sir Oliver Lodge and Sir Arthur Conan Doyle. Her
story offers us a different route into American Indian cultural history, one
that considers how passions for art and writing were used to promote equality for Indian women; she appears in this book as a friend and correspondent of Montezuma.[46] During Pokagon's time there were also Native writers
like Sarah Winnemucca and Alexander Posey and ethnologists like Francis
La Flesche who offer other entry points into the history of Native intellectual production and the various networks they created and navigated.
Indeed, there were still more Native people who were active as performers,
writers, and activists during the early twentieth century, and although not at
the heart of this project, all of them make appearances in the chapters that
follow.

I have chosen to contain and limit my study to these four individuals
because they give us particular opportunities to juxtapose different professional worlds, like that of Hollywood and the medical profession. The
different performative strategies Standing Bear (who wore a feathered headdress for public talks) used as compared to Montezuma (who opted for the
tuxedo instead) reveal the range of strategies Native intellectuals might use
to make political arguments as public speakers. Another point of comparison that engages with differing discourses pertaining to both race and gender comes into clearer focus when considering public perceptions of Bonnin
as a classically trained violinist at Carnegie Hall in contrast to Standing Bear
as an "authentic" Indian reenacting scenes from America's Wild West. Their
collective story explicates the often ambiguous and complicated matrix
of ideas, performances, and practices in which these particular intellectuals engaged over the course of their lives. By tracing out the circulation of

their ideas, and delineating the various networks they shaped and formed, I highlight how they shared ideas about culture and politics that gained currency within educational and literary institutions to have an impact on world events.[47]

The biographical dimensions of this project engage the personal contours of each figure's life to illustrate how their political ideals changed over time in the context of their personal relationships and professional efforts. In addition to using the lens of biography and tracing these individuals through various networks and circuits as a collective, I have organized my analysis through four main themes. Each chapter, therefore, focuses on one figure as an exemplar in relation to a specific theme that was visible in that figure's life, and yet also visible in the lives of many Indian people from this period. In pairing Eastman with the theme of education, Chapter 1 considers occasions when higher education was ripe with racist discrimination while providing the tools for uplift. Turning to epistolary culture and Montezuma's correspondence and newsletter suggests the critical links Native readers made between their own literacy and the power of private and public arenas for letter writing.[48] Although all four were actively publishing their work, Bonnin more than the others helps showcase the opportunities that arose by working closely with patrons of the literary arts who might support her political reform agenda as much as her poetic craft. The fourth theme of performance equally runs throughout this entire project, but comes to the fore in Standing Bear's chapter given his work in all types of westerns and as cofounder, with Jim Thorpe, of the Indian Actors Association.

This thematic structuring and engagement with particular cultural theories and historiographies are driven by three central research questions. How did the first generation of urban Indian intellectuals mobilize and revise definitions of citizenship, assimilation, and modernity to fight for changes in federal policy? How did these individuals create and maintain ties to pan-Indian networks while crafting their own individual positions that balanced the concerns of various Native publics with those of white readers? How did the cultural productions of these Indian people, as performers and power brokers, shape and challenge American national policy?[49]

It has been too easy to look at Eastman, Montezuma, Bonnin, and Standing Bear – as well as their contemporaries, Arthur C. Parker, and so forth – and label them "assimilationist" or "accommodationist" because of the ways their writings seemed to capitulate to a progressive, American version of civilization defined by hierarchical rhetoric regarding race, class, and gender. It is more productive, in my view, to refer to the historically contingent strategies they used to engage in an Indianness discourse. I see this discourse as mutable and ever-present, so that each figure grappled with it in her, or his, own way. In a similar fashion, I examine processes of racialization and gendering (whether social, political, or cultural) concerning rhetorical, political, and performance choices made by all four of these Native intellectuals. This approach amplifies the ways this cohort was exceptional but not entirely unique given that Native people have always used diverse sets of ways to access and shape modernity.[50]

This history of Indian intellectuals reflects important shifts in Native and American print culture. Therefore, my approach to framing and reading the texts this generation of Native intellectuals produced draws on the work of literary scholars working within Native American and indigenous studies.[51] Robert Warrior's approach to Native writing in *Tribal Secrets: Recovering American Indian Intellectual Traditions* (1994) and *The People and the Word: Reading Native Nonfiction* (2005), and Philip Round's engagement with bibliographic/print culture in *Removable Type: Histories of the Book in Indian Country, 1663–1880* (2010) both assert the central importance of Native writings and the development of an intellectual tradition that has tribal-national roots as well as pan-tribal crossings. Warrior, for instance, looks to an earlier era and figures such as William Apess to assert "that the history of Native writing constitutes an intellectual tradition, a tradition that can and should inform contemporary work of Native intellectuals."[52] My focus on intellectuals and their use of networks builds on Warrior's engagement with "intellectual trade routes" by pointing to the origins and dimensions of a Native intellectual tradition rooted in nonfiction writing (autobiographies, critical essays, communally authored texts, and political documents), as well as the emergence of literary and performance texts.[53]

My emphasis on published writings and spoken performances suggests that these were cultural sites of resistance that Native people used to fight the encroachment of white cultural practices and beliefs as well as political oppression. Round's study, if earlier than mine regarding time period, also examines the history of Native intellectual writing as a type of resistance. He notes, "Nineteenth-century Indian resistance did not merely take the form of plains warriors on horseback; Indian people authored books that often argued for Indian rights and criticized land theft. In addition to publishing books, many of these authors engaged in other rhetorical acts such as national speaking tours lobbying for Native rights."[54] Moving forward in time, this book builds on Round's examination of earlier generations of Native American writers, "for whom the material properties of texts, as well as the manner in which they were produced and consumed, would become an important component of their creative and expressive efforts," by pairing close readings of texts with the contexts in which they were produced and consumed as well as their cultural and political impact. These texts are often written but are also based on speeches and other forms of public performance. I move out of the 1880s, when the first generation of professional Indian writers was just entering school, Bonnin at White's Manual Institute in Indiana and Luther Standing Bear at Carlisle, to follow the histories of their variegated educational experiences. For Eastman, Montezuma, and Bonnin were all able to showcase their work within national periodicals like the *Atlantic Monthly* and *Harper's*, a point that furthers my claim that they participated in a Native high cultural edge of modernism, and that builds on previous historical inquiries by Hazel Hertzberg, Lucy Maddox, Alan Trachtenberg, and Frederick Hoxie.[55]

Keywords in Native American Studies

This book takes an interdisciplinary approach to writing a cultural history of Native America that requires thoughtful consideration of several keywords. *Keywords*, a concept I borrow from American studies, organize vast quantities of complex information. They do lots of conceptual, descriptive, and sometimes argumentative work. The keywords that return again and again throughout this book include *citizenship, intellectual, blood,* and *Indianness*. All four inform and shape one another and contribute to the political work and cultural production possibilities and representational strategies that characterize this generation of Native intellectuals. A central issue for Native people at the turn of the twentieth century, like today, was the idea of citizenship. Although many Native people called for, or maintained, separation from the United States with regards to indigenous sovereignty and tribal nationalism, still more during this era sought to claim the rights of American citizenship so that they might more productively intervene in the body politic; certainly this was the case for Eastman, Montezuma, Bonnin, and Standing Bear.[56]

Citizenship can be defined in both political and cultural terms. Since the founding of the United States it has remained a contested category: to be a citizen often reflects the existence and permanence of national boundaries that delineate who can and cannot participate in shaping the nation. This idea of access has been coded in gendered, classed, and racialized terms given that the ability to become a citizen has also functioned as a litmus test for social fitness. For writers and activists like Eastman, Montezuma, Bonnin, and Standing Bear, access to political citizenship in the United States was of paramount importance, not because they aimed for integration into American society but rather because they saw political equality as a means for reshaping the settler-colonial nation that continued to intervene in the affairs of their people and in their lives. As Beth Piatote notes regarding the intervention of the "settler-national" state into the domestic sphere of Indian lives, "The mechanism of citizenship through which individuals come to belong to a nation works through the personal to produce the national."[57] This cut both ways for the Native intellectuals who are at the center of this book in that they used their personal stories and positions to speak on behalf of Indian people as one race, almost as one distinct nationality, with the hope of unsettling dominant discourses concerning fitness for citizenship within the United States. As intellectuals, they were eager to participate in shaping American culture. As Indians, they were equally committed to reshaping national narratives that had disavowed the roles Indian people played in the United States. Therefore, they viewed citizenship as one way to gain access to revising these dominant narratives. Their attachment to citizenship also arose out of progressive reform efforts from the late nineteenth century as well as a politics of racial uplift. Indeed, pan-tribal political organizing was made possible by the emergence of Native leaders who drew on their educational training, social status, and the appeal of their cultural work among American audiences to become ambassadors on behalf of Indian people in general.[58] The path toward equality – visible through citizenship – was never clearly defined or easy, and yet these individuals found ways to embrace the notion of racial uplift and the idea of citizenship while remaining critical of the national apparatus that had given birth to these concepts.[59]

Certainly citizenship was neither a panacea for social conflict between Indian and white people, nor could it correct for a long history of political disenfranchisement. In some ways, it runs against the grain of contemporary sovereignty discourse, which asserts that Indian nations are distinct political and cultural entities apart from the United States with their *own* citizenry. Yet citizenship remained a central concept and concern in the work of these four Native intellectuals, and as one avenue through which to effect change. They navigated the uncertain waters between citizenship on one hand and racial uplift on the other. For them, the U.S. Constitution's parameters for defining nationhood and nationalism through the bodies of its citizens proved critical to their political reform efforts. As Jean O'Brien argues in *Firsting and Lasting*, the long history of political disenfranchisement and the failure of non-Indians "to accord Indian peoples a legitimate place in modernity" have their roots in New England histories from earlier in the nineteenth century.[60] My discussion of the kind of "dual citizenship" this later generation of Indian intellectuals imagined builds on O'Brien's analysis of how William Apess personified Indian resistance in New England. In particular, she argues that his *Eulogy on King Philip* aimed "to undo the replacement narrative" in order to advance "a revolutionary idea: that Indians could both exercise self-determination as Indian peoples and become citizens, that is, the notion of dual citizenship."[61] The efforts of Eastman, Montezuma, Bonnin, and Standing Bear aligned with some of the assertions made by Apess in that they saw themselves as citizens of *both* Indian Country and the United States, and this sort of "dual citizenship" became central to the type of work they could do as public Native intellectuals.[62]

One might wonder exactly what we mean when we cluster individuals into a category called "Native Intellectuals." As a term, *intellectual* brings with it tacit understandings of power, identity, and cultural capital. *Intellectual* is of recent, twentieth-century origin and has been applied retrospectively to earlier centuries as well as to contemporary contexts. In its earlier usage, the term described those of different occupations in professions who claimed or were credited with the right to speak over and above particular interests on matters of general philosophical, ethical, and aesthetic importance. What gives intellectuals this role is their own expertise and the authority of reason and truth guiding intellectual discourse. Certainly, the intellectuals of this book were inheritors of Enlightenment reason and a product of modernity. They were at the same time critical of the social and political effects of this inheritance, and also guided by indigenous intellectual traditions derived from their personal experiences and a longer and broader Native writing, reading, and speaking history. I also take up the term *intellectual* by drawing on Edward Said's discussion of "the intellectual in exile," which he defined in part based on Theodor Adorno's thinking that "the hope of the intellectual is not that he will have an effect on the world, but that someday, somewhere, someone will read what he wrote exactly as he wrote it." Building on this idea requires one to rethink the notion of "exile" for Native Americans at the turn of the twentieth century who would, as Said suggests, be "necessarily ironic, skeptical, even playful – but not cynical" in their intellectual work. Furthermore, I use *intellectual* because in many instances this is how these figures, and their supporters, defined and thought of their roles.[63]

Many white and Indian people supported the careers of a substantial number of Indian intellectuals, in part because they understood the efficacy of an intellectual speaking on behalf of a minority ethnic group. An Indian intellectual in the early twentieth century became someone defined as uniquely educated and cultured, and therefore better positioned to perform in public as a face and voice for all Indian people. Just as Eastman, Montezuma, Bonnin, Standing Bear, and others traveled between varying social and cultural spaces to find particular ways of managing white expectations regarding intellectualism and Indian people, circumstances changed from the 1880s to the 1930s. Each mobilized the very notion of an Indian as an intellectual to fight for an increase in social, cultural, and political rights for *all* Native people. Ultimately, citizenship, racial uplift, and intellectualism were central components to the representational politics members of this cohort articulated.[64]

For all four of them, the quest to redraw the boundaries of American citizenship and revise the history of the United States in intellectual terms could not succeed without recognizing and adjusting to politics defined by blood. In material and metaphorical ways *blood* was a cultural ideology they had to confront. More specifically, they often encountered the concept "full-blooded" that could be used to justify their status as representative Indians. Since the 1830s, the discourse of blood has been used, in various places and for specific purposes, to classify Indian identity in political and racial terms across the United States. After the Dawes Act of 1887 and in the decades preceding the Indian Reorganization Act of 1934, a growing number of Indian intellectuals took up this discourse to assert that any drop of Indian blood qualified them to represent Indian America. Although an Indian "one-drop" rule functioned in this way, more often than not, what also mattered to Indian and non-Indian people alike was whether one could claim "full-blooded" status as an Indian person. These different notions of blood in relation to identity occurred simultaneously, and although contradictory their discursive power could be harnessed by many Indian people in strategic ways.[65]

For Indian intellectuals, the rhetoric of blood became part of a politics of recognition and useful as a tactic to illustrate a key argument: the more Indians among Americans in the United States, the better for the country as a whole, and the better for the world. Such an argument also clearly resisted a dominant narrative that presupposed all Indians would vanish by either assimilation or death. Throughout the early twentieth century, the vast majority of public lectures and writings by Indian intellectuals used this "full-blooded" language to argue for social and political inclusion in tandem with more cosmopolitan perspectives, which reflected the fluidity of both culture and identity. Eastman, for instance, became a sought-after public speaker. He was continually framed in terms of his elite connections and educational status (as cosmopolitan) and equally so through the fact of his "full-blooded" subjecthood as an Indian. Eastman therefore used both concepts to demonstrate that he was best positioned to speak about "real" Indian issues and on behalf of *all* Indian people. This rhetoric of "blood" also became part of a broader discourse that I refer to as *Indianness*.

These Native people were public figures who were as concerned with their own self-fashioning as they were with how to represent other Indian people. My aim here and throughout this book is for readers to see representational politics as a sort of shorthand for the dynamic interplay of Native self-presentation and how individual Indians sought to speak for Indian Country more generally; *Indianness* was a key to this practice. For instance, as Indian speakers, members of this cohort could represent a public face of Indian identity that could be read within their individual bodies and voices. As they drew strategically on an essentialist, white view of Indianness to speak for a collective race of Indian people, each could self-reflexively shape their own subjectivity in ways to signal the specific, as an example of Native progress, on the individual scale. All four took part in public performances where, whether they wanted to or not, they were interpellated as Indians by their audiences. In these instances the urge to "play Indian" became a strategy whereby they could *represent* and also *intervene* in a discourse of Indianness.[66] Indianness, then, is critical as a keyword given that it operated during this era as a productive and destructive discourse gesturing to all things Indian. For Native people, Indianness indexed sites of possibility regarding performativity and identity whereby they could use their bodies, voices, clothing, and writings to conform to dominant white expectations regarding Indianness *or* do just the opposite.[67] The reality is that most found strategic ways to do both. By engaging with various tropes of Indianness, Native people could simultaneously gain the attention of white supporters and progressives while destabilizing the boundaries of Indian subjectivity, for example when they altered their mode of *address* to conflict with their mode of *dress*.[68]

During the late nineteenth and early twentieth centuries, stereotypical associations between romantic narratives regarding the Plains and nature as well as noble savagery permeated white cultural formations and expectations. For any of these Native intellectuals to have a voice in changing Indian political affairs and American cultural formations, they needed to be legible as Indian people, which often meant working within fraught permutations of Indianness. As a concept, Indianness traveled, perhaps paradoxically, because of both its stability and fluidity. On one hand, it was understood as locatable in the bodies of actual Indian people, and on the other, also in narratives about how to be Indian that were often drawn from earlier representations, novels by James Fenimore Cooper or paintings by George Catlin. Both of these understandings of Indianness grew out of and were reinforced by white cultural expectations. This book examines how Indian people strategically participated in performances to consider how they engaged Indianness, a seemingly essentialist discourse, to "play Indian" for mixed purposes.[69]

Indian Play

Like Pokagon before them, this cohort of Native intellectuals grappled with the politics of performativity. By this I mean how to use speech, language, and other nonverbal forms of expressive action to intervene in American culture and politics. For them, public appearances often required a speaker to perform (or play) Indian, to visually and rhetorically represent oneself in terms that conjured a strategic sort of ethnic authenticity. The problem in this type of performative move came at particular moments. For Eastman, I consider how his use of certain forms of costuming fed into a self-perpetuating market for Indianness. Despite his education and literary achievements, Eastman was continually asked throughout his life to "dress up" and "play" the part of Dartmouth's College's famous Indian graduate, or to even play the part of Samson Occom (1723–92), the foundational Native figure associated with the College. In the case of Montezuma, his engagement with performativity and an Indianness discourse ran in a different direction from that of his peers. He relied less on visual tropes (a feathered headdress, for instance) and more on rhetorical twists and turns to play the part of a "proper" Indian citizen. For example, he drew on the faulty logic of an American democratic society that defined citizenship through the U.S. Constitution without recognizing the legitimacy of Indian people as members of the nation. His article and speech "Life, Liberty & Citizenship" provided multiple readings of the song "America" to critique U.S. history, and because it was printed in *Wassaja* for Indian readers and also presented publicly to a mostly white audience in Chicago, Montezuma succeeded in circulating his ideas to a range of publics interested in Indian reform issues. For Bonnin the fact that her Indian blood needed to be made visible for white audiences who asked her to dress up as an "Indian princess" while she lectured was an important problem. So much so that despite her own feelings of uneasiness she repeatedly submitted to requests to see her as an Indian maiden or princess, with the hope of gaining allies in her quest for wider acceptance of Indian people as members of American society, who could then perform their own articulations of Native dress, language, and culture. Bonnin remained increasingly concerned with how others might trade on this type of "Indian play," and Chapter 3 reveals how she wrote regularly to her Indian friends about how best to counteract the "work" being done at the time by "false" Indians, like Red Fox St. James and Princess Chinquilla.

Luther Standing Bear recognized the power inherent in having Indian actors "play" Indian onscreen when he argued in favor of hiring "real" Indians to portray Indian people in shows and in film. Although his writings and letters demonstrate concern regarding the misrepresentation of Indian people, his work with the Indian Actors Association (IAA) in some ways reified an Indianness discourse that was still guided by rules set by the Bureau of Indian Affairs, policies such as allotment and the racialized logic of blood quantum. Relying on such practices to define an Indian's personhood did not necessarily disentangle them from the structures of power that reproduced the very misrepresentations Standing Bear sought to correct, and that decades earlier Pokagon had brought to center stage in his appearance at the World's Fair in Chicago.

A Native Intellectual Network Emerges

Just six years after Pokagon had strolled the fairgrounds during Chicago Day, on February 7, 1899, Richard Pratt, a white progressive activist, wrote to Carlos Montezuma about the death of their mutual friend, Chief Simon Pokagon. Pratt's letter highlighted the emergence of an Indian intellectual network that he thought was critical to the future success of the Carlisle boarding school and the cause of Indian citizenship, the latter of which depended on the legibility of accomplished Indians as exemplars for a white American public. Pratt's letter makes clear that he considered Montezuma one of these figures. Pratt also refers to books, like *Queen of the Woods* by Pokagon that had been published posthumously that same year, as examples of what an educated Indian might achieve and that could also serve as cultural tools for educating white Americans. In addition, Pratt's letter urged Montezuma to visit Carlisle for commencement. In this instance, Montezuma was being called on to provide physical proof for the school's recent graduates of just what an accomplished Indian could do for himself and for his race. It would seem he was being asked to play the part of an Indian intellectual.[70]

Returning to the site of Chicago and the 1893 Fair, we can see how the future of America relied both on remembrances of America's past and to some extent on the role of Indian people in that past. Pokagon's visage as he rang the Liberty Bell worked as part of a language of types that had emerged during this period regarding the role of race in American society. As Americans mourned the end of particular versions of America, certain types became increasingly mythologized in order to properly mourn this passing. For example, the cowboy and the "wild" Indian, which Fair visitors could see performing just outside the fairgrounds where William Cody had his Wild West troupe set up, as well as the true woman and the original Puritan, were typologies that could be mobilized to assert popular conceptions of identity, often based on social evolutionary theory. These ideas took hold most visibly and spectacularly at the Fair through the Midway Plaisance. Visitors there could take a visual accounting of different "types" of ethnicities presented in such a way as to suggest a progression toward Americanness, culminating in the monolithic whiteness signified by the White City at the Fair – the site Pokagon criticized in his opening address.[71]

The White City as the beacon of American progress and the Fair as a call to cultural enrichment helped foster social and cultural hierarchies by marking distinctions around social types and cultural practices. Pokagon found ways to maneuver through this hierarchization, just as the Indian writers and readers who followed him did. Charles Eastman and Gertrude Bonnin's participation in the expanding book and periodical market enabled them to use print culture as the site through which to enter a national discussion about the corrosive aspects of acculturation and the language of types. Still, this language created an illusion of stability for class-based and race-based hierarchies. Therefore, many Indian authors attempted to disrupt this imaginary rigidity by defining Indianness on their own terms even when faced with publishers and reviewers who aimed to define and market them as ethnic, exotic others.[72] Of course Indian writers, like their white, immigrant, African American, Latino, and Asian American contemporaries during this period, varied in their responses to the language of "types" and debates regarding U.S. imperialism and national identity, just as Pokagon and Eastman presented different sorts of speeches at the 1893 Fair.[73] Some Native writings invariably shored up hegemonic cultural practices, while others challenged laws, policies, films, novels, and performances. Pokagon's speech and the circulation of his pamphlet at the World's Fair offer a couple instances of these sorts of strategic practices.

Despite the coercive technologies involved in the Fair's design, Pokagon's appearance as an Indian intellectual enabled him to, in a speech and in a published "rebuke," resist the racialized logic of the Fair to remind visitors of an Indian past, present, and future.[74] His representational politics illustrates the different strategies Native intellectuals used to respond to white culture's demands. Although it is tempting to recall only the pageantry of Pokagon's performance at the Fair, for him the politics underlying this moment were of the utmost importance. All Indian intellectuals during this period wrestled constantly with similar problems regarding self-representation and Indianness within an array of public spectacles and international events, like a world's fair. In Pokagon's case, his well-choreographed movements at the Fair, from ringing the bell, to making a speech and then selling a keepsake, arose out of different institutional demands and expectations regarding his position as a Potawatomi leader, a supporter of interracial political projects, and a temperance worker. The Fair was not wholly about illustrating U.S. supremacy as much as it was also about creating it. Thus, Pokagon played a lead role at the Fair, where he did and also did not do what the organizers had planned. Such an opportunity for Native performance illustrates how Pokagon's appearance was a critical precursor for the cultural and political work that would be possible for Eastman, Montezuma, Bonnin, and Standing Bear, as well as other members of their generation's intellectual cohort. For many Native people, this was the beginning and not the end of a quest to redraw boundaries pertaining to indigenous citizenship and nationalism.

Notes

1   *Zitkala-Sa: American Indian Stories, Legends, and Other Writings*, edited by Cathy N. Davidson and Ada Norris (New York: Penguin Books, 2003), 182.
2   Although President Grover Cleveland officially opened the Fair on May 1, 1893, the largest single day of attendance was Chicago Day with over 700,000 visitors.
3   For more on the history of the 1893 World's Fair in Chicago see: Hubert Howe, *The Book of the Fair* (Chicago: Bancroft, 1893); David F. Burg, *Chicago's White City of 1893* (Lexington: University of Kentucky, 1976); Chicago. World's Columbian Exposition, 1893. *Report of the President to the Board of Directors of the World's Columbian Exposition* (Chicago: Rand McNally, 1898); Chicago. World's Columbian Exposition, 1893. *World's Columbian Exposition, 1893: Official Catalogue* (Chicago: Conkey, 1893); Rossiter Johnson, ed., *A History of the World's Columbian Exposition Held in Chicago in 1893* (New York: Appleton, 1897–8); U.S. World's Columbian Commission, *Classification of the World's Columbian Exposition, Chicago, U.S.A., 1893* (Chicago: Donohue and Henneberry, 1891); Trumbull White and William Ingleheart, *The World's Columbian Exposition, Chicago, 1893* (Philadelphia: Historical Publishing Co., 1893).
4   John Low, "The Architecture of Simon Pokagon," in *Queen of the Woods, Ogimakwe Mitigwaki, a Novel by Simon Pokagon*, with a foreword by Philip J. Deloria (Lansing: Michigan State University Press, 2011), 9.

5   The relationship between Harrison and Pokagon is explicated further by C. H. Engle, the editor of Pokagon's book *Queen of the Woods* (1899), whose introduction provides a brief biography of Pokagon. An important Native literary contemporary, Joseph Nicolar, produced a text that appeared around the same time in 1893; see: *The Life and Traditions of the Red Man: A Rediscovered Treasure of Native American Literature*, edited by Annette Kolodny (Durham, NC: Duke University Press, 2007).

6   Frederick E. Hoxie offers one of the first accounts of Pokagon's work at the Fair through the distribution of his booklet titled "The Red Man's Rebuke" in *Talking Back to Civilization: Indian Voices from the Progressive Era* (New York: Palgrave Macmillan, 2001). Cornelia Hulst notes the importance of Pokagon's speech titled "Red Man's Greeting" in *Indian Sketches: Père Marguette and the Last of the Pottawatomie Chiefs* (orig. 1912, reprinted in 2010). Hoxie and Hulst disagree regarding the clothing that Pokagon wore at the Fair. The former includes a photograph of Pokagon in a suit noting, "This ... was taken about the time he delivered his *Red Man's Greeting* at the Chicago World's Columbian Exposition," whereas the latter refers to a painting captioned "Chief Pokagon, In his tribal attire as he appeared at the World's Fair on Chicago Day." My narrative aligns with accounts based on newspaper reports about Chicago Day, which is the same conclusion John Low draws in his essay "The Architecture of Simon Pokagon" (2011).

7   For Native intellectuals see: David Martinez, ed., *The American Indian Intellectual Tradition: An Anthology of Writings from 1772–1972* (Ithaca, NY: Cornell University Press, 2011) and Robert Warrior, *The People and the Word: Reading Native Nonfiction* (Minneapolis: University of Minnesota Press, 2005). For an important overview, if not exhaustive list, see the following for literary and print histories pertaining to Native people before 1890: Philip H. Round, *Removable Type: Histories of the Book in Indian Country, 1663–1880* (Chapel Hill: University of North Carolina Press, 2010); Lisa Brooks, *The Common Pot: The Recovery of Native Space in the Northeast* (Minneapolis: University of Minnesota Press, 2008); Maureen Konkle, *Writing Indian Nations: Native Intellectuals and the Politics of Historiography, 1827–1863* (Chapel Hill: University of North Carolina Press, 2006); Barry O'Connell, ed., *Son of the Forest, and other Writings by* William Apess, *a Pequot* (Amherst: University of Massachusetts Press, 1997).

8   For the context in which Pokagon, as a Potawatomi, appeared at the Fair see: Hulst, *Indian Sketches*.

9   *Talking Back to Civilization: Indian Voices from the Progressive Era*, edited with an introduction by Frederick E. Hoxie (Boston, MA: Bedford/ St. Martin's, 2001), 32.

10 For a printed version of Simon Pokagon's speech at the 1893 World's Columbian Exposition see: James E. Seelye and Steven Alden Littleton, eds., *Voices of the American Indian Experience* (Santa Barbara, CA: ABC-CLIO, 2013), 381–2.

11 Modernity can be understood as a condition, rather than the designation for some particular period of time. Aspects of the modern condition may arise at any time and place, but they are most generally associated with historical trends from Cartesian philosophy, industrial capitalism, revolutionary politics, and cultural changes from the turn of the nineteenth century. Modernity as a

theoretical concept has been used by many different scholars within American studies. Cultural historians have used definitions for modernization (rather than modernity) as a historically contingent process in their work. Some key texts that help to illuminate the difference between thinking through modernity and the modern as a condition versus modernism as a marker for a specific period of modernization, and modernism versus postmodernism are: Matei Calinescu, *Five Faces of Modernity: Modernism, Avant-garde, Decadence, Kitsch, Postmodernism* (1987); David Harvey, *The Condition of Postmodernity: An Enquiry into the Origins of Cultural Change* (1991); and Fredric Jameson, *Postmodernism, or, The Cultural Logic of Late Capitalism* (1992). This generation of Indian intellectuals had to contend with modernity as a concept with ideological roots (pertaining to ways of thinking and acting), and in reference to a certain historical period marked by the rise of industrial capitalism.

12 See: Gerald Vizenor, *Manifest Manners: Postindian Warriors of Survivance* (Hanover, NH: University Press of New England, 1994), 51.

13 There were Native writers and intellectuals before Pokagon who prefigured the type of work he did and the range of writing and political strategies later used by Eastman and his colleagues, such as William Apess. See: Barry O'Connell, ed., *On Our Own Ground: The Complete Writings of William Apess, a Pequot* (N.P.: University of Massachusetts Press, 1992); Konkle, *Writing Indian Nations*; Brooks, *The Common Pot*; David J. Carlson, *Sovereign Selves: American Indian Autobiography and the Law* (Urbana: University of Illinois Press, 2006); Andy Doolen, *Fugitive Empire: Locating Early American Imperialism* (Minneapolis: University of Minnesota Press, 2005); Eileen R. Elrod, *Piety and Dissent: Race, Gender, and Biblical Rhetoric in Early American Autobiography* (Amherst: University of Massachusetts Press, 2008); Karim M. Tiro, "Denominated 'Savage': Methodism, Writing and Identity in the Works of William Apess, A Pequot," *American Quarterly*, American Studies Association, 1996.

14 For a theoretical study of performance and intersectionality see: Jose Esteban Muñoz, *Disidentifications: Queers of Color and the Performance of Politics* (1999). For Indian performance strategies from an earlier historical period see: Joshua David Bellin and Laura L. Mielke, eds., *Native Acts: Indian Performance, 1603–1832*, Afterword by Philip J. Deloria (2011).

15 For more regarding early Native American writers and leaders, such as Samson Occom, Joseph Brant, Hendrick Aupaumut, and William Apess, see: Brooks, *The Common Pot*.

16 For one of the earliest scholarly accounts examining the history of the "noble savage" see: Robert Berkhofer, *The White Man's Indian: Images of the American Indian from Columbus to the Present* (New York: Vintage, 1979).

17 For the history of Native American performance with an emphasis on the post-1960s context see: S. E. Wilmer, ed., *Native American Performance and Representation* (Tucson: University of Arizona Press, 2009), 3–4. Also see: Christy Stanlake, *Native American Drama: A Critical Perspective* (Cambridge,: Cambridge University Press, 2009), who contends, "Performance venues, such as theatre, cinemas, dime museums, wild-west shows, and world's fair exhibitions, capitalized on the exotic allure of the 'vanishing race.' ... These stereotypes of Noble/Savage for men or Princess

(ready-to-die-for-her-love-of-the-white-man)/Squaw (sexually ravenous savage) for women, weave throughout American history and, in so doing, persist in media representations of Native peoples, even today"(4). For work on the earlier generations of Native American writing traditions and intellectual legacies see the following: O'Connell, ed., *On Our Own Ground* and *A Son of the Forest and Other Writings* Konkle, *Writing Indian Nations;* Warrior, *The People and the Word;* Brooks, *The Common Pot;* Matt Cohen, *Networked Wilderness: Communicating in Early New England* (Minneapolis: University of Minnesota Press, 2009); Jean O'Brien, *Firsting and Lasting: Writing Indians Out of Existence* (Minneapolis: University of Minnesota Press, 2010); Scott Lyons, *X-Marks: Native Signatures of Assent* (Minneapolis: University of Minnesota Press, 2010); and Round, *Removable Type.*

18   Regarding westward expansion, as well as race, nation, and empire pertaining to the United States, see: Michael Hardt and Antonio Negri, *Empire* (2000); Amy Kaplan, *The Anarchy of Empire in the Making of U.S. Culture* (2005); Laura Wexler, *Tender Violence: Domestic Visions in the Age of U.S. Imperialism* (2000); Ann Stoler, *Carnal Knowledge and Imperial Power: Race and the Intimate in Colonial Rule* (2002); Anne McClintock, *Imperial Leather: Race, Gender, and Sexuality in the Colonial Contest* (1995); Paul A. Kramer, *The Blood of Government: Race, Empire, the United States, and the Philippines* (2006); and Penny von Eschen, *Satchmo Blows Up the World: Jazz Ambassadors Play the Cold War* (2004).

19   For white perceptions of Indian people see: Sherry Smith, *Reimagining Indians: Native Americans through Anglo Eyes, 1880–1940* (Oxford University Press, 2000). Smith examines a group of Anglo-American writers whose books about Native Americans helped shape Americans' understanding of Indian peoples at the turn of the twentieth century. These writers produced work celebrating Indian cultures, religion, and artwork and revealed their own doubts about the superiority of Euro-American culture. Moving from the East to the West, these writers' work also encouraged cultural relativism, pluralism, and tolerance in American thought.

20   Mark Smith argues that the transcendent symbolic and aural power of bells is critical to American culture in *Listening to Nineteenth-Century America* (2000). In specific regards to the term *Indianness*, I use it to refer to a discourse that circulated throughout America and could be both oppressive toward Indian people and open to modification by them. As Scott Richard Lyons points out, "even now discourses of Indianness are generated by institutions, the state, and the market" (*X-Marks,* 24).

21   "The Red Man's Rebuke" (Chicago: Self-published, 1893), 2, Bentley Historical Library, Ann Arbor, MI.

22   Robert W. Rydell, *All the World's a Fair: Visions of Empire at American International Expositions, 1876–1916* (Chicago: University of Chicago Press, 1984) explicates the roles that exhibitions were to play as ideological displays and the specific ties to disciplinary knowledge, which buildings and designs of the Fair were meant to convey with regard to ideas of evolution, ethnology, and popular amusements. Figure 1: "The Red Man's Rebuke," booklet cover, courtesy of the Bentley Historical Library, University of Michigan.

23 Kelsey and other literary scholars argue that Pokagon's "Rebuke" can be read within the context of the eastern woodlands method of recordkeeping and its epistemic function. I acknowledge this framework, but situate my reading instead in the context of the Midwestern geography and culture that Pokagon found familiar and his awareness of the urban site of Chicago and the Fair where he intended to circulate this pamphlet. For more from her analysis see: Penelope Myrtle Kelsey, *Tribal Theory in Native American Literature: Dakota and Haudenosaunee Writing and Indigenous Worldviews* (Lincoln: University of Nebraska Press, 2008), 3.

24 As a result of a typeset printing process, Pokagon's "Rebuke" gave the appearance of *both* handwork and mass production. The object masqueraded as a tourist commodity – which it was. And yet, by typing his message onto the ephemeral outer skin of the birch tree, Pokagon aimed to make both a material and metaphorical gesture to Indian people, indeed "his own people." At the Fair, most visitors would be drawn to the material itself and then forced to confront the story imprinted on it. Such a strategy was not unique to Pokagon. Decades earlier, during the 1840s and 1860s, Sojourner Truth had sold images of herself, to support her lecture tours, in the form of carte-de-visite with the caption: "I sell the shadow to support the substance." She aimed to draw attention to herself and to the evils of racism and later sexism in the United States. For the comparison to Sojourner Truth I look to Nell Painter's *Sojourner Truth: A Life, A Symbol* (1996).

25 "The Red Man's Rebuke," 2.

26 For other work on Pokagon that views the limits of his positioning see: James Clifton, *The Prairie People: Continuity and Change in Potawatomi Indian Culture, 1665–1965* (1998) and A. LaVonne Brown Ruoff, "Simon Pokagon," in *Dictionary of Native American Literature*, edited by Andrew Wiget (1994).

27 Gertrude Bonnin speaks on behalf of her race in 1918 when writing her editorial comment on the work of the Society of American Indians in its periodical *American Indian Magazine*, from which the epigraph for this introduction is taken.

28 Robert Warrior, *Tribal Secrets: Recovering American Indian Intellectual Traditions* (Minneapolis: University of Minnesota Press, 1995), xx.

29 Simon Pokagon, "The Red Man's Rebuke" (Published in 1893 by C. H. Engle and Michigan Historical Society), 1, which is sometimes confused with the address Pokagon gave at the fair, called "The Red Man's Greeting." In fact, these are quite different in tone and content. Cheryl Walker's *Indian Nation, Native American Literature and Nineteenth-Century Nationalisms* (1997) offers a recent printing of "The Red Man's Rebuke." My reading is based off of a facsimile of the original birch-bark pamphlet from the Bentley Historical Library, University of Michigan, as well as Walker's reprint.

30 Pokagon, "The Red Man's Rebuke."

31 African Americans were also noticeably absent as participants in the construction of Fair exhibitions, although Frederick Douglass was there as a "representative" for Haiti. Together with Ida B. Wells they circulated "The Reason Why the Colored American Is Not in the World's Columbian Exposition"; for more see: Gail Bederman, *Manliness & Civilization* (1996).

32   Elizabeth Hutchinson, *The Indian Craze: Primitivism, Modernism, and Transculturation in American Art, 1890–1915* (Durham, NC: Duke University Press, 2009).

33   From the "International Folk-lore Congress Chicago, IL," *World's Columbian Exposition* (1893), later published by Charles H. Sergel Co. in Chicago, 1898. Reprinted by (series) Archives of the International Folk-lore Association, v. 1 (inside on Google books, "The number of copies of this book is limited to six hundred, of which this copy is No. 146"), page 220.

34   Ibid., 227.

35   For Pokagon's white patrons and benefactors see: Low, "The Architecture of Simon Pokagon," 5.

36   For more on performing Indians and William "Buffalo Bill" Cody's enterprise see: L. G. Moses, *Wild West Shows and the Images of American Indians, 1883–1933* (1999) and Joy Kasson, *Buffalo Bill's Wild West: Celebrity, Memory, and Popular History* (2001).

37   Warrior, *Tribal Secrets* and *The People and the Word*; Round, *Removable Type*; Kelsey, *Tribal Theory in Native American Literature*, 44.

38   Hoxie, *Talking Back to Civilization* and Cathleen D. Cahill, *Federal Fathers & Mothers: A Social History of the United States Indian Service, 1869–1933* (Chapel Hill: University of North Carolina Press, 2011). O'Brien, *Firsting and Lasting*.

39   Berkhofer, *The White Man's Indian*; Brian Dippie, *The Vanishing American: White Attitudes and U.S. Indian Policy* (Lawrence: University Press of Kansas, 1991); Philip J. Deloria, *Playing Indian* (New Haven, CT: Yale University Press, 1999) and *Indians in Unexpected Places* (Lawrence: University Press of Kansas, 2004); and Beth Piatote, *Domestic Subjects: Gender, Citizenship, and Law in Native American Literature* (New Haven, CT: Yale University Press, 2013).

40   Although *pan-tribal* was not a contemporary term for these figures, the concept predates them by over 100 years. In fact, as Lisa Brooks and others have shown, the earliest recorded Native usage of *Indian* in North America seems to have emerged from the Algonquian coast in recognition of "the need for an intertribal alliance some time before the emergence of King Philip and long before Tecumseh." For more see Brooks' essay in *Reasoning Together: The Native Critics Collective*, edited by Craig S. Womack, Daniel Heath Justice, and Christopher B. Teuton (Norman: University of Oklahoma Press, 2008), 243.

41   I refer to networks throughout this book and am indebted to the work of Matt Cohen in *Networked Wilderness*, and to Brooks, *The Common Pot*. Both are helpful in analyzing the types of networks that Native people created and maintained, even if some were later lost.

42   Piatote, *Domestic Subjects*, 2.

43   I use collective cultural biography as a genre and an analytical framework to make an argument regarding a particular cohort of twentieth-century Indian intellectuals. This approach is my own; however, for another model with a similar method, see: John Stauffer, *The Black Hearts of Men: Radical Abolitionists and the Transformation of Race* (Cambridge, MA: Harvard University Press, 2002).

44   *Circuit* is also used productively throughout Adria L. Imada, *Aloha America: Hula Circuits through the U.S. Empire* (Durham, NC: Duke University Press, 2012);

also see her article "Hawaiians on Tour: Hula Circuits through the American Empire," *American Quarterly* Vol. 56, No. 1, March 2004.

45 Cahill, *Federal Fathers & Mothers*, 230.

46 For more on Wa-Wa Chaw see: Carlos Montezuma Papers, Wisconsin State Historical Society, Madison, Wisconsin.

47 My approach to studying these particular individuals and the larger cohort of Indian people of which they were a part builds on earlier work of scholars, such as: Hazel Hertzberg, *Modern Pan-Indian Movements* (1982); Hoxie, *Talking Back to Civilization*; Lucy Maddox, *Citizen Indians: Native American Intellectuals, Race, and Reform* (2005); Deloria, *Indians in Unexpected Places*; and Martinez, ed., *The American Indian Intellectual Tradition*.

48 For more on the relationship between letter writing and publishing in connection with the creation of a public sphere see: Jurgen Habermas, *The Structural Transformation of the Public Sphere: An Inquiry into Bourgeois*, translated by Thomas Burger (Cambridge: Massachusetts Institute of Technology Press, 1991).

49 I consulted Michel Foucault, *Discipline and Punish* (1977) and *Power/Knowledge* (1980) to theorize Indian intellectuals as agents of change through the transformation of social, political, and disciplinary networks and the work of discourse.

50 See note 39.

51 Since the mid- to late 1990s, certain methods of interpreting Native writing have become customary for scholars working within Native American and indigenous studies. They include: tribal nation specificity and American Indian literary nationalism, the former arguing for a move away from identity, authenticity, hybridity, and cross-cultural mediation to the Native intellectual, cultural, political, historical, and tribal national contexts from which indigenous literatures emerge. By moving away from the ethnographic methodologies that generated questions about identity and cultural authenticity that dominated American Indian literary studies during the "Native American Renaissance" (1968–95), this book builds on the approaches of post-1995 literary critics who accept that tribal national and community-specific contexts are important points of critical reference for interpreting Native texts, including work by Robert Warrior, Elizabeth Cook-Lynn, Gerald Vizenor, Jace Weaver, Craig Womack, and others. At the same time, the mobility of the four figures who are the center of this project and their own pan-tribal and "Indian" racial rhetoric suggests that I also engage their work through a Native literary lens that focuses on identity that is always contingent on place, whether urban or rural, Native or not, and how political issues on the local and federal levels impacted the places and cultural spaces that these four intellectuals worked in and through as writers and activists. I am aiming for an expansive approach to thinking about Native identity and politics that is also mindful of the specific histories of tribal nations and communities as they intersected with the United States as a settler-colonial nation.

52 Warrior, *The People and the Word*, xiii.

53 Warrior asserts that such nonfiction writing has been the primary form used by American Indians in developing a relationship with the written word – reaching far back in Native history and culture, and his scholarship lays the groundwork upon which this current project can stand.

54 Round, *Removable Type*, 3.

55 Ibid., 5. Also see: Hazel Hertzberg, *Modern Pan-Indian Movements* (1982), which defines American Indians in terms of other American minorities. I aim, instead, to recast Indian people not within the rhetoric of minority discourse but as distinct citizens of tribal nations and as figures who wrestle with how to position themselves within the broader national context of the United States. Lucy Maddox's *Citizen Indians* (2005) also focuses on the early twentieth-century period and the pan-tribal activities of this generation of Native intellectuals, in particular their work with Native organizations like the Society of American Indians but also with white progressive groups like the Indian Rights Association. Alan Trachtenberg's *The Incorporation of America: Culture and Society in the Gilded Age* (2007) offers an interdisciplinary analysis of American culture during the late nineteenth century, which contributes to how I frame the period within which these figures emerged. Frederick Hoxie's *Talking Back to Civilization* focuses on the period from 1893 to the 1920s, with a focus on primary documents produced by Native American reformers who, he argues, aimed to "talk back" to the civilization that had intervened in their lives and stolen much of their land, while also attempting to steal or destroy their culture. Hoxie's more recent *This Indian Country: American Indian Activists and the Place They Made* (2012) is a new and useful contribution to Native American studies that offers a counter-narrative to conventional U.S. histories. Hoxie argues for the centrality of American Indian history and the work of specific Native people, such as Sarah Winnemucca and Thomas Sloan, as political activists who entered into dialogues with other activist movements.

56 For the historical development, usage, and theorization of "keywords" see: Raymond Williams, *Keywords: A Vocabulary of Culture and Society* (New York: Oxford University Press, 1985); Bruce Burgett and Glenn Hendler, eds., *Keywords for American Cultural Studies* (New York: New York University Press, 2007). For a related study of how concepts travel in interdisciplinary projects and are meaningful when they help us to understand our object of study see: Mieke Bal and Sherry Marx-Macdonald, *Traveling Concepts in the Humanities: A Rough Guide* (Toronto, Canada: University of Toronto Press, 2002).

57 Piatote, *Domestic Subjects*, 8.

58 Cathleen D. Cahill suggests that work in the Indian Service, for many Native people, enabled the formation of a modern intertribal Indian identity that was built around a shared identity to organize a national cultural and political movement (*Federal Fathers & Mothers*, 7).

59 For more on the ways that individual Native people found to engage in a project of racial uplift see: Alan Trachtenberg, *Shades of Hiawatha: Staging Indians, Making Americans, 1880–1930* (New York: Hill and Wang, 2004). In particular, Trachtenberg devotes a chapter to the work of Luther Standing Bear as a young man employed by Wanamaker's Department Store that emphasizes some of the ways that Native youth entered the world of market capitalism and the racism they encountered when doing so.

60 O'Brien, *Firsting and Lasting*, 145.

61 For more on earlier periods when Indian intellectuals claimed "dual citizenship" see: ibid., 148.

62 Regarding the mutually constitutive relationship between American and Indian identity see: Deloria, *Playing Indian*, and Shari M. Huhndorf, *Going Native: Indians in the American Cultural Imagination* (2001). For studies of late nineteenth-century culture in America, and the intersecting categories of race, gender, and class, see: Susan Harris Smith and Melanie Dawson, eds., *The American 1890s: A Cultural Reader* (2000) and Gail Bederman, *Manliness & Civilization: A Cultural History of Gender and Race in the United States, 1880–1917* (1996).

63 Drawing selectively from a wide range of scholarly approaches to conceptualize the term *intellectual*, I consulted: Antonio Gramsci, *Prison Notebooks* (London: Lawrence and Wishart, 1971), 5–23; C. L. R. James, *C.L.R. James Reader edited by Anna Grimshaw* (1995), 245; Michel Foucault, "Truth and Power," an interview with Alesandro Fontana and Pasquale Pasquino (New York: Pantheon, 1977, 1980); Edward Said, *Representations of the Intellectual: The 1933 Reith Lectures* (New York: Vintage, 1994), 61; Warrior, *Tribal Secrets*; Martinez, ed., *The American Indian Intellectual Tradition*; Gerald Vizenor, *Fugitive Poses: Native American Indian Scenes of Absence and Presence* (Lincoln: University of Nebraska Press, 2000).

64 Regarding representational politics see: Joel Pfister, *Individuality Incorporated: Indians and the Multicultural Modern* (2004) and Deloria, *Indians in Unexpected Places*. For national narratives and citizenship and the relation between nationally defined communities versus more culturally or locally defined ones see: Benedict Anderson, *Imagined Communities: Reflections on the Origin and Spread of Nationalism* (1983), and Homi Bhabha's edited collection *Nation and Narration* (1990).

65 For the political and cultural importance of "blood" in a Hawaiian context see: J. Kehaulani Kauaunui, *Hawaiian Blood: Colonialism and the Politics of Sovereignty and Indigeneity* (Durham, NC: Duke University Press, 2008). For a contemporary account of questions of Native identity related to DNA testing see: Kim Tallbear, *Native American DNA: Tribal Belonging and the False Promise of Genetic Science* (Minneapolis: University of Minnesota Press, 2013). For more on "full-bloodedness" as problematically essential to defining Indian identity in New England during the early nineteenth century see, O'Brien, *Firsting and Lasting*.

66 As Jace Weaver has noted, "History of white/Native interaction told largely or exclusively from the perspective of the settler colonizers is not Native American Studies" because "ultimately the story being told is about white people." See: Jace Weaver, *A Miner's Canary: Essays on the State of Native America* (Albuquerque: University of New Mexico Press, 2010), 4–5. In addition, two books complicate this dynamic: Philip J. Deloria's *Playing Indian* and Shari Huhndorf's *Going Native*. I have consulted both to help me theorize and articulate the concept of an Indian "playing Indian" within American culture. Playing Indian is a phenomenon that is not unlike blackface minstrelsy as examined by Eric Lott. In *Love and Theft: Blackface Minstrelsy and the American Working Class* (Oxford University Press, 1995), Lott argues these shows were "an index of popular white racial feeling in the United States"(5). By examining how white people engaged with performing and performances of blackness, we can look at how "this articulation took the form of a simultaneous drawing up and

crossing of racial boundaries"(6). As Lott's title references, when white men played black in minstrel shows during the antebellum period, they both celebrated and exploited blackness. This sort of racial performance, as Lott further suggests, was "an encapsulation of the affective order of things in a society that racially ranked human beings"(6). Playing Indian, by white men and women, in the nineteenth and twentieth centuries was similar as a cultural phenomenon. Native performers had inherited these associations with the stage and race play, which they used strategically to affirm but also critique the terms on which racial difference was marked through Indian bodies and embodiment. Wild West shows were often marketed as attractions to be seen alongside minstrel shows, and Wild West traveling entertainments appealed to so many different audiences that these shows, like the minstrel shows of the antebellum era, could blur the boundary between high and low cultures; in the process, these shows commoditized Indianness, which is apiece with Lott's examination of blackface minstrelsy as a form of popular entertainment in the nineteenth century.

67 Performance theory is a useful methodological tool for any history accounting for Native participation in print and political culture in the Americas. My readings of speeches, and other performances of Indianness, for this cohort draws on this scholarship, especially the work of queer theorists and Native American studies scholars. Drawing on Jacque Derrida, Judith Butler writes that "performativity cannot be understood outside of the process of iterability, a regularized and constrained repetition of norms. And this repetition is not performed by a subject; this repetition is what enables a subject and constitutes the temporal condition for the subject." See: Judith Butler, *Bodies that Matter: On the Discursive Limits of Sex* (New York: Routledge Press, 1993), 95. Also see: Bellin and Mielke, eds., *Native Acts*. *Native Acts*, as Deloria summarizes in his afterword, focuses on very early examples of cross-cultural performance where the authors examine both the materiality of embodied performance and the written and spoken narratives that can also perform and produce claims about identities and subjectivities as well as so-called truths and authenticities, to include "new intercultural possibilities, and in the end, power relations themselves" (310).

68 See: Wilmer, ed., *Native American Performance and Representation*; Stanlake, *Native American Drama*; Jill Lane, *Black Face Cuba, 1840–1895* (Philadelphia: University of Pennsylvania Press, 2005); Laura G. Gutierrez, *Performing Mexicanidad: Vendidas Y Cabareteras on the Transnational Stage* (Austin: University of Texas Press, 2010); Gayatri Gopinath, *Impossible Desires: Queer Diasporas and South Asian Public Cultures* (Durham, NC and London: Duke University Press, 2005). Also see Michelle Wick Patterson, "'Real' Indian Songs: The Society of American Indians and the Use of Native American Culture as a Means of Reform," *American Indian Quarterly* Vol. 26, No. 1, Winter 2002, 44–66. Patterson uses specific examples of staged performance by Indian people involved with the Society of American Indians. I find Jose Esteban Muñoz's theorization of disidentification especially helpful with regards to these Native intellectuals' using certain types of clothing for specific audiences and venues.

69 For a more thorough historical account of this concept see: Deloria, *Playing Indian*.

70 From R. H. Pratt to Carlos Montezuma, Letter, Ayer MMS collection, Box 3, Newberry Library, Chicago, IL.

71 For a literary history concerning social divisions in the United States see: Richard Brodhead's *Cultures of Letters: Scenes of Reading and Writing in Nineteenth-Century America* (1993). For a study of cultural change in relation to cultural hierarchy see: Lawrence Levine, *Highbrow/Lowbrow: The Emergence of Cultural Hierarchy in America* (1988). For how the "White City" depicted whiteness and racial harmony through technological advancement see: Alan Trachtenberg's final chapter in *The Incorporation of America* (2007). In regards to studies of critical race theory and postcolonial studies I have consulted: Franz Fanon, *Black Skin, White Masks* (1967); Gloria Anzaldua, *Borderlands/La Frontera, the New Mestiza* (1987); Homi K. Bhahba, *The Location of Culture* (1994); Paul Gilroy, *There Ain't No Black in the Union Jack: The Cultural Politics of Nation and Race* (1987); *Black Atlantic: Modernity and Double Consciousness* (1993) and *Against Race, Imagining Political Culture beyond the Color Line* (2000); Lisa Lowe, *Immigrant Acts: On Asian American Cultural Politics* (1996); Barbara Christian, *Black Feminist Criticism: Perspectives on Black Women Writers* (1985); Kimberle Crenshaw, ed., *Critical Race Theory: The Key Writings that Formed the Movement* (1995); Diana Fuss, *Essentially Speaking* (1989); and Harry Justin Elam, ed., *Black Cultural Traffic: Crossroads in Global Performance and Popular Culture* (2005).

72 Gertrude Bonnin, "An Indian Teacher" in *American Indian Stories*, edited by Dexter Fisher (Lincoln: University of Nebraska Press, 1985), 98.

73 See: Carrie Tirado Bramen, "East Meets West at the World's Parliament of Religions," in *Uses of Variety: Modern Americanism and the Quest for National Distinctiveness* (2001); Edward W. Said, *Culture and Imperialism* (1993); Robert Christopher Reed, *All the World Is Here!: The Black Presence at White City* (2000); and Julie K. Brown, *Contesting Images: Photography and the World's Columbian Exposition* (1994).

74 In regards to the development of whiteness see: David R. Roediger, *The Wages of Whiteness: Race and the Making of the American Working Class* (1999); Matthew Frye Jacobson, *Whiteness of a Different Color: European Immigrants and the Alchemy of Race* (1999); and George Lipsitz, *The Possessive Investment in Whiteness: How White People Profit from Identity Politics* (1998).

A Global Mission

The Higher Education of Charles Eastman

It is the impression of many people who are not well informed on the Indian situation that book education is of little value to the race, particularly what is known as the higher education. The contrary is true. What we need is not less education, but more; more trained leaders to uphold the standards of civilization before both races.

– Charles Eastman, *The Indian To-Day* (1915)[1]

Introduction

On December 5, 1905, an array of literary figures, celebrities, and political elites gathered at an extravagant private party at New York City's Delmonico's Restaurant. Opened in 1830, Delmonico's by the turn of the twentieth century had become a pinnacle of haute cuisine and the embodiment of upper-class New York society, especially given the social status of its clientele. The spectacular party that winter was arranged by Colonel George Harvey, the president of Harper and Brothers Publishing Company, to celebrate Mark Twain's seventieth birthday.[2]

Over 170 friends and fellow writers attended the festivities, which featured a forty-piece orchestra as well as fifteen speeches and formal toasts. After a brief introduction by author, editor, and critic William Dean Howells, Twain set a convivial tone for the evening by punctuating his speech with satirical aphorisms. He remarked, "I have had a great many birthdays in my time. I remember the first one very well, and I always think of it with indignation; everything was so crude, unaesthetic, primeval. Nothing like this at all."[3]

One of Twain's birthday gifts that evening was a book of photographs featuring guests around their tables. In one, Doctor Charles A. Eastman (Sisseton-Wahpeton Sioux) sits prominently next to Alice MacDowan, James Rodgers, and Mrs. A. D. Chandler. Certainly the most ebullient at his table, Eastman wears an elegant tuxedo and toothy grin. The picture appeared in the next day's *New York Times*, accompanied by a story about the historic nature of the event, claiming that "never before in the annals of this country had such a representative gathering of literary men and women been seen under one roof." Indeed, guests came from all across the United States. Eastman was alone in representing Minnesota, but, perhaps more important, he was also the only Native American author in attendance. As a budding writer, he was in good company at Twain's party, where he mingled with new authors like Willa Cather and Charles Chesnutt.[4]

Although the *Times* reporter did not mention the presence of either Eastman or Chesnutt, despite the fact that both Native Americans and African Americans were scarcer than women at the banquet, the survival of the photograph featuring Eastman signifies twin facets of his life: his career as an Indian intellectual, and opportunities that brought him into contact with people who could shape print culture, politics, and public opinion. Indeed, Twain's party is but one example of a cultural space where Eastman could build a powerful relationship between his intellectualism – as he understood it and as it was defined by those who read his books and saw him speak – and literary networks to promote his educational mission.[5] Ultimately, Eastman aimed to teach Americans about the history of his people, the Sioux, and through this teaching to argue in favor of citizenship for Indian people in the United States.[6]

Just six years later, Eastman attended another historic event, although it was no party. Instead, Eastman was asked to represent Native Americans as part of an international congress on race at the University of London. The first Universal Races Congress was, according to one reporter, meant to be "a distinctly new and novel proposition." The United States, among other nations, was expanding its imperial reach beyond domestic borders into places like Guam and Puerto Rico, and it made sense for Americans to attend an international event that aimed to encourage interracial goodwill on a global scale. The universal mission of such a congress was to make "special reference to bringing about friendlier relations between Occident and Orient." Out of the ten Americans invited to present, two delegates stand out from the event's program because they were there to speak on behalf of interracial relations at home. Both were public intellectuals who were well-positioned to represent their races using a global platform.[7]

One was Dr. W. E. B. Du Bois, the prominent African American sociologist, who read a paper titled "The Negro in America." The other was Eastman, who gave a paper on "The American Indian." What brought Du Bois and Eastman, as intellectuals and members of ethnic minority groups in America, to London in 1911? According to the *New York Tribune*, they may have believed in its mission as one committed to the productive discussion of race by prominent sociologists and anthropologists from around the world. In fact, the Congress organizers were supported by the political heads of the British Empire and "many members of the permanent court of arbitration of The Hague," as well as "the council of the Interparliamentary Union," to organize this international forum to discuss race relations.[8]

As literary scholar Brent Hayes Edwards and others have demonstrated, Du Bois's 1911 speech echoed the rhetoric established in *The Souls of Black Folk* (1903). Edwards has argued that in Du Bois's appearance, one can see the outlines of not simply a "Black Atlantic," but also a diasporic black intellectual internationalism. Although Eastman was part of a similar, if less well-developed global circuit, his mission at the Congress almost certainly reflected a different history of Indian people in relation to European colonialism. He was there to speak on behalf of American Indians in the context of an increasingly globalized world.[9]

Each man also chose to speak for his "race" because of deep-seated concerns regarding the future of racialized and ethnic minorities within the United States.[10] Eastman, like Du Bois, was well educated, highly traveled, and a skilled orator. He understood that an international event of this type would be a great opportunity for him to present his own ideas about the current conditions Native Americans faced. Both men, along with Franz Boas, spoke on the panel "devoted to the question of the *modern* conscience in relation to the negro and the American Indian."[11] Given Eastman's quest to educate the American public about Indian people as modern citizens of the United States, the panel's emphasis on "the modern conscience" resonated with his cultural politics. Still, the question such a panel provoked did not give Eastman carte blanche to speak without certain reservations.

One reporter from the *Tribune* predicted that this panel would succeed in presenting ideas on race and humanity while also avoiding "all bitterness towards parties, peoples, and governments." In the context of these concerns, Eastman and Du Bois faced a tall order. Could Eastman include a historical critique of colonialism and conquest in his remarks on the "modern conscience" in relation to the American Indian? Could Du Bois refer to the history of slavery and Jim Crow in the United States? As each speaker prepared his remarks, they turned not to the specifics of these histories, but instead to the more future-oriented language that Du Bois used to characterize the color line. The panel showcased the modernist psychological language of "the veil" and "double-consciousness" for Du Bois, and the fact of "full-bloodedness" and the "Real" rather than primitive Indian for Eastman. Du Bois's assertion seemed precise and accurate; the problem of the twentieth century was indeed the problem of the color line. Eastman understood this problem differently from Du Bois, however, seeing the color line primarily in terms of Indian-white relations, and his speech aimed to improve interracial harmony with specific regards to Indian people's concerns.[12] Eastman used the opportunity the Congress gave him, like he used Twain's party, to present not only on behalf of Indians in America but for himself, so he could make new contacts with influential networks of scientists, writers, and politicians.[13]

Eastman's ability to address multiple publics exemplifies his success in accessing different networks to embody a public face for Indianness during the early twentieth century. Looking closely at his speeches, costumes, and audiences reveals Eastman's politics of representation to highlight the interconnectedness of his education with his literary work, aspects of epistolary culture, and performance that undergirded the dynamic ways he then fashioned himself as an educator. For Eastman, the theme of education plays out in terms of how his status as an educated Indian mattered and also in terms of his desire to provide an education to others.[14]

A Public Face for Indianness

Speaking at the London Congress in 1911, Eastman's address on "The North American Indian" offered both a general accounting of the geographic, linguistic, political, and religious traditions of indigenous peoples in North America prior to European contact, and specifics that were significant to his current position at the international gathering. Overall, he structured his remarks to reflect the mind of an educator and an intellectual with the ideals of a reformer. He made references to political organization and social laws in order to build cross-cultural understanding that could once again affirm the centrality of Indian people in the making of America, as arbiters of its unique history and as contributors to its growth in the modern age.

At the outset Eastman claimed that "The government of the first North American was the simplest form of democracy."[15] This bold statement reimagined not only an Indian past but an Indian present. By this time, the rise of pan-Indian organizations, the decline of living conditions for most Indians on reservations, and public criticism toward the U.S. Indian Bureau shaped what Eastman could say about the "modern conscience" as it pertained to Indian peoples. Eastman linked American democracy with earlier forms of governance used by Native people to do two critical things. First, he drew an ideological through-line from an earlier indigenous time to the modern that suggested democracy was as much Indian as it was American; in this instance, the question of citizenship for Indian people living in the United States would be thrust to the fore and the fact of their presence, rather than absence, in the body politic was no longer in question. Second, by making reference to how democracy functioned in this earlier era, Eastman recalled a different sort of presence in the past, one that highlighted the fact of sovereignty and nationalism that predated the formation of the United States. This precondition enabled Eastman to challenge America's desire to manage and control Indian people and their land. He was able, once again, to assert a modern place for Native Americans within the United States and across the world.[16]

Eastman's rhetorical strategy

It was not easy for Eastman to put Native institutions at the center of U.S. history while simultaneously offering a critique of that history. He needed first to debunk racialist discourse that used science and culture to place Indians, and other people of color, on the lower rungs of America's social and political system. Given the academic tone of his address, Eastman could speak plainly about how although "the physical character[istic]s of the race are assumed to be well known," they are "often incorrectly described."[17] As a published author, physician, and Dartmouth alumnus, Eastman could rely on his elite status as an intellectual platform from which to argue, "American historians have constantly fallen into error by reason of their ignorance of our democratic system, truly a government of the people, one of personal liberty and equal rights to all its members."[18] This rhetoric strategically mirrored American political discourse with regards to freedom and civilization. Considering that the formal qualities of Eastman's lecture offered a well-structured account of the past conditions of Indian peoples, which emphasized his knowledge of modern Western thought and belief in democratic principles, it is even more critical to note how he addressed contentious topics like exploitation under capitalism, the reservation system, and fears associated with miscegenation.

At this international meeting, Eastman defined American, not Native, democracy as intimately linked to material progress promised by market capitalism. Relying on this link, he could criticize U.S. colonialism and imperialism by remarking on how American civilization necessarily depended on breeding dishonesty and greed, and "the love of possessions."[19] Eastman argued this desire to own property and obtain objects ran counter to "freedom" as Indian people defined it. In particular, he offered that Native men were not well equipped to desire participation in capitalism because historically women owned all property, and it was "considered effeminate in a warrior" to desire possessions.[20] Thus, European colonization brought with it not only changes in thinking related to economic structures but to gender as well.

Eastman's speech tracked the ways Indian people, because of their distinct cultural characteristics, thrived before European colonists came and corrupted their pristine living conditions; "the pollution of streams, the destruction of forests, and the leveling of hills" were thought of by Natives as "a sacrilege" and too high a price to pay for civilization.[21] In drawing on this binary, and referring to European influence using a rhetoric of corruption and contamination, Eastman's speech conformed to certain tenets of social evolutionary theory that were prevalent at the time. He suggested that "it was equally inevitable that the vices of the more sophisticated race [white] should be imitated by the simpler [Indian]." In this instance, Eastman explains that a failure of early traders and Christian missionaries to learn from indigenous peoples resulted in the transfer of European cultural values that included European vices. Underpinning Eastman's argument is a cultural logic that understood race as produced by culture given that "the simpler" Indian race was without vice *prior* to their contact with a different, more sophisticated (in Eastman's words), European culture. This point of view is underscored by Eastman's simplistic depiction of "the savage philosopher" whose naturally and necessarily "strong religious sentiment forbade any effort on his part to deface mother nature."[22] Such a notion conformed to dominant (and white) expectations that located Native peoples not only in America's premodern past but in the landscape itself, both as closer to nature (rather than culture) and as the earliest environmentalists. By drawing on this relationship between racial identity and cultural formations in his speech, Eastman began to hone one of the ideas that would become central to his representational politics, which was how to present himself as the embodiment of a modern Native *and* American subject.[23]

Ultimately Eastman's speech argued that American civilization must correct its flaws to improve the current situation of the American Indian who lives in a "beggarly" state on reservations, which operate like prisons. Eastman asserted that in this new space the federal government of the United States had created a "pauperizing effect," and the graft of petty officials had led to the final eclipse of the Indian man, who lives like "a wild animal confined in a zoological garden."[24] Descriptions like these offered his audience a powerful and provocative parallel by defining wildness in relation to the primitive and animal-like state of Indian manhood now mutually constitutive with the construction of the reservation, which was itself a project of white Americans. Certainly, Eastman understood that Native men, like him, could move beyond the limits set forth by a reservation system.[25] Given the context in which he gave this speech, Eastman detailed the material ways that Indian people had been forced to live in a state of wildness due *not* to their inherent otherness, simplicity, or primitivism but rather due to the constraints imposed on them by a government intent on managing their development. His critique thus intends not to fault Native people for living like wild animals but to fault the larger systems that aim to "capture" them so that this would seem to be one of the only ways to live.[26]

In order to rally more support from his audience, Eastman used an important rhetorical strategy in his speech. By using "we" throughout his discussion of the "reservation policy" that "was a mistake," which led to "the fruits of a radical misapprehension of the red man's native capacity," he prompts his listeners to see themselves as part of the problem and also the solution.[27] By focusing on the irony of designing social and political structures meant to celebrate freedom that have, in fact, undermined the mobility and achievement of Indian people, Eastman urged his audience to reconsider the history of U.S. expansion. In addition, because his speech looked to the future it articulated new arenas that could promote the "development of the 'new Indian'" in America. He pointed to two explicitly: the first was educational policy, which he saw as moderately successful, and the second was

massive reform of the Bureau of Indian Affairs. The latter entailed the abolition of the reservation system and distribution of tribal funds held in trust
to individuals to benefit "the manhood and full independence of the Indian
citizen."[28] This second option aligned with some of the ideology promoted
by the Dawes Act of 1887, which aimed to divide reservation lands into
individual allotments.[29] Both solutions stressed the incorporation of Native
peoples into the social, economic, and, ultimately, political structures produced by the United States. Incorporation for Eastman was not the same as
integration, but rather a means of asserting a presence in the face of a vanishing Indian narrative that was pervasive during this period. For Eastman,
another cultural avenue for change that also related to incorporation was
interracial marriage, or as many would have it in 1911, miscegenation.

Given the premise for the Universal Races Congress, Eastman was in
good company to make a case for the benefits of interracial unions. He had
also been married to his white wife, Elaine Goodale Eastman, for nearly
twenty years by this time, so making this point was as much a personal issue
as a political one. Eastman's speech referenced the racism experienced not
only by interracial couples but by their offspring. He described a common
slur attributed to "mixed-blood" children that defined them as doomed to
having "the vices of both races and the virtues of neither," and confirmed
such an idea as "absolutely unjust."[30] Perhaps paradoxically, Eastman's celebration of mixed-race marriages had the added effect of confirming a future
for Indian people that simultaneously accepted "race amalgamation [a]s the
only final and full solution of the problem" in regards to the American Indian
being a dying race. Like many of his Native contemporaries who spoke to
similar audiences throughout their careers, Eastman argued for wider acceptance of marriages like his so that his offspring could be viewed as both
American and Indian. At the same time, he relied on his own "full-blooded"
status as a tool of authentication to advertise his public talks.

"The North American Indian" speech from 1911 was one of many that
Eastman gave between the 1890s and the 1930s, as he traveled throughout the United States and the world.[31] "The subjects of his many talks
ranged from 'The School of Savagery,' 'The Real Indian,' 'The Story of the
Little Big Horn,' to aesthetic topics such as, 'Indian Wit, Music, Poetry and
Eloquence.'"[32] During this time, he also wrote ten books, which circulated
to a range of reading publics, many of them white and some of them Indian.
As Eastman worked on his writing and lecturing, he also maintained volu-
minous correspondence ranging from the alumni of Dartmouth College to
white women's reform organizations and other leading Indian intellectuals.
All the while he saw himself as part of a larger educational mission with
Indian identity and citizenship at its center.[33]

Because Eastman initially promoted himself as an author writing mostly
fictional and folkloric pieces for children, many readers were first drawn
to Eastman's work by Indianness, and yet they ended up learning as much

about his views on Indian boyhood, nature, spirituality, and tradition as they did about the politics surrounding the past and present circumstances of Native-white relations in the United States. Locating the connections between Eastman's lifework and that of other Indian intellectuals and their non-Indian allies hinges on considering their involvement with a literary world and a political one.[34] Bringing the two together was of critical importance for Native intellectuals during the early twentieth century given the out-of-date ways social critics of this era often discussed the value of Native culture. Novelist and critic Waldo Frank, who actually visited Native American settlements in New Mexico in 1918, concluded the following in his manifesto for a new generation of American artists in *Our America* (1919):

The uncorrupted Indian knows no individual poverty or wealth. All of his tribe is either rich or poor. He has no politics. He has no dynastic or industrial intrigue – although of course personal and fraternal intrigue does exist. His physical world is fixed. And in consequence all his energies beyond the measure of his daily toil rise ineluctably to spiritual consciousness: flow to consideration of his place and part in Nature, into the business of beauty.[35]

What is telling in Frank's desire to create a romantic-democratic role for intellectuals as prophets of a new American culture is his erasure of Native participation in modern society, industry, and art – and that what appealed to him about Indian culture was a seeming lack of politics.[36] For Eastman, the stakes were personal and fraternal, to be sure, but also much larger. He, like Carlos Montezuma, Gertrude Bonnin, and Luther Standing Bear, knew that changing the social, economic, and political status of Indian people within American society had to take place through culture as much as through politics. Certainly the two could not be easily parsed for any Native intellectual during this period. And thus, Twain's party was not the only high society affair Eastman attended, nor was the Universal Races Congress his only opportunity to cross the Atlantic. Before and after these two events, Eastman was active in fashioning himself as an Indian intellectual. This meant an educated person and one who – in Eastman's version – teaches and leads by example.[37]

For Eastman and other Native intellectuals, modernity became critical to how they defined themselves and how they were viewed by those around them. As Indian people, they sought to recast dominant understandings of Indianness not as antithetical to, but rather, as mutually constitutive of Americanness. The modern world that Eastman, Montezuma, Bonnin, and Standing Bear lived in was one in which ideas about ethnicity, race, gender, and citizenship intertwined, and often reflected how modernity and the idea of the modern was experienced. Therefore, as federal Indian policies changed and new cultural forms were created, Indian intellectuals found openings to effectively engage in modern American society, and through that engagement they demonstrated the power of Indian people as shapers of modernity. Furthermore, by considering the shifting terrain of Indian policy in relation to Eastman's cultural politics, we can see the limits and possibilities he faced as a leading Indian intellectual during this period. Changes in his thinking with regards to allotment and citizenship were reflected in his work as a writer who utilized multiple genres, from autobiography to folklore to polemic, to convey his ideas. Through these textual examples, Eastman's mission to educate Americans and the global community about Native political concerns reflect not only changes in his beliefs but also broader social and political changes in U.S. society and Indian Country. His gift for the spoken word enabled Eastman to reach a useful array of audiences, whether he spoke to local women's clubs or foreign dignitaries. His oratorical training began early as a student at Dartmouth College.

Vox Clamantis in Deserto

Much of Eastman's early life as an undergraduate at Dartmouth College shaped his philosophy and his ability to work as a physician, author, and lecturer. As much as Eastman benefited from the time he spent at Dartmouth, so too did the College draw on its association with Eastman as a means for reaffirming its founding mission.

"The voice of one crying in the wilderness" was Dartmouth's motto since its founding in 1769. Established by Congregational minister Eleazar Wheelock (1711–79), partly with funds raised by Native American preacher Samson Occom (1723–92), the College considered its primary mission that of acculturating and Christianizing Native Americans. Despite this founding mission, the College graduated only nineteen Native Americans during its first 200 years.[38] After an extended period of financial and political struggles, Dartmouth emerged from relative obscurity in the early twentieth century – and it did so with considerable assistance from Charles Eastman, the cultural descendant of Occom.

According to *The Aegis* (Dartmouth's yearbook, founded in 1859), the freshman class of 1887 was distinguished by its only Native American student: Charles Alexander Eastman. His athletic and scholarly achievements were many and his listings include: a football captain, the Dartmouth Baseball Association, the Dartmouth Gun Club, a member of the Webster Chapter, the Phi Delta Theta fraternity, and the Missionary Committee. Not only was Eastman the only Indian at Dartmouth at this time, but he also came to Hanover, New Hampshire from the small town of Flandreau, located in Dakota Territory. His classmates, on the other hand, hailed mostly from New England, New York, Pennsylvania, and Ohio. Eastman's distinguishing achievements took place within the context of a Northern and New England social community completely foreign to him. Throughout his life, Eastman nonetheless maintained an association with Dartmouth's prestigious and vast alumni network to elevate the public profile of the College as one committed to the education and incorporation of Indian people within American society.[39]

Throughout Eastman's undergraduate years, Indianness remained a pivotal component of how others perceived him and how he in turn perceived himself. During this period, studies of race continued to shift despite the discourse's emphasis on biological definitions. A half-century earlier, in 1839, naturalist and craniologist Samuel George Morton (1799–1851) produced *Crania Americana* to provide detailed descriptions of racial difference for American readers, helping to define the term *scientific racism*. In many ways, Morton's work shaped how Americans thought about the connection between the idea of race and the materiality of the body. As "Dartmouth's Indian," Eastman could not escape the association others made between his Indianness and his body, which took shape in *blood*.[40]

Beginning in the 1880s, Eastman and others defined his position as an intellectual through the linked discourse of blood and education. More specifically, as an Indian student, he was celebrated by Dartmouth as its "most picturesque figure." *Picturesque* is a term that originates from the Italian word *pittoresco* or "as if in a picture"; it has been used to describe certain properties of landscape and garden views in reality or as depicted in visual arts. The category of picturesque objects has also been defined and redefined since its invention. In the late seventeenth and early eighteenth centuries, the picturesque beauty was a positive expression; to call something picturesque was a compliment. Edmund Burke (1729–97) developed a theory on beauty and the sublime, but the picturesque was not clearly defined because it was an irrational "pleasing" synthesis of often contradicting categories. The picturesque then described all those subjects that did not fit into the realms of beauty on one side and the sublime on the other. Thus, the picturesque became an aesthetic category that filled the gap between definitions of beauty and the sublime. This ability to "fill the gap" demonstrates the ways that the picturesque figure of an Indian represented one notion of Indianness that could fill a different type of gap, one between nature and civilization given that Indians were believed to be both human, and yet, as "noble savages," part of the natural world – a world white, mostly male society meant to control and tame as its own. Like the imaginary Indian of American culture, Eastman, as Dartmouth's "most picturesque figure," had an openness that enabled the concept to survive. It is the very nature of the picturesque to incorporate contradictory aspects and objects in a new aesthetic, and like Indianness, it becomes an expansive concept that is always in search of new elements. Despite his many achievements and the many changes in American society, an obituary written after his death highlighted Eastman's association with Dartmouth. He could not escape having once been its most picturesque figure; in death he was now famous as the College's "full-blooded" student.[41]

In 1939, Manchester's *Union* provided an extensive obituary titled "Dartmouth's Most Famous Indian Grad Dies in Detroit, Dr. Charles Eastman '87, a Full-Blooded Sioux Known as Ohiyesa, Recognized as Most Learned Member of Race." The headline itself positions Eastman in terms of race as a cultural *and* biological category. Indianness is figured through his education, reflecting cross-cultural possibilities in a way that reemphasizes racial difference. At the same time, the headline notes he was a "Full-Blooded Sioux," a seemingly biological statement that actually rested on cultural assumptions. Throughout his life, Eastman was forced to navigate this complex and often contradictory representation of Indianness, at once cultural and also biological. Ultimately, he turned to education as a political lens through which to recast this shifting image. He sought to revise how the majority of Americans conceived of Indian people by operating as a living exemplar of the modern Native subject.

Eastman's later writings and lectures articulated his Indian identity as one rooted in biology and marked by his link to Dartmouth. As Colin Calloway has shown, "Eastman's experience at Dartmouth reflects the complex and tension-filled relations between Indian people and the United States at that time. Surviving Dartmouth in the 1880s, like surviving the United States, exacted a heavy toll on an Indian."[42] In fact, as the college's "most famous Indian," Eastman continually negotiated the issue of Indian dress as a representational strategy when he chose which clothes to wear in order to confirm or refute biological destiny and perform more culturally rooted ideas about race.[43]

On one occasion at Dartmouth, during his undergraduate career from 1883 to 1886, Eastman's decision to wear certain types of clothing intersected with hegemonic ideas about race and racialization in America. In this instance, English cultural critic Matthew Arnold (1822–88) had been invited to give a lecture on literature "as an antidote to materialism in a democracy" at the College. Upon his arrival, Arnold "asked to see the famous Indian student." Arnold was then amazed when "Ohiyesa appeared in faultless evening clothes and not in war paint and tribal regalia." Arnold's remarks and his reaction to Eastman's appearance, *not* "in war paint and tribal regalia" but instead in "faultless evening clothes," carries the weight of white expectations regarding Indianness and also the power of performance. Arnold could have been awed by Eastman dressed in regalia, yet it was a different awe generated by Eastman in fine evening attire.[44]

Eastman may have, at first, appeared as an object for Arnold's consumption because he was Dartmouth's "famous Indian student." But on closer inspection Arnold came to understand that his preconceptions regarding Dartmouth's Indian did not align with Eastman's cultural persona. At the College, Eastman was distinguishing himself not only because of his Indianness but also because of his athletic prowess as a captain of the football team and champion distance runner, as well as a competitor in basketball, tennis, and boxing. In addition to sports, Eastman participated in fraternity life at Phi Delta Theta and enrolled in the Latin scientific curriculum that required courses in English, Latin, French, Greek, and linguistics. He also took classes in zoology, botany, chemistry, physics, natural history, political science, philosophy, and geometry.[45] In addition, because Eastman was so amiable, the two men met and spoke as equals. This meeting proved a propos given that Arnold's lecture encouraged his audience to seek out intelligent idealism in service to reshape society.[46]

Reports regarding the details of Arnold's meeting with Eastman circulated well beyond the small New Hampshire town. Such reports focused on the encounter as an aberration on two fronts. On one hand, Eastman was celebrated for exceeding his famous visitor's expectations. On the other hand, Arnold was portrayed as embarrassed in his desire to see Dartmouth's Indian in Native "regalia" and his failure to imagine Eastman in any other way. Perhaps Arnold's desire to see Eastman *as* an Indian in primitive and romantic terms offered the potential for a kind of homoerotics of loving and desiring improper racialized subjects?[47] This report, and the absence of Eastman's voice regarding their encounter, provided American readers an opportunity to play the role of Arnold at Dartmouth. They could imagine ways to locate Indians within different modes of dress and to recognize (as Arnold did with shock) the limits of their own imagination. For these readers, like Arnold, Eastman's racialized "otherness" could be desired because he was distinctly lesser than Euro-American white culture and society and, yet, if clothed in the right sort of Indian dress also romantic and noble in his "savagery." At the same time, these reports enabled American readers a chance to enjoy a laugh at the expense of an elite English intellectual. Although Eastman never commented on how he perceived Arnold, it seems likely that he was well aware of the gaffe that such a distinguished visitor made.

Years later, Dartmouth continued to celebrate its most famous Indian by memorializing him in an oil painting by Julius D. Katzieff (1892–1957). This portrait captured *not* the "real" Eastman of Arnold's encounter, but the imagined and properly "full-blooded" Eastman adorned "in full tribal dress." Today it hangs in the College museum as a gift commissioned by the class of 1887. Even though Eastman did not honor Arnold's expectation, he did acquiesce to his classmates' demands to memorialize him in regalia and oil paint. Eastman's decision to dress one way on the occasion that he met Arnold and in different costume for this portrait demonstrates the range of strategies open to him within Dartmouth's past and America's future. Furthermore, Eastman's ability to dress up as an Indian, or not, enabled him to address diverse audiences and their expectations.[48]

After graduating from Dartmouth, Eastman moved south to study medicine at Boston University. Not long after receiving his medical degree, he worked as a physician in the Indian Service. Although initially assigned to work at Fort Berthold, and later Standing Rock, after much back and forth between Eastman, his benefactor Frank Wood, and Thomas Jefferson Morgan (commissioner of Indian Affairs), Eastman finally started work at Pine Ridge in South Dakota. He arrived there during the first week of November 1890, and was struck by the starkness of his new surroundings. Two crucial events would take place during his time at Pine Ridge that would forever shape the landscape of Eastman's life and his career: he would meet and marry his wife,[49] Elaine Goodale, and together they would come face to face with the atrocities the Sioux suffered at the hands of the American military.[50]

Just a month after his arrival, Eastman was first on the scene to attend to Native victims of the Wounded Knee Massacre of December 29, 1890. In a makeshift hospital at the Episcopalian mission chapel, he treated wounded and mutilated survivors of the 200 to 300 Sioux who were shot down. The pews were ripped out and the floor covered with hay and quilts to lay the patients down. On New Year's Day, 1891, Eastman and others went out to the "battlefield" site in search of more survivors. "He found a woman's body three miles from the site of the massacre and 'from this point on we found them scattered along as they had been relentlessly hunted down and slaughtered while fleeing for their lives.'"[51] In fact, the accounts Eastman and Elaine Goodale gave of the massacre became widely cited as the most accurate narratives regarding the experiences of Native women, men, and children.[52]

Charles and Elaine were, at first, romantic partners who shared a desire to solve the so-called Indian Problem of the late nineteenth century. Over the course of their life together (before they separated in 1921), both were active writers and speakers.[53] But the differences in their backgrounds and the ways the world around them treated men and women would lead to irreconcilable differences. Elaine had been raised in a stable, middle-class home in the Berkshires of western Massachusetts. She had worked, as a young adult, at Hampton Institute in Virginia before she found her calling as a teacher among the Dakota.[54] Based partly on interviews with Eastman descendants, Raymond Wilson has asserted that Charles resented his wife's interference with his writing and her supposedly domineering manner.[55] Surprisingly, Elaine wrote and said little about her marriage, despite the fact that their relationship was often held up as a model for the benefits of white uplift. For she, as a white woman, was well poised to help her Indian husband assimilate into American society. Perhaps what led to their separation was that Elaine did not sympathize with the limited options that Charles faced due in large part to his status as an Indian man.[56] As Charles became more disenchanted with white civilization and Christianity, Elaine generally maintained support for the assimilation agenda; neither their writing nor their relationship could reconcile this split in thinking.[57]

For Eastman, time at Pine Ridge signaled an important loss in terms of the Indian wars of the nineteenth century and the place where he met the mother of his children, his often helpful copyeditor, and friend. Later, Eastman could look back on this time with a different sense of loss for his marriage as well. Even though Elaine would work with her husband to produce nine books, and write the foreword for his second autobiography, *From the Deep Woods to Civilization,* in 1916, their literary collaborations could not ameliorate deeper issues, not the least of which was their grief over the premature death of their daughter Irene in 1918 during the influenza epidemic. Although they never divorced or publicly commented on their separation, after 1921, they lived apart for the remainder of their lives.

Following his work as the physician at Pine Ridge, much of Eastman's later lectures were useful opportunities for him to recount the details of Wounded Knee and to mourn those who had perished. No doubt bearing witness to such unprovoked and widespread violence inspired and shaped the activist work he would take on in the decades that followed. Although Eastman traveled to different reservations in search of work as a doctor, he eventually abandoned a career in medicine for a more lucrative one in the world of publishing.

Imagining the Indian of Today

Eastman's most overtly political book, *The Indian Today,* maps changes in his thinking with regards to federal policies and his cultural politics pertaining to class, race, and gender. His support for allotment, for example, appears tied to white reform groups, which he saw as critical to the success of pan-tribal activism, and his ultimate goal for Indian people, which was to have their voices heard as citizens in American society. What is more, because this text was intended to reach both Native and non-Native readers alike, it emerges as one of Eastman's strongest pedagogical pieces and represents him as an Indian intellectual and educator. His particular interest in the problems of race leadership also comes to the fore and connects Eastman with other Native intellectuals from this period. These intellectual and political relationships illuminate the scope and strength of pan-tribal networks that emerged as critical sites for redefining Indianness by Indian activists during the early twentieth century.

The Indian Today: The Past and Future of the First American was first published by Doubleday in 1915. Unlike Eastman's autobiographies, *Indian Boyhood* (1902) and *From the Deep Woods to Civilization* (1916), which alternate between casting him as author and subject, and the more spiritually focused *The Soul of the Indian* (1911), as well as his turn to folklore in *Red Hunters and the Animal People* (1904) and *Wigwam Evenings: Sioux Folk Tales* (1909), *The Indian Today* articulates a new philosophy for

Eastman's readers. Considering the far-reaching influence of captivity narratives that cast Native people as abductors, and popular history books that framed the violence on America's frontier as a consequence of Indians threatening white people, Eastman aimed to teach his readers history and traditions of Indian people to counter these narratives. He wrote against the fictional worlds that celebrated Indianness rather than actual Indian achievements fabricated by writers like Henry Wadsworth Longfellow and James Fenimore Cooper. Indeed, *The Indian Today* challenged white notions about Indian history by offering a social-scientific approach to defining the modern Indian subject, as embodied by the educated Indian who participates in industrial capitalism. Throughout his text, Eastman uses this definition as a political argument in and of itself. He argues that readers see the necessity of full citizenship rights for all Native Americans, which at the time (1915) was still an extremely high priority for many Indian intellectual leaders.[58]

Eastman's narrative engaged different publics in order to create a groundswell of support for citizenship within Indian communities and America. For tribally distinct Indians, he aimed to teach about shared accomplishments and histories as well as an emerging pan-Indian movement. For white Americans, he spoke to the particular efforts of reformers and progressives. He called on individuals and organizations committed to Indian issues to become central in creating what would later be the Indian New Deal. A year later in his autobiography, *From the Deep Woods to Civilization*, Eastman continued to reach white audiences by parroting dominant views of white Americans who assumed the future for a "barbarous" race was limited. Eastman continued to emphasize education, explicitly noting that the "true character" of the American Indian is present when recognizing the "deep demoralization" Indian people had suffered because of the white man. He writes:

My chief object has been, not to entertain, but to present the American Indian in his true character before Americans. The barbarous and atrocious character commonly attributed to him has dated from the transition period, when the strong drink, powerful temptations, and commercialism of the white man led to deep demoralization. Really it was a campaign of education on the Indian and his true place in American history.[59]

This passage reflects a critical component of Eastman's strategy to seemingly embrace a civilizationist discourse, while the last sentence urges readers to pause to consider how such a campaign of education would lead to the "true place" for Indian people in American history. This text, like *The Indian Today*, represents Eastman's journey from "Dartmouth's Indian," to a physician, a folklorist, and, finally, a public educator about Indian rights. His work as a political activist required negotiating civilizationist thinking and rhetoric while recognizing indigenous sovereignty, so that he could attract the support of white progressives *and* Native leaders.[60]

Eastman's argument regarding Indian rights in *The Indian Today* has five central elements: policy, reform efforts, education, networks of Indian intellectuals, and "the problem of race leadership." By examining each of these elements, one sees how Eastman described and defined the parameters of Indian policy in America. Unlike his earlier writings, which demonstrated his educational philosophy through various forms of practice, this book lays out reform ideas in conversation with preexisting networks developed by white progressives and Indian activists. At the same time, education remains central to his thinking. For example, he focuses on Indian schools and considers the roles college-educated Indians can play in the fight for citizenship. Finally, what emerges as Eastman's greatest concern is an ideology that cuts across various ethnic groups: "the problem of race leadership."

To instruct his readers toward shaping the future of Indian policy in the United States, Eastman initially turns to the past.

It must always be borne in mind that the first effect of association with the more advanced race was not improvement but degeneracy. I have no wish to discredit the statements of the early explorers, including the Jesuit priests; but it is evidence that in the zeal of the latter to gain honor for their society for saving the souls of the natives it was almost necessary to represent them as godless and murderous savages – otherwise there would be no one to convert! Of course they were not angels, but I think I have made it clear that they were a God-fearing, clean, and honorable people before the coming of the white man.[61]

Chronicling a history of colonialism and conquest vis-à-vis relocation, the reservation system, and allotment, Eastman emphasizes the changing status of Indian people within the United States. He argues that the pitfalls of the federally run Agency System under the Bureau of Indian Affairs has remained largely unchanged since colonial times. This was a problem because, as Eastman notes, the U.S. government's right of "eminent domain" did not necessarily deny Indian people the "right of occupancy," but did impose limits on tribal sovereignty through the use of treaties, acts of Congress, and executive orders. By 1915, the sovereignty of tribal nations was under threat given the Dawes Act of 1887 and a push for universal citizenship for all Indian people in the United States. Eastman understood these circumstances and looked to individual rather than treaty rights as a new source of power for Indian people.[62]

Eastman's text highlights the problems inherent in U.S. Indian policy (to Indian and non-Indian readers alike) to point out the fundamental ambivalence on which later policies were overlaid. He argues that if Indian tribes could be understood as independent nations, then the policies that encouraged practices of elimination and resettlement would *not* be justified given their right of occupancy. At the time, Indian people had neither been recognized as members of sovereign nations nor been given the right of occupancy. Thus, clearly and consistently, the U.S. government mismanaged the welfare of Indian people. This is the history that was critical for Eastman because he knew how the development of the United States, as a democratic nation, rested on the political separation of Indian tribes and the rest of American society. In this sense, Eastman's text is in close dialogue with W. E. B. Du Bois and the integrationist politics of justice espoused by African American intellectuals, rather than his own intellectual descendants who turned to the notion of collective rights. Eastman's argument centered on an American contradiction, the same dilemma that drove Du Bois: How could Indian people participate in a democracy that was itself so undemocratic with particular regards to them?[63]

Du Bois was led by a long history of social integration matched with political powerlessness. Political integration – that is, citizenship – seemed a logical way of putting that social integration into an equitable practice. Indian history led someplace else. Rather than a long history of intimate social integration, Indian people had a history of treaty making and political independence. The contradiction, then, looked a bit different to Eastman than it did to Du Bois.

The Indian Today represents how Eastman grappled with the fraught history of U.S. colonialism in the context of his efforts as a reformer. He focused on the processes of dispossession and political independence while simultaneously arguing for the political incorporation of Indian people. "In less than a century 370 distinct treaties were made with the various tribes, some of them merely friendship agreements, but in the main providing for the right of way and the cession of lands, as fast as such lands were demanded by the westward growth of the country and the pressure of population." Eastman's account of this history recognized how dispossession was complicated and specific to each indigenous nation. In addition, the ward-ship system, developed out of treaties and the practical administrative apparatus of the government, succeeded in separating vast numbers of Indian people from important tracts of land. Indian lands were "set aside not only by treaty" but also "by act of Congress" and "executive order" for the settlement of white Americans. Even though much of Eastman's rhetoric favored incorporation through citizenship, he also argued that the future of Indian policy reform must take into account the specificity of this history of dispossession.[64]

As Eastman outlined the stages used to eradicate a preexisting population in order to make room for a new one, he used this history to argue for citizenship. What proves troubling is that Eastman must showcase the problems inherent in the reservation system to argue for its dissolution. This is a stance he argued from as early as 1911, in London at the Congress on Race. *The Indian Today* reveals his interest in converting Indian readers to the erasure of this system. Eastman wanted to encourage Indian people to embrace individual pursuits of work and property *because* these were part of the path toward full citizenship – and citizenship was his end goal.

Eastman advocated reform not through collective action and acts of tribal sovereignty via treaties, but through individual voices and votes.[65]

In order to strengthen his case for U.S. citizenship (as opposed to tribal nationalism), Eastman pointed to corruption within the reservation system. Although Indian businessmen "have developed traits that are absolutely opposed to the racial type," when they work for the Indian Service, "they become time-serving, beggarly, and apathetic," Eastman asserted. In this case, the intentions of a system may be positive but the execution falls short when American principles are hidden under the shield of a corrupt agent. Indians who try to avoid being corrupted by resisting the abuses of the government system are ironically labeled "incorrigible savages." In these instances, Indians who are the most aligned with better American principles cannot escape being seen as "Other." Here, Eastman highlights the failures within the system itself, and recognizes that individual Indians can help stall the growth of corruption within U.S. society. Eastman argues, ultimately, that Indian people who are corrupted by the system of the Indian Bureau are responding to harsh practices, which are part and parcel of that system. His text aims to convince nonnatives that this bureaucracy is riddled with problems that must be solved. Because rations of "cheap blankets and shoddy clothing" contribute to a decline in self-respect among Indians, then white Americans must seek out ways to reform U.S. policy with regards to Indian affairs.[66]

The larger problem, according to Eastman, was that capitalism and market impulses bred corruption among white men, which in turn spread to the Indian businessmen they encountered. Furthermore, because of out-of-date farming equipment and impracticable schooling, the political economy of reservations was neither self-sustaining nor in dialogue with the market logic outside of these reservations. In many senses, Eastman saw reservations as prisons for Indian people because they limited Indians' ability to advance materially, socially, and politically within the United States. Although the question of how Americans and Indians could escape the trap of corruption remained, Eastman was committed to noting how Indian people could participate in the world of modern capital with the hope that they would not be corrupted by it.[67]

Eastman strongly favored citizenship and the elimination of the Office of Indian Affairs (the official name of the bureaucracy until 1947, when it was renamed the Bureau of Indian Affairs) as possible solutions to corruption born from capitalism, and he advocated a new sort of policy.[68] This shift relied on a strategic alliance between white and Native reformers to manage modern capitalist expansion. Part of this management required the embrace of spiritual beliefs. This ideology emerged out of the work of white progressives who were active in the Lake Mohonk Conference, which met frequently between 1883 and 1916 to discuss Indian matters and to make recommendations.[69] For them, reform took the shape of stopping land speculators and others on "frontier" settlements in the United States from taking advantage of Indian people. These reformers sought legislation that would find a way to promote the progress of Christian settlement. Indeed, the keyword here is *Christian*. Their reformist agenda was built on Christian teachings. Eastman held both Dakota beliefs and Christian ones. As these white reformers supported Eastman, he became part of the body politic. In turn, Eastman reconciled his inclusion in the political structures of the United States by presenting himself as a case study to gain the support of white activists and as a model ripe for emulation by Indian people.[70]

In many ways, Eastman's ideas aligned with those espoused by "eastern sentimentalists." Because *The Indian Today* aimed to reach white Americans who might be sympathetic to the cause of the Indians in America and to show Indian people that white reform organizations were essential to the future of the Red Man, it celebrated what Eastman had learned from specific groups of "eastern sentimentalists." He names three groups as especially helpful: The Boston Indian Citizenship Committee (est. 1879), The National Indian Association (org. 1879), and The Indian Rights Association (org. 1882).[71] Eastman makes clear that "To all three of these bodies, as well as to the Board of the Indian Commissioners, belongs much credit for urging the reforms which triumphed, in 1887, in the 'Dawes bill,' the Emancipation Act of the Indian." As Eastman affirmed the merits of these reformers, he also celebrated, rather than critiqued, certain aspects of the allotment policy. In time, his ideas about the Dawes Act would shift to reflect a consensus among Indian communities regarding the disenfranchisement and poverty that followed in the wake of such a policy. At this time, however, Eastman was eager to "mend fences" separating white reformers who held political sway in Washington from an emergent pan-tribal movement whose power was growing.[72]

For Eastman, then, reform needed to occur in two directions. First, the corrupt agent system had to be addressed. This was an American and governmental problem. Second, Indian people needed to be educated. For Eastman, education meant skilled training that would enable Indians to participate in market capitalism, and Christian ideals that could help them avert corruption. His conception of education here fits within certain assimilationist logics that underpinned Indian policy during this period. However, Eastman did not view himself as pro-assimilation. Instead, he wanted to highlight education's merits so that schools and systems of education could be overhauled to benefit Indian students.

Eastman turned to a specific site to support his conclusions about the power of education: Dartmouth. He pointed to his alma mater and the figure of Samson Occom as a case study for "the most famous educated Indian of his day." Occom had traveled widely to promote Congregational minister Eleazer Wheelock's "Indian Charity School," but Wheelock used any funds Occom acquired to found Dartmouth College instead. Eastman used this case to argue that "individual red men were able to assimilate the classical culture of the period, and capable, moreover, of loyalty toward the new ideals no less than the old." Eastman celebrated Occom somewhat mistakenly given that he and Wheelock had a falling out after Occom learned what had happened to his funds, and the power of education through this example. Still, Occom's success as an educated reverend and a member of the Mohegan nation in the eighteenth century made him an apt subject to honor, according to Eastman's argument regarding the relationship between education and racial uplift. In his overview of "Early Mission and Contract Schools" and the Carlisle Indian Industrial School, Eastman again used Indian education to argue in favor of assimilation, although he understood it as a means of accessing politics rather than as a tool of manipulation and oppression.[73]

Despite his own feelings about inclusion, Eastman recognized that many Indians felt the debilitating effects of forced assimilation, oppressive educational institutions (like Carlisle), and paternalism based on racism that characterized much of the Indian service. Certainly, Eastman's citizenship was not theirs. But because he was an interlocutor between white society and Indian Country, Eastman also recognized the centrality of class in making an argument for citizenship. He understood the contradictions surrounding class, race, and citizenship. "Among the thinking and advanced class of Indians there is, after all, no real bitterness or pessimistic feeling. It has long been apparent to us that absolute distinctions cannot be maintained under the American flag." With these words, Eastman asserts a belief in an elite class and in the possibility of transcending racist practices through class mobility in America.[74]

For educated and middle-class Indians, according to Eastman, racism was not a roadblock to entering the body politic of the United States, which enabled him to make a critical distinction between citizenship and cultural assimilation. The latter was understood by white and Indian progressives as a means for shaping the traditions, practices, and politics of Indian people, so that they better aligned with dominant American society. This point of view was not shared by all Indian people. Part of Eastman's aim was to convince other Native leaders to see education as a means to an end because advanced schooling could ameliorate some of the differences and prejudices that separated Indian people from white Americans given hierarchical understandings of class and race. Still, Eastman remained aware that educated Indians could easily be misrepresented to white society, and he blamed the news media for these errors. "Whenever an Indian indulges in any notorious behavior, he is widely heralded as a 'Carlisle graduate,' although as a matter of fact he may never have attended that famous school, or have been there for a short time only.... Obviously the statement is intended to discredit the educated Indian."[75] Regardless of their socioeconomic status to begin with, a Native person who became educated, Eastman believed, gained skills necessary to successfully maneuver within American society.

While Eastman argues that more education can elevate Indian people's political and cultural positions within American society, he also returns to the race question, suggesting that Indian blood holds a special quality. He establishes a tenuous link between social mobility, political access, and ethnic essentialism. In particular, he uses the figure of Theodore Roosevelt to make a point about racial formation in America. According to Eastman, Roosevelt "would give anything to have a drop of Sioux or Cheyenne blood in his veins." Eastman does not discuss *why* it is that Roosevelt would "give anything" to have Indian blood. Instead, he positions Roosevelt within a narrative that argues it is the Indian who is the first and real American. In this case, Roosevelt's belief in an Indian one-drop rule enables white people to still be white without having to contend with racism, even while becoming Indian enough to *feel* their primitivist desires converted into authentic selfhood. Ultimately, Eastman uses Roosevelt to illustrate that "the intelligent and educated Indian has no social prejudice to contend with" because "His color is not counted against him." This is an important point to make regarding Indian blood as a celebration of authentic Americanness, as the rightful property of Indian people, and as distinct from the one-drop rule that worked to disenfranchise African Americans during this period. According to Eastman, one drop of Indian blood does not *taint* one's character as would one drop of African American blood, quite the opposite.

Eastman goes a step further by positioning himself against Booker T. Washington, who, Eastman notes, has been "in the habit of saying jocosely that the negro blood is the strongest in the world, for one drop of it makes a 'nigger' of a white man." Eastman misreads the irony of Washington's statement to argue that "Indian blood is even stronger, for a half-blood negro and Indian may pass for an Indian, and so be admitted to first-class hotels and even to high society."[76] Not only is one drop of Indian blood different than that of "a half-blood negro," but it is in fact *stronger* with regards to passing for white. His comparison rests on a fluid and fragile link between primitivist affection, Indian education, and class mobility. Such a link informed the cultural logic that underpinned Eastman's career as a writer and lecturer, and therefore in this moment he is also making an argument about himself. This example does not reflect Indian reality given that many Indian people experienced racism. Ultimately, the anecdote expresses aspiration rather than realism, but it does showcase the different ways Native intellectuals could navigate a world where ideas about Indianness could be fluid even when they appeared fixed.

Considering these two examples of Eastman's representational politics, we can see how he moves his readers to think about the "real" versus "imagined" power of blood in terms of policy, possibilities for reform, access to education, and race leadership. He asks readers to consider whether race is a biologically rooted or a culturally constructed category. This is a turning point in the narrative to prepare readers for what follows: a discussion of networks and the Indian intellectuals who navigate and manage them.[77]

Eastman emphasizes how "Some Noted Indians of To-day" constitute a network of intellectuals who will shape pan-tribal reform. He is among the first to make this point explicit. His catalogue of successful Indians points to the types of individuals he recognized as most influential within their Indian communities and who could come together to affect change across the United States. He groups them according to profession: doctors, lawyers, ministers, writers, teachers, and notable scientists, as well as artists, businessmen, and athletes. He then turns to two more groups of Indian intellectuals as essential members of the newly forming pan-tribal political groups: anthropologists and writers. In regard to the former, he refers specifically to the careers of William Jones, Arthur C. Parker, and Francis La Flesche. All three were important interlocutors for Eastman because they worked within social scientific disciplines studying contemporary Indian people. Parker was also a close, lifelong friend of Eastman's. Parker had professional success as the director of the Rochester Museum of Arts and Sciences from 1924 to 1945, and was made an honorary trustee of the New York State Historical Association. In 1935, he was elected first president of the Society of American Archaeology.[78]

Looking at Parker, one sees an example of a specific network of Native people who joined Eastman as participants in modernity. Parker recognized that the distinctive character of various tribal nations was a challenge to any pan-Indian movement and why pan-Indian institutions were "largely sponsored by mixed bloods." According to Parker, Indian leaders of mixed-heritage "have perspective; they see over the hills; they see the reasons and the romance. Perhaps, too, they see the shadow that will soon mean the setting of the racial sun."[79] Eastman refers to Parker as an Indian activist who has struggled with these issues. Indeed, Parker's mixed heritage could make him more *or* less Indian in the eyes of others. In this way, Parker and Eastman shared an ethos regarding their educational missions because each aimed to bridge not only divisions between Native and white societies but those within Native communities.

In terms of prominent Native writers, Eastman refers to Francis La Flesche (who worked as an ethnologist with Alice C. Fletcher), as well as Gertrude Bonnin and John Oskison.[80] La Flesche is notable for his anthropological work and his book, *The Middle Five*, which presented a critique of on-reservation schooling. Gertrude Bonnin was a regular interlocutor for Eastman through her work with the Society of American Indians (SAI), and because she traveled in similar publishing and literary circles. Surprisingly, Eastman's mention of Bonnin is brief, despite her accomplishments as a teacher, musician, writer, and public speaker during this period. He prefers to highlight her work as a public speaker and because of her higher

education. He writes that she "attended a Western College, where she distinguished herself in an intercollegiate oratorical contest." Although Eastman
and Bonnin were well acquainted and they both made a good living publishing and giving public talks, he says little more about her in this book.
Her gender may have been an influential factor for him. Finally, Eastman
recognizes the accomplishments of John Oskison as similar to those of
Bonnin. He notes that Oskison was "the winner in an intercollegiate literary
contest" and currently works "on the staff of *Collier's Weekly*," where he is
"praised for his literary work." Eastman uses these three writers to emphasize the importance of individual careers, but also to point out the various
non-Indian social networks that Native intellectuals, as writers, accessed to
promote their careers and their politics.[81]

In addition to doctors, lawyers, ministers, and writers, educators are the
backbone of Indian civilization as Eastman sees it. Through specific examples of other Native leaders, Eastman's voice emerges not as exceptional,
but rather as characteristic of a larger trend in American society. In fact, a
significant number of the Indian intellectuals that he mentions operated as
a network for political leadership. Eastman's text makes explicit the reach
and depth of these Native networks.[82]

After emphasizing how particular Native intellectuals shaped American
society, Eastman turns his analysis to "problems of race leadership." Race,
in this context, means something like "race" as we might understand it
today and something like a quasi-"national" identity for Indian people.
Race leadership, for Eastman, is not tribal leadership. Indeed, the two
might exist in some tension. He points to the diversity and complexity
of Indian peoples, their distinct cultures, and histories. Yet, despite this
diversity Eastman is invested in a narrative that knits together different
Indian tribes so that they may preserve their "distinct languages, habits,
and traditions" while they overcome "old tribal jealousies and antago-
nisms" to form a newly powerful pan-tribal historical bloc.[83] Eastman suggests that the "arbitrary power" put in the hands of the "Indian Bureau"
is the main problem facing modern pan-Indian movements, rather than
tribal differences. Therefore, "race leadership" depends on overcoming a
history of paternalism and a failing bureaucratic system, so that the Indian
"is allowed to take a hand in his own development" – a hand that is
both tribal (without the interference of corrupt government agents) and
pan-Indian (all Indians can participate in this process). Furthermore, during the Progressive Era, race leadership signified a desire to uplift oneself
in material terms while working within a social system that defined race
and class status based on white supremacy.[84]

Throughout his text, education remains pivotal in Eastman's assessment
of race leadership. He sees it as the means through which proper training will
produce "leading Indians," and then identifies "the founders of the Society
of American Indians" as precisely these "leading Indians": Dr. Coolidge,

Dr. Carlos Montezuma, white ally Professor F. A. McKenzie, Thomas Sloan, Charles E. Dagenett, Henry Standing Bear, and Laura Cornelius. The SAI was a progressive group formed in Columbus, Ohio, in 1911 by fifty Native Americans. Most were middle-class professionals. The SAI was established to find ways to improve health, education, civil rights, and local government for Indian people. The SAI also produced its own journal and publicized the accomplishments of famous Native Americans, like Olympic gold medalist Jim Thorpe.

In addition to a journal and conferences, staged Indian performances proved an important strategy for the leaders of the SAI in promoting their organization. Both Eastman and Montezuma were active participants in these sorts of activities. At their fourth annual conference in 1914, Montezuma suggested mounting a scene complete with an old Indian, an interpreter, and an agent to represent a slice of reservation life for a largely white audience, who he believed was ignorant of "real" Indian culture. Such an entertainment aimed to capture white interest by presenting Native culture not only in *real* terms but in appealingly *primitive* and familiar ways. Eastman's reform efforts for the SAI took full advantage of both the stage and the page. In an article for the SAI's journal and Hampton's *The Southern Workman*, he describes Native contributions to American art, stressing the dangers of allowing traditional methods and ideas to die out with the passing of older generations.[85] Through Eastman's work with the Camp Fire Girls, one of his many attempts to offer "Indian culture" as an antidote to modern American disenchantment, he promoted goals of civil rights, fair treatment, and respect through the strategic engagement of Indian culture. He also invited this group to perform at SAI conferences, and his daughter Irene in turn performed as a singer of "American Indian Melodies" at Camp Fire Girls ceremonies.[86] Irene Eastman had her own brief performance career that capitalized on her musical talents.[87]

Like other Native women of the early twentieth century, Irene was often marketed as an "attractive" and "charming" "Indian" girl. Like her father, she wore different costuming for specific occasions, as the musical program for one of her concerts shows. On the front cover, Irene's supposedly non-Native clothing represents middle- to upper-class fashions for white women during this period. The back cover of the program notes that "Miss Eastman has a musical voice, and, in her Indian dress, a fine presence." The interior image depicts Irene in the "Indian dress" she used for her concerts. As "Taluta," Irene performed at a myriad of public meetings and gala occasions, including those put on by the Daughters of the American Revolution and other women's clubs. For the leaders of the SAI, their attempts to use Native cultural performances to advance their political and social goals were apiece with the strategies used by both Eastmans and other Native intellectuals who sought large white audiences to hear their pleas for fuller recognition of Indian rights.[88]

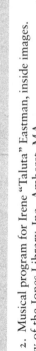

MISS IRENE EASTMAN   Soprano

The wild, appealing folk-music of the North American tribes, as recorded and harmonized by Troyer, Burton, Lieurance, Cadman, and other American composers, is rendered with exceptional fidelity and charm by Irene Eastman.

It should be said that Miss Eastman is unusually well fitted by inheritance, temperament, and training, to interpret to cultivated audiences the poetry and pathos of her father's people, now beginning to be appreciated as never before by white Americans.

She not only sings their melodies with distinction, but tells movingly some remarkable folk-tales of the race, reproducing by means of costume, gesture, and facial expression the characteristic atmosphere of the scenes she depicts.

Miss Eastman, though only a girl, has appeared more than thirty times within the past few months before clubs and schools, in churches and drawing-rooms, either alone or with her father, the Sioux Indian lecturer. She has sung in Boston, New York and Philadelphia; in Pittsburg and Scranton, Pa.; Hartford, Bridgeport, Waterbury and New London, Conn.; Concord, Worcester, and Spring-field Mass; Montpelier, Vt.; Nashua, N. H.; and many other cities and towns. She has also filled several return engagements.

Her program is peculiarly appropriate for public meetings or gala occasions of Camp Fire Girls and Daughters of the American Revolution, also for guest night at Women's Clubs.

A limited number of engagements will be accepted for the coming season.

WHAT PEOPLE SAY.

"Miss Irene Eastman, daughter of Dr. Charles A. Eastman, the Sioux physician, author, and lecturer, and Elaine Goodale Eastman, poet and essayist, gave an Indian song recital in Concord the evening of March 6. Miss Eastman has a splendid soprano voice, which she uses with very little effort. Every one was delighted with her program, which was composed of characteristic Indian melodies, showing the wild poetry and pathos of the native American. Her ceremonial robe of white deerskin, beaded in symbolic designs, has been made especially for her by expert Sioux needle women."

The Enterprise, Concord, Mass.

"Miss Irene Eastman, the attractive and charming Indian girl, appeared last evening in Montpelier under the auspices of the Camp Fire Girls. The audience was delighted with the entertainer, who has a rich, sweet

FIGURE 2. Musical program for Irene "Taluta" Eastman, inside images. Courtesy of the Jones Library, Inc., Amherst, MA.

Despite varied efforts toward reform, the SAI's influence dwindled after
1923. The organization finally disbanded in the 1930s. Although the Society
did not last long, it provided a forum for Indian leaders and a basis for later
attempts to improve conditions for Native Americans. By 1915, Eastman
had served briefly as the SAI's president and succeeded in organizing new
members while strengthening ties to white reform groups. Based on the politics he asserts throughout *The Indian Today*, we can see Eastman is express-
ing concerns within the SAI regarding methods for leadership. Although
Eastman's involvement in the SAI decreased as he focused on his speaking
career, he continued to support its efforts. Through his success as an author
and speaker, Eastman increased his visibility as a public intellectual; with
this increase in visibility, he could "help his race" in ways that stretched
beyond the scope of the presidency of the SAI.[89]

How to Market an Indian Author

The most indelible marks about Indianness that Eastman left as an educator
can be found in his published works. By looking more closely at the circulation of his texts and the reception of some of his ideas within key pieces, we
can access how Eastman made a living as a writer and, more importantly,
what his cultural and political aims were. Like his invitation to Mark Twain's
birthday party, the world of books offered opportunities for Eastman to connect with publishing and reading networks, which would not have been possible through Dartmouth, medicine, or pan-tribal organizations like the SAI.
Indeed, some of the particularities of his career as a writer add to how one
reads his spoken performances and other political projects. Eastman was
marketed as an Indian author, often in racialized terms, which enabled him
to gain support from fellow writers and white reformers.

Just a year after the photo of Twain's party was snapped, Eastman again
appeared in a tuxedo jacket. This time, Charles Harvey was the photographer capturing Eastman holding a book while seated in a high-backed
and ornately carved chair. Harvey's photograph appeared in the *American
Monthly Illustrated Review of Reviews* in 1906. It offered readers a rare
glimpse of Eastman not as the "full-blooded," authentic Sioux Indian wearing buckskin and feathers, but rather as a modern man, a reader, and a member of elite American society. This image positioned Eastman as an author,
like the author's portrait Little Brown and Company used in 1916 on the
inside of his second autobiography, *From the Deep Woods to Civilization*.[90]
Images like these framed Eastman more in terms of an upper-class and
educated cultural space as opposed to the spectacle of the lecture platform where Eastman gave talks about "full-blooded" Indians while wearing Sioux regalia, costumed according to white expectations of Indianness.
Eastman was an author whose work circulated to white reading publics
through well-worn intellectual networks. The doors to these networks often

FIGURE 3. Charles Eastman: Author's portrait (1916).
Archives and Special Collections, Frost Library, Amherst College, Amherst, MA.

opened to Eastman because of popular interest in Indian folktales *as told by* an Indian. As much as Eastman's books aimed to educate young readers and their parents about Sioux culture and history, he also needed to earn a living as a writer given that his medical practice was unprofitable. Both these economic concerns and demands to see Eastman required that he live a peripatetic life as a writer, reformer, and public speaker.

A large part of Eastman's educational mission that has often been over-looked are his efforts to teach America's youngest citizens. By writing for and speaking to white children, Eastman could reverse the Indian boarding school dynamic in critical ways. His desire to teach children (whether white or Indian) *before* they became fully entrenched into one particular culture enabled Eastman to shape how they thought about race, class, and nation. This type of approach was in dialogue with the emergence of the scouting movement in America. During this time, Ernest Thompson Seton (1860–1946), a noted author, wildlife artist, and founder of the Woodcraft Indians, began promoting the establishment of the Boy Scouts of America (BSA). Eastman worked with Seton, who was heavily influenced by Lord Baden-Powell (the founder of scouting in general). Eastman chose scouting and similar back-to-nature movements, like the Camp Fire Girls, to further his argument that white American children lacked Indian ties to nature and the spiritual properties of those ties. Eastman's stories for children, along with his first autobiography, *Indian Boyhood*, represented the philosophical ideals that underpinned scouting practices, namely that moral and spiritual development could be fostered through outdoor activities such as camping and hiking. All three men embraced the belief that American Indian culture should be a central component of the BSA. This aspect of American culture implied one possible audience.[91]

Eastman's books were marketed across the United States to all types of readers: boys eager to read tales of adventure similar to familiar pulp or dime novels, folklorists who wanted to own a piece of Native culture, and white bohemians living in cities who sought out examples of primitivism to save them from their increasingly modernist selves. These audiences were participating in an "Indian craze" that was in full swing by this time. As Elizabeth Hutchison defines it, the "Indian craze" was a type of collecting that connected "Indian things" to arts and crafts societies, museum exhibitions, and world's fairs. Furthermore, Hutchinson sets the "Indian craze" against the backdrop of American primitivist and reformist engagement with tribal peoples and in the context of an emergent American consumer culture.

Eastman and his publishers exploited the market for "Indian things" by navigating racialized expectations for Indian writers and advertising his books in order to garner the widest possible readership. Two advertisements for *Indian Boyhood*, from McClure, Phillips and Company, emphasize the authenticity of Eastman's story and its cross-generational appeal: "Boys will delight in this book, because it tells how real Indian boys lived and played; grownups will find it interesting, because it is the only story of Indian life ever written from inside." This sort of marketing was not limited to the Northeast. An ad from the *San Francisco Chronicle* notes, "In fact, it would be difficult to name a book containing so much of interest to boys as 'Indian Boyhood,'" while the *Milwaukee Sentinel* told readers that for a postpaid price of $1.73 they could not only buy Eastman's book as "an unique contribution to literature," but they could also own it as a piece of American history. These types of ads framed Eastman's narrative as a distinctly indigenous story that was also a part of a larger American narrative. For many white readers, *Indian Boyhood* was "the first time Indian life" could be "presented from the inside" to them. Thus, they might embrace the notion that Eastman's book was "of distinct value as a rare human document" because it was an Indian's contribution to American literature. The success of *Indian Boyhood* suggests that Native peoples were not outside of capitalism, but instead an integral part of capitalist and gendered forms of reproduction. Eastman recognized this sort of interplay and used it to his advantage through his work as a lecturer, where he could condemn the pitfalls of capitalism while drawing a salary based on market-driven demands to see and hear a "real" Indian speaker. As a writer, he was also able to sell his books as "unique" because they were written "from the inside" and then tell a personal story that celebrated aspects of his Indian upbringing as well as his life as a modern American.[92]

Eastman's narrative throughout *Indian Boyhood* focuses on his childhood to argue for the successful conversion he made from living the wildness of Indian youth to becoming an educated member of modern and white American society. On one hand, by contextualizing his story in primitivist terms, Eastman could reach a white youth market interested in figuring Indians and Indianness as authentic when viewed through the lens of noble savagery. On the other hand, Eastman's adult readers could embrace him as an Indian doctor; in this position, Eastman's authorial voice carried within it a narrative of education, modernity, and assimilation as well as the types of contributions he sought to espouse.[93]

Among the wide range of people who read Eastman's books were other American authors interested in writing about Indian subjects. One of the best known, who became an ally of Eastman, was Hamlin Garland. Although it is not clear how Garland and Eastman first became acquainted, they met on a number of occasions. Both were living in Boston during the 1880s and had attended and presented talks at the World's Columbian Exposition in Chicago in 1893. During this period, Garland was the first, together with Thomas J. Morgan (then commissioner of Indian Affairs) to promote a project to rename the Sioux in order to resolve any legal complications resulting from enforcement of the Dawes Allotment Act of 1887. It was Garland who thought to select Eastman to help in the renaming process, and so he was hired to work for the Office of Indian Affairs in this capacity from 1903–9. During this time, Eastman continued to pursue his writing career, perhaps because he had the support of a fellow writer like Garland.[94]

Around 1901, Garland sent an enthusiastic letter to Eastman about *Indian Boyhood*. Garland expressed that he had found it a "most delightful" book, which could have been even longer. He wrote to Eastman, "You must have a great deal more to say." Garland's remarks here refer more to politics than literary craft. Specifically, he encourages Eastman to go a step further with his next book by writing for a wider adult audience on the topic of racial prejudice: "This book is, in a sense, a book for young people. I would like to see a book from you addressed to men of like minds. Men to whom race prejudice is a survival of no better pass." Garland's letter recognizes both the marketable quality of Eastman's work for young readers and the political possibilities now open to Eastman if he were to address adult readers. This particular intellectual exchange augured the production of Eastman's second autobiography, *From the Deep Woods to Civilization*, which did have a more mature tone and would reach adults in favor of Indian rights.[95]

Like his exchange with Garland, many of the personal letters that Eastman received celebrated his career as a writer. These materials, along with an extensive set of book reviews, are objects of epistolary culture that demonstrate the circulation of his books and his contribution to print culture during this period. In addition, the reviews reflect changes in Eastman's work as well as how readers responded to those changes in the context of a broader American literary tradition.

The majority of book reviews for *Indian Boyhood* appeared in periodicals based in New York, Pennsylvania, and Massachusetts, and other urban areas like Atlanta, Chicago, and Rochester; with a few circulating to less-populated regions in California and Minnesota. In addition, a smaller sampling of reviews appeared in locally situated outlets like the *Sioux City Journal, St. Paul News, Pittsburgh Gazette, Kansas City Star*, and subject-specific journals, ranging from aesthetics to religion to politics, like *Book News, Art Interchange, Literary Digest, Missionary Review*, and *The Indian's Friend*. This range in publication of reviews for Eastman's most popular book demonstrates that his work appealed to urban as well as rural readers and those interested in American literary studies as well as progressive reform, whether secular or religious in nature. Overall, the social geography suggested by the circulation of these reviews indicates that there was a wide, perhaps diverse in terms of class, race, religion, and gender, audience for a "real" Indian's account of his life and the contemporary situation faced by Indian people living in America.[96]

Among the reviews a consensus appears regarding the value of *Indian Boyhood*: one ought to read it not only because an actual, "full-blooded Sioux Indian" wrote it, but also because it dealt with details of Indian life that paralleled familiar topoi in American literature. As one reviewer from the *Boston Post*, circa 1906, notes, readers could both recognize elements in *Indian Boyhood* and find something new: "It is claimed for this book that it is 'the only record in existence of Indian life as it is seen, not from the outside, by such poetic narrators as Longfellow, Cooper and Chateaubriand, but by one whose own boyhood was passed among the scenes described.'" These reviews, like Eastman's publishers, framed his writing using cultural authenticity and promoted it as the embodiment of the author, as from the "inside."[97]

As critics positioned Eastman within a larger literary history, they implicitly suggested he might be taken seriously as an author because his work could be read alongside that of more well-known writers like Henry Wadsworth Longfellow. However, they continued to rely on (and make explicit) an authority that referred to the raced/blooded body of Eastman as an author. His authority then depended on his status as an Indian, perhaps as Dartmouth's Indian, but still always as an Indian. The very avenue through which Eastman gained access to attention and, potentially, canonicity trapped him in the very expectations of Indianness that he worked his entire life to overcome. In the *Review of Reviews*, for example, Eastman and his work are described in just these terms. "Dr. Eastman, who is a full-blooded Sioux Indian ... embraced our civilization. 'Indian Boyhood' stands alone in our literature as a record of much that has passed beyond the range of human experience, never to return." For both Eastman and his book, the "range of human experience" is "never to return." Thus, time for Native people is separated out from the imperial machinations of the British, the French, and the Spanish. Certainly Eastman knew this colonial past was long gone. Although his writings gesture to an American nostalgia for this past, his primary goal was to convince Americans to recognize the lasting relevance of Indian people, not to relegate them to the past.

A review from the *Chicago Inter-Ocean* understood Eastman's larger point, and sought to reimagine Indian people based on Eastman's narrative. "It also appears that the Indian is not a stoic by nature, but is made stoical by his training. Nor is he ever the stoic that he appears. He has a keen sense of humor, and laughs as heartily as any one. He has affections the same as any one else, and loves his parents and his family, his pony, and his dog.... In short, according to Dr. Eastman, the Sioux is a good deal of a man and a very decent member of the community after his own rights." This review, like so many others, emphasized to readers that "Indians are human too." Indeed, it seems that because the Indian is "not stoic by nature" but can be "made stoical" by some sort of training, Eastman's texts might be read for Indianness that is both fluid and stable.[98]

Even though it was crucial to Eastman's work to negotiate the fine line between definitions of American identity and Indian identity, many reviews still celebrated *Indian Boyhood* in explicitly racialist terms. One review from the *Boston Herald* serves as a representative sample: "The book is unique, besides being full of information about the vanished civilization; but it is the author's pride in his race that makes it worth while." Another review, in the *New York Tribune*, uses even more paternalistic rhetoric: "An Indian boyhood as this Indian describes it was full of action and entertainment. The little Indian studied mankind and nature as the little Caucasian studies books."[99] This reviewer sets up a binary separating Indian children from the domains of "white" culture given that they are more inclined toward the study of "mankind and nature" whereas white children put their energies toward "books." Read even more closely, Eastman's childhood is not without study even if his autobiography is to be taken as a work of "entertainment" rather than a crucible for change. There were many who read Eastman's work, as Hamlin Garland did, and knew that he had the tools to revise white expectations that situated Indianness in nature, apart from civilized society and the world of books. This reviewer at least, ironically, elides Eastman's current status as both an Indian and an author. These were tenuous observations at best and destructive ones at worst. The specific pathos of the Indian boy so easily collapsed into an ethnological frame and simultaneously defined as entertainment contributed to celebrating the type of Indian that Eastman sought to revise. He was all too aware of its corrosive power within American imagination; despite his best literary efforts, this sort of Indianness survived, and paradoxically reinforced some of the representations he aimed to destroy.[100]

A discourse of Indianness tied to intellectualism emerges further through several reviews that position Eastman in the company of other Native writers, demonstrating an emergent network built and maintained by these writers, their publishers, and readers. One article from *Book-Buyer*, titled "Recent Writings by American Indians," defines notable Native writers as contributing to the formation of a uniquely American literature. The critic observes:

Of Late years we shall call ourselves Americans, but, after all, are only foreigners "changed by the climate," have had opportunities to read a small amount of purely American literature in the writings of some of the educated American Indians. Three authors in particular – Dr. Eastman, Mr. La Flesche, and the Indian girl Zitkala-Sa – have notably enriched our records of the characters and customs of their people.

In this case, Eastman, La Flesche, and Zitkala-Sa (Gertrude Bonnin's popular pen name) are incorporated into a new American literature where the line separating the genre of ethnography and literature is blurred. This fuzziness produces a different sort of genre that promised readers authentic tales by real Native writers. In *Before Cultures*, Brad Evans focuses his analysis on the intersection between anthropology and American literary history with examples of writers who were interested in culture in an anthropological sense, and who published in literary periodicals, much like Eastman did. As Evans notes, popular magazines such as *Century Illustrated Monthly* published Frank Hamilton Cushing's anthropological studies as articles alongside literary pieces by authors like Henry James. For these writers, having their work appear within a print culture that embraced the literary and the anthropological was helpful in promoting their work, if also misleading given that they could then be framed as natural anthropologists whose writings would enrich white readers with "records of the characters and customs of their people."

Looking more closely at the gendered and hierarchical language this critic used to describe these Indian writers reveals a rationale behind why Eastman was listed first. The title of "doctor" suggests he was given top billing not just because of the popularity of his books but also because of his status as a physician and a man. Notably, of the three only Zitkala-Sa is framed first by her race and then her gender. Restating the fact of being an Indian highlights the important pairing of Indianness with femaleness to suggest an underlying desire for the exotic Native princess. And yet she is framed within a colonialist discourse that genders her not as an adult woman, but rather like Pocahontas, as decidedly childlike by using the diminutive "girl." Neither Eastman nor La Flesche is framed using this paternalistic rhetoric.[101]

In addition to classifying these writers based on the ethnographic dimensions of their work as well as their race, gender, and class, the *Book-Buyer* article argues for the critical role to be played by Indians as intellectuals. As Robert Warrior and others have shown, the writings of Indian people pushed at the boundaries drawn by scholars in academia, and by white publics who could not imagine the possibility of indigenous contributions to an American literature.[102] From today we can look back to this earlier moment to reconceptualize American literary history. All three, Eastman, La Flesche, and Bonnin, mention the benefits of white civilization while also valuing Indian traditions.

> It is interesting to observe that each of them has emphasized the finer aspects of the old order – which, for them, has changed forever – with a pride that cannot fail to be recognized by the casual reader, even where it is accompanied by the most courteous acknowledgement of the merits and advantages of civilization.

As *Book-Buyer* notes, Indian writers worked as cultural in-betweens when they preserved "the old order" to retain the finer aspects, even if the same reviewer asserts that any cause for racial pride is now complicated given that the old order "has changed forever."

Looking to *how* reviewers categorized Eastman as an author and the content of his work in terms of genre and audience gives us a window into the world of print culture and his impact on it.[103] These reviews also point out the wide-ranging appeal and attention that Eastman's books generated within local, regional, national, and international literary markets. For example, on November 2, 1911, Eastman received a letter from Florence, Italy, and another, in French, from Castres, France. Both letters requested copies of *The Soul of the Indian*. As a narrative about Native spirituality, it attracted a diverse array of responses. Theodore Stanton, the writer from France, expressed interest in the book because it constituted a remarkable "oeuvre" unto itself. In addition, Stanton asserted that it was unique because it was drawn from Eastman's life experiences, and therefore, he wished to purchase additional copies because of its educational value for the public of France. Eastman must have been pleased to receive this sort of affirmation in that it confirmed his larger aim, which was to educate not just Americans but the world about Dakota spirituality in an effort to increase public support for Native issues.[104] Indeed, some of his later work, like *From the Deep Woods to Civilization* published by Little, Brown and Company of Boston in 1916, reached popular and influential readers who subscribed to sources such as *The Dial*, *Vogue*, and *The Nation*, as well as periodicals that highlighted Indian issues, like *The New York Times*, *The Chauttaqua*, *North American Review*, *The Red Man*, and *The Southern Workman*.[105] The majority of reviewers positioned Eastman as authentic in the sense that his writing lay somewhere between the tropes of primitivism and the ideals of literary intellectualism.[106] From the standpoint of publishers like Alfred McIntyre, Eastman's books were viewed more simply as commodities. In fact, in 1916, McIntyre was anxious to get *Deep Woods* out by that fall, so he offered Eastman "an advance of $250.00 on account of a royalty of [twelve and a half percent] on the first two thousand copies sold, and fifteen percent on sales thereafter." After *From the Deep Woods to Civilization* was published, McIntyre wrote to Eastman to celebrate the power of the new book: "We ... congratulate you on a splendid piece of work, which would do much to give people a better understanding of the Indian."[107] In addition to support from publishers, Eastman received a plethora of letters from friends, fellow writers, and interested readers who loved what he had written and urged him to write more.

Considering the ways Eastman's publishers promoted his books, the reactions he received from his friends and political supporters, along with how book reviews represented him as an author, suggest that Eastman reached many different types of readers and that he contributed to building a different, distinctly Native sort of literary history for this period. The ways Eastman's books were marketed and read by young people, white writers, and critics, as well as how he portrayed himself through these writings and imagined different audiences for his ideas reveal a complex author's portrait; an image that dovetailed with his career as a professional speaker. A different circuit through which Eastman produced knowledge about Indian history, culture, and politics, and where his efforts toward reform turned on the power of public performance, took full advantage of the lecture platform.[108]

Performance Politics: Body and Blood

Based on the professional and personal networks he was able to access, Eastman was often invited to give talks throughout the Northeast. Two trustees of Wellesley College, Mr. and Mrs. Frank Wood, with whom Eastman lived while attending medical school at Boston University, helped launch his college speaking tour by writing to their friend, President Palmer, of Wellesley College.[109] In addition to women's colleges, Normal Schools became primary venues for supporting Eastman's lecturing career. By this time, Normal Schools had formed to train high school graduates to become teachers. The label "Normal School" itself stemmed from the French use of *ecole normale* in the nineteenth century. These institutions provided a model school with model classrooms in order to offer "hands-on" training to their would-be teachers. Given Eastman's own experiences with higher education and his mission to educate Americans, it is no surprise that he would so often choose to speak in front of audiences filled with future teachers.[110]

In 1908, the principal of Worcester's Normal School, Mr. E. H. Russell, celebrated the power and excitement surrounding Eastman's visit to his school. Russell's letter confirmed the important role Eastman could play as an Indian intellectual by noting, "The secret of your power I cannot fathom, but I suspect it is in part that you do not give the lecture, but you are the lecture." Russell's reference to a merger between the messenger and his message reflects sentiments shared by other letter writers, friends, and newspaper reporters during this period. Although Russell did not actually understand the "secret" of Eastman's "power," he recognized that performance was at work when Eastman dressed up to give talks on the topic of the "Real Indian." Russell linked the content and form of Eastman's talk plainly. "You seem for the time to be the embodiment of your race, and that in its best state."[111] Indeed, this letter raises an important question: What was the power of Eastman as the embodiment of his race? One answer lies in the power of performance itself.

Russell understood that there was some power inherent in a public performance by an Indian man who presented himself as both the representative of Indian people and Indianness as a cultural category. However, Russell could not fully fathom the extent to which Eastman's talks succeeded in linking cultural aesthetics with political consequences. In the context of Russell's reading of Eastman's lecture, one can imagine that the Native ceremonial dress Eastman wore was as important to gaining the attention of audiences as were modulations in his voice and the positioning of his body. Dress, the cadence of one's voice, and bearing always play some role in convincing listeners to take one's speech to heart. Yet there was more at play when a "real Indian" gave a public talk about the future of "The Red Man in America." The difference for Eastman was that he designed the content of his talks to disrupt the expectations of his white audiences. For example, in 1928, Eastman participated in a speaking tour in England where he was encouraged to wear "Sioux regalia." Such a request suggested his audiences desired he *play* Indian for them, at least with regards to costuming, which he did. And yet Eastman took advantage of this engagement and others to speak on behalf of Indian people and argue their spirit had a real and lasting impact on American society. Wearing regalia could signify the past, but Eastman's words spoke to the future.[112]

Eastman's 1908 trip to the Worcester Normal School proved so successful that Russell argued more talks would be required. Russell went so far as to say that "a larger and larger hearing year by year" should take place, "until the remarkable characteristics of your race, now so little known and so generally misunderstood, shall be fairly apprehended and appreciated by ours." Eastman must have been delighted to see that his educational mission was starting to take hold, and Russell was correct. Eastman was able to book more speaking engagements in the years that followed.

Eastman and other Indian intellectuals were often forced to navigate their public presentations of Indianness in complicated if also contradictory ways in the early twentieth century given the question of political message versus an imagined racial essence.[113] In fact, of the over forty-five articles that appeared throughout New England, the New York Tri-State area, and the Midwest from the early 1900s to the 1930s, featuring accounts of the lecture career of "Dr. Charles Eastman," the most popular topic was his interpretation and representation of "the real Indian."

Two studio portraits taken while Eastman was an undergraduate at Dartmouth College augured the performative nature of his speaking career, and some of the ways he would embrace and redefine Indianness. In one photo, Eastman wears a button-down shirt, tie, and suit jacket. This clothing was typical for him throughout his life. In the other, Eastman is pictured wearing a Sioux costume with a feathered headdress, holding a bow and arrows. Which Eastman could his audiences expect to see before them when he came to give an address on the subject of "the real Indian": the man in the suit or the man with a feathered headdress?

In many cases, Eastman chose to wear different sorts of buckskin shirts and pants, often with extensive fringed edges, and he would carry a hatchet and/or wear some sort of feathered headpiece. He chose most often to represent Indianness by adorning himself with clothing and symbols that would ring familiar to audiences. These were truly moments of performance given that he drew on visual tropes that aligned with expectations stemming from Western dime novels, Wild West shows, and later Western films. He was keenly aware of the power of performativity given the many requests that audiences made to see him appear in "real" Indian costume, rather than a tuxedo or everyday suit and tie.[114]

Many accounts of Eastman's lectures point to the intimate and powerful connection he made with audiences by blurring the line between the method and message of his talks because he dressed up in Native costume. More often than not, stories regarding Eastman's public appearances highlight that he appeared in "full Sioux regalia," even as they celebrate his *topic*, the "Real Indian," as one Americans needed to know. In these instances, Eastman *played Indian* for audiences in ways that enabled them to hear him. Ironically, the clothes that made him visible and audible to these audiences' expectations of Indianness also, in some ways, erased the reality of his present situation. The trade-off was that Eastman could argue that Native American people were fit for citizenship and integral to the making of modern America. Thus, his physical presence as an Indian dressed in Sioux clothing authenticated a particular definition of Indian culture for white publics. By using buckskin to signify Indianness, Eastman elided the fact that he usually wore tailored cloth suits. As an Indian intellectual, Eastman needed a performative costuming repertoire, from a tuxedo to full Sioux regalia, which he could draw on in strategic ways depending on the differing expectations of his audiences.[115]

By the late nineteenth century, the proliferation of powerful imagery of Indian people created by fiction writers had taken visual form in posters advertising "Buffalo Bill" Cody's Wild West and embodied performance by the Native actors Cody hired to join his troupe. The popularity of these representations may have prompted intellectuals like Eastman to find a variety of ways to authenticate themselves as Indians. Eastman crafted a public persona that was amenable to wearing a tuxedo as much as full Sioux regalia. In either instance, Eastman could showcase his own display of Indianness, and then use that same occasion to speak against hegemonic understandings of Indian-white history that relied on and reified the tropes that made his Native costume popular and spectacular. Eastman's public performances, in many ways, represent the high point of his career as an Indian intellectual and the coming together of his education, publishing work, and the negotiation of networks that linked Indian and white activists, intellectuals, and supporters. The question remains, though: How did specific performances and the discourses that were produced around these talks solidify a space for Eastman as an Indian intellectual in American history?[116]

Like Normal Schools, the Chautauqua Circuit offered Eastman a network of white publics interested in hearing his ideas regarding assimilation, history, and federal policy pertaining to Indian people. The Chautauqua Circuit was a traveling show that attracted communities to gather for several days in a festival tent setting. The Chautauqua Literary and Scientific Circle (CLSC) began in 1878 to provide those who could not afford to attend college the opportunity to acquire skills and essential knowledge of a college education. The circuit brought programs to rural Americans not only to educate, but also to inspire and entertain them. The Chautauqua experience was crucial in stimulating thought and discussion on important political, social, and cultural issues, and helped to plant them in the minds of citizens. This circuit was useful for Indian intellectuals like Eastman because through it they could tap into other arenas: women's clubs, elite men's societies, and religion-based reform groups.[117]

At 8:30 in the evening on Friday, February 23, 1912, Eastman was invited to present a talk about "The Nature Life of the Indian" at the annual meeting of the National Indian Association (NIA) at the Waldorf-Astoria Hotel. His performance that evening spoke to the concerns of the NIA by calling for a need to reform Indian policy in America. The Association was known as the Women's National Indian Association (WNIA) from 1879 until 1901 because it was founded by white female progressives during the 1880s. It is not surprising that the NIA was a largely female organization. The connection between white female activists and Indian issues had been widely established since the antebellum period, when women and clergy worked together to send petitions to the U.S. government to protest the forced removal of the Cherokee from Georgia to Oklahoma, and continued well into the late nineteenth and early twentieth centuries given the proliferation of all-female reform groups. Eastman's marriage to a white woman and his ability to charm his audiences no doubt would have made him a popular speaker among these types of organizations.[118]

Initially, WNIA's efforts included approaches to end the encroachment of white settlers on land set aside for Native Americans because of the Dawes Act of 1887. They used a petition to address the obligation of treaties (without a hint of irony given that allotment aimed to break up tribally held land) between the United States and American Indian nations. Despite many members' support for assimilation practices and the spirit behind the policy of allotment, the NIA remained committed to treaties and the recognition of Native tribes as sovereign nations. They set an important legal-political and social precedent for the work of other progressive organizations. Eastman and the women involved in leading the NIA were interested in issues of sovereignty, power, and tribal nationalism, even if they also supported allotment and citizenship for Indian people. Eastman's participation in this meeting offers an example of how white reform groups allied with leading Native figures. National in its scope, such an event was attended by high-profile federal officials like Francis E. Leupp, then commissioner of Indian Affairs. Just two years later, and across the East River, Eastman was again the featured speaker at an equally opulent event, although his sponsors were not female and the theme of the evening had nothing to do with federal Indian policy.[119]

Given Eastman's work in the formation of the Boy Scouts and his regular association with members of the YMCA (he served as secretary for their International Committee from 1894–8), it makes sense that he parlayed these connections into an invitation to speak for the third annual sportsman's dinner, a highbrow affair sponsored by the Montauk Club of Brooklyn, a private men's social club founded in 1889. Eastman may have been surrounded by former Dartmouth classmates when he delivered his lecture on Monday, February 16, 1914.[120] Fraternal organizations of this sort offered white men spaces to "play Indian" and the funds to invite actual Native speakers to present at their events. The Montauk Club was a bit different in terms of gender given the separate spaces set aside for the wives and daughters of Club members so they "shall share with them all the enjoyments and pleasures which membership in the Montauk is expected to afford, and in this respect they set a very proper and commendable example."[121] Any attempt at gender inclusivity aside, race still played a critical role in how the Club positioned itself.

The naming of the Club was both a negation and affirmation of New York's indigenous history. Building on its Native association, the Montauk Club distinguished itself from similar sorts of social spaces in Europe. The architecture of the club made this sort of distinction clearer still. The Club House, designed by New York architect Francis H. Kimball and finally completed in 1891, was featured in an article printed in *Frank Leslie's Illustrated Newspaper* to highlight the architectural elements of the Club and to showcase the elite status of Club members, their contribution to society life in Brooklyn, and the larger cultural role such a space could play in the national imaginary. As the review from 1890 notes, "A grand balcony will extend around the building at the fourth story level, and underneath this will be a frieze, two and a half feet in width, consisting of a panorama in red and yellow terra-cotta, illustrative of the progress of American civilization." This review also celebrated the future contributions that could arise out of these new social spaces. "We hazard nothing in predicting that the Montauk Club will become a most influential factor in the social life of our sister city." [122]

By the late nineteenth century, other Brooklyn clubs – both men's and women's – sprang to life by the dozen: the Hamilton, the Crescent, the Union League, the Unity, the Germania, the Brooklyn, the Carlton, and many others. Indeed, Park Slope had begun to rival Brooklyn Heights as the borough's prime residential area. According to the 1890 census, Park Slope had the highest per capita income in the country and its residents were the leaders of Brooklyn society. It was within this changing social milieu that the men of the Montauk Club invited Eastman to present on current issues facing Native Americans in the United States. As *Brooklyn Life* reported, Eastman presented at: "A Memorable Sportsmen's Evening at the Montauk Club" dressed "in full regalia of a Sioux chieftain." He spoke "before an audience of what as a whole could be called typical up-to-date commercialized Americans," and reportedly succeeded in keeping "them spellbound." Indeed, the reporter speculated that members of the Club might struggle to reconcile Eastman's address on the merits of Native spirituality with the decline of their own spirit, "whether with all our marvelous achievements we had accomplished anything worth while when, by contrast, we seemed so pitifully small in spirit and defective in physical endurance beside the primitive, untutored aborigine." [123]

A reporter from the *Brooklyn Daily Eagle* also commented about the numerous stories recounted at the Club and the popularity of the event, noting that "three hundred members of the club" had been present to answer the "call of the wild" and in addition to dramatic tales of near-death experiences in pursuit of wild game the men were entertained by movies showing animals and fish in their natural habitat. After their dinner, stories, and movies, Eastman was, according to the *Eagle*, invited to talk as an "added attraction." The reporter framed Eastman's presence in terms of his status as a physician, his position as a graduate of Dartmouth College, and the authenticity of his Sioux regalia. Moving on to the substance of Eastman's talk, the article noted, "Dr. Eastman, glorifying the men of his own race, explained that, while the Indian was the greatest of all sportsmen, it was not the desire to slay wantonly that impelled him to hunt game." This apparently "sounded strange, coming from a redskin, after the other speakers had spoken so eloquently and enthusiastically of their achievements with the gun, but then they all knew and understood the big chief and he was roundly applauded when he concluded his interesting speech." The reporter's interpretation of the reception of Eastman's talk reveals two important things. First, Eastman used this opportunity to recall a time before colonization to highlight different approaches to hunting, to subtly critique the current practices of the white men he addressed whose own exploits had been touted that evening and no doubt fell under the category of wantonly killing game just for fun. Second, the sportsmen at the Montauk Club bore witness to an Indian who was skeptical about their contemporary hunting practices, and yet whose very presence signaled the primitivism they longed for, so they applauded Eastman's remarks to signal their understanding. What the reporter failed to articulate was the extent to which Eastman's speech was really "understood" from his vantage point and not just another interesting story told by a "big chief" who ought to be celebrated as an "added attraction" for the sportsmen's dinner.[124] This example parallels the many occasions in England when Eastman gave similar talks while dressed in costume, surrounded by elite white men in lavish venues that equally embraced and celebrated white understandings of a warrior aesthetic and primitive past that Eastman would then undermine through his spoken remarks.

Like he did during his experiences abroad, Eastman used his definition of the "real Indian" to denounce caricatures created by Cody's Wild West and later featured in Western films. Eastman questioned his audiences' familiar understandings of Indian people based on these fictional representations. In one lecture, he noted that the "real" aspects of being an Indian are separate from the "happy hunting grounds" that have been invented by a white man's imagination. Still, despite Eastman's attempts to revise dominant understandings of Indian peoples' lives as part and parcel of nature and divorced from the contemporary moment's technologies, ideas, and practices, many news reports emphasized that his talks were about "Folk Lore of the Indians," which were made even more appealing because he appeared "in Native Costume." In these instances and others, the "real Indian" rhetoric effaced the idea of indigenous peoples critiquing the history of colonization.[125]

One report in particular is representative of the kind of press that sought to define the limits and possibilities for Eastman as a Native speaker. According to Oregon's *Portland Argus*, the widespread appeal of the "Real Indian, Dr. Charles A. Eastman, A Full Blooded Sioux" who "Talks to the

Woman's Club" rested in Eastman's attire for the evening. He had been invited to address the Literature Department of the Woman's Literary Union in Portland. However, despite Eastman's career as an author, the reporter defined Eastman's expertise based on a description of his clothing:

Dr. Eastman was dressed in the full war costume of the real Indian, his head dress being a genuine war bonnet, and his costume decorated with the wonderful bead work which characterizes the best of these Indian costumes. It was not the costume of the Indian Reservation or the Indians of the frontier who commercialize their folk lore and their costumes, but it was an exact copy of the real North American Indian's costume.

Although this article focused on Eastman's appearance, it also recognized what was a "costume" and what was *not*. Eastman is figured as an authentic Indian even when his "real" Indian dress is a "copy" rather than the original "war costume." Despite the ways that the report locates Eastman in terms of ethnic authenticity, the recognition of costuming demonstrates a more nuanced understanding of Indian performance. This may have grown out of the development of cultural spaces in the United States that featured Indian people as performers. By 1910, a large number of Indian people were working in show business and performing according to certain racialized scripts, often reenacting the violence of the Western frontier. The vast majority of these actors had not actually experienced this sort of violence firsthand. They knew this, and in many cases so did their audiences; just as the *Argus* reporter knew that Eastman chose to wear "the full war costume of the real Indian" to reenact a historical imagining of Indianness rather than present himself in contemporary dress.[126]

In fact, the *Argus* reporter's reference to the reservation and the frontier locates contemporary Indian people within two distinctly different spaces. The first – the reservation – was a place in which government subsidies and surveillance attempted to regulate bodies, land, and practices of Indian people. And the other – the frontier – reflected an imagined and romanticized performance space in which Indian actors managed the expectations of their white audiences and the shows' organizers with commercialized "folklore" stories. In this cultural space, actors, like Eastman, wore copies of war regalia to draw on popular narratives for the purpose of entertainment. Unlike Eastman, they were not lecturing to a crowd interested in learning more about the "real Indian," but rather, they were performing part of an imaginary Wild West that dramatized events from the past.

In addition, the reporter's decision to discuss three different representations of Indians "in costume" and then to position Eastman outside of these forums does important cultural work. Eastman's exterior positioning confirms a certain form of authentically Indian perspective, one where his word is gospel by virtue of the fact that he is the real thing. In addition, the references to other types of performances where Indian people, culture, and history are reworked to function as entertainment suggests Eastman's educational lectures may have operated as moments of strategic performance. The question nonetheless remains: To what extent did Eastman's performances succeed in blurring the line between fact and fiction, so that his readers and the women who attended his talk might discern the rationale behind his decision to "play Indian" for them?[127]

Like Eastman, other Native American people were capable of transforming colonial concepts like authenticity through strategic performances of dress-up. The political ramifications of ideas about "real Indians" during the period when Eastman lived, wrote, and lectured often constructed Indianness based on a set of binaries: Indian/white, traditional/modern, and uncivilized/civilized. Those Indians who did not conform to these definitions for authentic Indianness, based on the interplay of these binaries, were often restricted by and challenged to think about how to "play Indian." Eastman's speeches invoked full-bloodedness to "play Indian" as a lecturer. But Eastman also used these forums to educate the American public. A centerpiece of his intellectual work relied on challenging Indianness as it had been articulated by writers like James Fenimore Cooper and by spectacular Wild West shows, but also by more dramatic staging produced by Indian operas, and those captured on film. Eastman took up this American cultural history of representing Indians to argue for the incorporation of Indian people as modern American citizens, to show the ambiguities surrounding these sorts of performances. Therefore, his lecture performances and writings encapsulated the strategic and accidental elements shaping his larger educational mission. Because he lectured with an awareness of the narrative imaginaries that defined Indianness, many representations of Eastman as a performer reflect strategic choices that worked as advertisements for his work, leaving a lasting impression of his success as an Indian intellectual.[128]

Many reports also assessed Eastman's performance through a discourse of the body. The *Pasadena Star*, for example, highlighted an event when Eastman did *not* dress up to align with certain expectations of Indianness. This report describes Eastman as speaking "with the unemotional nature of the Indian, clothed in the garb of the society paleface" who "kept his audience spellbound with the simple directness of his story." Still, Eastman in "the garb of the society paleface" is figured as an Indian who is racially distinct from his audience because of the "unemotional" affect of his countenance. The idea of the unemotional nature of the Indian subject indexes here gendered ideologies around violence, for Eastman's lack of emotion points to an overcoming of a past that required violence when white westward expansion met Indian armed resistance. The *Los Angeles Times* also describes him in bodily terms, noting that his "coal-black hair, his high cheek bones," and "his copper color, his majestic carriage" define him as a "thoroughbred Indian." These two examples help demonstrate how Eastman did not always wear a costume, and yet he remained racialized as other, as the proper embodiment of Indianness. Both the *Star*'s reference to "the unemotional nature of the Indian" and the *Times*' emphasis on his facial features, carriage, and skin tone elide the political effect of Eastman's clothes for these talks. In these moments, we can consider Eastman's body as a palimpsest, a destabilizing tactic with the tuxedo, where meaning shifts each time he dresses for a performance. His facial expression (or imagined lack of expressiveness) substitutes for Native costuming in these reports, and does its own symbolic work, perhaps suggesting that Eastman as stoic warrior had much to teach his audiences through the "simple directness of his story."[129]

Transatlantic Networks

Eastman's first crossing of the Atlantic in 1911, like that of Luther Standing Bear and others, maps his mobility within indigenous history as a part of the Atlantic world.[130] These movements reveal the power and possibility open to this cohort of Native people. For Eastman, the trip was possible because of the connections he had made through Dartmouth College, his work within the Indian Service for the Office of Indian Affairs, and his involvement in the publishing industry. He returned to Europe in the late 1920s as part of another important speaking tour. A series of letters exchanged between the autumn of 1927 and the spring of 1928 between Eastman and members of the Royal Colonial Institute of London showcases the types of lectures he gave while abroad. For Eastman, these events were the high point of his speaking career, and newspaper outlets from London, Liverpool, Bristol, and Wales outlined his itinerary to promote his trip to European audiences.[131]

Eastman's travels in 1928 would not have been possible without generous support provided by the Brooks-Bright Foundation of New York, established by Florence Brooks-Aten to foster good relations between English-speaking people in America and Great Britain. The Foundation funded him "for two months to speak before schools and societies." Naturally or perhaps ironically, a photograph from the *Daily Mirror* captured Eastman "in full regalia" during one of these tours. He stands next to Lord Dartmouth right before his primary speaking engagement at the Royal Colonial Institute. One among a number of colonial societies, the Institute was formed in the 1860s and was headquartered in London at King Street, St. James. It aimed to "provide a meeting place for gentlemen interested in colonial and Indian affairs," the latter referring to the Indian subcontinent, *not* to Native Americans. This elite and storied location was an ideal setting for Eastman to begin an extensive tour, which enabled him to give lectures throughout England, Ireland, Scotland, and Wales. Certainly, Eastman's undergraduate career at Dartmouth College amplified the interest of his hosts. Many of them maintained personal if not ideological ties to the founding mission of the College, as a place dedicated to the education of Indian people in the Americas. As Colin Calloway has noted, Eastman's prominence at the turn of the twentieth century appears as an anomaly given that many saw the College as ignoring its founding mission until the 1970s. This distinction suggests his trip was even more critical.[132]

As the tour commenced, Eastman found many willing and curious local hosts. Charles Thomas of the Royal Colonial Institute in Bristol, for example, was "most anxious to entertain" Eastman at tea "at the Red Lodge Wigwam" before his scheduled lecture on March 9, 1928.[133] For this tea, appropriate "dress" was requested. Thomas wrote explicitly about what Eastman might wear. "We have been most interested to see the picture of yourself in the current issue of 'United Empire' and we do very greatly hope that you will honour us by bringing with you your ceremonial Indian dress." When Eastman arrived, he was ushered into a "wigwam" – a cultural space rich with American Indian (and other) curios and trophies. Eastman was, in a sense, a human trophy for the institute in Bristol as he wore his full regalia and performed Indian authenticity for Thomas and his colleagues from "The Savages Club." No doubt club members were enthralled by the presence of a former "savage" among them who played to their expectations regarding savagery. In the Wigwam, wearing "full Indian dress" and performing according to Thomas's expectation, if not outright obsession with "things Indian," Eastman took advantage of the Indian craze that had spread from the United States across the Atlantic to England.[134]

The market for Indian things was largely dependent on primitivist impulses, and rapidly manifested through the marketing of Indian commodities – including actual people saying actual words, like Eastman. As Elizabeth Hutchinson has shown, at the turn of the twentieth century there was a marketplace for Indian objects, stories, and photographs that depended on capitalist ideology and industry. In fact, Native American baskets, blankets, and bowls could be purchased from department stores, "Indian stores," dealers, and the U.S. government's Indian schools. Other activities related to this collecting emerged to include Native American artifacts in art exhibitions sponsored by museums, arts and crafts societies, and world's fairs, as indigenous handicrafts became models for nonnative artists. In this context, no matter what his philosophical claims, Eastman could not avoid participating in a marketing of his own ethnicity, for the "Indian craze" was becoming global in its scope.[135]

Indian intellectuals like Eastman found ways to participate in the "Indian craze" that developed and proliferated between the 1890s and the 1920s. Two consequences of this craze reflected changes in both culture and policy. The first was an increase in the demand to *see* and market Indianness, which fed into Wild West show business, dime novels, and films, as well as the increase in sales of Indian curios and a surge in popularity of Indian music – most of the parlor music that was sold was created by white composers imagining Indianized themes. This emergent market was one that both white and Native cultural producers could manage. In many instances,

Native people used an array of strategies to participate in the marketing of Indian wares and Indian performances, whether live or onscreen.[136] The second outgrowth of this "Indian craze" was an embrace of the ideology of primitivism in artwork, which necessitated the creation of art by Native people. By 1935, the success of Native cultural producers and the widespread effect of this market culminated in a shift in federal policy with the establishment of the Indian Arts and Crafts Act. Eastman's second trip to Great Britain took place during the height of this "craze" precipitating the Act.[137]

On Wednesday, March 7, 1928, radio listeners in England could tune in to hear "An Interview with Dr. Charles Eastman, Chief of the Sioux Indians." For many who happened to turn the dial this might be the first time they ever heard a Native person speak, and so eloquently too! Less than two weeks later, on Friday, March 16, 1928, the *Western Daily Press* out of Bristol reported that "The Red Indian" at the Colonial Institute, while dressed "in full native costume," had given a talk the night before during which he explained "the significance of the eagle's feathers" and other parts of his costume. Eastman's talk, titled "North American Indians," was about the history of the "Red Indians" in America. Audiences listened to him explain how, since 1894, he had represented the Indian nation in Washington, and that the costume he wore was given to him by those he represented. He went on to recall how in 1914, 2,000 Boy Scouts passed through his hands in Washington, where the first principle they were taught was "Indian honor."[138]

Eastman's agenda at the Colonial Institute was twofold: to provide his listeners with personal stories and anecdotes that noted how Indians had "evolved a high civilization without materialism," and to emphasize that despite a history of conquest and displacement, "the Indian spirit was having an influence in America to-day." Eastman used lyrical phrasing as he described the important teachings Indian mothers passed on to their sons. Through this depiction, Eastman's crafting of Native families aligned with normative notions of gender promoted and protected by a white patriarchal society; indeed, however much Native people ought to be viewed as equal, Native women should remain at home and in charge of the children. And yet Native mothers, he argued, taught their sons "that possession was a dangerous thing, and that they must divide with their neighbors." Ever aware of the global setting in which he spoke, Eastman criticized capitalist impulses and the detrimental effects of materialism on young people. At the same time, he wore authentic Indian dress, ironically drawing on the very materiality of his costume to enthrall his audience and add weight to his argument and his place as a commodity.

Eastman's lecture took place in the context of increasing industrialization, which posed a very real threat to workers, strained urban social relations among strangers, and, as Eastman and others saw it, contributed to a decline in morality. Therefore, much of his speech emphasized the future roles to be played by girls and boys, who should be taught to be friendly to all of humanity. Like he had in his books for children, Eastman aimed to educate the world community about an Indian solution to the problems inherent in capitalist modernity; at the same time, he was able to argue that Native people still had critical roles to play in shaping the modernizing world. Any apparent conflict between his anti-materialist rhetoric and the spectacle of his own costume that evening reflected an uneven, if also powerful, strategy of representational politics for an Indian intellectual who was aiming to reach people across the world. Eastman's political aspirations while abroad revealed a highly stylized form of performance that mirrored his deep understanding of foreign desires to see him as the essence of Indianness and also as a cultural ambassador for America. The fact that he was speaking to a British audience, who were within a decade of the end of the First World War, is reflected in his concluding remarks, which recognized the value of peace and recalled an earlier era, his first trip to England in 1911 and the quest of the Universal Races Congress. Eastman, as transnational humanitarian, left the audience with this final thought: "Peace I bring you from America, peace not in the diplomatic sense, nor in the commercial sense, but in the deeper, spiritual sense, that of humanity." This second visit to England demonstrates the endurance of Eastman's commitment to racial uplift and harmony, even while his educational mission itself was made possible by a culture of capitalism that created a market for Indian people as public speakers.[139]

Eastman's travels throughout the United States and Great Britain from the 1890s and into the 1930s enabled him to make public speaking central in his mission to educate others about Indian history and politics. Whether looking at Eastman's early engagement with educational institutions, his foray into published authorship, or the various performances when he was a "real Indian lecturer," the complicated dialectical interplay between the method and message of his work shows how strategic he was in his representational politics. Whether he was mingling with aristocrats like Lord Dartmouth, Englishmen who "played Indian" at their savages clubs, or young people interested in joining the Boy Scouts, Eastman employed strategies that yielded powerful if uneven results.[140]

As Eastman lectured throughout Great Britain and the United States, reporters narrated the events of his talks in ways that sometimes ran counter to Eastman's agenda. For example, some reporters misrepresented the message of these talks when they ventriloquized Eastman. One reporter paraphrased Eastman's lecture, writing that "[he] laments the popularity of Fenimore Cooper's tales as conveying a false impression of the old Indian life" and "represents the Indians as they were when their life had been corrupted. The white man had placed a bounty on scalps, and a people normally peaceful [was] reduced to savagery." In this instance, the press surrounding Eastman's lecture reflects both his ideas and the ways that editors and reporters interpreted these ideas. In other words, a reporter's misreading could be intimately intertwined with Eastman's own representational strategies.

Eastman's language was not exactly the language of the reporters, but it was similar. Looking more closely at these reports, one traces a type of colonial shadow language that echoes, mimics, and engages and is *almost* the same. Eastman's ability to openly and persuasively critique Cooper's Indian, for example, while he is dressed "in Indian costume" participates in a counter-hegemonic performance that refigures Indianness. And yet, when Eastman plays the part of a "real Indian" dressed in authentic attire, he also points to particular origins for this sort of ethnic essentialism. Within this same moment, Eastman strategically captures the complicated set of representational politics he was forced to confront throughout his life as a representative of Indianness, and as a speaker on behalf of Indian people. Beyond the circuit of Normal Schools and international lecture tours are other performance sites where Eastman mobilized *and* challenged definitions of Indianness as a public figure.[141]

Through these different speaking engagements the very otherness of being an Indian in American society enabled Eastman to address a diverse array of audiences, and to perform both the role of the Indian philosopher and that of the ruggedly masculine warrior. Eastman's athleticism and Indianness were often linked together to fit into an American manhood characterized by an expression of strength in the physicality of the body. His ability to embody the best of white and Indian manhood certainly made Eastman an appealing speaker for white women's organizations, and for white fraternal groups who aimed to celebrate manliness through shows of strength that were inspired by Indian manhood. Both types of audiences were interested in Indian policy. The men's groups, however, were more interested in *playing Indian* through primitivist display than in lobbying for political change.[142] Throughout Eastman's life, he continued to draw on his early association with Dartmouth because there were many advantages to maintaining this relationship. On two separate occasions, separated by over two decades, Eastman was called on by his alma mater to reprise his role as Dartmouth's famous Indian graduate, to remind students and alumni of the power of Indianness in the College's foundational narrative.

Still Dartmouth's Indian

In late September 1904, Eastman received a letter asking if he would be "the guest of the College on occasion of the laying of the corner-stone of Dartmouth Hall." Not an unusual request for a distinguished alumnus. However, this invitation asked Eastman to participate in a double-performance. His presence was requested to recognize him as the most distinguished member of the class of 1887, and to reenact a scene from Dartmouth's founding moment. Thus, Eastman was asked to *play* Dartmouth's original Indian: Samson Occom. Dartmouth's president, W. J. Tucker (1893–1909), wrote to Eastman in reference to "a series of historical representations" that would take place to bring out "a good many dramatic points in the early history of the college." Tucker's request for Eastman to play Occom "especially in his audience with George the Third, or in Whitfield's church" was an unusual way to celebrate the achievements of Eastman's own life.[143]

By 1904, Eastman had already worked as a doctor, traveled widely with the Indian Service, and was beginning his career as an author and public speaker. In many ways, he was also beginning to assert his educational mission: to teach the world about the real history of Native people in the United States. Thus, returning to Dartmouth to portray Occom would have been strange not only because one Indian should not necessarily stand in for another, but also because Eastman clearly saw himself as apart from Occom's time and place. He was a modern exemplar of Dartmouth's continuing mission, which for Eastman rested not in civilizing indigenous peoples through the process of education, but rather in educating Americans about Indian civilization. Despite the oddness of Tucker's request, Eastman nonetheless acquiesced and continued his long and fruitful association with his alma mater, acting in the role of Occom in a series of tableaux staged by the Dartmouth Dramatic Club. It would not be the last time Eastman was asked to return to Dartmouth as a representative of Indianness. But, at least next time, he would be asked to play himself (for most of the time).[144]

Thirteen years later, in 1927, Eastman returned to Hanover, New Hampshire, to attend his fortieth college reunion. Throughout the reunion, several photographs of Eastman were taken. In all of them he is dressed in buckskin with a feathered headdress, and in one he appears seated atop a horse in a parking lot surrounded by a set of black automobiles. Taken in front of Dartmouth College's buildings, these portraits celebrate Eastman as "Dartmouth's Indian" from 1887. Another, more provocative image was taken with him posing next to his classmate, Stanley F. Johnson. This sepia print from 1927 includes some telling details on the back. It reads: "Eastman right, Stanley F. Johnson left, dressed in attire worn by his father on his honeymoon in 1847 (I kid you not!)." This comment about costuming and the past offers two critical elements to consider when examining the photograph more closely and most importantly in thinking about Eastman as a public face for Indianness in 1927.[145]

Eastman stands twisting slightly to the side as he looks off to the left, and is nearly out of the frame on the far right side. The focal point between the two men is occupied by foliage. Johnson lifts a cigar to his mouth with a fuzzy left hand and grips a cane with his right. Both men are dressed "in costume," but the note on the back refers only to Johnson and not to Eastman. Eastman wears moccasins, a long feathered headdress, and lots

FIGURE 4. Dartmouth College reunion photograph (1927).
Rauner Library, Dartmouth College, Hanover, NH. Courtesy of Dartmouth
College Library.

of fringed buckskin clothing brightly decorated with different colors and
shapes. A hatchet rests in the crook of his left arm.

   This photograph also displays particular kinds of gendered excess
intersecting with both whiteness and Indianness. A top hat, morning coat,
and bright white trousers for the former juxtaposed to intricately beaded
leatherwork, fringe, and feathers for the latter represent two different
forms of elite, elegant, if also extreme, manliness. One might see Johnson
and assume he plays the leisurely and empowered role of an upper-class
gentleman. Eastman's dress could be read as chiefly in its warrior aesthetic, suggesting not that he is a savage, menacing figure but rather a
well-positioned diplomat and interlocutor between Indian communities
and white America.

   Both men appear "dressed up," and yet onlookers may have interpreted
a top hat quite differently than a feathered headdress. Indeed, an alternative
reading of the foliage as a framing device situates Eastman within the realm
of nature, whereas Johnson's cane connects him solidly to both cement and
modernity, with pavement signifying industrial capital and the wealth born

out of modernization. But were these two men meant to be read in opposition to each other? Perhaps yes and perhaps no. This image offers one glimpse into Eastman's choice of self-presentation. No doubt there were others. By 1927, Eastman knew how to navigate the arenas of performance that were open to him in several ways. He had learned that his work as an educator might require he wear a tuxedo, for occasions like Twain's birthday party or a meeting with Matthew Arnold, whereas other appearances might require Sioux regalia depending on the invitation by his hosts, and still others would allow Eastman to wear his everyday suit as he spoke at a local YMCA or before a women's literary circle. It is likely that for this reunion photograph, he chose to adorn himself with clothes familiar to the audiences of his public talks, but also to his friends and other alumni equally familiar with his success as a public Indian intellectual. On this occasion, Eastman could not retreat from the expectation that he was Dartmouth's most "picturesque figure" because he was also an Indian. During the reunion, Eastman again played the part of Samson Occom to reenact the Mohegan's first meeting with Wheelock in 1743 and his sermon at the London tabernacle of George Whitefield in 1766.[146]

By 1930, the man who had once been "the hero of the Boston society girls" and who had "talked with Emerson, Longfellow, Francis Parkman, and many other men of note" left most of his public life behind him. Eastman retreated to a cabin along the northern shore of Lake Huron. This new life in the woods allowed Eastman to focus anew on writing. Once there, he started to work on a novel about Chief Pontiac of the Ottawa, based on a 1763 conspiracy and war against white colonial forces. Unfortunately, this novel never came to fruition. However, the fact that Eastman had begun this work suggests his optimism regarding how to change American culture had not waned. While he worked on his novel, Eastman occasionally practiced medicine and delivered lectures. During the colder winter months, he would move southward to the Detroit area, where he lived with his son, Ohiyesa. On January 8, 1939, at the age of eighty, Eastman died in a Detroit hospital and was buried nearby at Evergreen Cemetery.

As Eastman wrote in *The Indian Today* on the topic of Indian identity, the Native American man was a profound subject to study as "a man, a philosopher," and "a noble type both physically and spiritually." With these words, Eastman described himself as much as how to best define Indian manhood. After his passing, people cherished what they had learned from him as they sent scores of letters to his estranged wife, Elaine Goodale Eastman. Throughout these letters, like the many reporters and audience members who saw Eastman talk or who read his books, there is the sense that he was understood as the physical and intellectual embodiment of a modern Indian citizen. He was "symmetrical and finely poised in body" and without "the garb of deception and pretence." Indeed he was, in his own words, a "true child of nature" in the best possible sense.

His story is a compelling part of this earlier era given his work as an author, a doctor, and most profoundly as a voice for other Indian people who were challenged by demands for assimilation into American society and dominant expectations regarding cultural conformity. In the words of his second, and last, autobiography, *From the Deep Woods to Civilization*, Eastman leaves his readers with an ever balanced, if strategically ambivalent, image of himself that engages these challenges. "I am an Indian; and while I have learned much from civilization, for which I am grateful, I have never lost my Indian sense of right and justice. I am for development and progress along social and spiritual lines, rather than those of commerce, nationalism, or material efficiency. Nevertheless, so long as I live, I am an American."[147]

Notes

1   Charles Eastman, *The Indian To-Day: The Past and Future of the First American* (New York: Doubleday, 1915), 938.

2   By 1890, the Delmonico family restaurant business included four restaurants; the "Citadel" at 56 Beaver Street was the longest running, beginning in 1837. Today, it is one block from the National Museum of the American Indian. Eastman entered a building that was eight stories tall and featured, for the first time, electric lights with an entrance framed by Pompeii pillars and cornices. Joe O'Connell, "History of Delmonico's Restaurant and Business Operations in New York," at: http://www.steakperfection.com/delmonico/History.html.

3   The *New York Times*, the *New York Herald*, and *New York World* reported on the event, in: Charles Alexander Eastman Papers, 1891–1983, MS 829, Rauner Special Collections Library, Dartmouth College, Hanover, NH.

4   Ibid. This archive will be abbreviated as: CAE Papers, Dartmouth Collection. A special supplement to *Harper's Weekly* (December 23, 1905) published its speeches. Other notable figures: William Dean Howells, John Kendrik Bangs, Kate Douglas Riggs, Brander Matthews, Richard Watson Gilder, Andrew Carnegie, George Washington Cable, Hamilton W. Mabie, Agnes Repplier, Irving Bacheller, Rex E. Beach, and Hopkinson Smith. For more on Mark Twain's birthday party see the PBS Web site: http://www.pbs.org/marktwain/learnmore/writings_seventieth.html.

5   Raymond   Wilson,   *Ohiyesa: Charles   Eastman,   Santee   Sioux* (Champaign: University of Illinois, 1983). The following shaped my reading of Eastman's written work: David Martinez, *Dakota Philosopher: Charles Eastman and American Indian Thought* (Minnesota Historical Society, 2009); David H. Brumble, *American Indian Autobiography* (Lincoln: University of Nebraska Press, 2008); Peter L. Bayers, "Charles Alexander Eastman's 'From the Deep Woods to Civilization' and the Shaping of Native Manhood," in *Studies in American Indian Literatures* Vol. 20, No. 3 (Fall 2008), 52–73; Theodore D. Sargent, *The Life of Elaine Goodale Eastman* (Lincoln: University of Nebraska Press, 2008); Michael Oren Fitzgerald, ed., *The Essential Charles Eastman (Ohiyesa)*, Foreword by Raymond Wilson, Introduction by Janine Pease (Bloomington, IN: World Wisdom, 2007); Bernd Peyer, *"The Thinking*

Indian": *Native American Writers, 1850s–1920s* (New York: Peter Lang, 2007) and Bernd Peyer, ed., *American Indian Nonfiction: An Anthology of Writings, 1760s–1930s* (Norman: University of Oklahoma Press, 2007); David J. Carlson, *Sovereign Selves: American Indian Autobiography and the Law* (Urbana: University of Illinois Press, 2006); Harvey Markowitz and Carole A. Barret, *American Indian Biographies* (Pasadena, CA: Salem Press, 2005); LaVonne Brown Ruoff, "Eastman's Maternal Ancestry: Letter from Charles Alexander Eastman to H. M. Hitchcock, September 8, 1927," in *Studies in American Indian Literatures* Vol. 17, No. 2 (2005), 10–17; William R. Handley and Nathaniel Lewis, eds., *True West: Authenticity and the American West* (Lincoln: University of Nebraska Press, 2004); Malea Powell, "Rhetorics of Survivance: How American Indians Use Writing," *College Composition and Communication* Vol. 53, No. 3, February 2002, 396–434 and "Imagining a New Indian: Listening to the Rhetoric of Survivance in Charles Eastman's *From the Deep Woods to Civilization*," *Paradoxa*, August 2001 (Special Issue on Native American Literatures, guest ed. Kate Shanley), 211–26; Erik Peterson, "'An Indian … An American': Ethnicity, Assimilation, and Balance in Charles Eastman's *From the Deep Woods to Civilization*" in *Early Native American Writing, New Critical Essays*, edited by Helen Jaskoski (Cambridge: University of Cambridge Press, 1996); Carol Lea Clark, "Charles A. Eastman (Ohiyesa) and Elaine Goodale Eastman: A Cross-Cultural Collaboration" in *Tulsa Studies in Women's Literature* Vol. 13, No. 2 (Autumn 1994). Also see: Penelope Myrtle Kelsey, *Tribal Theory in Native American Literature: Dakota and Haudenosaunee Writing and Indigenous Worldviews* (Lincoln: University of Nebraska Press, 2008) for her chapter on Charles Eastman that argues he engages with Native epistemologies as a method for defending Native rights, and specifically Dakota worldviews. I disagree with Kelsey's oversimplification of the critical contributions of scholars such as David Brumble, Arnold Krupat, Dexter Fisher, and Bo Scholer given that Kelsey asserts they "overlook the subversive potential" of Eastman's work. Although these scholars do not emphasize Eastman's rhetorical strategies as methods of resistance, they do offer compelling portraits of him as an author that allow for nuance and complexity.

6 Lucy Maddox, *Citizen Indians: Native American Intellectuals, Race & Reform* (Ithaca, NY: Cornell University Press, 2005), points to how representations of Indians in the 1880s can be traced back to the earlier years of the nineteenth century and the roots of Indian-white cultural interactions between performers and audiences. Also see: Rosemarie K. Bank, *Theatre Culture in America, 1825–1860* (Cambridge: Cambridge University Press, 1997).

7 Out of fifty-four presenters at the First Universal Races Congress, ten men were from the United States. Five of these were photographed in this order: W. E. B. Du Bois, Prof. Earl Finch (Wilberforce University), Dr. Franz Boas (Columbia University), Dr. Paul S. Reinsch (University of Wisconsin), and Charles Eastman. See: *New York Tribune* (1911), CAE Papers, Dartmouth Collection.

8 In September 1911, Saint Nihal Singh articulated the mission of the Congress as "trying to solve the world's problems of race." Singh's article argues that humanity must be led by the demand "of the yellow, brown, and black races that the 'white' folk treat them in accordance with the Golden Rule," a demand that aligned with the work of both Du Bois and Eastman because they saw themselves

as leading figures with regard to racial politics in the United States. Saint Nihal Singh, "Trying to Solve the Problems of Race," *The American Review of Reviews* Vol. 44, No. 3, September 1911, 339–44.

9   See: Kate Flint, *The Transatlantic Indian, 1776–1930* (Princeton, NJ: Princeton University Press, 2008), which argues Native perspectives are critical to our understanding of transatlantic relations in this period and the development of transnational modernity. Also see: Jace Weaver, *The Red Atlantic: American Indigenes and the Making of the Modern World, 1000–1927* (Chapel Hill: University of North Carolina Press, 2014), which defines the Red Atlantic as the movement of western hemisphere indigenes and indigenous wealth, ideas, and technology around the Atlantic basin from 1000 C.E. to 1927.

10 See: Robert Berkhofer, *The White Man's Indian: Images of the American Indian from Columbus to the Present* (New York: Random House, 1978); Tom Holm, *The Great Confusion in Indian Affairs: Native Americans & Whites in the Progressive Era* (Austin: University of Texas Press, 2005), 51.

11 Emphasis mine.

12 "Racial Problems," in *Irving Church* (1913) was an article that announced panelists' papers would be published by the World Peace Foundation. CAE Papers, Dartmouth Collection.

13 See: Frederick Hoxie, *A Final Promise: The Campaign to Assimilate the Indians, 1880–1920* (Lincoln: University of Nebraska Press, 2001) and *Talking Back to Civilization: Indian Voices from the Progressive Era* (Boston, MA and New York: Bedford/St. Martin, 2001). For progressivism see: Richard Hoftstadter, *The Age of Reform: From Bryan to F.D.R.* (New York: Knopf Publishing, 1955). And the work of: Norman Pollack, C. Vann Woodward, and Lawrence Goodwyn in Robert Wiebe, *The Search for Order, 1877–1920* (New York: Hill and Wang, 1966).

14 Alan Trachtenberg, *Shades of Hiawatha 1880–1930* (New York: Hill and Wang, 2004), 33, 10.

15 Charles Eastman, "The North American Indian" in *Universal Races Congress*, edited by Gustav Spiller (London: P. S. King and Son; Boston, MA: The World's Peace Foundation, 1911), 367.

16 Ibid., 1–2. The World Peace Foundation was founded by Edwin Ginn of the Boston Ginn and Company publishing house (1868). Like Eastman, Ginn was situated at the nexus of two types of white networks that enabled Indian intellectuals to circulate their ideas to influential white publics. See: World Peace Foundation, records, 1899–1993, Digital Collections and Archives, Tufts University. Peter Filene, "The World Peace Foundation and Progressivism: 1910–1918," *The New England Quarterly*, Vol. 36, No. 4 (December 1963), 478–50.

17 Eastman, "The North American Indian" 367.

18 Ibid., 368.

19 Ibid., 369.

20 Ibid., 369.

21 Ibid., 369.

22 Ibid., 369.

23 For politics of representation see: Homi Bhabha, *The Location of Culture* (New York: Rutledge Press, 1994), 247. Bhabha theorized hybridity, that which arises out of the culturally internalized interactions between "colonizers" and

"colonized" and the dichotomous formation of these identities, as constructing a shared culture. Bhabha has argued that colonizers and colonized are mutually dependent within a "Third Space of Enunciation" where cultural systems are created. The advantage, then, for someone like Eastman was that he could be more aware of the construction of culture and the invention of tradition. Similarly, as public speakers, Native intellectuals from this period could embody hybrid positions to strategically reject claims of boundedness within race, language, and nation, as they constructed their own politics of representation. Eastman's very existence could then exemplify a merger of Dakota traditions with values and skills gained through association with elite circles of American society.

24 Eastman, "The North American Indian" 374.

25 For manhood as a gendered discourse that intersected with class and race see: Gail Bederman, *Manliness & Civilization: A Cultural History of Gender and Race in the United States, 1880–1917* (Chicago: University of Chicago Press, 1996).

26 Eastman, "The North American Indian" 6.

27 Ibid., 374.

28 Ibid., 376.

29 Congress passed the General Allotment Act in 1887, the same year that Eastman graduated from Dartmouth. Named after Senator Henry Dawes of Massachusetts, who introduced the legislation, the Act required reservations to be surveyed and divided into 160-acre sections, which were then allotted to individual families for improvement. Any "surplus lands" would then be open for sale to non-Indian settlers. Allotment would terminate communal ownership and, its supporters believed, liberate Indian people from the hold of tribe and community, where kinship obligations and reciprocal generosity governed individual conduct. For Eastman's involvement see: Colin Calloway, *The Indian History of an American Institution: Native Americans and Dartmouth* (Hanover, NH: Dartmouth College Press, University Press of New England, 2010), 120.

30 Eastman, "The North American Indian" 375.

31 Eastman first gained experience lecturing during college by giving speeches before groups and at the Lake Mohonk Conference of Friends of the Indian. See: Lake Mohonk Conference, eighth session, 1890, 46.

32 Wilson, *Ohiyesa*, 141. In fact, after the publication of *Indian Boyhood* in 1902, Eastman accepted a lecture invitation from the Twentieth Century Club in Brooklyn, New York for $100. There he met Major James B. Pond, a lyceum manager, who helped book further speaking dates. See ibid., 140–7.

33 Eastman, "The North American Indian," 7 and 9.

34 Eastman made his greatest impact as a writer with early sketches of his childhood that were first published by *St. Nicholas: An Illustrated Magazine for Young Folks* and later incorporated in his first book, *Indian Boyhood*, published in 1902. See: Wilson, *Ohiyesa*, 131. For Indian intellectuals as writers see: Robert Warrior, *Tribal Secrets: Recovering American Indian Intellectual Traditions* (Minneapolis: University of Minnesota Press, 1995); Maureen Konkle, *Writing Indian Nations: Native Intellectuals and the Politics of Historiography, 1827–1863* (Chapel Hill: University of North Carolina

Indigenous Intellectuals

Press, 2004); Kelsey, *Tribal Theory in Native American Literature*; and David Martinez, ed., *The American Indian Intellectual Tradition: An Anthology of Writings from 1772–1972* (Ithaca, NY: Cornell University Press, 2011).

35 Waldo Frank, *Our America* (New York: Boni and Liveright, 1919), 113–14.

36 Casey Nelson Blake, *Beloved Community: The Cultural Criticism of Randolph Bourne, Van Wyck Brooks, Waldo Frank, and Lewis Mumford* (Chapel Hill: University of North Carolina Press, 1990), chapter 5, "The War and the Intellectuals," 174–5.

37 The Royal Commonwealth Society formed in June 1868, and was named the Royal Colonial Institute in 1870. See: Trevor R. Reese, *The History of the Royal Commonwealth Society 1868–1968* (London: Oxford University Press, 1968) and R. Craggs, "Situating the Imperial Archive: The Royal Empire Society Library 1868–1945," *Journal of Historical Geography* Vol. 34, No. 1 (2008), 48–67. See: CAE Papers, Dartmouth Collection.

38 For more on the history of educating Native American students at Dartmouth see: "About the Native American Program" from Dartmouth College's Web site: http://www.dartmouth.edu/~nap/about/.

39 *The Aegis* (1885), Rauner Special Collections Library, Dartmouth College, Hanover, NH. Phi Delta Theta was founded in 1884. Eastman's life at Dartmouth revolved around athletics as much as academics. At an 1883 track meet, he ran the two-mile race in 11 minutes and 56 seconds, not quite fast enough to break the College record, but an impressive showing for that day. Off the field, Eastman, like many Dartmouth men, grew acquainted with several people living in Hanover. In 1887, he sent a letter to a young elementary schoolteacher, Miss Clarke, to accept her invitation for a game of whist. To Miss Clarke from Charles Eastman, April 13, 1887, Letter, CAE Papers, Dartmouth Collection. Such a letter was donated by Katherine B. Evertitt, niece of Miss Freelove A. Clarke, who, "in 1887, was a young Teacher in the Hanover graded schools," February 2, 1964 (Winchester, NH).

40 As Ann Fabian and others have noted, early nineteenth-century American inquiries into race and racial characteristics often relied on collecting and dissecting the bodies of Native Americans. Ann Fabian, *The Skull Collectors: Race, Science, and America's Unburied Dead* (Chicago: University of Chicago Press, 2010).

41 William Gilpin's *Three Essays: On Picturesque Beauty; On Picturesque Travel; and On Sketching Landscape: to which is Added a Poem, On Landscape Painting* were published in London in 1792. Richard Payne Knight, *An Analytical Inquiry into the Principles of Taste* (1806); Uvedale Price, *An Essay on the Picturesque, as Compared with the Sublime and the Beautiful; and on the Use of Studying Pictures, for the Purpose of Improving Real Landscape*, revised edition (London, 1796). Dorothy Wordsworth wrote *Recollections of a Tour Made in Scotland, A. D. 1803* (1874). John Ruskin identified the "picturesque" as a genuinely modern aesthetic category in *The Seven Lamps of Architecture* (1849). In the twentieth century, see: Christopher Hussey, *The Picturesque: Studies in a Point of View* (1927). The picturesque idea continues to have a profound influence on garden and planting design. George P. Landow, *The Aesthetic and Critical Theories of John Ruskin* (Princeton, NJ: Princeton University Press, 1971), and John Dixon Hunt, *Gardens and the Picturesque: Studies in the History*

of Landscape Architecture (Cambridge: Massachusetts Institute of Technology Press, 1994).

42   Calloway, *The Indian History of an American Institution*, 113.

43   Ibid., 112. A chapter focused on Eastman argues that he was Dartmouth's "most famous Native son."

44   Ibid., 118.

45   For more on Eastman's life as a student at Dartmouth, see ibid., 116–18.

46   G. W. E. Russell called Matthew Arnold "the most delightful of companions" in *Portraits of the Seventies*. T. H. Warren described Arnold as "a voice poking fun in the wilderness." It was Arnold's introduction of a method of literary criticism that brought him attention. Arnold shifted from literary criticism to a more general critique of his age in *Culture and Anarchy* (written between 1867 and 1869), where he popularized the term *philistine* to describe the English middle class during the Victorian era. A common ground may have existed for Arnold and Eastman because both had to contend with misrepresentations of themselves and they enjoyed a shared interest in literature. See: Lionel Trilling, *Matthew Arnold* (New York: W. W. Norton, 1939); Park Honan, *Matthew Arnold, a Life* (New York: McGraw-Hill, 1981), 399; and Ian Hamilton, *A Gift Imprisoned: A Poetic Life of Matthew Arnold* (London: Bloomsbury, 1998).

47   Arnold does not just expect and want to meet Eastman because he is an Indian but he desires to see a certain type of racialized subject that enables him to fetishize Indianness as apart from himself, as the colonized "other." In this moment we might recognize in a flash the intersection of homoerotic desire with orientalism, even though Eastman as "subject" is from neither Asia nor the Middle East. A selective bibliography of scholarship that I have found helpful in regard to queer and postcolonial studies follows. Michel Foucault, *The History of Sexuality, Vol. 2: The Use of Pleasure* (New York: Vintage, 1985); David Halperin, *One Hundred Years of Homosexuality: And Other Essays on Greek Love* (New York: Routledge, 1989); Anne McClintock, *Imperial Leather: Race, Gender, and Sexuality in the Colonial Contest* (New York: Routledge, 1995); John C. Hawley, *Postcolonial, Queer: Theoretical Intersections* (Albany: State University of New York, 2001); Ann Laura Stoler, *Carnal Knowledge and Imperial Power: Race and the Intimate in Colonial Rule* (Berkeley: University of California Press, 2002); Gayatri Gopinath, *Impossible Desires: Queer Diasporas and South Asian Public Cultures* (Durham, NC: Duke University Press, 2005); Rahul K. Gairola, "White Skin, Red Masks: 'Playing Indian' in Queer Images from *Physique Pictorial*, 1957–67," *Liminalities: A Journal of Performance Studies* Vol. 8, No. 4, September 2012.

48   President W. J. Tucker to Charles A. Eastman, September 1904, Letters, CAE Papers, Dartmouth College.

49   Newspaper article: "Wedded to a Sioux Indian: The child poet of Sky Farm becomes Mrs. Charles Eastman," *The Sun*, Elaine Goodale Eastman Papers [hereinafter EGE Papers], Sophia Smith Collection, Smith College, Northampton, MA.

50   While Eastman attended Boston University, he lived with Mr. and Mrs. Frank Wood. The couple influenced Eastman in terms of Christianity, and as trustees of Wellesley College helped him to procure a speaking engagement there.

For more on their relationship see: Anna Lee Stensland, "Charles Alexander Eastman: Sioux Storyteller and Historian," *American Indian Quarterly* Vol. 3, No. 3, Autumn 1977, 199–208.

51 Calloway, *The Indian History of an American Institution*, 123; Wilson, *Ohiyesa*, 59–61; Charles Eastman, *From the Deep Woods to Civilization* (Little, Brown and Company, 1916), 11–14.

52 John G. Neihardt to Elaine Goodale Eastman, September 5, 1945, Letter, EGE Papers, Sophia Smith Collection, Smith College, Northampton, MA. Years later, in 1945, Elaine received letters from John G. Neihardt (director of information for the Office of Indian Affairs) and Arthur C. Parker (then president of the New York State Historical Association) that applauded her excellent article on "The Ghost Dance and Wounded Knee Massacre." Neihardt remarked, "I spent a great deal of time studying in that field, and I think yours is easily the best article I have seen on the subject."

53 Ruth Ann Alexander, "Elaine Goodale Eastman and the Failure of the Feminist Protestant Ethic," *Great Plains Quarterly* 8, 1988, 89–101; Elaine Goodale Eastman, "All the Days of My Life," *South Dakota Historical Review* 2, 1937, 171–84; Elaine Goodale Eastman, *Sister to the Sioux*, edited by Kay Graber (Lincoln: University of Nebraska Press, 1978).

54 Elaine was a poet and a writer before she became a teacher. Some of her earliest publications are available in the Jones Library Archives, Amherst, MA.

55 Wilson, *Ohiyesa*, 163–5; Margaret D. Jacobs, "The Eastmans and the Luhans, Interracial Marriage between White Women and Native American Men, 1875–1935," *Frontiers: A Journal of Women's Studies* Vol. 23, No. 3, 2002, 38.

56 According to Margaret D. Jacobs, Elaine's "vision of womanhood and manhood began to veer away from that of her husband's" ("The Eastmans and the Luhans," 40).

57 Kiara M. Vigil, "From Ohiyesa's 'Deep Woods' to the 'Civilization' of Charles: Critiquing and Articulating Native American Manhood in Eastman's Autobiography," Master's Thesis, Dartmouth College, Hanover, NH, 2006, 54–8.

58 *Indian Boyhood* (1902; McClure Philips and Company), *From the Deep Woods to Civilization* (1916; Little, Brown and Company), *The Soul of the Indian* (1911; Houghton Mifflin), *Red Hunters and the Animal People* (1904; Harper and Brothers), *Wigwam Evenings: Sioux Folk Tales* (1909; Little, Brown and Company).

59 Eastman, *From the Deep Woods to Civilization*, 187.

60 In the preface to *The Indian Today*, a biography of Eastman lists his educational path: two years at Beloit, then Knox College, IL, then Kimball Union Academy, NH, and Dartmouth College (1887), and a MD from Boston University in 1890. See: Eastman, *The Indian To-Day*.

61 Eastman, *The Indian To-Day*, 11.

62 "Eminent domain," also called "condemnation," is the legal process by which a public body (and certain private bodies, such as utility companies, railroads, and some others) are given legal power to acquire private property for a use that has been declared public by constitution, statute, or ordinance. Eastman, *The Indian To-Day*, 298.

63 For more on an African American intellectual tradition see: Edward J. Blum and Jason R. Young, *The Souls of W.E.B. Du Bois: New Essays and Reflections* (Macon, GA: Mercer University Press, 2009); W. E. B. Du Bois, *The Souls of Black Folk* (1903; repr., Oxford: Oxford University Press, 2009); Hazel V. Carby, *Reconstructing Womanhood: The Emergence of the Afro-American Woman Novelist* (New York: Oxford University Press, 1987); James West Davidson, *They Say: Ida B. Wells and the Reconstruction of Race* (New York: Oxford University Press, 2007); Angela Y. Davis, *Women, Race & Class* (New York: Vintage Books, 1981); Kevin Kelly Gaines, *Uplifting the Race: Black Leadership, Politics, and Culture in the Twentieth Century* (Chapel Hill: University of North Carolina Press, 1996); Alice Gambrell, *Women Intellectuals, Modernism, and Difference: Transatlantic Culture, 1919–1945* (Cambridge: Cambridge University Press, 1997); Paula Giddings, *When and Where I Enter: The Impact of Black Women on Race and Sex in America* (New York: W. Morrow, 1984); Evelyn Brooks Higginbotham, *Righteous Discontent: The Women's Movement in the Black Baptist Church, 1880–1920* (Cambridge, MA: Harvard University Press, 1993); Zora Neale Hurston, *Mules and Men* (1935; repr., New York: Perennial Library, 1990); Manning Marable and Vanessa Jones, *Transnational Blackness: Navigating the Global Color Line* (New York: Palgrave Macmillan, 2008); Tricia Rose, Kennell A. Jackson, and Harry Justin Elam, *Black Cultural Traffic: Crossroads in Global Performance and Popular Culture* (Ann Arbor: University of Michigan Press, 2008); Booker T. Washington, *Up from Slavery: An Autobiography* (1901; repr., Garden City, NY: Doubleday, 1963); Deborah G. White, *Too Heavy a Load: Black Women in Defense of Themselves, 1894–1994* (New York: W. W. Norton, 1999); E. Frances White, *Dark Continent of Our Bodies: Black Feminism and the Politics of Respectability* (Philadelphia: Temple University Press, 2001); Victoria W. Wolcott, *Remaking Respectability: African American Women in Interwar Detroit* (Chapel Hill: University of North Carolina Press, 2001).
64 Eastman, *The Indian To-Day*, 20.
65 Ibid., 304, 317. Eastman and other reformers were influenced by Helen Hunt Jackson's *A Century of Dishonor* (1881). For Native American history see: Francis Paul Prucha, *The Great Father: The United States Government and the American Indians* (Lincoln: University of Nebraska Press, 1986); Richard Slotkin, *The Fatal Environment: The Myth of the Frontier in the Age of Industrialization, 1800–1890* (Middletown, CT: Wesleyan University Press, 1986); Richard White, *The Middle Ground: Indians, Empires and Republics in the Great Lakes Region, 1650–1815* (New York: Cambridge University Press, 1991); Gregory E. Dowd, *A Spirited Resistance: The North American Indians' Struggle for Unity, 1745–1815* (Baltimore, MD: Johns Hopkins University Press, 1992); Alan Taylor, *American Colonies: The Settling of North America* (Boston, MA: Penguin, 2002); James Brooks, *Captives & Cousins: Slavery, Kinship, and Community in the Southwest Borderlands* (Chapel Hill: University of North Carolina Press, 2002); Jeffrey Ostler, *The Plains Sioux and U.S. Colonialism from Lewis & Clark to Wounded Knee* (New York: Cambridge University Press, 2004); Tiya Miles, *Ties that Bind: The Story of an Afro-Cherokee Family in Slavery and Freedom* (Berkeley: University of California Press, 2005).

66 Eastman, *The Indian To-Day*, 23.

67 Ibid., 373 and 379. See: Bederman, *Manliness and Civilization*; Hoxie, *Talking Back to Civilization*; and Alan Trachtenberg, *The Incorporation of America: Culture and Society in the Gilded Age* (New York: Hill and Wang, 2007).

68 With help from Hamlin Garland, Eastman was hired to work for the Office of Indian Affairs (between 1903 and 1909) to help in renaming the Sioux in order, he thought, to assist them in receiving allotments and other benefits from the Federal Government. For more see: Wilson, *Ohiyesa*, 120–9.

69 White leaders and reformers who allied with Eastman in working toward a policy of inclusion were: General Grant, Bishops Whipple and Hare, William Welsh and his nephew Herbert Welsh (of Philadelphia), Commissioner of Indian Affairs Smith, General Samuel Armstrong, General Richard Pratt, and many who created Chautauqua societies and women's organizations, as well as Albert K. Smiley, the founder of the Mohonk Conference. See: Eastman, *The Indian To-Day*, 435–49.

70 Eastman, *The Indian To-Day*, 435 and 449. Eastman credits "the influence of the missionaries and their converts" for "the practical education of the Indian children" (467). Smiley was also a member of the Board of Indian Commissioners.

71 The Boston Indian Citizenship Committee was an association for the protection of the rights of Indians; organized in 1879 because of the forcible removal of the Ponca. Chief Standing Bear, released on a writ of habeas corpus, went to Boston to note that signatures in favor of removal were fraudulent and to enlist the sympathy of Hon. John D. Long, then governor of Massachusetts. The committee then attempted to secure citizenship for Indians on the basis of the payment of taxes, a principle that was finally denied by the U.S. Supreme Court. After the Dawes bill was passed, the committee devoted its attention to securing honest allotment. See: Frederick Webb Hodge, *Handbook of American Indians North of Mexico* (Washington, DC: Government Print Office, 1906). The National Indian Association began as the Women's National Indian Association. The Indian Rights Association was a humanitarian group dedicated to federal U.S. Indian policy and protecting Indians of the United States. The first meeting of the Association was held on December 15, 1882 in Philadelphia, Pennsylvania, in the home of Herbert Welsh, who served as its executive secretary. Welsh, along with Matthew Sniffen and Lawrence Lindley, directed the group's efforts from 1882 to 1904, mostly out of Philadelphia. These figures were regular correspondents with Charles Eastman, Carlos Montezuma, and Gertrude Bonnin. For primary documents see: *Manuscript 061, The Indian Rights Association Pamphlets, Years: 1884–1985; bulk 1884–1934*, Center of Southwest Studies, Fort Lewis College, Durango, CO.

72 Eastman, *The Indian To-Day*, 486–90. The National Indian Association slogan: "Education; Land in Severalty; Citizenship!"

73 Eastman, *The Indian To-Day*, 543, 585, 591, and 944 for reference to Carlisle. Also see: Elaine Goodale, *Pratt: The Red Man's Moses* (Norman: University of Oklahoma Press, 1935). For more on Carlisle and other Indian schools see: Robert Trennert, *The Phoenix Indian School: Forced Assimilation in Arizona, 1891–1935* (Norman: University of Oklahoma Press, 1988); Tsianina K. Lomawaima, *They Called It Prairie Light: The Story of Chilocco Indian*

School (Lincoln and London: University of Nebraska Press, 1994); Devon Mihesuah, *Cultivating the Rosebuds: The Education of Women at the Cherokee Female Seminary, 1851–1909* (Urbana: University of Illinois Press, 1993).

74　Eastman, *The Indian To-Day*, 861.

75　Ibid., 939.

76　Ibid., 970–2, 975.

77　Ibid., 970–2, 975.

78　Arthur C. Parker to Elaine Goodale Eastman, July 13, 1945, Letter, EGE Papers, Smith Collection. Like Whitecloud, Bonnin, Deloria, and Eastman, Parker was himself of "mixed" descent. His family had both Seneca and Scots-English roots.

79　Ibid.

80　Alice C. Fletcher (1838–1923) worked for Frederick Ward Putnam and trained as an ethnologist under Franz Boas. She was the leader of "Friends of the Indians," and with WNIA introduced a system of making small loans to Indians, so they could buy land and houses. She published *Indian Education and Civilization* (1888), was a member of the Archaeological Institute of America (1879), and worked with the Omahas through the Peabody Museum of Archaeology and Ethnology at Harvard University. See: Joan Mark, "Fletcher, Alice Cunningham" in *American National Biography* (New York: Oxford University Press, 1999). See: The Papers of Alice Cunningham Fletcher and Francis La Flesche, National Anthropological Archives, Smithsonian Institution, Washington, DC.

81　Indian business leaders: General Pleasant Porter (president of a railroad line in Oklahoma), Mr. Hill (of Texas), Howard Gansworth (graduate of Carlisle and Princeton); Indian athletes: Longboat, Sockalexis, Bemus Pierce, Frank Hudson, Tewanima, Metoxen, Myers, Bender, and Jim Thorpe. See: Eastman, *The Indian Today.*

82　Eastman, *The Indian To-Day*. Eastman uses his brother John Eastman (minister) as an example of a less formally educated yet still influential Indian intellectual leader.

83　Although Eastman was no student of Antonio Gramsci, they did live during the same time period. It seems possible that some of Gramsci's thinking regarding the attainment of power through cultural hegemony may have reached Eastman's intellectual circles. In regards to Eastman's thinking, in *The Indian Today* we can see that his views align with Gramsci's notion that any class that wishes to dominate in modern society must move beyond its own narrow economic and corporate interests, to exert intellectual and moral leadership, and to make alliances and compromises with a variety of social forces. Gramsci defines this union as a "historic bloc," taking a term from Georges Sorel. Eastman was certainly invested in finding a way to assert power for Indian people within the preexisting social order, rather than through violent revolution. His ideas would in some ways reproduce the hegemony of the dominant class that had so long subordinated him and other Indian people, which was especially true when he first supported allotment and the Dawes Act, although his views on this policy would shift decades later.

84　Eastman, *The Indian To-Day*. See: "In Search of Progressivism" (1982) by Daniel Rodgers, who argues the pluralistic and political scientists' readings of Progressives moved the historiographical debate past the "essence" of progressive politics to focus on the context of the historical moment. In this reading, standardization and professionalization are the tools with which this rising middle class can grapple with social and economic dislocations of an increasingly industrialized, urbanized, and mechanized world.

85 Eastman, "My People," 181–2; Charles Eastman, "Life and Handicrafts of the Northern Ojibwas," *Southern Workman* 40, May 1911, 273–8.

86 Charles Eastman, *Indian Scout Crafts and Lore* (New York: Dover Publications, 1974); Marguerite Norris Davis, "An Indian Princess Comes into Her Own," *St. Nicholas* 50, July 1923, 939; "Men and Women Whose Lives Count for the Red Man's Cause: Irene Eastman, Taluta, Soprano," *American Indian Magazine* 5, October–December 1917, 263–4; "American Indian Melodies" (a program for Irene Eastman) in SAI Papers, reel 3.

87 For musical program, photographs of Irene Eastman, and other ephemera related to her performance career see: Eastman Folder, Jones Library Archives, Amherst, MA.

88 Sherry Smith has argued that many educated Native people "understood" that their world included interactions with white Americans and that their self-definition in particular could not exist outside of white society. Sherry Smith, *Reimagining Indians: Native Americans through Anglo Eyes, 1880–1940* (New York: Oxford University Press, 2000), 11. For more about SAI members' efforts to use staged productions of Indianness see: Michelle Wick Patterson, "'Real' Indian Songs: The Society of American Indians and the Use of Native American Culture as a Means of Reform," *American Indian Quarterly* Vol. 26, No. 1, Winter 2002, 44–66.

89 In *The Indian Today*, Eastman announces the fifth meeting of the SAI, gives a brief history of the organization, and recognizes Arthur C. Parker's contribution as secretary and treasurer. Members of the SAI were committed to reforming not only policies, but also perceptions of Indianness in America. For example, some lobbied against the use of derogatory terms such as *buck* and *squaw*; others wrote articles against the use of "show Indians" in Wild West entertainment spectacles. Unfortunately, reaching consensus proved difficult for the SAI and may have contributed to its decline. For example, Carlos Montezuma urged the SAI to openly criticize the Office of Indian Affairs for the mismanagement of reservations and called for its termination. As a result, he faced pushback from the majority of Society members for being too radical; after all, many Native people were employed by the Indian Service. Consequently, Montezuma turned his back on their efforts.

90 Figure 3: Charles Alexander Eastman, 1916, author's portrait for *From the Deep Woods to Civilization* (Boston, MA: Little Brown and Company, 1916), courtesy of the Kim-Wait/Pablo Eisenberg Collection of Native American Literature, Archives and Special Collections, Frost Library, Amherst College, Amherst, MA.

91 Brian Morris, *Ernest Thompson Seton, Founder of the Woodcraft Movement 1860–1946: Apostle of Indian Wisdom and Pioneer Ecologist* (Lewiston, NY: Edwin Mellen Press, 2007); David Witt, *Ernest Thompson Seton, The Life and Legacy of an Artist and Conservationist* (Utah: Gibbs Smith, 2010); Jay Mechling, *On My Honor: Boy Scouts and the Making of American Youth* (Chicago, IL: University of Chicago Press, 2001); Wilson, *Ohiyesa*; Charles Eastman, *Indian Scout Craft and Lore* (New York: Dover Publications, 1974).

92 Newspaper Clippings, CAE Papers, Dartmouth Collection.

93 McIntyre to Charles Eastman regarding *Indian Boyhood*, September 28, 1900, in CAE Papers, Dartmouth Collection. Publisher: "The rest of this is still in Mr. Phillips's hands who is so much interested in what he has read that he wishes to read every line of it. I think I could not send you a more favorable report."

94 Donald Pizer, *Hamlin Garland's Early Work and Career* (Berkeley: University of California Press, 1960) and Keith Newlin, *Hamlin Garland, a Life* (Lincoln: University of Nebraska Press, 2008). Also see: Wilson, *Ohiyesa*, 121.

95 Hamlin Garland to Charles Eastman, November 14 circa 1901–2, in CAE Papers, Dartmouth Collection. Hamlin Garland, *The Captain of the Gray Horse Troop* (New York: Harper and Brothers Publishers, 1901); second printing by Curtis Publishing Company in 1902. These two publication dates give us a sense of when this letter was sent.

96 See CAE Papers, Dartmouth Collection. I have found approximately seventy-five book reviews of *Indian Boyhood*. Most of the reviews are titled "Indian Boyhood" or "Book Review" or in some cases "A Sioux Indian's Autobiography" or Tales of Indian Boyhood Spent in a Sioux Tepee" (*Brooklyn Daily Eagle*).

97 For a different account of the politics of authenticity with regards to race, gender, and authorship see: Nell Irvin Painter, *Sojourner Truth: A Life, a Symbol* (New York: W. W. Norton, 1996).

98 CAE Papers, 1891–1983, MS 829, Rauner Special Collections Library, Dartmouth College, Hanover, NH.

99 CAE Papers, Dartmouth College, Special Collections, Hanover, NH.

100 Ibid.

101 Brad Evans, *Before Cultures: The Ethnographic Imagination in American Literature, 1865–1920* (Chicago, IL: University of Chicago Press, 2005) and Michael Elliott, *The Culture Concept: Writing and Difference in the Age of Realism* (Minneapolis: University of Minnesota, 2002) inform how I contextualize the ways that readers and reviewers sought to position Charles Eastman's writings.

102 Robert Warrior, *The People and the Word: Reading Native Nonfiction* (Minneapolis: University of Minnesota Press, 2005); Philip H. Round, *Removable Type: Histories of the Book in Indian Country, 1663–1880* (Chapel Hill: University of North Carolina Press, 2010); Maureen Konkle, *Writing Indian Nations: Native Intellectuals and the Politics of Historiography, 1827–1863* (Chapel Hill: University of North Carolina Press, 2006); Annette Kolodny, ed., *The Life and Traditions of the Red Man: Reading Line: A Rediscovered Treasure of Native American Literature* (Durham, NC: Duke University Press, 2007); Barry O'Connell, ed., *Son of the Forest, and other Writings by* William Apess, *A Pequot* (Amherst: University of Massachusetts Press, 1997); and Lisa Brooks, *The Common Pot: The Recovery of Native Space in the Northeast* (Minneapolis: University of Minnesota Press, 2008).

103 The handful of reviews of *Indian Boyhood* fairly represents the larger array of reviews for the book, and the other reviews that appeared between 1904 and 1916 featuring all of Eastman's work. Over ninety reviews were printed in 1904 about *Red Hunters and the Animal People*, over forty featuring *Old Indian Days* in 1907, and in the years that followed, twenty-seven about *Wigwam*

Evenings, and nearly sixty celebrating his spiritual work in *The Soul of the Indian*, with over forty each for: *Indian Scout Talks*, *The Indian Today*, and *Great Chieftains & Mighty Heroes*. See CAE Papers, Dartmouth Collection.

104   P. Roemarre to Charles Eastman, November 2, 1911, in CAE Papers, Dartmouth Collection. Theodore Stanton to Charles Eastman, October 2, 1913, in CAE Papers, 1891–1983, MS 829, Rauner Special Collections Library, Dartmouth College, Hanover, NH.

105   Charles A. Eastman as author for: *Red Hunters and Animal People* (Harper and Brothers, 1904); *Old Indian Days* (McClure Company, 1907); *Wigwam Evenings: Sioux Folk Tales Retold* (coauthored with Elaine Goodale Eastman) (Little, Brown and Company, 1909); *The Soul of the Indian: An Interpretation* (Houghton, 1911); *Indian Scout Talks* (Little, Brown and Company, 1914); *The Indian Today* (published by Doubleday, Page and Company, New York, originally priced in 1915 at sixty cents net). Book reviews from: CAE Papers, 1891–1983, MS 829, Rauner Special Collections Library, Dartmouth College, Hanover, NH.

106   In defining Eastman, and others, as a participant in literary intellectualism, I am building on the work of literary scholars whose primary focus has been the written work of Native American people, in both historical and contemporary studies. See: Daniel F. Littlefield Jr. and James W. Parins, *A Biobibliography of Native American Writers, 1772–1924* (1981); Paula Gunn Allen, *The Sacred Hoop: Recovering the Feminine in American Indian Traditions* (1986); Gerald Vizenor, ed., *Narrative Chance: Postmodern Discourse on Native American Indian Literatures* (1989); Arnold Krupat, *The Voice in the Margin: Native American Literature and the Canon* (1989); A. LaVonne Brown Ruoff, "Literature," in *Native America in the Twentieth Century: An Encyclopedia*, edited by Mary B. Davis (1994); Arnold Krupat, ed., *New Voices in Native American Literary Criticism* (1993); Arnold Krupat, *For Those Who Come After: A Study of Native American Autobiography* (1994); Gerald Vizenor, ed., *Native-American Literature: A Brief Introduction and Anthology* (1995); Lawana Trout, ed., *Native American Literature: An Anthology* (1999); Craig S. Womack, *Red on Red: Native American Literary Separatism* (1999); John L. Purdy and James Ruppert, eds., *Nothing but the Truth: An Anthology of Native American Literature* (2000); Jace Weaver, Craig S. Womack, and Robert Warrior, *American Indian Literary Nationalism* (2005).

107   Alfred R. McIntyre to Dr. Charles Eastman, May 9, 1916, in CAE Papers, 1891–1983, MS 829, Rauner Special Collections Library, Dartmouth College, Hanover, NH.

108   Elaine Goodale Eastman to Mr. Rugg, April 19, 1939, Letter, EGE Papers, Smith College, Northampton, MA. For an account of their marriage, with an emphasis on Elaine's perspective based on her letters see: Sargent, *Life of Elaine Goodale Eastman*.

109   Alice Freeman Palmer was only twenty-seven when she became president of Wellesley College.

110   For more on the first Normal Schools in the United States see: Charles A. Harper, *A Century of Public Teacher Education: The Story of the State Teachers Colleges as They Evolved from Normal Schools* (Westport, CT: Greenwood

Press Publishers, 1970) and Allen Ornstein and Daniel Levine, *Foundations of Education*, 9th ed. (New York: Houghton Mifflin Company, 1993).

111 E. H. Russell to Charles Eastman, 1908, Letter, CAE Papers, Dartmouth College Special Collections, Hanover, NH.

112 For my reference to the "Red Man in America" speeches that Eastman gave see: Newspaper Clippings, CAE Papers, Dartmouth Collection.

113 Letters sent to Eastman regarding lectures: E. H. Russell, 1908; Mr. W. A. Baldwin, March 26, 1909; Frank Fuller Murdock, February 8, 1909; Charles E. Bloch, March 2, 1910, The Free Synagogue, New York, April 10, 1919; from: CAE Papers, Dartmouth Collection.

114 Ibid.

115 Philip J. Deloria, *Playing Indian* (New Haven, CT: Yale University Press, 1999) and more recently in *Indians in Unexpected Places* (Lawrence: University of Kansas Press, 2006) chronicles the practice of "playing Indian" by white Americans as a desire to constitute their Americanness as distinct from Europe. In his later work, Deloria looks briefly to moments of performance that draw on this history but are different given the moments when Indian people "play Indian" for largely white audiences, which is the sort of "playing Indian" I reference here. Eastman's lecture career began as early as 1895. See: "Indian Spoke" in *Boston Journal*, October 28, 1895 in CAE Papers, Dartmouth Collection.

116 Elizabeth Hutchinson, *The Indian Craze: Primitivism, Modernism, and Transculturation in American Art, 1890–1915* (Durham, NC: Duke University Press, 2009). For Eastman, the craze for "Indian things" and "things Indian" offered him an opportunity to harness the intimate relationship between art and politics, and to make representation and subjectivity central to his speaking performances. Elin Diamond, ed., *Performance and Cultural Politics* (London and New York: Routledge, 1996); E. Patrick Johnson, *Appropriating Blackness: Performance and the Politics of Authenticity* (Durham, NC: Duke University Press, 2003) examines how blackness as an identity category is not always self-constituting, but like performance, "often defies categorization." Jose Esteban Muñoz, *Disidentifications: Queers of Color and the Performance of Politics* (Minneapolis: University of Minnesota Press, 1999); Judith Butler, *Gender Trouble: Feminism and the Subversion of Identity* (New York: Routledge Press, 1990) and *Bodies That Matter: On the Discursive Limits of Sex* (New York: Routledge, 1993).

117 Charles Eastman, "The Real Indian," the Stanley L. Krebs Lectures, Chautauqua Assembly, Connecticut Valley; Charles Eastman, "First Full Day of Work. Address by Dr. C. A. Eastman," *Republican* (no date); Charles Eastman, "Talks of the Real Indian," *Concord Monitor* (NH) Walker free lectures. See: CAE Papers, Dartmouth Collection.

118 For more on WNIA see: Papers of the Women's National Indian Association #9237, Division of Rare and Manuscript Collections, Cornell University Library. According to WNIA records, this convention was held regularly between 1911 and 1926.

119 Maddox, *Citizen Indians*, 82. According to Maddox, the NIA "early on" had chosen to direct "its energies toward missions and leave the political reforms

to male-dominated organizations such as the Indian Rights Association." She argues that leaders of the SAI needed financial and political support from outside of their own ranks.

120 *Brooklyn Daily Eagle* (Brooklyn, New York), Tuesday, February 17, 1914, page 7, Brooklyn Newsstand Collection, Brooklyn Public Library. For more on Eastman as Indian secretary of the YMCA see: Wilson, *Ohiyesa*, 82–9.

121 "The Montauk Club Brooklyn," in *Frank Leslie's Illustrated Newspaper*, November 1, 1890.

122 Ibid. Founded in 1889 by prominent Brooklyn residents like Charles Pratt, Richard Schermerhorn, and Edwin C. Litchfield, the Club hosted political figures and former U.S. presidents: Grover Cleveland, Herbert Hoover, Dwight D. Eisenhower, John F. Kennedy, and Senator Robert Kennedy. Named for the indigenous peoples of Long Island, NY, the Montauketts, the Club had a representative of the Montauketts, Chief Robert Pharoah, as a guest at the 115th anniversary celebration in May 2004. See: http://montaukclub.com/.

123 *Brooklyn Life Magazine*, February 1914, Brooklyn Public Library (Brooklyn, New York).

124 Ibid. For another example of an all-male audience see: "Indian Lecture Well Attended," *Republican*, CAE Papers, Dartmouth Collection.

125 Of the documented talks by Charles Eastman that I have found, twenty-five were presented to all-female groups, whereas five to ten seemed aimed at youth groups and ten to wholly religious organizations. CAE Papers, Dartmouth Collection.

126 *Portland Argus* report in CAE Papers, Dartmouth Collection.

127 For more on Wild West performance see: Joy Kasson, *Buffalo Bill's Wild West: Celebrity, Memory, and Popular History* (New York: Hill and Wang, 2000).

128 Paige Raibmon, *Authentic Indians: Episodes of Encounter from the Late-Nineteenth-Century Northwest Coast* (Durham, NC: Duke University Press, 2005), 12. See: Walter Benjamin, "A Short History of Photography," in *Classic Essays on Photography*, edited by Alan Trachtenberg (New Haven, CT: Leete's Island Books), 199–219.

129 *Los Angeles Times*, "'Ohiyesa' in Swallowtail. Courtly Sioux Tells Story of His People," and *Pasadena Star*, "The Eastman Lecture Big Success. Tells of His People, the Warlike Sioux. Story of the Little Big Horn and Death of Custer." CAE Papers, Dartmouth Collection (dates unknown).

130 Weaver, *The Red Atlantic*. Weaver shows how indigenous people from the Americas crossed the Atlantic as royal dignitaries, diplomats, slaves, laborers, soldiers, performers, and tourists. He argues these cosmopolitan agents acted as conduits for resources and knowledge to bring about international changes that shaped the world.

131 CAE Papers, Dartmouth Collection.

132 "Clipping," in *Westminster Gazette*, March 15, 1928, CAE Papers, Dartmouth Collection. Also see: Contract between "Mrs. Florence Brooks-Aten and Charles Alexander Eastman," January 1928, "Mensel Papers," CAE Papers, Dartmouth Collection. For more about the history of Indian students at Dartmouth see: Calloway, *The Indian History of an American Institution*.

133 For a foil to Eastman's appearance at the Redman's Wigwam in England see: Elliott Young, "Red Men, Princess Pocahontas, and George Washington: Harmonizing Race Relations in Laredo at the Turn of the Century," *Western Historical Quarterly* Vol. 29, No. 1, Spring 1998, 48–85.

134 "Engemmard" (difficult to read) to Eastman, March 9, 1928, Letter, CAE Papers, Dartmouth Collection.

135 For more on the history of representation and expectation in regards to Indian figures see: Philip J. Deloria, *Indians in Unexpected Places* (Lawrence: University of Kansas Press, 2004), 11. Deloria describes expectation as "a shorthand for dense economies of meaning, representation, and act that have inflected both American culture writ large and individuals, both Indian and non-Indian ... in terms of the colonial and imperial relations of power and domination existing between Indian people and the United States."

136 As Sherry L. Smith has shown in *Reimagining Indians: Native Americans Through Anglo Eyes, 1880–1940* (New York: Oxford University Press, 2000), there were many white writers who acted as spokespersons for America's West in their depictions of the region and Indian people they met. At the same time, Smith notes, "Native Americans involved themselves in the discourse about Indians, then, because they understood the connection between knowledge, ideas, and truth, on the one hand, and agency, power, and practice, on the other. They attempted to both shape ideas and exercise social power despite their limited access to political power. Moreover, Indians did not agree on either what constituted truth about themselves and their cultures, or on the proper goals of policy" (11).

137 On performativity see: Jose Esteban Muñoz, *Disidentifications: Queer of Color and the Performance of Politics* (Minneapolis: University of Minnesota Press, 1999) and Butler, *Gender Trouble*. Also, the Indian Arts and Crafts Act of 1990 made it a criminal offense "to sell a product as Indian" if it was not produced by someone other than an enrolled member of a federally or state-recognized tribe, or as an artisan certified by such a tribe. What follows is a selective bibliography of work in performance studies I consulted for performativity. S. E. Wilmer, ed., *Native American Performance and Representation* (Tucson: University of Arizona Press, 2009); Christy Stanlake, *Native American Drama: A Critical Perspective* (Cambridge: Cambridge University Press, 2009); Jill Lane, *Black Face Cuba, 1840–1895* (Philadelphia: University of Pennsylvania Press, 2005); Laura G. Gutierrez, *Performing Mexicanidad: Vendidas Y Cabareteras on the Transnational Stage* (Austin: University of Texas Press, 2010); Gayatri Gopinath, *Impossible Desires: Queer Diasporas and South Asian Public Cultures* (Durham: Duke University Press, 2005).

138 "To-day's Broadcasting" (March 7, 1928) and "The Red Indian: A Chief's Address at the Colonial Institute" (March 16, 1928), both in *Western Daily Press*, Bristol, England. The British Newspaper Archive.

139 "The Red Indian: A Chief's Address at the Colonial Institute" (March 16, 1928), *Western Daily Press*, Bristol, England. The British Newspaper Archive.

140 A photograph of Eastman in Indian regalia surrounded by men in "the wigwam" of the "Bristol Savages" is captioned: Frank Stonelake, C. E. Kelsey, A. C. Fare (president), Alderman J. Fuller Eberle, T. Kingston, E. H. Ehlers,

H. E. Roslyn, R. H. Pezzack, and Stuart Thomas, in CAE Papers, Dartmouth Collection.

141 Eastman was also described by the *Springfield Union*: "Indian Lectures in Northampton. Dr. Charles Eastman of Amherst Speaks under Auspices of Red Men. Is in Indian Costume. Portrays "The Real Indian" in Glowing Terms and Scores His Enemies," in CAE Papers, Dartmouth College. See: James Graves, "Charles Eastman," in *Bostonia* (alumni magazine, spring 1993 issue), 54.

142 Deloria, in his theorization of the concept in *Playing Indian*, makes a helpful specific reference to Eastman in regards to performance and authenticity related to dress: "When Eastman donned an Indian headdress, he was connecting himself to his Dakota roots But he was also – perhaps more compellingly – imitating non-Indian imitations of Indians ... [making] it ever more difficult to pinpoint the cultural locations of Dakotas and Americans, reality and mimetic reality, authenticity and inauthenticity," 123–4.

143 President W. J. Tucker to Charles A. Eastman, September 1904, Letters, CAE Papers, Dartmouth College.

144 Ibid.

145 Unknown photographer, "Stanley F. Johnson and Charles Alexander Eastman," 1927, CAE, Dartmouth Collection.

146 Calloway, *The Indian History of an American Institution*, 127.

147 For more on Eastman's role in Boston society, see James Graves's biographical essay "Ohiyesa" in *Bostonia* (alumni magazine, spring 1993). Eastman's obituary, *Bostonia* Vol. 12, No. 5, February 1939. Eastman, *The Indian To-Day*, 30 and *From the Deep Woods to Civilization*, 195.

2

Tracing Carlos Montezuma's Politics

Progressive Reform and Epistolary Culture Networks

To those who are familiar with his history, what a flood of memories are
awakened and what thoughts attend at sight or mention of the word Indian.
– Carlos Montezuma, "What It Is to Be an Indian"[1]

Introduction

Among the boxes of files, piles of letters, memoranda, and subscriber lists
for Carlos Montezuma's self-published newsletter, *Wassaja*, in the Wisconsin
Historical Society is one note, revealing in two important ways. The first
side of this scrap of paper has the imprint of just two words, now purple
rather than blue and nearly illegible, *Indian Journal*. Montezuma believed
the future of American Indians was contingent upon personal correspondence and periodicals, like the *Indian Journal* – the leading publication for
the Society of American Indians (SAI).[2] Through this reform group that
Montezuma helped found and through his contacts with prominent white
Chicagoans, as well as *Wassaja*, Montezuma addressed a range of topics
from the dismantling of the Bureau of Indian Affairs (BIA) and the need for
higher education for Indian people to changes in Indian cultural practices
and fictional narratives misrepresenting Indianness.

On the flip side of this small rectangle of faded green paper is an equally
important hand-scrawled message with two more words: "spurious citizenship." With these words, Montezuma named an issue that was central
to debates among Indian intellectuals and of the utmost concern to him.
Although he had achieved entrée into middle-class white society in Chicago
because of his work as a physician, Montezuma never gave up fighting for
more recognition and inclusion for himself and other Indian people. In
fact, the issue of American citizenship underpinned his work as a progressive reformer. This particular piece of archival ephemera is a metaphor for
the centrality of a culture of letters within Montezuma's intellectual work.

As a Native intellectual leader interested in reworking dominant tropes of Indianness and struggling to gain citizenship, Montezuma relied on circulating his ideas through a myriad of print media to reach a wide array of Native and white audiences.[3]

Taken together, the handwritten note and the stamped image evoke a critical aspect of Montezuma's representational politics: his ability to raise the level of public discourse concerning the future of Native America. As Montezuma worked to be read as a legible citizen-subject who was both Indian and American, the result was always a struggle over cultural and social representations of Indianness.[4] This scrap of paper also captures the central tensions in his life as a writer, doctor, and activist: a struggle to define Indianness for an emergent pan-Indian identity while avoiding the many problems inherent in the Euro-American concept of race, and his fight to attain the equal rights promised by American citizenship while preserving tribally based traditions and practices. An examination of print culture considers the rhetorical impact of these notations, his many letters, and the important published writings Montezuma produced over the course of his lifetime – to lend context to Montezuma's multifaceted career.[5] As the rich archive of Montezuma's personal papers reveals his thinking, these texts also point to strategic alliances he made with a diverse network of politicians, business leaders, taste makers, white reformers, and fellow Indians, which is reflective of an urban Indian experience that has been long overlooked. In particular, his publication of *Wassaja*, and his diligent correspondence with his readership and colleagues, provide a window into the various ways Montezuma mobilized a politics of racial uplift in his daily practices as an Indian intellectual leader.

Although born to Yavapai parents in Arizona Territory in 1865, Montezuma spent the majority of his life in Chicago. As a practicing doctor, he enjoyed some of the comforts of middle-class life, and attained, to a degree, the status promised by American citizenship, which was a useful position for accessing print culture to present himself as an exemplar for Indianness. He relied on the politics of racial uplift to argue for inclusion, which meant incorporating Indian people into American society not only as citizens, but also as capitalists. As much as Montezuma may have wondered for whom does "genuine" citizenship achieve its meaning, his life and work in Chicago remained distinct from the experiences of most Indian people during the early twentieth century. Like Eastman, his citizenship was not theirs, and yet his writings raise an important question: As an Indian living in America, in which contexts could one be viewed as more of a citizen – or less of one? The majority of his written and spoken texts engage this question to critically analyze the structures and people with the power to determine who was or was not a citizen. Ultimately, he remained committed to the idea that Indian people ought to have a voice in this decision regardless of their social class. Like Charles Eastman, Montezuma believed citizenship might bring with it the power to reshape American politics and culture from the inside out.

On October 5, 1912, Montezuma gave an address titled "The Light on the Indian Situation" at the annual conference for the SAI. In this context, he referred to "Indian matters" involving military service and citizenship to urge his fellow Indian intellectuals to "awaken and express ourselves" for these causes.[6] Then, during World War I, in 1917, Montezuma published an article in *Wassaja* that asked the world community to "see that all men are treated on an equal footing, equality and human rights must be upheld ... Indian Bureauism is the Kaiserism of America toward the Indians. It enslaves and dominates the Indians without giving them their rights."[7] These two examples, one an address and the other a printed text, represent the strident tone Montezuma often used throughout his work as a reformer, and how determined he was to make citizenship a political reality for Indian people. He did not and could not work alone to achieve his goals of citizenship, reforming the BIA, and reshaping how Americans viewed Indian people.

Throughout his lifetime, Montezuma used correspondence to remain actively connected to a wide array of Indian performers, activists, and political leaders. He exchanged letters with archaeologist, historian, and folklorist Arthur C. Parker; Cherokee journalist, writer, and magazine editor John Oskison; visual artist Wa-Wa Chaw; and pan-Indian organization activists like Gertrude Bonnin and Charles Eastman, as well as nationally recognizable and politically influential leaders like Plenty Coups. In addition, correspondence connected Montezuma to white progressives who were sympathetic to Indian causes. He wrote regularly to journalists like Helen Grey, who investigated the BIA and land deals, and bureaucratic leaders and educational reformers like Richard H. Pratt. Correspondence, and to a lesser extent publishing, function as material goods, as intellectual theses, and useful lenses for examining Montezuma's ideas regarding race and citizenship as well as the types of political and cultural networks he accessed, created, and maintained.

Also imbedded within epistolary culture are ephemeral items that reveal the subtlety of Montezuma's self-perception and his changing views on contentious topics such as Indian identity and cultural authenticity: countless notices from the SAI; leaflets from organizations like the Indian Fellowship League; circulars from the Order of Red Men; and more. Because of the diversity of this archive, I focus on visible discursive formations to showcase Montezuma's representational politics, his literary production, and his ability to interact with a plurality of white and pan-tribal publics. Furthermore, although epistolary writing has not been the major focus of scholarship on the Progressive Era, it has figured prominently in a number of studies from the earlier period in Native writing.[8] These studies inform my close readings of Montezuma's texts, whether written or spoken.

Like other Indian intellectuals, Montezuma navigated his own politics of representation to shape the cultural and political development of the United States during the early twentieth century. Montezuma's public and private writings contributed to a print culture emerging out of a white American imagining of Indian people and their history, and that of the readers and writers in Indian Country. Indeed, Montezuma's written and spoken texts became central to how Native publics and counterpublics were established.[9] More specifically, his personal letters and his public newsletter, *Wassaja*, hailed an expanding network of Native people during the Progressive Era. Certainly, his letters did different work from that of his more formal newsletter. Looking at both, however, as representative texts for intellectual circuits demonstrates the diverse networks that connected Indian writers and reformers with white Americans. When letters became pamphlets that became newsletters that became journals and magazines, Montezuma's ideas (and those of other Indian writers) traveled along an important continuum. For instance, the letters Native people sent to Montezuma when he was editor of *Wassaja* produced an important form of internal and national dialogue across Indian Country. Montezuma's personal letters and ideas expressed in *Wassaja* demonstrate an emerging pan-Indian public sphere that diverged from American representative democracy, even as individuals like Montezuma aimed to incorporate themselves into that system in order to reform it.[10]

Education: "The Public Knows Very Little of the Indian People in the Right Way."

Montezuma's life and writings were intimately connected to his educational experiences and the ways Indian education, in general, went about training Native people to become proper citizens of the United States. Such an argument rests on an understanding of education as performance based. Therefore, by considering his life in relation to education, one can see how his career as a physician afforded him a space and social capital to work as an activist and a writer. It is rarely an easy road from childhood to medical school, and for Montezuma it was rocky, to say the least.

Montezuma's parents named him Wassaja at his birth, but soon he would be known by another name. At a young age, Montezuma was captured by the Pimas, a neighboring tribe to the Yavapais, who in turn sold him to an Italian photographer, Carlo Gentile, who had been traveling throughout the Southwest taking pictures of Native peoples. According to Montezuma's own recollections, Gentile paid thirty silver dollars for the boy. It was a fairly common practice to sell captured women and children as slaves to other tribes, to Mexicans, and to white settlers in the Southwest during this period. Gentile named the boy after himself and the pair traveled around the United States before finally relocating to Urbana, Illinois. Once there, George W. Ingalls, the director of the Indian Department, personally selected a placement for the eleven-year-old Montezuma in the household of Reverend William H. Stedman, pastor of the First Baptist Church of Urbana. According to one biographer, Montezuma maintained a positive relationship with the Stedman family throughout his life, with Reverend Stedman presiding at his wedding in 1913.[11]

Montezuma's private education was supported by Stedman's hiring of a tutor to assist him in passing the entrance exam for the preparatory school of the University of Illinois, which he attended for one year. In 1880, at the age of fourteen, Montezuma entered the university. He graduated four years later. While he was enrolled in the College of Natural Science in the pharmaceutical program of the School of Chemistry, Montezuma's education was sponsored by the university YMCA. Fortunately, in his second year, because his grades were good enough, the University waived all fees. Montezuma was well liked and well known among his classmates, and he was elected president as well as secretary of the class of 1884. He also became the president of the Adelphic Debate Society, where he gained early training in public speaking. In fact, Montezuma's success as an Indian debater was reported by the student newspaper, *The Daily Illini*, on May 5, 1883, which noted that he gave "one of the rare treats of the evening on 'Indian's Bravery.' " Clearly Montezuma was successful in building financial and intellectual alliances while at college, as he distinguished himself among his classmates.[12]

On June 21, 1884, Montezuma entered the Chicago Medical College as its first Indian student. While earning his degree, Montezuma supported himself as a pharmacist. Like almost all Indian intellectuals, he also gave lectures on "the Indian" to a variety of audiences ranging from ladies' clubs to church organizations. He benefited from a tremendous proliferation of women's and church clubs that created a circuit for such lecturers, and Montezuma began earning extra money through these speaking engagements. In 1888, for example, he gave a speech titled "The Indian of Tomorrow" in front of the National Women's Christian Temperance Union in Chicago. It was one of many similar events.[13]

After graduation, and before he became nationally known for his political writing, Montezuma worked to establish his career as a doctor. Thomas Jefferson Morgan, the commissioner of Indian Affairs from 1889 to 1893 (also a Baptist minister and professional educator), saw in Montezuma, the Indian doctor, a model of achievement. He wrote to offer the young doctor a position as a physician in the Indian Service. "My friend, Captain Pratt, tells me that you have finished your medical studies, and have entered upon the practice of your profession.... I have recently appointed Miss La Flesche, who graduated from the medical school in Philadelphia, and subsequently had some hospital training, as physician among her own people, the Omahas." Montezuma promptly accepted Morgan's offer. "For my part, I am willing to do anything which will reform them and also to do all

I can to set them a good example.... I remain yours for justice in the Indian Affairs." Montezuma's ability to seemingly capitulate to the patronizing rhetoric commonly used by white progressives who had committed themselves to solving the so-called Indian Problem enabled him to claim that he could "reform them," meaning other Native peoples. His later speeches and writings indicate that Montezuma believed Native peoples were inherently capable of managing their own uplift, in a social and political sense, if given the right tools: such as access to higher education.[14]

On September 20, 1889, Montezuma began work at Fort Stevenson, close to the banks of the Missouri River in North Dakota.[15] By this time the "Fort" was no longer operating as a military facility, but rather as the Fort Berthold Indian Agency. After practicing in North Dakota for a few years, Montezuma moved to Carlisle, Pennsylvania, where he worked as the Carlisle Indian Industrial School's physician, and ended up traveling with the school's football team as its doctor. This time was likely formative in his thinking about both Carlisle and Indian children's welfare more broadly, especially given the huge cemetery at the school that marked the school's failure on the health front. This was also when Montezuma forged a personal connection to an institution that was central to the experiences of the era's Native leaders, including Charles Eastman, Gertrude Bonnin, and Luther Standing Bear. But this post was only temporary. Montezuma longed to return to Illinois and set up his own practice. In December 1895, he returned to Chicago and established a private practice in two locations. He continued working in the city until 1922.[16]

Despite his ties to Carlisle, Montezuma drew on experiences with the business community of Chicago and his upbringing with the Stedman family when formulating his ideas about the education of Native peoples. He writes in a letter from 1921, "A great work must be done to educate the public that an Indian is the same as they are" because, as Montezuma saw it, the vast majority of non-Indian people in the United States knew very little "of the Indian people in the right way." Montezuma's desire was twofold when it came to education. First, he wanted to retool reservation day schools and boarding schools in order to increase the numbers of Indian students who could attend college. Second, like Charles Eastman, he wanted these individuals to become like him and serve as representatives of their race to help educate the rest of America. This vision aligned with Eastman's educational mission in many respects. Indeed, the two men had similar experiences when it came to attending college and then medical school.

At the same time, Montezuma was better positioned than Eastman to highlight himself as a "success" because he earned a steady income as a doctor in Chicago. Eastman had struggled for years to set up a practice, and eventually gave up the idea that his main source of income would come from being a physician. Like other progressives, Montezuma took an approach to changing Indian education by being in dialogue with different reform organizations that aimed to find political and practical solutions to the "Indian Problem." His contacts with the business world of Chicago taught him that there was a preexisting network of white progressives who might be able to help. Many of these groups were established during the last two decades of the nineteenth century.[17]

In 1909, the National Indian Association (NIA) celebrated its thirtieth anniversary. Founded and run by white women, the NIA represented a significant strand of thought and activity that characterized national reform efforts aimed toward Indian affairs.[18] Critical to the work of these women was the circulation of their monthly magazine, *The Indian's Friend*. Montezuma, like other Indian intellectual leaders at the time, was a regular subscriber to the journal. It is likely he read reports in August of that year regarding the performance of *Hiawatha* that the NIA noted "was presented by forty-five of the Indian students of the Haskell Institute at Lawrence," as a play for the National Educational Association's meeting. For the majority of Americans, plays based on Indian stories, events, and histories provided easy access to learning about Indian people. This type of educational entertainment offered a different way of reframing how American audiences viewed Indianness but also drew on a longer history of performance that had replayed historical events involving Indians that had been popular in various parts of the United States since the early nineteenth century.[19]

The NIA and Montezuma shared the belief that the education of Indian people *and* the education of the American public about Indians were key reform issues.[20] However, the organization's reformers and Montezuma differed when it came to the power of performance. Montezuma saw himself as an educator who publicly scorned performances he thought separated Indian people from modern society by locking them into an imagined past. Shows like those promoted by "Buffalo Bill's" Wild West, for example, were, according to Montezuma, dangerous arenas in which Native actors could not only be taken advantage of but might end up taking part in devastating misrepresentations of Indian history.

More difficult for Montezuma to protest were events like the one sponsored by the NIA, where Haskell staged a production of *Hiawatha*. For Montezuma, this type of low-level Indianized performance, promoted by progressive groups to aid the cause of citizenship, was a powerful tool for imagining but also undermining Indianness. In the first issue of *Wassaja*, which appeared in April 1916, Montezuma publicly denounced such Indianized staged performances. Specifically, he attacked the celebration of American Indian Day that included its own elements of pageantry, which had been promoted by Arthur Parker and other members of the SAI. Montezuma called it "a farce" and warned *Wassaja* readers that such events would not help Indian people but rather "the Indians will be used as tools for interested parties. To the Indian it is a mockery because he does not enjoy freedom, but is a ward and is handicapped by the Indian Bureau."[21]

The stakes for Montezuma were high because he was determined to make Indian citizenship a reality, and he believed stereotypical and highly racialized performances and mismanagement of Indian affairs by the Bureau together threatened the future for Indian people.

Montezuma believed that full citizenship could not happen, as long as white America imagined Indian people in primitive and anachronistic ways. At the same time, to further his cause Montezuma needed to be legible as a citizen who was an American and an Indian. Thus, even though his "cause in favor of citizenship" was political, he also had to grapple with cultural and social representations of Indianness. As a doctor in an urban space, Montezuma was well positioned to argue for the inclusion of Indian people in the body politic of the United States. His membership in local Chicago business organizations run by white, middle-class Americans gave him social status and a sort of de facto citizenship.[22] Yet he needed to speak and write against a plethora of misrepresentations in popular performances, films, and novels that continued to marginalize Native people by limiting how others could imagine them.[23]

Other Indian intellectuals joined Montezuma in emphasizing the role of education in a public fight for recognition of Indian people as modern citizens of the United States, rather than icons of the Wild West or America's lost past. On September 6, 1918, Gertrude Bonnin, then the secretary and treasurer for the SAI, sent a letter to the "Honorable F.P. Keppel," the third assistant secretary of war. Bonnin's letter, perhaps inadvertently, recaptures earlier moments in American history when the military functioned as a critical site of engagement for Indian policy. In reality, the War Department had ceased to be the main avenue through which Indian affairs were managed after the establishment of the Department of the Interior on March 3, 1849. But it was also necessary because the Army still owned the buildings and the site used by the Carlisle School, and was reclaiming use of the property at this time as a war-related measure.[24]

Her letter begins straightforwardly enough. "I have the honor, in behalf of a small body of Americans, the Red Americans, to beg your forbearance in this request for a reconsideration of the non-continuance of the Carlisle Indian School. It is understood that the law of 1882 provides for the reversion of this property for military purposes." Bonnin introduces herself and her allies vis-à-vis the careful use of a comma. Her pause is an important one, as it punctuates two key tenets of the SAI ideology, as well as the SAI's particular interest in asking for a reconsideration of the matter involving the Carlisle School. The SAI's commitment to full citizenship rights for *all* Indian people comes across in Bonnin's rhetorical decision to define them as composed of "Americans, the Red Americans"; a description that signaled to Keppel how this particular organization conceived of itself as *both* American and Indian. These modes of articulation were politically and culturally salient for Bonnin given that, by 1918, vast numbers of Indian people had been encouraged if not forced to *become* American through the erasure of languages, traditions, and cultural practices that would mark them as Indians. Ironically, this process was most often carried out in the classrooms of places like Carlisle, against which she had written – a place Montezuma knew all too well. But in this letter, Bonnin speaks on behalf of the SAI. For SAI members like Montezuma, to be "Americans" and also "Red" provided them with a complex and distinctive status, and an opportunity to claim political citizenship (which many did not legally have) while simultaneously retaining their Indian identity. They neither wanted nor needed to advocate for full cultural assimilation into white American society, but could claim Carlisle on their own terms.[25]

Institutionally, Carlisle was at once, as Bonnin's letter notes, "the Red Man's University" and an old "barracks" the military had used during the Civil War. In actuality, it had been established as a military post in the late 1750s; some of the buildings dated to the eighteenth century. She makes plain how "this fact today bears directly upon Indian education and civilization to which our Government pledged itself in good faith." Her letter argues education is at the heart of this matter for Indian people because to close Carlisle "for military purposes" would result in the transfer of Indian students to "inferior schools," and, more importantly, "not make up to the race the loss of educational opportunities only Carlisle can give." In this sentence, "Carlisle" represents not only a specific educational vision, but also the U.S. government's role as a patron of Indian education and granter of political power through that education. Despite the devastating effects of a Carlisle education on Native pupils (the loss of language, cultural practices, and other markers of identity), Bonnin, like Montezuma and other Indian intellectuals of this period, believed that social uplift and education went hand in hand, even if Carlisle was one of the places where schooling would take place. She asserts this belief and also calls attention to the fact that despite schools like Carlisle, and the efforts of educated Indians like herself, "the sad fact" is that "approximately 20,000 Indian children eligible for school are still without schools in our America." Her use of "our" here claims a space of belonging within America, and a voice with which to change it. The work of the NIA and the SAI, as well as individual writers like Bonnin and Montezuma, exemplified the centrality of Indian education as a component of race and nation making, both facets of Montezuma's activist work. Like Eastman, Bonnin, and Luther Standing Bear, Montezuma found an ally in Carlisle's headmaster and social architect: Richard Pratt (1840–1924), the white progressive.

Dear Monte: Correspondence with Richard Pratt

Because Montezuma worked primarily as a physician and not an author, correspondence functions differently for him as a political organizing tool when compared to the efforts of Charles Eastman, Gertrude Bonnin, and Luther Standing Bear. Letter writing worked to bridge the publishing forum of *Wassaja* with different discursive formations of Montezuma's speeches and printed texts and reveals the progression and changes in his cultural politics over time. One of the primary examples of changes in his thinking emerges through an extensive set of correspondence between Montezuma and Pratt. As a former Union Army officer, Pratt was well known among white reformers for being vocal on behalf of educated Indians seeking citizenship. He became famous for repeating a slogan regarding education as a process of assimilation, which promised Americans citizens that schools like Carlisle could: "Kill the Indian, and save the man!"[26] Sounding outrageous today, this mantra in the context of his time appeared sympathetic toward Indian people, if also underpinned by a racist logic. In reality, Pratt was friends with many of his Native students, who went on to become teachers, as well as doctors, lawyers, missionaries, and actors. Their achievements highlighted, for Pratt, the fact that he never gave up the fight to solve America's "Indian Problem" and what he saw as the persistent marginalization of Indian people in economic, social, and cultural terms. Over the course of their letters, Montezuma and Pratt often agree about the best tools for the advancement of Indian people, even if Montezuma would never go as far as to say you had to "kill the Indian" to "save the man."[27]

Writing to Pratt, Montezuma maintained an important contact within the white "Friends of the Indian" reform circles that dominated national debates about the futures of American Indians. Montezuma and Pratt had built a dynamic friendship over a twenty-five-year period, as many of their letters demonstrate. Throughout these exchanges, themes emerge that reflect Montezuma's growing concerns regarding broader campaigns for justice related to education, allotment, and citizenship, as well as social issues pertaining to race. Writing to each other about these themes, the two discussed the ideal of the educated Indian, the public role of the ideal Indian, and the role that religion, specifically Christianity, ought to play in the lives of Indian people. Many letters showcase Montezuma's desire to dissolve the reservation system and the BIA, which was a frequent headline for issues of *Wassaja*. Sprinkled throughout their correspondence, too, are personal missives and friendly turns of phrase. Looking more closely at some key passages reveals the complexity of their relationship and the centrality of correspondence both in Montezuma's political career and as a tool for reconstructing the networks of possibility Indian intellectuals navigated using their letters.

Not long after leaving Carlisle and setting up his medical practice in Chicago, Montezuma put forth his own thoughts on the "Indian Problem" or the "Indian Question." In fact, his speech, "The Indian Problem from an Indian's Standpoint," was so well received by the Fortnightly Club on February 10, 1898 that it was printed as a pamphlet and distributed to interested Chicagoans. A similar version of the text was later published in

Current Literature in April 1898 and retitled: "An Indian's View of the Indian Question." For Montezuma, the "Indian Question" had not been adequately addressed by white America because it was not fully understood. "You are blinded and ignorant in the enjoyment of your civilized life; in the midst of your refinement and education you are without a trace of an idea of the facts of the Indian question." He goes on to argue in favor of an allotment policy that would "wipe out these dark reservations," and with any money earned in resettling these lands, he suggests, every Indian child could then be educated in the public schools of the United States. "Let them be brought up in and become citizens of the various States." Citing himself as an example, Montezuma suggests that Indian children become "civilized" if taken while they are very young to be "in direct relations with good civilization." In essence, he is arguing in favor of assimilation, and despite the paternalistic tone, he is also against the policies he believes have failed Native people now living on reservations, which he likens to demoralizing prisons. For Montezuma, the space of the reservation is emblematic of the larger failings of the federal system as a "barrier against enlightenment, a promoter of idleness, beggary, gambling, pauperism, ruin and death." Finally, Montezuma drives his point home by bringing up Pratt's methods of civilizing Native children by distributing them among white families, as part of Carlisle's outing program. Building on this strategy, Montezuma argues the same needs to be done with reservations, to "divide and civilize; attack the reservations, cut them up and educate the divided parts in turn." Ultimately, he is arguing in favor of integrating public schools. He writes, "I wish I could collect all the Indian children, load them in ships in San Francisco, circle them around Cape Horn, pass them through Castle Garden, put them under proper individual care in your public schools, and when they have been matured and moderately educated let them do what other men and women do – take care of themselves. This would solve the Indian question."

At this moment, Montezuma appeared adamant about how allotment and education represented "the only way to liberty, manhood and citizenship" for Native men. The narrowness and sexism of these views are of a piece with how white progressives imagined the future for Native people in America, and reflect Montezuma's endorsement of a capitalist ideology that measured achievement based on the work of the individual rather than the collective. For Montezuma, if Native children were able to go to public schools, like so many of the new immigrants arriving in the United States, they would be able to make something of themselves. Native people would no longer be in need of financial or other support from the federal government. Pratt most certainly agreed with these sentiments in 1898 when Montezuma's talk first appeared in *Current Literature*.[28]

The next year, on February 7, 1899, Pratt wrote to Montezuma about the death of their mutual friend, Simon Pokagon. Pratt referred to *Queen of the Woods*, which Pokagon had written and which was published shortly after his death, noting to Monte that "You can count on me to take a dozen copies of his book to begin with." His letter also highlights an emerging network of Indian intellectuals as critical to the success of Indian education and the cause of citizenship. The latter depended on the legibility of accomplished Indians as examples for the American public. Pratt considered Montezuma one of these representative figures. Pratt used books, like the one by Pokagon, as one example of what an educated Indian might achieve and as a tool that could inform other Americans. His letter urges Montezuma to visit Carlisle for commencement. If he made the trip, Montezuma could be used as physical proof for the school's recent graduates of just what an accomplished Indian could do for himself *and* for his race.[29]

In September of that same year, Pratt wrote again about the topic of accomplished Indians and referred specifically to Montezuma's emerging role as a leader. In this letter, one can see that affiliation, along with self-presentation and careful use of rhetoric, were key strategies Indian intellectuals used as political activists and leaders. Pratt writes, "Every Indian that can separate himself from the crowd and get out among the people in any way, moves in the right direction. I am glad to know that you will stand by [Frank] and get your friends in Urbana and Champaign to do so."[30] Frank was a young man Pratt sent to the University of Illinois by way of Chicago. While in Chicago, Montezuma assisted Pratt by offering fellow Indians a place to stay and an introduction to important people. Pratt helped to nurture this type of networking, as he sent additional money for room, board, and transportation to Montezuma. In this letter and many others, material concerns aligned with philosophical issues. The two would come to a head when it came to Montezuma's public presentations, his views on race, and how other Indian people chose to engage a politics of performativity. As the first decade of the twentieth century neared its end, Pratt would once again call on Montezuma to act as a leader and spokesperson for the Indian race.

On December 21, 1908, Pratt wrote to Montezuma about the future of educated Indians and the BIA. His letter suggested they "press upon Mr. Taft our ideas as to what should be done for the Indians."[31] Integral to their plan was the development and strengthening of a network of Indian intellectuals who could work in local and regional contexts toward changing national policy. Montezuma was one example, and in his letter Pratt points to another Indian intellectual they both knew well: Reverend Sherman Coolidge (Arapaho, 1863–1932). Coolidge had advanced professionally within the ministry and showed how Indian clergy could be central to progressive reform within contemporary Indian affairs. Pratt described him as "levelheaded" like other Indian religious leaders, such as Henry Roe Cloud (Winnebago, ca. 1884–1950) and Reverend Philip B. Gordon (Ojibwe and Catholic priest, 1887–1948). Cloud had published "The Future of the Red Man in America" in *The Missionary Review of the World*,[32] whose goal was to create an institution that would combine secular vocational training with an interdenominational Christian curriculum for Indian students. He sought to counteract the increasing loss of authority religious bodies were experiencing during this period with regards to the field of Indian education since the federal government began to discontinue the mission contract schools in 1897. In addition, Cloud's widely read autobiographical essay "From Wigwam to Pulpit," subtitled "A Red Man's Story of His Progress from Darkness to Light," appealed to white reformers like Pratt for its references to the uplifting power of Christian teachings for the advancement of Indian people. As some historians note, Cloud's "contributions to theological inquiry, the education of Native Americans, and the formulation of government policies contribute to his inclusion in any list of the most prominent Native Americans in history."[33] Like Cloud, Rev. Philip B. Gordon used publishing to assert his religious and political views. In fact, he started a monthly four-leaf newsletter, *The War Whoop*, but was unable to publish it because his superiors in the Catholic Church forbad him to do so. Montezuma was influenced by Gordon's efforts to print his own paper: *Wassaja*. Like Cloud, Gordon was a founding member of the SAI, and perhaps more than Coolidge and Cloud was able to succeed both as a religious leader and as a political activist. As a Christian, Montezuma may have admired Gordon's ability to remain active in his faith and politics.[34]

Pratt's letter authenticates the type of power embodied in Rev. Coolidge because of his education and Indianness. Pratt writes to Montezuma, "being like yourself, a full blooded Indian, highly educated, his views are entitled to the most serious consideration." Pratt's sentiments link discourses of the body with the mind by reconciling Indian blood with education. He also participates in a discussion of assimilation, a process he thought necessary for Native people to incorporate themselves into American culture. Pratt defines citizenship through a careful combination, rather than a synthesis, of an "authentic" Indian subjectivity tied to blood quantum, with a right to speak based on one's educational background. So assimilation broadly conceived could cut two ways. First, educated Indians could draw on the intersection of Indian subjectivity as defined by blood *and* education to assert a particular space for themselves as political activists. This is interesting and somewhat surprising for someone who wanted "to kill the Indian." Second, someone like Montezuma could use his class position to assert a unique right to speak on behalf of Indianness writ large. In other words, like Eastman, Cloud, and Gordon, Montezuma could fashion himself as one of the best Indian leaders, someone to be counted on because he was educated *and also* full-blooded, or at least he was being hailed to do so at Pratt's urging.[35]

On May 22, 1909, Pratt wrote again to Montezuma concerning the future of Indians in America by emphasizing the power of educated Indians to change policy. "I suggested to [Mr. Owen] that a petition to Congress coming from educated Indians would be a splendid thing to help him out and he agreed and suggested that I write it." Here Pratt conveys a world of possibility for Indian intellectuals, but highlights the roles to be played by white activists who were necessary to write the petition. He presses Montezuma to become personally involved in an effort to reform the BIA: "If you or some other intelligent Indian or Indians would take it up you would make a tremendous case. I don't believe the country would agree to let the Bureau go but the move could be made to compel the Indian bureau to come to time and perform its duty." Pratt gives up some of his white authority, for a moment, by urging Montezuma "or some other intelligent Indian" (implying one might easily be exchanged for another) to take up the petition. By this time, Montezuma had openly criticized the BIA in public talks and written pieces; he would no doubt have jumped at the chance to lead others in an assault on this arm of the federal government. Read another way, Pratt may also be trying to rechannel the venom of Montezuma's attacks into an effort to reform instead of completely abolish the BIA.[36]

In August of that same year, Pratt wrote to Dr. Carl E. Grammer, a professor at the Virginia Theological Seminary and the president of the Indian Rights Association (IRA), concerning Indian education and sent a copy of his letter to Montezuma. It was common practice among these activists to send each other copies of letters to compel action based on the letters as supplemental evidence. This particular letter shows the divide between efforts of white reformers like Grammer and Pratt about all-Indian educational institutions like Carlisle. Pratt writes, "You say 'it has seemed to me that eventually the need for such schools as Carlisle must cease,' but I do not understand the Indian Rights Association to favor any immediate steps in that direction." Here Pratt questions the efficacy of Grammer's organization as an advocate for fuller citizenship for Indian people if Carlisle must close. Unlike Pratt, Montezuma believed places like Carlisle needed to be abolished so Indian students could attend the same schools as white students, a point he had made strongly and clearly back in 1898 when speaking about the "Indian Problem." In this sense, Montezuma would have agreed with Grammer's assertion that "schools as Carlisle must cease." However, Montezuma would also have understood Pratt's view that the IRA was an organization that had failed to achieve this goal because Indian schools rather than integrated schools remained the norm and Indian education in general seemed beyond the reach of the IRA's efforts.[37]

Why did Pratt and Montezuma differ on this point regarding Indian education? Perhaps because they had different understandings of assimilation. Pratt's outlook was practical, much like that of Booker T. Washington's vision of advancement for black people, in that he saw schools like Carlisle as paving the way for Indians to get off reservations and to integrate into the white economy through low-paying service jobs, which would let them attain a working-class social status in the larger society. It was the Carlisle *Industrial School*, after all. A similar approach was applied to the education of foreign immigrants during the same period, and because of this it was seen in many educational circles as a "progressive" approach in terms of social reform. Montezuma had hoped integration would produce more Indian professionals like himself who could then work toward political influence through citizenship. He had succeeded because of his education, but his was not an Indian school education, but rather one based on being a part of white America's educational system.

The debate concerning where to properly educate Indian children, in public schools or places like Carlisle, reflected to some extent a longer history and a time when Indian education had been tied to practices of Christianization rather than efforts to obtain citizenship. For Pratt and Montezuma, both practicing Christians, religious instruction could be an important component of educating Native children. This enabled them to find some common ground in their differing points of view regarding the value of integrating Indians into public schools. Not all reformers believed in the merits of religious instruction as critical to assimilation, but Montezuma, who had found support for his own schooling from the YMCA, believed cooperation between Christianity-based reform organizations and educational institutions could lead to the success of Indian students. In fact, Montezuma received (from Pratt) copies of two letters that point out the early history of this type of cooperation. One letter, from July 5, 1895, was sent by C. K. Ober, a white Chicagoan (then the secretary of the International Committee of the YMCA), and the other, from June 28, was sent by Charles Eastman.[38]

Eastman's letter demonstrates how Indian intellectuals worked together with white missionaries and teachers. Ober's letter suggests that Eastman was an example of an educated Indian who embodied the possibilities of Indian education. Ober recommends that Dr. Eastman, because of his "experience in college athletics, and his medical training," is "admirably fit" as both a subject "for the study of this problem" regarding the direction of Indian education, and as a fellow reformer "for the direction of this new effort." In this example, the figure of the Indian athlete and the question of the body as well as gender seem critical to confirming Eastman's status as representative subject, when coupled with his medical education. Educated Indians, like Eastman and Montezuma, bore a heavy burden as public figures who had to demonstrate intellectual development, athletic accomplishment, and moral character. Ober's letter makes explicit that "healthful athletic sports" work "in place of the demoralizing heathen practices of the Indians," suggesting sports could be a more helpful and American way of channeling a supposedly primitive warrior instinct and practice. Thus, Indian men could harness and achieve a white and an American as well as a Christian and a muscular manhood *if* they received a proper athletic as well as an intellectual education. An individual like Eastman was "fit" for "the study of this problem, and for the direction of this new effort" because of both his intellectual and physical strength – a view in keeping with a muscular Christianity discourse during this period, which sought to define proper American manliness through the body as much as the mind. In this exchange, and in others throughout Montezuma's archive, manliness operates as the preeminent gender identity embraced by Indian and non-Indian male reformers and worthy of highlighting for political ends.[39]

Eastman's letter does not shrug off the role he must play. Instead, it draws together the work of missionaries and Christian teachers by defining them as "deeply in sympathy with our work." Writing from the standpoint of an Indian Service employee and intellectual, Eastman sees "our" here both in terms of the network he and Montezuma were building as Native (male) leaders and in the context of cooperation between Indian groups and white reformers. Taken together, these letters bring Montezuma into the fold of a relationship that was forming between these groups. Montezuma was a Christian Indian who had been raised by a Baptist family in Illinois. His experience of Christianization and education did not necessarily have deleterious effects on his Indianness. For Montezuma, being a Christian functioned in much the same way as being a doctor did; it afforded him entrée into middle-class white society, and from that class position he could do and say more on behalf of Native people.[40]

Wassaja's World in Print

As a Chicago physician, Montezuma participated in Masonic activities, belonged to the Press Club of Chicago, and subscribed to several medical journals, all while operating a successful medical practice for at least fifteen years. By 1914, however, many of his patients fell on hard times. They could not keep up with their payments, and things took a turn for the worse. By 1916, Montezuma had to close his downtown office, and he had started to publish *Wassaja: Freedom's Signal for the Indians.*

Montezuma used his self-published newsletter to promote his views on education and those of his readers, who wrote many letters to the editor. Within *Wassaja*, Montezuma combined different ideas of Indianness with a shared goal of citizenship. He used the newsletter to combat what he saw as pernicious stereotypes of Native Americans to offer an idealized vision of Indianness that was pan-tribal and compatible with full citizenship rights. The circulation of this periodical captured and shaped critical debates across Indian Country. Its subscriber lists reveal and document different networks through which Montezuma, other Indians, and his friends and white allies created and participated in a shared discourse concerning both tribal-national and American citizenship.

First published in April 1916, *Wassaja* remained in print until November 1922. In fact, the last issue appeared only two months before Montezuma died. Readers paid five cents per copy or fifty cents for a year's subscription. Montezuma also encouraged local distribution by providing 100 copies of an issue for only two dollars. Many subscribers listed show that

Wassaja circulated throughout different rural reservation communities in
the Southwest, the Great Lakes area, and the Plains States. In 1920, however, Montezuma was forced to double his subscription rates because of an
increase in printing costs, which may have lowered the number of readers
he hoped to reach.[41]

The impetus behind *Wassaja* was to remind Indians and Americans of the
history of abuse perpetrated against Indian people by the U.S. government.
The newsletter's title means "signaling" or "beckoning," which embodied
Montezuma's desire to create a national, Native American newspaper to "signal" fuller citizenship and participation in American society. Because he had
been named "Wassaja" at birth and was later renamed "Carlos Montezuma"
by his white adoptive parent, the act of naming the paper after his Yavapai
birth name enabled him to reclaim this part of his past. Like Bonnin and
Eastman, this double name claim was important to Montezuma's subjectivity and to the politics of his self-representation. Naming and renaming
remained critical tools that Indian people could use to contest oppressive
cultural practices they experienced, whether as students (as Luther Standing
Bear notes in his autobiographical account narrating how he selected an
English name off of a blackboard after coming to Carlisle) or later as adults
who wanted to be legible as Indians and Americans. Perhaps readers came
to recognize Carlos both as the Indian doctor "Montezuma" from Chicago
and as the writer "Wassaja" – the Indian advocate and political critic. It is
likely that many of his Native readers may have already been familiar with
the notion of using a persona to write about controversial subjects affecting
Indian Country, especially those who had read some of Alexander Posey's
writings as "Fus Fixico." A Creek journalist and poet living and writing in
Indian Territory at the turn of the century, Posey wrote letters under the
pseudonym Fus Fixico ("Heartless Bird"). These appeared in the *Indian
Journal* – the same name the SAI later used for its periodical – the newspaper Posey ran from Eufala, Creek Nation, from 1902 to 1908. Written in
an Indian-English dialect, the letters captured readers' imaginations with
their humor and commentary on contemporary events, making Posey "one
of the best Indian humorists of all time." One might then imagine a Native
writing and reading continuum that begins in the nineteenth century and
carries over into the twentieth, when increased literacy rates enabled growing numbers of Indian readers to consume both Posey and Montezuma's
newspapers.[42]

Following in the footsteps of Rev. Philip Gordon, who had edited two
newspapers – *War Whoop* (Lawrence, Kansas) in 1916 and *a-ni-shi-na-bwe
E-na-mi-ad* (Reserve, Wisconsin) in 1918 – Montezuma entered the newsletter business with a discourse that critiqued and defined Indianness in
America.[43] It is likely he used *Wassaja* in much the same way that Bonnin
used copies of letters (SAI memoranda, for example) for mass distribution of
critical ideas and platforms, a tactic shared by pan-tribal organizations such

as the Brotherhood of North American Indians, founded in Washington, DC by Richard C. Adams, a member of the Delaware Tribe in Oklahoma, in 1911.[44] With a mailing list that at times numbered 1,000 from across the United States, *Wassaja* reached an incredibly diverse public. The circulation of Montezuma's paper together with the copied letters Bonnin sent out reflect the connection these activists made between the political power of epistolary culture and the territory magazines and journals occupied in the context of an expanding print market during the early twentieth century. Both sent materials out to Indian people and white progressives. Both believed these audiences were eager to stay informed about efforts to reshape U.S. federal policy with regards to Indian affairs. Much of their intellectual labor, and that of others in their cohort, took the form of writing, copying, and mailing out a varied set of texts to engage Native and non-Native people alike.

Because many issues of *Wassaja* showcased letters from readers, the paper itself functioned as a critical site for public discussions by Indian people regarding national issues, such as policy and education, as well as more localized concerns, such as land rights and reservation management. In a typical issue, Montezuma might publish three to four letters from readers as well as his responses to previous letters. As an arena for exchange, *Wassaja* enabled Montezuma to strategically represent himself as an Indian intellectual with a desire to be seen as an Indian leader and facilitator, and a citizen. At the same time, it honored different representations of Indianness by including a range of Indian voices. He did this not to impose an essential Indian subjectivity, but rather to open the idea up for discussion in order to fight for citizenship, which he believed would allow for individual choices of how to be an Indian in America. In addition to including articles by other Indian intellectuals and letters to the editor from across Indian Country, Montezuma used an array of genres and literary styles throughout the pages of *Wassaja*. By including prose and poetry as well as liturgy and parody, *Wassaja* spoke to the tastes of a broad range of readers and invited them to discuss *all* things Indian in whichever mode struck their fancy. Montezuma used political cartoons and allegories, parody and sarcasm as tools to make his criticism both clear and lighthearted, so that his readers might better discern fact from fiction, and real Indians from the popular misrepresentations of them that figured so prominently in other public arenas.

Not every issue of his newspaper featured U.S. citizenship as a subject for editorial comment. But most did. In March 1918, Montezuma wrote: "[T]he country must first make him a free man, and then give him his citizenship. But to give him citizenship with conditions attached to it is not citizenship that is enjoyed by true American citizens. That is false freedom!" Like "spurious citizenship," Montezuma's "false freedom" rhetoric questioned the federal government's definition of citizenship. Indeed, the changing and uncertain nature of the relationship between the federal government and Indian tribes complicated the issue of citizenship for Native people during the early twentieth century. *Wassaja* became an important outlet where Montezuma and others voiced their discontent regarding this history and raised questions regarding sovereignty because the United States continued to break many treaty obligations.[45]

Like many problems that confronted and continue to confront American Indians, the denial of citizenship can be traced to the treaty-making system. During the colonial period, France, Spain, and Great Britain had distinctive ways of dealing with Indian tribes, but despite their differences they established a pattern of treaty making that provided the basis for dealing with these tribes as independent and sovereign nations. The United States continued this early treaty-making tradition until the landmark Supreme Court *Cherokee Nation v. Georgia* (1831) case, where Chief Justice John Marshall redefined tribes as having the fraught status of "domestic dependent nations." This ruling became fundamental for establishing a process by which Indians had to work through Congress in order to change the nature of their relationship to the federal government. This was a crucial precedent, as the Cherokee Cases of the early nineteenth century inaugurated a new era of diminished sovereignty for Indian nations, at least from the perspective of the U.S. government. In 1871, an act of Congress banned treaty making between tribal nations and the federal government, which further weakened the inherent sovereignty of tribes as independent and foreign nations. During this period, individual Indians were defined as citizens through their relationship to their tribe. Therefore, Indians were citizens of tribal nations, and in order to become a citizen of the United States, they had to give up the rights of citizenship established by their individual tribes, a trade-off many did not want to make.[46]

For those who voluntarily disassociated from their tribal nations, citizenship remained legally ambiguous until 1884, when John Elk (living in Omaha, Nebraska) tried to vote and was refused. In the case of *John Elk v. Charles Wilkins*, the U.S. Supreme Court upheld this decision and ruled that an Indian could not become a citizen of the United States by abandoning tribal allegiance without the consent and cooperation of the U.S. government. Only through an act of Congress would all Native people receive the rights of citizenship. Many pro-assimilation activists, both white and Indian, who worked through Indian reform organizations during the late nineteenth and early twentieth centuries, believed citizenship was needed to secure legal protection, which was essential to becoming part of American civilization. Despite the fact that the Dawes Act of 1887 supposedly granted citizenship to Indians who separated themselves from their tribes and began living on their own private property, most Indians involved in the allotment process were not actually eligible for citizenship *until* they received titles to their lands, which came after a twenty-five-year trust period. This sort of waiting is exactly the type of policy that angered Montezuma, and was fodder for the articles in *Wassaja*.[47]

For *Wassaja* readers, the racialization of citizenship remained an important sticking point, especially because of the peculiar, extra-constitutional position in which Native peoples were subject (or not) to U.S. law. For instance, the 1790 U.S. Naturalization Act limited citizenship to any "free white person," and in 1857, in *Dred Scott v. Sanford*, the Supreme Court confirmed that no one of African ancestry could be a citizen. Then the Fourteenth Amendment was passed to make African Americans citizens by granting citizenship to "all persons born or naturalized in the United States, subject to the jurisdiction thereof." But at the same time, the amendment denied citizenship to Native people because most Indians were regarded as not subject to the jurisdiction of the United States, but subject to the jurisdictions of their particular tribal nations. In 1883, in *Ex Parte Crow Dog*, the Supreme Court affirmed the exclusion of Natives under tribal government from the jurisdiction of the United States, and finally this jurisdictional exclusion began to break down with the seven major crimes act of 1885, which placed certain crimes committed on tribal lands under federal jurisdiction, but did not extend citizenship in any universal way to Native people. These restrictions regarding eligibility for citizenship were based on class and race, as much as gender given its invisibility as a category, which aimed to keep women outside of the new body politic as well. During Montezuma's lifetime, these sorts of exclusions remained a central concern of Native people who sought both political and social recognition. The roles Native people could play in American society dominated the debates they waged on the pages of *Wassaja*.[48]

One article, "Life, Liberty & Citizenship," written between 1917 and 1918 against the backdrop of World War I, offered a sentimental digest of the song "America." It had served as a de facto national anthem for the United States before the adoption of "The Star-Spangled Banner." Montezuma's text invokes the opening lines of "My Country, 'Tis of Thee" to point out how "Let freedom ring" rings differently for the colonized subject. Indeed, for him, an analysis of this song produces a cultural space where he charts the racialization of Indian people as different from white citizens. He suggests that when Montezuma and other Indians listen to the song, it cannot be heard without sadness coming to mind. He writes, "It is sad and it often makes tears come to my eyes, because the song carries me to my people, to the wigwam, to the reservation, and I see my race enslaved by those who sing this song of liberty." Here Montezuma criticizes those who sing this song to constitute an American nation for embracing what can only be understood as spurious liberty for the Indian in America. For Montezuma, the moment of listening becomes marked by apprehension. "When I hear this song it makes my heart grow and I wonder if it is true." Such wondering does not lead to wonderment but rather to the harsh reality that the song's title does not recognize how "'My country-' it was once" and the truth of Native peoples' dispossession.[49]

Montezuma's article continues working through other stanzas in "America" to expand on how the song takes him back to "the wigwam" and the space of the reservation to question the concept of liberty. He uses call and response to incite the reader to listen to the song, and to hear it as he does. "'Land where my fathers died-' that is true, but does 'Freedom ring from every mountain side?' – where are you and where am I as children of the real Americans?" In this passage, Montezuma points out the flaw in the song's aim to define America as unified by the principles of liberty, despite a history of conquest where he notes "*my* fathers died." He flips the genealogical logic of the founding moment of America by claiming Indian fathers as foundational figures rather than the white "fathers" of Washington, Jefferson, and the like. The fathers of his relatives then become the "real Americans" missing from the song's narrative about freedom because of their deaths. Montezuma's inversion supports his next claim, that this "Sweet land of liberty" is one in which Indian people "are not free; liberty is not ours to enjoy." Analyses and claims like this appear throughout other issues of *Wassaja*.[50]

The denouement to "Life, Liberty & Citizenship" evokes the concept of liberty framed through the prism of Montezuma's life as a young boy in Arizona. He engages his Indian readers more explicitly by shifting from first person singular "*I* remember the days when *I* was with my people in Arizona" (emphasis mine) to first person plural:

We lived out in the open air on mother earth. We drank the water from the spring, we lived on nature's provisions and killed game for meat. No one owned anything. There was no law. To us there was no such thing as time; we went where we pleased. No one disputed our claim. We all lived as one. That is liberty.

This moment enables Montezuma to recall the past in idyllic and precapitalist terms, especially given that U.S. "citizenship" would not have been an issue to confront given that "there was no law." In his utopian framing, *real* liberty is neither produced out of American civilization (and, we might surmise, documents that authenticate that civilization, like the U.S. Constitution), nor celebrated by a national anthem. Instead, liberty is identified with a people and a place apart from the United States, and one not yet claimed by the hegemonic practices of colonialism. Still, this conception of liberty is locked in the past, thus acknowledging the capitalist present and its shifting terrain for Montezuma.

As a Christian, he calls out to God to reestablish the missing link between liberty and citizenship for Indian people. His call indicts the United States as a Christian nation, by noting how Native people are caught in the grasp of American nationalism, but ironically, not entitled to any of its benefits. He writes, "God help us to redeem our people by being free, by gaining our liberty and by being citizens."[51] This call for redemption fits within Christian teachings, and is not just symbolic, but also material. Indeed, the act of redeeming can be one in which an individual (or a group) seeks recovery of something that has been pawned or mortgaged. It can also refer to the payment of an obligation. In this latter case, Montezuma implies that it is not *really* God so much as the U.S. government that must redeem Indian people, and by extension redeem the nation itself. His version aims to become the real national anthem. Here we get something of what Montezuma sees as the relationship between Christianity and citizenship. Like abolitionist William Lloyd Garrison, who saw the Constitution as "a covenant with death" and "an agreement with hell," he is appealing to an authority that is higher than the U.S. government to grant Indians their rights.[52]

Despite *Wassaja's* popularity and the power of its rhetoric, it was a costly enterprise for Montezuma to keep up. Each month, he spent at least $20 of his $200 income to keep the newsletter in print. In 1922, he wrote to Pratt complaining of the financial strain *Wassaja* had placed on his life. "I have to forego many things in order to get out the Wassaja. I want to take a rest in Arizona a month, but now I can see no way to do it. If I were wealthy I do not think I would think very much about my people, but being poor, my heart yearns for them." So despite his career as a doctor and a penchant for wearing tuxedos for public talks, Montezuma did not consider himself a wealthy man. He chose to use his personal income toward Indian activism; a consequence was that he cut back on other material goods. Like Bonnin, he put himself and his income to work on behalf of *all* Indian people.[53]

Montezuma's financial records for *Wassaja* include a collection of subscriber slips and sixteen pages of a mailing list. Although these records are not a complete accounting of Montezuma's readership, the range of his newspaper's circulation provides a window into the types of readers who paid for annual subscriptions, suggesting the range of publics *Wassaja* reached. For example, within these records William Bergen of Martin, South Dakota is listed as the earliest subscriber from June 1916, and He Dog of the Rosebud Agency (also located in South Dakota) is listed as a subscriber for December 1920, near the end of the paper's run. Within these four years, *Wassaja* fought a discursive battle against the Indian Bureau, called for widespread reform with regards to Indian citizenship, and celebrated the feats of Native American soldiers who fought in World War I. Between 1916 and 1920, times were not easy at Rosebud and other agencies across the United States in terms of employment opportunities, given the lack of sufficient government subsidies. At the same time, an increase in schooling also meant an increase in literacy, so there were many readers on reservations who may have been drawn to *Wassaja's* more radical politics and who favored the abolition of the BIA.[54]

Within his subscription list, it is well worth considering specific individual subscribers in order to assess *Wassaja's* influence and the different circuits through which Montezuma was able to address a range of publics. These figures are not meant to be representative of entire groups or movements, but nevertheless, the readership appears to have been very diverse in terms of race, geography, class, and gender, to suggest the reach of Montezuma's ideas, if not their acceptance. Still, knowing a bit more about who subscribed to *Wassaja* can suggest the particular ways Montezuma's ideas were understood. Looking at these readers also reveals the ways literacy contributed to establishing and maintaining different types of regional and national Native communities.[55]

Like Gertrude Bonnin, who commented that she "[w]as glad to refresh myself in reading the Wasaja,[*sic*],"[56] Indian activists and intellectual leaders Henry Roe Cloud, Henry Standing Bear, and Charles Eastman, founding members of the SAI, all subscribed to *Wassaja*. However, the vast majority of Indian people who subscribed did not necessarily know Montezuma personally, nor is there much evidence to suggest they were active in national politics with regard to Indian issues. Yet these are people who may have engaged in a discourse of pan-Indian activism through their reading of *Wassaja*. Harvey Ashue, a member of the Yakima Indian Nation who lived in Wapato, Washington, a town founded in 1885 by Indian postmaster Alexander McCredy, along with Moses Archambeau from Greenwood, South Dakota, and De Forest Antelope of Watonga, Oklahoma, were *Wassaja* subscribers between 1918 and 1919. De Forest Antelope, an 1895 graduate of Haskell Institute, commented that the paper was "a fine example of the educated, industrious and successful Indians."[57]

In addition to lesser known Indian men and women, there were also subscribers who stand apart from the figures already mentioned because of their unique circumstances. Two men in particular wielded different sorts of power within Indian Country and American history. The first is Jackson Barnett (1856–1934), a Creek from Henrietta, Oklahoma. Known as the "Richest Indian," he became an American folk figure because of the discovery of oil on his allotment in 1912. In 1920, Barnett married a white woman, and by 1923, he had left Oklahoma to live in a mansion in Los Angeles, California. The second is Chief Plenty Coups (1948–32), a Crow. Montezuma's mailing list locates him in Pryor, Montana, which in 1996 became a National Historical Landmark where visitors could see the chief's log house. Not far from "the Homestead of Chief Plenty Coups, one of the last and most celebrated traditional chiefs of the Crow Indians," is the Chief Plenty Coups Museum. More a political and cultural leader than a man of material wealth like Barnett, Plenty Coups became very visible in American society. He was well known for allying the Crow with whites out West against their traditional enemies, the Sioux and Cheyenne, who opposed white settlement of the area.[58]

Plenty Coups came to the attention of other Indian people and the wider American public when he was eulogized, by Scott Leavitt of Montana, in the House of Representatives on Saturday, March 5, 1932. Leavitt framed his remarks by noting it was "not customary" to announce the passing of a private citizen to Congress "unless he has achieved distinction of the first order." Leavitt began by speaking about his personal relationship with Plenty Coups and on "his history," written by Frank B. Linderman, "a Montana author." Leavitt celebrated as well as flattened the life of Plenty Coups in his eulogy by defining him as a product of Americanization, noting how he was "in truth a symbol of the absorption of the American Indian into the citizenship of the United States." This is an odd comment to make given how Plenty Coups' actions have often been interpreted as a strategic way of engaging with the forces of colonialism in order to guarantee Native survival, which is not quite the same thing as working toward or accepting the "absorption of the American Indian" into the United States. Both Montezuma and Plenty Coups were known for their ability to lead Indian communities and to productively engage white audiences. Both contributed to a discourse of Indian citizenship that sought political power while maintaining Indian cultures and traditions.[59]

Despite a large number of Native readers, non-Indian readers constituted the largest number of subscribers to *Wassaja*. From enthusiasts who collected "Indian things" to Indian agents working for the U.S. government, to vaudeville performers, business magnates, and progressives, a wide range of white readers was interested in what Montezuma had to say about Indian affairs. Fellow Chicagoan Edward E. Ayer, the uncle of Elbridge Ayer Burbank, who painted and sketched more than 1,200 Native Americans from 125 tribes, was a successful business magnate, museum benefactor, and avid antiquarian collector of books, original manuscripts, and materials relating to the history and ethnology of Native American peoples, and an devoted *Wassaja* reader. E. E. Ayer's collection, one of the founding donations to the Newberry Library in Chicago, contains a number of his nephew Elbridge's works, including the most complete collection of *Wassaja* issues. Both Ayer and Burbank were enthusiastic collectors of Indian artifacts, which included Native newspapers.

Another subscriber, John R. Brennan, was affiliated with the Oglala Sioux Indian Reservation. Brennan came to the Black Hills in 1876, and helped found Rapid City, South Dakota. Later he was appointed agent at the Pine Ridge Reservation on November 1, 1900. He served in this post until July 1, 1917. According to Montezuma's records, Brennan was a subscriber in 1919. However, it is likely he could have read *Wassaja* even earlier because the two men became acquainted in 1904 following a train accident in Chicago involving some "show Indians" from Pine Ridge who were traveling on their way to perform for William "Buffalo Bill" Cody's Wild West. Montezuma tended to the Native men injured in the crash and recorded details for their lawsuit against the railroad companies involved as a medical witness. One might imagine a situation where an Indian agent like Brennan picked up the paper and ended up reading polemical articles sought to undermine his very existence.

Life at Pine Ridge could have produced just such an occasion for Brennan, who could have discussed the issue with Native subscribers living on the reservation. Perhaps an even more unusual subscriber is Fannie Beane from Wagner, South Dakota. One of the earliest comediennes of vaudeville, Beane began her performance career in 1875 and later married Charles Gilday in 1883, after which they performed together. We might speculate that Beane's interest in *Wassaja* was based on her life in Wagner because there were many other subscribers from that town. Perhaps she wanted to participate in local debates and conversations about news from Indian Country. In addition, she may have subscribed because her performances were likely to involve some themes and events based loosely on Indian-white relations.[60] Another *Wassaja* reader who, like Beane, was interested in representations of Indians and their history was Joseph K. Dixon (1856–1926).

Dixon photographed American Indians between 1908 and 1923 on behalf of the Wanamaker Expedition sponsored by the department store of the same name. Today, the Wanamaker Collection holds over 8,000 images of individuals from over 150 tribes. Dixon was in charge of the "Educational Bureau" for his employer and sponsor, Rodman Wanamaker – son and partner of John Wanamaker, who founded both the Philadelphia and New York stores. Dixon's interest in Montezuma's newsletter was partially motivated by a desire to market Indianness. In addition to photographs, Dixon worked with the Wanamaker store to sell "goods" such as mages, artifacts, and recorded sounds that "explorers" brought back from Indian Country; such goods became part of elaborate displays and theatrical productions staged in both the Philadelphia and New York department stores, which capitalized on the myth of the vanishing Indian. One such production narrated "A Romance of the Vanishing Race." In 1914, four years before he subscribed to *Wassaja*, Dixon succeeded in publishing *The Vanishing Race* (with illustrations by R. Wanamaker), published in New York by Doubleday.[61]

One can imagine Dixon read *Wassaja* with mixed feelings. On one hand, he may have liked the idea that this particular Indian intellectual sought to incorporate Indians into America as proper capitalist citizens, and on the other hand, he may have worried about a loss of authenticity whereby "Indianness" disappeared under the cloak of American citizenship. In actuality, Dixon and Montezuma were fundamentally at odds in their goals: the former needed the large government apparatus of the reservation system to better navigate among Indian people in search of *real* Indian things to sell, and the latter was committed to abolishing the Indian Bureau because he saw its mismanagement and mistreatment of Indian people as a perpetual problem. For Montezuma, citizenship and capitalism remained central issues in the newsletter, and were useful sites of engagement for a white businessman like Dixon, who wanted to market Indian things and to learn how to market *to* Indian people. This latter aim fit neatly into the goals of Pratt and other white progressives, who understood Native incorporation into U.S. society as political, social, and also economic – and as much about production as consumption.

Another entrepreneur who read *Wassaja* was William Bishop from Port Townsend in northwest Washington. A logger and a capitalist, Bishop helped create the Northwest Federation of American Indians (NFAI) with his son Tom. The NFAI was organized in 1913 by landless tribes in Puget Sound to resolve their status as tribes and to assert their treaty rights. Thomas G. Bishop of the Snohomish tribe was their first leader. After the Treaty of Point Elliot in 1855, tribes such as the Duwamish, Samish, Snoqualmie, and Snohomish did not remove to the assigned reservations but instead continued to live along the shore, lakes, and rivers in the area. This was also the era of Gifford Pinchot and the Forestry Service's efforts to practice conservation in U.S. forests, which did reduce opportunities for exploitation of prime timber lands, so private timber companies had to look for other forested areas, which may have been another factor influencing these tribes to remain in their ancestral homelands.[62] They preserved their tribal identities despite the fact that the U.S. government declined to recognize them. Bishop was a *Wassaja* reader who would have been concerned about changes in federal policy affecting tribal nations in the Northwest, and he could use the paper to promote the work of the NFAI in 1919.[63]

Perhaps the most infamous subscriber was neither an Indian nor a performer, but certainly an entrepreneur and industrialist: Henry Ford (1863–1947). He may have celebrated the self-publishing work of Montezuma because of his own recent venture in publishing the *Dearborn Independent*, which he had acquired in 1918.[64] Ford may have even met Montezuma; the latter made frequent trips as a lecturer to towns in Michigan close to Ford's hometown of Dearborn. Without more to go on, it is difficult to know for sure why Ford, or any other readers for that matter, subscribed to this paper and to know what they took away from it. Perhaps Ford was attracted to Indians for what he saw as exemplars of a simpler and purer version of rural life. Reynold Wik makes clear that Ford idealized a preindustrial and rural American way of life while also promoting a machine that dramatically transformed rural America. Not only did he create Greenfield Village, he also promoted square dancing among workers in his plants to promote or preserve what he saw as traditionally American. In addition, in 1927, Ford traveled to the Amazon, where he built "Fordlandia." There his intention of growing rubber became an export of America itself, including golf courses, ice cream shops, bandstands, indoor plumbing, and Model Ts rolling down broad streets.[65] Perhaps the pull of nostalgia and the trappings of Indianness motivated Ford to read the paper. Montezuma was by no means against capitalism, and so it is possible that the two men saw eye to eye on matters of industry regarding both material production and the rights of the individual.[66]

Certainly the articles printed in *Wassaja* produced a marked increase in demand for Montezuma as a lecturer and writer in other arenas. Plus, the popularity and circulation of the newsletter expanded his already large volume of correspondence. One letter that Montezuma sent to Pratt mentions the 100 letters or so that Montezuma had received and his intention to answer every one. This flow of letters generated an epistolary culture, which ran beside and in relation to Montezuma's newsletter. By 1920, Montezuma received letters on a daily basis from Indian people located across the country. They were his readers. And he, as "Wassaja" (the editor), took on a sort of "Dear Abby" role within Indian Country using his newsletter whenever he published responses to their queries. Within this forum, Montezuma could listen to and address what his readers asserted in their letters. Many of them insisted on better living conditions, more educational and work opportunities, as well as a voice in how to shape the future of the Indian Bureau. As a cultural space, *Wassaja* represented a diverse array of Native voices. The paper was not just the vision of its creator; it became central to the work of other Native reformers during Montezuma's lifetime.

Epistolary Production in Relation to Print Culture

The epistolary culture networks that connected Indian leaders and white allies depended on regular correspondence as well as printed talks and articles. For Montezuma, these texts became the sites of political discourse that linked these forums with the publishing work of *Wassaja*. On average, Montezuma received letters daily from national pan-tribal reform groups like the SAI and the smaller and less well-known Brotherhood of North American Indians. Overall, most of the letters he received were at least a page long. It appears he kept up with the onslaught by writing back within a day or two, which could mean he sent and received upwards of fifty or more letters a year with each person who wrote to him. Within Montezuma's personal archive, there are three Indian cultural producers with whom he corresponded who represent distinctive voices, geographical areas, and political positions that showcase the significance of correspondence in shaping Montezuma's political work as well as the efforts and writings of other Indian intellectuals during the period. Like Montezuma, Arthur C. Parker (1881–1955), John M. Oskison (1874–1947), and artist Wa-Wa Chaw (1883–1966) succeeded in having their work published during the early decades of the twentieth century. They also wrote letters regularly to Montezuma and subscribed to *Wassaja*.

Parker was one of Montezuma's primary correspondents. In 1916, Parker published "The Civilizing Power of Language" in the *Quarterly Journal of the Society of American Indians*. This essay reflects many of the topics and concerns Parker and Montezuma articulated throughout their extensive correspondence. Parker's text meditates on the role language plays in culture and civilization. He argues using English as an inter-tribal language will help Indian people adopt "a new mental vision and new grasp of the world." Parker's argument is a provocative one. In one sense he is writing against a scientific discourse that suggested Indians had not yet evolved the skills to properly speak English, and revises it to suggest Indian intellectuals can use English to be the best leaders by communicating with each other and the wider world. His article lists contemporaries, like Rev. Sherman Coolidge and Charles Eastman, along with leaders from earlier eras like John Ross and Alexander Posey. Parker sees these men as examples of those who have successfully bridged the gap between savagery and civilization.[67]

According to Parker, language is the preeminent tool of culture and power. He writes, "The American Indian mind 'borrowing' an alien tongue uses it with all the power that civilization has given it. That tongue of a 'civilized' people compels a thought expression and *weave* consistent with civilized ideals." By learning to speak and write in English, Indians can harness the power of American civilization, which is to be more civilized and more American. Parker emphasizes how learning enables language acquisition to function as the site where history, tradition, and culture can be accessed: "Used to its fullest extent it brings the native mind a hold on the literature, rhetoric, history and science of the race that evolved the language." Parker also remains carefully ambivalent about the hegemonic power of language. He does not discount the possibility that an Indian's prior knowledge may inflect the ways he or she learns English. "*But* woven in the understanding and in the thought fabric of the Indian is a thread and often *warp* all his own, lending an embellishment that is distinctive" (emphasis mine). Relying on the metaphor of sewing, Parker is able to refashion the trope of the warp. Here the thought fabric of the Indian pushes against the more dominant, white grain by remaining embedded in new ways of speaking, reading, and thinking that have come about through learning English – a process that is itself a critical part of the colonial legacy of the United States. Furthermore, Parker reflects the common ground he shared with Montezuma regarding their work as Indian intellectuals within Indian Country and the United States. Both men used the tools of their education to reform the system that had forced Native children to abandon their indigenous languages to be educated only in English.[68]

Parker implies that the ways Indian people think are distinctive (warped, but in a good way), and that they cannot be lost or overcome by the process of learning English. Parker marks learning itself as a fluid and mutable process, and therefore, it becomes possible that an Indian using English may add a "warp all his own" to improve the language and larger (American) culture. When Parker suggests "language is the outward expression of the thought life of a culture" and he pulls words from that language like "savagery," "brutality," "barbarism," "civilization," "education," and "reason" to say these are "but ways of thinking," his logic balances two important notions. One is how language (as a tool of culture) can be used to educate and uplift an individual, and the other is how the best representatives of "the Red race" will become "active forces in civilization" through their eloquence and logical ways of speaking and thinking in English. Finally, the "hidden transcript" in Parker's message suggests English can represent the dominant culture and practices of oppression, and still be adopted and actualized to the benefit of those who seek to disrupt, overcome, or resist that dominant culture. In fact, he argues a special position of power may be occupied by the Indian speaker of English when he writes, "No Roman orator ever spoke with such vigor, no senator of our Congress ever clothed his speech with greater beauty than the orators and writers of the Red race who spoke or wrote in English." The direct comparison to the Roman orator and the U.S. senator enables Parker to frame the "orators and writers of the Red race" in the context of American culture as well as above it. The reference to Rome suggests Native people are the antiquity of American civilization and also living examples of its greatness who need to be recognized. This strategy is similar to Montezuma's rewriting of the song "America," and it seems likely that Montezuma would have agreed with Parker's comparison. In many ways, this way of engaging history and language was a primary goal of Montezuma's newspaper and a theme in his correspondence. Montezuma used letters to comment on current events, and he led by example. Both Parker and Montezuma believed Native intellectual leaders needed to be bold, eloquent, and logical in their command of English to make convincing arguments about their place in the world and their future, a notion that John Oskison would also have supported.[69]

Oskison was Cherokee, a political ally, and fellow writer. However, Oskison's early years diverged from Montezuma's in a number of ways that would influence the trajectory of his writing career. Born near Tahlequah (part of the Cherokee Nation West) as the son of John Oskison, an English immigrant, and Rachel Connor Crittenden, part Cherokee, he went to Willie Halsell College, where he met and became lifelong friends with Will Rogers. His first significant publication appeared early, in 1887, as a short story. Unlike Montezuma, Oskison was developing his writing craft before he went to college. After graduating in 1894, Oskison went to Stanford University, where he received a BA in 1898. A year later, while he pursued graduate work in English at Harvard, Oskison won a writing contest sponsored by *Century Magazine*, which marked the beginning of his professional career as a writer.

Between 1897 and 1925, Oskison published at least twenty stories, many of which circulated in popular American magazines such as *Frank Leslie's Monthly*, *McClure's*, and *Collier's*. Oskison frequently wrote about contemporary Indian affairs, although unlike Montezuma his writing reached a broader and mostly white American audience through his fiction pieces. Between 1906 and 1912, he worked as an editor for the *Ossining* (New York), *The Citizen*, the New York *Evening Post*, and as an associate editor for *Collier's*. In these positions, Oskison accessed different sorts of networks driven by print culture that were tied to the white publishing houses of the East Coast. Oskison also joined the Temporary Executive Committee of the American Indian Association in 1911, and later played an active role in the SAI, which may be when he first met Montezuma. Much of Oskison's career in journalism and creative writing was broken up by military service during World War I. Before the war he wrote regularly to Montezuma while he worked for *Collier's*. The tone of their exchanges is friendly and familiar, and the content is often political. Because creative rather than polemical writing appealed to Oskison, he soon turned to writing mainly novels. These fictional works still tackled social issues facing Native people. Before this latter part of his career, Oskison published a more overtly political essay that reflected the ideals he and Montezuma shared on the topic of race leadership.[70]

Written in 1917, Oskison's "The New Indian Leadership" focuses on language and the rise of Indian leaders. Unlike Parker, Oskison's text finds the utterance of English "halting" when "you realize that you are listening to an alien whose tongue fumbles the language." He also dramatizes the problem of Indian leadership at the time, an issue that consistently occupied pages of *Wassaja* and Montezuma's letters as well as annual meetings of groups like the SAI. In one passage, Oskison reflects on the interplay between different generations of Indian people as centered around the use of different languages at an Indian meeting where "the old Indians [were] giving up their ceremonial pipes and their right to speak the first word, and the younger people, equipped with the white man's language and instructed in his ways, [were] reaching forward timidly and awkwardly for the leadership." For Oskison, the young people "equipped" with English use it for utilitarian purposes, rather than for uplift as Parker and Montezuma suggested.[71]

Oskison describes an "unsmiling interpreter" who is a young graduate of Carlisle "with arms straight down at his sides" and a "mask-like" face. The role of the interpreter suggests a loss of understanding separating the two generations. A young man cannot understand the old chief without a translator, and the older generation cannot understand the necessity for these young people to speak English. Despite this distance, Oskison imbues the scene of translation with emotional power: "Even through the colorless rendering of the young interpreter, the old man's words get you by the throat, and you wonder at a power of self-control which permits of quiet talk of the day when he shall have 'passed over the border,' leaving a great weight of trouble for his people behind." We cannot know exactly what is left behind when one generation dies and another takes over. Oskison implies ambiguity is critical in how to read this reservation meeting as a gathering of the young and the old. Given that *Wassaja* was printed in English, and Montezuma wrote letters only in English, it seems likely that he saw himself as part of this new generation of Indian leaders, the ones who must speak English and might require an interpreter to speak with their elders. These young people were Montezuma's intended audience.[72]

Oskison's emphasis on loss in the essay further departs from the ideas of Parker and Montezuma given that both promoted the path of education in English (and white politics and culture) as integral to a future for Indian people in America. At the same time, Oskison's work is very much in dialogue with the forum Montezuma created with *Wassaja*, and many of the ideas he expresses in his personal letters. In particular, the explicit ways Oskison challenges the U.S. federal government and his call for new leaders are akin to the messages Montezuma conveyed to many of his correspondents. Montezuma continually wrote to other Native people about the need to increase the number of "leading Indians" among them because this had to happen if they ever wanted to put an end to the abuses of the Indian Office and the reservation system.[73]

Out of the West Coast, Montezuma found support for *Wassaja* from another Indian activist, artist Wa-Wa Chaw. Both the tenor and length of her letters demonstrate that she was also a dedicated friend. In addition, as a fundraiser for *Wassaja* she planned many of Montezuma's campaigns and spoke out for the needs he represented. Like Montezuma, Wa-Wa Chaw was separated from her birth parents and raised by a white woman. Born in Valley Center, California in 1883, Wa-Wa Chaw was given by her Luiseno mother to Miss Mary Duggan of New York City, who was traveling nearby at the time of Wa-Wa's birth. Duggan returned with the young girl to New York, where she raised Wa-Wa Chaw with the help of her brother, Dr. Cornelius Duggan. Wa-Wa Chaw developed her skills as an artist at an early age by doing medical sketches for Dr. Duggan. Later, she painted huge canvases in oil, some of which depict the social problems she observed. Wa-Wa Chaw became an advocate for Indian and feminist causes and was well known for her social writings as well as her art. She married a Puerto Rican businessman named Manuel Carmonia-Nunez who was active in the Cigar Workers' Union, and who shared some of Wa-Wa Chaw's leftist political beliefs. She died at the age of eighty-three, in May 1966, in the Greenwich Village neighborhood of New York City. Although Wa-Wa Chaw had grown up in New York City, she never lost sight of her California roots.[74]

During the 1920s, Wa-Wa Chaw published poetry and other writings in the *Magazine of the Mission Indian Federation*, a periodical created by an organization of the same name, headed by a white man, Jonathan Tibbets, of Riverside, California. This monthly magazine's slogan was "Loyalty and Cooperation with Our Government." The frontpiece for the September 1922 issue features a poem by Wa-Wa Chaw titled: "Haunted Brains."

The message of "haunted brains" reappears in every stanza, reminding readers that Indians, whether alive or dead, have "no rest" because they have "haunted brains." Wa-Wa Chaw's haunting refers to the "mysteries of unknown plans" that may visit "during the night." Inside the magazine, readers gain further insight into what these "unknown plans" are by reading an article by an author known only as "Grizzly Bear." This piece points out that in California Indians are forced to live on small reservations: "not by treaty but by simple agreement."[75] These tenuous agreements could certainly haunt one's brain, if not also impede social and economic stability and cultural vitality.

Wa-Wa Chaw's efforts were well supported by this magazine because, like the Indian Board of Cooperation, the Federation had a large body of Indian members, even if non-Indians dominated many of their meetings.[76] In addition, the reference to a piece by "Grizzly Bear" may point to another magazine, *The California Grizzly Bear*, which was published by the Native Sons of the Golden West – a group of Indians who were active in the San Francisco area. During the first half of the 1920s, they campaigned to publicize the needs of California Indians. There were many other groups active in the cause of the California Indians, which Wa-Wa Chaw would have found support through and made connections with, such as: the Indian Welfare Committee of the Federated Women's Clubs (who Bonnin corresponded with on a regular basis), the California Indian Rights Association, Inc., the Northern California Indian Association, and the Women's Christian Temperance Union.[77] It is no coincidence that these different groups had formed and become active in the early decades of the twentieth century. By 1909, the Commonwealth Club of San Francisco was investigating the matter of Indian rights and the lost eighteen treaties, which had come to light in 1905 and started to sway public opinion in favor of Indian sovereignty – over their land and culture. By maintaining correspondence with Wa-Wa Chaw, Montezuma would be able to access the Indian reform networks of the West Coast, which would help him publish pieces in *Wassaja* that would reflect Native issues from across the United States.[78]

Like *Wassaja*, many issues of the *Indian Mission Federation Magazine* focused on the future of Indian people, especially those in California and concerns related to land and treaty rights. The magazine also featured poetry and fiction pieces. One poem, "Courage," by Wa-Wa Chaw represented the Federation's aims as well as her politics:

> Joyful through hope your motto still be
> "Human Rights and Home Rule."
> What glories will Mission Indian Federation unfold to you.
> Be of good mind, and cheer – take courage.

Like the writings inside the magazine, Wa-Wa Chaw's poem reminds readers that "human rights and home rule" are intimately linked. In this sense, California Indians were fighting not only for suffrage but also for sovereignty, and one might speculate that readers of the magazine could have been *Wassaja* readers, and vice versa. Copies of several issues among Montezuma's personal papers suggest he was one such reader, indicating a print network that circulated from and between Indians living on the West Coast and in the Midwest. In fact, the September 1922 issue features an article by Carlos Montezuma about the "Evils of Indian Bureau System." The next issue (October 1922) included an article on "Indian Bureau Economy," where Montezuma argues the "Indian Bureau philanthropy is an economical farce." Montezuma's articles in the *Magazine of the Mission Indian Federation* expressed political views he and Wa-Wa Chaw shared. Both sought ways to preserve "human rights and home rule," although he opted for nonfiction and she poetry. Through their letters they wrote frequently to each other about such topics.[79]

In many cases, the letters Montezuma exchanged with Parker, Oskison, Wa-Wa Chaw, and other Indian activists and leaders, operated as material ways to organize a proliferation of Indian intellectual and cultural production during the early twentieth century that became part of broader networks of reform, and as a space to test out the ideas they would later make public in published pieces. By 1920, Montezuma corresponded regularly with the Yakima Indian Commercial Club and the American Indian Tepee Christian Mission – both were based in the state of Washington and both wrote about the essential role *Wassaja* played as a site for exposing the "naked truth."[80] These letters connect directly to Montezuma's newsletter and provide evidence that he and Charles Eastman were members of the American Indian Tepee Christian Mission's advisory board, an organization that functioned as an interdenominational home for Indian children while they attended public school. The local board of trustees was also led by Rev. Red Fox Skiuhushu and Lucullus V. McWhorter, the latter of which would later work closely with Luther Standing Bear as an editor and political ally for the actor's reform work based out of Los Angeles.[81] This is but one other example of how far-reaching pan-tribal efforts were toward social change and how political reform relied on the movement of epistolary culture across the United States. Montezuma often put himself at the center of this production and circulation.

Private and Public Opinion

By 1916, an increasing number of influential and highly educated Indians saw themselves as responsible for leading not only their specific tribal nations but *all* Indians, as one unified race. This was no easy task. Montezuma believed that promoting and maintaining pan-Indian organizations like the SAI was an important part of this undertaking, and because of this the need for continuous communication among members was critical. Using letters and circulars, individual organizers reached out to each other and new members, as well as like-minded organizations and publications. This type of circulation suggests an important link activists made between correspondence and the fight for citizenship, and better access to education as well as changes in how the BIA managed Indian people. SAI members and leaders also worked to maintain ties to white reformers who could be useful allies.

From 1916 to 1918, Gertrude Bonnin confirmed the need for racial unity in the letters that she sent to Montezuma. On December 10, 1916, while living in Fort Duchesne, Utah, Bonnin wrote to Montezuma regarding their shared work as members of the SAI. "I know you are doing all in your power to help our race. It saddens me, that in our earnestness for a cause, we do not take time to study our various views and to manage some way to unite our forces. All Indians must ultimately stand in a united body, for their own protection." Here Bonnin affirms a shared mission to continue the "earnestness" of their cause to fight for citizenship and reflects on the difficulties of pan-tribal organizing. Her repeated call for more unity represents a theme within Montezuma's own correspondence, his newsletter *Wassaja*, and the rhetoric of other Native periodicals during this period.[82]

Bonnin's letter also highlights the stakes of their representational politics as Indian intellectuals. She writes, "You are right about Indians standing together, for the best interests of our race. We must work this year as we have never worked before.... I am glad you have your *Wassaja* for October ready. You are wise to be very cautious. Every step must be sure. Wisdom can never be too wise." Caution and care were critical components of the work Montezuma, Bonnin, and other Indian intellectuals produced: articles, pamphlets, conferences, and public lectures had to be carefully crafted to educate the American public about broken treaties, the failings of the Dawes Act, and increasing poverty on reservations. At the same time, her reference to caution and the notion that "wisdom can never be too wise" suggests an awareness of the fine line separating an individual's presentation from the tactics she or he might use as an advocate for a larger pan-tribal Indian body.[83]

In a subsequent letter from October 1918, Bonnin again turned to issues of representation and racial leadership. "I am glad you wrote to assure The Tomahawk of our good will toward their interests." The Tomahawk Publishing Company was run by the Minnesota Chippewa from 1918 until 1926. *The Tomahawk* published articles about Indian citizenship, the administration of Indian affairs, and, in particular, specific issues related to Chippewa natural resources.[84] In addition to letters, articles, and poems by Chippewa writers like Theo H. Beaulieu and others like Leta V. Smart, *The Tomahawk* published materials promoting the SAI and the Tipi Order of America, which meant features written by Montezuma and Bonnin.[85] Montezuma's writing for *The Tomahawk* was a different example of his reach and the types of networks utilized by Native activists to promote social change during this time.

In addition to seeking and finding support from Native publications, Montezuma, like Eastman, Bonnin, and Standing Bear, wrote regularly to white reformers. Their time and money were critical for supporting Indian causes. A small handwritten note, perhaps a rough draft of a letter, from Montezuma addressed to Mr. and Mrs. Daniel Smiley at Mohonk Lake, New York makes plain why he was unable to present at their upcoming Lake Mohonk Conference. "As one of the members of the Society of American Indians I am forced by previous arrangement to forego the pleasure of accepting your kind invitation to present." Despite strong ties established and maintained through extensive letter writing, Montezuma's correspondence also reveals ambivalence and hesitation. Here he pulls back from becoming more involved with the Lake Mohonk Conference. This reformer circle had been established by Smiley as a space where white, often elite, Northeastern progressives shared strategies of "uplift" for the people of so-called less fortunate races. Since the 1880s, the Conference addressed the "Indian Question" by promoting assimilation through education and policy changes, like the Dawes Act. Contemporary to such a conference were other discussions, events, and conflicts that reflected how the "Negro" and "Oriental" questions were addressed within American society. Perhaps Montezuma's choice to forego attending the conference represented a shift in strategy and a move toward more independence from the white progressive movement. Such a move would make sense given Montezuma's distrust of large bureaucracies in contrast to individual efforts and localized approaches.[86]

By 1918, under the dark shadow cast by World War I and its hyper-patriotism, Montezuma received a letter emblematic of the strained relations that now existed between many Indian intellectual leaders and white progressives. Sent by Joseph K. Dixon, on behalf of the "National American Indian Memorial Association," the letter called on Montezuma and "every Indian" to manifest "a spirit of patriotism." In it, Dixon asks Montezuma to sign "The Patriotic Sentiment of the Indian." His definition of patriotism reflects his take on a Plains Indian vision, overtly heterosexist and male-centered – a view that dominated the national imaginary during this period. But for Dixon the hyper-masculine warrior aesthetic aimed to encourage Montezuma and other Indian men to sign.

In olden times warriors would go out and fight for their women, their children, their Tepees and their horses when attacked by the warriors of other tribes.... The warrior [who] risked his life in defending the women, the children, the home and common property of the tribe was "patriotic," and the women who urged the warrior to fight [were] "patriotic."

Dixon links this allegorical scene to the present situation (however fraught the connection) by calling attention to national security and World War I. His rhetoric seems wholly unaware of Montezuma's life as an urban

Indian and the fact that his own ancestors originated in the Southwest and would not have lived in tepees. The letter also asks if Montezuma would dare not defend the United States as a nation defined "along the Mexican borders, the Canadian borders, the Pacific Coast or the Atlantic Coast" or "an invasion of your tribe or your reservation." These references to borders imply reservation spaces were understood as within the U.S. nation, rather than as tribal-national sites that could refer to political boundaries based on indigenous sovereignty.

Certainly Montezuma would have read the letter with a great deal of skepticism. In particular, Dixon's passage "The land is one, and the protecting laws are for all, white people, Indians and negroes" would have felt false to Montezuma given that full citizenship was still largely unavailable to Indian people. At this time living conditions on reservations were regularly "invaded" by federal bureaucrats who seemed unable or unwilling to improve basic necessities. Despite these problems, Montezuma *may* have agreed with Dixon's letter concerning the idea of rewarding "rights" to Indians who joined the cavalry to fight for the U.S. military. Dixon assures Montezuma that the Wanamaker expedition was sent out "carrying the flag to all the tribes" and *not* to raise money for the Wanamaker department store, but rather to bring "freedom and prosperity to the Indian." Although this claim is not truthful, Dixon uses it to convince Montezuma to sign "The Patriotic Sentiment of the Indian," and, even more important, to work on his behalf to have other Indians sign it as well.[87] Dixon concludes his letter with somewhat of a request for a favor, by asking Montezuma to "Tell all my Indian friends very frankly that the signing of this document does not mean that they are enlisted … but that it will be an expression to the country of your feelings and … your loyalty to the Government"; one might surmise Montezuma raised an eyebrow in suspicion and wondered why loyalty did not cut both ways. He may have sent a response inquiring: To which Indian *friends* do you refer Mr. Dixon?[88]

Although Montezuma wrote frequently in public about his stance against the BIA, his private letters often reflect on a shared experience of oppression among people of color. As private forums, Montezuma's letters articulate the motives behind opinions he expressed in more public venues. In 1921, he wrote to Edward Janney, a fellow doctor, regarding his "Indian work."[89] He took this opportunity to comment on why he continued to attack the BIA. He also drew an unusual parallel between the Freedmen's Bureau (established in 1865 through the War Department to undertake post–Civil War relief programs and social reconstruction for freed people) and the Indian Bureau (or BIA).

You ask, why I want the Indian Bureau abolished. To give the Indians their freedom and citizenship. Just for the same reason that the Freedmen Bureau was abolished. That one act was the salvation of the Negro race. There is just as much hope in the destiny of the Indians, after the abolishment of the Indian Bureau, as there was with the black people. To-day the colored people challenge the world in their progress.[90]

Despite the fact that the Freedmen Bureau was responsible for and largely successful in providing assistance to tens of thousands of former slaves and impoverished whites in the Southern states and the District of Columbia after the Civil War, Montezuma's parallel offers an implicit critique of Reconstruction in the United States. At the same time, he suggests that despite any failures in the system to assist African Americans in achieving the benefits of full citizenship, Montezuma was inspired by how "colored people challenge the world in their progress" – while he failed to recognize the reach and impact of Jim Crow.[91]

In addition to fellow doctors and white reformers, Montezuma wrote to journalists, with whom he may have felt a special kinship given the challenges and opportunities available to newspaper writers. Throughout the second decade of the twentieth century, Montezuma corresponded frequently and at length with Southern journalist Helen Gilkison (1909–48), whose pen name was Helen Grey. Grey's career as a female journalist through the 1920s and into the 1940s "fell outside the social norm, for women in general, but remained firmly within the expectations for a female journalist." And Grey "wrote with a particular voice, or better, two particular voices. One was strictly informational; the second was chatty and accessible to her reader. These voices were a bridge between the reader and the political world." These two types of voices are present in the letters that Grey sent to Montezuma concerning her views on Indian affairs.[92]

Grey's many letters to Montezuma address him as both a friend and political ally. She often uses turns of phrase she may have read in *Wassaja*. In one letter, she discursively aligns herself with Montezuma by posing a rhetorical question. "Why in the world is an Indian different from any other human being?" They did share similar struggles as writers. Both were striving to publish politically charged articles that aimed to educate and incite Americans to action. Perhaps the frequency of their correspondence and a shared sense of purpose helped them form a distant type of friendship.[93] Grey concludes another letter by affirming this shared purpose, and strikes a less cautious tone than the one Bonnin used. She writes, "We have only now to keep watching and hit hard every time an opportunity offers." Although Grey worked primarily in Louisiana, her writing exposed corruption and injustices Indian people suffered at the hands of the U.S. government throughout the Southwest and Northwest, and her letters to Montezuma often ask for his help in these matters.[94]

Montezuma's letters also recognize Grey's efforts. One in particular discusses her work in support of the Crow and Plenty Coups. In "Congressional Hearings: Neglected Sources of Information on American Indians," Robert Staley uses the Crow as an illustrative case study regarding

Indian diplomacy with the United States. He notes that, beginning in 1908 and ending in 1920, the Crow sent several delegations to present at hearings in Washington, DC in regard to living conditions on the Crow Reservation. "The delegations included both traditional leaders like Plenty Coups as well as representatives of a new generation of educated Crows. Allied with the delegation were the Indian Rights Association, the Washington law firm of Kappler and Merillat, and Helen Grey, a journalist who prompted a separate investigation into conditions on the Crow Reservation." A letter from 1910, from Pratt to Montezuma, fills in the picture by showing the extent to which Montezuma understood Grey's work on behalf of the Crow. Pratt writes, "Mrs. Gray's [sic] efforts have probably done more than anything else to stop a grave wrong against the Crow people."[95] For both Pratt and Montezuma, this is a moment of recognition regarding the power of print. Had Grey not written stories for public consumption about the conditions on the Crow Reservation, it is uncertain whether their delegation to DC would have been met with as much seriousness.

The diversity of Montezuma's writerly contacts, whether they exchanged letters or shared drafts of articles or wrote in each other's publications, demonstrates the degree to which print culture greatly shaped his reform work and became the central venue through which he could express his private and more public thoughts on a range of issues affecting Indian people. In many ways, Montezuma's representational politics would be further tested when he was invited to give public lectures to white groups, as a representative of the Indian race. The following section asks: How and in what particular circumstances were Montezuma's public performances similar to and divergent from those of other Native performers and Indian intellectuals during the early twentieth century? And what are some important conclusions that might be drawn from these similarities and differences?[96]

The Lecture Platform *not* the Show Indian

Examining how Montezuma conceived of language as performative, as he engaged with both Americanization and Indianization discourses, requires a discussion of how performativity, for Montezuma, was a tool of resistance and criticism. Montezuma's views regarding Native performance as a political or even an economic strategy departed from and aligned with Eastman, Bonnin, and Standing Bear in some important ways. The networks this cohort accessed were contingent upon systems of patronage and patriarchy, so any success Montezuma and other Native intellectuals experienced was often the exception and not the rule for Native people in the United States. *Wassaja* offers one perspective into the lives of a large proportion of indigenous people, on reservations and elsewhere, given the large number of Indian readers who subscribed to the periodical. Montezuma's other writings and speeches also use a rhetoric that harkens back to a precontact utopia, which became a central theme that he used to account for change over space and time, and to argue for recognition and incorporation of Native people as American citizens. Rather than focusing on performance spectacles created by "Buffalo Bill" Cody, which required an "Indian play" that horrified him, Montezuma strove to use other kinds of texts – less showy, perhaps, but equally performative – to promote an ideal of "Indianness" that was not locked in the past but rather addressed the current problems confronting Indian peoples.[97]

It was through/by his own performances that Montezuma intervened in a racialized imaginary that had been created and dominated by white Americans. In shaping his ideal of Indianness through performance, Montezuma confronted, appropriated, and redeployed the concept of race to fashion his own articulation of Indian life – like Eastman he was the object and subject of his public talks and his written texts. Both types of performances circulated to audiences during a time of heightened desire and awareness of Indianness in the context of an "Indian craze," which Elizabeth Hutchinson dates from 1890 to 1915.[98]

In the early decades of the twentieth century, Indian people had in large part been separated from Indianness, as a series of powerful literary and visual representations of Indians had taken root in the minds of many Americans. It materialized on the bookshelves of schoolhouses and public libraries. It was the stuff of the Wild West shows and the ethnographic displays at fairs and was becoming a genre in the burgeoning film industry. Whether they saw a film, a popular entertainment show or an opera, or purchased a songbook or a novel, Americans and Indians participated in reproducing dominant expectations regarding what it meant to be an Indian. The problem for Montezuma and others arose when these expectations continued to trap Indian people within particular misrepresentations based on preexisting tropes and images, which denied them a modern presence in the making of America and the necessary political access points to revise the structures responsible for reproducing these misrepresentations.

During these years, Native American baskets, blankets, and bowls could be purchased from department stores as well as "Indian stores," dealers, and the U.S. government's Indian schools. At the same time, there was widespread enthusiasm for collecting Native American art and sponsoring exhibits that used indigenous handicrafts as models for non-Native artists interested in exploring formal abstraction and emerging notions of artistic subjectivity. Hutchinson argues the Indian craze succeeded in convincing policy makers that art was a critical aspect of "traditional" Native culture worth preserving. The notion of traditional Indian art became intertwined with a discourse of authenticity, which compressed Indian people into a particular time (the past) and space (the West) – which was reflected in the rhetoric used in Dixon's 1918 letter. This practice paralleled contemporary expositions of ethnological display that flattened out the complexity of indigenous experience when it grouped distinct aboriginal peoples together under one derogatory category of "savagery."⁹⁹

Aspects of these arts and cultural activities were also performative, and this troubled Montezuma. For him, the problem with both show performances and the preservation of Indian arts and crafts stemmed from the possibility that these activities might continue to trap Native people in particular times and spaces, which were anachronistic at best and mythical at worst. The irony of the Indian craze for Montezuma lay in the fact that although he condemned such performances, he also performed in all types of positions that drew on similar expectations for authenticity defined through Indian embodiment.

Although many Indian people contributed to the Indian craze as producers and consumers of art, there were still others, like Montezuma, who felt the discourse of authenticity surrounding this moment undermined alternative ways Native people could be viewed, especially as thoroughly modern citizens. Montezuma represents an Indian intellectual perspective that condemned popular entertainments, which exploited Indian performers. While he promoted a political position based on the definition of Indian people as *one* race, he was equally concerned about an Indian art market that relied on nostalgic representations of Indianness. Montezuma's views contrast with how many progressive whites and Indians supported the preservation of Indian culture, including Charles Eastman and Gertrude Bonnin, and to a different extent Luther Standing Bear. They believed such preservation could positively influence the American public and lead to widespread political reform in Indian affairs. Instead, Montezuma thought the best way to "awaken the public" about "the real condition and workings that are debasing and not improving" life for Indians was not through pageantry, film, or drama, but rather hinged on the power of oratorical prowess.¹⁰⁰

To counter these damaging performances, Montezuma became a performer of Indianness. Throughout his lifetime, Montezuma delivered many lectures on Indian affairs, Indian history, and his own life. As we have seen, he began lecturing as early as 1888 while a medical student, and continued to book engagements (at least upward of three times a year) until his death in 1923. Although he spoke in front of almost all Indian audiences at national meetings for the SAI and would travel out of Chicago to talk to local church groups and women's organizations in Michigan and other Midwestern states, he was most successful at booking local venues sponsored by Chicago businessmen and reform groups. The impact of Montezuma's oratory was based both in the moment of presentation itself and (for many cases) afterward when he published and circulated reprints of his speeches.

Read in the context of a contemporary, such as Charles Eastman, Montezuma's participation in a public performance of Indianness eschewed the use of "costuming," in a way that Eastman did not. Also, because he was a man, audiences' expectations turned on different fictions than those that

FIGURE 5. Carlos Montezuma portrait (circa 1915). Public Domain.
Carlos Montezuma, 1896, Photo Lot 73 06702900, National Anthropological
Archives, Smithsonian Institution.

Gertrude Bonnin would have confronted (such as the ever-popular Indian
maiden or princess). Montezuma understood that an Indian speaker's
authority was linked to a particular *image* of the Indian body and through
it the idea of ethnic authenticity, yet his response to this paradoxical connection was to wear Western clothes (most often the tuxedo as pictured,
which Bonnin chided him for) in the hope of distinguishing his performance from those by "show" Indians. Certainly his appearances were no
less performative.

For Montezuma, the recirculation of his speeches was as important as his
clothing in regard to his self-presentation and the reception of his ideas. For
example, in 1915 he delivered a speech, "Let My People Go," in Lawrence,
Kansas for the Society of American Indians' Conference, which was later
published in *The American Indian Magazine* (January–March 1916, Vol. 4,
No. 1), and then reprinted in various newspapers. It was also read during
the first session of the Sixty-Fourth Congress in 1916, and included in the
Congressional Record. Later editions of *Wassaja* depict Montezuma on the

front page holding up this pamphlet in one hand and pointing to the Statue of Liberty with the other. In these ways "Let My People Go" expanded past its original performance moment to embody Montezuma's representational politics within different forms of print culture. Furthermore, in this expansion one can see that although Montezuma did not rely on Indian dress as a performance tactic, he did harness another aspect of performativity, which was the strategic repetition and redistribution of his speech to different audiences.[101]

"Let My People Go" merges the genre of the sermon with that of a political treatise, and begins with a rhetorical flourish: "From time immemorial, in the beginning of man's history, there come echoes and re-echoes of pleas that are deeper than life." The use of "re-echoes" here is suggestive. "Re-echoes" represents the softer and perhaps more subtle reiteration Montezuma believed was necessary for narrating a long history of "man's inhumanity to man." This ethical narrative is central to how he frames the oppression of Indian people at the hands of European imperialists and American colonizers. The relation of one inhumanity to the next and conversely the relation of one claim for justice to those that have come before the original claim is made are heard through echoes, and heard again through "re-echoes." He aims to connect this oppression, the pleas that require reechoing to be truly heard, to a history that transcends the time and space of the United States. This technique enables him to simultaneously engage with the ethics of progressive Christian uplift and universalism defined by cultural pluralism to challenge strict and oppressive race and class categories defined through the body and biology.

Montezuma's message in "Let My People Go" quickly shifts from the more abstract idea of "re-echoes" to argue the SAI must do more than present papers, hear discussions, and shake hands each year to effect real social and political change in the lives of Indian people. He moves to a material claim to criticize the failings of the Indian Bureau.[102] When he refers to "the bloody and gloomy days of Indian history," he uses the moment of his speech, 1915, as one opportunity to remind his audience that "public sentiment was against the Indians." People had believed Indians "could not be civilized," nor could they be educated, because "they were somewhat like human beings, but not quite within the line of human rights." But, in 1915, this is no longer true. Like other Christian Indian political activists of the period, Montezuma characterizes this earlier era as devoid of spiritual influence because "the only hope was to let the bullets do the work, cover up the bloody deeds and say no more" because "God and humanity were forgotten." He relies on the faults of this past to distinguish himself – and his peers – as distinctly empowered, by themselves and by God, to do more for their people in the present.[103]

For members of the SAI, who were the first to hear his speech, this was a turning point in political activism among Indians from different tribes throughout the United States. A critical tool used by SAI members and represented by Montezuma is the privileging of the word "Indian" as a racial and political category over that of tribe/nation. Montezuma shores up his use of the term by another reference to the past: "Patient, silent and distant the Indian race has been these many years." By noting that "the Indian race" had been silent and distant *before* this historical moment, he suggests the "Indian race" is now at an important crossroads in its development.

Montezuma's strategic use of *Indian* as an essentialist trope highlights the founding objective of the SAI as a pan-tribal Indian organization. Both his titular nod to "My" people and comments throughout that make continuous references to Indians as one "people" unify individual Indians against a larger white "civilization." He urges his audience to see that "Our position as a race and our rights must not be questioned.... there is only one object for this Society of Indians to work for, namely – 'Freedom for our people.' " Although this strategy elides cultural, linguistic, economic, and geographic differences based on tribe and the issue of sovereignty for tribal nations, Montezuma still addresses the system of paternalism the U.S. government used to deal with tribes. Within this context, *Indian* is problematic as a monolithic and an ahistorical term, but also useful for bringing together distinct indigenous peoples into one group in order to guarantee citizenship for *all* Native people. In addition, with his call for freedom, the speech suggests a lateral connection to W. E. B. Du Bois and the work of the National Association for the Advancement of Colored People (NAACP). In this other context, the language of race, performed by black orators, is mapped onto the performance of Indian speakers, like Montezuma, for other purposes.[104]

According to Montezuma, another benefit of relying on the category of Indian to define people into one racial group is "to tackle prejudice." He suggests this begins by playing "the samecard [sic] as the other fellow." This process is further aided by eliminating "Indian Everything" and the perpetuation of misrepresentations of Indianness.[105] Montezuma recognizes how in order to put an end to these misrepresentations, Indian people will need to engage with an American society that sees them as "Indians" first and citizens second. He expresses a careful ambivalence regarding how SAI members might strike a balance between becoming part of American society while maintaining cultural positions as Indians when he writes: "Push forward as one of them, be congenial and be in harmony with your environments and make yourselves feel at home as one of the units in the big family of America. Make good, deliver the goods and convince the world by your character that the Indians are not as they have been misrepresented to be." This was a fraught strategy for many Indian intellectuals who tried to incorporate themselves into different parts of American society. SAI secretary Gertrude Bonnin's autobiographical writings express the struggles she encountered as an Indian and a woman traveling throughout elite circles of white society. Not a part of the SAI but tied to performance are Luther

Standing Bear's writings that recall his first experiences with white culture, new technologies, school, and work, with a mixture of excitement and fear. Indeed his life was necessarily performative, in that he could not escape white discourse. He had to perform it in order to be legible, which sometimes meant wearing regalia. For Montezuma, performativity was linked more to the politics of uplift and civilization. In each case, no matter how an Indian intellectual presented himself or herself there was an ideology to contend with and through which to frame their lives for their white audiences.[106]

Montezuma continued to struggle with the concept of Indian as a racial category and a discursive form in his speeches and his writings. In "What It Is to Be an Indian," produced around April 15, 1921, he engages with "Indian" for rhetorical effect and as an object of analysis. Montezuma represents Indianness in the abstract and how it has changed over time. He begins by referencing a distant, precontact utopia, and shared past, akin to "Let My People Go," when he writes that "the earth's surface" was a "wilderness prolific in all that marks the absence of civilization," where "an Indian" in an "untutored way, lived and loved another race of beings." Montezuma also refers to Columbus's arrival and his mistake in misnaming "these naked natives, Indians,"[107] to draw on a moment other Indian writers like Simon Pokagon and Charles Eastman used in their work. This beginning enables his narrative to focus on the fraught origins of the term *Indian* in ways familiar to both Indian and non-Indian readers.[108]

His essay does more than replay the Columbus story. Montezuma inserts himself into the narrative directly by addressing his audience and posing a question: "[W]ho in this audience tonight has looked at me without having the thought 'Indian' in mind?" This shift compels Montezuma's listeners to recognize the present rather than the past of Indian people. His readers can then consider how what "it [was] to be an Indian" confirmed or denied their expectations. Unlike Simon Pokagon, Charles Eastman, and Gertrude Bonnin, Montezuma was *not* dressed in "Indian costume" for any of his public lectures given that he opted for tuxedo jackets instead, and so his question immediately forced listeners to confront their own expectations for Indian speakers based on gender, race, and class. Certainly, the tuxedo is a type of formal wear and another sort of costume; one that embodied upper-class white mobility and Americanness. By wearing this "costume," Montezuma conformed less to expectations regarding Indianness and was more consistent with white expectations for elite style, even while he performed a revised articulation of Indian subjectivity. Although he wore a tuxedo, this moment of "dress up" distinguishes Montezuma from other Indian intellectuals who wore some sort of Native "costume." Despite his dress, Montezuma's speech recognizes other ways his audience *still* cannot see him without having "Indian in mind." Clearly he's performing a different narrative, with its own pitfalls and kinds of efficacy, given that he is still

Indian, even while clothed in the fine accoutrements of upper-class white modernity.[109]

Montezuma follows this question about appearance and identity with an important, if ambiguous, statement regarding his self-presentation, which is similar to Du Bois's notion of the double-consciousness. "I have the appearance of the life as we have divided it for the purposes of this occasion." The "we" in this sentence bears a heavy burden. Given that addresses like these were intended for diverse audiences, the "we-ness" being invoked can refer to a shared Indian history or the "we-ness" of American society. Or perhaps, the "we" and "this occasion" taken together serve as a bridge between different histories separating Indian and American audience members. The reference to "division" also lends an opaque quality to his statement given that both Indians and white Americans had (in their writings, speeches, performances, and other arenas) imagined a divide between the "untutored" Indian of the past and the "civilized" Indian of the present. For Montezuma, the concept of division was embodied in the figure of the educated Indian. Because he saw himself as a representative case study, one who had been "part of" an Indian community, but who now lived as a member of Chicago society, Montezuma would be legible as urban, modern, and also Indian, and his words told a story to make this clear to his listeners.[110]

Montezuma's speech continues to focus on division to explicate how Indians have been separated into two categories. He defines one as "The Columbus Indian," who is "highly endowed, first of all with a sense of appreciation of kindness manifested toward him" and who is "without any of those highly developed vicious traits and habits which mankind acquire in civilized life as a result of the competition which naturally grows out of the close relations the individuals sustained to one another in the social state as the communities became thickly populated." Montezuma defines the second category of Indian in terms of decline: "it is necessary to consider how little at this time he had advanced intellectually beyond that of a child." During the post-contact period, Montezuma argues, Indians can only be understood in terms of their relation to "the civilized pale face," and in this context, to be an Indian is to be "a child" – and later a ward of the state after the creation of the BIA.[111]

His text underscores the hierarchical relation between white and Indian peoples in describing the "meeting point, between the North American Indian" and the "pale face." He recognizes how both parties were "ignorant of the nature and character of the other," while he examines the shortcomings of the "pale face." Montezuma's speech shifts at this point from an analysis of the term *Indian* to a critique of the white settler "with all of his pride of ancestry and conceit of wisdom." He emphasizes how the characterization of Indians as savage was a project of colonialism whereby white people lacked "true knowledge of the Redman, whom he called a savage after having made him such." Montezuma's key phrase "having made him such" unveils the discursive work being done to define the Indian in uncivilized terms. Furthermore, by pointing out the constructed nature of the term *Indian*, located in the figure of "the pale face" who was "dominated by his insatiate greed and his haste to profit at the expense of the simple-minded and unsuspicious native," Montezuma challenges his audience to sympathize with the mistreatment of Indian people because of the oppressive reach of capitalism and colonialism.[112]

Montezuma further highlights how characterizing Indians as savage justified the dispossession of their rights. He underscores this point by noting that "the selfish and unfeeling pale face pioneer" was flawed because he "neither knew nor cared" about the "virtues which are characteristic of the good man of civilization" and were "endowed" in "this native man." Like Montezuma's other spoken and written texts, "What It Is to Be an Indian" attacks oppressive practices associated with settler colonialism by not only pointing to physical violence and material loss but by emphasizing how these were buttressed by language loss and renaming. His arguments as an Indian intellectual contribute to a larger war of words that other Indian writers participated in during the period.[113]

Montezuma's speech concludes with a direct assault on white supremacy. He writes, "Prior rights of occupancy, or even the right to live, are not to weigh against the wishes of the pale face." By 1921, he argues, the Indian has a "still keener sense of how his life is shaped and checkered by the fact that he is known as an Indian. He is tainted with a name." This return to Indian as both a name (signifying a particular referent) and a word (an abstract noun) links Indianness as a discursive formation with the materiality of the body, but in problematic terms: "The word carries with it a sort of 'attainder of blood.' It is full of meaning strongly impressed on the memory of those who are inclined to accept the one-sided stories which make up so much of the tales of Indian life." Memories and the imagination are central vectors through which an Indian person may be understood as an Indian. Individual Indians must struggle against certain expectations and previous representations of Indianness (however false or flawed). At the same time, each has to contend with the corporeal and genetic stakes of being an Indian in America.[114]

For Montezuma, "Indian" could be narrativized and biological. Through the doubling of his names, he is Indian as Dr. Montezuma and also as "Wassaja." Bringing these two realms of knowledge together, he works to unseat the power of each and blur the line separating them. Importantly, his speech emphasizes the power of an Indian subject to speak back to the biological category of Indian (as measured and defined by blood quantum, which was a common practice during this period, especially in the era of eugenics), to the constructedness of the word as a container for an array of narratives and tropes, and to the inevitability of a life lived as a performance.

For Montezuma, putting on his tuxedo to make a speech to a white audience was a choice to perform, but also to think about being Indian because there were people watching and sitting in judgment.

Montezuma argues an Indian man is limited by the frames through which Indian bodies become legible because he "is scarcely recognized without his feathers, paint and warlike accoutrements," visual markers Montezuma chose never to use himself. In this instance, Montezuma uses recognition in a double sense.[115] On one hand, he suggests "Indianness" is recognizable only if certain visual economies are put into play, and on the other, he argues Indian and non-Indian people alike recognize the occasions when Indians dressed in feathers and paint are performing certain representations of Indianness that may not align with lived realities. In this sense, performance itself becomes a strategy through which Indian people can negotiate various expectations of Indianness. The ways performing Indianness can be strategic calls to question the notion of ethnic authenticity as well. Indeed, to be an authentic Indian, for Montezuma, took discursive form when the actual bodies of Indian people served to authenticate them as representing Indianness. What remained up for discussion was who judged and how to judge the authenticity of Indian performances.[116]

Although Montezuma succeeded in constructing his own representations of Indianness and worked to shift how both Indians and non-Indians conceived of the political and social realities of Indian people in America, he also operated within a particular historical moment. In that moment, representations limited the definition of "Indian" because of the production and consumption of things Indian and Indian things.

Montezuma believed the modern Indian subject (citizen) "was willing to draw the veil between the past and present and to make the most of the opportunities that were open for the improvement to his condition," and yet he could not escape "the indifference of the civilized pale face." The veil, of course, is integral to Du Bois's notion of the double-consciousness, which on the level of rhetoric acts like an echo in Montezuma's speech. Furthermore, the result of indifference, Montezuma suggests, leaves the Native "un placed among men." To be "un-placed" figuratively invokes a history based on the dispossession of Indian land, resulting in other losses of culture, political agency, and language. To be unplaced is to struggle for recognition regarding a larger problem of access to social standing, cultural relevance, and political freedom. What again remains at the center for Montezuma is the issue of citizenship.[117]

Wassaja's Departure

In December 1922, after living for twenty-six years near the South Side, Carlos Montezuma left Chicago. He had witnessed the cityscape change from being dominated by horses to being filled with automobiles. He had traversed neighborhoods, interacting with immigrants from Northern Europe, and then with people of Slavic and Mediterranean backgrounds before his own neighborhood became populated with black migrants from the South. In fact, during the last years of his life, the sociopolitical atmosphere of Chicago was one of ethnic tension due to competition among these different groups. One might wonder how Montezuma experienced the Chicago Race Riot of 1919, a major racial conflict beginning on July 27 and continuing until August 3. Dozens of people died and hundreds were injured during what many considered the worst of approximately twenty-five racially motivated riots during the "Red Summer of 1919" – so named because of the violence and fatalities across the nation. Perhaps Montezuma's awareness of this violence helped sharpen his critique of the United States and the provocative parallel he had already drawn between Kaiserism and Indian Bureauism in an article he wrote for *Wassaja* in 1917.[118] As a large number of Indian men joined the U.S. military to fight in World War I, despite the fact that they still faced legal and social discrimination, Montezuma's commitment to citizenship only strengthened. As a highly educated doctor and practicing Protestant, he saw himself, in the words of Charles Eastman, as "an Indian" and also "an American." He wanted others to have this same right.[119]

After reading through hundreds of Montezuma's personal letters, it is easy to recognize his handwriting and why "spurious citizenship" was important enough for him to write down, if only on a scrap of green paper. Both the note and the object he wrote it on serve as reminders of the sometimes fleeting but also critical battlegrounds where Indian intellectuals honed their positions to fight for citizenship and to weigh in on debates about cultural authenticity and Indian identity. Reading more carefully into Montezuma's engagement with epistolary culture reveals how Indian writers and readers were integral to this fight, and how they worked together to change not only American policy and society, but the future of Indian Country as well.

Decades after his death in 1923, Native people would pay tribute to Montezuma's voice and activism in the "Wassaja Award," provided by the Native American Journalists' Association (NAJA) to individuals who make extraordinary contributions to Indian journalism. The award was named after Montezuma's monthly newspaper because of "his strong editorial stand."[120] Rupert Costo, who was known to some, if not many, of NAJA's founders, named his own paper "Wassaja" (published in the 1960s and 1970s) after Montezuma's periodical.[121] These forms of recognition demonstrate Montezuma's legacies as a leading Indian intellectual, rabble rouser, and journalist whose contributions to print culture and political activism were crucial during the early twentieth century.

Notes

1   Carlos Montezuma, "What It Is to Be an Indian," in Carlos Montezuma Papers [hereinafter CM Papers], Box 9, Folder 3, Newberry Library, Chicago, IL.

2   For two excellent histories that focus on the SAI and that include information about white reformers' groups, see: Lucy Maddox, *Citizen Indians: Native American Intellectuals, Race & Reform* (Ithaca, NY: Cornell University Press, 2005) and Hazel Hertzberg, *The Search for an American Indian Identity: Modern Pan-Indian Movements* (Syracuse, NY: Syracuse University Press, 1971).

3   Although relatively little has been written about Carlos Montezuma, there are two biographies that reconstruct much of his life. See: Peter Iverson, *Carlos Montezuma and the Changing World of American Indians* (Albuquerque: University of New Mexico Press, 1982) and Leon Speroff, *Carlos Montezuma, M.D.: A Yavapai American Hero* (Portland, OR: Arnica Publishing, 2004).

4   President Calvin Coolidge signed the Indian Citizenship Act into law on June 2, 1924, a year after Montezuma died. The Act was proposed by Representative Homer P. Snyder (R) of New York. Although the Fourteenth Amendment guarantees citizenship to persons born in the United States, this does not apply to those who are "subject to the jurisdiction thereof," a clause that excluded indigenous peoples and made the "Snyder Act" necessary.

5   My framing of Montezuma's writings and speeches relies on scholarship from the history of the book and print culture; see the following. David Martinez, ed., *The American Indian Intellectual Tradition: An Anthology of Writings from 1772–1972* (Ithaca, NY: Cornell University Press, 2011); Robert Warrior, *The People and the Word: Reading Native Nonfiction* (Minneapolis: University of Minnesota Press, 2005); Philip H. Round, *Removable Type: Histories of the Book in Indian Country, 1663–1880* (Chapel Hill: University of North Carolina Press, 2010); Lisa Brooks, *The Common Pot: The Recovery of Native Space in the Northeast* (Minneapolis: University of Minnesota Press, 2008); Maureen Konkle, *Writing Indian Nations: Native Intellectuals and the Politics of Historiography, 1827–1863* (Chapel Hill: University of North Carolina Press, 2006); Barry O'Connell, ed., *Son of the Forest, and other Writings by William Apess, a Pequot* (Amherst: University of Massachusetts Press, 1997).

6   Carlos Montezuma, "The Light on the Indian Situation," an address for the Society of American Indians Conference, at Ohio State University, October 5, 1912, CM Papers, Wisconsin State Historical Society, Madison, WI.

7   Carlos Montezuma, *Wassaja*, June 1917 (microfilm) courtesy of the Newberry Library, Chicago, IL.

8   For more on this earlier period of Native writing see the following: Brooks, *The Common Pot*; Eve Tavor Bannet and Susan Manning, eds., *Transatlantic Stories and the History of Reading: Migrant Fictions 1720–1810* (Cambridge: Cambridge University Press, 2011); Phillip Carroll Morgan, "'Who Shall Gainsay Our Decision?' Choctaw Literary Criticism in 1830," in *Reasoning Together: The Native Critics Collective*, edited by Craig S. Womack, Daniel Heath Justice, and Christopher B. Teuton (Norman: University of Oklahoma Press, 2008), 126–46.

9   Michael Warner's theorization of the poetic character of public discourse situates my reading of Montezuma's writings and those of other Indian intellectuals

during this time period given that publics and counterpublics emerge through the production of discourses that both affirm and contradict themselves. Building on the theoretical work of Jurgen Habermas and Nancy Fraser, Warner's *Publics and Counterpublics* (Cambridge: Zone Books, 2002) offers a way of thinking about "the public," especially in connection with modernity. Warner distinguishes between audience and public, and notes that in both cases, anonymity (the sociality of strangers) is a key component for distinguishing between publics/counterpublics and groups/audiences that might be defined as "private."

10 In addition to Warner, I refer to Benedict Anderson, *Imagined Communities: Reflections on the Origin and Spread of Nationalism* (London: Verso Books, 1991) for how nations and nationalisms are constituted through the circulation of ideas in print and how different readers create nationalist communities through the collective practice of reading shared texts and discourses.

11 Carlo Gentile was an Italian photographer (b. 1835 in Naples). For a history of captivity and exchange in the U.S. Southwest, see: James Brooks, *Captives & Cousins: Slavery, Kinship, and Community in the Southwest Borderlands* (Chapel Hill: University of North Carolina Press, 2002). A 1951 novel, *Savage Son*, by Oren Arnold, presents a romanticized account of Montezuma's early life, his capture by the Pimas, his adoption by Carlo Gentile, and his eventual Christianization; see: Oren Arnold, *Savage Son* (Albuquerque: University of New Mexico Press, 1951). Also, for more on the relationship between Gentile and Montezuma, see Speroff, *Carlos Montezuma, M.D.*, 27, 89.

12 The School of Chemistry offered the following vocational programs: pharmaceutical, chemical, agricultural, and metallurgical. Montezuma emerged as a writer during his college years. *The Daily Illini* printed an essay he wrote on Aztec civilization on March 4, 1881 and another on "Our Indians" on March 10, 1884. See: Speroff, *Carlos Montezuma, M.D.*, 87–127. This school newspaper was named after the indigenous peoples who originally inhabited (but were forcibly relocated out of) the state of Illinois. Since 1871, The *Daily Illini* has been a mainstay on the University of Illinois campus. Today it is one of the country's largest student-run newspapers, and distributed free throughout Champaign-Urbana. The University also appropriated the "Illini" as a symbol and sports mascot beginning in 1926, and ending in 2007 when the fictional character named "Chief Illiniwek" was retired. The state of Illinois is named for the Illinois River, and by French explorers after the indigenous Illiniwek people, a consortium of Algonquian tribes (also known as the Illinois Confederation consisting of twelve to thirteen tribes from the Upper Mississippi area). *Illiniwek* can be translated to mean "those who speak in the ordinary way," although it is often mistranslated as "tribe of superior men." For more on symbols used by the State of Illinois, see its Web site: http://www2.illinois.gov/about/Pages/default .aspx (accessed June 30, 2010).

13 The Chicago Medical College later became Northwestern University School of Medicine. Susan La Flesche Picotte (a member of the Omaha tribe) graduated from the Women's Medical College of Pennsylvania in Philadelphia just two weeks before Montezuma. Rosa Minoka Hill was another contemporary

woman physician. For more on Montezuma's life as a medical student and doctor, see: Speroff, *Carlos Montezuma, M.D.*, 100.

14 Iverson, *Carlos Montezuma and the Changing World of American Indians*, 12.

15 Fort Stevenson was established on June 14, 1867 by Major Joseph N. G. Whistler of the 31st U.S. Infantry with troops from Fort Berthold. It served as a supply base for Fort Totten, and to protect navigation of the Missouri River and also to help manage Indian populations. By 1889, when Montezuma arrived, it was no longer operating as a military fort. Fort Stevenson had been abandoned on July 22, 1883, but a small detachment remained until August 31, 1883 to dismantle the fort and dispose of public property. The garrison was transferred to Fort Buford and the fort was turned over to the Fort Berthold Indian Agency on August 7, 1883. The Interior Department took possession of the fort on November 14, 1894. For more on this history see: Robert W. Frazer, *Forts of the West* (Norman: University of Oklahoma Press, 1965).

16 Montezuma was a member of the Chicago Medical Society, the Illinois State Medical Society, and the American Medical Association. His five dollar annual membership protected him from malpractice suits and blackmail. He subscribed to the *Illinois Medical Journal*. In Chicago, the challenge was to attract patients in a competitive environment, and so Montezuma developed a special salve, which was a mixture of Vaseline and menthol, a preparation that later became "Vicks VapoRub." This tincture was popular with his patients, who often wrote to him requesting it. For more on his work as a physician, see: Speroff, *Carlos Montezuma, M.D.*, 67, 68, 179, 184.

17 Carlos Montezuma to Mr. Edward Janney, September 26, 1921, Letter, CM Papers, Wisconsin State Historical Society, Madison, WI.

18 For more on the origins of the NIA, which began as the Women's National Indian Association (WNIA), see: Papers of the Women's National Indian Association #9237, Division of Rare and Manuscript Collections, Cornell University Library.

19 Combining education and entertainment with regards to Indian history and reform was not a new phenomenon. Throughout the nineteenth century, various plays narrated events that featured Indian people, sometimes as peacemakers and other times as warriors. Jill Lepore's *The Name of War: King Philip's War and the Origins of American Identity* (New York: Knopf, 1998) argues that acts of war generate acts of narration and both are joined in a common purpose: defining the geographical, political, cultural, and sometimes racial and national boundaries between peoples. She analyzes how different generations of Americans remembered King Philip's War through popular performances of "Metamora or The Last of the Wampanoags" in the 1830s and 1840s. These plays and later performances that featured "Hiawatha" became popular in the late nineteenth century, prefiguring the genre of the Hollywood Western, and existed alongside more spectacular public outdoor events that reenacted battles between whites and Indians. For more on the history of "show Indians" and Indian shows see: Joy Kasson, *Buffalo Bill's Wild West: Celebrity, Memory, and Popular History* (New York: Hill and Wang, 2000) and L. G. Moses, *Wild West Shows and the Images of American Indians, 1883–1933* (Albuquerque: University of New Mexico Press, 1996).

20 For more on specific Indian schools see the following. Robert Trennert, *The Phoenix Indian School: Forced Assimilation in Arizona, 1891–1935* (1988); Tsianina K. Lomawaima, *They Called It Prairie Light: The Story of Chilocco Indian School* (1994); Brenda Child, *Boarding School Seasons: American Indian Families, 1900–1940* (1998).

21 Hertzberg, *The Search for an American Indian Identity*, 141–2.

22 Ephemera in Carlos Montezuma's personal papers includes membership dues, event announcements, and invitations from the Press Club of Chicago, the YMCA, and other organizations, as well as evidence that he was a member of the Chicago Medical Society and the Illinois State Medical Society. See: CM Papers, Wisconsin State Historical Society, Madison, WI.

23 Philip J. Deloria, *Indians in Unexpected Places* (Lawrence: University Press of Kansas, 2004). Deloria focuses on the notion of expectation to critically analyze why Indians "as sports heroes" or "in automobiles" startled a public that expected them either to disappear or to remain frozen in an earlier time. I use this term to point out how popular culture produces political and social meanings, and how expectation reflects power relations that are defined through colonial and imperial relationships between Indian people and the United States.

24 For Indian policy histories see the following. Francis Paul Prucha, *Indian Policy in the United States* (1981); Lawrence Kelly, *The Assault on Assimilation: John Collier and the Origins of Indian Policy Reform* (1983).

25 A degree from Carlisle was equivalent in education to about two years of high school. Curricula were augmented by half of each day being devoted to training in carpentry, shoemaking, printing, blacksmithing, tinsmithing, farming, and other trades. By 1915 the teaching of trades was limited to blacksmith, carpenter, mason, painter, and farmer. One of the more useful sites for uncovering how Indian students responded to their education at Carlisle are the weekly school newspapers; these polemical texts spread the message of Carlisle and confirmed its success. Copies of these papers were sent to every member of Congress, all Indian agencies and military posts, and to most American newspapers. Their distribution helped engage the American public in the issue of Indian education and encouraged Indians outside of Carlisle to track the work being done there. For more on Montezuma and Carlisle, see: Speroff, *Carlos Montezuma, M.D.*, 55.

26 Elaine Goodale Eastman, *Pratt, the Red Man's Moses: The Civilization of the American Indian* (Norman: University of Oklahoma Press, 1935), 196.

27 Some scholars have characterized Montezuma as either an assimilationist or an accommodationist. His views are then taken as aligned with a dominant discourse that argued for the elimination of indigenous languages and political systems, educational and spiritual teachings, as well as cultural and economic practices. For many whites and some Indians, indigeneity was representative of primitivism, and Indian people who refused to "civilize" were defined as inferior Americans because they existed outside of industrial capitalism, Christian doctrine, individualism, and democratic government. I argue Montezuma cannot be framed in terms of this binary because of the complexity of assimilation itself as a set of practices, and because of the presupposition that there is one stable American culture to assimilate into.

28　Carlos Montezuma, "An Indian's View of the Indian Question: Chicago Record," in *Current Literature* Vol. 23, No. 4, American Periodical Series, 1898, 370.

29　Richard H. Pratt to Carlos Montezuma, Letter, Ayer MMS Collection, Box 3, Newberry Library, Chicago, IL.

30　Richard H. Pratt to Carlos Montezuma, September 1899, Letter, Ayer MMS Collection, Box 3, Newberry Library, Chicago, IL.

31　Richard H. Pratt to Carlos Montezuma, December 21, 1908, Letter, CM Papers, Wisconsin State Historical Society, Madison, WI.

32　(July 1924): 529–32.

33　For more see: David W. Messer, *Henry Roe Cloud: A Biography* (Lanham, MD: Hamilton Books, 2009). Also see: Renya A. Ramirez, "Henry Roe Cloud: A Granddaughter's Native Feminist Biographical Account," *Wicazo Sa Review* Vol. 24, No. 2, Fall 2009.

34　Bernd C. Peyer, *American Indian Nonfiction: An Anthology of Writings, 1760s–1930s* (Norman: University of Oklahoma Press, 2007). For a recent biography see: Joel Pfister, *The Yale Indian: The Education of Henry Roe Cloud* (Durham, NC and London: Duke University Press, 2009). I refer to Henry Roe Cloud as a "religious leader" because he was ordained as a Presbyterian minister in 1913.

35　Sherman Coolidge was a founding member of the SAI. He wrote an essay titled "The Function of the Society of American Indians," originally published in *The Quarterly Journal of the Society of American Indians* Vol. 2, No. 1, January–March 1914, 186–90. Reprinted, with a biography of the author, in Peyer, *American Indian Nonfiction*. The speeches of Charles Eastman and the writings of Gertrude Bonnin also illustrated that educated Indians could speak as representatives for Indianness on a national scale.

36　Richard H. Pratt to Carlos Montezuma, May 22, 1909, Letter, CM Papers, Wisconsin State Historical Society, Madison, WI.

37　Richard H. Pratt to Carl E. Grammer, August 18, 1909, Letter, CM Papers, Wisconsin State Historical Society, Madison, WI. For more on Dr. Carl E. Grammer see *Recollections of a Long Life* by Joseph Packard, edited by Rev. Thomas J. Packard (Washington, DC: Byron S. Adams, 1902), 323. On June 8, 1896, the *New York Times* reported that Grammer gave the annual commencement address before the YMCA of Roanoke College. See Charles Howard Hopkins, *History of the YMCA in North America* (1951). The IRA was founded in Philadelphia in 1882 as an American social activist group dedicated to the well-being and acculturation of Native Americans. The IRA remained influential in American Indian policy through the 1930s and involved as an organization until 1994. The management of the IRA fell almost entirely to: Herbert Welsh, Matthew Sniffen, Lawrence E. Lindley, Charles C. Painter, and Samuel M. Brosius, all of whom corresponded with Montezuma. Unitarian minister/journalist Jonathan Baxter Harrison published several books and articles regarding this reform work. See: Jonathan Baxter Harrison, *The Colleges and the Indians, and the Indian Rights Association* (Philadelphia: The Indian Rights Association, 1888) and William Thomas Hagan, *The Indian Rights Association: The Herbert Welsh Years, 1882–1904* (Tucson: University of Arizona Press, 1985).

38 Ober was a representative for the international committee for the YMCA and a missionary leader. He published "The American Association in Foreign Lands – Their Responsibility and Opportunity – Part III" (YMCA journal, *The Watchman*, 1889, 758). Jon Thares Davidann, *A World of Crisis and Progress: The American YMCA in Japan, 1890–1930* (Cranbury, NJ: Associated University Presses, 1998); see: Mary Ann Irwin and James F. Brooks, eds., *Women and Gender in the American West* (Albuquerque: University of New Mexico Press, 2004) for references to Eastman and Ober's correspondence. Also see: Francis Paul Prucha, *American Indian Policy in Crisis: Christian Reformers and the Indian, 1865–1900* (Norman: University of Oklahoma Press, 1976) and *The Great Father: The United States Government and the American Indians*, vol. 2 (Lincoln: University of Nebraska Press, 1984); Margaret Jacobs, *Engendered Encounters: Feminism and Pueblo Cultures, 1879–1934* (Lincoln: University of Nebraska Press, 1999); Bonnie Sue Lewis, *Creating Christian Indians: Native Clergy in the Presbyterian Church* (Norman: Oklahoma University Press, 2003).

39 For more on gender discourse with regards to manhood at the turn of the twentieth century see: Gail Bederman, *Manliness & Civilization: A Cultural History of Gender and Race in the United States, 1880–1917* (Chicago: University of Chicago Press, 1995) and Mark C. Carnes, *Secret Ritual and Manhood in Victorian America* (New Haven, CT: Yale University Press, 1989). On making manhood and the nation, from the Revolutionary War to the 1850s, see: Dana D. Nelson, *National Manhood: Capitalist Citizenship and the Imagined Fraternity of White Men* (Durham, NC: Duke University Press, 1998).

40 Robert Berkhofer Jr., *Salvation and the Savage: An Analysis of Protestant Missions and American Indian Response, 1787–1862* (Lexington: University of Kentucky Press, 1965); William McLoughlin, *Cherokees and Missionaries, 1789–1839* (New Haven, CT: Yale University Press, 1984); Ramon Gutierrez, *When Jesus Came the Corn Mothers Went Away: Marriage, Sexuality and Power in New Mexico, 1500–1846* (Palo Alto, CA: Stanford University Press, 1991); Clyde Holler, *Black Elk's Religion: The Sun Dance and Lakota Catholicism* (Syracuse, NY: Syracuse University Press, 1995).

41 Subscription lists show a rise from fifty cents to one dollar beginning in 1920, CM Papers, Wisconsin State Historical Society, Madison, WI. For more print culture during this period see: Cathy N. Davidson, ed., *Reading in America: Literature & Social History* (Baltimore, MD: Johns Hopkins University Press, 1989); Richard Ohmann, *Selling Culture: Magazines, Markets and Class at the Turn of the Century* (London: Verso, 1996); James Danky and Wayne Wiegand, eds., *Print Culture in a Diverse America* (Urbana: University of Illinois Press, 1998); Gregory M Pfitzer, *Popular History and the Literary Marketplace, 1840–1920* (Amherst: University of Massachusetts Press, 2008).

42 Although Montezuma's Yavapai parents named him Wassaja at birth, he was renamed "Carlos Montezuma" by Carol Gentile after his "adoption" from the Pimas. Posey's persona writing has been the subject of several studies; see: Leona G. Barnett, "Este Cate Emunev; Red Man Always," *Chronicle of Oklahoma* 46, Spring 1968, 20–40; Linda Hogan, "The Nineteenth Century Native American Poets," *Wassaja/The Indian Historian* 13, November 1980, 24–9; Daniel F. Littlefield Jr. and James W. Parins, "Short Fiction Writers of the Indian Territory," *American Studies* 23, Spring 1982, 23–38; Daniel F. Littlefield

Jr., *Alex Posey: Creek Poet, Journalist, and Humorist* (1992); Daniel F. Littlefield Jr. "Evolution of Alex Posey's Fus Fixico Persona," *Studies in American Indian Literatures* 4, Summer/Fall 1992, 136–44; Sam G. Riley, "Alex Posey: Creek Indian Editor/Humorist/Poet," *American Journalism* 1, Winter 1984, 67–76; Craig S. Womack, *Red on Red: Native American Literary Separatism* (Minneapolis: University of Minnesota Press, 1999); Tereza M. Szeghi, "'The Injin is civilized and aint extinct no more than a rabbit': Transformation and Transnationalism in Alexander Posey's Fus Fixico Letters," *Studies in American Indian Literatures* Vol. 21, No. 3, Fall 2009, 1–35.

43   Peyer, ed., *American Indian Nonfiction.*

44   See: Steven Crum, "Almost Invisible: The Brotherhood of North American Indians (1911) and the League of North American Indians (1935)," *Wicazo Sa Review* Vol. 21, No. 1, Spring 2006, 43–59. Crum usefully notes, "Native American people established intertribal or pan-Indian organizations throughout the twentieth century. Existing scholarship has made us familiar with several, including the Society of American Indians (1911), the American Indian Federation (1934), the National Congress of American Indians (1944), the National Indian Youth Council (1961), and the American Indian Movement (1968). On the other hand, there are others we know very little about. Two such organizations are the Brotherhood of North American Indians (1911) and the League of North American Indians (1935), also called the League of Nations, Pan-American Indians" (1).

45   See March 1918 issue, *Wassaja: Freedom's Signal for the Indians,* Special Collections, Newberry Library, Chicago, Illinois. For more on citizenship as an issue for Native people during the Progressive Era see: Tom Holm, *The Great Confusion in Indian Affairs: Native Americans & Whites in the Progressive Era* (Austin: University of Texas Press, 2005).

46   For an account of the early imperial battle for control over "Native" America see: Richard White, *The Middle Ground: Indians, Empires and Republics in the Great Lakes Region, 1650–1815* (1991). For legal history and cases effecting sovereignty see: William McLoughlin, *After the Trail of Tears: The Cherokees' Struggle for Sovereignty, 1839–1880* (1993); Sidney Harring, *Crow Dog's Case: American Indian Sovereignty, Tribal Law, and United States Law in the Nineteenth Century* (1994); Jill Norgren, *The Cherokee Cases: Two Landmark Federal Decisions in the Fight for Sovereignty* (1996); Blue Clark, *Lone Wolf v. Hitchcock: Treaty Rights and Indian Law at the End of the Nineteenth Century* (1999); Tim Garrison, *The Legal Ideology of Removal: The Southern Judiciary and the Sovereignty of Native American Nations* (2002). Beth Piatote shows how Native women in particular, in the case of Canada, lost property and personal rights if they married white men. Such a marriage, according to Canadian law, made them and any children no longer Native. They were now the property of their white husband. See: *Domestic Subjects: Gender, Citizenship, and Law in Native American Literature* (New Haven, CT: Yale University Press, 2013), 17–48.

47   Speroff, *Carlos Montezuma, M.D.,* 8. For the history of the Dawes Act see: Frederick Hoxie, *A Final Promise: The Campaign to Assimilate Indians, 1880–1920* (1984); Janet McDonnell, *Dispossession of the American Indians, 1883–1933* (1996). In regards to John Elk's case see: John C. Eastman, "From

Feudalism to Consent: Rethinking Birthright Citizenship, Legal Memorandum No. 18," Heritage Foundation, Washington DC, March 30, 2006.

48 See: U.S. Constitution, Article 1, Section 2, available online since 1995 at www.usconstitution.net/index.html (accessed May 27, 2011). Also see: Laurence H. Tribe, *The Invisible Constitution* (Oxford: Oxford University Press, 2008).

49 Carlos Montezuma, "Life, Liberty & Citizenship," proof, "Drafts & Galley Proofs," Misc. Writings, CM Papers, Wisconsin State Historical Society, Madison, WI. For more on how African Americans have appropriated "America" see: Eric J. Sundquist, *King's Dream* (New Haven, CT: Yale University Press, 2009). In chapter 5, "Whose Country 'Tis of Thee?" he considers both the historical context in which Samuel F. Smith adapted the melody of "God Save the Queen" to a new set of lyrics in 1831, and the various interpretations, parodies, and performances that have referenced this song in relation to African Americans fighting against slavery, and later segregation.

50 Montezuma, "Life, Liberty & Citizenship."

51 A moment of religious self-recognition in this text appears when he writes, "I remember when I was christened. I saw the Father in his garb, the cross and candles. I did not comprehend what it meant, but after years I accepted the Son of God as my personal Savior, and the Spirit of God works within me. That is the higher freedom that enlightens our souls from God. It teaches us to be faithful to our Creator, be loyal to our country, be helpful to our neighbor and true to ourselves. That is 'Freedom, Liberty and Citizenship.'" The four main figures in this book identified as Christians; however, this moment stands apart because Montezuma explicitly expresses the significance of Christian belief and practice in shaping his thinking.

52 Paul Finkelman, "Garrison's Constitution: The Covenant with Death and How It Was Made," in *Prologue Magazine* (National Archives, Winter 2000), Vol. 32, No. 4.

53 Carlos Montezuma to Richard H. Pratt, Letter, October 4, 1922, Reel 5.

54 Nearly 400 subscribers paid to read these types of stories and well over 50 percent were men, and nearly one quarter were Indian. Although it is difficult to know for sure who may or may not have identified with a particular tribal nation, many subscribers listed addresses that place them in a city or space within reservation boundaries in South Dakota, Oklahoma, and Montana. Individual subscribers also lived throughout the United States in cities like Chicago and New York as well as in newly settled areas of Alaska and Hawaii. CM Papers, Wisconsin State Historical Society, Madison, WI.

55 In addition to individual subscribers, Montezuma's records indicate that news outlets and religious organizations paid for regular subscriptions. These ranged from: the *Arizona Magazine* (based in Phoenix) and the *Dearborn Independent* (in Michigan) to the editors of the *Daily Press* and *Daily Enterprise* of Riverside, California and small rural papers like the *Fargo Farmer* of North Dakota, the American Christian Missionary Society (Cincinnati, Ohio), the Christian Temple (Muskogee, Oklahoma), the Baptist Indian Mission (Lodge Grass, Montana), and the Central Christian Church (San Diego, California). Other subscribers include: the Commercial State Bank of Wagner, South Dakota, the Oklahoma Historical Society, the California Women's Club based in San Francisco, College

Library of Hillsdale, Michigan, and the Bureau of American Ethnology. CM Papers, Wisconsin State Historical Society, Madison, WI.

56 Gertrude Bonnin to Carlos Montezuma, January 24, 1919, Letter. Also, regarding the circulation of *Wassaja* see: two letters from Gertrude Bonnin to Carlos Montezuma, August 26, 1918 and March 12, 1919, CM Papers, Wisconsin State Historical Society, Madison, WI.

57 For references to Harvey Ashue see: "Blind Tribesman Is Injured When Car Plunges off Road Embankment," in *Ellensburg Daily*, April 18, 1930, and for Moses Archambeau see: "Indian Wills, 1911–1921: Records of the Bureau of Indian Affairs," by Nancy Bowen and Jeff Bowen (Baltimore, MD: Clearfield Company, 2007), 174; and for De Forest Antelope see: *The Native American* (an illustrated weekly published by Phoenix Indian School), Vol. 15, 104.

58 See: NPS Form 10–900, page 4, description of present and historic physical appearance: "Chief Plenty Coups Home," U.S. Department of the Interior, National Park Service (1966). Also see: Glendolin Damon Wagner and William A. Allen, *Blankets and Moccasins: Plenty Coups and His People the Crows* (Lincoln: University of Nebraska Press, 1933), 276.

59 "Eulogy of Chief Plenty Coups of the Crows: Speech of Hon. Scott Leavitt of Montana in the House of Representatives," *Congressional Record Seventy-second Congress, First Session* (March 5, 1932). Also see: Frederick Hoxie, *Parading through History: The Making of the Crow Nation in America, 1805–1935* (Cambridge: Cambridge University Press, 1995), especially "Part Two, Making a Nation, 1890–1920," 167–294.

60 For John Brennan as agent see: Richard E. Jensen, *Voices of the American West: The Settler and Soldier* (Lincoln: University of Nebraska Press, 2005).

61 For more on Dixon and Wanamaker with regards to Indianness see: Alan Trachtenberg, *Shades of Hiawatha: Staging Indians, Making Americans, 1880–1930* (New York: Hill and Wang, 2004), chapter 5: "Wanamaker Indians," 211–77. For Dixon's work with Indians in collaboration (beginning in 1920) with the Office of Indian Affairs see: Susan Applegate Krouse, *North American Indians in the Great War* (Lincoln: University of Nebraska Press, 2007), 13.

62 For more on Gifford Pinchot and an environmental history of land use debates see the following. Brian Balogh, "Scientific Forestry and the Roots of the Modern American State: Gifford Pinchot's Path to Progressive Reform," *Environmental History* Vol. 7, No. 2, 2002, 198–225; John M. Meyer, "Gifford Pinchot, John Muir, and the Boundaries of Politics in American Thought," *Polity* Vol. 30, No. 2, 1997, 267–84; Char Miller, *Public Lands, Public Debates: A Century of Controversy* (Corvallis: Oregon State University Press, 2012) and *Gifford Pinchot and the Making of Modern Environmentalism* (Island Press, 2004); Gifford Pinchot, *Breaking New Ground* (Washington, DC: Island Press, 1998).

63 For more on William Bishop and Port Townsend see: Noel V. Bourasaw, ed., *Skagit River Journal of History & Folklore* (Sedro-Woolley, Washington, 2000 to the present), at http://www.skagitriverjournal.com/ (accessed February 22, 2015). For more on the NFAI, see: Cesare Marino, "History of Western Washington Since 1846," in *Handbook of North American Indians, Vol. 7, Northwest Coast* (Washington, DC: Smithsonian Institution, 1990), 169–79;

by David Wilma, August 8, 2000. During the 1950s, the landless tribes of the NFAI joined forces with landed tribes in the Inter-Tribal Council of Western Washington.

64 Henry Ford bought the *Dearborn Independent* (est. 1901) from Marcus Woodruff and added *The Ford International Weekly* to its banner in 1918. It was published using a press Ford purchased and installed in a tractor plant as part of the River Rouge. They began printing in January 1919, and attracted notoriety in June due to coverage of a libel lawsuit between Henry Ford and the *Chicago Tribune*, because stories written by reporters E. G. Pipp and William J. Cameron were picked up nationally. The paper reached a circulation of 900,000 by 1925 (only the *New York Daily News* was larger), due to promotion by Ford dealers and a quota system. Additional lawsuits regarding anti-Semitic material caused Ford to shut down the paper, and the last issue was published in December 1927. For more on this history see: Richard Bak, *Henry and Edsel: The Creation of the Ford Empire* (2003); Douglas G. Brinkley, *Wheels for the World: Henry Ford, His Company, and a Century of Progress* (2003); Robert Lacey, *Ford: The Men and the Machine* (1986); Henry Ford, *My Life and Work: An Autobiography of Henry Ford* (Alvin, TX: Halcyon Classics, 2009, orig. published 1922).

65 Greg Grandin, *Fordlandia: The Rise and Fall of Henry Ford's Forgotten Jungle City* (New York: Picador, 2010).

66 Reynold M. Wik, *Henry Ford and Grass-Roots America: A Fascinating Account of the Model-T Era* (Ann Arbor: University of Michigan Press, 1973).

67 There were other Indian writerly correspondents during this period. I have chosen three as representative examples of their intellectual work because of their different relationships with Montezuma. There were certainly others such as John Ross (1790–1866), a Christian Cherokee intellectual who envisioned the annexation of the Cherokee Nation as an independent state of the union, and Alexander Posey (1873–1908) (along with Charles Gibson), a prominent and talented humorist and poet known for his "Fus Fixico Letters" published between 1902 and 1908. See: Peyer, ed., *American Indian Nonfiction*; Daniel F. Littlefield Jr. and Carol A. Petty Hunter, eds., *The Fus Fixico Letters, Alexander Posey: A Creek Humorist in Early Oklahoma* (Norman: University of Oklahoma Press, 1993); Jace Weaver, *That the People Might Live: Native American Literatures and Native American Community* (New York: Oxford University Press, 1997).

68 Originally published as "Editor's Viewpoint: The Civilizing Power of Language," *The Quarterly Journal of the Society of American Indians* Vol. 4, No. 2, April–June 1916, 126–8. For more on Parker see: Lawrence M. Hauptman, "The Iroquois School of Art: Arthur C. Parker and the Seneca Arts Project, 1935–1941," *New York History* 60, July 1979, 253–312 and *The Iroquois and the New Deal* (Syracuse, NY: Syracuse University Press, 1981); Joy Porter, *To Be Indian: The Life of Iroquois-Seneca Arthur C. Parker* (Norman: University of Oklahoma Press, 2001).

69 James Scott's *Domination and the Arts of Resistance: Hidden Transcripts* (New Haven, CT: Yale University Press, 1990) defines *public transcript* as the open, public interactions between dominators and oppressed. He defines *hidden transcript* as an example of the critique of power that power holders do

not see or hear. Different systems of domination (political, economic, cultural, or religious) have aspects that are not heard that go along with their public dimensions. I argue that Parker used English, which he believed to be part of a system of domination, to communicate a critique of that domination. Writers like Parker published their writings in public papers, and presented their ideas at public events. Some scholars see "hidden transcripts" in opposition to the Gramscian notion of hegemony, as evidence that "subaltern" peoples have not consented to their own domination. I complicate this by considering what happens when the "hidden transcript" is published and circulated among various publics, and thus, how context constitutes it; in other words, when it emerges as a practice that contests and defines the hegemonic system from which it originates.

70 *Daily Oklahoman* (Oklahoma City), February 27, 1947. Mary Hays Marable and Elaine Boylan, *A Handbook of Oklahoma Writers* (Norman: University of Oklahoma Press, 1939). More recently, a previously unpublished novel by Oskison has been uncovered from university archives and reprinted. Edited by Melinda Smith Mullikin and Timothy B. Powell with an introduction by Jace Weaver, *The Singing Bird: A Cherokee Novel* (Norman: University of Oklahoma Press, 2007), might be the first historical novel written by a Cherokee. Set in the 1840s and '50s, when conflict erupted between the Eastern and Western Cherokees after their removal to Indian Territory, Oskison's novel focuses on the adventures and tangled relationships of missionaries to the Cherokees, including the promiscuous, selfish Ellen, the "Singing Bird" of the title. Fictional characters are intermingled with historical figures such as Sequoyah and Sam Houston, embedding the novel in actual events.

71 John M. Oskison, *The American Indian Magazine* Vol. 5, No. 2, April–June 1917, 93–100.

72 Ibid.

73 Ibid. Oskison's views foreshadow the philosophy of the National Indian Youth Council that was founded in Gallup, New Mexico in 1961 by college-educated Indians who sought to mend the gap between the generations by establishing more connections with reservation elders. See: Peyer, *American Indian Nonfiction.* At the same time, Montezuma's reference to "leading Indians" echoes Eastman's sentiments, and those of W. E. B. Du Bois, who stated: "The Negro race, like all races, is going to be saved by its exceptional men. The problem of education, then, among Negroes must first of all deal with the Talented Tenth; it is the problem of developing the Best of this race that they may guide the Mass away from the contamination and death of the Worst, in their own and other races." W. E. B. Du Bois, "The Talented Tenth," from *The Negro Problem: A Series of Articles by Representative Negroes of To-day* (New York: J. Pott and Company, 1903).

74 Stan Steiner, *Spirit Woman: The Diaries and Paintings of Benita Wa Wa Calachaw Nunez* (San Francisco, CA: Harper and Row, 1979). Wa-Wa Chaw came in contact with many white intellectuals and leaders of the day, including Sir Oliver Lodge and Arthur Conan Doyle. She wrote for many publications until the time of her death, and sold her paintings in sidewalk shows in Greenwich Village. She was passionate about using art and writing to promote equality for Indian women.

75 In 1848, California became a part of the United States. Under the terms of the Treaty of Guadalupe Hidalgo, California's Native peoples were to become citizens of the United States with their liberty and property rights given full protection under U.S. laws. However, the government failed to live up to these terms and Indian people suffered horrendously during the next several decades. In 1905, Indians became more involved in matters concerning them, and with the rediscovery of the eighteen lost treaties Indians and their supporters began a drive for land, better education, the rights of citizenship, and settlement of the unfulfilled treaty conditions. See: Alfred Louis Kroeber, *Handbook of the Indians of California* (Washington, DC: Government Printing Office, 1925); Robert F. Heizer, et al., *Handbook of North American Indians: Vol. 8* (Washington, DC: Smithsonian Institution, 1978); and "Five Views: An Ethnic Historic Site Survey for California," http://www.cr.nps.gov/history/online_books/5views/5views1.htm (accessed June 25, 2013).

76 Heizer, et al., *Handbook of North American Indians*, 715.

77 Kenneth M. Johnson, *K-344; or the Indians of California vs. United States* (Los Angeles, CA: Dawson's Book Shop, 1966), 36.

78 "Five Views: An Ethnic Historic Site Survey for California."

79 For copies of this magazine and materials related to Wa-Wa Chaw see: CM Papers, Wisconsin State Historical Society, Madison, WI.

80 Yakima Indian Commercial Club to Dr. Montezuma, Letter, August 30, 1920 (approximate), CM Papers, Center for Southwest Studies, Fort Lewis College, Durango, CO.

81 Rev. Red Fox to Carlos Montezuma, Letter, March 26, 1920, CM Papers, Center for Southwest Studies, Fort Lewis College, Durango, CO.

82 G. Bonnin to Montezuma, December 10, 1916, Letter, Box 3, Folder 4, CM Papers, Wisconsin State Historical Society, Madison, WI.

83 G. Bonnin to Montezuma, October 1918, Letter, Box 4, Folder 1, CM Papers, Wisconsin State Historical Society, Madison, WI.

84 G. Bonnin to Montezuma, October 22, 1918, Letter, CM Papers, Wisconsin State Historical Society, Madison, WI. After 1926, *The Tomahawk* continued to publish some White Earth news, but dropped its pro-Indian stance and ceased publication later that year. By 1927, this paper moved to Calloway, Minnesota and was renamed *The Calloway Tomahawk* edited by A. H. Lockwood. See: Daniel F. Littlefield Jr. and James W. Parins, *American Indian and Alaska Native Newspapers and Periodicals, 1826–1924 Vol. 1* (Westport, CT: Greenwood Press, 1984).

85 It is worth noting that the fraternal organization called the "Tipi Order of America" (also spelled "Teepee") was led by Red Fox St. James, a Montana rancher who claimed Blackfoot ancestry. He was of concern to Bonnin and others who doubted his Indian status. Both Cari Carpenter (*Detecting Indianness*, 2005) and Hazel Hertzberg (*The Search for American Indian Identity*, 1971) point to Arthur C. Parker's papers as a source for locating Red Fox as the leader of this group.

86 Chapter 1 includes an extensive historiography for the Progressive Era, which also defines progressivism, and progressive reform tactics, organizations and the roles of Indians within this framework.

87 The National American Indian Memorial was proposed in 1909 as a monument to American Indians embodied in a statue of an Indian warrior overlooking

the main entrance to New York Harbor. On December 8, 1911, Congress set aside federal land for the project but did not provide for expenses. In 1913, with President William H. Taft, they broke ground; approximately thirty-three American Indian chiefs, including Red Hawk and Two Moons, were present. Sculptor Daniel Chester French and architect Thomas Hastings came up with a general concept for the memorial, which included a 165-foot-tall Indian statue on an Aztec-like pyramid base atop an Egyptian Revival complex of museums, galleries, and libraries, surrounded by a stepped plaza and formal gardens with sculptures of bison and Indians on horseback. The project was never completed and there are no physical remains. See: "Ends Peace Trip to the Indians, Wanamaker Expedition Returns after Obtaining the Allegiance of All Tribes" for more about the "ground-breaking" exercises in the *New York Times* (December 1913).

88 Dixon to Montezuma, circa 1918, Letter, CM Papers, Wisconsin State Historical Society, Madison, WI.

89 Carlos Montezuma to Mr. Edward Janney, September 26, 1921, Letter, CM Papers, Wisconsin State Historical Society, Madison, WI.

90 Montezuma to D. Edward Janney, regarding "Indian work," September 26, 1921, Letter, CM Papers, Wisconsin State Historical Society, Madison, WI.

91 This private missive does important dialogic work for Montezuma because a personal letter, unlike a newspaper article, is designed with two-way communication in mind. Montezuma may be writing about a topic that he was still thinking through, and that he may have considered important for inclusion *or* strategic exclusion from his public writings. In addition to doctors like Janney, Montezuma wrote to fellow writers and journalists as well as other Indian activists and white allies. Many of these letters reveal his influence on others.

92 Angie Pitts Juban, MA Thesis: "Insiders: Louisiana Journalists Sallie Rhett Roman, Helen Grey Gilkison, Iris Turner Kelso," presented to the faculty in the Department of History at Louisiana State University, chapter 2, "Helen Grey Gilkison: Social Insider." *Helen Gilkison Papers, Mss. 1901, 2175*, Louisiana and Lower Mississippi Valley Collections, LSU Libraries, Baton Rouge, LA (bulk 1925–48) and see: Genevieve Jackson Boughner, *Women in Journalism: A Guide to the Opportunities and a Manual of the Technique of Women's Work for Newspapers and Magazines* (New York: D. Appleton and Company, 1926) H. Gilkison was born in Louisiana and a graduate of Louisiana State University, Baton Rouge.

93 Throughout Montezuma's correspondence, the question of intimacy appears in the meaning of "friend" and "friendship" that he and others use to talk about their relationships. Certainly, the networks of reform that he was involved in required a certain level of intimacy and trust between peers and fellow travelers. See: Amy Carla Kaplan, *The Erotics of Talk: Women's Writing and Feminist Paradigms* (New York: Oxford University Press, 1996).

94 Juban notes, "Helen Grey Gilkison lived and worked in a politically charged atmosphere. Huey P. Long influenced the university she attended, and she entered the journalistic world at the height of his power in the state of Louisiana." See: Juban, "Insiders," 44. Also see H. Grey to Montezuma, Letter, CM Papers, Wisconsin State Historical Society, Madison, WI.

95 Robert A. Staley, "*Congressional Hearings: Neglected Sources of Information on American Indians,*" *Government Information Quarterly* 25, 2008, 520–40. Available online April 18, 2008. Staley argues that over the past three decades, discussion of government documents on American Indians has emphasized federal agency documents and archival records, despite the fact that Congress has the ultimate authority in Indian affairs. He uses examples from early twentieth-century legislative and oversight hearings to show that there is significant untapped research content on American Indians in congressional hearings. "Between 1919 and 1920 the House Committee on Indian Affairs published 25 hearings on the condition of the Indians in the Southwest and Northwest." The Pratt quote included in this paragraph is from Richard H. Pratt to Carlos Montezuma, March 1, 1910, Letter, Ayer MMS Collection, Newberry Library, Chicago, IL.

96 From Pratt to Montezuma, Letter, Ayer MMS Collection, Box 3, Newberry Library, Chicago, IL.

97 For work in Native American studies regarding white interpretations of Indian history, cultural practices, and the range of representations that have dominated the white imaginary in terms of Indian people and Indianness, as well as questions of performance, authenticity, and a history of representation see the following. Philip J. Deloria, *Playing Indian* (New Haven, CT: Yale University Press, 1998); Robert Berkhofer, *The White Man's Indian: Images of the American Indian from Columbus to the Present* (New York: Vintage, 1979); and Brian Dippie, *The Vanishing American: White Attitudes and U.S. Indian Policy* (Lawrence: University Press of Kansas, 1982).

98 In many ways, the "craze" for the production, consumption, and marketing of Indian things during this period built on narratives from the 1820s and 1830s in the United States by James Fenimore Cooper, Lydia Maria Child, and Catharine Sedgwick as well as the dramas Jill Lepore studies. For more on the modernist obsession with Indianness see: Elizabeth Hutchinson, *The Indian Craze: Primitivism, Modernism, and Transculturation in American Art* (Durham, NC: Duke University Press, 2009); Carter Jones Meyer and Diana Royer, eds., *Selling the Indian: Commercializing & Appropriating American Indian Cultures* (Tucson: University of Arizona Press, 2001); Trachtenberg, *Shades of Hiawatha*.

99 For one of the earliest texts dealing with the historical and narrative use of savagery in regards to civilization see: Roy Harvey Pearce, *Savagism and Civilization: A Study of the Indian and the American Mind* (Baltimore, MD: Johns Hopkins University Press, 1953).

100 Carlos Montezuma to Mr. Edward Janney, September 26, 1921, Letter, CM Papers, Wisconsin State Historical Society, Madison, WI. Montezuma's title "Let My People Go" also references the history of enslavement of African Americans and the spiritual "Go Down Moses," which uses "Let My People Go" as a rallying cry. Initially, this was an anthem for the Contrabands at Fort Monroe around 1862. The sheet music states the song is from Virginia, from around 1853, and was published as "Oh! Let My People Go: The Song of the Contrabands" arranged by Horace Waters. L. C. Lockwood. For more on this song and a history of black music in America see: Eileen Southern, *The Music*

of Black Americans: A History (New York: W. W. Norton, 1971) and Samuel
A. Floyd Jr., *The Power of Black Music: Interpreting Its History from Africa to
the United States* (New York: Oxford University Press, 1995).

101 See: *Congressional Record*, 64th Cong., 1st sess., vol. 53, no. 123 (Friday,
    May 12, 1916). Also see: Peyer, *American Indian Nonfiction*, which includes
    a reprinted version of "Let My People Go"; See: Larner, The Papers of Carlos
    Montezuma, Microfilm Ed., Reel 5, The Indian Problems from an Indian's
    Standpoint; Reel 5, An Indian's View of the Indian Question; Reel 2, August
    2, 1906, Reel 2, May 16, 1909, Reel 3, February 27, 1914. Figure 5: Carlos
    Montezuma, 1896, Photo Lot 73 06702900, National Anthropological
    Archives, Smithsonian Institution.

102 In this speech, Montezuma references white organizations, such as the Mohonk
    Conference, Indian Rights Association, Indian Friends, and "other similar
    organizations," that he believes have evaded the issue of the Indian Bureau.

103 Carlos Montezuma, "Let My People Go" (1) in *The Papers of Carlos Montezuma,*
    M.D. [microform]: including the papers of Maria Keller Montezuma Moore
    and the papers of Joseph W. Latimer / edited by John William Larner Jr.,
    Scholarly Resources, Inc. 1983 through the Newberry Library, Chicago, IL
    (collection abbreviated as: PCM, Larner, 1983).

104 I have read through W. E. B. Du Bois letters that have been published; see: Herbert
    Apthekar, ed., *Correspondence of W.E.B. Du Bois Volume 1, Selections,
    1877–1934* (Amherst: University of Massachusetts Press, 1973). I did not
    uncover a material connection between him and Carlos Montezuma despite
    the fact that Du Bois was invited to attend an SAI annual meeting. For more
    on the ways discourses of race may have mapped onto each other with regards
    to the political movements of both African Americans and Native Americans
    during this period see the work of Heidi Ardizzone, from "Representing
    Race: Activism and Public Identity in the Early Twentieth-Century," presented
    October 16, 2008 at the American Studies Association's annual meeting.

105 See Carlos Montezuma, "Let My People Go," where he notes, "Keep in mind
    that Indian Bureau, Indian Reservations, Indian Schools, Indian College, Indian
    Art, Indian Novels, Indian Music, Indian Shows, Indian Movies, and Indian
    Everything creates prejudice and do not help our race." ... "To fight is to for-
    get ourselves as Indians in the world. To think of one-self as different from the
    mass is not healthy." PCM, Larner, 1983.

106 See: Simon Pokagon, "The Red Man's Rebuke" (published by C. H. Engle,
    1893); Charles Eastman, *The Indian To-Day: The Past and Future of the First
    American* (New York: Doubleday, 1915).

107 For more on the hailing and psychology of being instantiated as a brown sub-
    ject through the identification of one by others as Indian see: Frantz Fanon,
    Black Skin, White Masks (1952).

108 Carlos Montezuma, "What It Is to Be an Indian" (3). PCM, Larner, 1983.

109 For Figure 5, see "Photograph of Carlos Montezuma" (not dated, circa 1915),
    Carlos Montezuma's Papers as part of the Edward E. Ayer Collection, The
    Newberry Library, Chicago, IL.

110 Montezuma, "What It Is to Be an Indian" (3).

111 Ibid. (7).

112 Ibid.

113 Ibid. (10).

114 Ibid. (14 and 20).

115 Ibid. (21).

116 See: Shari M. Huhndorf, *Going Native: Indians in the American Cultural Imagination* (Ithaca, NY and London: Cornell University Press, 2001) and her chapter: "Imagining America: Race, Nation, and Imperialism at the Turn of the Century," which examines the displays of Indianness and the involvement of actual Indian people at the 1893 World's Fair in Chicago, Illinois.

117 Montezuma, "What It Is to Be an Indian" (12).

118 Carlos Montezuma, *Wassaja*, June 1917 (microfilm) courtesy of the Newberry Library, Chicago, IL.

119 Speroff, *Carlos Montezuma, M.D.*, 174. Charles A. Eastman, *From the Deep Woods to Civilization* (originally pub. Boston, MA: Little, Brown and Company, 1916; repr. New York: Dover, 2003), see page 109 of Dover edition for full quotation.

120 For more see, "Awards file" (uncatalogued) of the NAJA collection, Sequoya National Research Center, Little Rock, Arkansas. Special thanks also to Daniel F. Littlefield for investigating this history to find an undated memorandum from Laverne Sheppard (Shoshoni-Bannock), then executive director of NAJA, that reads: "The Wassaja Award is named after a monthly newspaper published in Arizona by a San Carlos Apache man Dr. Carlos Montezuma Jr." Sheppard also notes the name was chosen because of Montezuma's strong editorial stand, and although she had a few of the facts wrong, her statement verifies the source of the award's name.

121 Speroff, *Carlos Montezuma, M.D.*, 382. In 2000, the New York University Department of Journalism nominated *Wassaja* for consideration as one of the top 100 works of journalism in the United States during the twentieth century. Even though Montezuma's paper did not make the final list, the nomination shows the extent to which he contributed to a history of print culture as a leading Indian intellectual from the early twentieth century.

3

Red Bird

Gertrude Bonnin's Representational Politics

We come from mountain fastnesses, from cheerless plains, from far-off
low-wooded streams, seeking the "White Man's ways."
– Gertrude Bonnin, "Side by Side"[1]

Introduction

Born in 1876, Gertrude Bonnin entered the world in the same year as "The
Battle of the Little Bighorn," or as many Native people referred to it: "The
Battle of Greasy Grass." This event was an indicator of Indian triumph followed quickly by American military victories and the containment of most
Sioux people to reservations. This was also the era marked by systematic
violation by the U.S. government of the 1868 Treaty of Laramie, which
established Native rights and control over the "Great Sioux Reservation,"
including parts of South Dakota, North Dakota, Montana, and Wyoming.
The legacies of these events shaped Bonnin's childhood and the types of
short stories she would write, as well as the political work she would do
later in her life. Known as Gertrude to family and close friends, Bonnin gave
herself the nom de plume Zitkala-Sa, meaning Red Bird, after attending
Earlham College in 1897. Although the name is Sioux in origin (Lakota),
it is not from her Native dialect (Nakota). She certainly signed some letters
with this new name, but for most of her life she went by her married name
of Bonnin.[2]

Bonnin grew up on the Yankton Sioux Reservation in South Dakota.
Missionaries visited her family and convinced Bonnin's mother, Ellen Tate
Iyohinwin, to send her daughter away to school. From 1884 to 1888, she
studied at White's Manual Labor Institute in Wabash, Indiana – a school
founded and run by Quakers. Then, from 1889 to 1890, she attended the
Santee Normal Training School – founded by the Reverend Alfred Riggs, a
Congregational missionary, in 1870 – which became a center of education

for all Sioux. After only a few brief visits home, Bonnin went away again to Earlham College in Richmond, Indiana from 1895 to 1897.[3] Although she did not graduate because of an unexplained illness, her studies at Earlham prepared Bonnin for work as an educator.[4] She taught at the Carlisle Industrial Training School in Pennsylvania from 1897 to 1899. Unfortunately, she was soon at odds with the school's founder and headmaster, Richard Pratt, and by 1900 Bonnin relocated to Boston, where she was able to study violin at the New England Conservatory.[5] Many of Bonnin's writings from 1900 to 1902 refer back to these formative educational experiences.[6] In addition to education, her work reflects on the historical consequences of changes in U.S. Indian policy and the end of violent resistance efforts by Native people. She focuses on an education policy that aimed to assimilate Indian people and in the process erase the distinctive character of students' backgrounds with regard to culture and language. Relying on her schooling, Bonnin wrote stories for white audiences and successfully combined literary and political work to produce counter-narratives about Indian identity and the history of settler-colonialism in the United States.

Higher education, fictional and polemical writing, personal correspondence, and public performance all permeated Bonnin's life choices, choices that reflected a desire she shared with a larger cohort of Indian people. They wanted to show how their collective story considered questions related to citizenship, sovereignty, and performance. Her writings and political activism demonstrate the ways Indian intellectuals negotiated modernity and worked to change policies affecting their lives and the future of Indian Country. Bonnin sought ways to maintain the centrality of her gender and race as a voice for Native womanhood, in the context of an ever-changing and expanding United States. She created a dynamic public persona as an engaging writer and speaker to become central to the cause of citizenship that other Indian leaders fought for during this time.

Many popular and dominant representations Bonnin wrote against worked to memorialize the white and Indian warfare that was discernible during her childhood, but was no longer a factor as she grew up because violence against Indian people had shifted terrain from the frontier to include boarding schools, broken treaties, and mismanagement of Native lands by members of the Indian Office. Still, physical violence characteristic of the western frontier remained popular within an American cultural imaginary, especially through episodes represented in the "dime novel," a cheap, readable, and easily circulated book.[7] Bonnin's work had broad appeal because it could interest readers of dime novels as much as highly educated and wealthy persons who counted themselves among elite sections of American society.

In 1896, while attending Earlham College, Bonnin wrote her first essay for public consumption: "Side by Side." Initially delivered as a speech, it responded to the different ways white and Indian relations had been narrated during the 1890s. "Side by Side" offers an early indication of Bonnin's sophisticated thinking concerning major issues surrounding Indian people and how she might engage in representational politics by working through American cultural forms, like literature.[8] Bonnin won second place in the Indiana state oratorical contest for "Side by Side," demonstrating her successful debut as a public speaker. In a similar fashion to Charles Eastman, she used this moment to teach her audience about important intercultural themes. These themes illustrate Bonnin's concern for Indian people's power, which she viewed as continually threatened by white settlements and by federal policy. At the heart of her critique of American culture were the ways narratives had mischaracterized Indian people in telling the story of colonization. Her essay offers a rhetorical response to the literary texts, newspaper accounts, and Wild West performances during the period that chronicled and celebrated the Indian Wars of the nineteenth century. These dominant narratives denied the harsh reality of inequality and disenfranchisement that lay beneath colonial encounters between European powers and Indian nations. Bonnin understood the implicit power of narrative and this denial. She was part of a generation of Native female intellectuals like Sarah Winnemucca, S. Alice Callahan, and E. Pauline Johnson who, unlike past generations from the early nineteenth century, sought equality and enfranchisement given the broken treaties they had witnessed. Bonnin and her contemporaries aimed for "dual citizenship" and "rhetorical sovereignty" because they recognized that indigenous spaces could be independent from the United States because at the moment tribal nations were not necessarily being treated fairly or viewed through the paradigm of a nation-to-nation relationship with the United States.[9]

Bonnin managed, throughout her life, to navigate a fine line that divided but also linked her criticism of American culture with her celebration of it. Her understanding of education, policy, cultural formations, and the power of public performance shaped the ways she would position herself, as a Yankton woman, writer, musical performer, and political activist. In "Side by Side," Bonnin synthesizes rhetorical devices with political ideas and cultural aesthetics in a way that is characteristic of her later work.

"Side by Side" relies on romantic symbols ("we come from mountain fastnesses") and paternalistic tropes ("seeking the White Man's ways") reminiscent of James Fenimore Cooper's narratives, so Bonnin can maneuver these metaphors to connect stories about Indian origins and issues of cultural belonging to a biting critique of the "White Man's ways." This rhetorical strategy came to dominate her literary and political writing, and became part of a larger trend among other Indian intellectuals' work during the turn of the twentieth century, as Beth Piatote illustrates in *Domestic Subjects: Gender, Citizenship, and Law in Native American Literature.* Piatote examines writings by indigenous women in Canada and the United States who were able to use literature as a forum in which to critique legal systems that sought to undermine their sovereignty in personal and tribal-national terms.[10]

Because Bonnin's essay originated as a speech, she uses repetition as a device to highlight central themes and main points. She repeats "seeking" to draw her white audience into her rereading of American society. She also uses "we" (in reference to Indian people) in combination with "seeking your skill in industry and in art." She then provides a list to define both industry and art. She places Indians in a position of supplication, a position implying social hierarchies of superiority and inferiority, to appeal to a largely white audience. At first, her listeners may have taken pride in hearing this young Indian woman celebrate how she and other Indian people were seeking labor and knowledge as entrée into American culture and politics. A more attuned listener may have heard something else because of Bonnin's repeated use of "seeking" throughout her speech.

According to Bonnin, her speech was so not well received. "There, before that vast ocean of eyes, some college rowdies threw out a large white flag, with a drawing of a most forlorn Indian girl on it. Under this they had printed bold black letters words that ridiculed the college which was represented by a 'squaw.' Such worse than barbarian rudeness embittered me."[11] Her speech was an indictment of white society and its hypocritical uses of Christianity, a message that may have been lost on these "college rowdies." Bonnin's repeated phrasing juxtaposed two groups where the "we" of Indian people and the "your" of American society became dialectical opposites, and were set "side by side." Her religious critique would have been clear given the biblical language she used in the speech.

To-day the Indian is pressed almost to the farther sea. Does that sea symbolize his death? Does the narrow territory still left to him typify the last brief day before his place on Earth "shall know him no more forever?" Shall might make right and the fittest alone survive? Oh Love of God and of his "Strong Son," thou who liftest up the oppressed and succorest the needy, is thine ear grown heavy that it cannot hear his cry? … Look with compassion down, and with thine almighty power move this nation to the rescue of my race.[12]

Here Bonnin's appeal to Christian teachings enables her to urge her white listeners to do the rescuing that their God seems so unable to do, to quell the spread of settler-colonialism. Her deft use of questions suggest that death is neither the foregone conclusion for Native people, nor is further dispossession. Her queries aim to have listeners question whether might ought to make right concerning the issue of pressing Indian peoples to the farther sea.[13]

Use of "side by side" in the essay shows how she structured it around not one, but *two* tropes. Along with "seeking," Bonnin speaks continually of two peoples standing "side by side." Therefore, Bonnin's "seeking" enables her to celebrate and criticize the nation in which these groups exist side by side, where her "seeking" also takes place. Her speech clearly portrays an underlying tension in American society between social hierarchy (seeking) and social equality (side by side), which came to the fore for Indian people within U.S. history.

The majority of white Americans in the audience may have interpreted and experienced the rhetorical effect of "seeking to" *do* this and *do* that in Bonnin's speech as congruent with a nationalist impulse to elevate America and Americanness. Bonnin uses these phrases to reclaim and subvert an exceptional notion of America. As much as her speech seeks the "genius of your noble institutions," in the same breath it seeks "a new birthright to unite with yours our claim to a common country." Thus Bonnin lauds American "genius" as a strategy to lay claim to its power as part of a shared (common) country, and something equally Indian as it is American.

As her speech links Indians and Americans together through the nation, it also retains a necessary distance between Indian people (ours) and the rest of America (yours), which captivated the contemporary discourse at the time based on social evolutionary theory. By maintaining the use of "we" versus "you," Bonnin sidesteps one of the deepest fears in white American society – miscegenation. At the same time, she plays with language to bring disparate peoples together. Her speech established a rhetorical space in which Indians and white Americans could be different, separate, and yet equal with regard to their claim to "a common country." This shared claim and the notion of difference came to dominate Bonnin's later work, as she argued for equal protection under the law for Indian people *and* also their ability to maintain sovereignty over tribal traditions, lands, and culture.[14]

Bonnin's speech also positions Indian people alongside white Americans: "We may stand side by side with you in ascribing royal honor to our nation's flag." She is therefore also claiming to speak for other Indian people, many of whom did not necessarily share a sense of "our" nation signifying the United States. The physical proximity of white and Indian bodies standing "side by side" indexes Bonnin's desire for fuller inclusion in the body politic – a position that would hopefully enable her to critique and reshape federal Indian policy from the inside. For her audience, it may have seemed as if *we* and *you* united to form an "our" through the patriotic symbol of the flag. Yet Bonnin uses this coming together to displace the original "yours" of a white, colonized America. Furthermore, by maintaining a distance between we (Indian people) and you (everyone else) – however fictional this distance was for urban Indians and white settlers living in towns bordering reservation fence lines – Bonnin capitalizes on a racial discourse of 1896, which demands this separation.[15] At the same time, she invokes "our nation's flag" to push against the limits of this discourse; as a possible harbinger of U.S. imperial machinations in the Philippines, Cuba, and Puerto Rico, three places in which the rights guaranteed by the Constitution did not follow the flag, especially for those racialized as yellow, brown, and red. This form of rhetorical resistance operated not only in this speech, but in her published work, personal letters, and public lectures.

Later in her life, Bonnin would work more closely with tribal communities to have their voices heard through her reform organization, The National Council of American Indians. "Side by Side" is where Bonnin first used the racial discourse of imperialism strategically to argue for Indian peoples' freedoms, and when she first began promoting herself as a public intellectual. In addition, in this speech and her other texts, historical events and context remained paramount to how Bonnin, as a Native woman and political reformer, could use cultural practices to address audiences and express her views on Indian policy. These moments enabled her to confront racism and patriarchy while also relying on white patronage to book appearances and publish her work.

As cultural historian Philip Deloria has shown, an ideology that defined Indianness in terms of violence gave way to one that focused on pacification in the post–Wounded Knee era of U.S. history. The threat of possible violence became mutually constitutive of the impossibility of such violence by Indian people. By the 1890s, U.S. Indian policy became linked to the increasingly mismanaged and corrupt bureaucracy of the reservation system, which was buttressed by an American culture that aimed to place Indians into safe spaces (reservations) while simultaneously finding new ways to displace them (forced acculturation through education). Following the General Allotment Act of 1887, federal bureaucrats sought ways to define and manage Indian people in physical space.[16] At the same time, white cultural producers focused on the closing of the western frontier as a means for romanticizing the vanishing Indian and the end of violence along that frontier. The end of the Indian Wars offered a way to redefine American empire by imagining Indian people as permanently trapped within a primitive past and locked out of the benefits of modernity and any need to be a part of the U.S. nation.

This strange linkage created narratives about Americanness and Indianness that enabled figures like Bonnin, on one hand, to claim her separateness from American society (as an inferior "seeker"), and on the other, to assert her desire for an equal share of an American future where Indian people could reshape society (because they could live "side by side" with Americans). If we return, then, to Bonnin's speech and Indian people as part of "our claim to a common country," we can see how she navigates a complex set of expectations regarding Indian peoples' roles in a modern(izing) nation; a nation that viewed them, ironically, as separate (biologically inferior) but also ripe for assimilation (physically adjacent by permission), because now pacified they could live "side by side" with white settlers, many of whom were new immigrants who found themselves similarly interpellated into a system of Americanization.[17]

"Side by Side" is but one example of Bonnin's representational politics in a written and spoken text. It was important not only because of the arguments she made but because she presented them as a public speaker. This is the earliest example of how self-promotion enabled Bonnin to assert her own ethnic female literary identity, while gesturing toward broader categories (Indian and American) to speak for *and* to large groups of people. For her, Indianness cut two ways: it was a racial or ethnic category as understood by white America and also a political identity that implied certain rights. Bonnin's work as a lecturer was akin to her female contemporaries', successful and courageous activists, many of whom were African American, such as Ida B. Wells-Barnett, whose pamphlets exposed lynching in the South; Anna Julia Cooper, a prominent author, educator, and speaker; and suffragist Mary Church Terrell, a daughter of former slaves who was one of the first African American women to earn a college degree; as well as feminists from all backgrounds who participated in reform through the Women's Christian Temperance Union, formed in Cleveland, Ohio in 1874.[18] In the years that followed Bonnin's participation in the oratorical contest from 1896, she worked frequently as a lecturer. She would often draw on expectations of Indianness to present her unique political insights.

In 1908, Bonnin sought to reimagine Indianness in cultural terms by working with William Hanson to produce *The Sun Dance*, an opera based on Native history and themes. This was somewhat unusual given that opera, at the time, was most often associated with the Metropolitan Opera House in New York City and a few newer venues in Boston and Chicago. It premiered at the Orpheus Hall in Vernal, Utah in February 1913. For Hanson and Bonnin, this debut was quite an achievement given the relative newness of the genre to American audiences.[19] Through opera Bonnin combined music and performance to articulate a political vision that resisted colonialist narratives and celebrated Native culture, history, and identity.[20] Because most opera audiences were from elite social circles, the genre itself guaranteed future possibilities for wealthy patronage in support of Indian issues. In addition, the site of Vernal helped connect the white settler population with the local Shoshone people, who were featured as performers in the premiere. Three years later, Bonnin moved from Utah to Washington, DC, and from harnessing the power of cultural aesthetics to working largely in the realm of politics. She became the secretary for the Society of American Indians (SAI), and through this early pan-Indian organization she found many Native allies. While in the capital, she also worked with publishers to have her earlier writings (from 1900–2) collected and published as *American Indian Stories* in 1921. Bonnin lived in the city with her husband, Raymond T. Bonnin, for the remainder of her life. Together they founded and ran the National Council of American Indians (NCAI), with her serving as the president and him as secretary from 1926 until her death in 1938.[21]

School Days: An Indian Teacher among Indians

Among the legends the old warriors used to tell me were many stories of evil
spirits. But I was taught to fear them no more than those who stalked about
in material guise. I never knew there was an insolent chieftain among the bad
spirits, who dared to array his forces against the Great Spirit, until I heard this
white man's legend from a paleface woman.[22]

– Gertrude Bonnin, *School Days*

After leaving Earlham, Bonnin worked within the classroom to educate herself and others about the positive ways schooling might be an avenue for
change within Indian America. Her views on education appear explicitly
in her essay "An Indian Teacher among Indians," published in 1900 by the
Atlantic Monthly. Bonnin articulated misgivings she harbored about the
American educational system that aimed to "civilize" Native children using
schools and teachers. She emphasizes feelings of loss and confusion based
on her experiences and the students she had taught at the Carlisle School.
Along with her essay "The School Days of an Indian Girl," Bonnin created a
series of vignettes that focuses on the roles of teachers and boarding schools
to argue for changes in educational policy concerning Indian pupils.

In "School Days," Bonnin recalls her arrival at school with a mixture
of hope and sadness. "I had arrived in the wonderful land of rosy skies,
but I was not happy," she writes, pointing to a space of possibility because
it is ostensibly wonderful and rosy. Still, she was not happy because "My
tears were left to dry themselves in streaks, because neither my aunt nor
my mother was near to wipe them away."[23] Her sadness refers to the dislocation experienced by Native students forced to attend boarding school.
Tsianina Lomawaima and others have emphasized the type of violence such
forced assimilation did to Indian children and their families.[24] Bonnin was
right to focus on the pain associated with boarding school. These schools
had been designed to work in tandem with settler-colonial policies, as Beth
Piatote and other scholars have shown. Piatote writes, "The restructuring
of Indian economies, reassignment of labor, and reshaping of gender roles
extended from the paired workings of allotment and boarding schools."
Reading in the context of this fraught history, and of Bonnin's references
to longing for family and "home," white readers of the *Atlantic Monthly*
piece may have found it appealing because of its sentimental tone. Bonnin's
longing also signaled to Indian readers that educational policies could be
as harmful to their existence as a Hotchiss gun. Closer examination of
vignettes from "School Days" and "An Indian Teacher among Indians"
reveals how Bonnin engaged with sentimentality and nationalism to argue
that Indian children are left out of the nation that supposedly aims to educate them into it.

Bonnin's narrative in "An Indian Teacher among Indians" is driven by
a thematic tension between her views of "the East" and "the West." These

regions of the United States operate as important figurative and material vectors in this series of stories, especially when she begins by chronicling her travels in terms of a *return* to the land of "red apples." This return functions within a post–Dawes Act reality where Bonnin must go to the East in order to reshape Indian Country in the West. Unlike the westward movement of white settlers, Indians moved eastward to reshape the possibilities open to them in the West. Bonnin writes, "there had been no doubt about the direction in which I wished to go to spend my energies in a work for the Indian race."[25] Bonnin's recognition that she may be more influential if she lives in the East reflects her awareness of Northeastern white progressive political reform circuits. Given the vanishing Indian myth that had become popular in the East, especially under the influence of narratives like Cooper's *Last of the Mohicans*, Bonnin may also have recognized that a Native presence in the East was especially warranted and helpful to refute the familiar stories of disappearance. Bonnin constructs "an Eastern Indian school" as a site of possibility, despite the fact that this school, and many others, undermined Native identity formation and cultural preservation. The schoolhouse then becomes a "both/and" site, one in which Native students feel threatened while they are taught new tools, and yet many, like Bonnin, use these same tools to produce new cultural understandings for the future of Indian Country and the United States.

Bonnin's story about the "land of red apples" (from "School Days") describes the place where she will be educated as one of strange sights and sounds. The title recalls the familiar folktale about Johnny Appleseed working his way across the Midwest planting apple trees as a symbol of national unity, but Bonnin relies on this familiarity to invert the popular narrative. For her, this land is where her long hair will be cut; it is a place marked by bedlam where "my spirit tore itself in struggling for its lost freedom."[26] Bonnin's spirit stands in for nationalist fervor, and suggests the Indian boarding school was an ambivalent and harmful cultural space that could not represent freedom. Readers could look to this childhood story and sympathize with the challenges Bonnin faced, and those still being faced by Indian children who were forced to live according to the rules of an unfamiliar and unforgiving white society.

Because Bonnin's vignettes set up a critical tension between the East and the West, we might read these spaces not necessarily through the well-worn tropes of civilization and savagery, but rather as cultural spaces that Bonnin feels she has less or more control over. For her, the East is a space of institutional control and misunderstanding in which "paleface" women teach Indian children how to assimilate into American society. The West embodies not the free and untamed frontier imagined by white writers and readers but a real place of return where Bonnin can visit with her family. But Bonnin also romanticizes the West as a place that she unfortunately cannot actually visit except in her "happy dreams of Western rolling lands and un-lassoed

freedom," which in turn enables her to write against the trope of domestica-
tion of Indian people.[27] The idea of "un-lassoed freedom" in the West partly
aligns with a dominant understanding from a white American imaginary,
but her longing points to the ongoing process of settler-colonialism that
forecloses her ability to return home, except in her dreams.

Through the contrast Bonnin creates between East and West in "School
Days," she is able to highlight what she has lost and gained by her studies
in the East. In the sixth chapter, Bonnin describes how "after my first three
years of school" she finally returns to "Western country," which unfortunately results in "four strange summers." The strangeness is due to her pain,
a feeling of dislocation within the site of the familiar, as she finds a brother
who "did not quite understand my feelings" and a mother who "had never
gone inside a schoolhouse, and so she was not capable of comforting her
daughter who could read and write." Her experience, of loss, of lack of com-
fort and understanding, is important because it is not unique to Bonnin.[28]

A large number of Indian people who had attended boarding schools
found it difficult to return home to families who still lived on reservations
and who may not have had the same sort of access to white education.
Charles Eastman wrote about the struggle to define himself while visiting
relatives or traveling in Indian Country as an educated Indian and a physician. Certainly, there was a growing divide between generations of Indian
people due to different educational experiences as well as changes brought
about by new technologies and economies. Indian cultures were as fluid
and changeable as any other, and the embrace or resistance to change often
resulted in diverse worldviews and loaded interactions. Eastman, Bonnin,
and others who attended schools far from home and those who went to college found that they did not necessarily speak the same cultural language as
the Indian people who did not share in these types of experiences.

By 1900, when Bonnin first published in the *Atlantic Monthly*, the
Bureau of Indian Affairs (BIA) had increasingly intruded into the lives of
Indian peoples. Communally managed reservation lands were divided up
into smaller parcels designed to be owned by individual families. Both the
Dawes Act and later the Curtis Act aimed to use this sort of division to open
up supposedly "surplus" lands to white settlement. Along with allotment,
large-scale armed resistance by Indian nations against the encroachment of
white settlers and the U.S. military was no longer possible. These concur-
rent factors also deepened generational divides among many Indian people.
As land ownership became less tribally rooted, Indian leaders, who traveled
between rural and urban and Indian and non-Indian spaces, were forced to
imagine new possibilities for how Indian people could engage in the making
of Indian Country in America.[29]

As an autobiographer and a narrator, Bonnin embodied the position of
a traveler. She also played the role of trickster as she described a struggle
to redefine Indian agency and sovereignty in "School Days." Through her

invocation of the familiar image of the wild Indian, Indian readers might have recognized that she was writing herself into the trickster's role. Writing as an Indian woman traveling between different cultural spaces, Bonnin describes herself thusly: "I was neither a wee girl nor a tall one; neither a wild Indian nor a tame one. This deplorable situation was the effect of my brief course in the East, and the unsatisfactory 'teenth' in a girl's years."[30] Bonnin's trickster operates on two levels in this example. She recognizes the implicit power of colonial oppression through the notion that Indians could only exist within an either/or binary, but then actually twists this into a neither/nor situation, that is because of her "brief course in the East." The fact that she is "neither" but also "both" allows Bonnin to frame her "brief course in the East" in both affirmative and critical terms to create a new intercultural space. Hers is not a class gender trickster identity (like a warrior woman), but instead one that identifies with her family, her home, *and* the new places she encounters while remaining critical of the shortcomings of all three. Indeed, her trickster is not purely an either/or position, but a both/and one that enables Bonnin's text to convey the fluidity, mutability, and contingency of a modern subject, thus offering readers a glimpse into how this text is part of a self-fashioning project.[31]

This fluidity is productive because it allows Bonnin to critique the "deplorable situation" that might force an Indian person to feel pulled between two extremes: one of wildness and the other of tameness, and by extension one defined by the reservation and the other by the city. Certainly these are categories that are produced by her colonial education, and in either one, she is seemingly figured as an animal. At the same time, because Bonnin *can* articulate an unfixed position read through lenses of biology and culture, her use of ambiguity connects schooling with coming of age in some productive ways. At this moment in her essay, as in her other stories, Bonnin makes repeated references to the particular pitfalls that befell her because she was an Indian and because she was an educated young woman. She is determined to write past the extremes of wildness and tameness that others would associate with her race, gender, and age.[32]

The school operates as a foundational site for the self-making that Bonnin critiques. Narrating an encounter between herself, as a teacher, and the school's headmaster, "the imposing figure of a stately gray-haired man" (that likely represents Pratt from Carlisle), the new teacher is framed in patriarchal terms. For it is the headmaster who introduces her to the reader by his exclamation that "you must be the little Indian girl who created the excitement among the college orators!" This statement at once celebrates Bonnin as an orator but also forces her into the diminutive role of a child as "the little Indian girl." Further confirming the difference in their roles with regards to power, the headmaster orders Bonnin back West "to gather Indian pupils for the school." In this instance, the male headmaster acts as the father figure of the school and the embodiment of the paternalism

underpinning a long history of colonization, which had been put into practice through missionaries who went West. Bonnin's depiction of these events
enables her to use his character to link the Indian education system directly
to a larger project of highly gendered colonialism. The Indian Teacher is a
figure through which Bonnin can showcase the complicated, even paradoxical, roles educated Indian women played within the changing cultural landscape of American society and Indian Country.

As an Indian Teacher who makes return trips to visit her family, Bonnin
showcases in her narrative the gulf of misunderstanding that was created
between her and her family because of practices like forced education
and allotment. When she recalls a visit home and her mother's caution to
"beware of the paleface" because they are the source of death "of your sister
and your uncle," one gains more insights into the costs of forced assimilation. In this same story, Bonnin appears unsure about how to interpret her
mother's concerns. She describes how her mother's "outstretched fingers"
pointed toward "the settler's lodge, as if an invisible power passed from
them to the evil at which she aimed."[33] Her mother seems almost to play the
role of superstitious older woman and spiritual soothsayer. Following this
depiction, Bonnin herself comes to terms with the possibility that "the large
army of white teachers in Indian schools" might not be as benevolent as she
once thought. The settler's lodge and the school become linked as cultural
and physical symbols of westward expansion. They stand in for the intima-
cies of colonial contact and cultural interaction, not unlike the marriages
between white men and Indian women and the indoctrination of Indian
children by Christian missionaries, again highlighting gender and nation as
critical themes in her writing.

Bonnin's mother, and the generation of Indian people that she represents,
oppose the Eastern world of "white teachers" in both a literal and figurative sense, whereas Bonnin and the next generation can recognize that these
teachers "had a larger missionary creed than I had suspected." Her position
as a teacher is a contradictory and unstable one. She articulates a subjectivity that has been shaped by teaching and yet does not perceive herself as
having taken on all the aspects of the white system that her mother finds
so threatening. Her story augurs a future full of dislocation (because she
cannot remain with her people) *and* possibility given the new political and
cultural places that she will soon be able to travel to as an Indian activist.[34]

Throughout these stories, Bonnin moves between physical and metaphorical spaces. Ultimately, she leaves her white readers with a feeling of uneasiness regarding the future of boarding schools and a gendered history of
education where white, female teachers and male schoolmasters attempted
to assimilate both Indian teachers and children. Bonnin is able to use the
site of the schoolhouse to bring into relief the power of misunderstanding when Christian "palefaces" observe her classroom. She writes that these
people were "astounded at seeing the children of savage warriors so docile

and industrious."[35] Her depiction of these visitors mocks their progressivist logic, a key theme that underpinned many of her writings, which gave her reason to question the motives of any white allies.

Given that a large portion of her white readers may have seen themselves as reformers "cut from the same cloth" as the visitors in the classroom scene, we might speculate how they understood descriptions like this one.[36]

Examining the neatly figured pages, and gazing upon the Indian girls and boys bending over their books, the white visitors walked out of the schoolhouse well satisfied: they were educating the children of the red man! They were paying a liberal fee to the government employees in whose able hands lay the small forest of Indian timber.[37]

Bonnin continues by expanding the picture to illuminate flaws in the larger system of Indian education: "In this fashion many have passed idly through the Indian schools during the last decade, afterward to boast of their charity to the North American Indian. But few there are who have paused to question whether real life or long-lasting death lies beneath this semblance of civilization."[38] Bonnin's assertion that "few ... have paused to question" what will happen to Indian children educated in this fashion leaves open the possibility of both death and life. In this moment, she hints at her own troubled subjectivity, as an Indian Teacher who understands the progressive vision regarding education and yet worries about how effective it is for *all* Indian people. On another level, these statements reflect the intermittent friction that occurred between Bonnin and Pratt – one of the leading figures in Indian education.[39]

Pratt responded to "School Days of an Indian Girl" and "An Indian Teacher among Indians" by publishing an anonymous review (although Bonnin would have known it was him), in *The Red Man*, one of Carlisle's school newspapers. His reviews suggest Bonnin created a misleading portrayal of Indian schools. Despite the disagreement between these two figures, they maintained a strained relationship for a time. Not long after Bonnin worked as a teacher at Carlisle, Pratt asked her to play with the school's band. According to one scholar, Pratt's rationale behind Bonnin's participation was to capture her and keep her "on our side" – the pro-assimilation, allotment, and progressive white reformers' agenda. Bonnin's performance as "Zitkala-Sa" with the Carlisle Indian School Band kept her close enough to Carlisle that it appeared she could be captured and contained.[40]

It is equally likely that Bonnin had strategic reasons for traveling with the Carlisle Indian School Band. Her choice to maintain a connection with Pratt enabled her in the short term to perform for large audiences, which helped her develop as a professional musician. In the long term, Bonnin's political work benefited from contact with Pratt given his influence on federal policy and his personal contacts. The Carlisle Indian School Band was not wholly bad for Bonnin because she continued to study music and pursue performance as a helpful avenue for self-promotion and political activism.

Bonnin's formal training for her musical career began in 1899, after she left her teaching post at the Carlisle School and moved to Boston, Massachusetts. There she met Ho-Chunk artist Angel De Cora. Their friendship offered both Native women support as fellow artists. By 1899, De Cora, who had recently graduated from the School of Art at Smith College in Northampton, had already established an art studio for herself at 62 Rutland Square, conveniently located within a mile of her art school and the Museum of Fine Arts in Boston. For De Cora, the decision to live in Boston at the turn of the century "meant she wanted to paint to the pulse of her generation."[41] For Bonnin, the decision to study music at the New England Conservatory demonstrated a similar desire to explore new places and make new contacts. Like writing, music provided Bonnin with an artistic outlet to express some of her deepest desires. It seems extraordinary that this young Yankton woman would be able to pursue studying the violin in Boston, and yet the city made a lot of sense for her as a writer. It seems likely that her decision to live in one of the publishing centers of the United States was a strategic move as well, because it was a helpful place for her to further her writing career.

By 1901, De Cora and Bonnin partnered together to publish *Old Indian Legends*, with Bonnin writing the text and De Cora creating the illustrations to accompany it. This was part of De Cora's career as an illustrator for Native authored texts. She had already created the frontispiece for Francis La Flesche's *The Middle Five: Indian Boys at School*, which had been published by Small, Maynard and Company out of Boston in 1900. De Cora would later work with her husband, William "Lone Star" Dietz, to do the illustrations for Elaine Goodale Eastman's *Yellow Star: A Story of East and West*, which was also published in Boston, by Little, Brown and Company in 1911. Both Bonnin and De Cora were encouraged by Bostonian Joseph Edgar Chamberlain and his wife. Chamberlain was a columnist for the *Boston Evening Transcript* and editor of the *Youth's Companion*. He was widely recognized in the city as a leading journalist. In fact, Bonnin did much of her early writing in the summer of 1899 at Chamberlin's summer home in Wrentham, Massachusetts. Chamberlin even wrote to the editors of the *Atlantic Monthly*, urging them to publish Bonnin's pieces.

These formative years in Boston fostered a personal friendship between the two women that yielded professional results due to important networks in the city and the artistic achievements of both Bonnin and De Cora. Their collaboration, and others between De Cora and La Flesche, demonstrate the degree to which Native artists were able to help one another in support of their careers. These professional relationships fostered opportunities for Native intellectuals to discuss a host of political concerns as well. Soon De Cora would leave Boston to teach art at the Carlisle School for nine years, from 1906 to 1915, where her autobiography appeared in an issue of the *Red Man* in 1911. In it, De Cora asserted a position on Native art that, as Anne Ruggles Gere has shown, was repeated in speeches she gave to the National Education Association, the SAI, the Lake Mohonk Conference of the Friends of the Indian, and Quebec's International Congress of Americanists. As Gere further argues, "Operating from a constrained racial and gendered position, this artist-teacher engaged with white-dominated approaches to Indian art to transform them for her own and future generations."[42] The two women would collaborate again, and for an expressly political purpose, in 1919, when the spring volume of the SAI's journal featured Angel De Cora Dietz on the cover and Bonnin as editor. Bonnin had left teaching to try her hand at music and writing, with the hope of circulating her work to a wide range of audiences. In Boston, she succeeded in cultivating a more national profile, one made possible through publishing in periodicals like the *Atlantic Monthly*.

Sioux Indian Woman: Author and Lecturer

The first Boston-based publishing house to promote Bonnin as a writer was Ginn and Company.[43] Ginn published Bonnin's first book, *Old Indian Legends*, in 1901. A year later, the *Atlantic Monthly* published her essay "Why I Am a Pagan." Soon other pieces followed, circulating in *Harper's* and *Everybody's Magazine* as well as journals distributed in various Indian communities across the United States, including the SAI's *American Indian Magazine*. The stories serialized by the *Atlantic Monthly* were later collected and printed together in 1921 by Hayworth in Washington, DC; all told Bonnin produced an impressive array of literary and political texts from "Side by Side" in 1896 to *Oklahoma's Poor Rich Indians: An Orgy of Graft, Exploitation of the Five Civilized Tribes, Legalized Robbery* in 1924.

Given the content of her autobiographical writings, Sioux Indian stories, and her later political writings, it is a challenge to position Bonnin's work with regards to genre. She was a writer with a well-cultivated literary talent.[44] She was also a political activist who sought and maintained connections to powerful networks. Her literary art became necessarily entangled with a desire to protest elements in American society that continued to oppress Native peoples. Many of Bonnin's writings suggest the fight for Indian political rights should be linked to the preservation of distinctive cultural identities – an idea that arose with nineteenth-century ethnography. Her upbringing contributed to producing an individual with a mix of beliefs that although internally consistent, could appear contradictory to outside observers. She favored American citizenship for Native peoples, for example, but was also committed to promoting Native sovereignty regarding writing practices, artistic expression, and musical traditions.

Read as social reform, Bonnin's work addressed themes from her own life that she saw as applicable to other Indian people, including the tension between indigenous spirituality and Christian theology, and the management of intergenerational and intertribal differences that were based on varied educational and social experiences. As a writer, she borrowed romantic language and tropes from sentimentality that were recognizable to many readers of American literature.[45] Some scholars have argued that Native women engaged with sentimentality in their work to varying degrees. Cari Carpenter notes that while anger is a neglected element in a variety of sentimental texts, it should be recognized as a salient subject in the early literature of Native American women.[46] Any anger Bonnin expressed was based on personal experience, and many of her characters were similarly based on real events. These figures often represented white and Indian worldviews. As a folklorist, Bonnin celebrated certain aspects of Sioux culture. Although she openly criticized the work of Christian missionaries in her writing, she was well versed in a number of faiths. She read *The Book of Mormon*, and *Science and Health* by Mary Baker Eddy, and no doubt a number of other religious texts.[47] She remained overtly critical of Christian conversion as a means of assimilating Native people into American society – even as she fought *against* the right of Native people to use Peyote for religious purposes. The different genres Bonnin used and certain contradictions she articulated demonstrate that her written work dealt with conflicts between literature and politics, as well as tradition and assimilation.

Although some scholars have labeled her a "transitional" writer, for Bonnin, such a label eschews the possibility for fluidity within her work.[48] Categories of identity – race, class, gender, religion – intersect to mutually shape one another.[49] In this case, ambiguity and ambivalence in Bonnin's work are productive in that she allows for various categories to remain unfixed. For her and other Indian intellectuals, the idea of "tradition" itself was up for debate at the turn of the twentieth century. One might be tempted to locate her in a liminal space, trapped somewhere between aesthetic creation and political commitment or between the supposedly separate worlds of Christianity and Native American religion. But it makes more sense to consider her literary writings as always contingent, in dialogue with her political projects. For many Indian readers, Bonnin's ability to express confusion about how to find a cultural home while she fights for political freedom might have been familiar and reflected shared concerns. This sort of apparent confusion could exist alongside a story that asserted a worldview as entirely coherent and at least *internally* consistent enough for her.[50]

Bonnin had enough professional and personal space to imagine her own political goals and because of the support of friends, colleagues, and her husband, Raymond T. Bonnin. They met in 1902, when Gertrude Simmons was working as a teacher at the Standing Rock Reservation in North Dakota. They married that same year, and then moved to the Uintah and Ouray reservation in Utah. They lived there until 1916, after which they relocated to Washington, DC. From 1916 until Gertrude's death in 1938, the Bonnins lived in the capital, where they were well positioned to direct their energies toward Indian reform. One of Bonnin's greatest achievements as an activist with the SAI was editing the organization's journal. Beginning in the fall of 1918, she edited four issues of the *American Indian Magazine: A Journal of Race Progress*, published by SAI members.[51] Meanwhile, Raymond Bonnin went to work as a law clerk while Gertrude acted as a lobbyist in support of Indian citizenship. By 1926, Gertrude Bonnin had made political contacts and reshaped Indian policy in order to found her own political organization, the NCAI. Writing and speaking proved integral to this type of political work, and Raymond nurtured his wife's efforts by becoming the secretary for the NCAI during her presidency.[52]

In addition to her marriage, Bonnin found encouragement for her efforts from various all-female reform groups. In 1920, she was an active member of the League of American Pen Women. Her association with this organization makes sense because Marian Longfellow O'Donoghue, who had ties to both Boston and Washington, DC, had established the League in 1897 as a "progressive press union" for female writers. Other white journalists, like Margaret Sullivan Burke and Anna Sanborn Hamilton, were involved in promoting the League to recruit not only members of the press but artists and composers as well. By September 1898, the League boasted over fifty members from Maine to Texas and New York to California. By 1921, the association had officially become the National League of American Pen Women with thirty-five local branches across a number of states. Its membership increased during the 1920s and 1930s. No doubt Bonnin was compelled by the activist origins of the association because its first members believed women writers should always be compensated for their work.[53]

Bonnin's work found support from the professional connections she made as a member of not only the League of American Pen Women, but a myriad of other all-female organizations. Through her correspondence with women involved in these sorts of groups and other Native writers, artists, and activists, like De Cora, Bonnin worked to promote both her political ideals and sales of her books. Writing from New York City in April 1922, fellow author Princess Blue Feather inquired about how she might obtain a copy of Bonnin's *American Indian Stories*. Blue Feather also wrote about her own work, which consisted of "many poems of our race, but as yet [I] have not had them published." This statement was not wholly true given that several of Blue Feather's pieces had already appeared in Montezuma's newsletter, *Wassaja*, which was "a great compliment" because his paper "is such a vitally important medium to reach those who are ignorant of the conditions regarding our race."[54]

Bonnin's reply to Blue Feather on May 2, 1922, offers a glimpse into how candid she was when writing to other Indian women about how to defend

the good name of "our people." These types of exchanges were as important to the creation and maintenance of Indian political reform networks as
much as Indian publications and artistic creations. Bonnin's postscript refers
to a newspaper clipping Blue Feather had enclosed, and reveals something
critical to both of them. She writes, "The clipping only shows how ignorant
many White Americans are about the real Indian people of our country. They
have much to learn!" This remark demonstrates Bonnin's openness to a new
friend and her strategic inversion of the "real Indian" discourse that permeated news reports during this period, especially with regard to Eastman's
work as a public speaker. In many cases, these reports supported an ethnic
authenticity discourse built on white expectations for Indianness. Bonnin's
use of "real Indian" here refers instead to an understanding she and Blue
Feather share regarding who they are versus how others might see them.[55]

In addition to Native women like Blue Feather, there were several
long-time white supporters of Bonnin's publishing career. Principal among
them was Marianna Burgess. Scholarship on the Carlisle School has
pointed to Burgess as central to the regime of surveillance there given that
she used her editorship of the school's paper to exert control over Indian
students. It seems likely she and Bonnin became acquainted through their
time at Carlisle. As Jacqueline Fear-Segal argues, Burgess adopted a fictional persona as the "man-on-the-band-stand," enabling her to construct
a panopticon-like power mechanism designed to intimidate and subdue
Carlisle's students through the columns of the newspaper.[56] Burgess also
authored *Stiya: A Carlisle Indian Girl at Home*, a deeply offensive novel
portraying Native people and Native communities as filthy and backward.
But despite this history and Burgess's earlier experiences and views, Bonnin
and Burgess regularly exchanged letters throughout the early decades of
the twentieth century on the topic of Indian uplift. Perhaps Burgess had a
change of heart. Her friendship with Bonnin may have been integral to a
shift in Burgess's politics.

On May 6, 1922, Burgess wrote to Bonnin from Los Angeles regarding the
California State Federation of Women's Clubs (CSFW). This group had supported John Collier's work with the American Indian Defense Association
(AIDA), another reform organization that emerged out of the Southwest
during this period. According to Burgess, the CSFW was important and useful because it was trying "to keep the Indian to the front." In particular, one
of the ways the CSFW aimed to educate the public about Indian reform
was through dramatic performance. However fraught this forum might be,
Burgess wanted to share this strategy with Bonnin.[57]

Virginia Calhoun tried so loyally to present in out-door drama an archaic story of
the true character of the primitive Indian. She is a playwright of considerable prominence. There were actual trees set out for a forest background. The scheme was
grand. The whole Indian program shows your work in Salt Lake. But dear oh me,
how ignorant the educated are![58]

The way Burgess reconstructs the performance space as the arena in which to highlight "the true character of the primitive Indian" fits well within the realm of dominant expectations regarding spectacular displays of Indianness. These performances reproduced "reality" so that audiences might crave the spectacle again and again, rather than learn more about the rights and situations of actual Indian people. Still, Burgess knows enough to also note that despite using "actual trees," these sorts of primitivist displays may not have been that accurate when she says: "how ignorant the educated are!" How true. In addition, Burgess's remarks on Bonnin's own foray into dramatic performance through her "work in Salt Lake," a reference to the 1913 performance of *The Sun Dance* there, suggests she may be writing to Bonnin in search of expertise regarding Native-themed performances. However, the main aim of Burgess's letter is not about performance but rather to promote the sale of Bonnin's books. Burgess writes, there is "a fine display of your books in one of the best book-stores in town"; it seems possible that "this display" will result in "good sales." The success of Bonnin's books certainly had something to do with white desires to see Indianized performances. Bonnin recognized that she could work within dominant, mostly white expectations regarding Indian performance in order to ultimately change them.

The collaboration between Bonnin and Burgess is not wholly dissimilar from the patronage relationships of the nineteenth century between abolitionists and freed slaves in sponsoring slave narratives, as well as the "as told to" genre created by white writers, especially anthropologists, who recorded and published the life stories of Native informants.[59] The partnership of these women, to promote and sell a Native author's books, was not unusual by the early twentieth century. Many white writers supported Indian policy reform and paired up with Native authors to promote their careers. Luther Standing Bear worked closely with Earl Alonzo Brininstool and Christine Quintasket collaborated with Lucullus McWhorter to produce and promote their books in the late 1920s. Both McWhorter and Brininstool were eager to support Indian people beyond the realm of culture by becoming members of political reform groups, such as the National League for Justice to American Indians. Similarly, Eastman traveled widely during this period to give public lectures about Indian history, *and* to promote himself as an author; his success hinged on an ability to tap into white expectations and cultural networks, and to work closely with white progressive reformers.

As writers, Eastman and Bonnin had in common their connection to the Boston publishing world. Eastman, for example, found support from Little, Brown and Company, which was clearly interested in promoting the work of *Indian* writers given that it had begun publishing legal documents related to the United States during the first half of the nineteenth century. Many of these documents concerned treaties, court cases, and conflicts between Indian people and the United States. By 1925, the company agreed to publish all *Atlantic Monthly* books; with this agreement came an opportunity to publish work by, not just about, Indian people. Through publishing Eastman and Bonnin traveled along similar if not also overlapping writing circuits. Bonnin's *Old Indian Legends* (1901), with illustrations by Ho-Chunk artist Angel De Cora, was published by the Boston-based firm Ginn and Company.[60]

This publishing house was established by Edwin Ginn, a graduate of Tufts University. Ginn had created the company with textbooks in mind and he saw an opening with the establishment of the Federal Bureau of Education to begin creating schoolbooks on a range of topics. The company sought out work by Native authors like Bonnin. Her autobiographical essays and folktales fit neatly into Ginn's ideology of education. Ginn "saw millions of children trooping to elementary schools throughout the land and the tens of thousands of earnest students who would be enrolled in the high schools and in state and private colleges" with books provided by his company.[61] Ginn's beliefs grew out of a discourse common during the nineteenth century that tied literacy and literature to nation building and market capitalism. His choice to include Native authors in such a project helped to promote their histories, ideas, and stylistic choices as integral to the United States rather than locating them solely in the past or in the imaginaries produced by white authors. Ginn was also a supporter of the International Congress on Race, which had featured Charles Eastman on the American panel with W. E. B. Du Bois and Franz Boas. Ginn's interest in Native American issues is most explicit in his support of both Eastman and Bonnin.

When Ginn and Company published *Old Indian Legends* in 1901, it represented the ideals of a publishing house interested in "building up the list of elementary, high-school, college, and technical books."[62] The book became part of the company's legacy of promoting English-language texts as part of a uniquely American literary history as it turned toward publishing modern language books. This move was important for Ginn and for Bonnin in that the company started marketing books outside of the United States. It was probably no surprise to Bonnin when she received a letter on June 8, 1926 from Ginn that stated, "A German lady desires to translate Old Indian Legends into German. Are you willing that she should do so?" Bonnin responded promptly by June 11, noting that she had "no objections whatever to the translation" because indeed such a request "indicates the growing interest in the American Indian generally and in a measure encourages me to write other Indian Legends of which I have sometime ago written you."[63] The educational and political reach of *Old Indian Legends* was celebrated by Bonnin and her publishing house. In 1930, she wrote to the company again to inquire about a school reader, which had been produced to include her stories. In this instance, Bonnin's remarks showcase that it was not only white progressives and adults who were interested in reading her work, but children as well. She writes, "It has been my pleasure to be told by children here in Washington, and others in Virginia that one of my stories is in the School reader they are using today."[64] These comments reflect an important cultural shift from the nineteenth century when Native authors were mostly publishing "legends" for children because by this time Bonnin referred to her work specifically as "stories."

Bonnin's books were not only marketed to schools and libraries, but to wider reading publics as her publisher advertised her texts in national periodicals. At the same time, Bonnin remained committed to circulating her work among an Indian reading community that crisscrossed tribal-national boundaries and America's political geography. In 1919, while working as the general editor for *American Indian Magazine*, Bonnin published a short but timely and provocative article titled "America, Home of the Red Man." The title itself signaled a shift in this period to the singular and the racial. The notion of home in the piece provided several meanings for Indian readers to wrestle with.

In "America, Home of the Red Man," Bonnin plays with the association between home and nation to make a larger claim regarding citizenship. As Piatote argues, from the late nineteenth century into the early twentieth, conflicts between Native people and the "settler-national" state had shifted to the space of the Indian home: "A turn to the domestic front, even as the last shots at Wounded Knee echoed in America's collective ear, marked not the end of conquest but rather its renewal."[65] For Bonnin, home must be contested when considering the experiences of Native soldiers who had fought in the First World War. She provides them as an example for whom "home" resonated on a number of levels. Bonnin's article also uses allegories to enliven and inspire fellow Indians to reconsider what home means to them as Native people living always under the threat of U.S. settler-nationalism.[66]

Bonnin's essay deftly shifts between third and first person narration, as she describes a chance encounter with another traveler. Bonnin, as a character (and also as narrator) is "en route West" to assist with the SAI annual conference in Pierre, South Dakota. While traveling, she meets a white stranger who looks at the service pin she wears and asks, "You have a relative in the war?"[67] This question and Bonnin's response in the story is personal and direct, but underlying the exchange is the issue of patriotism and the tension between Native veterans who have fought a war on behalf of a nation that still does not consider them citizens, but rather domestic subjects.[68] Bonnin's response is as follows: "the star is for my husband, a member of the great Sioux Nation, who is a volunteer in Uncle Sam's Army."[69] By framing her husband's citizenship through the Sioux Nation first and then gesturing to his service to the United States (Uncle Sam), Bonnin raises a specter that haunted Indian Country during this period: how to reconcile military service with continued practices of oppression by the federal government toward Native people. Her use of the word "nation" here also does important dialogic work in terms of Indian treaties through the implication of citizenship in the Sioux Nation and not yet the United States for Native soldiers.

Bonnin's response also strategically positions the Sioux Nation on equal footing with the United States by referring to the army in familial and familiar terms rather than purely nationalist ones. Yet the moment seems uncanny because the traveler is struck by Bonnin's assertion. She describes him thus: "A light spread over the countenance of the pale-faced stranger. 'Oh! Yes! You are an Indian! Well, I knew when I first saw you that you must be a foreigner.'"[70] Such a remark urges readers to recognize issues of containment and racialization that Native people had to confront. That he is unnamed and only signified through race and strangeness enables Bonnin to offer a subtle critique of settler-nationalism given that although he labels her a foreigner, he is a stranger to her and by extension the space they both occupy. With these remarks, spoken thoughtlessly, the stranger disappears. He vanishes rather than staying to debate with her, "dropped like a sudden curtain behind which the speaker faded instantly from my vision."[71] The disappearance of the stranger and his remarks regarding her foreignness perpetuate the feeling of the uncanny in this moment. Bonnin uses this strangeness as part of an abrupt transition to actual foreign places from the First World War.

Readers are jolted into another reality as the narrative suddenly shifts to European battlefields, where "ten thousand Indian soldiers are swaying to and fro ... [so] that democracy might live."[72] Here Bonnin uses the war in Europe and the fact of Native service, to such a grand degree too (ten thousand!), in order that Indian readers might consider a different battlefield. Indeed, the image of Indian soldiers "swaying to and fro" in defense of democracy enables Bonnin to move from Europe to the home front in the United States, and the war over citizenship she wishes to fight. Bonnin highlights the sacrifices Indian soldiers made on behalf of a nation where many Indian people are recognized as foreigners, as she is by the "pale-faced stranger," to debate the terms of their military service, and by extension the terms of their service to American culture and politics.[73]

Her article then pointedly argues that "The Red Man of America loves democracy and hates mutilated treaties." By drawing on the sentimental and making overtly political comments, following her encounter with a curious stranger and an almost dreamlike scene of European battlefields, Bonnin sets the stage for criticizing U.S. democracy, on which these moments turn. She writes:

Time and distance were eliminated by the fast succession of pictures crowding before me. The dome of our nation's Capital appeared. A great senator of Indian blood introduced upon the floor of the United States Senate a resolution that all Indian funds in the United States Treasury be available to our government, if need be, for the prosecution of the war. From coast to coast throughout our broad land not a single voice of the Red Man was raised to protest against it.[74]

Not every reader would have had access to the same education, nor would he or she have the same cultural or political commitments to Indian rights as Bonnin defines them. However, her rhetoric aims to unify Indian people under the banner of "America" as a shared "Home." Moreover, her reference to "a great senator of Indian blood" may be both a reference to Cherokee senator Robert Latham Owen, Jr. from Oklahoma,[75] who served in the U.S. senate from 1907 to 1925, and her pride in how far Native people had come as participants and shapers of American democracy. Bonnin makes the connection between America and home explicit by defining America as the Home of the Red Man and the Home of Democracy. Her use of "and" seems strategic here, as an attempt to suggest these two homes exist side by side and may also overlap, at least through the space of the home. In this instance, she is challenging the concept of Indian fidelity and allegiance to democracy unless it is also a part of their home. In addition, in this context, Bonnin urges her Indian readers to raise their voices in protest. She calls for a response to the injustice of using Indian funds to prosecute a war in Europe by asking an important question: "When shall the Red Man be deemed worthy of full citizenship if not now?" In other words, why fight a war on behalf of a home that is not fully ours to use as we please? This question, of course, is doubly ironic when reading World War I as an imperialist endeavor rather than a democratic one.[76]

In the context of a world war that had affected many people in Indian Country, Bonnin urges former soldiers and their supporters to fight for "home" within the political arena of the United States. Her text mobilizes loaded feelings of patriotism to ask for a renewed commitment to citizenship. This story illustrates Native peoples' beliefs in and support of America, but also how they must fight for their rights within and against it. In this case, Bonnin's call for citizenship aims to be heard throughout Indian Country and the United States.[77]

Bonnin's narrative ends with a return to the paleface stranger. In what seems like a fantastic encounter, she highlights the quotidian and American aspects of their exchange, using the frame of the book market. "From the questions with which I plied him, he probably guessed I was a traveling book agent.... Slowly shaking his head, the stranger withdrew cautiously, lest he be snared into subscribing for one or all of these publications."[78] This framing is significant given Bonnin's identity as an author and her status as an educated Indian who knew this market all too well, even if she did not sell books herself. Keeping this denouement in mind, one can imagine that Indian readers followed the unusual workings of this story to their logical conclusion: that America was indeed theirs for the taking, but the question remained as to how the Indian could engage the paleface in this project. Bonnin looked to the many letters that came across her desk on a daily basis in order to answer such a question.

Epistolary Culture Networks

Interspersed throughout memoranda, letters, and writings that would have occupied Bonnin's office are materials that reflect her intimate relationship with the inner workings of the Office of Indian Affairs, white progressives, and other Indian intellectuals. Her success as a writer and public speaker, for example, did not go unnoticed by members of the Department of the Interior.

In September 1922, Chief Clerk C. F. Hauke sent Bonnin a letter regarding a new edition of *Indian Legends*, which he wanted to include in the office library. According to Hauke, "This library is maintained, with the exception of the purchase of a few law books, by contributions of various authors and publishers, and it has been thought that you may desire to have a copy of your publication upon the Library shelves."[79] How would Bonnin have reacted to the clerk's letter? At first she may have been surprised and even laughed to express mixed feelings of frustration and bemusement. Certainly, there were any number of reasons the Office of Indian Affairs might write to her. Without a copy of her response it is impossible to know for sure how she met Hauke's inquiry. This particular letter is important, however, because it acknowledges Bonnin's work and expertise while it maintains a careful distance that suggests politics and culture should not necessarily be connected, at least within the Office of Indian Affairs.

Hauke's letter explains that the library may serve political and public interest regarding Indian affairs when he writes:

In connection with the library work a miscellaneous correspondence desk is maintained, where numerous inquiries relative to Indian customs, history, legends, etc., are answered, and it is often advisable to refer the correspondent to various publications on the subjects concerning which inquiry is made, quoting, where available, price and publisher.[80]

Hauke's request points to Bonnin's cultural work as a useful reference tool, and his reference to "miscellaneous correspondence" that is "relative to Indian customs" and so forth seems to suggest some ethnographic projects sponsored by the Office of Indian Affairs that might be under way. His letter also suggests that Bonnin might be able to sell a few books through her association with their library. Hauke's letter also connects Bonnin to an important social reform network, which many Indian intellectuals of this period participated in as interlocutors with or employees of the Indian Service, which was a part of the Office of Indian Affairs. This was one of several reform-based networks that Bonnin worked through during her lifetime.

Six years later, on September 24, 1928, Bonnin sent a six-page letter to Miss Vera Connolly of New York about the "present Indian movement." Bonnin wrote, "My whole life has been devoted to the Indian cause, but more ostensibly my relationship with the ... movement" began in 1921, when "at my plea" the General Federation of Women's Clubs (GFWC) took up the cause of Indian welfare.[81] Indeed, her work with the GFWC enabled Bonnin to give a series of public talks to women's clubs across the United States for several years. However, Bonnin's ability to participate in these public lectures decreased as she gave more "attention to legislation of Congress on Indian affairs." By this time in her life, Bonnin was married with one son, and had already published sets of short stories and nonfiction pieces. All the while, she continued to build personal and professional relationships bolstered by letter writing. In this particular letter, Bonnin includes a biographical sketch of her life and a copy of the "Constitution and By-Laws for the National Council of American Indians." She notes that "Our letterhead symbolizes the reunion of the tribes pitching their lodges in the circular camp ground." This excerpt embodies the centrality of correspondence in creating and strengthening pan-tribal networks throughout this decade and demonstrates the leading role Bonnin played in creating and maintaining these connections through her work with white reformers.[82]

Examining a few representative letters from Bonnin's extensive personal collection reveals the types of networks she accessed to benefit her career and to promote Indian activism. Following the letter from Hauke and the one Bonnin sent to Connolly, exchange with Carlos Montezuma and Bonnin's white female friends and supporters, Marianna Burgess and Stella Atwood, illustrate the ways women's organizations were essential to the work Bonnin sought to accomplish. Ultimately, she emerges as one among a cohort of Indian intellectuals, unique but not solitary in her aims, one who relied on alliances with white progressive organizations to gain widespread support for reforming Indian policy.[83]

In the winter of 1915, as Gertrude and Raymond Bonnin prepared to leave Utah and move to DC, Gertrude found herself "under a big load of correspondence" that had accumulated and needed her immediate attention. Drawing a letter out of the pile, Bonnin began writing to "Monte," a term of affection she used to refer to her friend and fellow Indian reformer Carlos Montezuma. Bonnin wrote about the development of the SAI, which was nearly five years old at the time. Monte and Gertrude had been engaged several years before. During this time they exchanged many letters that reveal both their romantic relationship and their shared interest in promoting Indian citizenship. In several letters, she teases him, using a list of attributes that he does not possess and explaining why she is therefore better off without him. Overall, these letters reveal a relationship based on mutual respect and understanding that survived despite a broken engagement. My interest, however, is with the specific instances in which Bonnin and Montezuma wrote about politics rather than romance. Therefore, I focus on the letters written after they broke off their engagement and had each married other people.

The SAI reached the zenith of its influence in the world of Indian affairs and the history of American Indian writing as Bonnin began her tenure as secretary. In many ways, this work enabled her to act as a critical interlocutor for SAI members and as a voice for then President Charles Eastman. She also became a memorable and fashionable public face for Indian womanhood through the SAI. When she wrote to Montezuma, she wanted to discuss ways they could strengthen the efforts of this pan-tribal organization.

In 1915, Bonnin was reaching out to political activists in DC who were interested in Indian issues. She was especially focused on increasing the membership and influence of the SAI. She calls on Montezuma to be strategic, and applauds him, saying, "I am glad you have been writing some good letters."[84] She writes again in 1918 about the importance of content and style for any correspondence related to the SAI.

> Dr. Eastman, like you, is planing [*sic*] a letter to his friends, both Indian and White, asking them to take interest in our society and become members. Why don't you write two letters, one to Indians and one to the Whites and have these letters multigraphed; send them out by the hundreds! They will bring results.[85]

Within Bonnin's plea for activity is strategic planning and the enthusiasm that Indian intellectuals felt with regards to using emergent technologies to reach multiple reading publics. The multigraphing process demonstrates her awareness of a useful connection between epistolary culture and newsletter production. During this same time, Montezuma was circulating *Wassaja*, which aimed to reach Indian audiences interested in political reform and to respond to a white-dominated press. Montezuma could have easily put Bonnin's suggestions into immediate practice.

Like other members of the SAI, Bonnin and Montezuma understood the power of rhetorical effect and the necessity of crafting different messages for different audiences. And, unlike other members, Bonnin and Montezuma shared an emotional intimacy because the two had once been engaged to be married. By the time they were both active in the SAI, however, their courtship had ended, with Bonnin breaking the engagement because she found Montezuma unsuitable as a romantic partner. Now, as friends and political allies, they corresponded more about their lives as writers and readers living in urban settings. Both had easy access to an array of periodicals, which may have served as models for ways to engage white readers. Curiously, jotted at the bottom of a typed letter she sent to Monte is a handwritten afterthought, revealing another expression of intimacy where Bonnin urges him to "Read 'Drifting Cloud' in November Cosmopolitan!"[86]

Bonnin's note reveals the eye of a well-trained writer and avid reader, someone who recognizes the relationship and political potential within letters and publications. It is not surprising that both she and Montezuma read magazines like *Cosmopolitan* and other national periodicals.[87] In 1918, Bonnin would have paid two dollars for her yearly subscription, if she did not happen to stop by a local newsstand to buy an issue of the magazine for twenty-five cents. The article, briefly referenced in her postscript, was actually titled "Drifting Smoke." Written by Gouverneur Morris, with illustrations by Lejaren A. Hiller, it appeared alongside pieces by writers like Jack London in that month's *Cosmopolitan*. The title refers to protagonist Oliver Pigeon, a Harvard-"educated Indian" with a "very tender" heart, which seemed to appeal to Bonnin (and she imagined it might appeal to Montezuma too).[88]

The representation of Oliver Pigeon is contrasted with that of his grandfather, a man who bore a heavy burden because he "was a connecting link between the Kansas prairies of 1900 and the Atlantic seaboard before the white men came."[89] Although Oliver is the hero of this story because of his educational achievements and athletic prowess, Morris emphasizes Oliver's one weakness, which is his "hatred" for an Indian agent named Mr. Ross. Ross is cruel and corrupt, a man who has "bled the Indians under his care in every conceivable way … All the Indians knew it; but they couldn't prove it." Both men are ultimately undone by the corrupt behavior of this agent.[90]

The climax of this story about contagion and the pitfalls of contact features a now "sickened" Oliver paying a nighttime visit to Ross's daughter. He creeps into her bedroom while she is asleep, planning to scalp her. Oliver is described ambivalently, "at once a figure dreadful and ludicrous" when some "curious and wonderful thing happened."[91] Ross's daughter is a symbol of white womanhood indicated by the purity of her face, the only hint of color coming from her rosy cheeks. As Oliver gazes on the sweetness of her countenance, she reaches out for his hand. In this instance, the young woman's hand becomes a metaphor for the outreach of civilization, salvation, and the type of reform Bonnin both sought and questioned when she worked with white female reformers. With this gesture Oliver's fate is changed. He cannot scalp the girl after having received the "gift" of her touch; and by extension, Indian people can no longer resist the encroachment of U.S. society into their lands and cultures. Oliver retreats from the girl's bedroom, drifting like smoke into the night air.

The story ends with Oliver sitting in the front yard of the Ross house: "A naked Indian, his legs stretched out, sat under the tree, his back against the tremendous stem. Across his knees was a bow and quiver of arrows. Upon his head a crown of eagle-feathers. His cheeks were streaked with dead white and vermilion."[92] Oliver's appearance, especially the war paint, represents a futile attempt to reunite with his Indian culture, which he has lost by going east and attending Harvard. Agent Ross, kept awake night after night by Oliver's distant coughs outside his home, then approaches the tree to see Oliver. Both men seem plagued by the reality of each other. Oliver's "sickness" in the story makes him mad, so that he leaves his family to live in the woods, where he plots to kill Ross and his daughter; an Indian desire to destroy a white future, perhaps. While Ross cannot escape the fact of Oliver's distant coughs, he is haunted by the omnipresent ghostliness of Indians and cannot sleep. Their proximity throughout the story and at the end offers an implicit critique of the uneasy relationship between Indian agents and their wards. The paternal nature of such a relationship is further emphasized by the fact that Oliver is a young man and Ross a father.

When at last Oliver dies from his mysterious sickness, lying beneath a tree by the Rosses' house, Agent Ross approaches and he too falls ill and dies. However, the story does not end there. The final image that we are left with, and that may have captured Bonnin's attention, is of Ross's daughter and her fiancé, Mr. Gilroy. Together they make breakfast and discuss where Mr. Ross might be. They will soon be married and become a family, a potential metonym for the U.S. nation. The fact that the young white couple is blissfully ignorant of two dead men (one white, and one Indian), whose bodies lie just beyond the home's kitchen, further suggests the nation must remain ignorant of the violence that has accompanied colonialism and racial conflict, resulting in the dispossession of so many Indian people, incidents that were never far from the supposed tranquility of domestic spaces.[93]

What might Bonnin have thought about this story's fallen Indian man, who seems at first to occupy a position not unlike her own? Oliver is "one member of his race" who "might enjoy an equally glorious future" and yet, perhaps because of his education in the East, he ends up as an "emaciated body." The negative portrayal of Ross, the corrupt Indian agent, would have appealed to both Bonnin and Montezuma given their criticism of the mismanagement of Native lands by the Office of Indian Affairs. The sentimental depiction of Oliver as "a full-blooded Indian descended from chieftains" may also have appealed to Bonnin as an author who drew on similar imagery. It is likely she saw the tragedy of his death as a useful allegory for his failure to fully return to "the land and the ways of his people" because of his education. She would have bristled at the white author's suggestion that the future domestic space of the United States could only lie with the young white couple.[94] The depiction of the agent as a transitional figure helping shape the nation, like Natty Bumpo in Cooper's tales, who must die or fade into the past signals the successful destruction and assimilation of Native people. Bonnin's recommendation of this story to Montezuma demonstrates the variety of texts Indian intellectuals read and how they engaged with different discourses and representations of Indianness circulating around them.

Bonnin's other letters communicated more mundane business, the highs and lows of personal life. Looking at these exchanges reveals the ways Indian activists criticized and disagreed with one another. On June 30, 1919, Bonnin expressed a mixture of concern and excitement in a letter she sent to Montezuma about federal legislation and an Indian appropriation bill. Central to her concern was the problem of not having enough activists to aid in the fight. "Right now, I have been too tired to relax; and suffer from sleeplessness.... I hope for the day to come when we shall have more workers; when the work may be divided and not have it hung too heavily upon any one."[95] This hope for more hands to share the burden of political reform remained central to Bonnin's life.

Throughout her work as SAI secretary Bonnin promoted messages of solidarity and unity in order to lighten the load of political reform that she must have felt. She also promoted unity to ameliorate personality clashes and disagreements over political tactics among members of the SAI. This was around the same time that Montezuma was advocating getting rid of the BIA entirely, a topic for debate within the organization over whether change "from within" could be most effective. In writing to Montezuma, she responds to his dismissal of the work of Indians in Washington, whom he sees as just sitting around in offices, rather than doing more overtly political work. She writes, "I am sure that you never meant to charge me with 'sitting in my office' indifferent to Congressional Acts."[96] This retort both pushes back against Montezuma's idea of what Indian reform work can look like and also uses a friendly tone to remind him that "we're in this together" after all. This sort of building and maintaining of alliances may have fallen more on Bonnin than other members of the SAI not merely because she was the secretary for the group but also because she was a woman. She is never explicit about the challenges she faced that may have differed from those faced by men like Eastman and Montezuma, but one can imagine that she managed patronage and patriarchy because of her gender. Apart from gender, Montezuma's work as a physician in Chicago brought him into contact with different sorts of personal and political issues than those Bonnin was familiar with. In this context, one can see how they had to negotiate diverse points of view because of their unique positions due to class, as well as gender and race. Because Bonnin was based out of Washington, DC, she had better access than Montezuma to certain political networks, and her note aims to keep him in the fold of SAI activities originating out of DC, not Chicago. She makes her alliance plain to him: "Let us not blame the Society of American Indians for failure to dictate to the American Congress."[97] Bonnin is aware they must collaborate in their efforts to gain more Indian and non-Indian supporters for their efforts. She emphasizes this point when she writes, "You tell me to gather up 'forces' that are not in existence unless they are spirits!"[98] Her phrasing throughout the letter represents a pragmatic and emphatic approach to dealing with the negative aspects of failed policies, like allotment, and how to amend a failing educational system that might have partially succeeded in educating Native children, even as it attempted to strip them of their languages and cultures by forcing them into white society. These political goals, Bonnin asserted, required regular maintenance of the bonds uniting Indian activists.[99]

Not only did Bonnin delicately suture together opinionated figures, like Montezuma, with other Indian activists, she also found ways to access other political networks based on her friendships with white female reformers;

perhaps most useful among them was Marianna Burgess.[100] Burgess's commitment to Indian reform, however fraught, began while she worked at the Carlisle School. By the 1920s, however, Burgess was living "all alone" and working in downtown Los Angeles, in an area later known as Westlake. Burgess had done well for herself in the "gold selling game,"[101] and she aimed to use any free time or resources to help Native people in California. Burgess was just one of a large number of white female reformers active in Southern California during this period. Burgess openly favored "the abolishment of the Bureau" of Indian Affairs; perhaps she was a subscriber to Montezuma's *Wassaja*.

Throughout most of 1921, while Bonnin wrote to Burgess, she lived a transient life on the road. Bonnin was busy surveying living conditions among Indian people across the Plains and Southwest, gathering data to provide Congress with concrete examples of the suffering and abuse that resulted from poor living conditions created by the General Allotment Act of 1887 and the Curtis Act of 1898.[102] She gathered this evidence in order to advocate for changes in federal Indian policy when it came to who could own and sell land and how to acquire U.S. citizenship. The correspondence of Burgess and Bonnin focused on the political goals Bonnin wanted to accomplish, and the inspirational role Burgess believed Bonnin should play.

Glad you are going to find your RIGHT place. Opportunities will be plenty, and you are going to be the intellectual and spiritual Joan of Arc of your people, not in a sensational way, but a way that will TELL for their good.[103]

Bonnin's "RIGHT" place, according to Burgess, positioned her at a critical juncture between leading Indian people and representing them to the larger world. Comparing her to Joan of Arc suggests there is something revolutionary and inherently powerful embodied within Bonnin's public profile at this moment. And at the same time such a comparison was also a warning – must Bonnin become a martyr for her cause? Was that always already the fate of an outspoken woman? Moreover, the bringing together of the intellectual with the spiritual recognizes Bonnin as a Christian and successful writer. Despite the drama, Burgess seems intent on moving away from sensationalism and toward the facts that enabled Bonnin to search for steady streams of income in support of her activist work. While the two women exchanged letters, Bonnin was constantly traveling as a lecturer to promote the "Indian cause," maintaining her writing career while also pursuing research to lobby for policy reform. She also sought new ways to increase sales for her books and to have her older works reprinted. Burgess understood the financial costs of activist work for someone like Bonnin, becoming one of the writer's benefactresses.

Burgess promoted Bonnin as an "intellectual and spiritual Joan of Arc" for Indian people among white networks of power. Such networks grew out of a plethora of local and national women's organizations, created to address social ills. In letters to her Indian allies, Bonnin often expresses skepticism and resignation regarding the support of these white women's groups. Still, she understood that nonwhite women needed to tap into a range of networks and harness various representational strategies to produce lasting political change. She relied on the financial and public support of white women's organizations to further her career as an author, Indian spokesperson, and lobbyist. In November 1921, Burgess encouraged Bonnin to make a trip to California, where she "could arrange for ten lectures at $50.00 [each]" as much as $600 today.[104] Such alliances between Native and white women could be both politically and financially advantageous.[105]

Relying on the strength of her relationship with Marianna Burgess, Bonnin sent a letter to Marianna's brother, Dr. C. A. Burgess, who lived in Chicago. Bonnin was set to speak at the Chicago Culture Club, Rogers Park Woman's Club, the Arche Club, and the Tenth District meeting, from January 9 through 16, 1921. Her letter asks if Dr. Burgess might arrange for her to speak at his "Church of Spirit Healing." She broaches the matter by referring explicitly to Marianna, who "suggested that arrangements might be made for me to speak in your Church." Bonnin's letter draws on a personal connection between herself and Marianna and that of a sister and brother.

In her letter to Dr. Burgess, Bonnin writes both within and against primitivism as an ideology defined in opposition to modernity. She casts it as both positive and negative. Bonnin does this by framing herself and her talk in racialized terms that rely on the oppositional relationship between the primitive and the modern. She writes: "I am an Indian (Sioux) and my subject is the Indian."[106] Bonnin is clearly self-conscious about how to represent Indianness according to white expectations. She adds this important detail concerning her appearance for the talk: "I usually speak in my Native costume, unless otherwise requested."[107] For Bonnin, this meant purposefully wearing a Yankton buckskin dress.[108] This comment on costuming and performance worked within the logic of cultural practices embodied by Indian women who were performers during the early twentieth century. Other scholars, like Beth Piatote and Frederick Hoxie, have written about the different literary and political strategies Native female writers like E. Pauline Johnson and Sarah Winnemucca used to critique white civilization. In this sense, Bonnin is building on a preexisting network of Native female performance, much of it literary, to draw the attention of white reformers and benefactors.[109]

In terms of staged performance, Bonnin was also not alone in her ability to self-consciously represent Indian womanhood for a white audience. Tsianina Redfeather, Creek/Cherokee (ca. 1882–1985), listed on the Creek rolls as Florence Evans, enjoyed a successful career as a professional singer and entertainer that enabled her to participate in Charles Wakefield Cadman's opera *Shanewis*. "Princess Watawaso," also known as Lucy Nicolar, Penobscot

(1882–1969), was employed by the "Redpath Chautauqua Circuit," where she performed generic "Indian" entertainments. These two women were well known to white audiences for their musical talents and their ability to embody characteristics of an imaginary Indian princess. Like Bonnin, they were strategic about when and how to promote themselves in relation to their talent or in relation to their Indianness. As performers on the operatic stage who *also* participated in public speaking tours, Redfeather and Watawaso had to navigate different understandings about Indian womanhood. They played Indian in ways that aligned with what other Indian performers were doing with nostalgia and the reenactment of historical events that were popularized through Wild West shows and appealed to white audiences because of the romances written during the nineteenth century. They certainly had to make choices about what clothes to wear and how to embody Indian womanhood whether they were performing in a musical or giving a public lecture. Indian women were most often narrated as savage exotics who existed outside normative ideals of white womanhood, and genres of sentimentality and the romance of late nineteenth-century womanhood.[110] Ideas regarding a savage Indian woman or Native princess were created and popularized by non-Indian actors and actresses who "played Indian." Even more damaging, perhaps, was that these ideas were recirculated by actual Indian performers who reenacted nostalgic historical conflicts as part of a Wild West frontier fantasy. It is difficult to calculate the degree to which the reenactment of historical violence by Indian people may have perpetrated cultural violence against Indian people given that these performances maintained a flawed national imaginary that stripped Native people of their cultural specificity, personhood, and agency.[111]

All three of these women relied on and to some extent were able to reshape the market for Indianness as a performance. Within this market the real and imagined came together. When Bonnin references wearing "my native costume," she suggests the performative nature of her talk and mobilizes a particular politics of representation. She also recognizes that her costume was not that of an imaginary Indian princess. Regardless of the imagined Indianness on which lecture success hinged, the material reality for Bonnin lay in the fact that she was well paid for these performances and put her earnings toward "support of the cause."[112]

Through participating in this market, Native women became increasingly attuned to balancing cultural performance opportunities with their political reform work. Ella Deloria, Yankton Sioux (1888–1971), worked as a "national field representative" from 1919 to 1925 for the YWCA's Indian Bureau, and several years later, in 1940 and 1941, produced a community pageant for the Indians of Robeson County, North Carolina. Like Deloria and Bonnin, Ruth Muskrat Bronson, Cherokee (1897–1981), educated at Mount Holyoke College in 1925, later worked as a guidance and placement officer for the BIA's Education Division in 1930, and became active in the National Congress of American Indians, founded out of Chicago in 1944. Deloria and Bronson were not exactly the cultural performers that Redfeather and Watawaso were, and yet these women's activities illustrate the different networks Native women accessed and shaped. Politics and performance operated at the center of what they aimed to do and what they could do. These networks of Native women were often intimately tied to white women's reform work, as we have seen with Burgess and Bonnin.[113]

Indeed, as Burgess helped Bonnin make contacts in Chicago that would add to her work as a public lecturer, she also connected Bonnin to a network of women's organizations that emerged out of the West Coast. Together, Bonnin and Burgess promoted a pan-Indianist cause by selling Bonnin's books and arranging speaking engagements for her in Los Angeles, San Francisco, and Pasadena, as well as Portland and Seattle.[114] The combination of writing and speaking was critical to Bonnin's success as an interlocutor between pan-Indian reform groups and those of white women. Stella Atwood, also out of California, worked as the state chairman of the Division of Indian Welfare, a part of the Department of Welfare under the aegis of the California Federation of Women's Clubs out of Riverside, and she helped Bonnin pursue shared reform goals.[115] Atwood and Bonnin were similar in that they each became known as social and political brokers for Indian people. Of course an important distinction resides in Atwood's status as a white woman.[116]

The friendship and political alliance between Bonnin and Atwood was no coincidence. Because Atwood had worked as a "clubwoman" in California for some time, she drew on her relationships with Indian activists to influence other women in these clubs, as well as reformers like John Collier. As historian Karin Huebner has shown, alliances that formed between California clubwomen, Collier, and the Indians of the Southwest from 1917 to 1934 were based on a mutual interest in Indian reform despite differences in gender, class, and ethnicity. Huebner also shows the extent to which California clubwomen effectively waged political campaigns aimed at supporting Indian religious freedom, protecting tribal lands, and Native self-determination. As historian Margaret D. Jacobs has argued, important parallels existed between clubwomen's philosophy and work in Indian reform with the ideas expressed by antimodern feminists such as Mabel Dodge Luhan. These women sought out Native cultural ideals and practices in their quest for personal redemption; in effect they celebrated Indian primitivism as defined by communalism, spiritualism, and a close relationship to the land as the antidote to the moral decay and corruption they believed necessarily accompanied modernity.[117]

Many Indian people did not miss out on opportunities to form alliances with white supporters when threatened by federal legislation that sought to undermine their claims to land. During the early 1920s, Bonnin and Atwood exchanged letters focused on two main goals. The first was to promote the

use of Bonnin's writings, especially *American Indian Stories*, in club programs, an activity that worked in tandem with their second goal, which was
to gain club members in support of Indian reform efforts. On December 30,
1921, Atwood wrote to Bonnin to convey that she was "anxious to have
a fine Indian Exhibit and if this Indian Arts and Crafts Society is what it
should be, it will be a great opportunity for them also" at the biennial meeting of the California Federation of Women's Clubs (CFWC) in Chautauqua,
New York to be held in June 1922. Bonnin and Atwood's twin goals came
together when club members and Indian activists united for this meeting.[118]

In 1922 and 1923, two pieces of legislation, the Bursum and Lenroot
bills, were put before Congress; these bills aimed to settle disputes regarding land titles and water rights between Pueblos and non-Indian claimants. In effect, the Bursum bill would dispossess Pueblos of land without
legal recourse to fight non-Indian claimants. Atwood and Collier worked
together with Indian reform organizations and the Pueblo Indians to campaign against the Bursum bill. Testimonies before the House Committee on
Indian Affairs on January 15, 1923 succeeded in stopping the bill's passage.
As Huebner shows, the GFWC, with Atwood as chairwoman, was a critical
force in defeating this type of legislation. In addition, Tisa Wenger notes that
the organization of Indian people of the Southwest, through the Council of
All of the New Mexico Pueblos, was also critical in protesting and stopping
the Bursum bill.[119]

A year after the defeat of the Bursum bill, John Collier formed the AIDA.
Atwood, along with other officers and members from the CFWC, served on
the executive board. This alliance was timely given that 1923 was devoted
to the defeat of the Lenroot bill. This bill aimed to correct major flaws in the
Bursum bill, but it was not one Collier supported because he believed any
non-Indian encroachment onto Indian lands since 1848 (in the Southwest)
had been illegal.[120] Although the Lenroot bill promised to create a three-man
Pueblo land board that would deal with contested land claims and bring any
disputes over title to federal court, this was not a bill that most Indian people
supported. In fact, members of the All Pueblo Council actively opposed the
Lenroot bill. Unfortunately, representatives from the New Mexico branch of
the Indian Rights Association (IRA), which was a white reform organization
familiar to Bonnin, argued in support of the Lenroot bill. Apparently settlers' advocates in New Mexico had convinced the IRA to "tacitly" endorse
the bill.[121]

Early on the morning of January 3, 1924, Stella Atwood sent an urgent
telegram to Gertrude Bonnin asking for her help to defeat the Lenroot bill.
It read: "I am sending you special delivery letter which will explain why
I want you to attend a board meeting at headquarters please plan to dress
in costume and be there as much as possible I am worried as to outcome
if you aren't here." The aforementioned letter, which Atwood surely must
have sent in haste, urges Bonnin to visit with members of the Board because

the "New Mexico group have been perniciously busy poisoning the minds of everyone possible." Although neither the telegram nor the letter make specific mention of the effort to stop the Lenroot bill, it seems likely that Atwood enlisted Bonnin to help convince Board members to oppose this bill alongside members of the AIDA and the All Pueblo Council. The "New Mexico group" that was "poisoning" people's minds may be a coded reference to a branch of the IRA. Atwood's letter further suggests that Bonnin could best represent Indian people at the meeting if she would "dress up in your costume and go over to Headquarters the day before the meeting and see what you can find out."[122] With this request, Atwood appealed to Bonnin as a successful political organizer and a representative for Indian people in general, and specifically because of her ability to perform Indianness in strategic ways.

Another letter, sent to Raymond Bonnin from Mrs. Felix T. McWhirter, president of Woman's Department Club (1922–4), also emphasizes Bonnin's ability to win over the hearts of clubwomen "by her charming personality, her appealing voice and her sincere message for her people."[123] Like so many of Bonnin's letters and public performances we see a mixing of method and message in this compliment. Surely Bonnin was successful because she was an Indian woman advocating for "her people." At the same time, it was equally likely that she captivated audiences because she possessed well-honed performance skills.

Performance Opportunities: Photography, Music, and Indian Play

Bonnin engaged with performativity as an avenue through which she might not only represent herself, but also Indianness writ large. In two 1898 photographs taken by Gertrude Kasebier (1852–1934), Bonnin appears not in the garb of an opera performer or a Wild West show entertainer, but in modest, sometimes Edwardian, dresses with her hair loosely tied at the back (Figures 6 and 7). In one she holds a violin, and in the other a book rests lightly in her lap. Kasebier aimed to create an alternative archive of images. She wanted to portray Bonnin and other Indian subjects in contemporary frames, wearing clothes and holding objects that depicted their interests and aptitudes, as opposed to the vast majority of publicity materials and photographs taken during this time to promote the careers of Indian actors and performers – images that largely relied on costuming meant to reify a primitivist aesthetic.

Bonnin and Kasebier met when Bonnin was just beginning to promote herself as "Zitkala-Sa," an Indian author, while she was busy traveling between Boston and New York. The image with the violin represents Bonnin's love of music and her recent course of study at the New England Conservatory. It reveals a young, yet savvy woman who is keenly aware of

FIGURE 6. Gertrude Bonnin portrait by Gertrude Kasebier (circa 1898) –
Smithsonian, Washington, DC.
Gertrude Kasebier Photograph Collection, Division of Culture & the Arts,
National Museum of American History, Smithsonian Institution.

the power of her representation. Holding her violin with a penetrating gaze
and slightly turned head, Bonnin looks right into the eye of the camera.
Her straight gaze, tilted head, and slouching body convey a subtle desire to
engage the viewer. As she draws us in to consider her pose, the more relaxed
position of her body calls into question some of the strict conventions of
portrait photography from this period.[124]

FIGURE 7. Gertrude Bonnin portrait by Gertrude Kasebier (circa 1898) – Smithsonian, Washington, DC.
Gertrude Kasebier Photograph Collection, Division of Culture & the Arts, National Museum of American History, Smithsonian Institution.

Most portraits aimed to define their subjects according to class and gender norms. Women, regardless of race or actual legal status (like Native people and colonial populations such as Puerto Ricans), were encouraged to represent themselves as proper citizens whose virtue was defined by acceptable forms of deportment. Bonnin also succeeds in drawing in the viewer without relying on any Indian topos. The violin and bow appear as framing devices, creating a V that is echoed in the lines of her dress and perhaps even her hair, which, because of the turn and slouch, hangs to her left side; her head then looks somewhat out of proportion to the rest of her body. Considering these aspects and the lack of smile I wonder: To what extent was she aware of or did she seek to control this representation of her self? Did she choose the dress, the violin, and the posture? How might this portrait exemplify self-determination?[125]

Regardless of her choices, Bonnin (and Kasebier) had to work within a medium, which during the late nineteenth century was "understood to represent the world objectively," that helped "stabilize cultural notions of race," which this photograph disrupts.[126] The indexicality of photography further suggests that these images speak to the experiences of the person in front of the camera. Portraiture in particular is open to multiple readings given that there is both the intention of the sitter and the photographer to consider. As art historian Elizabeth Hutchinson asserts, Bonnin was familiar with the popular visual culture of her day, and for her, visual self-presentation, especially using clothing, "was an important means of communicating cultural identity in both Native and mainstream American society."[127] Because these photographs were created during a period in which photography was used to fix rather than blur racial categories, Bonnin and Kasebier destabilized the concept of race as biologically determined to contradict race-based expectations for Indian women. The image of Bonnin with the violin denotes an interest in music as an elevated Western art form (although violins were also fiddles, and the most common instrument among settlers living along the frontier lines of white civilization), conveying a commitment to high culture marking her as a "civilized" and a specially educated Indian. The two images here are from a set of nine; each portrait is simple. Bonnin is either sitting or standing, her hair sometimes loose and other times bound with wide ribbon or beads. She holds a violin in four and reads a book in two of the images, while clasping a basket to her chest in one and empty-handed in the rest. Both Bonnin and Kasebier were at the beginning of their careers, the former about to make a name for herself through music and writing (thus the prominence of the violin and the book as props) and the latter a recent art school graduate now running her own commercial portrait studio in lower Manhattan.

The second image shows Bonnin holding a book. This object seems to represent her commitment to writing and to reading. Her Edwardian dress allows Bonnin to embody femininity, culture, and success on her own Indian and modern terms. These two portraits may represent Bonnin's sense of herself as much as they reveal Kasebier's commitment to photographing Native people *neither* in costume *nor* with surroundings that might romanticize or sentimentalize them.[128] Taken out of these cultural ideologies Bonnin's portraits reflect modernity and individuality and the future not the past of its Native sitter. Indeed, close looking at the shadowing produced for viewers a racial ambiguity that points to fluid thinking regarding womanhood, while the floral prints float in the background and suggest more Victorian gender conventions.

For Kasebier, and also Bonnin, Indianness was fluid and not necessarily tied to the scripts of either the Wild West or the well-worn tropes of James Fenimore Cooper's (1789–1851) narratives and George Catlin's (1796–1872) paintings. Still, the messages Kasebier's images conveyed have been occluded by later experiences and accounts Bonnin and others gave regarding the occasions when she seemed to have no choice but to appear dressed in "full Indian regalia." At this time, regalia had become a marker not only of fixed racial categories but also a certain understanding of ethnic authenticity, which Kasebier's images seem to work against, offering more authentic self-representation. These accounts suggest that Bonnin understood, in complicated ways, the how, when, and why of audiences and the possibilities she had for controlling the ways she represented herself to them.[129]

Returning to the portrait of Bonnin with the book in her lap, with her face half hidden by shadows, the darkness seems to, at least partially, obscure her beauty as well as her expression.[130] This ambiguity produces a gap to be filled in by the imaginative eye of the viewer. There is an ease to her posture, which reminds us of the constructed nature of a photograph. The book on her lap indicates leisure and literacy rather than domestic labor, although she may be read as the ideal wife and homemaker ready to perform tasks identified as intrinsically female, or as something else.[131]

The handkerchief she grasps in her left hand produces associations with sentimentality that position Bonnin within normative discourses based on whiteness, womanhood, and middle-class American values, subordinating the truth to desire emotional effect. Thus, one way of reading her holding the handkerchief is as cynical; the actual significance is not with the object but with the emotional impact of that on oneself. It would suggest a collaboration between Bonnin and Kasebier to push back against an oppressive cultural system that linked properly empowered womanhood always to whiteness. The floral backdrop evokes a domestic home scene and simultaneously alludes to the natural wilderness that exists in opposition to the space of the home. Taking the dress and the wallpaper together, Bonnin is linked to white, middle-class American cultural frames for defining her identity, which elide her Yankton Sioux heritage.

Reading the image within a literary realist framework produced by authors like Mark Twain, William Dean Howells, and Henry James, the photograph becomes unremarkable, just a simple portrait of the quotidian, contemporary, and true reality of banal middle-class womanhood.[132] Viewed as a mundane representation of a domestic space or read more ideologically as a reflection of reality, the book in her lap seems an apt symbol for Bonnin's intellectual work as a teacher and writer. The photograph is remarkable because it has a racialized indigenous woman at the frame's center. Together, Bonnin and Kasebier created an ambivalent, yet powerful image. Bonnin is presented within her historical moment as the embodiment of Indian womanhood. Indianness appears cloaked considering the power of representations produced by popular narratives that defined Indian people in terms of ahistorical settings, primitive clothing, and often culturally inappropriate objects and make-up. Such representations of "Wild West-ness" were intended to be spectacular and out of the ordinary, whereas Kasebier's portraits were designed to be realistic, if also personal and intimate. Looking at these particular images of Bonnin, one can peer into the past and see a moment of possibility regarding her self-representation. In these instances, Bonnin challenges dominant narratives about Indian women. For Euro-American viewers, these portraits are a departure from the types they would have seen in public venues, depicting educated Indians "contrived to portray a mixture of 'savagery' and 'civilization' that would communicate their status."[133]

The time and care put into constructing and designing these images is useful for highlighting Bonnin's recognition of the possibilities of a particular kind of representation, and how she built on these sorts of experiences to complicate the stage performance brand of self-representation. Looking at her career, as one that required public presentations (both written and spoken), it is possible to point to several important vectors of performance. Indeed, the ways Bonnin represented her Native and feminine "self" responded to white ideological expectations for Indian people, the marketing of primitivist desire in the form of commodities and fashion, as well as civilization and gender discourses, all of which fed into the question of recognition by audiences.

In concert halls and on lecture platforms, Bonnin spoke about her ideas regarding public debates surrounding the "Indian Question." During these talks, Bonnin often wore clothing that embodied a "primitivist" aesthetic, one embraced by cosmopolitan whites who sought ways to nostalgically avoid and culturally reform the modern world they lived in. Within these contexts, Bonnin's long, beaded dresses made of animal skin and her jeweled necklaces made by Indian hands were deemed by most audiences as "traditional" and authentically Indian. In a quotidian sense, these were not Bonnin's typical clothes. Although Bonnin may have been read as more exotic and more Indian because of such costumed appearances, more and more Americans were able to purchase these items from local crafts dealers and through mail-order catalogs. Thus, Bonnin's "Yankton dress" reflected not only a particular expression of Indian culture but reinforced (perhaps accidentally) a market system structured by the desire to see, produce, and consume the aesthetics of this culture and to reify a generic Indian in the national imaginary.[134]

While Bonnin's costume reinforced certain white expectations regarding "traditional" Native clothing, it also enabled her to become a living advertisement for the marketing of Indianness. In addition, it ran against the grain of the representational politics she seemed to have established when working with Kasebier. In these later instances, performance itself became a meaning-laden arena. On stage Bonnin might find herself in a double-bind: trapped within certain representations of femininity and Indianness. Yet within this predicament she found ways to participate in and also revise discourses of American civilization. As a performer, not unlike Eastman and other Indian intellectuals at the time, Bonnin developed important strategies for how to be recognizable as an *Indian* writer and activist, so that she might rewrite what it meant to be an Indian woman.

Bonnin remarked in several personal letters that she recognized the necessity, if also the danger, of having to dress in costume to "play Indian," especially in her letters concerning "Princess Chinquilla" and "Red Fox St. James." No doubt, her brief career as a violinist exposed Bonnin to the opportunities and the limits that accompanied any public Indian performance. After she trained with Austrian violinist Eugene Gruenberg (1854–1928) at the New England Conservatory in Boston (1899–1900),[135] Bonnin made memorable appearances as a soloist with the Carlisle Indian School Band. In March 1900, she received a warm reception at Philadelphia's Association Hall and again when the band performed at Carnegie Hall in New York City. Advertisements for this concert promised audiences a mix of high art and Indian spectacle: "Zitkala Sa, the Indian Girl Violinist from the Boston Conservatory." This popular tour culminated with performances at the Paris Exposition. These sorts of moments showcase Bonnin's accomplishments as much as they demonstrate how her ethnic identity became entangled with her cultural work. In the years that followed, the two became mutually constitutive as she took on the name "Zitkala Sa" to promote herself as an author, and later as a political activist. Another photograph from later in Bonnin's career exemplifies how complicated performance was for Native activists.[136]

On March 9, 1926, members of the NCAI assembled in Washington, DC to take part in a ceremony for unveiling a statue of Sitting Bull. The statue was made for the Wyoming Historical Society and paid for by contributions from white schoolchildren in Pennsylvania. NCAI members gathered around the statue's sculptor, Mr. U. S. J. Dunbar, with their president and NCAI founder, Gertrude Bonnin, on Dunbar's left. A photographer snapped away to document all who were present. In the process, a range of Native costumes was captured, from all different nations, including Bonnin in her Yankton buckskin dress.[137]

There is a double monument to Indianness present in the image captured that day. It suggests the productive potential of representations by and about Indian people, and the underlying performative nature of such representations. Sitting Bull himself is an apt symbol to embody the changing relationship between Indian people and mediated forms of representation, which centered on them in public performances. His short-lived alliance with William F. Cody as a member of "Buffalo Bill's" Wild West touring company enabled both men to improve their financial and political futures. The contract that Sitting Bull negotiated with Cody also demonstrated the Indian leader's awareness of the power and influence show business and celebrity could bring to Indian participants. Unlike many Indian performers, Sitting Bull's notoriety among American audiences, the government, and the military enabled him to simply "play himself" as a part of Cody's enterprise. Furthermore, his involvement with Cody's company allowed Sitting Bull to improve the material circumstances of himself and members of his tribe. This was especially crucial given that Sitting Bull was imprisoned under the supervision of James McLaughlin (the agent in charge of the Standing Rock Reservation), and yet Sitting Bull managed to use his affiliation with Cody to make diplomatic visits to Washington, DC, consequently frustrating McLaughlin.[138]

The image's caption lists the tribesmen of the Sioux, Assiniboine, Yakima, Miami, Kiowa, Apache, and Osage who were present at the unveiling of the statue to honor Sitting Bull – we might further assume that those in "Native costume" were representing their individual tribal nations. A handwritten note adds another level of context for those who might have viewed and circulated such a photograph. Bonnin writes, "To Miss Julia A. Thomas, With Love, Zitkala Sa (Gertrude Bonnin)." The photograph and Bonnin's signature, followed by a parenthetical reference to herself as Gertrude Bonnin, point to her understanding of key discourses that authenticated Indian performance. In this case, her choice to use "Zitkala Sa" first and then Bonnin highlights her role as an author first and an activist second. Bonnin's Sioux regalia matched the tribally specific dress of the other female members of the NCAI. Their clothing would have appealed to white primitivist aesthetics and could generate more attention to support their work. Bonnin's costuming and the use of Zitkala-Sa represent her strategic choices to be associated with Sioux culture and heritage. In addition, her use of parentheses in writing to Julia Thomas demonstrates an awareness of multiple publics that could read her as either Zitkala-Sa (Indian author and performer) and/or Gertrude Bonnin (political activist, wife, and mother). Moreover, her use of parentheses seems more strategic than ambivalent and less a matter of confusion about her identity than a matter of recognition regarding the multiple ways Indian intellectuals could be visible.[139]

Bonnin was not alone in using parentheses in strategic ways. Eastman, for example, often signed his letters as Ohiyesa, and his publishers would name him as the author Charles (Ohiyesa) Eastman. In a similar way, Carlos Montezuma produced a newsletter and editorial alter ego using the name "Wassaja." Renaming oneself and when and how to use certain names parallels the ways Indian intellectuals performed public identities, and wore more or less "authentic" clothing representing Indianness. For Bonnin, performances could be manipulated and mobilized to play off nostalgic tropes and (anti)modernist longings for primitivism. She could then open up spaces to argue for wider recognition of Indian people as cultural and political participants in shaping American society, as she reshaped it herself.[140]

One arena in which Bonnin first attempted to rework how white Americans imagined Indian history, people, and culture was through her collaboration with music professor William Hanson to produce *The Sun Dance* opera. The name Sun Dance derives from the Sioux identification of it as Wi wanyang wacipi, translated as "sun gazing dance." The ceremony is highly variable because its performance is intimately connected to the guidance of visions or dreams that establish an individual relationship between one or more of the central participants and one or more spirit persons. In all cases, however, the primary meaning is understood to be the performance of acts of sacrifice in ritual reciprocity with spiritual powers, so the welfare of friends, family, and the whole people is enhanced. The Arapaho, Cheyenne, Blackfoot, and Sioux nations all practiced sacrificial acts of piercing the flesh. Others, such as the Ute, Shoshone, and Crow nations, performed sacrificial acts of embodying their spiritual intentions through fasting and intense dancing, but not through piercing. The central concern of the Sun Dance was to establish and maintain kinship with all peoples, including animals, and plants.[141]

In 1912, Bonnin and Hanson set to work on designing a story, sets, and costumes to produce an opera loosely based on the Plains Sun Dance ritual. The opera debuted on February 20, 1913, in Vernal, Utah, and later was performed with two separate productions at Brigham Young University in Provo in May and December 1914.[142] These later productions featured mostly undergraduates of the University, where Hanson was employed. Bonnin wrote the libretto and also made many public costumed appearances in Utah to advertise it. Her participation in making and promoting this show was one way to advance politics, which traded heavily on the work of culture. Despite her efforts, the *Sun Dance* remained relatively obscure, although it was popular among Utah audiences.[143]

One May 26, 1914 review from the *Deseret Evening News* notes that "the libretto is by Zikala Sa (Mrs. R. T. Bonnin) a highly educated Sioux woman, and the music is by William F. Hanson, a young man of Vernal, and instructor in the Uinta Stake Academy of that place." This same article describes the opera as "one of the most melodious and interesting representations of western aboriginal life ever seen on the local stage ... in the Salt Lake theater." Other reviews highlight the collaboration between Bonnin and Hanson, while also placing Indianness itself at the center of their analyses of the opera. This same review comments on how "weird Indian melodies" are arranged by a production that features both white and Indian singers and dancers. As P. Jane Hafen illustrates: "Part of the success of The Sun Dance Opera was the incorporation of local Ute performers. At various times, the opera would come to a dead halt as the Native performers entered the stage to sing and dance. Because the Utes practiced the Sun Dance, it is easy to draw the conclusion that, knowing the topic, they performed their own ritualistic songs and dances."[144]

The opera could be read on multiple levels. It played to audiences who expected and embraced romantic tropes and nostalgic narratives about Indian people, and who would be entertained by a love story about two young braves competing to court Winona, "a lovely Shoshone maiden." The opera also provided little in the way of action and instead sought to teach white audiences about the local Ute population. As one review noted, "the chief value of the tale lies in the opportunity it offers for emphasis on Indian customs and superstitions, and for the use of authentic aboriginal tunes." As Hafen further points out, the Ute songs and dances were not part of the score of the opera even though they were integral to the performances.[145]

Another review framed the educational impact of the performance through the body of Bonnin herself, noting how she "in a pretty five-minute address, explained the Indian customs and legends incorporated in the opera." Despite Bonnin's accomplishments in writing the libretto, her musical training at the New England Conservatory, and her work as an author, she could not (and would not) escape being framed within a discourse of ethnic authenticity that defined her and Indianness as invoking a necessary realism for the opera. Reporters framed Hanson as authentic as well because he had visited the Ute and studied their ceremonies and melodies. Together they worked within a sphere of understanding Native performance that was not wholly dissimilar from the productions of Wild West touring companies. Except, by using opera as their genre, Hanson and Bonnin appealed to middle- and upper-class audiences, as opposed to the Wild West, which relied on the humor, fast pace, and spectacle traditions of Vaudeville coupled with the fact of real Indians' participation to authenticate the stories and rituals that were used. Despite its pretention toward high society, *The Sun Dance* opera was celebrated for being both "instructive" and "at times dramatic" because of the representations about and by the Ute people. As an American opera, sung entirely in English, with mostly Native cast members, it was a genre unto its own.

As a form of political resistance, the opera was an ingenious creation given that there had been U.S. laws from the 1880s that prohibited the performance of the Sun Dance. It seems likely that Bonnin might have intended to make a political statement in naming the opera *The Sun Dance* given her Yankton background. Mark Rifkin argues in his reading of Ella Deloria's novel *Waterlily*, written during the early 1940s but published in 1988, that Deloria recognizes her political context of post-IRA policy and Collierian discourse by acknowledging the earlier era's restrictions on Native practices. "However, in what seems to me impossible to construe as merely coincidence, the novel addresses all the practices targeted by the code of Indian offenses in the 1880s – the Sun Dance, polygamy, the presence of medicine men, giving away property as part of a mourning ritual, and traveling away from one's reservation – weaving its story in and through these elements in Dakota sociality."[146] It is not an understatement to say that the ritual of the Sun Dance is an important centerpiece for Deloria's novel. Furthermore, the fact that polygamy, as practiced by both Natives and Mormons, was under attack and still illegal when Bonnin was working with Hanson in the heart of Mormon and Native areas in Utah, suggests other forms of resistance may have been at play in the opera they made together.

A December 21, 1914 publicity photo of Hanson and Bonnin and her subsequent talks that explained the customs and legends incorporated into *The Sun Dance* show the ways that Bonnin used the opera as a platform to educate white audiences about Ute life, even if she embraced certain primitivist tropes. The publicity shot features both opera producers dressed in costumes that place them into the narrative they imagined for their opera. Indeed, the dress that Bonnin is wearing in the photo is quite similar to what she would wear several years later as the president of the NCAI witnessing the unveiling of Sitting Bull's statue. This publicity photo and reviews following the first performances of the opera served to celebrate and authenticate it as a cultural work because of Hanson's close association with Indian people and Bonnin's identity and performance as a "full-blooded Sioux."[147]

Following the modest success of *The Sun Dance* in Utah, the Bonnins relocated to Washington, DC and Hanson set to work on other cultural productions that capitalized on the Indian representations he and Bonnin had put into their opera. He created *The Bear Dance*, which claimed to feature "medicine songs, scalp dance songs and burial songs" from the Ute. Throughout the 1920s, newspapers reported that Hanson traveled with Utah Indians around the state to affirm the authenticity of their performances. With the support of local Indian people and public interest in seeing these performances, Hanson formed the Hanson Wigwam Company. According to the company's promotional materials they created compositions that aimed to transport listeners "back one hundred years" so that they might "get a picture of those original roamers of western hills and valleys, and see more than books of history ever tell."[148] The educational impetus behind the original collaboration between Bonnin and Hanson seemed to be carried on in these later productions.

Although Bonnin was no longer involved with the promotion of *The Sun Dance* after she left Utah in 1916, Hanson remained active in producing Indian-themed works. In fact, he worked to revive their opera, making some alterations to the score in the process.[149] By 1938, after Bonnin had died, Hanson brought a new company to present *The Sun Dance* for its New York premiere at a Broadway theater. This new version of the opera featured Yakima actor and singer "Chief Yowlachie," also known as Daniel Simmons, whose career in film would bring him into close contact with

Luther Standing Bear's political activities based in Los Angeles during this same time.[150] A May 15, 1938 article in *Musical Courier* celebrated the work as "a new romantic American Indian opera."[151] By this time there was nothing new about the use of Indian themes in operatic productions, especially because Charles Wakefield Cadman's Indian-themed opera *Shanewis (The Robin Woman)* had premiered as the first American opera to play two seasons at the Metropolitan Opera house in New York City in 1918.[152] Still, the article refers to these "typical themes" and their "racial flavor" as central to the opera's appeal, and attributes them to Hanson rather than Bonnin. Despite her erasure from the review, the opera's message, which was also hers, of "the heart throbs, the National Voice of the Indians of the mountains" could now reach a new white audience, and be celebrated as the American opera of the year.[153]

After relocating to Washington, DC to pursue political work, Bonnin left behind many of the Indianized themes that would make Hanson famous to present a different sort of national voice for Indian people in the United States. As an author and activist, she was constantly aware of the power of representation and how best to appeal to different sorts of audiences. Over the next two decades, Bonnin was invited to give public talks on "Indian Affairs" throughout the United States because of her work as secretary for the SAI and because of the alliances that she made with white women's groups. Bonnin was able to connect to a range of different networks be they local or national, overtly political, or more cultural in their focus. Bonnin was repeatedly applauded for her presentation style and her appearance at these gatherings. In 1927, at the Nation Dinner in New York City, newspaper reporters commented on her "Indian dress," which was as forceful in making an argument about the validity of Native concerns as the tone of Bonnin's voice. She and her attire made a statement. Although Bonnin no longer took to the musical stage as a venue to educate American audiences, she did not entirely give up the use of a costume or cadence to make a point.

Bonnin became, especially as the president of the NCAI, a representative figure of Indianness and voice for Indian affairs. The NCAI was created in February 1926 "to establish Local Lodges in Indian country for self-help and study" among Indians "to use their new citizenship," so that "the Indian may become a producer and not a consumer only" in American society. As the "Constitution and By-Laws" notes in article 3, the NCAI will be headquartered in Washington, DC along with "various branches" that "shall be located in the respective communities wherein they are created."[154] As president of the NCAI, Bonnin's duties were also outlined in this document. "It shall be the duty of the President to preside over all meetings of the National Council of American Indians and meetings of the Board of Directors or Advisory Board." In addition to these meetings, the "By-Laws" is explicit that Bonnin would also sign and execute any documents required and authorized by the Board of Directors, she would require all officers and

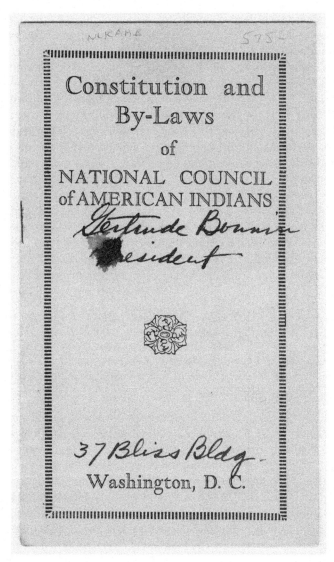

FIGURE 8. NCAI: Constitution and by-laws (circa 1926).
Archives and Special Collections, Frost Library, Amherst College, Amherst, MA.

committees to make reports on an annual basis, she would maintain regular and proper means of communications between the various officers, boards, and committees, and "from time to time cause the issuance of bulletins or other notices to all members whereby information on important matters will be given to the members of the organization."[155] As president, Bonnin did all of these things, and from the extant letters and memoranda in her personal papers, it is clear she probably did even more. As president of the NCAI she was still a writer, but with a much different purpose and a much different audience.[156]

Bonnin's work with the NCAI – smaller in national scope and influence in Indian affairs than the SAI – gave her ample opportunities to work with other Native activists "to help our Indian people find their rightful place in American life."[157] Throughout her work as a public face for Indian people, Bonnin confronted a new sort of issue that was connected to expectations for Indian performances and performers. She started to be on the look-out for individuals who were making public presentations, while "playing Indian," but whom she believed were not Indian at all.

As she traveled to promote the NCAI, Bonnin worried, privately in her letters, about the negative influence that imposter Indians would pose to her efforts. This worry came from her own practice – dressing up to make her Indianness visible could encourage imposters to "play" Indian using similar methods. On April 18, 1927, she wrote to friend and former SAI president Reverend Philip Gordon about her concerns related to these "inauthentic" Indians.

During the time I served the Society of American Indians as Secretary, I had some correspondence with Dr. Montezuma about Red Fox and his workers. Arthur Parker, previous to our activities in the SAI, had written Red Fox up quite to his utter exposure as an imposter; so I mentioned that to Dr. Montezuma; Red Fox naturally did not relish my attitude; and when later he was in Washington, D.C. for a short time, he FAILED to call at the SAI office.

Bonnin points out how pan-Indianist groups like the SAI, and probably to a lesser extent the NCAI, could manipulate public expectations regarding Indianness while at the same time fearing their own legitimacy might be threatened by charlatans who adopted their practice by posing as Indians. These sorts of exchanges showcase the ways Indian intellectual leaders saw themselves uniquely positioned to not only speak on behalf of Indian people in general, but also to act (however dangerous and fraught this may be) as "culture cops" to police the boundaries of what *proper* Indianness looked and sounded like. For Bonnin, the issue was largely about what the political consequences of these deviations might mean for their activist work.[158]

Bonnin writes more to Rev. Gordon with details regarding the problem of Red Fox.[159] Apparently, Red Fox had collected money from the general public "for Indian work" and then a white man named "Black Hawk" disappeared with the money. Bonnin also mentions that concerns about Red Fox have extended to include various Indian figures involved with the SAI. For her, a particular concern arose regarding "Princess Chinquilla," whom Bonnin met in New York City. After that meeting, she wrote again to Gordon that "a clipping was sent me," and it read: "'Princess Chinquilla and Dr. Skiuhushu a Blackfoot, organized the club under the auspices of the American Indian Association for the benefit of the 200 Indians living in New York.'" Bonnin apparently dropped the matter after writing to Chinquilla and receiving a reply that stated the "Princess" had not started any such organization, but rather thought it was a continuation of the SAI. At best, Red Fox and Chinquilla are problematic examples of Indians "playing Indian." At worst, they are con artists, scammers, and grafters who bring other Indian people down with them. In either case, all of these figures operated within influential cultural networks, which often relied on white people "going Native."[160]

Bonnin's concerns regarding Indian Play seem firmly rooted in suspicions surrounding imposter Indians who used Indianness for the express purpose of making money. In fact, she maintained professional relationships with white organizations like the IRA, despite their own practices of Indian Play. This all-white and male political reform group had members that supported and celebrated fraternal clubs and childrearing organizations, like the Boy Scouts, which gave American men opportunities to "Play Indian" when they were young, so that they might become better Americans as they grew up. Bonnin's concerns regarding the "American Indian Order, Inc." that listed among its principal officers "Dr. Red Fox St James" and "Skinhushu, Wampum Keeper" with Rev. Red Fox (Skinhushu) Executive Chief, etc." was that they might succeed in tarnishing the reputation of legitimate organizations like the SAI and the NCAI.

Additional correspondence with other friends, among them Charlotte Jones, a new member of the NCAI, confirm that Bonnin's suspicions were correct. Princess Chinquilla, et al. were not necessarily Indians per se and were indeed using "Indian Play" for the purposes of fame and financial gain. Throughout Bonnin's correspondence she expresses concerns regarding "false Indian" figures who threatened to undermine her ability to "play Indian." As Cari Carpenter, Ruth Spack, Dorothea M. Susag, and P. Jane Hafen have shown, Bonnin was a figure who could manipulate genres and identities available to her. In particular, Carpenter argues, "Bonnin's correspondence with Charlotte Jones gives us insight ... into the ways that such prominent American Indians were producing and revising their public Indianness in the 1920s."[161] Rev. Gordon's reply to Bonnin's original inquiry validates her worst fears: "I had occasion to meet Princess Chinquilla a while back. Somehow or other, she does not ring quite true to me and I am inclined to 'hae ma doots' in regard to her." As Gordon *plays Irish* he mocks and questions the authenticity of Chinquilla's ethnicity. He goes on to argue that she is also guilty by association. "In the first place she is tied up with Red Fox St. James who, I am convinced is a fake, as are also a great many of the people he has with him."[162] The strength of white imaginaries that associated Indian women with images of princesses, like the one that Chinquilla was performing, remained critical to the political work Bonnin did because she had to negotiate these troubling cultural frameworks. Bonnin managed to embody Indian femininity in different ways at different times. No doubt deciding which network to tap into influenced how she would represent herself and her politics.

After 1924 and the Indian Citizenship Act

Throughout the 1920s and early 1930s, Bonnin remained active as a writer. She wrote speeches to give at public events organized by philanthropic groups and white reformers. In these public venues, she drew on work as a pan-tribal activist that had begun with the SAI and continued with the NCAI.[163] Like Eastman and Montezuma, Bonnin allied with white reformers committed to Indian issues in order to expand the networks of influence she saw as necessary to nourishing pan-Indian political activity. Not unlike Luther Standing Bear, Bonnin was able to find allies for her political concerns in a range of places. Along with women's clubs, she maintained ties to white fraternal groups like the IRA because many of their members held sway in Washington. In turning to the IRA and its leader, Matthew K. Sniffen, as well as Charles Faben (one of the heads of Collier's AIDA), Bonnin set to work on an important political piece. In 1924, the three of them published *Oklahoma's Poor Rich Indians: An Orgy of Graft and Exploitation of the Five Civilized Tribes – Legalized Robbery.*[164] This became an influential political treatise that led to the formation of the Meriam Commission and the appointment of IRA leaders to the top two positions in the BIA by President Herbert Hoover.

For Bonnin, *Oklahoma's Poor Rich Indians* represented a departure from her more literary work and an example of how she could directly influence federal policy. In that same year, all Native Americans were incorporated into the United States as full citizens, while the Johnson-Reed Immigration Act became federal law and limited the annual number of immigrants who could be admitted to the country, further restricting entry by Southern and Eastern Europeans and East Asians and Asian Indians. Ironically as the United States sought to stop the influx of certain types of immigrants, federal law finally recognized the original inhabitants of the Americas as citizens.[165] Although the Indian Citizenship Act was an important turning point in federal Indian policy, it remained a thorny issue in relation to tribal sovereignty. For Bonnin, 1924 marked a turning point in her quest for citizenship and the culmination of her research for *Oklahoma's Poor Rich Indians*, and yet she was not fully satisfied with these achievements. During the remainder of her life, Bonnin remained committed to turning changes in policy into changes in material circumstances.

From 1926 until her death in 1938, the best way for Bonnin to remain politically active was through her role as president of the NCAI. This type of commitment makes sense given that the first three decades of the twentieth century were marked by critical changes in federal Indian policy as well as a significant increase in public interest regarding Indian arts and crafts and Indian performances. Like her contemporaries, Bonnin navigated the intersections of art and policy as an author, a performer, and an activist. The power of her representational politics shifted in different contexts, from when she was a college student to a teacher, and as she managed her public persona within a literary marketplace and different performance venues, ranging from concert halls to political organizing meetings. Within these specific areas Bonnin mobilized a range of strategies to position herself within established reform networks, as she worked to create new ones. She succeeded in refashioning a public image that could represent Indianness in ways that were legible to white, middle-class society. As a writer and an advocate for Indian people, she spoke the languages of literature, music, and policy. Given her many achievements Bonnin may seem unusual, but she was not alone. There were others: Native women and men who aligned themselves with Indian causes while strategically cultivating tenuous relationships with white progressives. The legacy Bonnin left in relation to literature and politics creates a compelling window through which to examine the past of Indian Country and America. Her story told in the context of a larger cohort of Indian intellectuals offers a new understanding of early twentieth-century cultural history and the central role Native women played in it.

Notes

1   Gertrude Bonnin, "Side by Side," *The Earlhamite* 2, March 16, 1896, 178–9. MSS 1704, Gertrude and Raymond Bonnin Collection, 20th–21st Century Western and Mormon Americana, L. Tom Perry Special Collections, Harold B. Lee Library, Brigham Young University.
2   I use Bonnin rather than Zitkala-Sa (or both) throughout this chapter for consistency.
3   Roy W. Meyer, *History of the Santee Sioux* (Lincoln: University of Nebraska Press, 1993).
4   See: P. Jane Hafen, ed., Zitkala-Sa, *Dreams and Thunder: Stories, Poems, and the Sun Dance Opera* (Lincoln: University of Nebraska Press, 2005), xvii.
5   "Class Card" for Gertrude E. Simmons, New England Conservatory Archives, Boston, MA.
6   Several sources focus on Gertrude Bonnin. I have consulted: Betty Louise Bell, "If This Is Paganism …': Zitkala-Sa and the Devil's Language," in *Native American Religious Identity: Unforgotten Gods*, edited by Jace Weaver (Maryknoll, NY: Orbis, 1998), 61–8; Dexter Fisher, "The Transformation of Tradition: A Study of Zitkala-Sa and Mourning Dove, Two Transitional American Indian Writers" (Diss., City University of New York, 1979); Lisa Laurie, "The Life Story of Zitkala-Sa/Gertrude Simmons Bonnin: Writing and Creating a Public Image" (Diss., Arizona State University, 1996); Ruth Spack, "Revisioning American Indian Women: Zitkala-Sa's Revolutionary *American Indian Stories*," *Legacy* Vol. 14, No. 1, 1997, 25–43, and "Zitkala-Sa, *The Song of Hiawatha*, and the Carlisle Indian School Band: A Captivity Tale," *LEGACY* Vol. 25, No.

2, 210–24; Margaret A. Lukens, "The American Story of Zitkala-Sa," in *In Her Own Voice: Nineteenth-Century American Women Essayists*, edited by Sherry Lee Linkon (New York: Garland, 1997), 141–55.

7 Many agree that the term *dime novel* originated with the first book in Beadle & Adam's *Beadle's Dime Novel* series, *Maleaska, the Indian Wife of the White Hunter*, by Ann S. Stephens, dated June 9, 1860. This series ran for 321 issues, establishing many of the conventions for the genre, from the lurid and outlandish storylines to melodramatic double titling that were used into the 1920s. For more on this print culture history see: Helen C. Nelson, "Navigating Nineteenth Century Novels: Linking Historical and Literary Perspectives to Explore the influence of Dime Novels in Nineteenth Century America" (MA Thesis, Humboldt State University, 2005).

8 Cari Carpenter, *Seeing Red: Anger, Sentimentality, and American Indians* (Columbus: Ohio State University Press, 2008); Dorothea M. Susag, "Zitkala-Sa (Gertrude Simmons Bonnin): A Power(ful) Literary Voice," *Studies in American Indian Literatures* Vol. 5., No. 4, Winter 1993, 3–24.

9 For more on "rhetorical sovereignty" see: Scott Lyons, *X-Marks: Native Signatures of Assent* (Minneapolis: University of Minnesota Press, 2010), 449–50.

10 Beth Piatote, *Domestic Subjects: Gender, Citizenship, and Law in Native American Literature* (New Haven, CT: Yale University Press, 2013); A. Lavonne Brown Ruoff, "Early American Women Authors: Jane Johnston Schoolcraft, Sarah Winnemucca, S. Alice Callahan, E. Pauline Johnson, and Zitkala-Sa" in *Nineteenth-Century American Women Writers: A Critical Reader*, edited by Karen L. Kilcup (Malden, MA: Blackwell, 1998); Susan Bernardin, "The Lessons of a Sentimental Education: Zitkala-Sa's Autobiographical Narratives," *Western American Literature* Vol. 32, No. 3, November 1997, 212–38; Martha J. Cutter, "Zitkala-Sa's Autobiographical Writings: The Problems of a Canonical Search for Language and Identity," *MELUS* Vol. 19, No. 1, Spring 1994, 31–45; P. Jane Hafen, "Zitkala-Sa: Sentimentality and Sovereignty," *Wicazo Sa Review* Vol. 12, No. 2, Fall 1997, 31–42; Roseanne Hoefel, "Writings, Performance, Activism: Zitkala-Sa and Pauline Johnson" in *Native American Women in Literature and Culture*, edited by Susan Castillo and Victor M. P. DaRosa (Porto, Portugal: Fernando Pessoa University Press, 1997), 107–18.

11 Gertrude Bonnin, *American Indian Stories* (London and Lincoln: University of Nebraska Press, 1985), 79.

12 *The Earlhamite*, MSS 1704, LTPSC.

13 Hafen, ed., *Dreams and Thunder*, xvi. Tom Hamm, "Side by Side: Zitkala-Sa at Earlham 1895–1897: From Campus to the Center of American Indian Activism," *The Earlhamite* (winter 1998).

14 My reading of "side by side" and "seeking" here draws on Jacques Derrida's theorization of difference, in particular, his usage of *différance* (as a neologism) to signal to the reader multiple meanings and intentions. Among these is the possibility for multiple signifiers that take into account how both difference and deferral can be at play at once. In Bonnin's speech, I see a similar logic in her rhetorical choices. She uses seeking and side by side to critique the structures of power within the United States that delimit who is or is not a part of the nation; at the same time, she strategically plays with these words within the logics of

this structure to position herself as legitimately within (seeking) and distant from (side by side) the nation. See: Jacques Derrida, *Writing and Difference* (Chicago: University of Chicago Press, 1978), translated by Alan Bass.

15 The year 1896 stands out in terms of public discourse regarding race, racialization, and political rights given the "separate but equal" doctrine set forth by the ruling in *Plessy v. Ferguson*, 163 U.S. 537. "Separate but equal" remained standard doctrine in U.S. law until its repudiation in the 1954 Supreme Court decision *Brown v. Board of Education*.

16 Piatote, *Domestic Subjects*.

17 Philip J. Deloria, *Indians in Unexpected Places* (Lawrence: University Press of Kansas, 2004); Tom Holm, *The Great Confusion in Indian Affairs: Native Americans and Whites in the Progressive Era* (2005); Frederick Hoxie, *A Final Promise: The Campaign to Assimilate Indians, 1880–1920* (1984).

18 For more on a literary history of female ethnic identity and the connections made by women during this period with regard to authenticity and authorship see Mary V. Dearborn, *Pocahontas's Daughters: Gender and Ethnicity in American Culture* (New York: Oxford University Press, 1986).

19 Although opera had been popular in Europe since its debut in the sixteenth century, in turn-of-the-century America it was still relatively new to most audiences. Dramas composed of vocal pieces with orchestral accompaniment, overtures, and interludes, opera reached the United States in the era of vaudeville, Tin Pan Alley, and ragtime, all of which were far more popular. However, with the patronage of New York high society, eager to experience this elegant European import firsthand, the first fully staged opera performance took place in New York in 1825. An Italian opera troupe was imported for the premiere of Rossini's *The Barber of Seville*.

20 *The Sun Dance* was a collaborative project between Gertrude Bonnin and William Hanson. See: P. Jane Hafen, "A Cultural Duet: Zitkala Sa and The Sun Dance Opera," *Great Plains Quarterly* Vol. 18, No. 2, 1998, 102–11.

21 Although the NCAI disappeared after Bonnin's death, a similar organization, the National Congress of American Indians, was founded in 1944. This later group responded to the Indian Reorganization Act of 1934 and the termination policies of the 1940s and 1950s.

22 In 1900, the *Atlantic Monthly* published several essays by "Zitkala-Sa." Among them were "The School Days of an Indian Girl" and "An Indian Teacher among Indians." For more on two other Indian intellectuals who achieved public success during this period see: Linda A. Waggoner, *Fire Light: The Life of Angel De Cora, Winnebago Artist* (Norman: University of Oklahoma Press, 2008) and Joel Pfitzer, *The Yale Indian: The Education of Henry Roe Cloud* (Durham, NC: Duke University Press, 2009). Also see: Charles Hannon, "Zitkala-Sa and the Commercial Magazine Apparatus," in *"The Only Efficient Instrument": American Women Writers and the Periodical, 1837–1916*, edited by Aleta Feinsod Cane and Susan Alves (Iowa City: University of Iowa Press, 2001), 179–201.

23 Gertrude Bonnin, "The School Days of an Indian Girl" in *American Indian Stories* (Lincoln: University of Nebraska Press, 1985), 47–80. Originally published: Washington, DC: Hayworth Publishing House, 1921. In this narrative, Bonnin combines sentimentality and anger in ways that mirror the work of

her predecessor Sarah Winnemucca (1844–91) in *Life among the Piutes: Their Wrongs and Claims* (1883), and the later modernist work of *Cogewea the Half-Blood: A Depiction of the Great Montana Cattle Range* (1927) by Mourning Dove (Christine Quintasket) (1888–1936).

24 Tsianina Lomawaima, *They Called It Prairie Light: The Story of Chilocco Indian School* (Lincoln and London: University of Nebraska Press, 1994), 99. For more on Indian education in the United States see also: Brenda Child, *Boarding School Seasons: American Indian Families, 1900–1940* (1998); Devon Mihesuah, *Cultivating the Rosebuds: The Education of Women at the Cherokee Female Seminary, 1851–1909* (1993); Robet Trennert, *The Phoenix Indian School: Forced Assimilation in Arizona, 1891–1935* (1988); and Penelope Kelsey, "Narratives of the Boarding School Era from Victimry to Resistance," *Atenea* Vol. 23, No. 2, 2003, 123–37.

25 Bonnin, "An Indian Teacher among Indians," in *American Indian Stories* (London and Lincoln, University of Nebraska Press, 1985), 81.

26 Bonnin, "School Days," 52.

27 Ibid., 65.

28 Ibid., 69. Scholars in critical race and ethnic studies have engaged with Lacanian psychoanalytic theory to potentially rectify the flawed ways ethnic and racialized subjects have been conceptualized in North America since the mid-twentieth century. For more see: Antonio Viego, *Dead Subjects: Toward a Politics of Loss in Latino Studies* (Durham, NC: Duke University Press, 2007). Also influencing how I read the loss Bonnin suffers after leaving home to receive a boarding school education is Anne Anlin Cheng, *The Melancholy of Race: Psychoanalysis, Assimilation, and Hidden Grief* (Oxford: Oxford University Press, 2000). Cheng considers race a melancholic construction that has the power to imprison both dominant and marginal subjects in haunted relations of identification and loss. Cheng also examines the social and psychological costs of racism that is imaginative and uncompromising.

29 For more about the Dawes Act era see: Leonard Carlson, *Indians, Bureaucrats, and Land: The Dawes Act and the Decline of Indian Farming* (1981); Emily Greenwald, *Reconfiguring the Reservation: The Nez Perces, Jicarilla Apaches, and the Dawes Act* (2002); Frederick Hoxie, *A Final Promise: The Campaign to Assimilate Indians, 1880–1920* (1984).

30 Bonnin, "School Days," 69.

31 Ibid.

32 Ibid.

33 Bonnin, "An Indian Teacher among Indians," 93.

34 Ibid., 93, 94–5.

35 Ibid., 98.

36 Ibid., 98.

37 Ibid., 98.

38 Ibid., 99.

39 The Carlisle Indian Industrial School produced a variety of newspapers and magazines, which provided Pratt with a platform from which to publicize his experiment and perpetuate his views on education. These newspapers were popular among locals, available at the post office and by subscription throughout the country; they became a small source of income to supplement funding

by the government. News of former students, often in the form of letters to "Dear Old Carlisle," made its way into these papers on a regular basis. For more see: Records of the Cumberland County Historical Society, and the Richard Henry Pratt Papers, WA MSS S-1174, Beinecke Rare Book and Manuscript Library, Yale Collection of Western Americana, Yale University, New Haven, CT.

40 For more about Pratt and Bonnin with regards to a the notion of captivity see: Spack, "Zitkala-Sa, *The Song of Hiawatha,* and the Carlisle Indian School Band."

41 Waggoner, *Fire Light,* 91. For more about Angel De Cora and her relationship to Smith College see: "Paying Tribute to Smith's First Known Native American Graduate," Jan McCoy Ebbets, http://www.smith.edu/newssmith/fall2003/decora.php (accessed September 26, 2014).

42 Anne Ruggles Gere, "An Art of Survivance: Angel De Cora at Carlisle," *American Indian Quarterly* Vol. 28, No. 3 & 4, Summer/Fall 2004, 649–84.

43 This section heading refers to an advertisement, most likely produced by Ginn and Company, to promote Bonnin as the author of "American Indian Stories," "Americanize the First Americans," and "Old Indian Legends." From: MSS 1704; Gertrude and Raymond Bonnin Collection, 20th–21st Century Western and Mormon Americana, L. Tom Perry Special Collections, Harold B. Lee Library, Brigham Young University [hereinafter MSS 1704, LTPSC].Thomas Bonaventure Lawler, *Seventy Years of Textbook Publishing: A History of Ginn and Company* (Boston, MA: Ginn and Company, 1938).

44 Bonnin, "An Indian Teacher among Indians"; "Impressions of an Indian Childhood," *Atlantic Monthly* 85, 1900, 37–47; "School Days of an Indian Girl," *Atlantic Monthly* 85, 1900, 185–94; *Old Indian Legends* (Boston, MA: Ginn and Company, 1901); "Soft Hearted Sioux," *Harper's Monthly,* New York (1901); "The Trial Path," *Harper's Monthly* Vol. 103, October 1901; "A Warrior's Daughter," *Everybody's Magazine* (1902); "Why I Am a Pagan," *Atlantic Monthly* 90, 1902, 801–3; *American Indian Stories* (Washington, DC: Hayworth Publishing House, 1921).

45 By "romantic language," I refer to romanticism as it emerged and took shape in England and the United States from the 1830s to the 1860s, which was characterized by: sensibility; primitivism; love of nature; sympathetic interest in the past, especially the medieval; mysticism; individualism; and figured in opposition to neoclassicism. The romantic period in American literature coincided/emerged out of the Jacksonian Era and the Civil War as the United States sought to redefine itself as a nation embroiled in debates over Indian removal and slavery. Three major literary figures exemplified this Romantic movement: William Cullen Bryant, Washington Irving, and James Fenimore Cooper. Overlapping with this sort of literary production was the emergence of the sentimental novel. This form deviated from realist writings produced by Herman Melville, Henry David Thoreau, and Mark Twain. Whether understood in terms of sympathetic relations or of manipulative influence, sentimentality was mobilized by several women writers for political and personal reasons. Sentimentality also became linked to the intimate details of women's private lives. Although this form was most popular in early and mid-nineteenth-century America, it has often been overlooked in literary histories until recently.

46 Carpenter, *Seeing Red.*

47 Esther Whitmore (?) to Zitkala-Sa, June 3, 1930, Letter, MSS 1704, LTPSC. Whitmore notes, "I am sure you are studying Science and Health, you are gaining new and better views than ever of God," and links another Indian figure to Christian Science – "I have just written Tsianina. She tells me that she is earnestly studying Christian Science." This refers to Tsianina Redfeather, the great singer, who we can see is part of Bonnin's network of Native women artists, activists, writers, and performers. Redfeather remained a devoted Christian Scientist for her entire life. Also in a letter (July 9, 1921) sent to Bonnin by Adam Bennion, the superintendent of the Commission of Education of the Church of Jesus Christ of Latter Day Saints notes, "I am happy in the thought that you are reading the *The Book of Mormon*, and trust that you will enjoy it." Bonnin wrote critically about the negative effects of forced Christianization on Indian people, especially schoolchildren, and yet she distinguished between positive aspects of Christian reformers and the problems perpetuated by "so-called Christian Americans."

48 There has been ample scholarship about Gertrude Bonnin's literary work. What follows is a selective bibliography. Susan Bernandin, "The Lessons of a Sentimental Education: Zitkala-Sa's Autobiographical Narratives," *Western American Literature* Vol. 32, No. 3, 1997, 212–38; Vanessa Holford Diana, "'Hanging in the Heart of Chaos': Bi-Cultural Limbo, Self-(Re)Presentation, and the White Audience in Zitkala-Sa's American Indian Stories," *Cimarron Review* 121, 1997, 154–72; Jessica Enoch, "Resisting the Script of Indian Education: Zitkala-Sa and the Carlisle Indian School," *College English* Vol. 65, No. 2, 2002, 117–41; Cutter, "Zitkala-Sa's Autobiographical Writings"; Robert Allen Warrior, "Reading American Indian Intellectual Traditions," *World Literature Today* 66, 1992, 236–40; Dexter Fischer, "Zitkala-Sa: The Evolution of a Writer," *American Indian Quarterly* 5, 1979, 229–38; Lukens, "The American Story of Zitkala-Sa"; D. K. Mesenheimer Jr., "Regionalist Bodies/Embodied Regions: Sarah Orne Jewett and Zitkala-Sa," in *Breaking Boundaries: New Perspectives on Women's Regional Writing*, edited by Sherrie A. Inness and Diana Royer (Iowa City: University of Iowa Press, 1997), 109–23; Julianne Newmark, "'Writing (and Speaking) in Tongues' Zikala-Sa's American Indian Stories," *Western American Literature* Vol. 37, No. 3, 2002, 335–58.

49 For more on the feminist sociological approach to theorizing intersectionality see: Kimberle Crenshaw, "Mapping the Margins: Intersectionality, Identity Politics, and Violence against Women of Color," *Stanford Law Review* 43, 1992, 1241–2.

50 Kristin Herzog, "Gertrude Bonnin," in *The Heath Anthology of American Literature* (fifth edition), edited by Paul Lauter.

51 Arthur C. Parker was the editor of the SAI's journal from the summer of 1916 until the summer of 1918. The look and feel of the journal changed markedly between 1916 and 1917, from matte paper to a more glossy cover that often featured a photographic portrait of a prominent Indian member, such as that of Angel De Cora in 1919 under Bonnin's editorship.

52 Bonnin was not alone in gaining support from organizations that were run by white women and in working with Native organizations. Laura Cornelius Kellogg (1880–1947) was a founding member of the SAI who was committed to self-sustaining economic development on Native reservations. Ruth Muskrat

Bronson (1897–1982) was the first Indian woman to graduate from Mount Holyoke College (MA) in 1925. Bronson received national attention when she became the first American Indian student delegate at the World Student Christian Federation's annual conference, in 1922 in Beijing, China. A year later, she presented her views on Indian affairs to the Committee of 100 meeting in Washington, DC, and in 1930, Bronson accepted an offer to fill the newly created position of guidance and placement officer for the BIA. In 1944, Bronson published *Indians Are People Too* (New York: Friendship Press). Charles Eastman also worked with the Women's National Indian Association (WNIA, founded in 1879), which had formed to fight the encroachment of white settlements onto Indian lands. Less politically oriented groups also arose out of artistic communities. Mabel Dodge Luhan, for example, moved to Taos, New Mexico (1919) to start a literary colony inspired by (and supportive of) nearby indigenous peoples' cultural traditions and practices. An outgrowth of this colony was the formation of the AIDA by John Collier in 1923 to fight to protect religious freedom and tribal property rights for Native Americans in the United States. The General Federation of Women's Clubs (GFWC), founded in 1868 by Jane Cunningham Croly (1829–1901), was also devoted to Indian issues. In 1921, the GFWC created the Indian Welfare Committee, which worked toward improving both education and health facilities on reservations, as well as preserving Native American culture. In addition, other Indian and non-Indian women activists became involved with reformist agendas by becoming active in the YWCA.

53 On March 8, 1920, Bonnin received a receipt from the League of American Pen Women for her yearly dues; for the receipt see: Box 2, Folder 11, MSS 1704, LTPSC. For more about the National League of American Pen Women see: http://www.americanpenwomen.org/history/history.cfm (accessed September 26, 2014). There is little within Bonnin's personal papers to show the concrete connections that she may have formed with other members of the League, although it is likely that members who lived in DC might have found occasions to meet, at least informally.

54 Princess Blue Feather to Gertrude Bonnin, April 1922, Letter, MSS 1704, LTPSC.

55 Gertrude Bonnin to Princess Blue Feather, May 2, 1922, Letter, MSS 1704, LTPSC.

56 See: Patricia Okker, *Our Sister Editors: Sarah J. Hale and the Tradition of Nineteenth-Century American Women Editors* (Athens: University of Georgia Press, 1995).

57 In the 1920s, Antonio Luhan, a member of the Taos Pueblo, showed John Collier the living conditions among American Indian communities in the surrounding area, which provided evidence necessary for Collier to found the AIDA. In 1933, President Franklin D. Roosevelt appointed Collier as the new commissioner of Indian affairs, which almost immediately led to the Indian Reorganization Act (1934). For more on the AIDA and John Collier see: John Collier Papers (MS 146), Manuscripts and Archives, Yale University Library. Also see: Ken R. Philp, *John Collier's Crusade for Indian Reform, 1920–1954* (Tucson: University of Arizona Press, 1977) and Lawrence C. Kelly, *The Assault on Assimilation: John Collier and the Origins of Indian Policy Reform* (Albuquerque: University of New Mexico Press, 1963).

58 Marianna Burgess to Zitkala-Sa, May 6, 1922, Letter, MSS 1704, LTPSC.
59 Arnold Krupat, *For Those Who Come After: A Study of Native American Autobiography* (Berkeley: University of California Press, 1985); John Sekora, "Black Message/White Envelope: Genre, Authenticity, and Authority in the Antebellum Slave Narrative," *Callaloo* No. 32, Summer 1987, 482–515; Winifred Morgan, "Gender-Related Difference in the Slave Narratives of Harriet Jacobs and Frederick Douglass," *American Studies* Vol. 35, No. 2, Fall 1994, 73–94.
60 Lawler, *Seventy Years of Textbook Publishing*, 10.
61 Ibid., 150.
62 Ibid., 150.
63 Ginn and Company to Gertrude Bonnin, June 8, 1926, Letter, and Gertrude Bonnin to Ginn and Company, June 11, 1926, Letter, MSS 1704, LTPSC.
64 Gertrude Bonnin to Ginn and Company, June 19, 1930, Letter, MSS 1704, LTPSC.
65 Piatote, *Domestic Subjects*, 3.
66 For more on settler-nationalism in connection with domesticity see ibid., 4.
67 Gertrude Bonnin, "America, Home of the Red Man," in *The American Indian Magazine* Vol. 4, No. 4, 165.
68 For more discussion and theorization of the historical situations where Native people are not quite citizens yet find themselves defined within the boundaries of the United States as a nation see: Piatote, *Domestic Subjects* and Mark Rifkin, *Manifesting America: The Imperial Construction of U.S. National Space* (Oxford: Oxford University Press, 2009).
69 Bonnin, "America, Home of the Red Man," 165.
70 Ibid., 165.
71 Ibid., 165.
72 Ibid., 165.
73 Ibid., 165.
74 Ibid., 166.
75 For more about Robert Latham Owen Jr. see: Wyatt W. Belcher, "Political Leadership of Robert L. Owen," *Chronicles of Oklahoma* 31, Winter 1953–4, 361–71. Kenny L. Brown, "A Progressive from Oklahoma: Senator Robert Latham Owen, Jr.," *Chronicles of Oklahoma* 62, Fall 1984, 232–65, and "Robert Latham Owen, Jr.: His Careers as Indian Attorney and Progressive Senator." PhD dissertation (Oklahoma State University, 1985). Edward Elmer Keso, *The Senatorial Career of Robert Latham Owen* (Gardenvale P.Q., Canada: Garden City Press, 1938). As well as the following written by Owen. Robert Latham Owen, *The Federal Reserve Act* (New York: Century Co., 1919); "The Origin, Plan, and Purpose of the Currency Bill," *North American Review* 19, October 1913, 556–69; *The Russian Imperial Conspiracy, 1892–1914: The Most Gigantic Intrigue of All Time* (Baltimore, MD: Sun Book & Job Printing Office, 1926); "What Congress Should Do to Develop an American Mercantile Marine," *Proceedings of the Academy of Political Science* 6, October 1915, 48–60; and *Where Is God in the European War?* (New York: Century Company, 1919).
76 Rather than offer an extensive historiography of World War I, I want to acknowledge changes in historical scholarship following World War II. By the 1950s, many historians (American, but European as well) viewed World War

I as caused by powerful forces that were pushing Europe into war: nationalism, imperialism, militarism, and the system of alliances. However, other scholars returned to an older idea that German imperial ambitions were to blame – "[The German] bid for continental supremacy was certainly decisive in bringing on the European War." See British historian A. J. P. Taylor, *The Struggle for Mastery in Europe* (1954). In this latter sense, the causes behind World War I were certainly imperial in nature while U.S. rhetoric claimed to fight in defense of democracy.

77   Bonnin, "America, Home of the Red Man," 166.
78   Ibid., 167.
79   C. F. Hauke to Gertrude Bonnin, September 1922, Letter, MSS 1704, LTPSC.
80   Ibid.
81   Gertrude Bonnin to Vera Connolly, Letter, September 24, 1928, MSS 1704, LTPSC.
82   Ibid. For a detailed discussion of the letterhead also see: Ada Mahasti Norris, "Zitkala-Sa and National Indian Pedagogy: Storytelling, Activism, and the Project of Assimilation," *Dissertation Abstracts International, Section A: The Humanities and Social Sciences* Vol. 65, No. 1, 2004, 147.
83   Harry C. James to Gertrude Bonnin, Letter, July 6, 1921, MSS 1704, LTPSC. James writes on behalf of the National Association to Help the Indian (Headquarters: Dark Cloud Lodge, Los Angeles, CA). This inquiry relates to H.R. Bill 2432 and "this little Association of ours" that "is to form an Association of influential people interested in helping the American Indian ... to secure absolute religious liberty for the Indian, citizenship and economic independence ... I would like very much to have your ideas about the Association."
84   Gertrude Bonnin to Carlos Montezuma, December 27, 1915, Letter. In another letter (December 6, 1918), Bonnin writes extensively about the need to use telegrams rather than letters to conduct business. "That wire to the President was simply one of many ways in which this matter must be pressed for consideration and action by the American people." For more on the confusion and tension white Americans expressed regarding Indian people using technology see Philip Deloria's chapter on "Technology" in *Indians in Unexpected Places*.
85   G. Bonnin to C. Montezuma, October 26, 1918, Letter, see: Carlos Montezuma Papers (CMP), Center for Southwest Studies, Fort Lewis College, Durango, CO.
86   G. Bonnin to C. Montezuma, December 27, 1915, Letter. G. Bonnin to C. Montezuma, October 26, 1918, Letter; see: CMP, Center for Southwest Studies, Fort Lewis College, Durango, CO.
87   For more on literary historical examines of the context in which Bonnin would have been part of wider readerly and writerly communities during the turn of the century see the following: Richard H. Brodhead, *Cultures of Letters: Scenes of Reading and Writing in Nineteenth-Century America* (Chicago: University of Chicago Press, 1993); George Shumway, *Creating American Civilization: A Genealogy of American Literature as an Academic Discipline* (Minneapolis: University of Minnesota Press, 1994); Anne E. Boyd, *Writing for Immortality: Women and the Emergence of High Literary Culture in America* (Baltimore, MD: Johns Hopkins University Press, 2004); Susan Mizruchi, *The Rise of Multicultural America: Economy and Print Culture, 1865–1915* (Durham: University of North Carolina Press, 2008).

88 *Cosmopolitan* Vol. 65, No. 6, November 1918, Hatcher Graduate Library, University of Michigan, Ann Arbor, MI.

89 Gouverneur Morris, "Drifting Smoke," *Cosmopolitan*, November 1918, 63.

90 Ibid., 64.

91 Ibid., 118.

92 Ibid., 119.

93 This story also echoes James Fenimore Cooper's *The Pioneers: The Sources of the Susquehanna* (1823). Also see: Susan Scheckel, *The Insistence of the Indian: Race and Nationalism in Nineteenth-Century American Culture* (Princeton, NJ: Princeton University Press, 1999). Scheckel examines the Supreme Court's decision on Indian land rights and Cooper's frontier romance *The Pioneers* to argue that both worked to legitimate American ownership claims over indigenous lands while also seeking to diminish any guilt related to violent conquest by attempting to incorporate Indians into America's political "family."

94 Morris, "Drifting Smoke," 67.

95 Gertrude Bonnin to Carlos Montezuma, June 30, 1919, Letter, CMP, Center for Southwest Studies, Fort Lewis College, Durango, CO.

96 Ibid.

97 Ibid.

98 Ibid.

99 "The earliest appropriations bills were written by select committees on instruction from the Committee of the Whole House, and later ones by the standing Committee on Ways and Means. As the appropriation requirements of the government became more complex, the number of separate appropriation bills prepared each year grew from one in 1789 to as many as 21 during the 1850s" (3.2). "Between 1877 and 1885 eight appropriations bills were transferred from the jurisdiction of the Appropriations Committee to the committees with legislative jurisdiction. The agriculture bill, army bill, navy bill, Indian bill, District of Columbia bill, post office bill, rivers and harbors bill, and diplomatic and consular bill were given to the appropriate authorizing committees, while the Appropriations Committee retained jurisdiction of the fortification, legislative, executive and judicial, pension, sundry civil, and deficiency bills only" (3.4). "Petitions from the 1890s and into the 20th century primarily concern the education of young Indians and call for the reorganization of the Government's less-than-successful efforts to provide services to the Indian tribes.... The number of petitions among the records of the committee diminishes dramatically after the late 1920s, and, for some Congresses, no petitions are present"(13.32). From: "Chapter 3. Records of the Committee on Appropriations," in *The Guide to Records of the U.S. House of Representatives at the National Archives, 1789–1989* (Record Group 233).

100 For more on the formation of race, sexuality, and gender with regards to imperial practices and colonial ideology see: Mary Louise Pratt, *Imperial Eyes: Travel Writing and Transculturation* (New York: Routledge, 1992); Anne McClintock, *Imperial Leather: Race, Gender, and Sexuality in the Colonial Contest* (New York: Routledge, 1995); Margaret Jacobs, *Engendered Encounters: Feminism and Pueblo Cultures, 1879–1934* (Lincoln: University of Nebraska Press, 1999); Laura Wexler, *Tender Violence: Domestic Visions*

in an Age of U.S. Imperialism (Chapel Hill: University of North Carolina Press, 2000).

101 For more on California in relation to "Club Women" like Burgess see: Kevin Starr, *Inventing the Dream: California through the Progressive Era* (Oxford: Oxford University Press, 1986); Mike Davis, *City of Quartz: Excavating the Future in Los Angeles* (New York: Vintage, 1992); Edward W. Soja, *Thirdspace: Journeys to Los Angeles and other Real and Imagined Places* (Oxford: Basil Blackwell, 1996); Norman Klein, *The History of Forgetting: Los Angeles and the Erasure of Memory* (New York: Verso, 1997).

102 The Curtis Act of 1898 aimed to amend the Dawes Act by extending allotment policies, whether they wanted it or not, to the Five Civilized Tribes (Cherokee, Choctaw, Chickasaw, Muscogee, and Seminole) in the Indian Territory (present-day Oklahoma), For more on this policy history see: Francis Paul Prucha, *Indian Policy in the United States* (Lincoln: University of Nebraska Press, 1981).

103 Marianna Burgess to Gertrude Bonnin, October 20, 1921 and November 8, 1921, Letters, MSS 1704, LTPSC. Membership records from Chicago Monthly Meeting show Mariana Burgess was present. Quaker Monthly Meeting Minutes (May 10, 1914).

104 Gertrude Bonnin to Marianna Burgess, December 1921, Letter, MSS 1704, LTPSC.

105 In 1921, $200 had the same buying power as approximately $2,400 has in 2009. Fifty dollars in 1921 would amount to $599 today, suggesting that Bonnin and other speakers had to hustle to supplement their earnings from publishing and elsewhere with speaking engagements.

106 Gertrude Bonnin to Dr. C. A. Burgess, December 30, 1921, Letter, MSS 1704, LTPSC.

107 Ibid.

108 Carol Kort, "Zitkala-Sa," *A to Z of American Women Writers, Revised Edition, A to Z of Women* (New York: Infobase Publishing, Jan. 1, 2007), 364. Also see: P. Jane Hafen, "Zitkala Să," in *Encyclopedia of North American Indians*, edited by Frederick E. Hoxie (Boston, MA: Houghton Mifflin, 1996), 708–10; Renee Melissa Henderson, "Gertrude Simmons Bonnin, Zitkala-Sa," Voices from the Gaps. http://voices.cla.umn.edu/vg/Bios/entries/bonnin_gertrude_simmons_zitkalasa.html (accessed January 24, 2007); Liz Sonneborn, "Gertrude Simmons Bonnin," *A to Z of American Indian Women, Revised Edition*, 20–4. New York: Facts On File, 2007.

109 Piatote, *Domestic Subjects* and Frederick E. Hoxie, *This Indian Country: American Indian Activists and the Place They Made* (New York: Penguin Press, 2012).

110 See note 8 for sources on sentimentality, and see note 45 for more on romance and sentimentality in relation to the discourses pertaining to late nineteenth-century womanhood.

111 Philip J. Deloria on "Music" in *Indians in Unexpected Places* points to how promotional materials for Tsianina's performances turned on her authenticity. "Tsianina, one brochure proclaimed, was not a made-up Indian. Rather, she was 'full blooded' and a Native 'aristocrat' (a descendent of Tecumseh, no less)" (213). Michael V. Pisani also connects playing Indian with music and the stage in "'I'm an Indian Too': Playing Indian in Song and on Stage,

1900–1946," in *Imagining Native America in Music* (New Haven, CT: Yale University Press, 2005). Also see: Nicole M. Guidotti-Hernandez, *Unspeakable Violence: Remapping U.S. and Mexican National Imaginaries* (Durham, NC: Duke University Press, 2011) for more on examining notions of citizenship, silence, violence, and discipline by revisiting histories where nonwhites participated in violence against indigenous peoples. Although Guidotti-Hernandez is referring to actual battles, it seems logical to consider the way cultural violence was committed through the perpetuation of a national imaginary that distorted Native history and agency.

112 Gertrude Bonnin to Dr. C. A. Burgess, December 30, 1921, Letter, MSS 1704, LTPSC.

113 My brief references to the work of Ella Deloria and Ruth Bronson rely on David L. Moore's excellent overview of critical archival sources. See: David L. Moore, "'The Literature of this Nation': LaVonne Ruoff and the Redefinition of American Literary Studies," in *Studies in American Indian Literatures* Vol. 17, Iss. 2, New York, Summer 2005, 63–70, 113. For more on Ella Deloria in a comparative context see: Maria Eugenia Cotera, *Native Speakers: Ella Deloria, Zora Neale Hurston, Jovita González, and the Poetics of Culture* (Austin: University of Texas Press, 2008). For a brief biography of Ruth Muskrat Bronson see: Mount Holyoke Historical Atlas Research Project; also for more on Bronson and other Native students at Mount Holyoke see: Mount Holyoke College. Students and Alumnae Profiles and Statistics Collection, Archives and Special Collections, Mount Holyoke College, South Hadley, MA.

114 M. Burgess to G. Bonnin, December 20, 1921, Letter, MSS 1704, LTPSC.

115 Other committees operating under Public Welfare by this club included: Child Welfare, Public Health, and Industrial and Social Conditions.

116 For more on the complicated history of all-female organizations' activist work see: Anne Firor Scott, *Natural Allies: Women's Associations in American History* (Champaign: University of Illinois Press, 1992); Lori D. Ginzberg, *Women and the Work of Benevolence: Morality, Politics, and Class in the Nineteenth-Century United States* (New Haven, CT: Yale University Press, 1992); Ellen Carol Dubois, *Feminism and Suffrage: The Emergence of an Independent Women's Movement in America, 1848–1869* (Ithaca, NY: Cornell University Press, 1999).

117 For more on Stella Atwood and John Collier as cultural relativists who aimed to revise assimilation ideology and were critical to implementing elements of white culture that they viewed as positively shaping Indian policy see: Karin L. Huebner, "An Unexpected Alliance: Stella Atwood, the California Clubwomen, John Collier, and the Indians of the Southwest, 1917–1934," in *Pacific Historical Review* Vol. 78, No. 3, 2009, 337–66.

118 For more on reform activities in California and the Indian New Deal see: Kenneth R. Philp, *Termination Revisited: American Indians on the Trail to Self-Determination, 1933–1953* (Lincoln: University of Nebraska Press, 1999). Also see Lawrence C. Kelly, *The Assault on Assimilation: John Collier and the Origins of Indian Policy Reform* (University of New Mexico, 1983).

119 Tisa Wenger, "Land, Culture, and Sovereignty in the Pueblo Dance Controversy," in *Journal of the Southwest*, Summer 2004, 381.

120 For more about the Lenroot bill in the context of the Bursum bill and the Omnibus bill and regarding Collier's perspective see: Donald Lee Parman, *Indians in the American West in the Twentieth Century* (Indianapolis: Indiana University Press, 1994), 79.

121 Tisa Joy Wenger, *We Have a Religion: The 1920s Pueblo Indian Dance Controversy and American Religious Freedom* (Chapel Hill: University of North Carolina Press, 2009), 131.

122 Stella Atwood to Gertrude Bonnin, January 2, 1924, Letter, MSS 1704, LTPSC.

123 Mrs. Felix T. McWhirter to Major R. T. Bonnin, March 6, 1924, Letter, MSS 1704, LTPSC.

124 Figure 6: Photograph by Gertrude Kasebier (ca. 1898); "Gum-bichromate: 'Zitkala-Sa' holding a violin" (Kasebier Collection, Smithsonian Images, no. 2004–57782). Important to note is Laura Wexler's work in *Tender Violence: Domestic Visions in an Age of U.S. Imperialism* (Chapel Hill: University of North Carolina Press, 2000), in which she reads some of Gertrude Kasebier's photographs. Her reading implicates Kasebier, as it does other white female photographers, in reproducing a middle-class white cultural logic regarding presentation that is meant to signify America and imperialism. For Wexler, Native American subjects who sat for these photographs were part of U.S. imperialism because of efforts to assimilate and misappropriate them, regardless of their agency. My reading runs against this grain a little to suggest that Bonnin's familiarity with Kasebier, and other white women like her, enabled Bonnin to have a hand in the types of images created to portray her. I also read Kasebier's portraits of Bonnin as attempting to position Bonnin in opposition to, or as an alternative to, the type of imagery that was being created to market Indian actors who performed with shows like Buffalo Bill Cody's Wild West. Also, given that Bonnin performs the role of an "Indian maiden" in a play at the Carlisle School's commencement ceremonies in 1899, just a year after she sat for Kasebier, one can see the extent to which Bonnin uses different modes of dress to appeal to different audiences for specific occasions. Also see: Elizabeth Hutchinson, "Native American Identity in the Making: Gertrude Käsebier's 'Girl with the Violin,'" Exposure," *Exposure Special Issue on Photography, Race and American Society* Vol. 33, No. 1/2, Fall 2000, 21–32.

125 For conventions regarding photographic portraits see: Alan Trachtenberg, *Reading American Photographs: Images as History, Mathew Brady to Walker Evans* (New York: Hill and Wang, 1990).

126 Hutchinson, "Native American Identity in the Making."

127 Ibid.

128 Early American writers, heavily influenced by Chateaubriand and Rousseau's ideas, brought sentimentality and romance together to do ideological work in their treatment of "the noble savage." For more about how this idea developed and spread see: Robert Berkhofer, *The White Man's Indian: Images of the American Indian from Columbus to the Present* (New York: Vintage, 1979) and my discussion in note 46.

129 Photographer and critic Joseph T. Keiley (1869–1914) also took photographic portraits of Gertrude Bonnin in 1898, which were first exhibited in Philadelphia

and later became part of Alfred Stieglitz's (1864–1946) collection. In July 1899, Alfred Stieglitz published five of Kasebier's photographs in *Camera Notes*, declaring her "beyond dispute, the leading artistic portrait photographer of the day." Alfred Stieglitz, "Our Illustrations," *Camera Notes* Vol. 3, No. 1, July 1899, 24. Keiley celebrated her rise to fame: "a year ago Käsebier's name was practically unknown in the photographic world ... Today that name stands first and unrivaled." "The Philadelphia Salon: Its Origin and Influence," *Camera Notes* Vol. 1, No. 3, January 1899, 126. I use Kasebier's portraits given her interest in presenting Indian people as they lived versus the images created by photographers like Edward Curtis (1868–1952), who sought to memorialize Indian people by framing them within a "vanishing American" narrative. For more on the problematics of this narrative see: Brian Dippie, *The Vanishing American: White Attitudes and U.S. Indian Policy* (Lawrence: University Press of Kansas, 1982).

130 Figure 7: "Platinotype: Sioux girl, 'Zitkala-Sa,' with book in her lap; floral wallpaper in background," by Gertrude Kasebier (ca. 1898) (Kasebier Collection, Smithsonian Images, no. 2004–57783).

131 Most middle-class American women of the late nineteenth century lived in the domestic realm caring for small children, tending to ill or aged adults, and managing the daily chores of the household. As Angel Kwolek-Folland has shown, domesticity itself became idealized such that it could be moved (via objects) from place to place vis-à-vis the materiality of the home. A desire to stabilize and standardize American social institutions played out within late Victorian home culture that was physically and spiritually designed and guided by women. See: Angel Kwolek-Folland, "The Elegant Dugout: Domesticity and Moveable Culture in the United States, 1870–1900," *American Studies* Vol. 25, No. 2, Fall 1984, 21–37.

132 For American literary realism see: Patricia Okker, "Native American Literatures and the Canon: The Case of Zitkala-Sa," in *American Realism and the Canon, edited by* Tom Quirk and Gary Scharnhorst (Newark: University of Delaware Press, 1994), 87–101; Amy Kaplan, *The Social Construction of American Realism* (Chicago: University of Chicago Press, 1988). For the distinction between realism and naturalism see: June Howard, *Form and History in American Literary Naturalism* (Chapel Hill: University of North Carolina Press, 1985).

133 Hutchinson, "Native American Identity in the Making," 27.

134 Elizabeth Hutchinson, *The Indian Craze: Primitivism, Modernism, and Transculturation in American Art, 1890–1915* (Durham, NC: Duke University Press, 2009).

135 Eugene Gruenberg was a graduate of the Vienna Conservatory, where he was a close friend of conductor Arthur Nikisch (1855–1922). In 1878 he joined the orchestra of the Leipzig Opera under Nikisch. In 1889, Gruenberg left to play in the Boston Symphony Orchestra (BSO) now under Nikisch. When Nikisch left the BSO to return to Germany in 1895, Gruenberg became head of the violin department at the New England Conservatory of Music, where he remained for the rest of his life. In 1897, Gruenberg published *The Violinist's Manual*, which was revised in 1919 under the title *Violin Teaching and Violin Studies*

with a preface by Fritz Kreisler. For more on Gruenberg see: Eugene Gruenberg Papers (MS Mus 234.2). Houghton Library, Harvard University.

136   *The Sun*, March 25, 1900 (New York), Library of Congress: www.loc.gov/ chroniclingamerica (accessed September 26, 2014).

137   In regards to the fashion history of Native Americans I consulted the following: Theodore Brasser, *Native American Clothing: An Illustrated History* (Firefly Books, 2009); Josephine Paterek, *Encyclopedia of American Indian Costume* (New York: Norton, 1994); Smithsonian Institution, *Identity by Design: Tradition, Change, and Celebration in Native Women's Dresses* (Washington, DC, 2007). The aforementioned photograph was printed by Underwood & Underwood, MSS 1704, LTPSC.

138   For more about the life of Sitting Bull see: Robert M. Utley, *Sitting Bull: The Life and Times of an American Patriot* (New York: Holt, 1993); Stanley Vestal, *Sitting Bull: Champion of the Sioux* (1931, reprinted 1989); Ernie LaPointe, *Sitting Bull: His Life and Legacy* (Layton, UT: Gibbs Smith, 2009). For more details regarding the professional relationship between Cody and Sitting Bull see: Louis S. Warren, *Buffalo Bill's America: William Cody and the Wild West Show* (New York: Knopf Doubleday Publishing, 2005). Also see: Joy S. Kasson, *Buffalo Bill's Wild West: Celebrity, Memory, and Popular History* (New York: Hill and Wang, 2000) and L. G. Moses, *Wild West Shows and the Images of American Indians, 1883–1933* (Albuquerque: University of New Mexico Press, 1996).

139   It seems likely that this photograph was given as a token of friendship by Bonnin to Miss Julia Thomas, MSS 1704, LTPSC.

140   For more on costuming in Bonnin's life as well as that of her contemporaries, see: Waggoner, *Fire Light*: "Wearing inappropriate Indian dress came back to haunt Gertrude Simmons Bonnin later in life. When she and Pratt lobbied against peyote use (and its advocate, ethnographer James Mooney), Mooney pointed out to those attending the 1916 Senate Peyote Hearings that Bonnin 'claims to be a Sioux woman. [H]er dress is a woman's dress from some Southern tribe, as shown by the long fringes. The belt is a Navajo man's belt. The fan is a peyote fan, carried only by men, usually in the peyote ceremony'" (288). For an account of Bonnin's counterattack on Mooney see: L. G. Moses, *The Indian Man: A Biography of James Mooney* (Lincoln: University of Nebraska Press, 1984), 200–10.

141   The Sun Dance is a distinctive religious ceremony central to the cultural life and identity of the indigenous peoples of the Great Plains. It developed among the horse-mounted, bison-hunting nations during the eighteenth and nineteenth centuries. The nations at the core of its practice and that have continued it into the contemporary period include the Arapahos, the Cheyennes (Southern and Northern), the Blackfoot (who include the Siksikas or Blackfoot proper, the Bloods or Kainahs, and the Northern and Southern Piegans or Pikunis), and the Sioux (including in particular the westernmost Sioux, who are the seven tribes of the Lakota nation, but also including the Yanktons and Santees, who comprise the six tribes of the Dakota nation). From these four nations, the Sun Dance ceremony spread to the Kiowas and Comanches, who ranged the Southern Plains, and to Northern Plains nations such as the Plains

Crees of Saskatchewan and the Sarcees of Alberta, as well as other Plains peoples, including the Arikaras, Assiniboines, Crows, Gros Ventres, Hidatsas, Mandans, Pawnees, Plains Ojibwas, Poncas, Shoshones, and Utes. David J. Wishart, *Encyclopedia of the Great Plains* (Lincoln: University of Nebraska Press, 2011). Also see: Frances Densmore, *Teton Sioux Music and Culture* (Lincoln: University of Nebraska Press, 1992); George Amos Dorsey, *The Arapaho Sun Dance: The Ceremony of the Offerings Lodge. Field* Columbian Museum Publication, no. 75 (Chicago: Field Museum of Natural History, 1903); William E. Farr, *The Reservation Blackfeet, 1882–1945: A Photographic History of Cultural Survival* (Seattle: University of Washington Press, 1986).

142 Catherine Parsons Smith, "An Operatic Skeleton on the Western Frontier: Zitkala-Sa, William F. Hanson, and The Sun Dance Opera," *Women and Music*, January 2001, 1.

143 There were several "Indianist" operas by white composers in the early twentieth century such as: Arthur F. Nevin (1907). *Poia*, grand opera performed at Carnegie Hall; Charles Wakefield Cadman (1912). *Daoma: Ramala (Land of Misty Water)*, written in collaboration with Francis LaFlesche, opera in four acts performed at the Metropolitan Opera, New York; Eleanor Everest Freer (1927). *The Chilkoot Maiden*, opera in one act performed at Skagway, Alaska; Ernest Trow Carter (1931). *The Blonde Donna: The Fiesta at Santa Barbara*, opera comique performed at the Heckscher Theater, New York; Julia Frances Smith (1939). *Cynthia Parker*, opera in one act performed at North Texas State University, Denton.

144 Hafen, *Dreams and Thunder*, 127.

145 Review, *Deseret Evening News*, May 26, 1914, MSS 299; William F. Hanson Collection; University Archives; L. Tom Perry Special Collections, Harold B. Lee Library, Brigham Young University. Hafen, *Dreams and Thunder*, 127.

146 Mark Rifkin, *When Did Indians Become Straight? Kinship, the History of Sexuality, and Native Sovereignty* (Oxford: Oxford University Press, 2011), 222. For more on the history of U.S. legal prohibitions against indigenous social and cultural practices and "technologies of power" see: Thomas Biolsi, *Organizing the Lakota: The Political Economy of the New Deal on the Pine Ridge and Rosebud Reservation* (Tucson: University of Arizona Press, 1992), 7–10.

147 Bonnin's engagement with strategic essentialism in this period parallels the way identity as performance has been theorized in postcolonial, queer, gender, and performance studies. My thinking has been informed by: Gayatri Spivak (*In Other Worlds*, 202–15; *Outside*, 3–10) and "Can the Subaltern Speak?" in Cary Nelson and Lawrence Grossberg's *Marxism and the Interpretation of Culture* (1988); Diana Fuss, *Essentially Speaking: Feminism, Nature, and Difference* (1989); Edward Said, *Culture and Imperialism* (1993); Homi K. Bhahba, *The Location of Culture* (1994); Jose Esteban Munoz, *Disidentifications, Queers of Color and the Performance of Politics* (1999). Another useful way of thinking about identity stems from Satya Mohanty's critique of Spivak. See; Satya Mohanty, "The Epistemic Status of Cultural Identity," in *Reclaiming Identity: Realist Theory and the Predicament of Postmodernism*, edited by Paula Moya and Michael Hames-Garcia (Berkeley. University of California

Press, 2000). In postpositivist realist theory, according to Mohanty, understanding emerges from past and present experiences and interactions as interpreted in sociopolitical contexts. Understanding identity is relative to one's experiences as a raced, gendered, classed, nationalized, etc., being. For Bonnin and other oppressed peoples to define and articulate their social, economic, and political realities in their own terms becomes part of an ongoing movement to show how structural forces shape their lives and how they act within the context of such forces. In short, identities are both constructed and real, identities are mediated through cognitive and social processes, knowledge garnered in the context of oppression should be afforded epistemic privilege, and the power of individual and collective agency should be part of discussions of identity.

148   MSS 1704; Gertrude and Raymond Bonnin Collection; 20th–21st Century Western and Mormon Americana; L. Tom Perry Special Collections, Harold B. Lee Library, Brigham Young University. MSS 299; William F. Hanson Papers; L. Tom Perry Special Collections; Arts & Communications Archives; 1130 Harold B. Lee Library; Brigham Young University.

149   Pamela Karatonis and Dylan Robinson, eds., *Opera Indigene: Re/presenting First Nations and Indigenous Cultures* (Ashgate Publishing, 2013), 199.

150   New York Light Opera Guild advertisement for "The Sun Dance" featuring Erika Zaranova and Chief Yowlache [*sic*]. MSS 299, LTPSC. Yowlachie (or Daniel Simmons) was born in Washington in 1891 and died in 1966 in Los Angeles. A member of the Yakima tribe in Washington, he began as an opera singer, but in the 1920s switched to film. Over the next twenty-five years he played roles ranging from Apache chief to comic relief sidekick, notably in *Red River* (1948), where he traded quips with veteran scene stealer Walter Brennan. Yowlachie also appeared as Geronimo in the 1950s syndicated television series *Stories of the Century* starring Jim Davis as a railroad detective, and as I note in Chapter 4, he was a featured performer at an evening event Luther Standing Bear designed in 1931 to promote the National League for Justice to American Indians, a white and Indian reform group based in Southern California.

151   L. T. "Picturesque Indian Customs Form Basis of The Sun Dance, New American Opera," in *Musical Courier*, May 15, 1938, MSS 299; William F. Hanson Collection; University Archives; L. Tom Perry Special Collections, Harold B. Lee Library, Brigham Young University.

152   Charles Wakefield Cadman Collection, 1905–36, HCLA 1460, Special Collections Library, Pennsylvania State University.

153   The New York Light Opera guild was founded in the spring of 1931, and incorporated in the fall of the same year as a nonprofit educational and cultural institution. According to its own record and under general director and conductor John Hand, from 1931 to 1927, the aims of the Guild were: "to establish an adequate season of Light Opera, in Standard English, in New York City, to become self-sustaining, to provide additional opportunities for debuts before the public and press for young American singers, to provide singers in minor roles, as well as members of the ensemble, with the advantages of lectures and systematic instruction in the school of Light Opera and the histrionics of the stage … advancement in their singing careers, and to support the

American composer through the rendition of established works of new compo-
sitions." MSS 299; William F. Hanson Collection; University Archives; L. Tom
Perry Special Collections, Harold B. Lee Library, Brigham Young University.
Further abbreviated as: MSS 299, LTPSC. Also see: New York Light Opera
Guild, Inc. to Editor, November 29, 1937, Letter, MSS 299, LTPSC, regarding
"The Sun Dance" by William F. Hanson. "After careful study of many works,
the Guild now sends you the enclosed article announcing the selection of "The
Sun Dance," a romantic American Indian opera by William F. Hanson, an
American Composer from Utah, for production."

154 "Constitution and By-Laws of National Council of American Indians,"
Kim-Wait/Pablo Eisenberg Native American Literature Collection, Archives
and Special Collections, Frost Library, Amherst College, Amherst, MA.

155 Ibid.

156 Gertrude Bonnin to Miss Charlotte Jones, March 3, 1927, Letter, MSS 1704,
LTPSC. Also see: Gertrude Bonnin to Rev. Philip Gordon, April 13, 1927,
Letter. She notes, "Last summer, Capt Bonnin and I travelled 10.600 miles by
auto visiting Indian reservations. We started about 25 Local Lodges. During the
Short Session of Congress, the National Council of American Indians cooper-
ated with the Indian Defense Association. We received numerous letters com-
mending our work." Bonnin makes reference to key differences between the
NCAI and the SAI, which "was top heavy, without any body," whereas "the
National Council has its Local Lodges in the field, and these discuss and han-
dle their own local problems,–then unite their forces in the Washington D.C.
Headquarters for general, mutual aid before Congress and the Departments."
Image is courtesy of Frost Library, Archives and Special Collections at Amherst
College.

157 Gertrude Bonnin to Miss Maud B. Morris, January 10, 1927, Letter, MSS 1704,
LTPSC. Another letter, from Bonnin to J. R. H. King, April 5, 1927, offers an
expanded discussion of the NCAI's formation and its progress to "help Indians
very materially."

158 Although my example is a historical one, the issue of policing identity with
regards to Native Americans concerning nationalism and modernity remains a
critical arena for discussion and scholarly analysis. For more on the phenomena of culture cops as a contemporary practice see: Lyons, *X-Marks*.

159 Carpenter, "Detecting Indianness." I focus on Bonnin's correspondence and
also her musical career and her political activism as three different modes of
performance that she integrated into her life as an Indian intellectual.

160 Gertrude Bonnin to Rev. Philip Gordon, April 13, 1927 Letter, MSS
1704, LTPSC.

161 For more on Bonnin's investment in determining Chinquilla's real identity to
"define and assert her own" see: Carpenter, "Detecting Indianness." For a different reading of Bonnin and performance see: Spack, "Zitkala-Sa, *The Song of
Hiawatha*, and the Carlisle Indian School Band."

162 Rev. Philip Gordon to Gertrude Bonnin, April 1927, Letter, MSS 1704, LTPSC.

163 Laura I. Fletcher to Gertrude Bonnin, March 13, 1921, Letter, Box 2, Folder
19, MSS 1704, LTPSC.

164 Gertrude Bonnin, Matthew K. Sniffen, and Charles Faben, *Oklahoma's Poor Rich Indians: An Orgy of Graft and Exploitation of the Five Civilized Tribes – Legalized Robbery* (Office of the Indian Rights Association, 1924).

165 For a comparative history that examines the construction of an American identity based on Indian people and immigrant groups see: Alan Trachtenberg, *Shades of Hiawatha: Staging Indians, Making Americans, 1880–1930* (New York: Hill and Wang, 2005).

4

Luther Standing Bear

Staging U.S. Indian History with Reel Indians

The land was ours to roam in as the sky was for them to fly in. We did not think of the great open plains, the beautiful rolling hills, and winding streams with tangled growth, as "wild." Only to the white man was nature a "wilderness" and only to him was the land "infested" with "wild" animals and "savage" people.

    – Luther Standing Bear, *Land of the Spotted Eagle*

Introduction

Late in May 1931, not far from the back lots of Hollywood's burgeoning film industry, a coterie of writers, political reformers, and Native American actors gathered at the home of Marian Campbell. They came to Buckingham Road that evening for several reasons. Some came to meet and mingle with screen celebrities such as Bill Hart, who had, a couple decades earlier, established his career as a silent film cowboy.[1] Others came to see the less well-known Indian actors who were present, such as Nipo Strongheart, Chief Yowlachie, and Luther Standing Bear. Still others came to see a performance. Standing Bear, with help from his adopted niece May Jones, had personally arranged the evening's entertainment. Given his experiences as both a performer and an advocate for Indian actors, he was well positioned to manage white expectations for Indian performance.

First, guests gathered to see Sioux and Hopi dances. Next, they listened to songs sung by young children, like the Chickasaw girl Pakali, followed by a duet featuring contralto Lou-scha-enya and tenor Martin Napa. Their performance was based on an excerpt from *The Seminole* – an operetta composed by their hostess, Campbell, a few years earlier. Next, guests were surprised and excited to see Chief Yowlachie (or Daniel Simmons) perform with his wife, Whitebird. Both were becoming recognizable for the roles they played in movies and as members of Hollywood's Indian acting community. Like many high-profile Native actors during this period, Yowlachie had been given the honorary title of "Chief" to use before his name. This title was less tribal-national in origin and more a way for Hollywood to signify his status as an important player. Yowlachie's acting career is impressive. He appeared in several films ranging from *Ella Cinders* in 1926 to *Red River* in 1948 and *The FBI Story* in 1959. He also became well known for his portrayal of Geronimo in the television series *Stories of the Century*.[2] Yowlachie's presence as a performer and guest signifies how Standing Bear and Campbell could capitalize on the cultural power of Native celebrity by building a network consisting of Indian activists who made their living primarily through the entertainment business.

Although Standing Bear had designed the program to center on Indian folk songs and traditional dances, he drew on his history with Wild West touring companies to create a dramatic end to the evening by invoking a popular narrative trope – the covered wagon – familiar to fans of Western-themed movies and books.[3] The attack on the covered wagon – and the iconography of the wagon itself – had long been a key scene in William "Buffalo Bill" Cody's Wild West. Less than a decade earlier, in 1923, James Cruz and Paramount Pictures produced a popular film titled *The Covered Wagon* that asserted its authenticity and cinematic power based on the realism of scenes featuring Native extras. One program promoting the film noted, "The attack of a thousand Indians on the two-mile wagon train is one of the greatest thrills ever staged. These Indians were brought from reservations hundreds of miles away to appear in this episode."[4]

By employing a real covered wagon that evening, Standing Bear implored guests to consider both the symbolic power of these sorts of performances, and the fraught history of Native and white interactions they aimed to represent. No doubt guests were already familiar with filmic stories that featured covered wagons on their way westward, and what that journey entailed for both settlers and Native people. Standing Bear's awareness of the romantic, heroic, and tragic ways images of covered wagons had been used in an American cultural imaginary enabled him to utilize the wagon in his own staged performance to strategically thrill his guests. As an Indian actor who had lived in the actual West of the late nineteenth century depicted by Hollywood's Westerns, and as an activist situated in Los Angeles during the 1930s, Standing Bear needed to be careful in his deployment of a public "self." He could use performances like this one to negotiate the complex interplay between cultural aesthetics and political organizing as mutually constitutive, rather than oppositional, categories.

The evening's entertainment thus concluded when an old covered wagon emerged in Campbell's garden driven by young white men dressed as cowboys, accompanied by Bill Hart. After receiving robust applause, Hart dispensed refreshments of Indian corn soup and hard tack. As Hart began doling out soup to the audience, the show became a truly interactive experience, a film narrative come to life. Hart was simultaneously acting as a cowboy and an ambassador of the Western film, engaging guests in a shared performance space framed by Western themes.[5]

This moment offers a poignant example of how Standing Bear, like film directors and traveling show entrepreneurs before him, designed a spectacle that capitalized on and transformed imagery from America's Wild West to command the attention of his audience. Like those earlier showmen, Standing Bear reworked the imagery in order to make an argument about politics and history. Set in the context of Hollywood, Standing Bear offered a complex reimagining of the wagon as an iconic prop. His decision to use the wagon *and* Bill Hart demonstrates not only a keen awareness of Western tropes, but also of the powerful association Americans made between their own identities as citizens and an idealized America built on westward expansion. His choices for the performance reflect how the Wild West had already been adapted into films. Standing Bear also seemed to recognize his Hollywood setting as a site ripe for ironic self-referential humor – and for powerful cultural politics. Despite the problematic ways Indian people were often misrepresented in Western stories, Standing Bear reproduced the powerful imaginary surrounding conquest and the slow disappearance of the Indian. He did so, however, as part of a larger political strategy driven by the social activism of Indian people working in Southern California. This opening anecdote is emblematic of both the role of performance in mobilizing public interest in Native issues and the significance of the political networks created by performers in Hollywood in the 1930s, networks that could include Chief Yowlachie and Bill Hart, as well as Marian Campbell and Luther Standing Bear.

After the performances and the food, Campbell and Standing Bear turned to the business of the evening. They needed to add members to their newly formed political organization, the National League for Justice to American Indians (NLJAI). For Standing Bear, reform and performance were not mutually exclusive; although Charles Eastman and Gertrude Bonnin "performed" their own versions of Indianness, it is clear that the movie images Standing Bear and his fellow actors created – dynamic, generic, heroic, romantic – were slightly different from the Victorian poses of the early twentieth century, and a cultural world apart from Chicago, where Carlos Montezuma donned a tuxedo for his public appearances. Although promoted with the trappings of Hollywood, the League was strictly political in its aims. It built its platform on articles from the U.S. Constitution – namely, the First, Fourth, Fourteenth, and Fifteenth Amendments. Because the League identified itself as part of America's democratic mission, it could argue in favor of guaranteeing rights to Indians as citizens of the United States. Readers of contemporary Native American politics will note that Standing Bear ignored the Sixth Amendment, one of the articles key to claiming tribal sovereignty. Like many of his peers (including Montezuma, Bonnin, and Eastman), Standing Bear was more interested in the question of citizenship, which made sense given his urban context and career. The League's claims to America and Americanness resonated with Standing Bear's use of Western motifs in the performances for the evening meeting, even as the organization actively revised and resisted the underlying logics of conquest supporting such motifs of imperialist expansion.[6]

The League articulated five aims as critical to its mission:

- First: to "publish a true history of the American Indian."
- Second: "to render assistance to the American Indians in marketing their wares."
- Third: "to promote a study of the legal rights of American Indians as citizens."
- Fourth: "to secure the admittance of Indian children to public schools throughout America."
- Fifth: to make "known to the peoples of the world the present conditions and needs of the various tribes and nations of American Indians, whether on reservations or elsewhere."

The fifth and final aim was a familiar objective for progressive reformers during this period, and the last clause was especially relevant to urban residents like Standing Bear, Strongheart, and Yowlachie. The fact of Indian people living in cities and working as actors "marketing their wares" was an important component of the League's goals given that it wanted to increase *both* employment and political opportunities for Native people. Its emphasis on education and publishing a "true history" represented its desire to change how the majority of Americans imagined Indian people and Indianness as part of American culture. Such an education might push back against the often derogatory and purely fictional representations that characterized most silver screen Indians.[7]

The president of the League was Marian Campbell. As a white woman, her role is not surprising given that she was a veteran of reform work in California focused on Indian rights, where she had collaborated with various women's organizations. In addition, years before Campbell moved to Los Angeles from Cleveland, she had begun work on her light opera based on Indian themes.[8] As a composer interested in Indian culture, Campbell's music aligned with the work of white Indianist composers and performers as well as with the proliferation of an Indian curio market that sold Native crafts or Native-themed crafts to white consumers through dealers and catalogues across the United States.[9] Not long after divorcing her first husband, a wealthy car manufacturer from Ohio, Campbell married Nipo Strongheart; it is likely that a large part of her interest in promoting Native rights was based on their relationship. As president, Campbell often spoke on behalf of the League in public. In an interview with the *Los Angeles Times* a week following the first meeting of the League, Campbell stated bluntly that "we are the only Indian welfare organization seeking the abolition of our age-old

Bureau of Indian Affairs [BIA] and demanding that the American Indian be recognized as an American citizen, treated as such, educated as such."[10] Although Campbell spoke the words, Standing Bear shared the desire for recognition and the abolition of the BIA. His political vision for Native people underpinned his participation in the League and reflected ideas articulated by Native intellectuals like Eastman and Bonnin. The abolition of the BIA was a prominent topic in the pages of Montezuma's *Wassaja*.

As first vice president of the League, Standing Bear worked as an advocate for Native people who shared similar views. In addition to Campbell, other white Americans joined the League to assist in their mission. Bill Hart was named second vice president. Two white writers interested in Western history, with a particular fondness for Native people, became members of the League's advisory board: E. A. Brininstool and Lucullus McWhorter. Both were part of a broad and critical network of Indian publication and performance.

Three years earlier, Brininstool had worked with Standing Bear as an editor for his book *My People the Sioux*, which when published in 1928 featured an introduction by Bill Hart. McWhorter's involvement grew out of his connection to a Native author, writer Christine Quintasket, who was known by the pen name "Mourning Dove."[11] McWhorter had helped with editing and publishing of her novel, *Cogewea: The Half-Blood*, in 1927.[12] Consider the network active at Campbell's home that night: singers, including Yowlachie, who would go on to a Hollywood career; white and Native actors Hart, Strongheart, and Standing Bear; and the editorial voices of McWhorter and Brininstool, two writers and editors with strong ties to the publishing business. Music, Hollywood, Publishing. Here is a network that incorporated Indian performance, the film industry, and the literary and editorial work of Native and white activists.[13]

In addition to white activists, celebrities, and writers, high-profile Native figures were crucial for the League's success. Nipo Strongheart, a well-known actor and activist in his own right, was elected to serve as the executive secretary and historian for the group. Strongheart actively recruited fellow Indian performers to become members of the League, which is perhaps why Yowlachie had been invited to perform at their first meeting at Campbell's home. In the years following their first meeting, Strongheart and Campbell, together with Standing Bear and May Jones, traveled throughout California to promote the League by giving a series of public lectures.[14]

As an activist, a writer, and a performer, Standing Bear offers a narrative for understanding the path Native people could take from Carlisle in the 1880s to Los Angeles in the 1930s. The reform work that Standing Bear became part of when he and Campbell invited friends to join the NLJAI signals one specific example of a wider trend. There is no question that changes in federal Indian policy that occurred in the 1930s were launched from the West Coast. John Collier had in fact "discovered Indians" after he moved from New York to California.[15] The Association on American Indian

Affairs had its roots in New Mexico and California, and the chief political supporters of the Indian New Deal were (at least initially) people familiar with the multicultural scene in the West.[16] The reforms of the 1930s were not so much products of tribal engagement (although that would come later with groups like the National Congress of American Indians[17]) as they were expressions of broad popular beliefs about Indians as inherently communal (hence tribal) and consensual (hence governed by "councils" with no separation of powers). While continuously debated, the Collier reforms seem more from above than from below, which is why highlighting Standing Bear's career helps emphasize the roles that Native people could play on-screen and off, personally and politically.

Native Actors as Activists

Experiences in the film world led Strongheart and Standing Bear to the political work surrounding citizenship. Two decades later, Strongheart reflected back on these moments. In a piece for *Wisconsin Magazine*, "History in Hollywood," Strongheart comments on his life as a Native American performer and criticizes the role of historical research within the movie industry. He notes the various historic and ethnic misrepresentations and misinterpretations perpetuated by most Hollywood films. Strongheart had worked as an advisor to filmmakers in order to argue for the importance of accurate historical study and the procurement of "live material" to guarantee authenticity within a given motion picture. His recollections offer a glimpse into the costs and benefits for Indians of pitching themselves as the "live material" that would grant ethnic authenticity to the emergent medium of film. Like Eastman, Bonnin, Montezuma, and others, leading "Hollywood Indians" were part of a network of Native intellectuals trying to develop an authoritative voice with which they might speak to white Americans. Arguably, Standing Bear was among one of the first to develop such a voice, demonstrated by his political reform efforts, autobiographical texts, and acting career. Standing Bear was not alone in these efforts because Strongheart had served as a historical ethnologist and technical director for multiple productions, including at least seven films made between 1905 and 1952.[18]

As Native actors, Standing Bear and Strongheart aimed to use their positions in Hollywood to reshape some of the ways audiences might view and desire Indian bodies portrayed on screen. Part self-promotion and part history lesson, Strongheart's *Wisconsin Magazine* piece raised the specter that haunted and defined performativity for Indians in Hollywood: the vexed question of authenticity. The desire to portray "real Indians," and in effect to have audiences experience "authentic" Indianness on-screen, enabled directors and producers to support the careers of a large number of Indian actors. This often meant a great deal of material gain for Indian people as well as an authoritative role for Native experts. As early as 1911, a large number of

Native people (many of them Sioux from the Great Plains) lived in Southern California and worked in film. For many viewers, such Indian lives – wage-workers in Hollywood, living far from ancestral homelands – would be defined as "inauthentic." And yet a discourse of "ethnic" authenticity as a means for defining Indianness permeated the productions involving these Indian people, as the promotional materials for Cruze's *The Covered Wagon* made clear.[19]

Throughout Standing Bear's lifetime, authenticity (as opposed to performance) appeared as a discourse embedded thoroughly in the context of Wild West shows, films, and even literary writing. These concepts – one focused on the wide world of the imaginary; the other on the wage-working material practice of that same imaginary – tied discussions of "real" Indians to the employment of actual Natives. In some significant ways, such avenues for performance existed in tension with the types of images created by Eastman, Montezuma, and Bonnin. Certainly all these Native writers, like Standing Bear, engaged with questions surrounding authenticity. Their politics of racial uplift and those of the Society of American Indians (SAI), of which Henry Standing Bear (Luther's younger brother) was a founding member, led them to create local plays and pageants representing historical accuracy and "ethnological truth."[20] But many SAI members believed that the "barbaric" dances and violent clashes performed in Wild West narratives – whether live or on-screen – would hurt Native American chances for acceptance into American society.[21] Of course, these images of barbarism were bread and butter for the Hollywood film industry. But even as they performed such images, Standing Bear and other Native actors and activists like Strongheart and Yowlachie, and later Jim Thorpe, understood the SAI complaint. They took up the mantle of authentic Indianness to claim positions of authority within cultural performance venues, to use that authority to assert their own points of view. Standing Bear lived an extraordinary life that represented the subtleties and complexities of strategic performances of ethnic authenticity. His texts, whether written or spoken, at times replicated dominant understandings of Indianness, while at other times criticizing practices of domination carried out by white cultural producers and political reformers. Always, Standing Bear resisted opportunities that automatically foreclosed the possibility of Indian people to participate in shaping modern U.S. society.[22]

As a film advisor, Standing Bear often spoke as an Indian expert to confirm the authenticity of a film's sets, costumes, and plot. His insights did not always result in more nuanced portrayals of Indian characters on-screen, nor did his interpretation of Native history, culture, language, and behavior always contradict dominant expectations of a director's imagination or a writer's narrative when it came to representing Indian people. These performances and the work of Native people within them raise important questions. What was the relationship between authenticity as a self-identity that generated wages in performance and a kind of self-authenticity that led one to political commitments, writing, and efforts to change the structures of representation? What kinds of things could compromise both the public and private aspects of these performances of Indian self? By interrogating particular moments in Standing Bear's life, we begin to answer these questions and pinpoint specific aspects of his life that might be representative of how other Native performers experienced acting and activism during this period. For Standing Bear, entertainment became the realm where he could perform Indianness *and* advocate for more control over these performances to shift dominant expectations regarding the portrayal of Indian people within American culture. Popular demands to see Indians in Westerns could then mean opportunities for Native actors to put on their own public meetings and "shows" to engage audiences in different narratives regarding the West, conquest, and nationalism.

The issue at hand for any Native actor was the simplicity of filmic representations of Indianness, which resulted in diminishing the complexity of historical realities, and the cultural specificity and diversity that has always existed among and between indigenous peoples. As "Plains Indians" became a type in movies the cultural particularities of peoples like the Apache, Crow, Arapaho, and Cheyenne were erased – by lumping them into one simple category – viewers might learn names like Sioux and Comanche as easily as they forgot Cherokee, Ojibwe, and Wampanoag.[23] Nevertheless, Standing Bear made an argument in favor of indigenous difference and political agency. He was able to empower Indian actors through the Indian Actors Association (IAA) and to spur the formation of reform groups, such as the NLJAI during a time when Southern California became a place many Native people associated with new career opportunities. The better wages film offered enabled many Indian actors to escape the paternalism and poverty characteristic of reservations in the 1920s and 1930s.[24] Coming to Hollywood also enabled Native people to engage with performativity to build distinct networks that necessitated the "real Indian" performances they were hired to portray. One way to connect Standing Bear to other Native actors and Indian intellectuals during this period is to identify both the employment and activist networks he navigated, to point out the limits and possibilities emerging for him through these networks.

The Road Ahead for Luther Standing Bear

By the time he was sixty-three, Standing Bear had traveled far and wide from the Nebraska Territory where he was born in 1868. His final home, in Huntington Park, California, was where, at age fifty, he put pen to paper to write his first book: *My People the Sioux*, published in 1928. As a writer, Standing Bear aimed to educate his readers about "the truth" regarding the first Americans. His first book, like the three that would follow, *My Indian*

FIGURE 9. Chief Standing Bear full-length portrait.
Public Domain, Date: ca. 1919. Subject: Standing Bear, Luther, 1868?–1939.
Indians of North America – Clothing & dress – 1910–1920.

Notes: J236948 U.S. Copyright Office. Copyright by William Charles Thompson,
Alhambra, California. Format: Portrait photographs 1910–1920. Photographic
prints 1910–1920.

Source: Library of Congress.

Boyhood (1931), *Land of the Spotted Eagle* (1933), and *Stories of the Sioux* (1934), asserted such an aim in the preface. "I trust that in reading the contents of this book the public will come to a better understanding of us, I hope they will become better informed as to our principles, our knowledge, and our ability. It is my desire that all people know the truth about the first Americans and their relations with the United States Government."[25] His autobiography focuses on the early years of his childhood growing up on the Plains before he attended the Carlisle Industrial School in Pennsylvania from 1879 to 1885. Through various recollections Standing Bear describes his first home, a teepee, and how his parents called him Ota K'te, or "Plenty Kill." Later at school, he "was told to take a pointer and select a name for myself from the list written on the blackboard" and gave himself the name "Luther." His younger brother Henry, born around 1869, also went on to study at Carlisle from 1883 to 1891. According to school records, the older Standing Bear arrived as "Kills Plenty" and the younger as "Kills Little" before both took their new English names.[26] This renaming policy was a common practice for Native pupils at boarding schools. In this case, the erasure of the brothers' Lakota names works to undo the relational and descriptive character of their Sioux names.[27]

Writing about his time at Carlisle, Standing Bear's autobiography frames him as a Native exemplar. According to *My People the Sioux*, from the beginning of his time at the school, Standing Bear was viewed by the school's headmaster, Richard Henry Pratt, as someone other students should emulate.[28] Pratt's views may have been guided by the fact that Standing Bear recognized in himself a sense of status because he was the son of a chief. Through this, and his self-described "boyish willingness" to live up to the standards of Pratt's educational ideology, Standing Bear was sent to work at the Wanamaker department store. Once there, he believed he was more than a mere employee; Standing Bear was a representative of his family, his tribe, and the rest of Carlisle's students. His text emphasizes the moment Pratt selected him to go to work at Wanamaker. "As I rose everybody turned to look at me. It seemed as if I was walking on air. My feet did not seem to touch the floor!"[29] These feelings of exaltation make Standing Bear exceptional. Not every Indian kid might feel this way. His feelings of pride as a Native representative echo similar emotions conveyed by the writings of Eastman, Montezuma, and Bonnin. By the time Standing Bear is writing about these early moments he had already been speaking on behalf of fellow Sioux, first for Cody's Wild West and later when he worked for filmmaker Thomas Ince. The narrative from *My People the Sioux* continues to refer explicitly to racial uplift and Pratt's aims in sending Standing Bear to Wanamaker. " 'My boy, you are going away from us to work for this school, in fact, for your whole race.' "[30] It was true. By age seventeen, Standing Bear was indeed acting as a representative of an entire "race," whether he liked it or not. A few years earlier, Pratt had succeeded in exposing the young Standing Bear to other opportunities to travel with other Native students beyond Carlisle to demonstrate to the world the success of the school's mission in educating indigenous youths.

Performing for Carlisle and Wanamaker

On May 24, 1883, at the age of fifteen, Standing Bear made his first trip to New York City and his first public appearance. He lined up with fellow classmates in City Hall Park, in lower Manhattan, to lead the Carlisle School's marching band across the new Brooklyn Bridge. "When the parade started I gave the signal, and we struck up and kept playing all the way across the great structure."[31] The Carlisle band had been invited to play as part of an American ceremony, a cultural ritual to celebrate the bridge, the great city of New York, and the U.S. nation.[32] The desire for Indian participation in this ceremony harkened back to Simon Pokagon's role during the opening of Chicago Day at the 1893 World's Fair.[33] The first readers of *My People the Sioux* would sense a great deal of irony surrounding this "national" moment of celebration and musical performance. Although the band played for largely non-Indian audiences, Standing Bear narrates its experience through a claim to Americanness and citizenship. "So the Carlisle Indian band of brass instruments was the first *real American band* to cross the Brooklyn Bridge, and I am proud to say that I was their leader" (emphasis mine).[34] His use of "real" before American here denotes an inscription of indigenous peoples into the U.S. nation as its founders, a subversive revision of the historical moment that Pratt had designed for his school's band to help celebrate the Brooklyn Bridge as the symbol of American modernity. No matter how grand a performance it was, the students were given no break, as their trip around New York continued. With several engagements throughout the city, including the Fifth Avenue Baptist Church, the band moved on to play at large churches in Philadelphia before finally making its way back to Carlisle, Pennsylvania. Such a variety of locales suggests Pratt aimed to showcase the talents of his Indian students to a range of audiences who wanted to witness the now *civilized* Native musicians, thereby affirming Carlisle's assimilationist success.

Although less enamored with Carlisle and Pratt, Gertrude Bonnin had also seen her performance career take off through her association with the school's band less than a decade after Standing Bear's appearance at the Brooklyn Bridge. Highly critical of Pratt's strict discipline and the forced Christianization of Native students, Bonnin only taught at the school for two years. As a gifted Native female singer, Bonnin was called on by Pratt to perform with the school band in 1900 for a concert in Paris.[35] That same year, Bonnin left her teaching position to attend the Boston Conservatory of Music. Her decision to leave and study the violin made a lot of sense given how critical Bonnin had become of Pratt's assimilation methods. Both Bonnin and Standing Bear found some success as musicians performing for large nonnative audiences eager to see civilized Indians playing Western rather than tribal music.[36] These sorts of performative moments, for Standing Bear and Bonnin, were analogous to events where Eastman and Montezuma spoke in public but with an important difference: although the audiences were similar, the performers were not standing in as singular representatives of their race, but as members of a group showcasing Indian musical talent and skill. Carlisle's Indian band demonstrated the promises of American education and possible futures available for Native youth who could now master musical aspects of white American culture. Whether they liked it or not, they were participating in an effective advertising campaign Pratt designed to sell his fellow Americans on the assimilation success of Carlisle.

As Standing Bear's schooling drew to a close, later in 1885, he went, as promised, to work as a clerk at the Wanamaker department store in Philadelphia. Pratt had been asked by Mr. Wanamaker to send the very best students in his school. He told Standing Bear, "Go, and do your best. The majority of white people think the Indian is a lazy good-for-nothing. They think he can neither work nor learn anything; that he is very dirty. Now you are going to prove that the red man *can* learn and work as well as the white man."[37] So Standing Bear's first real job was framed according to the rhetoric of racial uplift. Whether performing for the band or working for Wanamaker, Standing Bear learned from a young age that wherever he would go he might be viewed as a representative of his race, and soon all Indian people in America became his concern.[38]

Such labor did not come without emotional costs. Indeed, there are two types of labor happening in these scenarios: the ostensible labor of serving customers and the actual labor of being on display for an audience. Experiencing both, Standing Bear reflected in his work at Wanamaker the patronage and patriarchy governing Indian employment in performance industries. When outlined within the emergence of a display culture characterizing department stores at the turn of the twentieth century, his appearance at Wanamaker suggests a different, racialized interpretation of display,[39] which fit all too easily within the rise of consumer capitalism "Where Almost Anything May Be Bought."[40]

Standing Bear understood the fraught racial politics surrounding his work in Philadelphia. He recalled Pratt's instructions clearly: "I was to prove to all people that the Indians could learn and work as well as the white people; to prove that Carlisle School was the best place for the Indian boy."[41] For the most part, his experience at Wanamaker went well, although his classmate Clarence Three Stars did not find it so "tolerable" and complained saying, "Luther, my work is not to my liking … as I go behind the counters the clerks all call me 'Indian,' and I don't like it; it makes me nervous."[42] Three Stars' exposure to racial discrimination pushed him to return to life on his reservation.[43] Standing Bear was unable to convince Three Stars to stay, and with him gone he "worked all the harder" at the store.[44]

Despite Standing Bear's initial enthusiasm regarding his work at Wanamaker, times grew tough once Three Stars left. One day, Standing Bear was called up to the first floor, where a little glass house had been built. He was asked to sit inside the house rather than behind the clerk's counter. "So everyday I was locked inside this little glass house, opening the trunks, taking out the jewels and putting price tags on them. How the white folks did crowd around to watch me!"[45] He understood these white onlookers were under the impression that "an Indian would steal anything he could get his hands on."[46] In his autobiography, Standing Bear further highlights these negative attitudes and concludes that despite being put on display, he at least received a promotion with more pay once he was working inside the glass house. This is an important assertion, especially in the context of autobiography as a self-reflexive genre, because it recognizes a need and desire for material well-being. Both *My People the Sioux* (1928), where this incident is reported, and *Land of the Spotted Eagle* (1933) are autobiographies narrating challenging personal experiences that can be read as complicated written performances. They may not accurately reflect lived experience so much as narrate key moments Standing Bear used to define his life and his philosophy, from the position of a writer living in the late 1920s and early 1930s.[47]

While working for Wanamaker, Standing Bear first came into contact with Cody's Wild West and the great Lakota leader Sitting Bull (1831–90). Their encounter was a strange one. One evening, going home from work, Standing Bear:

> bought a paper, and read that Sitting Bull, the great Sioux medicine man, was to appear at one of the Philadelphia theaters. The paper stated that he was the Indian who killed General Custer! The chief and his people had been held prisoners of war, and now here they were to appear in a Philadelphia theater. So I determined to go and see what he had to say, and what he was *really* in the East for (emphasis mine).[48]

Standing Bear strategically remembers how there must have been another reason for Sitting Bull to make such an appearance; something else was taking place that evening in a Philadelphia theater, which ran against the grain of the newspaper's statement regarding Custer's killer. After paying fifty cents to enter, Standing Bear witnessed "many Indian trappings" inside the theater. With a stage before him, he saw four Indian men, one of whom was Sitting Bull, seated. Part of the strangeness of the encounter lay in its context. The other was an issue of mistranslation.

Standing Bear's autobiography focuses on this moment by remembering the translator for Sitting Bull and the ways he misrepresented the great leader's speech. This remembering of mistranslation raises the question of how language enabled American understandings of indigenous lives. As Sitting Bull talked about peace and education, his interpreters wrongly told the crowd he was describing the Battle of the Little Big Horn. Standing Bear's text lays bare this blatant mistranslation to highlight its intended effect of entertainment, as opposed to accurate historical testimony, for a mostly white audience. His narrative actually remembers Sitting Bull's testimony by laying bare the chicanery of the translator and the show's operators that evening.

Framing the event and his memory of it with a keen sense of the representational politics at stake, Standing Bear's text reengages the original purpose of Sitting Bull's appearance as a performance playing to white expectations. Standing Bear's examination of the deeper event of mistranslation allows him to urge white readers to consider the possibility of inaccuracy. Because the real Sitting Bull is there, the evidence of authenticity is right in front of the audience, hard to deny, and yet the story as translated is completely false. The "representational politics" here are a set of historically contingent actions involving the creation and distribution of culture and political views that Standing Bear remembers on his own terms, offering a revised historical narrative. By calling out the act of mistranslation and his awareness of it, Standing Bear showcases a moment of pan-Indian solidarity. When Standing Bear tells the story of mistranslation, he maps his representational politics onto Indian identity, as something imbricate, fluid, and perpetually changing – both in relation to an individual's sense of self, and to how he or she interprets the expectations of the social context through which he or she moves. Writing about this event, Standing Bear locates a moment of solidarity given that his identity in the store as an Indian worker is equally performative and open to white misreadings. Sitting Bull is similarly positioned, but because of the mistranslation, he does not have the same opportunity to correct the record. So Standing Bear's narrative, written in California over forty years after the event, demonstrates how the two examples, Standing Bear in the glass house and Sitting Bull on the stage, are connected. Standing Bear's narrative makes the case speak to the larger issue of pan-Indian solidarity. He considers the importance of their encounter as a pedagogical opportunity to show the next generation of Indian leaders what it meant for him to see Sitting Bull at "work" for Cody. Years later, Standing Bear as an author enjoys the benefit of hindsight, and through it, he emphasizes Sitting Bull's performance as a strategy. Sitting Bull had worked for Cody to support his tribe and to resist the surveillance of the Indian agency that sought to confine and limit him. Although empowered in this way, Sitting Bull's testimony could still be willfully misrepresented and the white audiences seemingly thrilled to hear about Custer's demise.[49]

Standing Bear especially remembers how the translator "told so many lies that I had to smile."[50] The gesture of the smile refers to his memory and the power relations of the moment itself. At the time of writing, Standing

Bear's description that he "had" to smile recalls this moment to signal cha-
grin, if not outrage, over the translator's deception. This affective response
toward the translator's lies suggests Standing Bear could use humor to tem-
per the violence of misrepresentation apparent in this scene. He writes further about how two Indian women received his smile. "One of the women
on the stage observed me and said something to the other woman, then both
of them kept looking at me."[51] They knew that he knew, thus creating the
possibility for a shared Indian critical consciousness.

This inversion of the power relations arranged on the stage makes
Standing Bear's understanding of the *real* message Sitting Bull means to send
visible to white members of the audience as well as the other Indians that
were present. When the Indians on the stage witness Standing Bear's smile,
they can read it as an act of opposition. They might also read his smile
as a recognition of the necessity and triumph of defeating Custer. Just as
Sitting Bull's narrative is overwritten by a mistranslation, Standing Bear's
text reflects on the act of mistranslation that has taken place and his smile
acknowledges the hegemonic practices of white paternalism and colonization occurring through mistranslation. His smile also figures possibility for
subverting these practices by drawing attention to his own understanding
of the mistranslation. Standing Bear's smile places him with all Indian people, symbolically standing on stage with Sitting Bull and the other Indians.
Moving beyond symbolic and toward literal solidarity, Standing Bear's text
describes how he approached the stage, "not intending to say a word," but
then speaking Sioux with "the woman who had first noticed me smiling
from my seat."[52] Such a moment of recognition, from one Indian to another,
"of course caused some excitement among the crowd of white people."[53]
Next, Standing Bear is called on by Sitting Bull and the others to act as their
translator for the rest of their brief stay in Philadelphia. Standing Bear's narrative is quite explicit about the ramifications of this experience.

As I sit and think about that incident, I wonder who that crooked white man was,
and what sort of Indian agent it could have been who would let these Indians leave
the reservation without even an interpreter, giving them the idea they were going to
Washington, and then cart them around to different Eastern cities to make money
off them by advertising that Sitting Bull was the Indian who slew General Custer! Of
course at the time I was too young to realize the seriousness of it all.[54]

His explicit references to the "crooked white man" and the "Indian agent" as
well as how these Indians were used to "make money," for readers in 1933,
recognizes the ongoing practices of settler-colonialism and the moments
when authentic, real Indians are novel relics of an American past represented
through the successful conquest of the West. The fact that Sitting Bull and
the others were misled regarding the purpose of their trip enables Standing
Bear to further critique the corruption and oppression inherent both in the
misrepresentation of history and in the mismanagement of Native people by
the federal government. The scene prefigures later moments within Standing

Bear's text, when he will again work as a translator both for William Cody's troupe and Thomas Ince's film company.

Standing Bear's depiction of the white translator and the excitement of the white crowd who did not expect a young Native man in their midst encourages readers of *My People the Sioux* to pause and consider the deleterious effects of mistranslation on people, cultures, and history itself.[55] This scene is further highlighted by the fact that another Indian, who understands and speaks Lakota, *must* be present to witness and re-translate this history. Standing Bear's presence as an Indian neither on display nor on the stage, but among the audience, offers readers a subtle revision of assimilation practices from this period that claimed an Indian would either assimilate or die, whereas in this case he could be sitting in the audience.[56]

Work for the Office of Indian Affairs

Not long after he left Wanamaker, on July 6, 1885, Standing Bear graduated from Carlisle and made his way back to South Dakota and the Pine Ridge Reservation in search of a job. By 1891, Standing Bear was in a bit of a predicament. Although he had been offered a position as a teacher, the job was at Rosebud rather than Pine Ridge, where his father and the rest of his family lived. Given the extreme poverty many Indian people were facing, Standing Bear could not refuse the position of assistant teacher at the Rosebud Agency. His longing for Pine Ridge aside, Standing Bear distinguished himself as an excellent teacher. Ms. Wright, the head teacher of the school, noted that he was "diligent and faithful, persevering and trustworthy" and you could "depend upon his word."[57] Standing Bear also reflected on his teaching, but in less celebratory terms. "At that time, teaching amounted to very little. It really did not require a well-educated person to teach on the reservation. The main thing was to teach the children to write their names in English, then came learning the alphabet and how to count. I liked this work well, and the children were doing splendidly."[58]

Despite sending many inquiries to the Office of Indian Affairs (OIA), Standing Bear was unable to receive official support to move back to Pine Ridge and rejoin his family. This did not stop him. He moved there anyway and began building a home. Although the upper-level administrators of the Indian Service, many of whom lived in Washington, DC, did not grant permission for a transfer to Pine Ridge, Standing Bear found local support from the acting agent, Charles G. Penny. He viewed Standing Bear favorably because of the young man's connection to the Carlisle School and a glowing recommendation from Pratt.[59] By November 1891, Penny sent his third letter to the OIA to argue for Standing Bear's relocation to Pine Ridge.

He is a young man who has been educated in the East, and it is becoming that great consideration should be shown him.... To force him back to Rosebud Agency, against his will, will tend to dishearten him and to make him discontented. His desire to reside here with his father, brothers and sisters, is natural, laudable and will be productive of good results.

The "desire to reside" aspect of Penny's explanation for Standing Bear's request refers, in part, to the emotional life of his Indian ward. That closeness to Standing Bear's family would "be productive of good results" suggests contentment and happiness afforded to Standing Bear, at least in this moment, and suggests he was somewhat privileged because of his mobility. Penny's endorsement may have been welcome even if his paternalistic tone conformed to a politics of uplift that defined Standing Bear's character in terms of an education in the East – itself a tool of the government to reshape Indian people into "fit" citizens. Similarly, Penny's discussion of Standing Bear's desires as tied to family, not the tribal-national unit, as "natural" and "laudable" worked to position his ward as a part of a white discourse of civilization. In just two years, federal Indian policy makers would successfully argue for assimilating Native people through allotments that promised individual heads of household private land ownership and eventual citizenship in the United States.[60]

As an employee, Standing Bear both challenged and reinforced the power of the OIA. His move from Rosebud back to Pine Ridge revealed the complicated, multilevel, and contradictory inner workings of the OIA. He found allies within the system who judged him worthy of "great consideration," as Penny did. They too wrote in support of his request for a transfer. This phrase comes out of the many exchanges made between OIA officials. One might read it as a remark on his class position given that Standing Bear was an educated Indian and trying to make himself more American, thereby effacing his race. Such an effort, the OIA agents thought, should be rewarded. Standing Bear's move from one reservation to another was hotly debated among administrators of the OIA. These officials' letters not only represent a debate regarding Standing Bear's request but also the extent to which the U.S. bureaucracy designed to manage Indian affairs was enmeshed in the daily lives of Indian people.

As these officials calculated the line dividing what they thought would be best for their administration of land and people, as opposed to what would be best for an individual, they invoked familiar, if troubling rhetoric regarding the fitness of Indians to become part of the Indian Service.[61] This issue of autonomy dogged many of the graduates of Carlisle and the other Indian schools. In theory, their education should have conveyed, not simply "consideration" from the OIA, but actual control over their own lives.

By the summer of 1892, Standing Bear was settled on Pine Ridge. During this period, many educated Indians were returning to reservations from boarding schools to live and work among their people. In this instance, because he was viewed as a "very competent educated mixed blood" by the white officials working in the Indian Service, Standing Bear could negotiate the terms of his employment in ways other Native people could not. At the same time, there remained a concern among white progressives working within the OIA that education itself would not necessarily create material and cultural change among Native people, and therefore, those who returned to their reservations but did not take up farming, teaching, or owning a business of some sort were in danger of going "back to the blanket." This reference to a blanket aimed to further patronize and infantilize Native people, confirming they were doomed to perish if they did not give up their "old" (primitive, antimodern, and blanket-wearing) ways in favor of those they had learned at school.[62] Despite support from the OIA and some success as a teacher, Standing Bear would not remain at Pine Ridge for long.

Performance: A Family Affair

In October 1900, Luther's brother, Henry Standing Bear, was living in New York City and working as an actor. In 1903, along with a number of other Indians, he performed in a show at Coney Island as part of the Steeplechase Amusement Park.[63] The opening of George C. Tilyou's Steeplechase Park in 1897 marked the beginning of Coney Island's era as "the Nation's Playground" and was the precursor to the modern-day amusement park. Named for Coney Island's horseracing tradition, initiated by the Brighton Beach Racetrack in 1879, the Park drew in an estimated 90,000 visitors a day during its peak years. As a Native performer, Henry was fortunate to have more than one option. Both Pawnee Bill's "Wild West Show and Great Far East Show" and Fred T. Cummins' "Indian Congress and Life on the Plains" were sanctioned by the U.S. government to entertain Park visitors at this time.[64]

While Henry Standing Bear worked as an Indian performer in Coney Island, Luther performed with Cody's Wild West. After this, Luther would join the Miller Brothers' "101 Ranch" where, like Henry, he "enjoyed mixing with the swarms of visitors." It is important to situate the brothers geographically in what became a fully bicoastal arrangement. Henry regularly worked at Coney Island, the most significant amusement park on the Atlantic, and Luther was employed on the West Coast at Venice Pier, one of the original mass entertainment venues in the Los Angeles area. In addition to "playing Indian" as a movie extra and actor, Luther Standing Bear operated an archery concession on the pier to supplement his wages. According to one historian, Standing Bear's capabilities with a bow and arrow were put to the test at the pier one day when several Japanese tourists challenged him to a shooting contest. Fortunately for his career, Luther won.[65]

The opportunity to work in entertainment could be highly gendered; as men, Luther and Henry were privileged to construct lives apart from their families when they went to work at either Coney Island or the Venice

Pier. Because they were *Indian* men, these opportunities equally turned on fictions of race, for they were expected to act the parts of noble savage, wild warrior, and authentic primitive all at once. Henry's "fitness" as an American man might have been called into question because he had left his family behind in South Dakota to pursue a career in show business. His wife, Nellie, even asked for help from Indian agent Charles E. McChesney to transfer her and their five children (Lily, Emily, Julia, Joseph, and Annie) from Pine Ridge to Rosebud because "my husband left me and I am without any means of support."[66]

By the time Luther moved to California, he too had chosen to abandon his wife. For both brothers, being apart from their families could not have been easy. At the same time, what sort of public acceptance might they have been able to find given dominant expectations for Native men to be Indian heroes? Was it heroic to leave one's wife and children at home, perhaps never to return? Moreover, how did their lives apart from their wives and children make them seem more or less fit as potential American (white) men? By the turn of the twentieth century, a white, middle-class masculinity affirmed men in terms of physical and mental fitness.[67] Although the Standing Bear brothers could easily claim the former as Indian men – and thereby natural warriors – the ease with which they traveled without much regard for their families made them look like philanderers. Still, the fluidity of their gender identities fit well enough into the cultural context of traveling circuses and vaudeville acts that were popular entertainment showcases during this period. These entertainment acts welcomed an especially diverse array of people, in regards to gender, race, and sexuality, as performers.[68] Also popular during this era were "medicine shows" that circulated throughout the United States. These shows offered Native people, both men and women, unique opportunities to travel and make money at the same time.[69]

The Kickapoo Indian Medicine Company, one of the largest and most successful medicine show operators in America from 1880 until the 1930s, hired many Indian spokespeople to attract audiences and sell its products. Headquartered in New Haven, Connecticut, the Company published a variety of booklets, posters, and other forms of advertisements to promote its products independently of the medicine show. The Kickapoo Company promoted the health benefits of its "natural tonics" as necessarily linked to the heritage and biological strength of Indian people. Many of its advertisements depicted Indian warriors "saving" young white women. This refashioned captivity tale promised to cure the sicknesses of white society by tapping into the inherent health of Indianness.[70] This advertising strategy was nothing new.

Since the early nineteenth century, various tonics, even dandruff remedies, were promoted by advertisements that featured Native imagery. The main difference for Kickapoo centered on gender. Earlier ads figured the Indian woman as a healer who had a reputation for healing white men.[71] Like

Wild West shows, the various medicine shows of the late nineteenth century capitalized on hiring "real Indians" to promote their products. Under the management of Healy and Bigelow, the Kickapoo Company was so named because it employed Indians, supposedly Kickapoos, to tour the country demonstrating Indian life and selling the medicines. By the late 1880s, as many as 300 Indians were living in the "principal wigwam" – the winter quarters in New Haven, Connecticut. It is easy to imagine that the advertisements medicine shows used circulated among white reading publics who were encountering a large number of ads for an Indian curio market and might be attending popular entertainments featuring Wild West experiences. It is equally plausible that some of the Native actors hired to work in Coney Island could have taken the train up to New Haven to act in the "principal wigwam" designed by the Kickapoo Company; perhaps Henry Standing Bear was among them.

The Wild West: Part and Parcel of American Culture

From 1882 to 1916, "Buffalo Bill" Cody produced a series of spectacular entertainments based on America's history of white-Indian violence. From the beginning, it was called "The Wild West" (or Buffalo Bill's "Wild West"), a name that both eschewed the use of "show" and confirmed it was neither mere display nor entertainment but ought to be identified with a specific time, place, and history. Notwithstanding protests by Indian activists and white progressives and members of the OIA, much of the show's authenticity was supported through letters from leading military officers published in the program handed out to audiences. These performances reinforced a nostalgic imagining of Indianness that reflected a romantic vision of Plains Indians. Cody's entertainments aimed to blur the line between history and fantasy and created oversimplified stories about white conquest and the Western frontier. Despite attending to authenticity and repeatedly advertising its realist approach, the Wild West, as Cody designed it, was history conflated with mythology.[72]

The repetition of these Wild West performances throughout the United States and in Europe further entrenched a blurred understanding of America's past for many audiences. It seems likely that there were savvy white viewers and Indian people among the audiences who understood that these performances were meant to celebrate America more than actually represent facts about its history. It is less clear whether these same viewers were able to successfully disentangle the underlying logic of Cody's narrative regarding the West, namely that violence and savage warfare were necessary components of American progress that coincided with the inevitable decline and destruction of Indian people.

Throughout these performances, Indians remained central to how Cody, as well as his white audiences, remembered, imagined, and expected Indian

people to be. Nor was Cody the only participant in this game. Throughout the
period, Native intellectuals like Charles Eastman sponsored Indian-themed
pageants that provided a different way for white audiences to access Native
culture. One pageant from Minneapolis (the "Paris of Indian life," according
to Eastman) featured "sun dances, barbecues, and frolicking in costume to
the music of tomtoms" by white participants.[73] Eastman praised the event
for the authenticity of its costumes and noted he would be "delighted to
help" plan similar sorts of engagements in the future.[74] These types of performances supported white expectations used to define Native identity and
culture, which were reinforced by white participation in presentations of
Indian song and dance. Entertainment of this type refused to emphasize the
violence characterizing Cody's performances, which might be why Eastman
participated in supporting these celebrations while criticizing the work of
show Indians. Perhaps Eastman's proximity to Native and non-Native participants gave him a sense of control regarding the ultimate message attend-
ees of the pageants might receive. Much of the excitement advertised by
Cody's version of the West centered on the reenactment of colonial violence whereby white settlers found themselves surrounded by hostile Indian
forces. This narrative of *the surround*, theorized by Philip Deloria, became
integral to American ideas regarding Indians and violence as well as the
cultural productions that drew on these ideas.[75]

The surround was a necessary part of American history that showcased
colonization. For Cody, the tension between whites and Indians was a
useful allegory for American imperialism and the heroism of the cowboy.
American manhood itself was constructed through these dramatic performances as white men represented the promise of a new, young, and virile
nation that defined itself against the primitive savagery of its Indian past.
These imaginings required Native men to represent a warrior aesthetic,
which typified a different sort of highly sexualized and raced masculinity.
Native men, no matter how valiant their efforts to fight white attackers,
were always already doomed to fail. This conquest narrative further undermined their strength as men, and by extension suggested Native manhood
was inherently inferior because it would always be threatened and overrun
by the power of American (white) manhood. However fraught this making
of modern America may have been for the Indian performers who joined
Cody's traveling troupes, their employment afforded many of them more
material benefits than they would have had if they stayed home. This fact
challenged the aims of assimilationists and some white progressives who
believed Native men must serve as the heads of families and live on individual allotments to ensure the proper acculturation of Indian people. As
the heads of their heterosexist households, as farmers or businessmen,
Native men could ensure the proper incorporation of Native families into
American society. That Luther Standing Bear, and for a time his brother,
Henry, eschewed this option in favor of more mobile and non-normative

employment suggests that life as a Native performer resisted as much as it also complied with colonial ideologies.[76]

Standing Bear had struggled to find gainful employment after Carlisle, first as a teacher and then a clerk at a dry goods store, so the opportunity to travel widely and make money was hard to pass up. The material benefits of show Indian work prompted him to leave Pine Ridge. As he recalled in his autobiography, "my wife was greatly pleased when I told her the news that we were going to have the chance to go abroad."[77] She would join him initially for their travels with Cody, but not when he went to California. Traveling with the family, at least at first, afforded the Standing Bears new opportunities for global travel.

The Standing Bear family's first journey with Cody was not entirely positive given prejudices within the company and without. Many of these experiences were marked by changes in policy that came with allotment in 1887 and the end of violent resistance by Indian nations following the massacre at Wounded Knee in 1890.[78] With the end of military conquest and the Dawes Act, most Americans understood that the frontier, once populated with Indians, was now closed. No more would white settlers *happen* to find themselves, as the minority, surrounded by a majority of Indian people. Instead, they came to see themselves as the guardians of American land. In terms of historical reenactments dramatized and popularized by Cody, the connection between Indianness and violence did not disappear with the end of the surround. Rather, Indian violence became refigured around a new, yet eerily familiar, narrative for audiences, which was the *outbreak*. In this sense, Indians were still defined as violent and locked into a struggle that once again doomed them to submit to the power of the white military figure, cowboy or pioneer, who in turn had to fight (sometimes even resist) the Indian outbreak.

The outbreak suggested Indians had been conquered and to some extent "tamed" and contained. But of course, containment by the OIA did not necessarily mean an end to resistance. Many of these narratives of Indian violence became part of the repertoire of touring companies and the Western genre of film. In both spaces, Indians had to perform. Now defeated, they had to reenact a moment when they historically did hold the power to surround and destroy white settlers and colonists. Now safely contained, they performed the possibility that they would escape and become violent (outbreak!).

So any one performance mixed these things together: pretending to be violent and powerful with the possibility that, although no longer powerful, Indian people could still become violent. Underneath this was an ideology of pacification, which meant that there was no way that Indians would actually become violent. Indian performers like Standing Bear were navigating the terrain of performativity marked by powerlessness in terms of changes in their own strategies of resistance and the cultural imagination of what they

could or would do. Standing Bear had been given a glimpse into these sorts
of narratives beginning with his containment in Wanamaker's glass box to
when he willfully broke out of Rosebud, but was ironically contained again
in Pine Ridge before he could leave to pursue a career in show business.

Although Cody's Wild West offered a historical program bent on playing
with racial categories requiring Indian actors like Standing Bear, imbedded
within many of these narratives was a strong identification with American
imperialism. This was perhaps best represented through the military elements within the show. Posters advertising "Buffalo Bill" Cody and his
"Rough Riders" served a double purpose as they displayed new models
of artillery that, as Richard Slotkin argues, eclipsed the more traditional
Western elements associated with the cowboy. The cowboy was transformed
into a soldier and the place of the Wild West became an even more mobile
concept that could represent new frontiers beyond the physical borders of
the United States in Pacific and Caribbean waters.

In 1899, before Standing Bear joined the troupe, Cody replaced "Custer's
Last Fight" with the "Battle of San Juan Hill" to celebrate the heroism of
Theodore Roosevelt and "The Rough Riders" as worthy of historical replay.
As Slotkin argues, this type of performance glorified the imperialization of
the American republic and through associations with Wild West imagery
could also democratize the imperial project. Then in 1901, San Juan's backdrop was traded in for the Battle of Tientsin to reenact the capture of that
city by the Allied army that had suppressed China's Boxer Rebellion to rescue "captives" from the Peking Legation Quarter. Indian actors were hired
to play the role of the Boxers as the soldiers, and cowboys in the rest of the
troupe now stood in for white civilization. This type of Yellowface performance, like minstrel shows, was not uncommon at the turn of the century.[79]
"Tientsin" remained a popular performance into 1902 before Cody's troupe
reprised their roles in "San Juan Hill" from 1903 to 1904. Because Standing
Bear was hired to work for Cody in 1902, it seems plausible that he may
have played the role of either a Boxer or a Spanish military officer, although
he does not confirm this in his autobiography. How might he have understood these roles in combination with or set against his work as a translator
and the times he "acted" the part of himself? As Cody's enterprise took on
international perspectives, he also hired people from Puerto Rico as well as
Hawai'i and the Philippine Islands. These new hires were incorporated into
performances and presented as curiosities. Not unlike the Native American
performers before them, they were useful as cultural brown "Others" and
"as memorials of an imaginative world distant in time and space."[80] For
Standing Bear, Cody's enterprise represented important life lessons about
business, commercialization, and performativity. Issues of class and race
intersected with the performative value of Native people, who were celebrated as the main attraction for shows where they *played* Indian and at
other times just *played* themselves.

1902: New York and London – *No Old Pancakes for the Indians*

Standing Bear's work with Cody would bring him and his family first to New York and later London for special performances to entertain British royal society.[81] While in Manhattan, they stayed in a hotel with another performer, named Black Horn. After dinner their first night, there was a meeting of all the Indian performers, and a man named Rock called on Standing Bear to say a few words. Standing Bear remembers this moment in terms of his dedication to helping "his people." He addressed the crowd, recalled here in *My People the Sioux*, as if they were a part of an extended Indian family.

My relations, you all know that I am to take care of you while going across the big water to another country, and all the time we are to stay there. I have heard that when any one joins this show, about the first thing he thinks of is getting drunk. I understand that the regulations of the Buffalo Bill show require that no Indian shall be given any liquor. You all know that I do not drink, and I am going to keep you all from it.[82]

Standing Bear praises Cody's commitment to temperance and confirms his status as a teetotaler, and therefore a protector of his fellow actors. This chapter of his autobiography details his trip to England while working for "Buffalo Bill," and reads as part celebration of Cody and part nostalgic remembrance of circumstances surrounding the beginning of his acting career.[83]

How Standing Bear and his fellow Indians perceive *and* are perceived operate as themes throughout his chapter about Cody's Wild West. He positions himself as "The Chief Interpreter of the Sioux Nation," who understands the complex relation between class and race as markers of power for Native performers. Because he speaks for other performers, his text highlights his rank among them, a reflection of *status*. Standing Bear's position of power is twofold in the text. As the narrator, he can remember and write about the past however he sees fit. As the "Chief Interpreter," he appears as a character in his own story who possesses a power akin to the translators he witnessed working with Sitting Bull in Philadelphia. Standing Bear connects a story about the ways Indian performers misread the status of a butler hired to make their beds with another about the power relations within the Wild West circuit, which involved, of all things, pancakes.

One morning everyone in the show was served pancakes for breakfast, with the exception of the Indian actors. Later that day, they were served the cold leftovers for dinner. Standing Bear "was very angry" about this incident. So much so that he "went over where Buffalo Bill and the head officials of the show were eating dinner" to let him know that serving old, cold pancakes to the Indians was not right. Standing Bear's sense of his own importance comes to the fore in this anecdote. He uses it to showcase an opportunity for activism when he describes how Cody scolded the cook regarding such ill treatment of his Indians. Cody's remarks highlight the performative value of his Indian troupe when he says, "they are the principal feature of this show, and they are the one people I will not allow to be misused or neglected. Hereafter see to it that they get just exactly what they want at meal-time."[84] In this moment the Native actors appear to have more important cultural capital than any other members of Cody's enterprise. Standing Bear's account does not include how far this sentiment went with regards to issues like actual pay, benefits, and the type of work Cody provided for Indian people.

The pancake story reflects how the cook assumed Indians were inferior; he thought they, like animals, would eat cold leftovers. Standing Bear's demand recognizes this prejudiced view. Cody concurs because Native performers were the heart of his business. By quoting Cody's reaction, Standing Bear suggests the Wild West might provide a complicated cultural space where Native people could be treated poorly by some while venerated by others, viewed as lesser socially even if they were valued for their economic potential.

Standing Bear's depiction of his work as a "show Indian" casts himself as a man of good character, largely through his refusal to drink alcohol and smoke tobacco. He is framed not only as an interpreter of language but as an arbitrator of morality and culture working on behalf of other Indian performers who were part of the show. This is, in part, an argument for the acceptability of their labor. He could speak for his fellow Indians as their translator, and he could keep in constant contact with Cody regarding their movements and any inappropriate activities related to alcohol and overspending of wages. He mediated their cultural interactions, whether in New York or London.

Standing Bear reflects on an interaction that took place in England with a butler that illustrates his cosmopolitan sensibility regarding dress codes and social status. This moment in and of itself is also about performance. He notes how the Native actors for Cody were amazed to find "a very finely dressed man, wearing a high silk hat, Prince Albert coat, kid gloves, silk handkerchief in his pocket, and carry cane" who was later seen "making up our beds." Their amazement stems from the fact that racial prejudice marked many of their experiences. The Native performers are amazed because the man wearing the "silk hat, Prince Albert coat, kid gloves" is not an aristocrat, or even a performer, but is there to serve them. Their perception, ventriloquized by Standing Bear's narrative, reflects a critical shift in their epistemological standpoint; that is, they were afforded mobility (and some kind of status) through their work as performers and yet their performances were severely limited to particular types of Indianness. Whenever they were not performing, some people saw them as lesser, as the kinds of people who would eat cold pancakes.

Through Standing Bear's account of the pancakes and the London trip one can see two more things: first, how he remembers his life as a Wild West performer; and, second, what he gleans from these experiences, which is the necessity of leading and advocating for other Indians, who are defined as a collective. In some sense, Standing Bear is similar to Sitting Bull – who built a small network through the performative aspects of his touring life. And yet Standing Bear is perhaps more exemplary as a primary builder of the next generation's network, significant wings of which would grow out of Carlisle, the Wild West circuit, and the politics of the SAI and other pan-tribal reform organizations. Standing Bear's early experiences at Carlisle, Wanamaker, and Pine Ridge play out in these two stories regarding his work for Cody's touring company. These accounts are tinged with anxieties about class and racial politics, while another brings these dynamics to the forefront by considering the nature of performance itself and just how far Cody would go to use actual Native bodies to promote his shows.

While on the road in London, Standing Bear and his wife, Nellie DeCory, became proud parents for the third time when their daughter, Alexandra Birmingham Cody, was born. Whether Cody congratulated the couple, offered them a gift, or passed out cigars Standing Bear does not say. But he does discuss how Cody saw the newborn infant as performance capital for his show; Cody quickly proposed to Standing Bear that Alexandra should be on exhibit as part of a sideshow. This idea was hardly novel. From the earliest exhibitions, through the 1893 Columbian Exhibition and the Wild West show era, children and infants had offered showmen a powerful marketing hook. Audiences gained an opportunity (not always taken) to humanize Indian people through the harmlessness and "uncultured" nature of children who had not yet been socialized into Native or white worlds. Children and infants offered possibilities for viewers to imagine possibilities for individual development rather than social evolutionary destiny – and these "performances" contributed to the cultural underpinnings of policies (including a Carlisle education) that focused on the individual, rather than the community. Of course, babies did not perform. They simply were. But the context in which parents and young children existed did not allow even everyday lives to be other than performative. As performances, they were always already signifying racial possibilities and destinies, gender hierarchies (it is worth remembering that Cody approached Luther – not Luther' wife – about exhibiting the baby), and even class dynamics.

Within that context, the Standing Bear family members made their own decisions. You might imagine Standing Bear's outrage at the thought of their newborn being put on display. Such might have been the case. But Standing

Bear writes about this event to suggest a more nuanced decision-making process and experience.

> My wife sat on a raised platform, with the little one in the cradle before her. The people filed past, many of them dropping money in a box for her. Nearly every one had some sort of little gift for her also. It was a great drawing card for the show; the work was very light for my wife, and as for the baby, before she was twenty-four hours old she was making more money than my wife and I together.[85]

His emphasis on the light workload for his wife and the earning potential of their baby suggests Standing Bear understood this performance as nothing more than a strategy of appeasement coupled with improved earning potential. But despite the increased financial security that was a boon to the Standing Bear family, it came at a cost. As large crowds of Londoners made their way to see the Wild West, they stopped to admire an Indian mother and child on their way to the show. These glimpses of a *real* Indian baby on display helped further a desire to see and market Indianness and confirmed the necessity of hiring Indian people to *play Indian* for such occasions.[86]

This sideshow experience was not wholly dissimilar from Cody's offer to patrons to come "back stage" after performances, so that they might meet and mingle with *real* Indians. In these instances, Native actors could decide the degrees to which they were still performing according to certain racialized scripts. For Standing Bear, the sideshow offered an occasion to both *play Indian* and play *with* Indianness, in that it muddled the usually clear division between the viewed and the viewer, because it was neither clothed in the accoutrements of myth nor the spectacle of reenactment, but rather the messy reality of poverty. According to *My People the Sioux*, the personal relationship between Cody and Standing Bear was mutually beneficial if also marked by certain racialized expectations regarding Native performativity. Standing Bear's recounting of the display of his wife and their newborn points to the pervasiveness and intimacy of Cody's desire to market historical "reenactments" using his Indian actors. Standing Bear's narrative reflects on the dire financial circumstances that undergirded their decision to use the baby, and at the same time he is explicit about Cody's request that they do so. Readers from 1928 and today might ask: Why would Standing Bear have consented to this type of public display? Perhaps, at first, he interpreted Cody's request as outside the bounds of proper performance given that there was neither a reference to history nor any educational merit to a sideshow. But, upon second thought, he acquiesced given the material gain.

For in addition to displaying their newborn, the Standing Bears' oldest son, Luther, was hired to play Indian as part of Cody's enterprise. Standing Bear describes preparing his son, who had to be "rigged up for the part he took in the show," in great detail. He also comments explicitly on his son's reaction to taking part in such a performance.

He had a full costume of buckskin, very much like the one I wore, and every day his face must be painted and his hair combed and braided for the two performances. The Indian boys seemed to think it was a pleasure to get the little chap ready for exhibition. After he was "all fixed up," he would stand outside the tipi, and the English-speaking people would crowd around to shake his hand and give him money. This he would put in a little pocket in his buckskin jacket, and when it was full he would refuse to accept any more, although the crowd would try to force it on him. Then he would leave, in apparent disgust, and come inside the tipi. He kept us all laughing.[87]

Given the undertones of these sorts of exhibitions and sideshows as cultural phenomena during this period, when a Native mother and child played "themselves," or a young Indian boy was paid for dressing in buckskin, they might be viewed as exotic at best, or as an exhibit of human oddities at worst by the crowds stopping to see them on display. Standing Bear's text offers three slightly different meanings pertaining to his son's "apparent disgust" following his performances. In fact, at first, one might wonder whether it was real disgust. Was it Luther Standing Bear's uncertainty about his perception of disgust? Or was it a performance of "disgust" for the white audience? That such a scene kept Standing Bear and the other performers "laughing" further signals to the reader that this ought to be read as a critique of the exhibition rather than a light-hearted take on exploitation. In some sense, their laughter is of a piece with Standing Bear's knowing smile in Philadelphia after he witnessed the mistranslation of Sitting Bull's remarks before a mostly white audience.[88]

The performance work of the Standing Bear family is but one example of how Indian people navigated the arenas of performance open to them. Certainly, there were other performer families like the Standing Bears who, however contested the work of "show Indians" may have been throughout this period, were able to make a decent living through these shows, and who may have even viewed their experiences in a favorable light. However, before Standing Bear could parlay work with Cody into future jobs in show business, he was involved in a devastating train accident that would put his career on hold. The accident exposed him to different sorts of racism and corruption, which suggested the critical necessity of pan-tribal efforts toward political reform.

1904–1911: "Indians Die in Wreck, Survivors Chant Death Song for Three Victims"

On the morning of April 7, 1904, the Omaha Express stopped near Melrose Park, a suburb of Chicago. An increasingly dense screen of fog covered the tracks that morning, stretching all the way from the banks of Lake Michigan to the west of Chicago's city limits. The fog made visibility exceedingly poor for the train operators. The weather, coupled with the fact that the Omaha was running twenty minutes behind schedule, contributed to a devastating collision between the Northwestern Fast Mail train and the Omaha Express. The "Express" had traveled all the way from San Francisco heading east to New York City. This same train had also picked up sixty-three Sioux performers from Rushville, Nebraska for their transatlantic trip to England as part of "Buffalo Bill's" Wild West. Luther Standing Bear was among the twenty-nine Indian actors injured during the train wreck, as he had just begun his second season with Cody's company.[89] Three members of the troupe, Kills A Head [*sic*], Philip Iron Tail Jr., and Thomas Comes Last, were crushed upon impact and died at the scene.[90] The serious injuries Standing Bear and the other performers suffered took a long time to heal. Yet it was not the physical suffering the group endured as much as a prolonged legal battle that created a lasting memory of the incident for Standing Bear.

Following the train wreck, Carlos Montezuma came to the aid of the Lakota actors as both their doctor and their advocate. Montezuma worked with Standing Bear and the rest of the troupe to sue the Chicago and Northwestern Railroad Company for compensation accounting for their injuries and the work they would miss. As a physician, Montezuma wrote detailed reports regarding the extent of individual injuries. He made a strong case that the injured parties ought to receive from $1,250 to $12,000 each, depending on the extent of their suffering. In contrast, the Railroad underestimated the passengers' injuries and offered a meager settlement of $100 to $2,500 per person. Ultimately, the court accepted the Railroad Company's terms.[91]

At this time, railroad corporate executives had reached the pinnacle of their economic power, so perhaps it should not be surprising that, although contested, they triumphed. Ironically, the Indians' employment with Cody hindered their claims for compensation. Pine Ridge agent John R. Brennan, who was working on behalf of the injured Indians, but who seemed more in support of the Railroad, defined the work of these Native performers as "un-American." The connection between the Indian actors and the world of show business framed them in terms of spectacle and excess. Such claims sought to undermine their social status by arguing that they should not be entitled to a higher settlement on account of their lost wages. Standing Bear and the others who sought damages were caught in a double bind. Their work for Cody helped to celebrate a narrative of American exceptionalism that depended on *real* Indian performers to reenact frontier life as it was in the Wild West but because they were Indians working for Cody rather than employed in more respected trades (like Montezuma, the doctor), they were less "fit" for citizenship, and somehow less entitled to receive money for any missed work.

Still, fitness for citizenship could be used to argue for or against the case these Native performers made against the Railroad. This case represents a paradox because the claimants were being kept out of the very society their performances aimed to celebrate because the type of work required for such celebration defined them as less manly, less white, and less advanced for inclusion into the body politic of the United States. On May 2, 1904, a copy of the settlement to be paid to those injured in the wreck and the claims related to the three men who had died was sent to W. A. Jones, the commissioner of Indian affairs. This agreement, between the Indians' representative, J. R. Brennan, the railroad companies, and the U.S. government, reflects not only a paltry sum regarding damages, but the even more damaging rhetoric characteristic of the racist and patronizing views of the parties involved in deciding how to handle the costs associated with the wreck.

It was hard to determine what the values of the lives of the three dead ones were. But taking everything into consideration, considering also that the Indians themselves are satisfied with these amounts, we concluded to recommend them. Two of the dead Indians had never done any work. One of them, Iron Tail, had done some work. The measure of damages in this State, as I suppose in all States, is based upon the ability and willingness of the deceased person to work.[92]

Why was it "hard to determine" the "values of the lives" of the three Native men who had perished? Framed within the logics of industrial capital and white supremacy, their Indianness disabled these men, except Iron Tail, who "had done some work," to be viewed as valuable contributors to American society, in essence as workers. The value of their lives lay in whether they were productive contributors to modern American capitalism, which certainly conformed to dominant ideologies of the time regarding racial uplift. In other words, these Native men, because they were Indians, could never have done much "work" to contribute to American society and thus, in death, their lives were *less* valuable than other, presumably white, citizens. And yet so important was the work of Native performers to Cody's enterprise that he was quick to hire replacements following the train crash so the season could continue without a hitch.[93] Montezuma's letter on May 6 protested the settlement with the Railroad, and despite his detailed account of the injuries suffered by the Native men involved, his protest fell on deaf ears and a new trial never took place.

For Standing Bear and Montezuma, this was an opportunity to consider extrajudicial means through which they might challenge social expectations that limited the power and position of Indian people. Perhaps the two men swapped notes on organizing while Standing Bear was in Chicago. Soon after this, Montezuma would work closely with Henry Standing Bear and the SAI. Perhaps Montezuma gave Luther a copy of *Wassaja* and added him to his subscription list. Both men were interested in how Native people could obtain the rights of full citizens in the United States. At the time, both agreed that the reservation was not the best site through which Native people could gain these rights or more power; both would later change their minds to see the benefits of Native spaces. Although no additional records from the train accident exist to show how this moment marked a turning point in the lives of the doctor and the actor, what remains clear is that they worked together to fight for the Indians injured in the crash. As Standing Bear would later assert in *My People the Sioux*, he had learned that reform work beyond the reservation was necessary, and it required a pan-tribal approach to reshaping politics and culture.

With all my title of chieftain, and with all of my education and travels, I discovered that as long as I was on the reservation I was only a helpful Indian, and was not considered any better than any of the uneducated Indians – that is, according to the views of the white agent in charge of the reservation.... If I tried to better the condition of my people, while on the reservation, I found it was an utter impossibility.[94]

Throughout the pages of *Wassaja*, Montezuma's writing echoes this rhetoric and calls for the abolition of the Indian Bureau and the reservation system. Despite agreement over the dangers associated with the OIA, the two men did not necessarily agree with regards to Indian performance.

As an outspoken member of the SAI, Montezuma often criticized Native actors in Wild West shows for furthering negative stereotypes. Montezuma's public and private writings reveal that he was less interested in performing according to primitivist expectations for Indians. He opted not for the war bonnet but rather the tuxedo when invited to give public talks or appear at important functions in and around Chicago.[95] Still, the experience of treating and advocating for actual Indian performers, employed by Cody no less, may have forced Montezuma to reconsider his views concerning the costs and benefits of Native performance. Perhaps Standing Bear told Montezuma about the travel opportunities and economic gains he and his family received by working in show business.

After he recovered from the crash, in 1907, Standing Bear left Pine Ridge again in an attempt to reignite his career in show business. At this time, his brother, Henry, was going to New York City with a party of Indians to appear in an act at the enormous Hippodrome Theater. From November 1906 to August 1907, audiences came in droves to enjoy "Pioneer Days: A Spectacle Drama of Western Life."[96] This show was massive, employing upward of 100 Lakota adorned in feathers, face paint, and war bonnets. They battled soldiers, attacked stagecoaches, and reenacted the Ghost Dance against a magnificent orange moon. Although on a grander scale, such pageantry was similar to Cody's Wild West and no doubt would have been familiar to Luther and his brother.

Working in this show, both brothers met other Native entertainers like the married couple Red Wing (born Lillian St. Cyr) and James Young Deer. Like the Standing Bear brothers, Red Wing, who was Ho-Chunk, had attended the Carlisle School, graduating in 1902. She married James Young Deer, whose ancestry is less clear given that some records suggest he was mixed race, perhaps white, African American, and Nanticoke from Delaware.[97]

Regardless of his background, for the purposes of the show and his future career in film, Young Deer positioned himself as Ho-Chunk like his wife. Given the racial prejudice against African Americans as this time it is not surprising that Young Deer claimed a fully Native identity to escape the pervasive oppression of Jim Crow. The two were married on April 9, 1906, just shortly before their performance at the Hippodrome. Like Luther Standing Bear, Young Deer's work in silent film was shaped and made possible by earlier types of entertainments that employed Indians, such as Barnum and Bailey's circus and the Miller Brothers' 101 Ranch Wild West show. In 1909, the New York Picture Company established Bison Motion Pictures, in the Los Angeles neighborhood of Edendale, then the center of West Coast film production. There they began producing Westerns that Young Deer would go on to direct. The first Native American film in 1909 was *The Falling Arrow*, co-starring Red Wing.[98] Thus, a network of Indian performers emerged to reach across the United States, from New York to Los Angeles, and across tribes and families.

Luther had a six-month contract in New York, and during this time he would meet Red Wing and Young Deer at the Hippodrome. He could also make contacts with other Native actors – who would also become central to the film industry on the West Coast.[99] Economic reasons also helped Luther Standing Bear decide to stay in the City.

I concluded to stay and see if I could make my living among the white people. I appeared in theaters and side-shows. I lectured, and did any sort of work I could find. While lecturing I met many people who were really interested in learning the truth in regard to the Indians. I determined that, if I could only get the right sort of people interested, I might be able to do more for my own race off the reservation than to remain there under the iron rule of the white agent.[100]

While in New York, Standing Bear began to experience the political power of performance in much the same way that Eastman and Bonnin did in their public lectures. As an actor, he participated in a network created and driven by Indian performers. After New York, Standing Bear moved to Bliss, Oklahoma to join the Miller Brothers' 101 Ranch show. This spectacular entertainment was an outgrowth of the Miller brothers' 110,000-acre cattle ranch. Joe, Zack, and George L. Miller were busy working as cowboys before their neighbor, performer "Pawnee Bill" (Major Gordon W. Lillie), showed them how to make a better living by retelling the conquest of the West, which had made their ranch possible in the first place.[101]

In 1905, the Millers began producing a local show. These shows functioned like mobile company towns, offering a limited form of mobility to the Native actors they employed. By 1907, the Millers were on the road performing outside of Oklahoma at places like the Jamestown Exposition in Virginia and Brighton Beach in New York – where they cast Native actors like Henry Standing Bear to play Indian. These heritage sites were already popular tourist destinations, so it seems likely that shows featuring Native performers sought to take advantage of already captive audiences. During these performances, the captivity tale was inverted again, but this time, the experience of white audience members was structured by a market for their continued desire to see the primitive, wild, yet also romantic Indian as an ethnic other. Such performers could capture white spectators again and again.[102]

Given that the 101 Ranch show was a latecomer to the Wild West-themed enterprise it is not surprising that they suffered financially with the invention of motion pictures. Despite this setback, they succeeded in profiting from the popularity of the Indian curio market.[103] Not unlike the Kickapoo Indian Medicine Company, the Miller Brothers marketed all kinds of Indian rugs, beaded belts, and silver jewelry manufactured in their novelty factory by Indian employees. Along with Indian-themed articles, a large assortment of souvenir leather goods such as cowboy belts, boys' chaps, and vests were made and sold to tourists.[104]

The Miller Brothers lost Standing Bear in 1912 when he applied to work with filmmaker Thomas H. Ince. Using train fare provided by Ince, Standing Bear joined the rest of the Sioux actors' crew in Inceville – located in the Palisades Highlands stretching seven and a half miles (12.1 km) up Santa Ynez Canyon, between Santa Monica and Malibu, California. This company town was built to house Native and other actors working on Ince's films. Throughout this period, the more vocal Indian actors attempted to expand their influence on the films under production at Inceville. Led by Standing Bear, they pointed out to Ince that his films would be even more authentic if he used more Indians in the major roles. Frustrated by the lack of three-dimensional characters for Indian actors, Standing Bear offered ideas for scripts and volunteered to serve as a language coach for the other Sioux actors. Perhaps his experiences as a translator for Cody empowered him to make suggestions to Ince. Unfortunately for him, Ince declined to accept any of his help.[105]

Perhaps the fact that Luther Standing Bear continued to work in show business and did not return to Pine Ridge like his brother, Henry, did after some years working in New York explains why he never became involved with the SAI like Eastman, Montezuma, and Bonnin. Despite direct involvement, Standing Bear's views regarding the Citizenship Bill of 1923, for example, resonated with many of the concerns the SAI's leaders shared in terms of whether "citizenship" would actually amount to material changes in the lives of Indian people. In his second autobiography, *Land of the Spotted Eagle*, Standing Bear writes about this issue explicitly, stating, "The signing of the bill changed not in the slightest measure the condition of the Indian."[106] According to Standing Bear, the failure of this bill was true because "not one agent was removed from office, Indian boys and girls are still segregated in school life and the reservation and reservation rule still exist."[107] Here his rhetoric echoes that of Montezuma and Eastman, both of whom sought fuller incorporation of Indian students into the American education system, and who greatly distrusted the corruption inherent in the reservation system. Standing Bear decided he would not return to live at Pine Ridge. Separated from the majority of his family, he found new ways to combine performance and politics so that he might dismantle the notion that "the Indian of the cheap magazine and the movie still remain as the best type of the First American."[108]

Film from the 1910s to the 1930s: "The White Man's Estimate of the Indian Is Established"

Long before Russell Means, Oglala/Lakota, AIM activist, became well known for playing the part of Chingachgook in *Last of the Mohicans* (1992) and narrating Walt Disney's *Pocahontas* (1995), Luther Standing Bear and other Native actors appeared in several silent and sound films, establishing the genre of the Western and the centrality of Native people within it. This first generation of Native people played an active role in establishing America's film industry. Standing Bear acted alongside Fay Wray, William Cody, Tom Mix, and William S. Hart, all of whom supported the careers of Indian actors. In addition, Standing Bear found he was not the only Carlisle student to gain employment in film. Jim Thorpe, Isaac Johnny John or "Chief John Big Tree," William Malcolm Hazlett, Richard Davis Thunderbird, and Lillian "Princess Red Wing" St. Cyr all worked in film after leaving Carlisle. Looking through the prism of Standing Bear's acting career reveals the connections between performativity and cultural politics for Indian actors. In this context, issues regarding ethnic authenticity, historical realism, and the history of Native American representations became critical factors for shaping the ever-evolving genre of the Western, as well as the stakes Indian actors faced in creating and maintaining the genre.[109] In 1921, there were an estimated 87,000 "cinematograph theaters" in the world, with 16,900 in the United States and just over 4,000 in Great Britain. During this period a number of Westerns, a genre defined by the setting of "the American West," the spirit of struggle, and the decline of the frontier, were produced to appear in these theaters.[110]

Many characteristics of Western films stemmed from popular Western literature of the late nineteenth century. Pulps were first printed in the 1880s and 1890s and continued well into the twentieth century, and with the violent backdrop of World War I and the rise of mafia-related violence and the image of the gangster in American cities, a fascination with the Old West continued to flourish within American culture. Part of the appeal of the Western was its simplicity. Westerns featured the pursuit of justice against forces of violence embodied by the savagery of Indians. "Outlaws" moved between the two extremes. Cowboys and Indians (like two armies or cops

versus robbers) were easily portrayed as oppositional figures – doubles that
enacted clear morality tales already familiar to audiences. Another part of
the genre's appeal was that one could easily predict the winners and the
losers. If the Western novel gave readers a certain myth of America and
its making, then the earliest Hollywood Westerns, from the 1910s to the
1930s, transplanted similar source material to make an even simpler and
more unbelievable narrative of nation making.[111]

Many of these early Westerns referred back to the Turnerian "frontier thesis" and relied on stock characters such as cowboys, gunslingers, and bounty
hunters, who were wanderers wearing Stetson hats, bandannas, spurs, and
buckskin. These figures were largely white, although there were a number
of Native characters, too, as well as Mexicans and Asians.[112] All groups
took part in performing westernness, and their portrayals were marked by
violence. They often used revolvers or rifles as everyday tools of survival.
Their way of life was characterized by mobility, not in a modern sense, but
in the horses they rode across vast stretches of uninhabited land. These trips
between small towns and cattle ranches could be interrupted by "hostile"
Indian forces, as the surround articulated in early books and shows. These
moments involved fighting sequences between the U.S. Calvary and Indian
warriors or a band of cowboys and a renegade tribe. Such representations
did not necessarily challenge the notion of westward expansion or the concept of "open" land so much as reify the expectation of Indian men who
were *always* out for blood, although it was *their* ultimate destruction that
was almost always the outcome of these violent encounters.

Western films were enormously popular in the silent era, and Standing
Bear built a career that straddled the transition from silent film to "talkies."
With the advent of sound in 1927–8, however, many of the major Hollywood
studios abandoned Westerns, leaving the genre to smaller studios and producers who churned out countless low-budget features and serials into the
1930s. By the latter part of the decade, the Western film occupied a similar
space to the early Western novels because both had declined in popularity.
However, the Western film was brought back to life in 1939 by the release
of John Ford's *Stagecoach*, one of the biggest hits of the year, and the vehi-
cle that propelled John Wayne into a major screen star. The year 1939 was
also when Standing Bear acted in his final film, *Union Pacific*. A review of
DeMille's masterpiece celebrated the director's achievements in producing a
new blockbuster: "For Mr. DeMille spares nothing, horses or actors, when
he turns his hand to Western history.... He stages a romantic dialogue on a
hand-car hemmed in by grunting bison, a tender farewell in a caboose surrounded by whooping redskins.... When he has a chance for real action, of
course, the sky's the limit – Indian raids, shooting scrapes, brawls, fist-fights,
train robberies, fires, chases and trestle-breaks."[113] Despite their ubiquity,
the reviewer only briefly mentions the Native cast members involved with
DeMille's film. Although Indian people were essential in adding to DeMille's

claims to realism and historical accuracy, Standing Bear and other extras spoke no lines. The scenes they shared with white characters reinforced the notion that Indians stood in the way of the transcontinental railroad and the progress of civilization. "Whooping redskins" and Indian raids did little to transform audiences' perceptions of Native people as violent, savage, and out of pace with modernity. Perhaps more telling than the film's over-the-top portrayal of "Western history" is the fanfare surrounding its premiere in 1939.

Screened in the middle of a four-day celebration known as "Golden Spike Days" in Omaha, Nebraska, DeMille's film debuted at the site of the Union Pacific headquarters. Along with parades of Omaha's residents dressed in period costumes for events, many Omaha men grew a beard and mustache to lend realism to their event costumes. These events, like the film, relied on pageantry and romance to perform and narrate an imagined Western past. Unfortunately, Luther Standing Bear did not live to see himself on-screen in *Union Pacific*. He also did not live to see that an "Indian Village" was part of the pageantry required to salute DeMille's revival of the Western genre. DeMille's "Indian Village" had been erected on the lawn in front of Omaha's courthouse, and no doubt employed some of the same Indian actors who had been cast in the film.

An important aspect of this history of representation with regards to Indianness in Westerns involved whether actual Indian actors were hired to portray the Indian characters on-screen. The question of bodily authenticity mattered to Cody. It continues to matter today.[114] And it mattered to Luther Standing Bear and his peers in the SAI. Debates among filmmakers and throughout Indian Country took place regarding whether it was possible to offer accurate portrayals of Indian life in these movies. As with Wild West shows, members of the OIA objected to certain features in these films, and Commissioner Robert G. Valentine (1909–12) promised he would help reform the industry. Certainly, for a pro-assimilation figure like Valentine, the romantic frontier narrative, where Indian people were cut off from the promise of white civilization (at best) or figured prominently as violent attackers (at worst), would be detrimental to his aim to incorporate Native people into American society. Through these performances the question emerged regarding the "authenticity" of the performance (desirable to mythmakers) and the degrading character of the performance in relation to cultural transformation and individual social mobility (desirable to policy makers). Two groups of white Americans collided on this issue. At least two groups of Indians did too: reformers, who echoed the white policy discourse in some ways, and performers who cared about authenticity in tandem with caring about their livelihoods. Despite protests by Indian activists, white policy makers, and white reformers, many Western filmmakers continued to seek out real Indian actors and natural locations to claim authenticity and historical realism.[115]

For Standing Bear in particular, the merger of Wild West show traditions (and their promise of realism) with the technological advance of film and its promise of broader distribution, became integral to the role he would play as an actor and an activist in Westerns and a growing film industry. By the end of 1911, the Bison Company had partnered with the Miller Brothers' 101 Ranch Real Wild West show to release elaborate historical recreations to film-going audiences. This merger was the idea of Thomas Harper Ince, who created a stock company employing a large number of technicians, artists, and cowboys in the Santa Monica Mountains overlooking the Pacific Ocean. He even signed an agreement with the federal government to secure a large group of Indians as employees. By 1913, Ince's Indian performers were earning seven to ten dollars a week, plus expenses. It is no wonder that Standing Bear found himself enticed to go to work in California at Inceville.[116]

Standing Bear made many films at Inceville between 1912 and 1915. He appeared in the second film adaptation of Helen Hunt Jackson's popular 1884 novel *Ramona* in 1916, directed by Donald Crisp, at the Clune Studio located at Bronson and Melrose Avenues. In 1921, he played the role of "Long Knife" in *White Oak*, directed by Lambert Hillyer and starring William S. Hart. Hart's success as an actor and director of silent films in Hollywood was useful for Standing Bear in that Hart could connect his Native friend to a different influential network that existed among white people involved in film production. *White Oak* was a story about revenge. In it, Hart played a gambler looking for a villain (played by Alexander Gaden) who had "ravished" his sister (played by Helen Holly). Gaden's villain also went after Hart's sweetheart, played by Vola Vale, before moving on to the daughter of his "partner in crime," an "Indian chief" played by Standing Bear. Written by Hart, the film suffered from a number of artistic and aesthetic shortcomings, not to mention a hyperbolic embrace of misogyny. Some of these reflected Hart's anachronistic view of the West (and those who populated it) while others arose because of elemental failings of the genre itself. By this time, Hart's career was in decline because his version of gritty melodramatic and low-budget Westerns were no longer popular among audiences. Still, Hart released three more films that year and one more in 1921, before retiring in 1925.[117]

Between 1916 and 1935, as his friendship with Hart strengthened, Standing Bear acted in at least thirteen films. He was busiest during 1935, appearing in four films: he played "Porcupine" in *Cyclone of the Saddle*, "Chief Black Hawk" in *Fighting Pioneers*, "Sioux Chief" in *The Circle of Death*, and "Chief Last Elk" in *The Miracle Rider*. All this activity fueled Standing Bear's interest in fairer wages for himself and the other Indian actors he met, especially given that they were continually competing with non-Indians for their roles. Apart from wages, Standing Bear was also interested in confronting representations of Indianness and the larger question of whether he could alter the representational politics of the films in which he acted. These two goals – meeting financial need and pressing his employers on their inadequacies – required balance, compromise, and calculation. In each of these films, Standing Bear had opportunities to make new connections, meet new people, and build new alliances to assist in the political reform work he did outside of film sets.[118] Working out of this context, Standing Bear met Yowlachie and Whitebird, among other Native actors, and encouraged them to attend the first meeting of the NLJAI. They were not alone in their efforts.

As a critical mass of Indian people came to live and work in Los Angeles, local, pan-tribal organizations emerged to support the development of an Indian community there.[119] For example, in the 1920s, the Wigwam Club formed to raise money for Indians in need. By 1935, the Los Angeles Indian Center was established as the primary meeting place and welfare agency for Los Angeles-area Indians, and it served their needs for the next five decades. Nipo Strongheart went on to become the president of the Center during the 1950s.[120] Other organizations also emerged based on the interests and participation of Native actors and activists, such as: the Native American League, the Pan American Indian National Organization Council, the National American Indian League, and the Association on American Indian Affairs (AAIA). Standing Bear and his "niece" May Jones traveled together to present public talks in connection with these organizations. Fortunately for Jones and Standing Bear, by the early 1920s, three new Indian reform organizations emerged in California in response to the Bursum Bill of 1922. This legislation aimed to settle land disputes between Pueblo Indians and non-Indians who settled after 1848 on Pueblo holdings in the Rio Grande Valley. White artists, anthropologists, and writers from Santa Fe, with strong ties to the local Pueblo community, organized the New Mexico Association on Indian Affairs (NMAIA) to oppose the bill. Similar opposition, although through a different network, emerged out of New York City, where residents formed the Eastern Association on Indian Affairs (EAIA) in 1922. The NMAIA and EAIA worked together, at first, to fight against the Bursum Bill. Gertrude Bonnin also assisted them in their efforts during this time. John Collier, a former social worker, also emerged in opposition to the bill and formed his own group, the American Indian Defense Association (AIDA), in May 1923. Headquartered in New York City, AIDA established branches on the West Coast to tie together networks of reformers, mostly white but some Indian, based along both coasts of the United States.

For advocates of Indian reform based out of Southern California, like Standing Bear, the work of NMAIA, EAIA, and AIDA represented a critical shift from prevailing assimilation goals of the earlier progressive groups. Although citizenship remained a goal, there was much more tolerance and celebration of Native cultures by members of these newer reform groups. Perhaps more important, these organizations were willing to attack the

OIA directly. As commissioner of Indian affairs from 1933 to 1945, Collier would try to overhaul the Office. Through an alliance between the National Association on Indian Affairs, formerly the EAIA, and AIDA (Collier's organization), the American Association on Indian Affairs was formed in 1937.[121]

Renamed the Association on American Indian Affairs in 1946, the AAIA promoted the rights of more than 300 Native American tribes throughout the United States and stood on the forefront of battles for Native American rights, protecting land and water resources and the right of self-determination as well as the right to worship freely and to secure equal educational opportunity for Native children. The Association was similar to the National League for Justice created by Standing Bear in that it embraced eight areas of concern to Native Americans: education, economic development, health and sanitation, land tenure, irrigation, preservation of culture and religion, tribal sovereignty, and youth. Also like the League, the AAIA represented a nexus of culture and policy. This link is perhaps most clearly seen in Oliver La Farge's work within the film industry and his leadership within the AAIA.[122]

As a white anthropologist and Pulitzer Prize–winning writer for his novel, *Laughing Boy* (1929), about the Navajo, La Farge was well positioned to become a prominent figure within Indian reform activities. At Harvard University, La Farge pursued an interest in American Indian culture, specializing in anthropology and archaeological research. Although highly respected in this field, La Farge abandoned his studies to publicize the Indians' dilemma. He rejected the popular sentimental image of the Indian in contemporary literature and countered it in his own writing. *Laughing Boy*'s theme of civilization's corruption of Indian culture seemed suitable for white liberals and reformers interested in reshaping popular conceptions of Indianness to counter a long history of misrepresentation of Indian characters. A filmic version of La Farge's novel was first attempted by Universal Pictures. The studio found vocal opposition to its efforts from Indian agencies, civic groups, and religious educators. B. D. Weeks, president of Bacone (Baptist) College in Oklahoma, condemned the movie industry for complete ignorance on the subject: "These films about white corruption of Indian people reflect badly upon the red man, and cheapen him in the eyes of the world."[123] Notwithstanding such protests, Metro-Goldwyn-Mayer took over production and released the film in 1934. Luther Standing Bear was among the cast. He played the part of "Quiet Hunter" in the film. Perhaps Standing Bear had been influenced by La Farge's *Laughing Boy* when he and Campbell drafted the goals of their League; their first aim was to "publish a true history of the American Indian," which could correct misrepresentations of Indian culture in literature and film. Despite MGM's best efforts, box office receipts and reviews from *Variety* suggest *Laughing Boy* was a commercial failure, regardless of star performers and a prize-winning story.[124] By the mid-thirties, the Western was fading in popularity and with it opportunities to make and promote well-intentioned Indian films. For Standing Bear and La Farge, Indian reform would have to take place off-screen.

Considering the work of the NLJAI and the AAIA as well as growing numbers of Native people working in California's entertainment industry, Standing Bear was well positioned to reshape American culture and policy. The unique character of his performative career alters our understanding of the cultural politics characterizing a significant group of pan-tribal intellectuals during this time. Standing Bear's life as a case study shifts the very notion of resistance and intellectualism to reflect a diverse set of strategies. Analysis of Native performance builds on Judith Butler's study of bodies as constituted in the act of description, whereby her examples of sex and gender are always (to some degree) performative. When Standing Bear is framed as a *real* Indian or a full-blooded Indian (rather than just, say, an Indian) or is given the title of "chief," such speech acts are illocutionary and performative. In the case of Yowlachie, the act of naming an Indian performer using "real Indian" or "full-blooded" or "chief" initiated a process by which Indianness gained symbolic power. While working in Hollywood, Standing Bear and other Native actors found strategic ways to resist or conform to these articulations of Indianness.[125]

Throughout the 1920s and 1930s, Hollywood filmmakers hired Indian actors to portray *real* Indians on-screen; in the process, Indian performers were often interpellated into a popular imaginary based on being full-blooded and authentic enough. Once the necessary proof of Indianness was provided, they could be hired again and again to *play Indian* for live audiences or in film, and could then reap the financial benefits from this employment.[126] The desire on the part of filmmakers and audiences to see *real* Indians portraying Indian characters also produced a norm whereby Indian actors were continually cited as real Indians. This chain of citationality helped reproduce frames for defining Indianness that aligned with dominant narratives and popular (mis)conceptions about Indians. In these cases, to label an individual as a *real Indian* was not a neutral act of description, but rather a performative statement that interpellated the Indian as such. For Native people, from various tribal nations, the IAA became a new space through they could shape the filmmaking process in terms of the types of roles they were offered and who was hired to play these roles.

Indian Actors Association, Founded in 1936

In addition to a desire for authenticity and improved working conditions and wages, the IAA was established in response to shifting demographics in Hollywood. By the 1930s, Syrians, Swedes, Arabs, Latinos, and Filipinos donned braided wigs and face makeup to *play* Indian for the camera. The influx of these ethnic groups, along with the onset of an economic depression

across the United States and a decline among the film-going public's interest in Westerns, forced many Indian people to rally together to assert their
rights as actors.[127] As an affiliate of the Screen Actors Guild, members of
the IAA demanded that only real Indians be hired to *play Indian* roles on
screen.[128] As a leading figure in the group, Standing Bear advocated for
Indian performers. His visibility as an author helped him to do so. In addition to casting *real* Indians, the Association argued for studios to hire Indian
people as technical experts, and it sponsored courses in Indian sign language
and pictography. Perhaps the biggest issue facing Indian actors was compensation. Through vocal protest IAA members won equal salaries for Indian
actors who had been earning half of what non-Indian extras got paid.[129] The
paradox of this "win" resides in the fact that *playing Indian* now depended
on being able to authenticate oneself as such. Casting and compensation
were most certainly linked.

Much of Standing Bear's success was owed to the efforts of Jim Thorpe,
who worked with the IAA to advocate for his fellow Indians. Thorpe's primary concern was how to guarantee that only *real* Indians portray Native
characters in films. Ironically, with the assistance of the Department of
Labor, Thorpe searched for undocumented Mexican and Italian immigrants
in Hollywood who posed as Indians in order to *play Indian* on-screen.[130]
Thorpe made a case that 40 percent of extras playing Indians were in fact
not actual Indians, but the U.S. attorney's office argued that studio hiring
practices were exempt from federal law, so any complaints Thorpe had on
behalf of the IAA went unheeded. To combat what he saw as a rising tide
of opportunistic Indian fakes, Thorpe established his own troupe of 250
professional Indian actors ready for hire. In 1936, Thorpe was disappointed
when Cecil B. DeMille chose to hire Indians from a reservation outside of
his control to act in *The Plainsman*.

Later, Thorpe was outraged when DeMille hired two non-Indians, Victor
Varconi and Paul Harvey, to play chiefs in the film. He protested to no avail,
but his concerns seem justified. A large number of talented Indian actors
was available for hire in Hollywood during this time. Many could speak
their Native language and ride bareback. Perhaps Thorpe's anger came
from personal experience, given the highs and lows associated with his own
fame and fortune. He had been born in 1887 of an Irish and Sac-Fox father
and part French and Potawatomi/Kickapoo mother, in the Indian Territory
of Oklahoma. After attending Carlisle, where Thorpe met famed football
coach Glenn S. "Pop" Warner, Thorpe went on to win two gold medals for
the pentathlon and decathlon at the 1912 Olympics in Stockholm, Sweden.
The Amateur Athletic Union revoked his medals in 1913 after accusations
that he had played professional baseball. Still, Thorpe's career in sports
remained active as he played both professional baseball and football. He
became the first president of the American Professional Football Association
(later renamed the National Football League). However, by the early 1930s,

Thorpe was living in Los Angeles digging ditches for only four dollars a day. A *Los Angeles Times* reporter observed, "His existence has been a series of ups and downs with the latter distinctly predominant."[131] While Thorpe struggled to make a living as a minor player in Hollywood films, he actively campaigned against studios that hired non-Indian actors.

Indian adventures and interracial romances, made popular in the early silent films, were no longer of interest to moviegoers by the time Thorpe protested DeMille's hiring practices for *The Plainsman*. The director had a different sort of Western adventure in mind, as he designed an epic to revive the flailing genre. By the mid-1930s, "cowboy and Indian" stories of conquest, taming, and expansion were becoming popular once again, now as big-budget pictures. The new blockbuster Western needed Native people once again to participate. Luther Standing Bear comments on the problem of representing Indianness in Westerns in *Land of the Spotted Eagle*. He writes that the Western stories "joined in glorifying the pioneer ... in their course of conquest across the country," and could only do so "by committing untold offenses against the aboriginal people."[132] Although new Westerns meant more employment opportunities for Native actors, a fact that pleased Thorpe given his dire financial straits, most roles were neither realistic nor helpful in curtailing myths about Native peoples. Both Standing Bear and Thorpe hoped things would change to reflect their realities to at best represent Indian people as members of modern American society and at worst provide more job opportunities for many out-of-work Indian actors. Their success in establishing the IAA reflects one aspect of Standing Bear's social reform agenda. He would continue to build and maintain the networks that began through his association with Carlisle and his work for Cody, and that were now built around rich sympathizers like John Collier and Oliver La Farge, as well as editors and publishers like E. A. Brininstool and Lucullus McWhorter. Standing Bear continued working as an actor, writer, and reformer before he found himself caught in a new world defined by rumor and scandal.

Rumor and Scandal: First His Blood, Then His Character

In 1930, Bill Hart wrote to Standing Bear, as his friend and fellow actor, to express how "astounded" he was "at certain calumny directed against you. How any man, woman, or child could question your standing as an upright American of the red or white race is beyond my comprehension."[133] This rumor had traveled all the way to Washington, DC and the OIA, where Commissioner C. J. Rhodes had to take time out of his busy schedule to address it. The buzz around town was regarding the "exact degree of Indian blood of Luther Standing Bear."[134] Once Standing Bear and others had made the case for Indian people playing Indian parts, the next logical question was how to identify Indians, and which Indians might be real and which might be fake. Blood quantum, a familiar frame for thinking about "authentic" identity, proved critical to the question. Hart was astounded to hear that an accusation was being made that Standing Bear had none. The world of Hollywood was full of actors acting, performers constantly performing, people shifting names and identities. Given the numbers of non-Indians playing Indian, it should come as no surprise that all "Indian" actors became open to identity policing – a concern for *any* Indian in Westerns, which could have profound consequences. It seems as if this accusation would have fizzled into minor gossip if the commissioner had not made the mistake of sending a letter to Mrs. Jeanne Cappel (who seemed most invested in verifying the rumor's charge) in 1932, in which he noted that Luther Standing Bear of Rosebud was "three fourths white and one fourth Indian."[135]

It turned out the inverse was true: according to other federal records, Standing Bear was three-fourths Indian and one-fourth white. Files from 1908 confirm that Standing Bear was a *real* Indian in the eyes of the government because he was counted as a member of the Sioux tribe within the Pine Ridge Reservation of South Dakota – and, most important then, entitled to an allotment of land. The distribution of his allotment had been approved by the secretary of the interior on October 20, 1906. Notably, it was the heavy surveillance of the U.S. government managing Indian people that appeared equally capable of affirming or denying the very Indianness of any particular individual; it carried such authority that a mistake could be terminal. In the context of Hollywood's film industry, the idea of ethnic authenticity for Indian actors was now crucial for promoting and maintaining their careers because groups like the IAA advocated for the right of Indian actors as one *above* those of non-Indians to *play Indian* parts. Any question about the fullness of Standing Bear's blood and Indianness was critical to his involvement with the IAA and other Indian advocacy groups at the time. Hart and other friends of Standing Bear were able to cast doubt on the rumor immediately by invoking indigenous sovereignty. As Hart put it, Standing Bear's birthright (his very Indianness) was clear because of his "nationality as a Sioux."[136] Such a claim to nationhood, recognized by Hart, performed a critical awareness of Standing Bear's identity as at once defined by the United States and also the Sioux Nation.

As this rumor made its way from Hollywood to DC, not only Standing Bear's race but also his position as "chief" was in question. As a consequence, Standing Bear sought supporters like E. A. Brininstool to counteract the "propaganda going around" Los Angeles. In letters and conversations around town, white and Indian friends testified to the fullness of Standing Bear's Indian blood and his character. Standing Bear was able to draw on networks built around performativity to come to his aid in this matter. He also turned to a different sort of network by relying on letters from the OIA to confirm his Indianness. Through these efforts, the rumor was squashed. No one, however, was prepared for the scandal that followed in its wake.[137]

Early in September 1934, Standing Bear sent a letter to John Collier, who had been newly appointed the commissioner of Indian affairs. In it, he asserted his concern that many of the Indians he had met with were "undecided" as to how to view the impending Wheeler-Howard Bill that Collier proposed would resolve the economic, social, and cultural issues resulting from the Dawes Act of 1887. Standing Bear sought Collier's help on a number of fronts. He wanted support for the practice of indigenous religions on Pine Ridge, especially given that he had witnessed Christian denominations working against the practice of the "Sun circle." He argued that "if my people could once more worship in the natural way of their fathers they would gain their strength much faster."[138] In addition, he wanted to resolve a personal concern that his sister, Mrs. Conroy, should have to pay taxes "as a white citizen" given that she is a "reservation Indian." Finally, Standing Bear aimed to confirm the promise made by "Mr. Collette" in California to procure money for California's Indian population based on land claims.[139]

These sentiments regarding religious freedom, individual rights, and how to manage the work of white reformers were no doubt still on Standing Bear's mind; he had described them in great detail just a year earlier in *Land of the Spotted Eagle*. Like *My People the Sioux*, this book was made possible through the support of a white patron, Melvin R. Gilmore – the curator of ethnology at the University of Michigan. Before coming to Michigan, Gilmore taught biology and zoology at Cotner University (1904–11), and worked as a curator at the Nebraska State Historical Society (1911–16), where he compiled information about Native American village sites, recorded Pawnee traditions, and grew plants of Native American origin. From 1916 to 1923, Gilmore was the curator of the State Historical Society of North Dakota, after which he worked at the Museum of the American Indian (1923–8). In 1929, he joined the Museum of Anthropology at Michigan and became the first curator of ethnology. Gilmore's career had enabled him to work closely with Native peoples and his collaboration with Standing Bear would have been known to Collier, and celebrated for their insights regarding Native American life and history.[140]

In *Spotted Eagle*, Standing Bear argues that Americans must be reeducated about Indian people and the history of the United States to alter their impressions of "the Indian of the cheap magazine and the movie." This produces a false sense of history, and he suggests, "the parents and the grade teachers of this land ... now fulfill the duty of demanding that true histories be placed in the hands of the young." Standing Bear goes a step further to argue that "a school of Indian thought" should be built, so that the nation might "be cognizant of itself" and through this recognition preserve its true identity.[141]

Standing Bear hoped his own books would aid in this cause. The first step was the publisher who could help promote Standing Bear's work. He turned to the well-known and influential Boston-based Houghton Mifflin

Company; it had, by the mid-nineteenth century, worked with an array of well-known American writers, including Henry Wadsworth Longfellow, Nathaniel Hawthorne, Ralph Waldo Emerson, Harriet Beecher Stowe, Mark Twain, Henry James, Sarah Orne Jewett, and Henry David Thoreau. By 1928, when the first edition of *My People the Sioux* was printed, Houghton Mifflin had also worked with other Native writers.[142] Standing Bear's ability to work with this publisher may have stemmed from his connection to Carlisle, as well as his collaboration with Western writers like Brininstool and with ethnologists like Gilmore. Through these different but related white networks, Standing Bear successfully marketed himself as a Native writer. As a published author, he carried an air of respectability with him when he wrote to political leaders like John Collier. How, then, would his readers, as well as collaborators (Gilmore and Brininstool) and political allies like Collier, have dealt with the news that Standing Bear was arrested for "making improper advances to a young half-breed Piute girl"?[143]

On May 6, 1935, the *Los Angeles Times* reported that Standing Bear had pled guilty to the charge of child molestation. According to records from Los Angeles County, Standing Bear was convicted under Penal Code 288 of "lewd acts on a minor under 14." There is little archival evidence available to clarify the details surrounding this case. The voice and identity of the eight-year-old girl, Standing Bear's accuser, remain hidden from the historical record. Yet the fact of his arrest and the ensuing activity of those who rallied to assert his innocence or condemn his actions fill in much of the historical context surrounding these charges.[144]

After pleading guilty, Standing Bear was sentenced to one year in jail "as a condition of five years' probation by Superior Judge Desmond" for this "sexual assault" offense. The same *Los Angeles Times* article featured a photograph of Standing Bear with a feathered headdress and a somber expression, as well as a list of his friends, all of whom begged for leniency from the court.[145]

Among his friends [were] John H. McGregor, superintendent of the Pine Ridge Reservation in South Dakota, where Standing Bear was born: Little Badger, White Bird, Young Beaver, Kuuks Walks-Alone, Weeping Star, Mrs. Bird Jack, Dana W. Bartlett, William S. Hart, Sitting Calf, Willow Birch, Little Horse and Marian Campbell, president of the National League for Justice to American Indians.[146]

White Bird, William S. Hart, and Marian Campbell all knew each other and Standing Bear through their work for the NLJAI. The others listed among this motley assortment were likely to be members of the IAA or white reformers. The *Times* article concluded by affirming the contributions Standing Bear had made regarding Indian political rights. "For many years Standing Bear was a leader in movements to aid American Indians of all tribes, according to letters received by the probation department."[147]

According to the *Times* and a slew of letters, Standing Bear was surrounded by people determined to help him. A network forged through the meeting of performance and political organizing included people who responded to his indictment with shock and horror, not because they believed the young Piute girl, but because they believed Standing Bear was incapable of such a charge. And yet he pleaded guilty, which suggests there is truth to his accuser's claims. The repeated assertions about the impossibility of his guilt are performative utterances that invoke his status as an Indian activist and older notions regarding the inherent innocence of Indians linked to primitivism. Supporters repeated details about his life "without tobacco and alcohol" to exonerate Standing Bear. They reminded the public, the court, and the OIA that he was a "good" Indian, not one of the "bad" ones corrupted by white civilization – ironic suggestions given that these definitions positioned him as akin to a child, proposing he had *not* been influenced by depraved behavior. But how could this be if he had molested the Piute girl?[148]

The paradox of the defensive rhetoric used to support Standing Bear seemed to forget the charge of misconduct against a child, while simultaneously interpellating Standing Bear into a position of innocence so often ascribed to children. This sort of framing invariably linked a discourse of racialization – whereby Indian people were wards of the U.S. nation-state – to their agency, or lack thereof. Rather than taking into account the complexity of Standing Bear's identity, the majority of his supporters relied on this history to argue he not be incarcerated within Los Angeles County, but released into the custody of his people at Pine Ridge. The desire of his supporters to have Standing Bear in the care of "his people" separated him from their social space, and by extension, *returned* him to live under the watchful eye of the federal government and the Indian Bureau. A familiar narrative began to emerge, which was because Native people had been pacified, a by-product of settler colonialism, the maintenance of a separate system to deal with Natives as wards of the state was necessary. Therefore, Standing Bear's allies thought they could use the Indian Bureau as a favorable substitute for their own penal system to deal with his misconduct. Certainly for many Native people during this period, reservation spaces could and did operate just like prisons.[149]

John Collier seemed especially confused as to how to interpret the events of 1934–5 with regards to Standing Bear's case. As letters of support poured into the OIA and Collier learned, as he put it, the "details of the case," he deferred help to "Judge Parker" and "local friends of Mr. Standing Bear" as "the only ones who really can help him."[150] Although Collier spent much time and effort to address Mrs. Cappel's accusation regarding the "quantity of Indian blood" of Luther Standing Bear, when it came to a statutory offense brought by a young girl, Collier would not be moved. He sent several copies of the same letter to individual supporters of Standing Bear redirecting them to local authorities in California, further distancing himself from the situation.

White residents of Los Angeles and friends of Standing Bear wrote to Collier in March 1935 recommending that "in the event that Standing Bear receives sentence" and given that "his whole life has been devoted in their interests and has done for them what no other Indian has done" by recording the history of the tribe, it would be a futile "gesture to place him in prison."[151] Moreover, despite Standing Bear's publishing career and royalties from Houghton Mifflin, he was in dire economic straits. This financial strain may have affected his access to legal representation and even the advice for his plea. He might have had bad counsel, and therefore, thought he would get probation if he copped a plea, instead of something longer if he did not and was convicted. The many testimonies about "his personal habits" as "meticulously careful and orderly; in his mental and moral habits even more so," and repeated references affirming his character based on the fact that he "never indulged in liquor or the use of tobacco in any form" were not enough to excuse him from standing trial. When his trial day came, it would seem Standing Bear was guilty – or induced to plead that way.[152]

In 1935, Laura W. Soldier, a Sioux woman, and, more important, the ex-wife of Luther Standing Bear, wrote to James H. Cook. Her letter was in response to his inquiry regarding the matter of Standing Bear's character and the child molestation case. Her remarks provide another picture of how some may have perceived Standing Bear's gender and sexual politics in response to the molestation charges. Soldier does not mince words in assessing her ex-husband. "It serves him right; he has been too selfish. I have never forgot nor forgave him, even tho' I'm trying to live a Christian life. He left one woman [Nellie] with 7 children, and left me when Eugene was 6 mo. old." This raises the issue of whether both Standing Bear brothers were able to make their way in the world, in part, by abandoning their familial obligations, further suggesting these choices were underpinned by masculine privilege and an abandonment of the role of hunter/provider that came out of an older, Lakota cultural practice. Soldier's statements in the letter do not confirm Standing Bear's guilt, but do claim that he "deserves punishment" because she always thought "he would get in bad some day; his weakness is women."[153] Such a weakness can be read as a negative evaluation of Standing Bear's gender politics at best and a confirmation of sexual abuse at worst.[154]

Perhaps two failed marriages, both resulting in abandonment of spouses and children, demonstrate the degree to which Standing Bear's views of gender reflected the heterosexual, patriarchal, and sexist ideologies commonly held by many men during this period. Or perhaps not. Just two years earlier, in 1933, Standing Bear expressed his understanding of gender and race publicly by dedicating *Land of the Spotted Eagle* to his mother. When readers turned the opening pages to begin, they would first encounter this dedication to: "My Indian mother, Pretty Face, who, in her humble way, helped to make the history of her race. For it is the mothers, not the warriors, who create a people and guide their destiny."[155] Some readers might pause to consider how "mothers, not the warriors" could be better guides for the Lakota people. Such a notion set women apart from Standing Bear, importantly so, as superior leaders of their people. Looking more closely, his reference to the "humble way" his mother and other women "helped" make Lakota history suggests Native women played ancillary, if also essential roles. On one hand, the dedication expresses the gratitude and love of a son for his mother, and on the other, it relies on vaguely paternalistic and patriarchal rhetoric to challenge the efficacy of women's roles in the making of history. Regardless of it truth value, Soldier's condemnation threatened not only to undermine Standing Bear's manhood but his career as an actor and an author.

James Cook sent a copy of Soldier's damaging letter to long-time friend and editor for Standing Bear's first book Earl Alonzo Brininstool, who was living in Los Angeles at the time of the trial. Brininstool had become popular as a Western historian and writer of "cowboy poetry." Born in Warsaw, New York, he moved with his wife to Los Angeles in 1895 so that he could pursue a career in journalism. Although he mostly wrote poetry involving Western themes, Brininstool also worked as a freelance writer and contributed articles to magazines such as *Hunter-Trader*, *Sunset*, *Frontier Times*, *Outdoor Life*, and *Winners of the West*. In fact, his most noted work was published well after Standing Bear passed away. During the trial and Standing Bear's incarceration, Brininstool remained readily available to help his friend.[156]

After receiving multiple requests for such help, Brininstool did not take Soldier's biting remarks to heart; instead, he supported Standing Bear's application for probation in April 1935. Then on May 8 of that same year, Brininstool received a letter from Robert J. Hamilton:

the Chief was granted probation this Friday morning, May 3, in Department 43 of the Superior Court of this County on condition first, that he serve a year in the County Jail, and on release therefrom [sic] return to the Indian Reservation in South Dakota, his former home, and where he has many relatives and friends.[157]

These events demonstrate how the man who had been elected to a two-year term as president of the American Indian Progressive Association and worked to reform Indian affairs during President Herbert Hoover and Franklin D. Roosevelt's administrations, could also be convicted of child molestation. Such a conviction and the limits of his probation did not result in a return to South Dakota. Instead, Standing Bear remained in Huntington Park, California, for the remainder of his life. He refused to relocate to live under the watchful eye of the federal government and was able to continue making movies up until his death.[158]

A Contested Will

On a particularly cold and windy day in late February Standing Bear traveled through Los Angeles to his suburban home after a long day of filming DeMille's *Union Pacific*. His work was mostly outside that day and the stormy weather did not help protect him against catching a cold. As evening came, he developed a severe fever. According to his nurse, Donna Hite, the elderly Standing Bear was quite ill, and yet May Jones Montoya/Sunflower insisted on moving him in the middle of the night to sleep at her house. Jones had been managing Standing Bear's affairs following his arrest in 1935. The move that night proved fatal, and on Monday, February 20, 1939, Standing Bear died at the age of seventy-one.

Later that same day, Indian friends in "full costume" attended a Christian funeral service followed by a Lakota service honoring Standing Bear's life. According to eyewitness accounts, a peace pipe was placed in his hands before he was laid to rest in Hollywood's Forever Cemetery. Perhaps he was buried wearing a costume from one of the many movies that he worked on, such as the elaborate feathered headdress, bear class necklace, and metal cuff he wears in Figure 10.[159]

During his funeral, Indian and non-Indian guests alike would have celebrated Standing Bear's refusal to submit to romantic and anachronistic representations of Indianness. These fictional representations existed within the same cultural and economic sphere that relied on the "fact" of Indian blood as a marker of one's status and right to portray an Indian on-screen. Just six years before his death, Standing Bear commented on this sort of complexity in *Land of the Spotted Eagle*.

Irreparable damage has been done by white writers who discredit the Indian. Books have been written of the native American, so distorting his true nature that he scarcely resembles the real man; his faults have been magnified and his virtues minimized; his wars, and his battles, which, if successful, the white man chooses to call "massacres," have been told and retold, but little attention has been given to his philosophy and ideals.[160]

These philosophical ideas have left as indelible a mark on American culture. Early on in this text, Standing Bear notes that "The Indian was a natural conservationist. He destroyed nothing, great or small."[161] While later he confirms, "The Lakota was a true naturist – a lover of Nature." These rhetorical choices reflect a desire to uplift the image of Native peoples and simultaneously critique "white America." Standing Bear continues, "The white man has come to be the symbol of extinction for all things natural to this continent."[162] These are biting remarks to be sure, far less ambivalent or strategic than how he remembered Wanamaker or Cody in his first autobiography. Times had changed by the 1930s, and as Standing Bear grew older his politics became more radical.

FIGURE 10. Luther Standing Bear actor's portrait.
Courtesy of Braun Research Library Collection, Autry National Center, Los
Angeles, CA; Photo # OP. 798.

But his books and his funeral are not the end of the story. Following
Standing Bear's death, Donna Hite and his son George E. Standing Bear,
who lived in Pawhuska, Oklahoma at the time, fought to regain control
over Standing Bear's estate from May Jones. Standing Bear and Jones were
friends and political allies. She had worked with him through groups like
the NLJAI, the Native American League, the Pan American Indian National
Organization Council, the National American Indian League, and the AAIA.
Jones was not just a political ally because she had taken control over the
publishing royalties Standing Bear received for his books from the Houghton
Mifflin Company. Despite financial straits that prompted the IAA to raise
money to cover the cost of Standing Bear's funeral and burial, Jones was
flush with cash because of book royalties. Why did Jones fail to cover the

costs of his burial? As the sole beneficiary in his will, Jones had a lot to lose if Hite and George Standing Bear succeeded in contesting the will.

They were unsuccessful. Jones retained her inheritance when the court found no legal reason to dispute the will. In tribute to Standing Bear's life, Jones continued the political and cultural work they had begun together by participating in public lectures for many years after his death. Two decades later, on September 22, 1959, Jones honored Luther Standing Bear by donating 145 Teton Sioux artifacts and clothing items – many made or owned by Standing Bear – to the San Bernardino County Museum. Included among them were the distinctive beaded ensembles and headdresses that he wore in most of his films. The dynamic of material authenticity in dialogue with discursive belief reproduced in these objects, both in their making and in their subsequent display, returns to the issue of authenticity in Native performance. Although these items have provenance, it is uncertain how *Indian* these artifacts may be given that many were made solely for the purpose of *playing Indian* as part of the film industry. Still, Standing Bear's beading ability to craft dance clothes may also be read as an exactly appropriate avenue for him to bring his knowledge of the Sioux world to the film industry. Looking at the donated garments, museum curators could appreciate Lakota artistry. Exhibited in the museum, visitors could gaze on these objects with a similar sort of appreciation mixed with curiosity, although probably less aware that Standing Bear approached the task of beading for a film with a different sensibility than he would if making these items for his family or his tribe. The aesthetics and work of beading do not necessarily change all that much because the garments being made are to be worn on-screen. Of course, ethnographic certification of a feathered headdress, for example, does offer a different sort of authenticity, one that may not require testimony or authentication by an Indian person, which is not exactly the type of authenticity that Standing Bear would have supported.[163]

Standing Bear was pleased about being an actor during a time when other Native leaders were not equally proud of the performative moments in their careers. Unlike other Indian intellectuals from this period, Standing Bear celebrated his acting career as an accomplishment. The positive position he stakes out in *My People the Sioux* not only reconciles his choice to work as a performer within entertainments that many Native people viewed with skepticism and concern, but dovetails with the role he played after he left Wild West shows and moved to Hollywood. Working in film provided Standing Bear time and resources needed to produce his books. *My People the Sioux* (published over ten years after Eastman's last book, *Indian Heroes and Great Chieftains*), as well as Standing Bear's other texts, raises issues of ethnic authenticity, how to confront a vanishing narrative, and how to correct misrepresentations of Indian history and identity – all themes that related to work in Western films. During the 1930s, Native people faced these issues on the eve of a dramatic shift in federal Indian policy with Collier's

Wheeler-Howard Act of 1934. Also known as the Indian Reorganization Act (IRA), it was designed by Congress to reverse the allotment policies of the 1880s and "to conserve and develop Indian lands and resources; to extend to Indians the right to form business and other organizations; to establish a credit system for Indians; to grant certain rights of home rule to Indians; to provide for vocational education for Indians; and for other purposes."[164] In *My Indian Boyhood* (1931), *Land of the Spotted Eagle* (1933), and *Stories of the Sioux* (1934) Standing Bear writes about Lakota traditions, beliefs, and cultural practices to reimagine the roles of Native people in American culture. These narrative claims are set against the shifting political climate of the 1930s, so that Standing Bear's writings work beyond the limits defined by the IRA to effect broader cultural change in American society. His books urge white readers to reimagine Native people and their histories. His writings seem to anticipate the failures of the IRA. As many historians have shown, the IRA was only mildly successful in reversing the negative effects associated with allotment.[165] For individuals like Standing Bear, who already lived outside of a reservation community in an urban center surrounded by Native people from a range of tribal nations, there were different issues at stake that had little to do with tribal sovereignty and land, although he was well aware of these issues for his family back home.

As a Los Angeles-based writer, Standing Bear aligned his political reform agenda more with progressives from the 1920s and 1930s, and especially the white activists whose efforts grew out of their relationship to the Pueblo people of New Mexico. Critical to Standing Bear's life and those of other Native actors in Southern California was how to negotiate a new, urban, pan-tribal Indian community. This is different from Collier's primitivist political ideas that formed the ideological basis of the Indian New Deal. For Standing Bear, political reform and literary production represented a turning point in Indian intellectual production, which built on the earlier writings of Eastman, Montezuma, and Bonnin, and now asserted a desire to move outside of federal bureaucracy. Read in the context of the Great Depression and the emergence of Hollywood as a central site for American cultural production and Native American participation in that production, Native actors, like Standing Bear, did more than just make a living through film – they used the connections produced by that industry to build a pan-tribal political community.

Perhaps Standing Bear's fellow activists celebrated the fact that May Jones felt it appropriate to donate his collection of artifacts and costumes to a local museum after his death. Through this type of public space, Native and non-Native people alike could learn more about his career and the legacies of Native performance, more broadly speaking. They might appreciate the struggles of Strongheart, who aimed to challenge the sort of ethnic "authenticity" required for *real Indians* to play Indian in some ways and not others. They might also come to see the aesthetics of these performances as intimately political as much as personal. If exhibited properly, the very notion of performance itself could be reevaluated to challenge Standing Bear's cautionary tale that the damage white writers did to discredit the Indian was "irreparable."

Notes

1   William S. Hart started acting in his twenties. At the age of forty-nine, he came west to Hollywood to start his movie career; he made more than sixty-five silent films, the last being *Tumbleweeds* in 1925. In 1921, Hart purchased a ranch house and surrounding property where he built a twenty-two-room mansion, which today houses Hart's collection of Western art, Native American artifacts, and early Hollywood memorabilia. Hart lived there for almost twenty years until his death in 1946. See: The Natural History Museum of Los Angeles County and William S. Hart Museum.

2   Chief Yowlachie (1891–1966) was born Daniel Simmons. He acted in several films including *Ella Cinders* (1926), *Bowery Buckaroos* (1947), *Red River* (1948), *Ma and Pa Kettle* (1949), *My Friend Irma* (1949), *Winchester '73* (1950), *Annie Get Your Gun* (1950), *The Painted Hills* (1951), *Hollywood or Bust* (1956), and *The FBI Story* (1959), and he portrayed Geronimo in the television series *Stories of the Century*.

3   Michelle Wick Patterson, "'Real Indian' Indian Songs: The Society of American Indians and the Use of Native American Culture as a Means of Reform," *American Indian Quarterly* Vol. 26, No. 1, Winter 2002, 50, argues that members of the Society of American Indians produced similar sorts of pedagogical entertainments. Such shows would celebrate traditional dances, music, and stories from Indian life while also suggesting historical accuracy and ethnological truth. Standing Bear's performance drew on similar logics while also referring to a long history of Native performance driven by imaginaries about America's Wild West.

4   Promotional materials and other ephemera related to *The Covered Wagon* (1923) available in the archival collection of the Autry Library, Gene Autry National Center, Los Angeles, CA.

5   *Los Angeles Times*, "Home, Club and Civic Interests of Women," May 31, 1931, ProQuest Historical Newspapers Los Angeles Times (1881–1987), 22.

6   I refer to "America" and "Americanness" to represent the rhetoric used by the League, which understood America as synonymous with the United States. This was especially true during the 1930s for American Indian people who would refer to their positionality by using both terms interchangeably to represent the U.S. nation, rather than, say, referring to America as a symbol for all three continents of North, Central, and South America.

7   "National League for Justice to American Indians," Pamphlet, Lucullus McWhorter Papers, Manuscripts, Archives, and Special Collections, Washington State University Libraries, Pullman, WA. An intriguing comparison can be drawn by looking to the East Coast, and what Alain Locke termed in his 1925 essay "The New Negro Movement." As a Howard University professor of philosophy, Locke described this movement as a transformation and departure from

older models to embrace a "new psychology." Central to this notion was the mandate to "smash" all of the racial, social, and psychological impediments that had obstructed black achievement. Six years earlier, black filmmaker Oscar Micheaux called for similar changes in his film *Within our Gates*. Micheaux represented a virtual cornucopia of "New Negro" types: from the educated and entrepreneurial "race" man and woman to the incorrigible Negro hustler, as well as others, from the liberal white philanthropist to the hard core white racist. Micheaux created a complex, melodramatic narrative around these types to develop a morality tale of pride, prejudice, misanthropy, and progressivism. For more on this history see: Henry Louis Gates Jr. "Harlem on Our Minds," *Critical Inquiry* Vol. 24, No. 1, Autumn 1997, 1–12, and Richard J. Powell, "Re/Birth of a Nation" in *Rhapsodies in Black: Art of the Harlem Renaissance* (Berkeley: The Hayward Gallery and the Institute of International Visual Arts, University of California Press, 1997), 14–34.

8   A "light opera" is shorter and of a light and amusing character, often created to appeal to children and sometimes referred to as an "operetta."

9   By "Indianist composers," I mean those white Americans who wrote music that in words and sound aimed to represent Native themes even if these songs were rarely based on actual Native music, but rather built on caricatures of the "Sound of Indian." For more on these specific histories see the chapter on music in Philip J. Deloria, *Indians in Unexpected Places* (Lawrence: University Press of Kansas, 2006) and see Michael Pisani, *Imagining Native America in Music* (New Haven, CT: Yale University Press, 2005).

10 *Los Angeles Times*, "Home, Club and Civic Interests of Women."

11 Lucullus McWhorter (1860–1944) from the Yakima River valley of Washington, became involved in preserving the cultural heritage of the first peoples of the Columbia Plateau. As an author, amateur historian, linguist, and anthropologist, McWhorter collected stories, artifacts, drawings, maps, photographs, and printed materials to preserve the history and culture of these indigenous peoples. He documented Indian-government relations in eastern Washington, including individual recollections of Indian wars such as the Nez Perce War of 1877 and the Yakima Indian War of 1855–8. McWhorter's published works include *Yellow Wolf: His Own Story* (1940), *Tragedy of the Wahk-Shum: Prelude to the Yakima Indian War, 1855–56* (1937), *Hear Me, My Chiefs! Nez Perce History and Legend* (published posthumously, 1952), and *The Crime against the Yakimas* (1913). See: Biographical description, Cage 55, Guide to the Lucullus Virgil McWhorter Papers, Manuscripts, Archives, and Special Collections, Washington State University Libraries, Pullman, WA.

12 *Cogewea* was largely autobiographical. Quintasket had gone to secretary school to learn how to type so she could draft her own novel. McWhorter's role as editor may have complicated matters by rewriting aspects of her text that would later require her disavowal.

13 For another example of collaborations between Indians and non-Indians see: Sherry Smith, *Hippies, Indians, and the Fight for Red Power* (Oxford: Oxford University Press, 2012).

14 Regarding the Stronghearts' activist work together see: *Los Angeles Times*, "Indian Chief Will Be Church Speaker," April 27, 1931, and *Los Angeles Times*, "Indian Chief Joins League: Nipo Strongheart, Yakima Leader, Speaks at Izaak

Walton Gathering; Urges Game Protection," October 26, 1929, both from ProQuest Historical Newspapers Los Angeles Times (1881–1987).

15 For more on John Collier up to the late 1920s see: Lawrence C. Kelly, *The Assault on Assimilation: John Collier and the Origins of Indian Policy Reform* (Albuquerque: University of New Mexico Press, 1983). For biographical details related to the Indian New Deal see: Kenneth Philp, *John Collier's Crusade for Indian Reform, 1920–1954* (Tucson: University of Arizona Press, 1977) and *John Collier and the American Indian, 1920–1945* (Lansing: Michigan State University Press, 1968). For more regarding Indian people, federal policy, and the American West see: Peter Iverson, *When Indians Became Cowboys: Native Peoples and Cattle Ranching in the American West* (Norman: University of Oklahoma Press, 1994).

16 For more on the Association on American Indian Affairs see: Association on American Indian Affairs Records, 1851–2013 (mostly 1922–95), Public Policy Papers, Department of Rare Books and Special Collections, Princeton University Library.

17 For more on the National Congress of American Indians (NCAI) see the following. *National Congress of American Indians: Constitution, By-Laws and Standing Rules of Order* from the official NCAI Web site states the purpose of the NCAI, different types of memberships, and rules and regulations. Also see: Vine Deloria Jr., *Custer Died for Your Sins: An Indian Manifesto* (New York: Avon Books, 1970); N. B. Johnson, "The National Congress of American Indians," in the *Chronicles of Oklahoma; Report of Activities, American Association on Indian Affairs, June 1945-May 1946*; Bradley G. Shreve, "From Time Immemorial: The Fish-in Movement and the Rise of the Intertribal Activism," *Pacific Historical Review* Vol. 78, No. 3, 2009, 403–34; Thomas W. Cowger, *The National Congress of American Indians: The Founding Years* (Lincoln: University of Nebraska Press, 1999).

18 Nipo Strongheart's career in film began with *The White Chief* (1905) and ended with *Lone Star* (1952).

19 For more on the connection between Wild West shows, like the Miller's 101 Ranch and Thomas Ince, as well as Inceville as the home for the Bison Film Company see: the "Research Center at the Oklahoma Historical Society," Oklahoma City, OK, http://www.okhistory.org/research/index.html (accessed May 5, 2011). Aamire Mufti, "The Aura of Authenticity," *Social Text* 64, Vol. 18, No. 3, Fall 2000, 87–103. See Mufti for more on the philosophical nature of authenticity as an aura, where certain cultural practices can be seen as resources for overcoming alienation produced through the colonial encounter (87).

20 Patterson, "'Real Indian' Indian Songs," 50. Patterson argues SAI members intended to push "forward the ideas that Indians could adapt to 'civilized' life," and these were best articulated through performances that sought out historical accuracy and ethnological truth, as opposed to the erroneous representations of Native cultures perpetuated by Wild West shows.

21 Ibid. "Some members defended the shows by arguing that they reached a broad spectrum of American society and provided Native people with opportunities to travel and earn money. The shows also provided an education for both the audience and the participants." Also see: Charles Eastman, "My People: The

Indians' Contribution to the Arts of America," *The Craftsman* 27, November 1914, 184–5.

22 Ethnic authenticity has been addressed within history, sociology, literature, and anthropology as well as in American studies and various critical ethnic studies fields. What follows is a selective list of key texts that engage and theorize the term. Sean Teuton, *Red Land, Red Power: Grounding Knowledge in the American Indian Novel* (Durham, NC: Duke University Press, 2008) and "Placing the Ancestors: Postmodernism, 'Realism,' and American Indian Identity in James Welch's Winter in the Blood," *American Indian Quarterly* Vol. 25, No. 4, 2002, 626–50; Paul Chaat Smith, *Everything You Know about Indians Is Wrong* (Minneapolis: University of Minnesota Press, 2009); Joane Nagel, "Constructing Ethnicity: Creating and Recreating Ethnic Identity and Culture," *Social Problems* Vol. 41, No. 1, Special Issue on Immigration, Race, and Ethnicity in America, February 1994, 152–76, and *American Indian Ethnic Renewal: Red Power and the Resurgence of Identity and Culture* (Oxford: Oxford University Press, 1996); Paige Raibmon, *Authentic Indians: Episodes of Encounter from the Late-Nineteenth Century Northwest Coast* (Durham, NC: Duke University Press); Shun Lu and Gary Alan Fine, "The Presentation of Ethnic Authenticity: Chinese Food as a Social Accomplishment," *Sociological Quarterly* Vol. 36, No. 3, June 1995, 535–53; Henry Staten, "Ethnic Authenticity, Class, and Autobiography: The Case of Hunger of Memory," *PMLA* Vol. 113, No. 1, Special Topic: Ethnicity, January 1998, 103–16. Staten's article focuses on Richard Rodriguez's autobiographical work in *Hunger of Memory* (1982) to unpack the ways that Rodriguez has been criticized as a "sell-out" to white bourgeois culture for rejecting his Chicano identity. Tim Oakes, "Ethnic Tourism in Rural Guizhou: Sense of Place and the Commerce of Authenticity," in *Tourism, Ethnicity, and the State in Asian and Pacific Societies*, edited by M. Picard and R. Wood (Honolulu: University of Hawaii Press, 1997), 35–70, is an overview considering the relationship between tourism, culture, and development. He suggests the process of commercial and cultural integration associated with tourism does not necessarily break down a place-based sense of identity or render it "flat" and inauthentic, but rather becomes an important factor in the ongoing construction of place identity. Sharmilla Rudrappa, "The Politics of Cultural Authenticity" in *Ethnic Routes to Becoming American: Indian Immigrants and the Cultures of Citizenship* (Brunswick, NJ: Rutgers University Press, 2004). Isabel Molina Guzman, "Mediating Frida: Negotiating Discourses of Latina/o Authenticity in Global Media Representations of Ethnic Identity," in *Critical Studies in Media Communication* Vol. 23, No. 3, 2006, 232–51.

23 I name these two nations not only because of the violence used against Indian people but because of the complexity of Native actions in both instances, as two distinct examples of colonial conquest, versus say the Indian Wars of the Southwest and Great Plains that are often depicted in Western films.

24 The vast majority of Native people who migrated to California for work sought better employment and living conditions than was possible for them given the failures of the reservation system. See: Nicolas G. Rosenthal, *Reimagining Indian Country: Native American Migration and Identity in Twentieth-Century Los Angeles* (Chapel Hill: University of North Carolina Press, 2012).

25　Luther Standing Bear, *My People the Sioux* (1928; repr. Lincoln: University of Nebraska Press, 1975), preface, xvi.

26　Carlisle school entry cards, Bureau of Indian Affairs, Record Group 75 for "Standing Bear, Luther" and "Standing Bear, Henry."

27　Luther Standing Bear, *Land of the Spotted Eagle* (Lincoln: University of Nebraska Press, 2006), 234.

28　Standing Bear, *My People the Sioux*, 177–9.

29　Ibid., 178.

30　Ibid.

31　Standing Bear, *My People the Sioux*, 171. After Standing Bear left Carlisle, Gertrude Bonnin also became deeply involved with the Carlisle band. In fact, from 1899 to 1900 she worked at the school teaching music and was able to perform with the band at the Paris Exposition of 1900.

32　Alan Trachtenberg, *Brooklyn Bridge: Fact and Symbol* (Chicago: University of Chicago Press, 1965, 1979).

33　Michael Warner, "Publics and Counterpublics," *Public Culture* Vol. 14, No. 1, Winter 2002, 49–90.

34　Standing Bear, *My People the Sioux*, 171.

35　Ruth Spack, "Zitkala-Sa, The Song of Hiawatha, and the Carlisle Indian School Band: A Captivity Tale," *Legacy* Vol. 25, No. 2, 2008, 211–24.

36　For an early twentieth-century history of Native Americans as musicians see John Troutman, *Indian Blues: American Indians and the Politics of Music, 1879–1934* (Norman: University of Oklahoma Press, 2012).

37　Standing Bear, *My People the Sioux*, 178.

38　Ibid. There are some similarities, at least on the surface, of a connection to Alain Locke and possibly W. E. B. Du Bois, to show "race men" at their best. Yet another way to think about Standing Bear's "self-fashioning" in this moment from his text is in regard to autobiography. For more see: Arnold Krupat, *Ethnocriticism: Ethnography, History, Literature* (Berkeley: University of California Press, 1992).

39　For more about the history of the Wanamaker department store and Luther Standing Bear's experiences there see: Alan Trachtenberg, *Shades of Hiawatha: Staging Indians, Making Americans, 1880–1930* (New York: Hill and Wang, 2004), 278–310.

40　Although Standing Bear's work for Wanamaker in 1880 complicates and adds to a culture of display windows developing during the late nineteenth and early twentieth centuries within similar sorts of department stores in major U.S. cities, such as W. F. Macy and Company, Marshall Fields, and Schuster's and Gimbels, my primary interest is how he interpreted his position given his recent experiences at Carlisle and his status as a young Native man. *New York Times*, "The Great Sixth-Avenue Bazaar; Opening Day at Macy & Co.'s – A Place Where Almost Anything May Be Bought," 1878, ProQuest Historical Newspapers.

41　Standing Bear, *My People the Sioux*, 179.

42　Ibid., 183.

43　Three Stars became one of the founders of Martin, South Dakota, and one of the first elected officials, working as the state's attorney during the early twentieth century; see: *Biennial Report of the Attorney General of the State of South*

Dakota, By South Dakota. Office of Attorney General, 556. Charles W. Allen, *From Fort Laramie to Wounded Knee: In the West That Was* (Lincoln: University of Nebraska Press, 2001).

44 Standing Bear, *My People the Sioux*, 183.

45 Ibid., 184.

46 Ibid., 184.

47 As many scholars have argued, autobiography may be a particularly modern and American genre of writing. James Olney notes the slipperiness of the genre: "But if autobiography is the least complicated of writing performances, it is also the most elusive of literary documents. One never knows where or how to take hold of autobiography: there are simply no general rules available to the critic." Also see: John Sekora, "Is the Slave Narrative a Species of Autobiography?" in *Studies in Autobiography*, edited by James Olney (New York and Oxford: Oxford University Press, 1988); Arnold Krupat, ed., *Native American Autobiography, An Anthology* (Madison: University of Wisconsin Press, 1994); Roy Pascal, *Design and Truth in Autobiography* (New York: Garland, 1985); Robert F. Sayre, "Autobiography and the Making of America" and Louis Renza, "The Veto of the Imagination: A Theory of Autobiography" in *Autobiography: Essays Theoretical and Critical*, edited by James Olney (Princeton, NJ: Princeton University Press, 1980); and Sidonie Smith, "Who's Talking/Who's Talking Back? The Subjects of Personal Narratives," *SIGNS: Journal of Women in Culture and Society* 18, Winter 1993, 392–407.

48 Standing Bear, *My People the Sioux*, 185.

49 Paul Gilroy's *The Black Atlantic: Modernity and Double Consciousness* (1993) conceptualizes the black Atlantic not as a fixed geographic space, but as a "rhizomorphic, fractual structure … [a] transcultural, international formation" (4). Gilroy's black Atlantic is an evolving, morphing cultural process, through which the Black diaspora, African-American and Afro-Anglo history is negotiated. For Indian intellectuals a similar dilemma was at hand as figures were striving to be both Indian and American. This striving must then be examined against a perpetually changing cultural network that was made and remade by Indian and non-Indian people alike and negotiated along with social and political concerns. Jace Weaver builds on and complicates Gilroy's work in *The Red Atlantic: American Indigenes and the Making of the Modern World, 1000–1927* (University of North Carolina Press, 2014).

50 Standing Bear, *My People the Sioux*, 185.

51 Ibid., 185.

52 Ibid., 186.

53 Ibid., 186.

54 Ibid., 187.

55 Ibid., 179–87.

56 Richard Slotkin, "Buffalo Bill's 'Wild West' and the Mythologization of the American Empire" in *Cultures of United States Imperialism*, edited by Amy Kaplan and Donald E. Pease (Durham, NC: Duke University Press, 1993), 171. As Joy Kasson notes, "Like Luther Standing Bear finding bitter amusement in the mistranslation of Sitting Bull's remarks during a performance in the 1880s, Indian spectators attending the Wild West could enjoy a joke when Sioux

performed Omaha dances, or understand a subversive monologue when Kicking Bear recited his deeds in Lakota." Joy Kasson, *Buffalo Bill's Wild West: Celebrity, Memory, and Popular History* (New York: Hill and Wang, 2000), 212. Richard White, *The Middle Ground: Indians, Empires, and Republics in the Great Lakes Region, 1650–1815* (Cambridge: Cambridge University Press, 1991), refers to the "middle ground" in historically contingent terms in his work, whereas my reference operates more in terms of figurative language.

57 Luther Standing Bear to Commissioner of Indian Affairs, August 24, 1891, Letter, and Daniel Dorchester to Commissioner of Indian Affairs, August, 3, 1891, Letter, "Letters Received," *Records of the Bureau of Indian Affairs* (Record Group 75), Federal Records in the National Archives of the United States, Washington, DC. From this point on, citations from this archive will be abbreviated as: LR, RG 75, DC.

58 Standing Bear, *My People the Sioux*, 192–3.

59 Throughout the Carlisle School records, part of Record Group 75, in the National Archives Pratt is called on again and again to testify as to the "fitness" of his former students as new Indian "citizens" of the U.S. nation.

60 Charles Penny to Commissioner of Indian Affairs, November 2, 1891, Letter, LR, RG 75, DC. For more on the complex history of the U.S. Indian Service see: Cathleen Cahill, *Federal Fathers and Mothers: A Social History of the United States Indian Service, 1869–1933* (Chapel Hill: University of North Carolina Press, 2011).

61 Charles Penny to Commissioner of Indian Affairs, November 2, 1891, Letter, LR, RG 75, DC.

62 "Luther Standing Bear Seeks Position in the School Service," July 24, 1892, "First endorsement," by Captain Brown given August 5, 1892, and Luther Standing Bear to Capt. George Brown, January 20, 1893, regarding "No. 20 Day School Corn Creek," Letter, LR, RG 75, DC.

63 Given the year Henry Standing Bear performed at Coney Island he could have worked either as part of Pawnee Bill's "Wild West Show and Great Far East Show" or Cummins' "Indian Congress and Life on the Plains," the only Wild West shows sanctioned by the U.S. government. From Henry's own letters we know he was working seasonally within the Steeplechase Amusement Park from 1903 to 1908.

64 Michael Immerso, *Coney Island: The People's Playground* (Piscataway, NJ: Rutgers University Press, 2002).

65 Wallis suggests that Luther Standing Bear won the "shooting contest" with the Japanese tourists. See: Michael Wallis, *The Real Wild West: The 101 Ranch and the Creation of the American West* (New York: St. Martin's Griffin, 1999), 373.

66 Nellie Standing Bear to Charles E. McChesney, October 1900, Letter, LR, RG 75, DC.

67 For more on gender studies related to manhood and different masculinities in the United States see: Gail Bederman, *Manliness and Civilization: A Cultural History of Gender and Race in the United States, 1880–1917* (Chicago, IL: University of Chicago Press, 1996); E. Anthony Rotundo, *American Manhood: Transformations in Masculinity from the Revolution to the Modern Era* (New York: Basic Books, 1994); Michael Kimmel, *Manhood in*

America: A Cultural History (Oxford: Oxford University Press, 1996); Simon J. Bronner, *Manly Traditions: The Folk Roots of American Masculinities* (Bloomington: Indiana University Press, 2005).

68 For more on vaudeville, burlesque, circus "shows," and other popular performance arenas where identity was also performed and altered along different lines regarding gender, race, class, and sexuality see the following: Robert C. Allen, *Horrible Prettiness: Burlesque and American Culture* (Chapel Hill: University of North Carolina Press, 1991); M. Alison Kibler, *Rank Ladies: Gender and Cultural Hierarchy in American Vaudeville* (Chapel Hill: University of North Carolina Press, 1999); Janet M. Davis, *The Circus Age: Culture and Society under the American Big Top* (Chapel Hill: University of North Carolina, 2002); Rachel Shteir, *Striptease: The Untold History of the Girlie Show* (Oxford: Oxford University Press, 2004); Gillian M. Rodger, *Champagne Charlie and Pretty Jemima: Variety Theater in the Nineteenth Century* (Urbana: University of Illinois Press, 2010); Nadine George-Graves, *The Royalty of Negro Vaudeville: The Whitman Sisters and the Negotiation of Race, Gender, and Class in African American Theater, 1900–1940* (New York: St. Martin's Press, 2000); Jayna Brown, *Babylon Girls: Black Women Performers and the Shaping of the Modern* (Durham, NC: Duke University Press, 2008).

69 Wallis, *The Real Wild West*, 373.

70 See U.S. National Library of Medicine for more on the history of the "medicine show" in American culture. Also see the chapter focusing on the Kickapoo Indian Medicine Company in Stewart Holbrook, *The Golden Age of Quackery* (New York: Macmillan, 1959), and Brooks McNamara, "The Indian Medicine Show," *Educational Theatre Journal* Vol. 23, No. 4, December 1971, 431–45.

71 Rayna Green, "The Pocahontas Perplex: The Image of Indian Women in American Culture," *The Massachusetts Review*, Vol. 16, No. 4, Autumn 1975, 698–714.

72 Slotkin points out that the Wild West was "not only a major influence on American ideas about the frontier past at the turn of the century, it was a highly influential overseas advertisement for the United States during the period of massive European emigration." Slotkin, "Buffalo Bill's 'Wild West,'" 164. For a different examination of the Wild West with regards to violence and justice see: R. Michael Wilson, *Frontier Justice in the Wild West: Bungled, Bizarre, and Fascinating Executions* (Guilford, CT: TwoDot, 2007). Also see: Don Russell, *Wild West or A History of the Wild West Shows* (Forth Worth: University of Texas Press, 1970) and *The Lives and Legends of Buffalo Bill* (Norman: University of Oklahoma Press, 1979); Louis Warren, *Buffalo Bill's America: William Cody and the Wild West Show* (New York: Random House, 2005); Kasson, *Buffalo Bill's Wild West*.

73 Philip J. Deloria, *Playing Indian* (New Haven, CT: Yale University Press, 1998), 115. Such a performance, two decades after Standing Bear's work for Cody's Wild West, serves as an example of "playing Indian." See Deloria for more on this important phenomenon and the mutually constitutive nature of modern/antimodern practices that typified touristic escape for white Americans through Indian play.

74 *Minneapolis Morning Tribune*, "Annual Celebration Built on Indian Lore and Settings Planned for City," October 5, 1919, sec. 1, p. 3, in *The Papers*

of the Society of American Indians, edited by John W. Larner (Wilmington, DE: Scholarly Resources, 1986), reel 10.

75 Deloria, *Indians in Unexpected Places*, 15–51. Deloria theorizes and discusses examples of the move from the "surround," where Indian people had more power to threaten and disrupt settlement, to that of "outbreak," where they were the ones now contained by a federal bureaucracy aiming to control, assimilate, or eliminate them.

76 L. G. Moses, *Wild West Shows and the Images of American Indians, 1883–1933* (Albuquerque: University of New Mexico Press, 1996) for more about the costs and benefits associated with employment in these shows for Indian people. Frederick Hoxie, *A Final Promise: The Campaign to Assimilate the Indians, 1880–1920* (Lincoln: University of Nebraska Press, 1984), in regards to the progressive era and pro-assimilationist views pertaining to the proper roles for Native men and women to play.

77 Standing Bear, *My People the Sioux*, 248.

78 Janet McDonnell, *The Dispossession of the American Indian* (Indianapolis: Indiana University Press, 1991), 1, for more about the Dawes Allotment Act of 1887. See: Robert M. Utley, *Last Days of the Sioux Nation* (New Haven, CT: Yale University Press, 1963) and *The Indian Frontier 1846–1890* (Albuquerque: University of New Mexico Press, 2003) for more about the massacre at Wounded Knee.

79 Julia Lee, *Interracial Encounters: Reciprocal Representations in African American and Asian American Literatures, 1896–1937* (New York: New York University Press, 2011), 22.

80 Slotkin, "Buffalo Bill's 'Wild West,'" 178–9 and Kasson, *Buffalo Bill's Wild West*, 253–5. Also see: Gretchen Murphy, *Shadowing the White Man's Burden: U.S. Imperialism and the Problem of the Color Line* (New York: New York University Press, 2010).

81 A marriage is listed to Millie Standing Bear in 1886, but it may be Nellie. See: Donovan Arleigh Sprague, *Images of America: Rosebud Sioux* (Great Britain: Arcadia Publishing, 2005), 40.

82 Standing Bear, *My People the Sioux*, 249.

83 Standing Bear, *My People the Sioux* and Kasson, *Buffalo Bill's Wild West*.

84 Standing Bear, *My People the Sioux*, 261.

85 Standing Bear, *My People the Sioux*, 266. This presentation of Standing Bear's wife on public display did not occur in a vacuum. Set in a broader context, this image might be put in conversation with other representations of Indian families. See: Ned Blackhawk, *Violence over the Land: Indians and Empires in the Early American West* (Cambridge, MA: Harvard University Press, 2009), 276.

86 Ruth J. Heflin, *"I Remain Alive": The Sioux Literary Renaissance* (Syracuse, NY: Syracuse University Press, 2000), 89. Heflin offers a productive, if short reading of the scene in Standing Bear's autobiography concerning the display of his wife and child as part of a sideshow related to their employment with Cody in England. See: L. G. Moses, *Wild West Shows*, 145. L. G. Moses comments on the negative reactions of reformer Indians against the display of Indians in sideshows during this period.

87 Standing Bear, *My People the Sioux*, 266.

88 Scott Richard Lyons, *X-Marks: Native Signatures of Assent* (Minneapolis: University of Minnesota Press, 2010). Lyons notes that a "discourse of Indianness" is "generated by institutions, the state, and the market," 25.

89 Train wrecks were among the greatest dangers members of traveling shows faced around the turn of the twentieth century. For more on this incident see: Cindy Fent and Raymond Wilson, "Indians off Track: Cody's Wild West and the Melrose Park Train Wreck of 1904," *American Indian Culture and Research Journal* Vol. 18, No. 3, 1994, 235–49.

90 *Chicago Daily Tribune*, April 8, 1904; *Los Angeles Times*, April 8, 1904; *New York Times*, April 8, 1904, ProQuest Historical Newspapers. "Indians Die in Wreck, Survivors Chant Death Song for Three Victims." *The Washington Post*, April 8, 1904, ProQuest Historical Newspapers.

91 Standing Bear, *My People the Sioux*, 271. Carlos Montezuma's personal papers list his original findings with regards to injuries and also his estimates for damages. See: Carlos Montezuma Papers, Center for Southwest Studies, Fort Lewis College, Durango, CO.

92 "Chicago and Northwest Railroad Company Memorandum of Agreement with Indians Injured in C & N.W. Wreck, near Melrose Park, Illinois, 7 April 1904," to W. A. Jones, Commissioner of Indian Affairs, Letter (copy), May 2, 1904, Carlos Montezuma Papers, Center for Southwest Studies, Fort Lewis College, Durango, CO.

93 Standing Bear, *My People the Sioux*, 272. Letter from William F. Cody to John R. Brennan, May 27, 1904, William F. Cody Archive, Buffalo Bill Historical Center, Cody, Wyoming.

94 Standing Bear, *My People the Sioux*, 277.

95 Two letters confirm the relationship established between Montezuma and Standing Bear surrounding the train accident. See: "Carlos Montezuma to Hon. William A. Jones," Commissioner of Indian Affairs, May 6, 1904, Letter, Carlos Montezuma Papers, Center for Southwest Studies, Fort Lewis College, Durango, CO; "Office of Indian Affairs to Carlos Montezuma et al.," May 24, 1904, Letter, Papers of Carlos Montezuma, Wisconsin State Historical Society, Madison, WI.

96 Angela Aleiss, "Who Was the Real James Young Deer? The Mysterious Identity of the Pathè Producer Finally Comes to Light," *Bright Lights Film Journal*, Issue 80, May 2013.

97 For more about the enigmatic aspects surrounding Young Deer's racial identity and his work in film see: Angela Aleiss, *Making the White Man's Indian: Native Americans and Hollywood Movies* (Westport, CT: Praeger Publishers, 2005), 1–2 and "Who Was the Real James Young Deer?"

98 Red Wing and Young Deer's film careers were mostly over by the 1920s. Young Deer worked in France making documentaries between 1913 and 1919. Red Wing worked as a college lecturer and civil rights activist. During the 1930s, Young Deer worked occasionally as a second-unit director on B-movies and serials. He died in New York City in April 1946. Red Wing died on March 13, 1974. For more on their careers in film see: Aleiss, *Making the White Man's Indian*.

99 Deloria, *Indians in Unexpected Places*.

100 Standing Bear, *My People the Sioux*, 278.

101 "Bliss" was later renamed Marland to honor Oklahoma governor E. W. Marland in 1922. The origins of the town continue to be disputed by its Native, primarily Ponca, residents.

102 The cast often included Bill Picket, Bessie Herberg, Bee ho Gray, Tom Mix, Jack Hoxie, Mexican Joe, Ross Hettan, and an elderly Buffalo Bill. Given that Henry Standing Bear lived in New York at this time and commented about his work at Brighton Beach it is likely that they could have cast him, but impossible to know for sure. See the Cherokee Strip Museum of Perry, Oklahoma, http://www.cherokee-strip-museum.org/index.html (accessed May 5, 2011).

103 Molly Lee, "Appropriating the Primitive: Turn-of-the-Century Collection and Display of Native Alaskan Art," *Arctic Anthropology* Vol. 28, No. 1, 1991, 6–15. Lee emphasizes the roles played by individuals rather than museums in her study of collecting along the Inside Passage of southeastern Alaska at the turn of the twentieth century. For more about curio markets in the Southwest see: Jonathan Batkin, *The Native American Curio Trade in New Mexico* (Santa Fe, NM: Wheelwright Museum of the American Indian, 2008); Bruce Bernstein, "The Booth Sitters of Santa Fe's Indian Market: Making and Maintaining Authenticity," *American Indian Culture and Research Journal* Vol. 32, No. 3, 2007, 49–79; Edwin L. Wade, "The Ethnic Market in the American Southwest, 1880–1980." in *History of Anthropology, Vol. 3 Objects and Others: Essays on Museums and Material Culture*, edited by George W. Stocking Jr. (Madison: University of Wisconsin Press, 1985). For more on the intersection of consumerism and ethnic identity construction see: Erika Bsumek, *Indian-made: Navajo Culture in the Marketplace, 1880–1940* (Lawrence: University Press of Kansas, 2008).

104 Wallis, *The Real Wild West*.

105 William J. Ehrheart, "Chief Luther Standing Bear II: Activist, Author, Historian," in *Persimmon Hill* (Autumn 1997). Later on Standing Bear taught sign language at the University of California Los Angeles and at the Southwest Indian Museum.

106 See Standing Bear, *Land of the Spotted Eagle*, 229.

107 Ibid.

108 Ibid.

109 Standing Bear, *Land of the Spotted Eagle*, 172. For a preliminary list of scholarship concerning Native people in film and as filmmakers see: Peter C. Rollins and John E. O'Connor, eds., *Hollywood's Indian: The Portrayal of the Native American in Film* (Lexington: University Press of Kentucky, 1998); Jacquelyn Kilpatrick, *Celluloid Indians: Native Americans and Film* (Lincoln: University of Nebraska Press, 1999); Beverly R. Singer, *Wiping the War Paint off the Lens: Native American Film and Video* (Minneapolis: University of Minnesota Press, 2001); Deloria, "Representation: Indian Wars, the Movie" in *Indians in Unexpected Places*; Aleiss, *Making the White Man's Indian*; Edward Buscombe, *'injuns!' native americans in the movies* (London: Reaktion Books, Locations Series, 2006); Michelle H. Raheja, *Reservation Reelism: Redfacing, Visual Sovereignty, and Representations of Native Americans in Film* (Lincoln: University of Nebraska Press, 2010); Denise K. Cummings, ed., *Visualities: Perspectives on Contemporary American Indian Film and Art* (Lansing: Michigan State University Press, 2011); LeAnne Howe, Harvey

Markowitz, and Denise K. Cummings, eds., *Seeing Red: Hollywood's Pixeled Skins* (Lansing: Michigan State University Press, 2013).

110 Regarding the genre of the Western I refer to the American Film Institute's definition for the Western from 1921. Also, Davidson Boughey, *The Film Industry* (London: Sir Isaac Pitman & Sons, 1921). For more about the ethos of the frontier drawn from Frederick Jackson Turner in film and American culture see: Peter C. Rollins and John E. O'Connor, *Hollywood's West: The American Frontier in Film, Television, and History* (Lexington: University Press of Kentucky, 2009).

111 The three biggest Western authors who helped define the contours of the genre were Zane Grey, Maxwell Brand, and Clarence Mulford. All seem to have drawn some inspiration from Owen Wister's *The Virginian* (1902), a romance and fictional account of the Johnson County War set in 1890s Wyoming. Based on their work many films adopted a similar narrative shape. Bob Herzberg, *Shooting Scripts: From Pulp Western to Film* (Jefferson, NC: McFarland, 2005) Also see: C. Courtney Joyner, *The Westerners: Interviews with Actors, Directors, Writers and Producers*, with foreword by Miles Swarthout (Jefferson, NC: McFarland, 2009) Postwar Western writers like Louis L'Amour harkened back to these types of works in search of stories that were about a simpler, more bucolic existence. See: Melody Graulich and Stephen Tatum, *Reading the Virginian in the New West* (Lincoln: University of Nebraska Press, 2003).

112 My reference to "Mexicans" here reflects the fact that a large number of Westerns often had at least one "stock character" understood to be Mexican, usually male, and almost always comic and corrupt in nature. Such representations were derogatory and threatening to actual people of Mexican or Mexican American, Chicano, or Mestizo descent, especially given that many of these characters were portrayed by white European actors.

113 Frank S. Nugent, "THE SCREEN IN REVIEW; Cecil Be De Mille Continues His Historical Roadwork With 'Union Pacific' Opening at the Paramount – 'Hotel Imperial' Is Shown," *New York Times*, May 11, 1939.

114 One contemporary example would be debates surrounding Johnny Depp's portrayal of "Tonto" in Disney's film *The Lone Ranger*. Months before filming began, Depp and studio representatives spoke with members of the Comanche nation, and had several leaders read and critique scripts. See: Tatiana Siegel and Pamela McClintock, "Why 'The Lone Ranger's' Johnny Depp Joined the Comanche Nation," *The Hollywood Reporter*, April 26, 2013: "For Chris Eyre, the highest-profile Native American director working in show business, Disney's move is a welcome change. 'I'm not looking to this movie to be the Native Schindler's List,' says Eyre. 'But I completely respect Johnny Depp for making this movie happen and for him to try and rewrite Tonto for a new generation.'" http://www.hollywoodreporter.com/news/why-lone-rangers-johnny-depp-435652 (accessed May 10, 2013).

115 Aleiss, *Making the White Man's Indian*, 10–13.

116 As Philip Deloria and Andrew Smith have shown, as early as 1909 the New York Motion Picture Company recruited Indian participants James Young Deer and Princess Red Wing to work on producing Westerns. The two moved to Los Angeles in November of that year to work as part of the Bison brand before being lured away to the French company Pathe Freres. And, in this new

context they produced a number of films for Pathe that offered portraits of race and gender that challenged some of the typical elements of cross-race romance offered by domestic melodramas. Unfortunately for Standing Bear, he did not work with Young Deer and Red Wing but rather found his entrée into Hollywood through the usual route offered to Indian actors – the connection between live-action, Wild West performance and the machinations of Thomas Ince. See: Deloria, *Indians in Unexpected Places.*

117 Ronald L. Davis, *William S. Hart: Projecting the American West* (Norman: University of Oklahoma Press, 2003).

118 Luther Standing Bear's other roles included: "Saka" in *Bolshevism on Trial* (1919), "Chief Sutanek" in *The Santa Fe Trail* (1930), "White Cloud" in *The Conquering Horde* (1931), "Indian Chief" in *Texas Pioneers* (1932), "Indian" – uncredited – in *Massacre* (1934), and "Quiet Hunter" in *Laughing Boy* (1934). See: Alan Gevinson, *American Film Institute Catalog: Within our Gates: Ethnicity in American Feature Films, 1911–1960* (Berkeley: University of California Press, 1997), and "Chief Standing Bear" in the Internet Movie Database. "Internet Movie Database," http://www.imdb.com/name/nm0822052/ (accessed February 15, 2011).

119 See: Rosenthal, *Reimagining Indian Country.*

120 Nicolas G. Rosenthal, "Representing Indians: Native American Actors on Hollywood's Frontier," *Western Historical Quarterly* 36, Autumn 2005, 329–52.

121 "The Association on American Indian Affairs Archives," Publications, Programs, and Legal and Organizational Files, 1851–1983, Filmed from the holdings of the Seeley G. Mudd Manuscript Library, Princeton University.

122 The Association on American Indian Affairs Archives. Among its major achievements was the Association's role as catalyst for the enactment of the Indian Child Welfare Act in 1978.

123 Aleiss, *Making the White Man's Indian*, 46.

124 Ibid., 48. MGM invested $518,000 and lost $383,000.

125 Judith Butler, *Gender Trouble: Feminism and the Subversion of Identity* (New York: Routledge, 1990) and *Bodies that Matter: On the Discursive Limits of "Sex"* (New York: Routledge, 1993).

126 Deloria, *Playing Indian.*

127 Aleiss, *Making the White Man's Indian*, 55–7.

128 Importantly, the issue of who was really Indian has lingered into the present. The American Indian Registry for the Performing Arts, which began in 1983, served as a civil rights organization and clearinghouse for Native American talent. Based in Hollywood, this agency attempted to clarify the issue of "real Indians" by screening members for tribal affiliation. For more on this organization's efforts concerning the issue of using only "real Indians" in film see: Aleiss, *Making the White Man's Indian*, 149. In particular she states, "The registry even created its own talent directory of Indian performers and technicians to encourage studies to hire Native Americans."

129 According to Angela Aleiss, non-Indian extras received $11/day whereas Indian actors received only $5.50.

130 "Iron Eyes Cody" (born Espera Oscar de Corti) may be the most well-known "Indian" non-Native actor who made a career in Hollywood playing solely

Native roles in film and television. Born to Italian immigrants but claiming Cherokee ancestry, Cody refashioned himself into an authentic Indian. In 1996, the *New Orleans Times-Picayune* reported Cody had Sicilian heritage, but he denied it. Angela Aleiss, "Native Son: After a Career as Hollywood's Noble Indian Hero, Iron Eyes Cody Is Found to Have an Unexpected Heritage," May 26. He lived his adult life claiming he was American Indian; his half-sister and other relatives in Louisiana stated he was of Italian ancestry. Cody supported American Indian-related causes most of his life. His two autobiographies disavow any Italian heritage and instead include fabricated family stories that lay claim to an indigenous past. See: Iron Eyes Cody and Collin Perry, *Iron Eyes: My Life as a Hollywood Indian* (Book Sales, 1984) and Iron Eyes Cody and Marietta Thompson, *Iron Eyes Cody: The Proud American* (Empire Publishers, 1988).

131 *Los Angeles Times*, September 2, 1940. Also see: Aleiss, *Making the White Man's Indian*, 96–9.
132 Standing Bear, *Land of the Spotted Eagle*, 227.
133 William S. Hart to Luther Standing Bear, August 11, 1930, Letter, Letters Received File 72636, Record Group 75, National Archives, Washington, DC. Abbreviated as: LR, RG 75.
134 C. S. Rhodes to Jeanne El Strange Cappel, January 5, 1932, LR, RG 75.
135 C. S. Rhodes to Jeanne El Strange Cappel, January 5, 1932, Letter, LR, RG 75.
136 William S. Hart to Luther Standing Bear, August 11, 1930, Letter, LR, RG 75.
137 LR, RG 75, 1908, Luther Standing Bear to E. A. Brininstool, August 9, 1930, Letter, Earl Alonzo Brininstool Collection, 1850–1945, Dolph Briscoe Center for American History, The University of Texas at Austin – abbreviated as EAB Collection.
138 Luther Standing Bear to John Collier, September 6, 1934, Letter, LR, RG 75.
139 Ibid.
140 "Melvin R. Gilmore Papers, 1905–1938," Bentley Historical Library, University of Michigan, Ann Arbor, MI.
141 Standing Bear, *Land of the Spotted Eagle*, 229.
142 Houghton Mifflin began in 1832 with William Ticknor and the Old Corner Bookstore in Boston with James Fields. In 1880, the firm became Houghton, Mifflin & Company, named after Henry Oscar Houghton (1823–95) and George Harrison Mifflin, who was co-partner in 1872. See: "Harvard College Class of 1877 Seventh Report" (Norwood, MA: Plimpton Press, 1917) and "Report of the secretary of the Class of 1865 of Harvard" (New York: P. F. McBreen, 1885). For more on the founding members of this company see: "Houghton Mifflin Hardcourt Company," http://www.hmco.com/company/about_hm/henryhoughton.html (accessed May 5, 2011). Standing Bear, *Land of the Spotted Eagle*, 227.
143 County of Los Angeles Probation Office records, EAB Collection. For legal codes see the Superior Court of California, Los Angeles, http://www.lasuperiorcourt.org/criminal/ (accessed February 16, 2011).
144 Ibid.
145 With regards to Penal Code 288, "Lewd Acts with a Child," the way one might be prosecuted for this offense varies greatly given that a hug and kiss to a child

that may not have been done in a "lewd or sexual manner" could still be prosecuted for this charge, according to the law.

146 *Los Angeles Times*, "Chief Standing Bear Given Year Term in County Jail," (1923–Current File), May 6, 1935, ProQuest Historical Newspapers *Los Angeles Times* (1881–1987), A1.

147 *Los Angeles Times*, May 6, 1935, ProQuest Historical Newspapers.

148 Many letters were sent to Collier's office in support of Standing Bear's character and requesting assistance. See: Mrs. Charles E. Burbee, Mrs. H. H. Burgess, Anne Ross, Chief Ralph Rojas, Nelson M. N. Wauls, Lucien Y. Maxwell, Mrs. Etta Cortas, Thelma Offet (Whiteflower) to John Collier, March 27, 1935, Letter, Olympia Houten, White Bird, Kuuks Walks Alone, Young Beaver, and Little Badger to John Collier, March 28, 1935, Letter, Mrs. May Jones to John Collier, April 5, 1935, Letter, LR, RG 75.

149 Frederick E. Hoxie, "From Prison to Homeland: The Cheyenne River Indian Reservation before World War I," *South Dakota History* 10, Winter 1979, 1–24; Jeffrey Ostler, *The Plains Sioux and U.S. Colonialism from Lewis and Clark to Wounded Knee* (New York: Cambridge University Press, 2004), 109; Roger L. Nicholas, *The American Indian Past and Present* (Norman: University of Oklahoma Press, 2008).

150 Mrs. Charles E. Burbee, Mrs. H. H. Burgess, Anne Ross, Chief Ralph Rojas, Nelson M. N. Wauls, Lucien Y. Maxwell, Mrs. Etta Cortas, Thelma Offet (Whiteflower) to John Collier, March 27, 1935, Letter, Olympia Houten, White Bird, Kuuks Walks Alone, Young Beaver, and Little Badger to John Collier, March 28, 1935, Letter, Mrs. May Jones to John Collier, April 5, 1935, Letter, RG 75.

151 Ibid.

152 Ibid.

153 Mrs. Laura W. Soldier to James H. Cook, April 23, 1935, copy sent to E. A. Brininstool, EAB Collection.

154 Standing Bear championed the rights of Indian actors. A large component of his fight aimed to replace romantic, simplistic, and nostalgic representations of Indianness that dominated American narratives about Indian people, the West, and the history of the nation and still influenced Indian policy decisions. Instead, Standing Bear sought ways to make Indians legible as a three-dimensional people. With this fight in mind I include this court case in my narrative about Standing Bear to avoid the danger of portraying him in simplistic terms, as either wholly good or wholly bad, but rather as human. Just as Collier referred those seeking assistance with the case against Standing Bear to local authorities, so too has this aspect of Standing Bear's personal life been ignored by many historians who have studied him. The dearth of material available to uncover the specifics of the case, especially the identity and voice of his accuser, may be one rationale behind these omissions. Certainly it is a striking, if not corrosive blemish on an esteemed record of service to Indian people and his contributions to American literary history, which further complicates Standing Bear's story enough that scholars would leave it out. But, as responsible scholars, one cannot memorialize all Indian activists like Standing Bear

as pure, unimpeachably moral, and uncomplicated. As troubling as this part of his past is to uncover, Standing Bear's humanity, indeed his Indianness in the best sense, goes partially unexamined without it. By failing to acknowledge the various dimensions of his life, the stakes of his life's political work remain on the margins as well.

155 Standing Bear, *Land of the Spotted Eagle*, dedication page.

156 E. A. Brininstool developed correspondence with participants in the Battle of Little Bighorn (1876), namely Walter Camp, Fred Dustin, William J. Ghent, Charles Kuhlman, and Col Graham. He also tracked down stories of so-called survivors from the Custer phase of the battle. Of the greater than seventy stories he collected, none was found to have much veracity. He wrote biographies of Crazy Horse, Red Cloud, and Dull Knife. See: EAB Collection.

157 County of Los Angeles Probation Office records, copy, and Robert J. Hamilton to E. A. Brininstool, May 8, 1935, Letter, EAB Collection.

158 I have focused on Standing Bear here more than his accuser because I was not able to obtain more material to uncover details regarding the experience, identity, and voice of this Piute girl. My hope is that drawing attention to the case's existence may open the door for more scholars to investigate the larger ramifications of this event for all parties involved.

159 Figure 10: "Luther Standing Bear," Braun Research Library Collection, Autry National Center, Los Angeles; OP.798.

160 Standing Bear, *Land of the Spotted Eagle*, 227.

161 Ibid., 165, 192, 166.

162 Ibid., 166.

163 Donna Hite to Office of Indian Affairs, April 8, 1939, Letter, LR file no. 23323, and George E. Standing Bear to Commissioner of Indian Affairs, May 26, 1939, Letter, LR file no. 35359, both in RG 75, National Archives, Washington, DC. William J. Ehrheart, "Chief Luther Standing Bear II: Activist, Author, Historian," in *Persimmon Hill*, Autumn 1997. Special thanks to Diana Fields from the Donald C. & Elizabeth M. Dickinson Research Center, the National Cowboy and Western Heritage Museum, Oklahoma City, OK.

164 For more about the IRA see: "Wheeler-Howard Act–exempt certain Indians: Hearings before the Committee on Indian Affairs, House of Representatives, Seventy-sixth Congress, third session, on S. 2103, an act to exempt certain Indians and Indian tribes from the provisions of the Act of June 18, 1934 (48 Stat. 984), as amended. June 10, 11, 12, 13, 14, 17, 18, 19, and 20, 1940," *United States Congress House Committee on Indian Affairs* (U.S. Government Printing Office, 1940).

165 For an investigation of federal Indian policy history and law I have consulted the following: Graham D. Taylor, *The New Deal and American Indian Tribalism: The Administration of the Indian Reorganization Act, 1934–45* (Lincoln: University of Nebraska Press, 1980); Vine Deloria Jr. and Clifford M. Lytle, *American Indians, American Justice* (Austin: University of Texas Press, 1983); Francis Paul Prucha, *The Great Father: The United States Government and the American Indians* (Lincoln: University of Nebraska Press, 1986); Blue Clark, *Lone Wolf v. Hitchcock: Treaty Rights and Indian Law at*

the End of the Nineteenth Century (Lincoln: University of Nebraska Press, 1999); Francis Paul Prucha, *Documents of United States Indian Policy: Third Edition* (Lincoln: University of Nebraska Press, 2000); Frederick E. Hoxie, *A Final Promise: The Campaign to Assimilate the Indians, 1880–1920* (Lincoln: University of Nebraska Press, 2001); David E. Wilkins and K. Tsianina Lomawaima, *Uneven Ground: American Indian Sovereignty and Federal Law* (Norman: University of Oklahoma Press, 2002).

Conclusion

The 1930s, Indian Reorganization, and Beyond

He looked toward the mountains in the east, and then upward to the fleckless
sky. Nowhere in the world, he imagined, was there a sky of such depth and
freshness. He wanted never to forget it, wherever he might be in times to come.
Yes, wherever he might be!
      – D'Arcy McNickle, *The Surrounded*[1]

D'Arcy McNickle (1904–77), novelist, Bureau of Indian Affairs (BIA)
administrator, and historian, grew up on the Flathead Reservation in
western Montana, created by the Treaty of Hellgate in 1855 in which the
Flathead, the Pend d'Oreille, and the Kootenai gave up millions of acres
of their land. The reservation space not only confined the three tribes who
signed the treaty, but other tribes as well, and kept them out of the way of an
onslaught of American settlers. McNickle was neither Salish nor Kootenai;
his mother was Canadian Cree. But he was born on the reservation in 1904
and enrolled as a member of the Flathead tribe in 1905. Like many other
Indian children during the first part of the twentieth century, he went to a
reservation grade school before transferring to an Indian boarding school.
At Chemawa Indian School, like most Indian boarding schools of the day,
McNickle experienced school as a military academy. Students wore military
uniforms and marched in formations. Like Gertrude Bonnin and Luther
Standing Bear, he later recalled how students were punished for speaking
to each other in Indian languages. Unlike many other Indian young people
during the first part of the twentieth century, however, McNickle was able
to attend college. At the University of Montana in Missoula he majored in
literature and history and joined the staff of the University's literary journal,
The Frontier, in which he published poetry and short stories. Although he
had learned a great deal at the University, he did not graduate. However, his
mentor, Harold G. Marriam, the head of the English department, encouraged McNickle to expand his horizons and suggested the possibility of earning his bachelor's degree at Oxford.[2]

Once abroad, McNickle found out Oxford would not accept all of his academic credit. Although he did not end up enrolling there, McNickle stayed on in England and attended lectures, explored the libraries, and took advantage of many opportunities to study on his own. Following this self-education abroad, McNickle returned to the United States determined to make his way in the publishing field. While living in New York City, McNickle took on a variety of freelance jobs, including writing, proofing, and book make-up. Also while in New York, he enrolled at Columbia University, where he studied American history, but with the pressures of trying to earn a living at the same time he was unable to complete his degree. More of an explorer than a finisher, McNickle still valued these varied academic experiences and the opportunities education could provide. He believed in making higher education more accessible and affordable for Indian people. "Bridging the generational gap between Progressive and post–World War II Indian intellectuals and activists, McNickle's work marks the boundary between pre-and post-1934 epochs in American Indian history, when indigenous communities began to realize their latent power as sovereign nations, long oppressed under the reservation system."[3] Throughout his life he would work as a writer and activist toward these goals.

In 1938, four years after Congress had passed the Wheeler-Howard Act (otherwise known as the Indian Reorganization Act, or IRA), McNickle published an article, "Four Years of Indian Reorganization," in the July issue of *Indians at Work*. He aimed to take stock of this major shift in policy. Because John Collier, then commissioner of Indian affairs, had designed the IRA to reverse the failures of the allotment policies following the Dawes Act of 1887, questions of citizenship, tribal sovereignty, and Indian labor were necessary components of McNickle's response.[4] McNickle had already worked for the BIA and the Federal Writer's Project (a part of the Works Progress Administration, or WPA, a New Deal arts program) while struggling to publish his first novel, *The Surrounded*.[5] The rhetoric of his article and the fact that it appeared in a magazine funded and printed monthly by the BIA shows that he sought to engage multiple publics, both Indian and white, to fuel discussion regarding the IRA. From the early 1930s through the mid-1940s *Indians at Work* had functioned as a "news sheet for Indians and the Indian service."[6] The publication of McNickle's piece represented a necessary turning point in the history of Indian intellectuals in America.[7] At the same time, McNickle's narrative reflected the political history and intellectual traditions he had inherited from an earlier generation of Native writers, including: Charles Eastman, Carlos Montezuma, Gertrude Bonnin, and Luther Standing Bear.

The life and writings of McNickle can be read as a bookend to the performative moment of Simon Pokagon's appearance at the opening ceremonies for Chicago Day at the 1893 World's Fair. Pokagon's presence at the Fair prefigured the types of successes and failures future generations of Indian people would encounter in American history in much the same way that McNickle's political activism, literary achievements, and impressive multi-faceted career confirmed the modern status of Indian people as reformers and writers in the United States during the 1930s. His work as a founder of the National Congress of American Indians (NCAI) and his assessment of the changes in national policy related to Indian people through the IRA offered a vision for the possible futures Indian people could have in the decades to follow. Given McNickle's later tenure as the founder and director of the Center for American Indian History and Indigenous Studies (that now bears his name) at the Newberry Library in Chicago, he not only figuratively but literally returned Native intellectual engagement with U.S. history to the site of Pokagon's "The Red Man's Rebuke." In other words, McNickle's work at the Newberry helped reinstate American Indian history as a focal point for research in the city and to remind Americans of the colonial history that Pokagon and the Potawatomi had experienced.

McNickle's article from 1938 begins in much the same way that Pokagon's speech from 1893 does: he recalls the history of Native America using broad, somewhat idealistic strokes. "In years past, the seasons came and went, and left the Indians untouched."[8] Here "the Indians" appears to capitulate to an aesthetic understanding of Indianness as almost always set in the past and tied to a primitivist ideal. The word "the" separates McNickle from his subject, or so he might have his readers assume. The notion that time flowed over Indian Country so that people remained "untouched" not only idealizes precontact America but hits his audience with familiar tropes. No doubt, as the seasons came and went, no one could remain untouched by acts of war, alliance, and the rise and fall of great civilizations. But McNickle means to be taken metaphorically, and he leans on the ideas of seasons and growth by referring to harvests reaped to sustain Native people through long winters. In 1938, McNickle was right to recognize that a change of season was "upon us" because "this year, for some Indians, there is a difference. There are grain fields growing. Hay is ripening. Calves and lambs are finding their legs."[9] By suggesting that the IRA was set in a moment of growth and prosperity, McNickle highlights how this shift in policy had stopped the practice of dividing Native American tribal lands into individual allotments, and encouraged tribes to establish their own formal governments under a written constitution, as well as introduced other reforms to promote Native American autonomy and to protect cultural traditions. So despite the economic challenges that still lay ahead, at least ideologically and to some degree structurally, Native America was reimagined by the federal government as more able to govern its own lands and affairs – liberating the BIA from more direct management of Native space. Given these changes, McNickle's article was also being literal because the Indians who had survived allotment were now seeing the differences the IRA promised them regarding the reconfiguration of tribal governments and land for self-development.

In effect, this "Indian" New Deal was a turning point in some important ways.[10] It was largely successful in reversing the Dawes Act's privatization of tribal holdings into individual parcels. It also restored the management of assets (mainly land) more directly into Indian hands. Had the law not been passed, the continuation of individual allotments might have resulted in the termination of the reservation system altogether. Under the law, about 2 million acres of land were added to Indian reservations over the following twenty years. Moreover, the IRA was reasonably successful in providing a mechanism for establishing stable tribal governments. Still, the IRA did not always work as intended and therefore has a complicated and fraught legacy. For example, the new tribal government system increased Indian dependence on the BIA, thereby actually decreasing tribal autonomy. Many Native communities also disagreed about who should be put in charge of these "new" governments, especially because many tribal nations had long-established traditions for governing that were working just fine without the federal government's intervention. Also, although the affirmative action preferences for employment with the BIA benefited particular individuals with the hope of minimizing the long-standing distrust of Native Americans toward the agency, these were modest gains given a lack of economic development and educational opportunities for large numbers of Indian people. In the end, the IRA was not as successful as Collier and others had hoped in reversing poverty and unemployment rates across Native America.

McNickle, as a former BIA and WPA employee, knew full well that Indian "reorganization" was necessary not only because of the allotment policy's threat to tribal sovereignty but also because of the Great Depression. His post-1934 article recognized what was new and what was not in the IRA. He writes:

In four years tribes have become organized and incorporated, money has gone into tribal treasuries, land has been purchased, students have secured loans to attend colleges and professional schools. For these, life will be different this year. Many of the things being done today through the agency of the Reorganization Act have been done in the past. Tribes have set up governing bodies before. Tribes have borrowed money from government.... The Indian Reorganization act, apart from certain legal developments, is primarily a training school in self-government and economic self-management.[11]

Although McNickle's article from 1938 seems to emphasize continuity rather than change, he continues by highlighting the new powers accorded to tribal governments. With this new type of recognition, certainly flawed given the already uneven dispersal of power between the federal government and Native nations, McNickle suggests Native people may be able to claim more authority over their own lives to limit the involvement of the commissioner of Indian affairs and his agents. More than tribal autonomy and an increased land base, McNickle emphasizes a critical cultural change that would result from the IRA's increase in educational support through a student loan program. With the help of such loans, more Native people could attend college and professional schools. In essence, McNickle celebrates the futures that might be possible through education because he is keenly aware of how his own education afforded him better opportunities as a writer, activist, and federal government employee.[12]

The final section of his 1938 article offers readers specific case studies for the implementation of the IRA, which is an important shift in the tactics characterizing Indian intellectual thought and reform work. From Hydaburg village in Alaska, the Hopi in New Mexico, the Tongue River Reservation and Blackfeet in Montana, as well as examples from the Jicarillas, Rosebud Sioux, and Flathead tribe, McNickle asserts, "The law must operate in the lives of men and women before it begins to have meaning."[13] He uses these case studies to show examples of this meaning, and includes these highlights to "indicate some of the currents that have been set up. They are not intended to indicate how far the trend has gone or how soon any one question will be answered. Something has started, and here is the general direction in which it moves."[14] McNickle's conclusion further refines what he means by "the general direction" as directly tied to types of education for Native communities. "Tribal governments have serious need of education in public administration, in Indian laws, treaties and regulations, and in the use of the powers embedded in their own constitutions. Failure to get this education may fairly well destroy the whole purpose of the reorganization program."[15] Less the cultural politics of the previous generation and more attuned to administration, policy, and law, McNickle only modestly plays the Indian cards of primitivism and exoticism in this piece. Instead, he opts for those of tribal governance and technical expertise, which signaled a shift in strategy to his Native readers.

McNickle further suggests that with a rising number of organized tribal governments the federal government will necessarily decrease the funds allotted for Indian reorganization purposes, which was in fact one of the rationales behind the Act in the first place. As much as this shift in policy aimed to reverse the Dawes Act to some extent, for others in Congress, the Act suggested a future where tribal funds would no longer be tied to the U.S. Treasury at all. In effect, self-government equaled self-sufficiency and a separation between the U.S. economy and Native-based ones. Such an issue has remained central to American Indian affairs. Certainly, McNickle's article was prescient given that less than twenty years later, Native people, and McNickle himself, would be working against another critical shift in Indian policy during the Termination Era of the 1950s, when the U.S. government sought to dismantle tribal sovereignty one nation at a time.[16]

During these decades, Congress adopted policies aimed at terminating federal obligations to tribes, in effect attempting to conclude with "reorganizing" Native people that had begun during the 1930s. The three main

tools the federal government used to accomplish this were the BIA relocation program, actual termination of some tribes, and the extension of state
jurisdiction into Indian Country through Public Law 280, which extended
state criminal and some civil jurisdiction into Indian spaces in certain named
states. Termination meant officially ending the process by which the federal government recognized certain tribes as national and sovereign entities.
Today many of these tribal nations are actively engaging with Congress in
order to regain recognition. At the time, McNickle's article fit within an
ideology of uplift promoted by the previous generation of Indian intellectuals like Charles Eastman, who often worked with Congress and dominant
white reform groups to promote social change and to fight for the future of
Indians in America. For McNickle, the future would build on, if also resist,
the efforts of the IRA through the arenas of politics and culture. Although
measured and abstract, McNickle's overall message from 1938 is one of
hope and possibility.

> The problems are many and certainly there is no intention of belittling them. It is
> possible, nevertheless, to realize that where in the past there have been only misgiv-
> ings and despair for the future of the Indians, today there is reason to be hopeful. For
> some Indians, at least, there is already a difference. Something has begun to happen.
> When this year's harvest comes around, some few Indians will have something to
> garner. That is a beginning.[17]

McNickle was right. The year 1938 was some sort of a new beginning. In
the years following, McNickle became very well known for another piece of
writing: *The Surrounded*, published by Dodd, Mead and Company in 1936.
In this novel, his fictional focus on the social and political effects shaping
Indian identity fit well into what anthology editors from the 1930s defined
as the connection between storytelling and the "folk." One reviewer at the
time stated, "Especially noteworthy about *The Surrounded* is that it's told
by one who is on the inside looking out."[18] His novel was well received
upon its initial publication as the literary product of an educated Indian.
And, although widely celebrated today for being one of the first of this
period by a Native author, it was not unlike work produced by McNickle's
contemporaries such as William Faulkner, Zora Neale Hurston, and Henry
Roth. His writing embraced modern literary styles such as realism and naturalism to engage Native and non-Native readers without relying on romantic
or sentimentalist approaches used by the majority of Native and non-Native
writers from the generation before him.

In *The Surrounded*, McNickle explores the relationship between violence, cultural memory, and Native identity. These themes play out as the
protagonist, Archilde, struggles to relate to his family and tribal community after returning home. As Paul Whitehouse argues, through a series of
violent episodes, Archilde is able to reconnect to "a symbolic, pre-colonial
past and, in that instant, both recognize and challenge the institutionalized,

legislative, and normative violence that has stifled his individual development and threatens to engulf the cultural identity of his wider Native community."[19] Whitehouse's reading suggests that McNickle's novel grapples
with the larger theme of systemic violence that Native Americans experienced in boarding schools, on reservations, and in other facets of American
society given the practices and policies of settler-colonialism. This theme
was not new for Indian writers and intellectuals. Certainly, Eastman understood the reach of systemic violence as a witness to the atrocities Indian
victims suffered after the massacre at Wounded Knee in 1890. Both Bonnin
and Standing Bear experienced a different, if equally destructive, sort of
violence as a teacher and student within the Indian boarding school system. Montezuma, sold as a young child by his parents to the Pimas before
he was sold again to Carlo Gentile (an Italian photographer), also experienced the violence of forced separation from his family and community.
For McNickle, the subject of systemic violence becomes manifest in his text
through brutal forms of physical violence perpetrated on or by various characters, as well as Archilde's mother's violent stand against cultural assimilation. For readers during the 1930s, McNickle offered a fictional account of
the negative effects of settler-colonialism on Native and non-Native people.
His novel in many ways was far bolder in its critique of white America than
McNickle's nonfiction writings, suggesting that he knew well how to engage
with different representational strategies contingent on genre and audience.

The figure of Archilde, many critics have surmised, may be a loosely
autobiographical representation of McNickle. At the same time, it seems
equally plausible that Archilde is a composite figure, representing the thousands of untold stories of generations of Indian children who were forced
to assimilate into American society and struggled with how to integrate
themselves back into their Indian communities after being away at school.
McNickle's story centers on Archilde's return to the reservation he grew up
on after being away for a few years at an Indian boarding school and having
some success in the white world as a violinist. This fictional account reflects
McNickle's own explorations to some extent, and also reads as an echo of
Bonnin's life given her early education, a stint at the New England conservatory, and well-publicized role as an Indian musician. Both Archilde and
Bonnin embraced the violin as a means of escape, liberation, and resistance.
McNickle may well have read her *American Indian Stories* and known
enough about her life as a musical performer to make his protagonist's pro-
fession that of violin player.

After writing *The Surrounded*, McNickle spent the remainder of his life
working for Indian people, often employed by the BIA. He also wrote several nonfiction books about Indian history: *They Came Here First* (1949,
1975), the still-in-print *Indians and Other Americans* (with Harold Fey,
1959, 1970), *Indian Tribes of the United States* (1962), *Native American
Tribalism* (1973), and a young adult book, *Runner in the Sun* (1954) – a

historical fiction story set in the time before any contact with Europeans in the Americas. During the 1930s, in academe, anthropology was at the center of what would later become Native American studies as it approached "the apogee of its rush to 'salvage' a supposedly vanishing Indian America in part through transcriptions of oral storytelling."[20] Like other leading Native intellectuals such as Vine Deloria Jr., McNickle responded to the work of professional anthropologists by using both fiction and nonfiction to offer counter-narratives for broader public consumption.[21] Since the nineteenth century Native people have had to contend with anthropological work that was both persuasive and pervasive in the claims it made about Indian people, culture, and history. For McNickle, anthropology needed to be claimed by Native Americans for intellectual as well as political purposes. As practitioners in this field, Native people might revise the types of methods used for studying indigenous communities.

In fact, McNickle built on his literary success through his political work to create meaningful and lasting bridges across Indian Country in the form of the NCAI. Like the Society of American Indians (SAI), the membership of the NCAI was pan-tribal and the group's earliest concerns related to redefining and reaffirming ethnic identity of Indian people to influence national politics and cultural change in America. McNickle and the other early founders Archie Phinney, Nez Perce, and Charles E. J. Heacock, Lakota, first began discussing the aims of the group in the late 1930s, mostly through writing letters. Along with other founding members, they met from May 25 to May 27 in 1944, in Chicago, to complete planning for their organization's first convention. Despite disagreements about membership and the scope of the organization, the NCAI thrived and has continued to function as one of the most important intertribal political organizations of the modern era, bringing together a wide range of Native peoples to fight the effects of termination as well as to create the Indian Claims Commission. The SAI was not only a precursor to the NCAI in terms of a public profile for what a pan-tribal activist organization would look and sound like, but at least four of the same members of the SAI were still alive and politically active in the early years of the NCAI, including: Albert Exendine, Jesse Rowlodge, Henry Standing Bear, and Arthur C. Parker.[22] These connections could be quite helpful.

Learning from some of the mistakes of the SAI, McNickle was able to raise funds to support the travel and attendance of Indians to the NCAI's conventions because otherwise many would not be able to afford to go.[23] By addressing these sorts of material concerns, the issue of uneven representation that Henry Standing Bear had found challenging in regards to the SAI (where reservation and rural Indians were largely cut off from the meetings of the larger body and the decisions made by the leadership) were anticipated and ameliorated. And like Henry, McNickle believed it was essential to bridge any gap between so-called urban Indians (like himself) and reservation-based members.

In addition to former SAI members, much of the NCAI's initial success was due to the same or similar sorts of Indian and white networks created and harnessed previously by activists like Eastman, Montezuma, Bonnin, and Standing Bear. For example, when the ad hoc committee met to complete plans to launch the NCAI, McNickle decided to invite the American Association on Indian Affairs (AAIA) to help. He also thought it was a good idea to avoid assistance from Indian reform organizations such as the Indian Rights Association and the Home Missions Council because they were less progressive and more interested in supporting coercive assimilation practices. Such a decision departed from the strategies of the earlier generation, who often had to rely on these types of pro-assimilation groups despite disagreeing with some of the main aims of white reformers – as we have seen with Bonnin who relied on the patronage of white women's organizations even while she remained critical of their ability to completely understand and support her more radical views. In this new era of the IRA, founding members of the NCAI were eager to promote tribal sovereignty concerns, and although the AAIA was a predominantly white reform group, McNickle believed it was truly sympathetic to Indian issues and different from white reform groups from the previous period.[24]

Building relationships across like-minded reform groups was a critical strategy that the earlier cohort of Indian intellectuals had used to organize their own pan-tribal groups and to promote themselves as individuals. Thus, many of the political and cultural strategies the NCAI members used were indebted to the reform work of figures like Eastman and Bonnin, among others. The multi-public networking that Luther Standing Bear drew on, for instance, as he combined politics with a performance career, continued into and well beyond the 1930s. McNickle and others found ways to build support for Native activism as well as cultural change given their ties to a range of publics, which stemmed from different arenas in print culture and public policy. Another similarity with regards to the formation of the NCAI and the earlier work of Native political reformers is that several had graduated from Carlisle and the Haskell Institute. And yet an important difference were the large numbers who had also attended four-year colleges. The majority, roughly 80 percent, also had some ties to the BIA. Following the passage of the IRA, many founding members had served on IRA-chartered tribal councils. So education and employment with the federal government, which were both components of the Progressive Era's engagement with the "Indian Question," remained critical factors for New Deal Native activists. Unfortunately, another similarity between the early years of the NCAI (from 1944 until 1955) and the previous generation's attempts at political reform was a stark gender disparity within the group's membership. In the beginning, only 10 percent of registered delegates were women. Fortunately, by the 1950s more than half of the membership was female.[25]

In addition to his work with the NCAI, and as the first director of the Newberry Library's Center for American Indian History, McNickle helped found the Department of Anthropology at the University of Saskatchewan, Regina. There he was able to continue his work as a self-proclaimed, vocal proponent of Native American rights to self-determination, cultural preservation, and continued access to higher education – all goals that he had articulated in his article from 1938. Most importantly he was able to reshape the field of anthropology to hold its practitioners more accountable for their work with Native communities. McNickle, like Standing Bear and others from the generation before him, had succeeded in urban America and remained self-identified with the life he had on the reservation. His voice and the stories he told represented Native verbal arts and tribal perspectives.

As an intellectual descendent of Eastman, Montezuma, Bonnin, and Standing Bear, McNickle sought ways to dramatically engage with white America so that he might push for better understandings of Indian politics, culture, and history. In fact, as much as this book is a collection of biographies and stories by distinct individuals, it is also a cumulative history of the ways these individuals influenced one another and collectively reshaped how Native and non-Native people alike would come to see the past, present, and future regarding Indian policy in the United States. Their efforts aimed to help everyone recognize the centrality of Native participation in American culture whether on the stage, on the screen, in the courtroom, or in the pages of a book.

All four intellectuals featured in this book, along with the networks of Indian and non-Indian supporters with whom they worked, were committed to reforming U.S. Indian policy as well as reshaping attitudes in American society with regards to Indian identity and history. They were also connected to each other through the rhetoric of uplift they used to push against denigrating portrayals of Indian people highlighted by the popularity of cultural work, like Western films and novels. Standing Bear's cultural politics connect to efforts made by Eastman, Montezuma, and Bonnin given how he championed and criticized aspects of U.S. citizenship as a means through which Native people could improve their situation in America. Similarly, Eastman and Bonnin both engaged literary audiences, mostly white ones, to read about Indian life based on their own experiences. They succeeded in not only garnering new sorts of attention for the literary worlds Native authors created at the turn of the twentieth century but demonstrated to other Indian readers how Native writers might use poetic work to make political arguments, sometimes overtly and sometimes not.

No doubt McNickle's cohort had read or were somewhat familiar with the works of the Native authors who preceded them. Perhaps they had ordered a copy of Montezuma's newsletter, *Wassaja*, or better yet their parents were among those who sent in letters to the editor that Montezuma later published. Sandwiched between Pokagon and McNickle, Montezuma was well positioned to engage in cosmopolitan circles of Chicago given his professional success as a physician and his consistent commitment to writing and speaking on behalf of Indian Country. As perhaps the most outspoken critic of the BIA among this early generation, Montezuma was more forthright in his critiques than Pokagon, but not as measured as McNickle. Nonetheless his presence in the city reminded those who read *Wassaja* and attended Montezuma's public talks that Native intellectuals were shapers of American modernity. In a similar way, Eastman, Bonnin, and Standing Bear fit within the Pokagon and McNickle generational bookends given their struggles to build careers as artists while working to represent Native American politics to the world.

The lessons all four figures taught McNickle, and the later generations who would tote Vine Deloria Jr.'s *Custer Died for Your Sins* around with them, are straightforward. Eastman led by example to tout the benefits of higher education as a writer and an accomplished public speaker. Montezuma used his newsletter, correspondence, and other forms of epistolary culture to create and participate in a range of Native and non-Native cultural and political networks. Bonnin's literary work, highly gendered and raced public performances, and political lobbying demonstrated the degree to which she needed to engage all three of these strategies to succeed in changing public opinion and federal policy regarding Indian affairs. And Luther Standing Bear's life as a professional performer helped him make inroads into different aspects of the entertainment industry to parlay his fame into a career as a writer and public voice for Indian rights. Like McNickle, these were Indian intellectuals who found ways to work through various reform organizations, many pan-tribal and interracial in nature, to reframe dominant expectations regarding the place of Indian people in America's past and also its present. Certainly they shared similar strategies when it came to the realm of performance and cultural politics. Their work through groups like the SAI and the National League for Justice to American Indians makes them the forerunners for Indian leaders who would create the NCAI and many who would become active participants in the Red Power movement. Both moments, that of the 1930s and that of the 1960s, required Native people to consider how best to garner public attention to find support for their political causes.

As much as the SAI and Eastman's generation had to rely on public events that often hinged on the popularity of Indian performativity to promote their political aims, bring in new members, and procure the support of non-Indian patrons, so too did the NCAI have to grapple with fraught representational politics. The stakes remained the same: how to critique representations of Indian people and Indian life that stemmed more from an American imaginary than a Native reality. For McNickle, this came to a head with an unauthorized publicity stunt organized by NCAI members George LaMotte and Dan Madrano, whom McNickle had disparagingly referred to as "phony publicity hounds."[26]

In May 1945, LaMotte arranged for the NCAI, along with local groups, to sponsor a reception, luncheon, broadcast, and parade to honor Ira Hayes, noted Pima war veteran, at Soldier Field in Chicago. Despite LaMotte's enthusiasm for public events to celebrate Indianness, no one from the executive committee of the NCAI had approved such an approach. LaMotte personally led the parade of seventy-five Indians dressed in traditional attire as they staged a reenactment of the flag raising at Iwo Jima in front of 60,000 people. This was not quite the same performance as Simon Pokagon ringing a copy of the Liberty Bell in 1893, or Charles Eastman's reenactment of Samson Occom to celebrate Dartmouth's founding mission. Still, embedded within the pageantry surrounding Hayes' public appearance were dominant, mostly white expectations regarding Native men as natural warriors who could represent an exceptional part of America's military fabric, even if they were not fully accepted into all sectors of American society. McNickle was not at all happy with such a stunt. He complained that Madrano and LaMotte had used the event for their own self-promotion. Furthermore, he argued it encouraged stereotypes and produced negative publicity for the NCAI. As a behind-the-scenes technician, McNickle was so upset he threatened to quit until NCAI president Johnson could control the two men. For McNickle, and many others in the NCAI cohort, the strategy of Indianized performance seemed out of date given that they were now more invested in organizing and lobbying and therefore moving away from the strategies of cultural politics that had characterized the generation before them. Following McNickle's outrage, Heacock tried to soothe the situation by saying that the "Hayes stunt" had actually led to positive publicity for the organization. Still, the issue at hand was an old one, which was familiar to previous generations of Indian activists and is still alive today, which is just how, if you are Native, to seek out public interest in your cause without relying on familiar, often derogatory, performative tropes.[27]

During the 1960s and 1970s, Native reformers reversed direction once again. And, to some extent, they returned to the strategies that had characterized the early twentieth-century cohort's politics of cultural representation. This was a departure from the NCAI members, who were less inclined to this approach even though they had set up the structure to allow for the alliance of culture and politics that characterized Indian activism in the 1960s. During the Red Power movement, most young Indian activists said no to inside game playing with lobbying and politicking; instead they took to the streets. A striking example of this strategy was the occupation of the deserted federal prison on Alcatraz Island in San Francisco Bay on November 20, 1969. Referring to the 1868 Treaty with the Sioux, a group of eighty-nine Native Americans, mostly college students, seized the island on behalf of "Indians of All Tribes." They demanded federal funds to remake the site into a cultural and educational center. This objective recalled the aims of both the NCAI and the SAI. Although unsuccessful in achieving the stated goals, the event raised the profile of what later became known as the Red Power movement.

At the forefront of Red Power was the American Indian Movement (AIM), founded in 1968 in Minneapolis, Minnesota. With young and militant leaders and a mostly urban Indian membership, AIM was organized to work for Indian civil rights in cities, not unlike the Black Panthers and Brown Berets. AIM was able to play a major role in building a network of urban Indian centers, churches, and philanthropic organizations. The visible actions of AIM members enabled them to attract attention from the news media and to inspire the creation of local chapters, as well as writing about American Indian political issues. Also during this time, many young Indians began to turn to their elders to learn tribal ways, including traditional dress and spiritual practices. Like the response to the IRA, Native leaders and community members wanted to maintain American Indian communities by promoting self-government at the tribal level.

After three and a half years of being in America's spotlight through a series of guerrilla theater tactics, AIM "could highlight a problem, but failed to make a compelling case for its own vision of change," according to Paul Chaat Smith and Robert Warrior in *Like a Hurricane: The Indian Movement from Alcatraz to Wounded Knee* – their landmark study of Red Power. Jerry Wilkinson, the executive director of the National Indian Youth Council (NIYC), also offered a critique of AIM's failure, citing two main weaknesses: "It did not create a tradition of people relentlessly, ceaselessly, and uncompromisingly pursuing a long-range goal," and it was "terribly anti-intellectual."[28] Wilkinson noted too that the telephone had replaced correspondence and that Indian leaders rarely wrote letters or articles anymore so that "intellectual growth in the Indian community over the last twenty years has been next to zero."[29] Wilkinson's critique was not entirely valid given that he was speaking from the vantage point of the 1980s, which had witnessed an impressive growth in Native American literary studies and the creation of Native American studies programs as well as major shifts in the field of American Indian history – all of which suggest intellectual ambitions remained salient components of Native life. Still, Wilkinson's critique is instructive. By reflecting on these two types of failings in activism and political organizing from the 1960s, it is easier to distinguish this period from the earlier era and a generation of Native leaders involved with the NCAI and those who had formed the SAI. Native reformers from both of these previous eras strongly emphasized education and intellectual frameworks as necessary components of pan-tribal reform work.[30]

The takeover of Alcatraz in 1969 and similar events also demonstrated that political theater was still a vital tactic for waging a war on American settler-colonialism.[31] The publicity surrounding this event provides a historical through-line connecting members of AIM with earlier Native reformers, especially the Indian intellectuals who figured most prominently in the early twentieth century, because they sought strategic ways to publicly engage Indianness for personal and also larger political purposes. Despite a decline in activity and extreme financial hardship (brought on by having to fight the federal government in legal battles that bankrupted the group), Smith and Warrior note, the AIM made important gains during this period: "It was also a season of struggle for power and respect, for treaty rights and personal validation, for economic and political justice. Most importantly, it gave thousands of Indians a raison d'etre, an opportunity to be important to their own communities."[32] Therefore, however cloudy the future would seem, the late 1960s and early 1970s marked a brief time when Indians did unexpected things to challenge American society with the hope of changing everything. Many of their strategies had their roots in the efforts of earlier generations, who knew well how to organize and promote a reform agenda using cultural tropes and highly visible public performances. Any failure of AIM to fully embrace an intellectual framework that could enable them to more adequately organize their activism into a fully fledged movement with a long-term goal seems to suggest that the lessons of McNickle and the NCAI as well as the multifaceted strategies and commitments of Eastman's cohort to education, networking, writing, and performance are all the more important to remember. Perhaps now the "edgy, unpredictable creature that challenged American power"[33] known as AIM might be re-envisioned and reactivated into a new movement that keeps the long history and traditions of Native intellectual work in their thoughts and their tactics.

Coda

Simon Pokagon and D'Arcy McNickle have become known for significant literary and political achievements. They lived several generations apart and were separated even further by different sets of cultural expectations for Indianness that they could navigate. Certainly, Montezuma might serve as a bridge figure given his work and political activity based out of Chicago during the early decades of the twentieth century. Examining the life, writings, and political activism of McNickle demonstrates the continued significance of the themes of education, epistolary culture, publishing, and performance in relation to Indian intellectual storytelling and political organizing. These four themes were critical factors in enabling McNickle to build a career for himself and, often, to become the spokesperson for the next generation of Indian people. In many ways, the story of McNickle's life functions as a through-line for readers of Indian history by moving from the political and cultural history of the 1880s to the 1930s and beyond.

Returning to 1893 and the World's Columbian Exposition in Chicago, could Pokagon ever imagined a future where his friend Montezuma would be a doctor and a political writer? Where McNickle would return to the same city several decades later to direct the Center of American Indian History at the Newberry Library, less than four miles from where Pokagon had addressed fairgoers on Chicago Day? We will never know. But the Native intellectual leaders who lived, wrote, and performed in the years in between understood why Pokagon had sought to rebuke his audience rather than celebrate the arrival of Columbus and the subsequent influx of white settlers along the shores of Lake Michigan. Like the students who seized Alcatraz, Pokagon reclaimed Chicago as his city to indigenize an American space. He stood on the stage that day to remind everyone present about the significance of this claim. His rhetoric necessarily engaged a nineteenth-century audience's ears and so he could not use the same bold statements made by leaders like Russell Means and Dennis Banks. But Pokagon spoke as an Indian nonetheless, and like Charles Eastman he spoke on behalf of the Red Man's race because there was a lot the world had to learn about Native American people.

Today, in the United States of America, debates among, between, and within Indian nations continue to focus on how to determine and define the boundaries of Indian ethnic identity and tribal citizenship. From the 1880s, following the passage of the Dawes Act and later the Curtis Act, and into the 1930s, after the Indian Citizenship Act (1924) and the "Indian New Deal" (1934), many Native people participated in similar debates as they confronted white cultural expectations regarding what it meant to be an Indian in modern American society. Anticipating contemporary discussions, Native intellectuals of the early twentieth century asked hard questions about ethnicity and authenticity, particularly in relation to their status as new citizens of the United States. Although separated by time, many contemporary debates resonate with the ways that this first generation of urban Indian intellectuals grappled with representational politics. Those politics centered on the ways they performed and narrated "Indianness" with regard to their individual subjectivities. These strategic performances had to grapple with essentialisms (like primitivism) – and derogatory racialized representations (like the noble savage) – which were part of larger discourses aimed to define and confine Indian people by relegating them to America's premodern past, suggesting their power lay in fiction, memory, and nostalgia rather than in history and politics. Charles Eastman, Carlos Montezuma, Gertrude Bonnin, and Luther Standing Bear each understood the contours of these discourses and found ways to mobilize them for their own advancement and on behalf of other Indian people in the United States. They wanted to change how everyone viewed Indian history and at the same time to increase Native participation in the political systems of their age. Their Indian-based dialogue has continued to influence contemporary concerns among and between tribal nations, the U.S. government, and diverse sets of ethnic and racial groups in American society, as well as the wider world beyond it.

Notes

1   D'Arcy McNickle, *The Surrounded* (1936), 5. Reprint published by Dodd, Mead, New York, 1964, 1978.

2   Dorothy R. Parker, *Singing an Indian Song: A Biography of D'Arcy McNickle* (Lincoln: University of Nebraska Press, 1992) and "D'Arcy McNickle," in *The New Warriors: Native American Leaders since 1900* (Lincoln: University of Nebraska Press, 2001). David Martinez, ed., *The American Indian Intellectual Tradition: An Anthology of Writings from 1772 to 1972* (Ithaca, NY: Cornell University Press).

3   Martinez, ed., *The American Indian Intellectual Tradition*, 269.

4   The IRA was perhaps the most significant initiative of John Collier Sr., commissioner of the BIA from 1933 to 1945. He had worked on Indian issues for ten years prior to his appointment, particularly with the American Indian Defense Association. He had intended to reverse some of the worst government policies and provide ways for American Indians to reestablish sovereignty and self-government, to reduce the losses of reservation lands, and to establish ways for Indians to build economic self-sufficiency. Various other interests effected changes to the legislation that reduced protections for Indians and preserved oversight by the BIA.

5   Several scholars have written about the literary contributions of McNickle's novel. This conclusion aims to point out the political connections between his text and his activist work as well as the cultural context that gave rise to McNickle himself and how he may in fact be an inheritor of the Eastman cohort. For more literary interpretations of McNickle's first work see: Paul Whitehouse, "Seeing Red: Violence and Cultural Memory in D'Arcy McNickle's *The Surrounded*," *Dandelion* Vol. 2, No. 1, 2011; Parker, *Singing an Indian Song*; John Purdy, *Word Ways: The Novels of D'Arcy McNickle* (1990); John Purdy, ed., *The Legacy of D'Arcy McNickle: Writer, Historian, Activist* (1996); James Ruppert, *D'Arcy McNickle* (1988); Robert Dale Parker, "Who Shot the Sheriff: Storytelling, Indian Identity, and the Marketplace of Masculinity in D'Arcy McNickle's *The Surrounded*," *Modern Fiction Studies* Vol. 43, No. 4, Winter, 1997, 898–932.

6   *Indians at Work* Vol. 4, No. 11, January 15, 1937, subtitle "A News Sheet for Indians and the Indian Service," Bureau of Indian Affairs, Smithsonian Libraries, Washington, DC.

7   Although the subtitle for the magazine varies, it has been "An emergency conservation news sheet for ourselves" as well as "A news sheet for Indians and the Indian Service." For more on the archives related to the magazine *Indians at Work*, see Records of the Bureau of Indian Affairs, Record Group 75.14.12, "Records of the Civilian Conservation Corps-Indian Division," National Archives, Washington, DC.

8   Martinez, ed., *The American Indian Intellectual Tradition*, 269.

9   Ibid.

10 There is already an impressive array of scholarship on the "Indian New Deal" era, and as such, this conclusion merely engages with the main sources in order to provide the political and cultural context of this period as the time when Charles Eastman (1939), Luther Standing Bear (1939), and Gertrude Bonnin (1938) died (Carlos Montezuma having passed away much earlier in 1923). Thus, what follows is not an exhaustive historiography but points to the main sources relevant for my readings in this chapter. Kenneth R. Philp, *John Collier's Crusade for Indian Reform, 1920–1954* (Tucson: University of Arizona Press, 1977); Lawrence C. Kelly, *The Assault on Assimilation: John Collier and the Origins of Indian Policy Reform* (Albuquerque, University of New Mexico Press, 1983); Robert Fay Schrader, *The Indian Arts & Crafts Board: An Aspect of New Deal Policy* (Albuquerque, University of New Mexico Press, 1983).

11 Martinez, ed., *The American Indian Intellectual Tradition*, 270.

12 Ibid., 272.

13 Ibid., 272.

14 Ibid., 274.

15 Ibid., 274.

16 Kenneth R. Philp, "Termination: A Legacy of the Indian New Deal," *The Western Historical Quarterly* Vol. 14, No. 2, April 1983, 165–80.

17 Martinez, ed., *The American Indian Intellectual Tradition*, 275.

18 J. MacMurrough, "From the Inside: The Surrounded, by D'Arcy McNickle," *The New Masses*, March 3, 1936, 24.

19 Whitehouse, "Seeing Red," 1.

20 Parker, "Who Shot the Sheriff," 1.

21 For some examples from Vine Deloria Jr. see: *Custer Died for Your Sins* (1969), *God Is Red: A Native View of Religion* (1972), and *Red Earth, White Lies: Native Americans and the Myth of Scientific Fact* (1995).

22 Thomas W. Cowger, *The National Congress of American Indians: The Founding Years* (Lincoln: University of Nebraska Press, 1999), 41.

23 Ibid., 40.

24 Ibid., 35.

25 Ibid., 41.

26 Ibid., 45.

27 For more on Hayes' stunt see: ibid., 46.

28 Paul Chaat Smith and Robert Allen Warrior, *Like a Hurricane: The Indian Movement from Alcatraz to Wounded Knee* (New York: New Press, 1996), 275–6.

29 Ibid.

30 For more on the roles American Indians played in Red Power see: Bradley Shreve, *Red Power Rising: The National Indian Youth Council and the Origins of Native Activism* (Norman: University of Oklahoma Press, 2011).

31 Smith and Warrior, *Like a Hurricane*, 269.

32 Ibid., 277.

33 Ibid., 279.

Afterword

During the summer of 2000 I took my first road trip to cross the contiguous United States. It began in Brooklyn, New York and ended in San Francisco, California. Like many road trips, this was not just a journey through time and across space, but an opportunity to explore new and old places. It was during the second week of driving that I and my fellow travelers began to explore South Dakota. Although we were taking a strategic combination of Interstates 80 and 90 for our east-to-west voyage, we made an important detour after we reached the city of Sioux Falls, which is where we spent the Fourth of July. So on July 5, we headed north up Route 29 toward Sisseton, a small town that sits at the intersection of Route 29 and State Road 81.

For the first time in my life I was about to visit the Sisseton-Wahpeton Reservation where my grandmother, Ethel Hemminger, had been born and where some of my more distant relatives still lived. I knew little about this place, given that Ethel and her parents, having received monetary compensation for their allotments from the Office of Indian Affairs, packed up most of the family and their belongings to move to Southern California during the 1920s. There, in different parts of Los Angeles County, they spent the remainder of their lives working in show business. As part of Hollywood's burgeoning film industry, they mostly played the parts of extras in Westerns, although later my great grandfather and great-uncle would find steady employment in Disneyland's "Indian Village," a focal point of Frontierland in the then brand new theme park. Working in film and for Disney enabled my relatives to earn a decent enough living to support themselves and their children and to meet a rising number of Native Americans who were themselves new to the Los Angeles area. In fact, as Indian people traveled from South Dakota they also came from Oklahoma, New Mexico, Maine, and Washington, among other places, to join the world that Luther Standing Bear and the earliest Native actors had begun to build a decade earlier. Well into the 1930s, '40s, and '50s a pan-tribal Native community was forming in Southern California, where my father grew up with memories of going to socialize at the local "Indian club." This story of Native intellectuals and the networks they traveled was not about the Indian world built in Hollywood, but rather the political, cultural, and economic conditions that necessitated the mass migration of my relatives and other Indian people across the United States. They left the Dakotas in the hopes of finding better career opportunities and living conditions in California, through film and other forms of popular entertainment.

Back in 2000, as we drove toward the BIA office at Sisseton, I had no idea what to make of this unfamiliar place. I felt strangely shy about asking anyone we saw for directions. Yet as I walked toward the BIA office I felt a vigorous sense of purpose. I knew there would be some information pertaining to my family's history somewhere in the agency's files. After all, this was an archive of sorts, with records of American imperialism as much as land holdings for the Hemmingers. After a couple of phone calls to my father, the immediate heir to our family lands and therefore the only one the BIA recognized to receive any information, the young woman at the desk gave me permission to view a large set of maps. Moving through each piece of paper in this pile of photocopies, she highlighted small squares, parcels really, which were subsections of collectively owned lands. It was dizzying and curious. What did I find when I looked at these maps? That my family could claim 1/54 of this piece of land over here, or 1/322 of this one over there, or perhaps a little bit more, perhaps even 1/16 of this section way over there. It was very confusing and unnerving.

After looking at the various highlighted sections and talking with the office staff, I learned that although we had these shares, so did other Native people. I began to consider how they might use these claims. Because much of this land was not useful for farming or anything else, the tribal government of the Lake Traverse Indian Reservation decided that a good way to administer the use of collectively owned lands was to lease it, and each of us would then be paid according to the fraction of our individual shares. I still get checks once a year (and they aren't big) from the U.S. Treasury for this purpose. What I learned that day was that the U.S. federal government was often (if not always) the highest bidder when it came to leases, so it was nearly always the primary lessees of my family's lands. Interesting and strange, I thought. As I stood there looking at my maps, I decided it was time to get on the road again and go look at some of this land with my own eyes, perhaps to figure out how one might use it. After a short drive (and some helpful directions from the BIA office) we went to check out a section.

What did I see? Lots of tall grass growing, and not much else. Apparently our tribal government had decided to lease these parcels for grazing. In reality, most of it was fallow, only useful as a crossroads, and none of it situated at the intersection of State and Main, but rather the type of liminal and placeless crossroads that no one was apt to travel through or to. What I wondered at that moment, scanning the horizon filled with scrubby little trees and miles and miles of grasses, was how all of this could have happened. How could it be that my people, my ancestors who had known and occupied vast stretches of the Great Lakes region as well as areas to the west and north (including parts of Canada) no longer really used their own land? How could it be that the economy of this particular reservation community was largely supported by two small and not so profitable casinos and the BIA? Why were the market's shelves mostly empty and only half of the fluorescent ceiling lights on? In addition, how could it be that after so many military and legal battles, the federal government still got to use this land however it wanted, even when that meant not using it at all?

I yearned to know more about the history of Indian affairs and policy, and also about the lives of the people who had once lived here and those who had left, as my grandmother had done. I wanted answers to help me figure out how I might interpret all the strange highlighted parts on this set of BIA maps and the cultural consequences of dividing up vast stretches that had once been known, used collectively, and mapped by Indian people in their own ways. It was this experience that inspired the research for this book, which led to a different sort of journey altogether.

The archival research necessary to write this collective cultural biography led me again to travel across the United States, but in a more purposeful way. In search of answers to these questions, I went to Dartmouth College for graduate school and found among the school's archives the personal papers of an important alumnus from the nineteenth century: Charles Eastman. I did not know then as I do now that Charles Eastman was, like my father and me, part of the Santee Dakota peoples. He had traveled across some of the same lands that I had just begun to know. Like my grandmother, he had also chosen to leave them. He left at a young age in search of an education and in search of answers, because not unlike today, the Dakota people of the nineteenth century were struggling to navigate cultural, economic, and polit-ical changes in their already uneasy relationship with the U.S. government. Eastman wanted to have a voice in those changes. He sought citizenship not because he wanted to pledge allegiance to the United States but because he wanted to have a stronger hand in changing the policies of a government that been intervening in the lives of Dakota people for far too long. And like him, Carlos Montezuma, Gertrude Bonnin, and Luther Standing Bear found ways to add their voices to discussions concerning Indian policy. They often, although not always, worked through culture to influence politics, in order to shift public perceptions of Indian history and Indian people. After several trips to different archives I discovered that the details of their lives and the larger frame for this cultural history began to emerge; it became clearer still that these four figures were not alone but rather were members of a larger network of Indian intellectuals.

Following the unexpected connection between Eastman's history and that of my own family, and in preparation to visit archives, I began to ask a new set of questions in regard to Eastman and his Indian contemporaries. I knew he could not have been alone in his pursuit of education, his use of publishing to teach Americans, or his ability to perform a particular politics on local and national stages across the United States and in Europe. How did an individual like Eastman maintain ties to pan-tribal networks as he crafted his own Indian subjectivity? In addition, how did he and other figures balance the concerns of Native publics with those of their white readers? Eventually, I set out to write a cultural history of the first generation of urban Indian intellectuals to trace their efforts in mobilizing and revising concepts like citizenship, assimilation, and modernity. With this collective cultural biography, I have begun to answer these questions. Moreover, I found that to tell the story of these writers, performers, and power brokers I needed to suture together just how their cultural work shaped and reflected their politics. All the time I was hoping to come to a better understanding of the highlighted maps that I had held in my hands back in the summer of 2000.

Indeed, the driving force behind telling a narrative based on Eastman, Montezuma, Bonnin, and Standing Bear was to examine them as members of a wider world of Indian people and a collective movement that could be mapped in material ways. In other words, looking at the actual times and places that these figures could have and did meet one can see the ways they moved through social, political, and cultural spaces, and how their mobility was critical to the creation of pan-Indian reform organizations and public meetings. Moreover, as powerful as they could each be in getting their ideas out to people through letters and through the publication of articles, newsletters, and books, they each had immense influence when they took to the public stage to give a lecture and address an audience in person. With this book I have aimed to map out their travels. I have also aimed to map out abstract concepts to illustrate the ways meaning takes shape and changes how Indianness was produced by expectations that Native and non-Native people generated during these moments of public performance. This book has offered close readings of texts, images, and public performances to point to the myriad ways these particular Indian figures made their own journeys across the United States throughout the 1880s and into the 1930s. It has signaled the other Native people they knew and worked with in regards to reforming politics as much as culture. Ultimately, my hope is that this story helps us uncover large portions of U.S. history that have remained on the margins of the historical record, both to bring me closer to understanding why my ancestors lost control over so much of their lands, and to bring all of us closer to understanding the centrality of American Indian people in the making of American culture and society.

Appendix

In writing this collective cultural biography a central point that has emerged is the fact that this cohort of Indian intellectuals participated (sometimes as members, at other times as leaders) in a number of reform organizations. Many of these groups had the same or similar-sounding names, which can lead to a bit of confusion. These Native leaders also sought out white progressive allies, and in these instances found support from reform groups composed predominantly of white men and women. In order to assist the reader in locating these different groups I have made the following table as a reference guide, and noted when organizations were primarily white; otherwise they were Indian.

Organization	Key Figures	Location	Period
Society for American Indians (SAI) Although primarily formed by and for Indians, many white allies also became associate members	Founded by: Charles Eastman, Henry Standing Bear, Carlos Montezuma, Laura Cornelius, Thomas Sloan, Charles Dagenett	First meeting: The Ohio State University Columbus, OH	1911–23
National Council of American Indians (NCAI)	Gertrude Bonnin, President Raymond Bonnin, Secretary	Washington, DC	1926–38

Organization	Key Figures	Location	Period
National Congress of American Indians (Although distinct from the "National Council" formed by Bonnin, this group is referred to by the same acronym of NCAI)	J. B. Milam D'Arcy McNickle Vine Deloria Jr.	Washington, DC	1944 to present
Northwest Federation of American Indians (NFAI) Formed by landless tribes living in Puget Sound	William Bishop	Port Townsend, WA (western Washington)	1913–?
Indian Actors Association (IAA) Formed as branch of the Screen Actors Guild (SAG)	Jim Thorpe Luther Standing Bear	Los Angeles, CA	1936–?
National League for Justice to American Indians (NLJAI)	Marian Campbell Luther Standing Bear William S. Hart E. A. Brininstool Lucullus McWhorter Nipo Strongheart	Los Angeles, CA	1931–?
Lake Mohonk Conference Also referred to themselves as the "Friends of the Indians" (An annual meeting mostly for white progressives)	Albert K. Smiley Alice C. Fletcher (ethnologist)	Lake Mohonk, NY	1883–1916
Indian Rights Association (IRA) (A white humanitarian group dedicated to federal U.S. Indian policy)	Herbert Welsh Matthew Sniffen Lawrence Lindley Charles C. Painter Samuel M. Brosius	Philadelphia, PA	1882–1986
Boston Indian Citizenship Committee (BCC) (mostly white organization)	Founded by Boston progressives interested in an association for the protection of the rights of Indians	Boston, MA	1879–?

Bibliography

Archival and Manuscript Material Abbreviations

CAE   Charles Alexander Eastman Papers, 1891–1983, MS 829, Rauner Special Collections Library, Dartmouth College, Hanover, NH

CM   Carlos Montezuma Papers, Wisconsin State Historical Society, Madison, Wisconsin

EAB   Earl Alonzo Brininstool Collection, 1850–1945, Dolph Briscoe Center for American History, The University of Texas at Austin

EGE   Elaine Goodale Eastman Papers, Sophia Smith Collection, Smith College, MA

LR, RG 75   "Letters Received," *Records of the Bureau of Indian Affairs* (Record Group 75), Federal Records in the National Archives of the United States, Washington, DC

MSS 1704, LTPSC   Gertrude and Raymond Bonnin Collection; 20th–21st Century Western and Mormon Americana; L. Tom Perry Special Collections, Harold B. Lee Library, Brigham Young University

MSS 299   William F. Hanson Collection; University Archives; L. Tom Perry Special Collections, Harold B. Lee Library, Brigham Young University

PCM, Larner 1983   *The Papers of Carlos Montezuma*, M.D. [microform]: including the papers of Maria Keller Montezuma Moore and the papers of Joseph W. Latimer / edited by John William Larner Jr., Scholarly Resources, Inc. 1983 through the Newberry Library, Chicago, IL

Other Archival Collections

Braun Library, Southwest Museum part of the Gene Autry National Center, Los Angeles, CA

British Newspaper Archive, Bristol, England

Brooklyn Newsstand Collection, Brooklyn Public Library, accessed April 21, 2014

Carlos Montezuma Collection, 1887–1980 (bulk 1887–1922), Department of Archives & Special Collections, Arizona State University Libraries, MS CM MSS-60

Carlos Montezuma Papers, Center for Southwest Studies, Fort Lewis College, Durango, CO

Cumberland County Historical Society, and the Richard Henry Pratt Papers, WA MSS S-1174, Beinecke Rare Book and Manuscript Library, Yale Collection of Western Americana, Yale University, New Haven, CT

Eugene Gruenberg Papers (MS Mus 234.2). Houghton Library, Harvard University, "Eulogy of Chief Plenty Coups of the Crows: Speech of Hon. Scott Leavitt of Montana in the House of Representatives," *Congressional Record Seventy-Second Congress, First Session* (Mar. 5, 1932).

Helen Gilkison Papers, Mss. 1901, 2175, Louisiana and Lower Mississippi Valley Collections, LSU Libraries, Baton Rouge, LA (bulk 1925–48)

John Collier Papers (MS 146), Manuscripts and Archives, Yale University Library

Lucullus Virgil McWhorter Papers, Manuscripts, Archives, and Special Collections, Washington State University Libraries, Pullman, WA

Melvin R. Gilmore Papers, 1905–1938, Bentley Historical Library, University of Michigan, Ann Arbor, MI

Manuscript 061, The Indian Rights Association pamphlets, Years: 1884–1985; bulk 1884–1934, Center of Southwest Studies, Fort Lewis College, Durango, CO

NAJA collection, Sequoya National Research Center, Little Rock, AR

Papers of Carlos Montezuma (1866–1923), Special Collections Library, University of Arizona, A-287

Papers of the Women's National Indian Association #9237, Division of Rare and Manuscript Collections, Cornell University Library, Ithaca, NY

Peter Iverson Collection, 1898–2002, Labriola National American Indian Data Center, ASU Libraries, MS LAB MSS-165

ProQuest Historical Newspapers: *Chicago Daily Tribune, Los Angeles Times, New York Times, Washington Post* (1881–1987)

Records of the Bureau of Indian Affairs, Record Group 75.14.12, "Records of the Civilian Conservation Corps-Indian Division," National Archives, Washington, DC

Seeley G. Mudd Manuscript Library, Princeton University, "The Association on American Indian Affairs Archives," Publications, Programs, and Legal and Organizational Files, 1851–1983. Filmed from the holdings of the Seeley G. Mudd Manuscript Library, Princeton University

Students and Alumnae Profiles and Statistics Collection, Archives and Special Collections, Mount Holyoke College, South Hadley, MA

Student Records, New England Conservatory Archives, Boston, MA

The Papers of Alice Cunningham Fletcher and Francis La Flesche, National Anthropological Archives, Smithsonian Institution, Washington, DC

Wassaja: Freedom's Signal for the Indians, March 1918, Special Collections, Newberry Library, Chicago, IL

William F. Cody Archive, Buffalo Bill Historical Center, Cody, WY

World Peace Foundation, records, 1899–1993, Digital Collections and Archives, Tufts University

Bibliography of Secondary Sources

Aleiss, Angela. *Making the White Man's Indian: Native Americans and Hollywood Movies*. Westport, CT: Praeger, 2005.

"Who Was the Real James Young Deer? The Mysterious Identity of the Pathè Producer Finally Comes to Light." *Bright Lights Film Journal* 80 (May 2013).

Alexander, Ruth Ann. "Elaine Goodale Eastman and the Failure of the Feminist Protestant Ethic." *Great Plains Quarterly* 8 (1988): 89–101.

Allen, Charles W. *From Fort Laramie to Wounded Knee: In the West That Was*. Lincoln: University of Nebraska Press, 2011.

"American's Women's History Online." *Facts on File*, 2007. http://www.fofweb.com/activelink2.asp?ItemID=WE42&iPin=AWWP0221&SingleRecord=True.

Anderson, Benedict. *Imagined Communities: Reflections on the Origin and Spread of Nationalism*. London: Verso Books, 1991.

Anzaldua, Gloria. *Borderlands/La Frontera, The New Mestiza*. San Francisco, CA: Aunt Lute Books, 1987.

Apess, William. *Son of the Forest, and Other Writings*. Edited by Barry O'Connell. Amherst: University of Massachusetts Press, 1997.

Apthekar, Herbert, ed. *Correspondence of W.E.B. Du Bois Volume 1, Selections, 1877–1934*. Amherst: University of Massachusetts Press, 1973.

Arnold, Oren. *Savage Son*. Albuquerque: University of New Mexico Press, 1951.

Bak, Richard. *Henry and Edsel: The Creation of the Ford Empire*. Hoboken, NJ: Wiley, 2003.

Baker, Lee D. *Anthropology and the Racial Politics of Culture*. Durham, NC: Duke University Press, 2010.

From Savage to Negro: Anthropology and the Construction of Race, 1896–1954. Berkeley: University of California Press, 1998.

Bal, Mieke, and Sherry Marx-Macdonald. *Traveling Concepts in the Humanities: A Rough Guide*. Toronto: University of Toronto Press, 2002.

Bank, Rosemary K. *Theatre Culture in America, 1825–1860*. Cambridge: Cambridge University Press, 1997.

Bannet, Eve Tavor, and Susan Manning, eds. *Transatlantic Stories and the History of Reading: Migrant Fictions 1720–1810*. Cambridge: Cambridge University Press, 2011.

Barnett, Leona G. "Este Cate Emunev; Red Man Always." *Chronicle of Oklahoma* 46 (Spring 1968): 20–40.

Barnum, P. T. *The Life of P.T. Barnum, Written by Himself*. Urbana and Chicago: University of Illinois Press, 2000.

Batkin, Jonathan. *The Native American Curio Trade in New Mexico*. Santa Fe, NM: Wheelwright Museum of the American Indian, 2008.

Bayers, Peter L. "From the Deep Woods to Civilization and the Shaping of Native Manhood." *Studies in American Indian Literatures* 20, no. 3 (2008): 52–73.

Bear, Luther Standing. *Land of the Spotted Eagle*. Boston, MA: Houghton Mifflin Company, 1933.

My People the Sioux. Boston, MA: Houghton Mifflin Company, 1928.

Bederman, Gail. *Manliness & Civilization: A Cultural History of Gender and Race in the United States, 1880–1917*. Chicago, IL: University of Chicago Press, 1996.

Bell, Betty Louise. "'If This Is Paganism…': Zitkala-Sa and the Devil's Language." In *Native American Religious Identity: Unforgotten Gods*, edited by Jace Weaver. Maryknoll, NY: Orbis, 1998.

Bellin, Joshua David, and Laura L. Mielke, eds. *Native Acts: Indian Performance, 1603–1832*. Lincoln: University of Nebraska Press, 2011.

Berkhofer, Robert. *Salvation and the Savage: An Analysis of Protestant Missions and American Indian Response, 1787–1862*. Lexington: University of Kentucky Press, 1965.

The White Man's Indian: Images of the American Indian from Columbus to the Present. New York: Random House, 1978.

Bernardin, Susan. "The Lessons of a Sentimental Education: Zitkala-Sa's Autobiographical Narratives." *Western American Literature* 32, no. 3 (November 1997): 212–38.

Bernstein, Bruce. "The Booth Sitters of Santa Fe's Indian Market: Making and Maintaining Authenticity." *American Indian Culture and Research Journal* 32, no. 3 (2007): 49–79.

Bhabha, Homi K. *The Location of Culture*. New York: Routledge Press, 1994.

Biolsi, Thomas. *Organizing the Lakota: The Political Economy of the New Deal on the Pine Ridge and Rosebud Reservations*. Tucson: University of Arizona Press, 1992.

Blackhawk, Ned. *Violence Over the Land: Indians and Empires in the Early American West*. Cambridge, MA: Cambridge University Press, 2009.

Blake, Casey Nelson. "The War and the Intellectuals." In *Beloved Community: The Cultural Criticism of Randolph Bourne, Van Wyck Brooks, Waldo Frank, and Lewis Mumford*. Chapel Hill: University of North Carolina Press, 1990.

Blum, Edward J., and Jason R. Young. *The Souls of W.E.B. Du Bois: New Essays and Reflections*. Macon, GA: Mercer University Press, 2009.

Bonnin, Gertrude. "A Warrior's Daughter." *Everybody's Magazine*, 1902.

"America, Home of the Red Man." *The American Indian Magazine* (Winter): 1919.

American Indian Stories. Washington, DC: Hayworth Publishing House, 1921.

American Indian Stories. Edited by Dexter Fisher. Lincoln: University of Nebraska Press, 1985.

"An Indian Teacher among Indians." *Atlantic Monthly* 85 (1900).

"Impressions of an Indian Childhood." *Atlantic Monthly* 28 (1900): 37–47.

Old Indian Legends. Boston, MA: Ginn and Company, 1901.

"School Days of an Indian Girl." *Atlantic Monthly* 85 (1900): 185–94.

"Soft Hearted Sioux." *Harper's Monthly*, 1901.

"The Trial Path." *Harper's Monthly*, October 1901.

"Why Am I a Pagan?" *Atlantic Monthly* 90 (1902): 801–3.

"Editor's Viewpoint: The Civilizing Power of Language." *The Quarterly Journal of the Society of American Indians* 4, no. 2 (June 2016): 126–8.

Boughey, Davidson. *The Film Industry*. London: Sir Isaac Pitman & Sons, 1921.

Boughner, Genevieve Jackson. *Women in Journalism: A Guide to the Opportunities and a Manual of the Technique of Women's Work for Newspapers and Magazines*. New York: Appleton, 1926.

Bowen, Nancy, and Jeff Bowen. *Indian Wills, 1911–1921: Records of the Bureau of Indian Affairs*. Baltimore, MD: Clearfield Company, 2007.

Boyd, Ann E. *Writing for Immortality: Women and the Emergence of High Literary Culture in America*. Baltimore, MD: Johns Hopkins University Press, 2004.

Bramen, Carrie Tirado. *Uses of Variety: Modern Americanism and the Quest for National Distinctiveness*. Cambridge, MA: Harvard University Press, 2001.

Brasser, Theodore. *Native American Clothing: An Illustrated History*. Ontario, Canada: Firefly Books, 2009.

Brinkley, Douglas G. *Wheels for the World: Henry Ford, His Company, and a Century of Progress*. New York: Penguin Books, 2003.

Brodhead, Richard H. *Cultures of Letters: Scenes of Reading and Writing in Nineteenth-Century America*. Chicago, IL: University of Chicago Press, 1993.

Brooks, James. *Captives & Cousins: Slavery, Kinship, and Community in the Southwest Borderlands*. Chapel Hill: University of North Carolina Press, 2002.

Brooks, Lisa. *The Common Pot: The Recovery of Native Space in the Northeast*. Minneapolis: University of Minnesota Press, 2008.

Browman, David L., and Stephen Williams. *Anthropology at Harvard: A Biographical History, 1790–1940*. Cambridge, MA: Peabody Museum Press, 2013.

Brown, Julie K. *Contesting Images: Photography and the World's Columbian Exposition*. Tucson: University of Arizona Press, 1994.

Brumble, David H. *American Indian Autobiography*. Lincoln: University of Nebraska Press, 2008.

Bsumek, Erika. *Indian-Made: Navajo Culture in the Marketplace, 1880–1940*. Lawrence: University of Kansas Press, 2008.

Burg, David F. *Chicago's White City of 1893*. Lexington: University of Kentucky Press, 1976.

Burgett, Bruce, and Glenn Hendler, eds. *Keywords for American Cultural Studies*. New York: New York University Press, 2007.

Burt, Ryan E. "'Sioux Yells' in the Dawes Era: Lakota 'Indian Play,' the Wild West, and the Literatures of Luther Standing Bear." *American Quarterly* 62, no. 3 (September 2010): 617–37.

Buscombe, Edward. *"Injuns!" Native Americans in the Movies*. London: Reaktion Books, Location Series, 2006.

Butler, Judith. *Bodies That Matter: On the Discursive Limits of Sex*. New York: Routledge Press, 1993.

——. *Gender Trouble: Feminism and the Subversion of Identity*. New York: Routledge Press, 1990.

Cahill, Cathleen D. *Federal Fathers & Mothers: A Social History of the United States Indian Service, 1869–1933*. Chapel Hill: University of North Carolina Press, 2011.

Calloway, Colin. *The Indian History of an American Institution: Native Americans and Dartmouth*. Hanover, NH: Dartmouth College Press, University Press of New England, 2010.

Carby, Hazel V. *Reconstructing Womanhood: The Emergence of the Afro-American Woman Novelist*. New York: Oxford University Press, 1987.

Carlson, David J. *Sovereign Selves: American Indian Autobiography and the Law*. Urbana: University of Illinois Press, 2006.

Carlson, Leonard. *Indians, Bureaucrats, and Land: The Dawes Act and the Decline of Indian Farming*. Santa Barbara, CA: Praeger, 1981.

Carnes, Mark C. *Secret Ritual and Manhood in Victorian America*. New Haven, CT: Yale University Press, 1989.

Carpenter, Cari. "Detecting Indianness: Gertrude Bonnin's Investigation of Native American Identity." *Wicazo Sa Review* 20, no. 1 (Spring 2005): 139–59.

Seeing Red: Anger, Sentimentality, and American Indians. Columbus: Ohio State University Press, 2008.

Cheng, Ann Anlin. *The Melancholy of Race: Psychoanalysis, Assimilation, and Hidden Grief*. Oxford: Oxford University Press, 2000.

Cherokee Strip Museum of Perry, Oklahoma. Accessed May 5, 2011. http://www.cherokee-strip-museum.org/index.html.

"Chief Standing Bear." *Internet Movie Database*, February 15, 2011. http://www.imdb.com/name/nm0822052/.

Child, Brenda. *Boarding School Seasons: American Indian Families, 1900–1940*. Lincoln: University of Nebraska Press, 1998.

Clark, Blue. *Lone Wolf v. Hitchcock: Treaty Rights and Indian Law at the End of the Nineteenth Century*. Lincoln: University of Nebraska Press, 1999.

Clark, Carol Lea. "Charles A. Eastman (Ohiyesa) and Elaine Goodale Eastman: A Cross-Cultural Collaboration." *Tulsa Studies in Women's Literature* 13, no. 2 (Autumn 1994).

Cohen, Matt. *The Networked Wilderness: Communicating in Early New England*. Minneapolis: University of Minnesota Press, 2010.

Cole, Douglas. *Franz Boas: The Early Years, 1858–1906*. Seattle: University of Washington Press, 1999.

Coolidge, Sherman. "The Function of the Society of American Indians." *The Quarterly Journal of the Society of American Indians* 2, no. 1 (March 1914): 186–90.

Cotera, Maria Eugenia. *Native Speakers: Ella Deloria, Zora Neale Hurston, Jovita González, and the Poetics of Culture*. Austin: University of Texas Press, 2008.

Cowger, Thomas W. *The National Congress of American Indians: The Founding Years*. Lincoln: University of Nebraska Press, 1999.

Craggs, R. "Situating the Imperial Archive: The Royal Empire Society Library 1868–1945." *Journal of Historical Geography* 34, no. 1 (2008): 48–67.

Crenshaw, Kimberle, ed. *Critical Race Theory: The Key Writings That Formed the Movement*, New York: New Press, 1996.

Crenshaw, Kimberle. "Mapping the Margins: Intersectionality, Identity Politics, and Violence against Women of Color." *Stanford Law Review* 43, no. 6 (July 1991): 1241–99.

Crum, Steven. "Almost Invisible: The Brotherhood of North American Indians (1911) and the League of North American Indians (1935)." *Wicazo Sa Review* 21, no. 1 (Spring 2006): 43–59.

Cummings, Denise K., ed. *Visualities: Perspectives on Contemporary American Indian Film and Art*. Lansing: Michigan State University Press, 2011.

Cummins, Maria. *The Lamplighter*. Boston, BA: John P. Jewett and Company, 1854.

Cutter, Martha J. "Zitkala-Sa's Autobiographical Writings: The Problems of a Canonical Search for Language and Identity." *MELUS: The Journal of the*

Society for the Study of the Multi-Ethnic Literature of the United States 19, no. 1 (Spring 1994): 31–45.

Danky, James, and Wayne Wiegan, eds. *Print Culture in a Diverse America.* Urbana: University of Illinois Press, 1998.

Davidan, John Thares. *A World of Crisis and Progress: The American YMCA in Japan, 1890–1930.* Cranbury, NJ: Associated University Presses, 1998.

Davidson, Cathy N., ed. *Reading in America: Literature & Social History.* Baltimore, MD: Johns Hopkins University Press, 1989.

Davidson, Cathy N., and Ada Norris, eds. *Zitkala-Sa: American Indian Stories, Legends, and Other Writings.* New York: Penguin Books, 2003.

Davidson, James West. *They Say: Ida B. Wells and the Reconstruction of Race.* New York: Oxford University Press, 2007.

Davis, Angela Y. *Women, Race & Class.* New York: Vintage Books, 1981.

Davis, Marguerite Norris. "An Indian Princess Comes into Her Own." *St. Nicholas* 50 (July 1923).

——— "Men and Women Whose Lives Count for the Red Man's Cause: Irene Eastman, Taluta, Soprano." *American Indian Magazine* 5 (December 1917).

Davis, Mike. *City of Quartz: Excavating the Future in Los Angeles.* New York: Vintage, 1992.

Davis, Ronald L. *William S. Hart: Projecting the American West.* Norman: University of Oklahoma Press, 2003.

Dearborn, Mary V. *Pocahontas's Daughters: Gender and Ethnicity in American Culture.* New York: Oxford University Press, 1986.

Deloria, Philip J. *Indians in Unexpected Places.* Lawrence: University of Kansas Press, 2004.

——— *Playing Indian.* New Haven, CT: Yale University Press, 1999.

Deloria Jr., Vine. *Custer Died for Your Sins: An Indian Manifesto.* New York: Avon Books, 1969.

Deloria Jr., Vine, and Clifford M. Lytle. *American Indians, American Justice.* Austin: University of Texas Press, 1983.

Densmore, Frances. *Teton Sioux Music and Culture.* Lincoln: University of Nebraska Press, 1992.

Derrida, Jacques. *Writing and Difference.* Translated by Alan Bass. Chicago, IL: University of Chicago Press, 1978.

Diamond, Elin, ed. *Performance and Cultural Politics.* London and New York: Routledge Press, 1996.

Diana, Vanessa Holford. "'Hanging in the Heart of Chaos': Bi-Cultural Limbo, Self-(Re)Presentation, and the White Audience in Zitkala-Sa's American Indian Stories." *Cimarron Review* 121 (1997): 154–72.

Dippie, Brian. *The Vanishing American: White Attitudes and U.S. Indian Policy.* Lawrence: University of Kansas Press, 1982.

Doolen, Andy. *Fugitive Empire: Locating Early American Imperialism.* Minneapolis: University of Minnesota Press, 2005.

Dowd, George E. *A Spirited Resistance: The North American Indians' Struggle for Unity, 1745–1815.* Baltimore, MD: Johns Hopkins University Press, 1992.

Du Bois, W. E. B. *The Souls of Black Folk.* Oxford: Oxford University Press, 1903.

——— "The Talented Tenth." In *The Negro Problem: A Series of Articles by Representative Negroes of To-Day.* New York: J. Pott and Company, 1903.

Dubois, Ellen Carroll. *Feminism and Suffrage: The Emergence of an Independent Women's Movement in America, 1848–1869.* Ithaca, NY: Cornell University Press, 1999.

Eastman, Charles. *From the Deep Woods to Civilization.* Boston, MA: Little, Brown and Company, 1916.

———. *Indian Scout Crafts and Lore.* New York: Dover Publications, 1974.

———. "My People: The Indians' Contribution to the Arts of America." *The Craftsman* 27 (November 1914).

———. *The Indian To-Day: The Past and Future of the First American.* New York: Doubleday and Company, 1915.

———. *Universal Races Congress.* Edited by Gustav Spiller. London and Boston, MA: P.S. King and Son; The World's Peace Foundation, 1911.

Eastman, Elaine Goodale. "All the Days of My Life." *South Dakota Historical Review* 2 (1937): 171–84.

———. *Pratt: The Red Man's Moses.* Norman: University of Oklahoma Press, 1935.

———. *Sister to the Sioux.* Edited by Kay Graber. Lincoln: University of Nebraska Press, 1978.

Ellensburg Daily. "Blind Tribesman Is Injured When Car Plunges off Road Embankment." April 18, 1930.

Elliot, Michael. *The Culture Concept: Writing and Difference in the Age of Realism.* Minneapolis: University of Minnesota Press, 2002.

Elrod, Eileen R. *Piety and Dissent: Race, Gender, and Biblical Rhetoric in Early American Autobiography.* Amherst: University of Massachusetts Press, 2008.

Enoch, Jessica. "Resisting the Script of Indian Education: Zitkala Sa and the Carlisle Indian School." *College English* 65, no. 2 (2002): 117–41.

Evans, Brad. *Before Cultures: The Ethnographic Imagination in American Literature, 1865–1920.* Chicago, IL: University of Chicago Press, 2005.

Fabian, Ann. *The Skull Collectors: Race, Science, and America's Unburied Dead.* Chicago, IL: University of Chicago Press, 2010.

Fanon, Franz. *Black Skin, White Masks,* New York: Grove Press (1967) 2008.

Farr, William E. *The Reservation Blackfeet, 1882–1945: A Photographic History of Cultural Survival.* Seattle: University of Washington Press, 1986.

Fent, Cindy, and Raymond Wilson. "Indians Off Track: Cody's Wild West and the Melrose Park Train Wreck of 1904." *American Indian Culture and Research Journal* 18, no. 3 (1994): 235–49.

Field Museum of Natural History. *The Arapaho Sun Dance: The Ceremony of the Offerings Lodge. Field Columbian Museum Publication, No. 75.* Chicago, IL: Field Museum of Natural History, 1903.

Filene, Peter. "The World Peace Foundation and Progressivism: 1910–1918." *The New England Quarterly* 36, no. 4 (December 1963).

Fisher, Dexter. "The Transformation of Tradition: A Study of Zitkala-Sa and Mourning Dove, Two Transitional American Indian Writers." Dissertation, City University of New York, 1979.

———. "Zitkala-Sa: The Evolution of a Writer." *American Indian Quarterly* 5 (1979): 229–38.

Fitzgerald, Michael Oren. *The Essential Charles Eastman (Ohiyesa).* Bloomington, IN: World Wisdom Inc., 2007.

"Five Views: An Ethnic Historic Site Survey for California." Accessed June 25, 2013. http://www.cr.nps.gov/history/online_books/5views/5views1.htm.

Flint, Kate. *The Transatlantic Indian, 1776–1930*. Princeton, NJ: Princeton University Press, 2008.

Floyd Jr., Samuel A. *The Power of Black Music: Interpreting Its History from Africa to the United States*. New York: Oxford University Press, 1995.

Flusser, Alan. *Dressing the Man: Mastering the Art of Permanent Fashion*. New York: Woodford: Harper Collins Publishers, 2002.

Forbes, Jack D. *The Indians in America's Past*. Englewood Cliffs, NJ: Prentice Hall, 1964.

Ford, Henry. *My Life and Work: An Autobiography of Henry Ford*. Alvin, TX: Halcyon Classics, 2009.

Foucault, Michel. *Discipline and Punish: The Birth of the Prison*. New York: Vintage, 1977.
　Power/Knowledge. New York: Vintage, 1980.
　The History of Sexuality, Vol. 2: The Use of Pleasure. New York: Vintage, 1985.
　"*Truth and Power*," an interview with Alesandro Fontana and Pasquale Pasquino. New York: Pantheon, 1977, 1980.

Frazer, Robert. *Forts of the West*. Norman: University of Oklahoma Press, 1965.

Fuss, Diana. *Essentially Speaking: Feminism, Nature, and Difference*. New York: Routledge Press, 1989.

Gaines, Kevin Kelly. *Uplifting the Race: Black Leadership, Politics, and Culture in the Twentieth Century*. Chapel Hill: University of North Carolina Press, 1996.

Gairola, Rahul K. "White Skin, Red Masks: 'Playing Indian' in Queer Images from Physique Pictorial 1957–67." *Liminalities: A Journal of Performance Studies* 8, no. 4 (September 2012).

Gambrell, Alice. *Women Intellectuals, Modernism, and Difference: Transatlantic Culture, 1919–1945*. Cambridge: Cambridge University Press, 1997.

Garrison, Tim. *The Legal Ideology of Removal: The Southern Judiciary and the Sovereignty of Native American Nations*. Athens: University of Georgia Press, 2002.

Gates Jr., Henry Louis. "Harlem on Our Minds." *Critical Inquiry* 24, no. 1 (Autumn 1997): 1–12.

Gere, Anne Ruggles. "An Art of Survivance: Angel De Cora at Carlisle," *American Indian Quarterly* 28, no. 3 & 4 (Summer/Fall 2004): 649–84.

Gevinson, Alan. *American Film Institute Catalog: Within Our Gates: Ethnicity in American Features Films, 1911–1960*. Berkeley: University of California Press, 1997.

Giddings, Paula. *When and Where I Enter: The Impact of Black Women on Race and Sex in America*. New York: W. Morrow, 1984.

Gilroy, Paul. *Against Race: Imagining Political Culture beyond the Color Line*, Cambridge, MA: Belknap Press, 2000.
　Black Atlantic: Modernity and Double Consciousness. Cambridge, MA: Harvard University Press, 1995. Originally published 1993.
　There Ain't No Black in the Union Jack: the Cultural Politics of Nation and Race, Chicago, IL: University of Chicago Press, 1987.

Ginzberg, Lori D. *Women and the Work of Benevolence: Morality, Politics, and Class in the Nineteenth-Century United States*. New Haven, CT: Yale University Press, 1992.

Gopinath, Gayatri. *Impossible Desires: Queer Diasporas and South Asian Public Cultures*. Durham, NC and London: Duke University Press, 2005.

Gramsci, Antonio. *Prison Notebooks*. London: Lawrence and Wishart, 1971, 5–23.

Graulich, Melody, and Stephen Tatum. *Reading the Virginian in the New West*. Lincoln: University of Nebraska Press, 2003.

Greenwald, Emily. *Reconfiguring the Reservation: The Nez Perces, Jicarilla Apaches, and the Dawes Act*. Albuquerque: University of New Mexico Press, 2002.

Guidotti-Hernandez, Nicole M. *Unspeakable Violence: Remapping U.S. and Mexican National Imaginaries*. Durham, NC: Duke University Press, 2011.

Gutierrez, Laura G. *Performing Mexicanidad: Vendidas Y Cabareteras on the Transnational Stage*. Austin: University of Texas Press, 2010.

Gutierrez, Ramon. *When Jesus Came the Corn Mothers Went Away: Marriage, Sexuality and Power in New Mexico, 1500–1846*. Palo Alto, CA: Stanford University Press, 1991.

Guzman, Isabel Molina. "Mediating Frida: Negotiating Discourses of Latina/o Authenticity in Global Media Representations of Ethnic Identity." *Critical Studies in Media Communication* 23, no. 3 (1996): 232–51.

Habermas, Jurgen. *The Structural Transformation of the Public Sphere: An Inquiry into Bourgeois*. Translated by Thomas Burger. Cambridge: Massachusetts Institute of Technology, 1991.

Hafen, P. Jane. "A Cultural Duet: Zitkala Sa and The Sun Dance Opera." *Great Plains Quarterly* 18, no. 2 (1998): 102–11.

——— "'Great Spirit Listen': The American Indian in Mormon Music." *Dialogue: A Journal of Mormon Thought*, 1985.

——— "Zitkala Sä." Edited by Frederick E. Hoxie. *Encyclopedia of North American Indians*. Boston, MA: Houghton Mifflin Company, 1996.

——— "Zitkala-Sa: Sentimentality and Sovereignty." *Wicazo Sa Review* 12, no. 2 (Fall 1997): 31–42.

Hagan, William Thomas. *The Indian Rights Association: The Herbert Welsh Years, 1882–1904*. Tucson: University of Arizona Press, 1985.

Halperin, David. *One Hundred Years of Homosexuality: And Other Essays on Greek Love*. New York: Routledge Press, 1989.

Hamilton, Ian. *A Gift Imprisoned: A Poetic Life of Matthew Arnold*. London: Bloomsbury, 1998.

Handley, William R., and Nathaniel Lewis, eds. *True West: Authenticity and the American West*. Lincoln: University of Nebraska Press, 2004.

Hannon, Charles. "Zitkala-Sa and the Commercial Magazine Apparatus." In *"The Only Efficient Instrument": American Women Writers and the Periodical, 1837–1916*, edited by Aleda Feinsod Cane and Susan Alves. Iowa City: University of Iowa Press, 2001.

Hanson, William F. *Sun Dance Land: A Survey of Sioux, Ute, and Shoshone and Other Related Religious Cultures in Sun Dance Worship*. Salt Lake City, UT: J. Grant Stephenson, 1967.

Harper, Charles A. *A Century of Public Teacher Education: The Story of the State Teachers Colleges as They Evolved from Normal Schools*. Greenport, CT: Greenwood Press, 1970.

Harring, Sidney. *Crow Dog's Case: American Indian Sovereignty, Tribal Law, and United States Law in the Nineteenth Century*. London: Cambridge University Press, 1994.

Harrison, Jonathan Baxter. *The Colleges and the Indians, and the Indian Rights Association*. Philadelphia, PA: The Indian Rights Association, 1888.

Harvard College Class of 1877 Seventh Report. Norwood, MA: Plimpton Press, 1917.

Hauptman, Lawrence M. *The Iroquois and the New Deal*. Syracuse, NY: Syracuse University Press, 1981.

——— "The Iroquois School of Art: Arthur C. Parker and the Seneca Arts Project, 1935–1941." *New York History* 60 (July 1979): 253–312.

Heflin, Ruth J. *"I Remain Alive": The Sioux Literary Renaissance*. Syracuse, NY: Syracuse University Press, 2000.

Heizer, Robert F. *Handbook of North American Indians: Vol. 8*. Washington, DC: Smithsonian Institution, 1978.

Hertzberg, Hazel. *The Search for an American Indian Identity: Modern Pan-Indian Movements*. Syracuse, NY: Syracuse University Press, 1971.

Herzberg, Bob. *Shooting Scripts: From Pulp Western to Film*. Jefferson, NC: McFarland, 2005.

Herzog, Kristin. *The Heath Anthology of American Literature*. Edited by Paul Lauter. 5th ed., n.d.

Hicks, Michael. *Mormonism and Music: A History*. Champaign: University of Illinois Press, 2003.

Higginbotham, Evelyn Brooks. *Righteous Discontent: The Women's Movement in the Black Baptist Church, 1880–1920*. Cambridge, MA: Harvard University Press, 1993.

Hodge, Frederick Webb. *Handbook of American Indians North of Mexico*. Washington, DC: Government Printing Office, 1906.

Hoefel, Roseanne. "Writings, Performance, Activism: Zitkala-Sa and Pauline Johnson." In *Native American Women in Literature and Culture*, edited by Susan Castillo and Victor M. P. Da Rosa. Porto, Portugal: Fernando Pessoa University Press, 1997.

Hoftstadter, Richard. *The Age of Reform: From Bryan to F.D.R.* New York: Knopf Publishing, 1955.

Hogan, Linda. "The Nineteenth Century Native American Poets." *Wassaja/The Indian Historian* 13 (November 1980): 24–9.

Holbrook, Stewart. *The Golden Age of Quackery*. New York: Macmillan, 1959.

Holler, Clyde. *Black Elk's Religion: The Sun Dance and Lakota Catholicism*. Syracuse, NY: Syracuse University Press, 1995.

Holm, Tom. *The Great Confusion in Indian Affairs: Native Americans & Whites in the Progressive Era*. Austin: University of Texas Press, 2005.

Honan, Park. *Matthew Arnold, a Life*. New York: McGraw-Hill, 1981.

Hoover, Herbert T. "The Sioux Agreement of 1889 and Its Aftermath." *South Dakota History* 19 (1989): 56–94.

Hopkins, Charles Howard. *History of the YMCA in North America*. New York: Association Press, 1951.

Houghton Mifflin Hardcourt Company, May 5, 2011. http://www.hmco.com/company/about_hm/henryhoughton.html.

Howard, June. *Form and History in American Literary Naturalism*. Chapel Hill: University of North Carolina Press, 1985.

Howe, Hubert. *The Book of The Fair*. Chicago, IL: Bancroft, 1893.

Howe, LeAnne, Harvey Markowitz, and Denise K. Cummings, eds. *Seeing Red: Hollywood's Pixeled Skins*. Lansing: Michigan State University Press, 2013.

Howley, John C. *Postcolonial, Queer: Theoretical Intersections*. New York: State University of New York, 2001.

Hoxie, Frederick E. *A Final Promise: The Campaign to Assimilate the Indians, 1880–1920*. Lincoln: University of Nebraska Press, 2001.

"From Prison to Homeland: The Cheyenne River Indian Reservation Before World War I." *South Dakota History* 10 (Winter 1979): 1–24.

Parading through History: The Making of the Crow Nation in America, 1805–1935. Cambridge: Cambridge University Press, 1995.

Talking Back to Civilization: Indian Voices from the Progressive Era. New York: Palgrave Macmillan, 2001.

This Indian Country: American Indian Activists and the Place They Made. New York: Penguin Press, 2012.

Huebner, Karen L. "An Unexpected Alliance: Stella Atwood, the California Clubwomen, John Collier, and the Indians of the Southwest, 1917–1934." *Pacific Historical Review* 78, no. 3 (2009): 337–66.

Huhndorf, Shari M. *Going Native: Indians in the American Cultural Imagination*. Ithaca, NY and London: Cornell University Press, 2001.

Hunt, John Dixon. *Gardens and the Picturesque: Studies in the History of Landscape Architecture*. Cambridge: Massachusetts Institute of Technology Press, 1994.

Hurston, Zora Neale. *Mules and Men*. New York: Perennial Library, 1935.

Hussey, Christopher. *The Picturesque: Studies in a Point of View*. London: Frank Cass, 1927.

Hutchinson, Elizabeth. "Native American Identity in the Making: Gertrude Käsebier's 'Girl with the Violin,' Exposure." *Exposure Special Issue on Photography, Race and American* 33, no. 1/2 (Fall 2000): 21–32.

The Indian Craze: Primitivism, Modernism, and Transculturation in American Art, 1890–1915. Durham, NC: Duke University Press, 2009.

"Illinois State Symbols." Accessed June 30, 2010. http://www2.illinois.gov/about/Pages/default.aspx.

Imada, Adria L. *Aloha America: Hula Circuits through the U.S. Empire*. Durham, NC: Duke University Press, 2012.

"Hawaiians on Tour: Hula Circuits through the American Empire." *American Quarterly* 56, no. 1 (March 2004).

Irwin, Mary Ann, and James Brooks, eds. *Women and Gender in the American West*. Albuquerque: University of New Mexico Press, 2004.

Iverson, Peter. *Carlos Montezuma and the Changing World of American Indians*. Albuquerque: University of New Mexico Press, 1982.

Jackson, Helen Hunt. *A Century of Dishonor*. Norman: University of Oklahoma Press, 1995. Originally published 1881.

Jacobs, Margaret D. *Engendered Encounters: Feminism and Pueblo Cultures, 1879–1934*. Lincoln: University of Nebraska Press, 1999.

"The Eastmans and the Luhans, Interracial Marriage between White Women and Native American Men, 1875–1935." *Frontiers: A Journal of Women's Studies* 23, no. 3 (2002).

Jacobson, Matthew Frye. *Whiteness of a Different Color: European Immigrants and the Alchemy of Race*. Cambridge, MA: Harvard University Press, 1999.

James, C. L. R. *C.L.R. James Reader*. Edited by Anna Grimshaw. Oxford: Wiley-Blackwell, 1995.

Jensen, Richard E. *Voices of the American West: The Settler and Soldier*. Lincoln: University of Nebraska Press, 2005.

Johnson, E. Patrick. *Appropriating Blackness: Performance and the Politics of Authenticity*. Durham, NC: Duke University Press, 2003.

Johnson, Kenneth M. *K-344; or the Indians of California vs. United States*. Los Angeles, CA: Dawson's Book Shop, 1966.

Joyner, C. Courtney. *The Westerners: Interviews with Actors, Directors, Writers and Producers*. Jefferson, NC: McFarland, 2009.

Juban, Angie Pitts. "Insiders: Louisiana Journalists Sallie Rhett Roman, Helen Grey Gilkison, Iris Turner Kelso." Master's Thesis, Louisiana State University, 2003.

Kaplan, Amy Carla. *The Erotics of Talk: Women's Writing and Feminist Paradigms*. New York: Oxford University Press, 1996.

The Social Construction of American Realism. Chicago, IL: University of Chicago Press, 1988.

Kaplan, Amy Carla, and Donald E. Pease. *Cultures of United States Imperialism*. Durham, NC: Duke University Press, 2003.

Kapler, Charles J., ed. "Chapter 289." In *Indian Affairs: Laws and Treaties, Vol. I, Laws*. Washington, DC: Government Printing Office, 1904.

Kasson, Joy. *Buffalo Bill's Wild West: Celebrity, Memory, and Popular History*. New York: Hill and Wang, 2000.

Kauaunui, J. Kehaulani. *Hawaiian Blood: Colonialism and the Politics of Sovereignty and Indigeneity*. Durham, NC: Duke University Press, 2008.

Kelly, Lawrence. *The Assault on Assimilation: John Collier and the Origins of Indian Policy Reform*. Albuquerque: University of New Mexico Press, 1983.

Kelsey, Penelope Myrtle. "Narratives of the Boarding School Era from Victimry to Resistance." *Atenea* 23, no. 2 (2003): 123–37.

Tribal Theory in Native American Literature: Dakota and Haudenosaunee Writing and Indigenous Worldviews. Lincoln: University of Nebraska Press, 2008.

Kilpatrick, Jacquelyn. *Celluloid Indians: Native Americans and Film*. Lincoln: University of Nebraska Press, 1999.

Klein, Norman. *The History of Forgetting: Los Angeles and the Erasure of Memory*. New York: Verso Books, 1997.

Knight, Richard Payne. *An Analytical Inquiry into the Principles of Taste*. Oxford University Press, 1806.

Kolodny, Annette, ed. *The Life and Traditions of the Red Man: A Rediscovered Treasure of Native American Literature*. Durham, NC: Duke University Press, 2007.

Konkle, Maureen. *Writing Indian Nations: Native Intellectuals and the Politics of Historiography, 1827–1863*. Chapel Hill: University of North Carolina Press, 2004.

Kroeber, Alfred Louis. *Handbook of the Indians of California*. Washington, DC: Government Printing Office, 1925.

Krouse, Susan Applegate. *North American Indians in the Great War*. Lincoln: University of Nebraska Press, 2007.

Krupat, Arnold. *Ethnocriticism: Ethnography, History, Literature*. Berkeley: University of California Press, 1992.

For Those Who Come After: A Study of Native American Autobiography. Berkeley: University of California Press, 1985.

Native American Autobiography, An Anthology. Madison: University of Wisconsin Press, 1994.

Kwolek-Folland, Angel. "The Elegant Dugout: Domesticity and Moveable Culture in the United States, 1870–1900." *American Studies* 25, no. 2 (Fall 2004): 21–37.

Lacey, Robert. *Ford: The Men and the Machine.* Little, Brown and Company, 1986.

Landow, George P. *The Aesthetic and Critical Theories of John Ruskin.* Princeton, NJ: Princeton University Press, 1971.

Lane, Jill. *Black Face Cuba, 1840–1895.* Philadelphia: University of Pennsylvania Press, 2005.

LaPointe, Ernie. *Sitting Bull: His Life and Legacy.* Layton, UT: Gibbs Smith, 2009.

Laurie, Lisa. "The Life Story of Zitkala-Sa/Gertrude Simmons Bonnin: Writing and Creating a Public Image." Dissertation, Arizona State University, 1996.

Lawler, Thomas Bonaventure. *Seventy Years of Textbook Publishing: A History of Ginn and Company.* Boston, MA: Ginn and Company, 1938.

Lee, Julia. *Interracial Encounters: Reciprocal Representations in African American and Asian American Literatures, 1896–1937.* New York: New York University Press, 2011.

Lee, Molly. "Appropriating the Primitive: Turn-of-the-Century Collection and Display of Native Alaskan Art." *Arctic Anthropology* 28, no. 1 (1991): 6–15.

Lepore, Jill. *The Name of War: King Philip's War and the Origins of American Identity.* New York: Knopf Publishing, 1998.

Levine, Lawrence. *Highbrow/Lowbrow: The Emergence of Cultural Hierarchy in America.* Cambridge, MA: Harvard University Press, 1988.

Lewis, Bonnie Sue. *Creating Christian Indians: Native Clergy in the Presbyterian Church.* Norman: University of Oklahoma Press, 2003.

Lewis, Herbert S. "The Passion of Franz Boas." *American Anthropologist* 103, no. 2 (2001): 447–67.

Lipsitz, George. *The Possessive Investment in Whiteness: How White People Profit from Identity Politics.* Philadelphia, PA: Temple University Press, 1998.

Littlefield Jr., Daniel F. *Alex Posey: Creek Poet, Journalist, and Humorist.* Lincoln: University of Nebraska Press, 1992.

"Evolution of Alex Posey's Fus Fixico Persona." *Studies in American Indian Literatures* 4 (Summer/Fall 1992): 136–44.

Littlefield Jr., Daniel F., and Carol A. Petty Hunter, eds. *The Fus Fixico Letters, Alexander Posey: A Creek Humorist in Early Oklahoma.* Norman: University of Oklahoma Press, 1993.

Littlefield Jr., Daniel F., and James Parins. *American Indian and Alaska Native Newspapers and Periodicals, 1826–1924 Vol. 1.* Westport, CT: Greenwood Press, 1984.

"Short Fiction Writers of the Indian Territory." *American Studies* 23 (Spring 1982): 23–38.

Lomawaima, Tsianina K. *They Called It Prairie Light: The Story of Chilocco Indian School.* Lincoln and London: University of Nebraska Press, 1994.

Lott, Eric. *Love and Theft: Blackface Minstrelsy and the American Working Class.* Oxford: Oxford University Press, 1995.

Low, John. "The Architecture of Simon Pokagon." In *Queen of the Woods, Ogimakwe Mitigwaki, a Novel by Simon Pokagon*. Lansing: Michigan State University Press, 2011.

Lowe, Lisa. *Immigrant Acts: On Asian American Cultural Politics*. Durham, NC: Duke University Press, 1996.

Lu, Shun, and Gary Alan Fine. "The Presentation of Ethnic Authenticity: Chinese Food as a Social Accomplishment." *Sociological Quarterly* 36, no. 3 (June 1995): 535–53.

Lukens, Margaret A. "The American Story of Zitkala-Sa." In *In Her Own Voice: Nineteenth-Century American Women Essayists*, edited by Sherry Lee Linkon. New York: Garland, 1997.

Lyons, Scott Richard. *X-Marks: Native Signatures of Assent*. Minneapolis: University of Minnesota Press, 2010.

MacMurrough, Jay. "From the Inside: The Surrounded, by D'Arcy McNickle." *The New Masses*, March 3, 1936.

Maddox, Lucy. *Citizen Indians: Native American Intellectuals, Race & Reform*. Ithaca, NY: Cornell University Press, 2005.

Marable, Manning, and Vanessa Jones. *Transnational Blackness: Navigating the Global Color Line*. New York: Palgrave Macmillan, 2008.

Marable, Mary Hanes, and Elaine Boylan. *A Handbook of Oklahoma Writers*. Norman: University of Oklahoma Press, 1939.

Marino, Cesare. "History of Western Washington since 1846." *Handbook of North American Indians* 7 (1990).

Markowitz, Harvey, and Carol A. Barrett. *American Indian Biographies*. Pasadena, CA: Salem Press, 2005.

Martinez, David. *Dakota Philosopher: Charles Eastman and American Indian Thought*. St. Paul: Minnesota Historical Society, 2009.

——— *The American Indian Intellectual Tradition: An Anthology of Writings from 1772–1972*. Ithaca, NY: Cornell University Press, 2011.

McClintock, Anne. *Imperial Leather: Race, Gender, and Sexuality in the Colonial Contest*. New York: Routledge Press, 1995.

McDonnell, Janet. *Dispossession of the American Indians, 1883–1933*, Bloomington: Indiana University Press. 1996.

McLoughlin, William. *After the Trail of Tears: The Cherokees' Struggle for Sovereignty, 1839–1880*. Chapel Hill: University of North Carolina Press, 1993.

——— *Cherokees and Missionaries, 1789–1839*. New Haven, CT: Yale University Press, 1984.

McNamara, Brooks. "The Indian Medicine Show." *Educational Theater Journal* 23, no. 4 (December 1971): 431–45.

Mesenheimer Jr., D. K. "Regionalist Bodies/Embodied Regions: Sarah Orne Jewett and Zitkala-Sa." In *Breaking Boundaries: New Perspectives on Women's Regional Writing*, edited by Sherrie A. Inness and Diana Royer. Iowa City: University of Iowa Press, 1997.

Messer, David W. *Henry Roe Cloud: A Biography*. Lanham, MD: Hamilton Books, 2009.

Meyer, Carter Jones, and Diana Royer, eds. *Selling the Indian: Commercializing & Appropriating American Indian Cultures*. Tucson: University of Arizona Press, 2001.

Meyer, Ron W. *History of the Santee Sioux*. Lincoln: University of Nebraska Press, 1993.

Mihesuah, Devon. *Cultivating the Rosebuds: The Education of Women at the Cherokee Female Seminary, 1851–1909*. Urbana: University of Illinois Press, 1993.

Miles, Tiya. *Ties that Bind: The Story of an Afro-Cherokee Family in Slavery and Freedom*. Berkeley: University of California Press, 2005.

Mizruchi, Susan. *The Rise of Multicultural America: Economy and Print Culture, 1865–1915*. Durham, NC: Duke University Press, 2008.

Mohanty, Satya. "The Epistemic Status of Cultural Identity." In *Reclaiming Identity: Realist Theory and the Predicament of Postmodernism*, edited by Paula Moya and Michael Hames-Garcia. Berkeley: University of California Press, 2000.

Moore, David L. "'The Literature of This Nation': LaVonne Ruoff and the Redefinition of American Literary Studies." *Studies in American Indian Literatures* 17, no. 2 (Summer 2005): 63–70, 113.

Morgan, Philip Caroll. "'Who Shall Gainsay Our Decision?' Choctaw Literary Criticism in 1830." In *Reasoning Together: The Native Critics Collective*, edited by Craig S. Womack, Daniel Heath Justice, and Christopher B. Teuton. Norman: University of Oklahoma Press, 2008.

Morgan, Winifred. "Gender-Related Difference in the Slave Narratives of Harriet Jacobs and Frederick Douglass." *American Studies* 35, no. 2 (Fall 1994): 73–94.

Morris, Brian. *Ernest Thompson Seton, Founder of the Woodcraft Movement 1860–1946: Apostle of Indian Wisdom and Pioneer Ecologist*. Lewiston, NY: Edwin Mellen Press, 2007.

Moses, L. G. *The Indian Man: A Biography of James Mooney*. Lincoln: University of Nebraska Press, 1984.

——— *Wild West Shows and the Images of American Indians, 1883–1933*. Albuquerque: University of New Mexico Press, 1996.

Mufti, Aamire. "Aura of Authenticity." *Social Text* 64 18, no. 3 (Fall 2000): 87–103.

Mullikin, Melinda Smith, and Timothy B. Powell, eds. *The Singing Bird: A Cherokee Novel*. Norman: University of Oklahoma Press, 2007.

Muñoz, Jose Esteban. *Disidentifications: Queers of Color and the Performance of Politics*. Minneapolis: University of Minnesota Press, 1999.

Murphy, Gretchen. *Shadowing the White Man's Burden: U.S. Imperialism and the Problem of the Color Line*. New York: New York University Press, 2010.

Nagel, Joane. *American Indian Ethnic Renewal: Red Power and the Resurgence of Identity and Culture*. Oxford: Oxford University Press, 1996.

——— "Constructing Ethnicity: Creating and Recreating Ethnic Identity and Culture." *Social Problems* 40, no. 1 (February 1994): 152–76.

"The National League of American Pen Women," n.d. http://www.americanpen women.org/history/history.cfm.

National Museum of the American Indian. *Identity by Design: Tradition, Change, and Celebration in Native Women's Dresses*. Washington, DC: Smithsonian Institution, 2007.

Nelson, Cary, and Lawrence Grossberg. *Marxism and the Interpretation of Culture*. Chicago: University of Illinois Press, 1988.

Nelson, Dana D. *National Manhood: Capitalist Citizenship and the Imagined Fraternity of White Men.* Durham, NC: Duke University Press, 1998.

Nelson, Helen C. "Navigating Nineteenth Century Novels: Linking Historical and Literary Perspectives to Explore the Influence of Dime Novels in Nineteenth Century America." Master's thesis, Humboldt State University, 2005.

Newlin, Keith. *Hamlin Garland, A Life.* Lincoln: University of Nebraska Press, 2008.

Newmark, Julianne. "'Writing (and Speaking) in Tongues' Zitkala-Sa's American Indian Stories." *Western American Literature* 37, no. 3 (2002): 335–58.

Nichols, Roger L. *The American Indian Past and Present.* Norman: University of Oklahoma Press, 2008.

Norgren, Jill. *The Cherokee Cases: Two Landmark Federal Decisions in the Fight for Sovereignty.* Norman: University of Oklahoma Press, 1996.

Norris, Ada Mahasti. "Zitkala-Sa and National Indian Pedagogy: Storytelling, Activism, and the Project of Assimilation." *Dissertation Abstracts International, Section A: The Humanities and Social Sciences* 65, no. 1 (2004).

O'Connell, Barry. *On Our Own Ground: The Complete Writings of William Apess, a Pequot.* Amherst: University of Massachusetts Press, 1992.

Oakes, Tim. "Ethnic Tourism in Rural Guizhou; Sense of Place and the Commerce of Authenticity." *Tourism, Ethnicity, and the State in Asian and Pacific Societies,* edited by M. Picard and R. Woods. Honolulu: University of Hawaii Press, 1997.

Ohmann, Richard. *Selling Culture: Magazines, Markets and Class at the Turn of the Century.* London: Verso Books, 1996.

Okker, Patricia. "Native American Literatures and the Canon: The Case of Zitkala-Sa." In *American Realism and the Canon,* edited by Tom Quirk and Gary Scharnhorst. Newark: University of Delaware Press, 1994.

Our Sister Editors: Sarah J. Hale and the Tradition of Nineteenth-Century American Women Editors. Athens: University of Georgia Press, 1995.

Ornstein, Allen, and David Levine. *Foundations of Education.* 9th ed. New York: Houghton Mifflin Company, 1993.

Ostler, Jeffrey. *The Plains Sioux and U.S. Colonialism from Lewis and Clark to Wounded Knee.* New York: Cambridge University Press, 2004.

Packard, Joseph. *Recollections of a Long Life.* Edited by Thomas J. Packard. Washington, DC: Bryson S. Adams, Publisher, 1902.

Painter, Nell Irvin. *Sojourner Truth: A Life, a Symbol.* New York: W. W. Norton, 1996.

Parker, Dorothy. *Singing an Indian Song: A Biography of D'Arcy McNickle.* Lincoln: University of Nebraska Press, 1992.

Parker, Robert Dale. "Who Shot the Sheriff: Storytelling, Indian Identity, and the Marketplace of Masculinity in D'Arcy McNickle's *The Surrounded.*" *Modern Fiction Stories* 3, no. 4 (Winter 1997): 898–932.

Parman, Donald Lee. *Indians in the American West in the Twentieth Century.* Indianapolis: Indiana University Press, 1994.

Pascal, Roy. *Design and Truth in Autobiography.* New York: Garland, 1985.

Paterek, Josephine. *Encyclopedia of American Indian Costume.* New York: Norton, 1994.

Patterson, Michelle Wick. "'Real' Indian Songs: The Society of American Indians and the Use of Native American Culture as a Means of Reform." *American Indian Quarterly* 26, no. 1 (March 2002): 44–66.

Pearce, Roy Harvey. *Savagism and Civilization: A Study of the Indian and the American Mind.* Baltimore, MD: Johns Hopkins University Press, 1953.

Peterson, Erik. "An Indian ... An American': Ethnicity, Assimilation, and Balance in Charles Eastman's From the Deep Woods to Civilization." *Early Native American Writing, New Critical Essays,* edited by Helen Jaskowski. Cambridge: Cambridge University Press, 1996.

Petri, Paula. "Parading as Millionaires: Montana Bankers and the Panic of 1893." *Enterprises & Society* 10 no. 4 (2009): 729–62.

Peyer, Bernd, ed. *American Indian Nonfiction: An Anthology of Writings, 1760s–1930s.* Norman: University of Oklahoma Press, 2007.

"The Thinking Indian": Native American Writers, 1850s–1920s.* New York: Peter Lang, 2007.

Pfister, Joel. *The Yale Indian: The Education of Henry Roe Cloud.* Durham, NC and London: Duke University Press, 2009.

Pfitzer, Gregory. *Popular History and the Literary Marketplace, 1840–1920.* Amherst: University of Massachusetts Press, 2008.

Philp, Kenneth R. *John Collier's Crusade for Indian Reform, 1920–1954.* Tucson: University of Arizona Press, 1977.

"Termination: A Legacy of the Indian New Deal." *Western Historical Quarterly* 14, no. 2 (April 1983): 165–80.

Termination Revisited: American Indians on the Trail to Self-Determination, 1933–1953. Lincoln: University of Nebraska Press, 1999.

Piatote, Beth H. *Domestic Subjects: Gender, Citizenship, and Law in Native American Literature.* New Haven, CT: Yale University Press, 2013.

Pisani, Michael V. *Imagining Native America in Music.* New Haven, CT: Yale University Press, 2005.

Pizer, Donald. *Hamlin Garland's Early Work and Career.* Berkeley: University of California Press, 1960.

Poignant, Roslyn. *Professional Savages: Captive Lives and Western Spectacle.* New Haven, CT: Yale University Press, 2004.

"The Making of Professional 'Savages': From P.T. Barnum (1883) to the Sunday Times (1998) in Photography's Other Histories." edited by Christopher Pinney and Nicolas Peterson. Durham, NC: Duke University Press, 2003.

Pokagon, Simon. *The Red Man's Rebuke.* C. H. Engle, 1893.

Porter, Joy. *To Be Indian: The Life of Iroquois-Seneca Arthur C. Parker.* Norman: University of Oklahoma Press, 2001.

Powell, Malea. "Rhetorics of Survivance: How American Indians Use Writing." *College Composition and Communication* 53, no. 3 (February 2002): 396–434.

Powell, Richard J. "Re/Birth of a Nation." In *Rhapsodies in Black: Art of the Harlem Renaissance,* 14–34. Berkeley: The Hayward Gallery and the Institute of International Visual Arts, University of California Press, 1997.

Pratt, Mary Louise. *Imperial Eyes: Travel Writing and Transculturation.* New York: Routledge Press, 1992.

Price, Uvedale. *An Essay on the Picturesque, as Compared with the Sublime and the Beautiful; and on the Use of Studying Pictures, for the Purpose of Improving Real Landscape.* London, 1796.

Prucha, Francis Paul. *Documents of United States Indian Policy: Third Edition.* Lincoln: University of Nebraska Press, 2000.

The Great Father: The United States Government and the American Indians. Vol. 2. Lincoln: University of Nebraska Press, 1984.

Purdy, John. *The Legacy of D'Arcy McNickle: Writer, Historian, Activist*. Norman: University of Oklahoma Press, 1996.

Word Ways: The Novels of D'Arcy McNickle. Tucson: University of Arizona Press, 1990.

Raheja, Michelle H. *Reservation Reelism: Redfacing, Visual Sovereignty, and Representations of Native Americans in Film*. Lincoln: University of Nebraska Press, 2010.

Raibmon, Paige. *Authentic Indians, Episodes of Encounter from the Late-Nineteenth-Century Northwest Coast*. Durham, NC: Duke University Press, 2005.

Ramirez, Renya A. "Henry Roe Cloud: A Granddaughter's Native Feminist Biographical Account." *Wicazo Sa Review* 24, no. 2 (Fall 2009).

Reed, Robert Christopher. *All the World Is Here!: The Black Presence at White City*. Bloomington: Indiana University Press, 2000.

Renza, Louis. "The Veto of the Imagination: A Theory of Autobiography." In *Autobiography: Essays Theoretical and Critical*, edited by James Olney. Princeton, NJ: Princeton University Press, 1980.

Report of the President to the Board of Directors of the World's Columbian Exposition. Chicago, IL: Rand McNally, 1898.

Report of the Secretary of the Class of 1865 of Harvard. New York: P. F. McBreen, 1885.

Research Center at the Oklahoma Historical Society. Accessed May 5, 2011. http://www.okhistory.org/research/index.html.

Resse, Trevor R. *The History of the Royal Commonwealth Society 1868–1968*. New York: Oxford University Press, 1968.

Rifkin, Mark. *Manifesting America: The Imperial Construction of U.S. National Space*. Oxford: Oxford University Press, 2009.

When Did Indians Become Straight? Kinship, the History of Sexuality, and Native Sovereignty. Oxford: Oxford University Press, 2011.

Riley, Sam G. "Alex Posey: Creek Indian Editor/Humorist/Poet." *American Journalism* 1 (Winter 1984): 67–76.

Roediger, David R. *The Wages of Whiteness: Race and the Making of the American Working Class*. New York and London: Verso Press, 1999.

Rogers, Daniel T. "In Search of Progressivism." *Reviews in American History* 10, no. 4 (December 1982): 113–32.

Rollins, Peter C., and John E. O'Connor, eds. *Hollywood's Indian: The Portrayal of the Native American in Film*. Lexington: University Press of Kentucky, 1998.

Hollywood's West: The American Frontier in Film, Television, and History. Lexington: University Press of Kentucky, 2005.

Rose, Tricia, Kennell A. Jackson, and Harry Justin Elam. *Black Cultural Traffic: Crossroads in Global Performance and Popular Culture*. Ann Arbor: University of Michigan Press, 2008.

Rosenthal, Nicolas G. *Reimagining Indian Country: Native American Migration and Identity in Twentieth-Century Los Angeles*. Chapel Hill: University of North Carolina Press, 2012.

"Representing Indians: Native American Actors on Hollywood's Frontier." *Western Historical Quarterly* 26 (Autumn 2005): 329–52.

Rossiter, Johnson, ed. *A History of the World's Columbian Exposition Held in Chicago in 1893*. New York: Appleton, 1897.

Round, Philip H. *Removable Type: Histories of the Book in Indian Country, 1663–1880*. Chapel Hill: University of North Carolina Press, 2010.

Rudrappa, Sharmilla. "The Politics of Cultural Authenticity." In *Ethnic Routes to Becoming American: Indian Immigrants and the Cultures of Citizenship*. New Brunswick, NJ: Rutgers University Press, 2004.

Ruoff, LaVonne Brown. "Early American Women Authors: Jane Johnston Schoolcraft, Sarah Winnemucca, S. Alice Callahan, E. Pauline Johnson, and Zitkala-Sa." In *Nineteenth-Century American Women Writers: A Critical Reader*, edited by Karen L. Kilcup. Malden, MA: Blackwell, 1998.

"Eastman's Maternal Ancestry: Letter from Charles Alexander Eastman to H. M. Hitchcock, September 8, 1927." *Studies in American Indian Literatures* 17, no. 2 (2005): 10–17.

Ruppert, James. *D'Arcy McNickle*. Boise, ID: Boise State University Press, 1988.

Ruskin, John. *The Seven Lamps of Architecture*, New York: Dover Mineola, 1849.

Russell, Don. *The Lives and Legends of Buffalo Bill*. Norman: University of Oklahoma Press, 1979.

Wild West or A History of the Wild West Shows. Fort Worth: University of Texas Press, 1970.

Rydell, Robert W. *All the World's a Fair: Visions of Empire at American International Expositions, 1876–1916*. Chicago, IL: University of Chicago Press, 1984.

Said, Edward. *Culture and Imperialism*. New York: Vintage Books, 1993.

Representations of the Intellectual: The 1933 Reith Lectures. New York: Vintage, 1994.

Sargent, Theodore D. *The Life of Elaine Goodale Eastman*. Lincoln: University of Nebraska Press, 2008.

Sayre, Robert F. "Autobiography and the Making of America." In *Autobiography: Essays Theoretical and Critical*, edited by James Olney. Princeton, NJ: Princeton University Press, 1980.

Schrader, Robert Fay. *The Indian Arts & Crafts Board: An Aspect of New Deal Policy*. Albuquerque: University of New Mexico Press, 1983.

Scott, Ann Firor. *Natural Allies: Women's Associations in American History*. Champaign: University of Illinois Press, 1992.

Scott, James. *Domination and the Arts of Resistance: Hidden Transcripts*. New Haven, CT: Yale University Press, 1990.

Sekora, John. "Black Message/White Envelope: Genre, Authenticity, and Authority in the Antebellum Slave Narrative." *Callaloo* 32 (Summer 1987): 482–515.

"Is the Slave Narrative a Species of Autobiography?" In *Studies in Autobiography*, edited by James Olney. New York: Oxford University Press, 1988.

Shumway, George. *Creating American Civilization: A Genealogy of American Literature as an Academic Discipline*. Minneapolis: University of Minnesota Press, 1994.

Siegel, Tatiana, and Pamela McClintock. "Why 'The Lone Ranger's' Johnny Depp Joined the Comanche Nation." *The Hollywood Reporter*, April 26, 2013. http://www.hollywoodreporter.com/news/why-lone-rangers-johnny-depp-435652.

Singer, Beverly R. *Wiping the War Paint off the Lens: Native American Film and Video*. Minneapolis: University of Minnesota Press, 2001.

Slotkin, Richard. *The Fatal Environment: The Myth of the Frontier in the Age of Industrialization, 1800–1890*. Middletown, CT: Wesleyan University Press, 1986.

Smith, Linda Tuhiwai. *Decolonizing Methodologies: Research and Indigenous Studies*. Dunedin: University of Otago Press, 1999.

Smith, Paul Chaat. *Everything You Know about Indians Is Wrong*. Minneapolis: University of Minnesota Press, 2009.

Smith, Paul Chaat, and Robert Allen Warrior. *Like a Hurricane: The Indian Movement from Alcatraz to Wounded Knee*. New York: New Press, 1996.

Smith, Sherry. *Reimagining Indians: Native Americans through Anglo Eyes, 1880–1940*. New York: Oxford University Press, 2000.

Smith, Sidonie. "Who's Talking/Who's Talking Back? The Subjects of Personal Narratives." *SIGNS: Journal of Women in Culture and Society* 18 (Winter 2993): 392–407.

Soja, Edward W. *Thirdspace: Journeys to Los Angeles and Other Real and Imagined Places*. Oxford: Basil Blackwell, 1996.

Southern, Eileen. *The Music of Black Americans: A History*. New York: W.W. Norton, 1971.

Spack, Ruth. "Revisioning American Indian Women: Zitkala-Sa's Revolutionary American Indian Stories." *Legacy* 14, no. 1 (1997): 25–43.

——— "Zitkala-Sa, The Song of Hiawatha, and the Carlisle Indian School Band: A Captivity Tale." *Legacy* 25, no. 2 (2008).

Speroff, Leon. *Carlos Montezuma, M.D.: A Yavapai American Hero*. Portland, OR: Arnica Publishing, 2004.

Sprague, Donovan Arleigh. *Images of America: Rosebud Sioux*. Great Britain: Arcadia Publishing, 2005.

Staley, Robert A. "Congressional Hearings: Neglected Sources of Information on American Indians." *Government Information Quarterly* 25 (2008): 520–40.

Stanlake, Christy. *Native American Drama: A Critical Perspective*. Cambridge: Cambridge University Press, 2009.

Starr, Kevin. *Inventing the Dream: California through the Progressive Era*. Oxford: Oxford University Press, 1986.

Staten, Henry. "Ethnic Authenticity, Class, and Autobiography: The Case of Hunger of Memory." *PMLA* 113, no. 1 (January 1998): 103–16.

Stauffer, John. *"The Black Hearts of Men: Radical Abolitionists and the Transformation of Race*." Cambridge, MA: Harvard University Press, 2002.

Steiner, Stan. *Spirit Woman: The Diaries and Paintings of Benita Wa Wa Calachaw Nunez*. San Francisco, CA: Harper and Row, 1979.

Stenland, Anna Lee. "Charles Alexander Eastman: Sioux Storyteller and Historian." *American Indian Quarterly* 3, no. 3 (Autumn 1977): 199–208.

Stoler, Ann Laura. *Carnal Knowledge and Imperial Power: Race and the Intimate in Colonial Rule*. Berkeley: University of California Press, 2002.

Stowe, Harriet Beecher. *Uncle Tom's Cabin*, Boston, MA: John P. Jewett and Company, 1852.

Sundquist, Eric J. *King's Dream*. New Haven, CT: Yale University Press, 2009.

Superior Court of California, Los Angeles, February 16, 2011. http://www .lasuperiorcourt.org/criminal/.

Susag, Dorothea M. "Zitkala-Sa (Gertrude Simmons Bonnin): A Power(ful) Literary Voice." *Studies in American Indian Literatures* 5, no. 4 (Winter 1993): 3–24.

Szeghi, Tereza M. "'The Injin Is Civilized and Aint Extinct No More than a Rabbit': Transformation and Transnationalism in Alexander Posey's Fus Fixico Letters." *Studies in American Indian Literatures* 21, no. 3 (Fall 2009): 1–35.

Tallbear, Kim. *Native American DNA: Tribal Belonging and the False Promise of Genetic Science*. Minneapolis: University of Minnesota Press, 2013.

Taylor, Alan. *American Colonies: The Settling of North America*. Boston, MA: Penguin, 2002.

Taylor, Graham D. *The New Deal and American Indian Tribalism: The Administration of the Indian Reorganization Act, 1934–45*. Lincoln: University of Nebraska Press, 1980.

Teuton, Sean. "Placing the Ancestors: Postmodernism, 'Realism,' and American Indian Identity in James Welch's Winter in the Blood." *American Indian Quarterly* 25, no. 4 (2002): 626–50.

——. *Red Land, Red Power: Grounding Knowledge in the American Indian Novel*. Durham, NC: Duke University Press, 2008.

Tiro, Karim M. "Denominated 'Savage': Methodism, Writing and Identity in the Works of William Apess, A Pequot." *American Quarterly*, 1996.

Trachtenberg, Alan. *Reading American Photographs: Images as History, Mathew Brady to Walker Evans*. New York: Hill and Wang, 1990.

——. *Shades of Hiawatha 1880–1930*. New York: Hill and Wang, 2004.

——. *The Incorporation of America: Culture and Society in the Gilded Age*. New York: Hill and Wang, 2007.

Trennert, Robert. *The Phoenix Indian School: Forced Assimilation in Arizona, 1891–1935*. Norman: University of Oklahoma Press, 1988.

Trilling, Lionel. *Matthew Norton*. New York: Norton, 1939.

"United States Constitution: Article 1 Section 2." Accessed May 27, 2011. www .usconstitution.net/index.html.

U.S. World's Columbian Commission. *Classification of the World's Columbian Exposition, Chicago, U.S.A., 1893*. Chicago, IL: Donohue & Henneberry, 1891.

Utley, Robert M. *Last Days of the Sioux Nation*. New Haven, CT: Yale University Press, 1963.

——. *Sitting Bull: The Life and Times of an American Patriot*. New York: Holt, 1993.

——. *The Indian Frontier 1846–1890*. Albuquerque: University of New Mexico Press, 2003.

Vestal, Stanley. *Sitting Bull: Champion of the Sioux*. Norman: University of Oklahoma Press, 2009.

Viego, Antonio. *Dead Subjects: Toward a Politics of Loss in Latino Studies*. Durham, NC: Duke University Press, 2007.

Vigil, Kiara. "From Ohiyesa's 'Deep Woods' to the 'Civilization' of Charles: Critiquing and Articulating Native American Manhood in Eastman's Autobiography." Master's thesis, Dartmouth College, 2006.

Vizenor, Gerald. *Fugitive Poses: Native American Indian Scenes of Absence and Presence*. Lincoln: University of Nebraska Press, 2000.

Manifest Manners: Postindian Warriors of Survivance. Hanover, NH: University Press of New England, 1994.

Wade, Edwin L. "The Ethnic Market in the American Southwest, 1880–1980." In *History of Anthropology, Vol. 3 Objects and Others: Essays on Museums and Material Culture*, edited by George Stocking Jr. Madison: University of Wisconsin Press, 1985.

Waggoner, Linda A. *Fire Light: The Life of Angel De Cora, Winnebago Artist.* Norman: University of Oklahoma Press, 2008.

Wagner, Glendolin Damon, and William A. Allen. *Blankets and Moccasins: Plenty Coups and His People the Crows.* Lincoln: University of Nebraska Press, 1933.

Wallis, Michael. *The Real Wild West: The 101 Ranch and the Creation of the American West.* New York: St. Martin's Griffin, 1999.

Warner, Michael. *Publics and Counterpublics.* Cambridge, MA: Zone Books, 2002. "Publics and Counterpublics." *Public Culture* 14, no. 1 (Winter 2002): 49–90.

Warner, Susan. *The Wide, Wide World.* New York: George P. Putnam, 1851.

Warren, Louis S. *Buffalo Bill's America: William Cody and the Wild West Show.* New York: Knopf Publishing, 2005.

Warrior, Robert. "Reading American Indian Intellectual Traditions." *World Literature Today* 66 (1966): 236–40.

The People and the Word: Reading Native Nonfiction. Minneapolis: University of Minnesota Press, 2005.

Tribal Secrets: Recovering American Indian Intellectual Traditions. Minneapolis: University of Minnesota Press, 1995.

Washington, Booker T. *Up from Slavery, An Autobiography.* Garden City, NY: Doubleday and Company, 1901.

Weaver, Jace. *A Miner's Canary: Essays on the State of Native America.* Albuquerque: University of New Mexico Press, 2010.

That the People Might Live: Native American Literatures and Native American Community. New York: Oxford University Press, 1997.

The Red Atlantic: American Indigenes and the Making of the Modern World, 1000–1927. Chapel Hill: University of North Carolina Press, 2014.

Wenger, Tisa Joy. "Land, Culture, and Sovereignty in the Pueblo Dance Controversy." *Journal of the Southwest* (Summer 2004).

We Have a Religion: The 1920s Pueblo Indian Dance Controversy and American Religious Freedom. Chapel Hill: University of North Carolina Press, 2009.

Wexler, Laura. *Tender Violence: Domestic Visions in an Age of U.S. Imperialism.* Chapel Hill: University of North Carolina Press, 2000.

White, Deborah G. *Too Heavy a Load: Black Women in Defense of Themselves, 1894–1994.* New York: W. W. Norton, 1999.

White, E. Frances. *Dark Continent of Our Bodies: Black Feminism and the Politics of Respectability.* Philadelphia, PA: Temple University Press, 2008.

White, Richard. *The Middle Ground: Indians, Empires and Republics in the Great Lakes Region, 1650–1815.* New York: Cambridge University Press, 1991.

White, Trumbull, and William Ingleheart. *The World's Columbian Exposition, Chicago, 1893.* Philadelphia, PA: Historical Publishing Company, 1893.

Whitehouse, Paul. "Seeing Red: Violence and Cultural Memory in D'Arcy McNickle's The Surrounded." *Dandelion* 2, no. 1 (2011).

Wiebe, Robert. *The Search for Order, 1877–1920*. New York: Hill and Wang, 1966.

Wilkins, David Eugene. *American Indian Politics and the American Political System*. Lanham, MD: Rowman and Littlefield, 2006.

Wilkins, David E., and Tsianina K. Lomawaima. *Uneven Ground: American Indian Sovereignty and Federal Law*. Norman: University of Oklahoma Press, 2002.

Williams, Raymond. *Keywords: A Vocabulary of Culture and Society*. New York: Oxford University Press, 1985.

Wilmer, S. E. *Native American Performance and Representation*. Tucson: University of Arizona Press, 2009.

Wilson, R. Michael. *Frontier Justice in the Wild West: Bungled, Bizarre, and Fascinating Executions*. Guilford, CT: TwoDot, 2007.

Wilson, Raymond. *Ohiyesa: Charles Eastman, Santee Sioux*. Champaign: University of Illinois Press, 1983.

Witt, David. *Ernest Thompson Seton: The Life and Legacy of an Artist and Conservationist*. Utah: Gibbs Smith, 2010.

Wolcott, Victoria W. *Remaking Respectability: African American Women in Interwar Detroit*. Chapel Hill: University of North Carolina Press, 2001.

Womack, Craig S. *Red on Red: Native American Literary Separatism*. Minneapolis: University of Minnesota Press, 1999.

Wordsworth, Dorothy. *Recollections of a Tour Made in Scotland, A. D. 1803*, 1874.

World's Columbian Exposition, 1893: Official Catalogue. Chicago, IL: Conkey, 1893.

Index

Lightning Source UK Ltd.
Milton Keynes UK
UKOW04f0716140118
316112UK00001B/37/P

9 781107 656550